Lecture Notes in Artificial Intelligence   1600

Subseries of Lecture Notes in Computer Science
Edited by J. G. Carbonell and J. Siekmann

Lecture Notes in Computer Science

Edited by G. Goos, J. Hartmanis and J. van Leeuwen

Springer

Berlin
Heidelberg
New York
Barcelona
Hong Kong
London
Milan
Paris
Singapore
Tokyo

Michael J. Wooldridge   Manuela Veloso (Eds.)

Artificial Intelligence Today

Recent Trends and Developments

Springer

Series Editors

Jaime G. Carbonell, Carnegie Mellon University, Pittsburgh, PA, USA
Jörg Siekmann, University of Saarland, Saarbrücken, Germany

Volume Editors

Michael J. Wooldridge
Queen Mary and Westfield College, University of London
Department of Electronic Engineering
London E1 4NS, United Kingdom
E-mail: m.j.wooldridge@qmw.ac.uk

Manuela Veloso
Carnegie Mellon University, Department of Computer Science
Pittsburgh, PA 15213, USA
E-mail: veloso@cs.cmu.edu

Cataloging-in-Publication data applied for

Die Deutsche Bibliothek - CIP-Einheitsaufnahme

Artificial intelligence today : recent trends and developments /
Michael Woolridge ; Manuela Veloso (ed.). - Berlin ; Heidelberg ;
New York ; Barcelona ; Hong Kong ; London ; Milan ; Paris ;
Singapore ; Tokyo : Springer, 1999
  (Lecture notes in computer science ; 1600 : Lecture notes in artificial
  intelligence)
  ISBN 3-540-66428-9

CR Subject Classification (1998): I.2

ISBN 3-540-66428-9 Springer-Verlag Berlin Heidelberg New York

© Springer-Verlag Berlin Heidelberg 1999
Printed in Germany

Typesetting: Camera-ready by author
SPIN 10704761   06/3142 – 5 4 3 2 1 0   Printed on acid-free paper

Preface

Artificial Intelligence (AI) is one of the most fascinating and unusual areas of academic study to have emerged this century, with its ultimate goal as the complete understanding and replication of human cognition, perception, and behavior.

This daring and challenging objective has given rise to controversial opinions about the field. For some, AI is a true scientific discipline, that has made important and fundamental contributions to the use of computation for our understanding of the nature and phenomena of the human mind. For others, AI is the black art of computer science.

It is not our intention to contribute to the AI debate. Our belief is that AI has led to a range of important results and techniques, which have significantly enriched the computer science field. In addition, AI can justifiably claim to have built bridges and contributed to other disciplines, of which philosophy, cognitive science, and logic are obvious examples.

The main motivating purpose of this book was to provide a showcase for the field of AI as it stands today. Twenty years ago it would have been realistic to present a survey of the entire field in a single book. Today, given the extremely wide range of issues addressed within AI, this would clearly be impossible. Instead, we aim at giving the reader a taste of the problems attacked and the solutions developed by contemporary AI researchers. We have not attempted to be comprehensive, but include both "traditional" areas of study, such as theorem proving, as well as ones that have emerged more recently, such as agents, AI and the Internet, and synthetic characters. The chapters themselves are a mixture of specialised research papers and authoritative survey papers.

The secondary purpose of this book is to celebrate Springer-Verlag's *Lecture Notes in Artificial Intelligence* (LNAI) series. LNAI volumes provide a rapid, low-cost way of publishing and disseminating research results, and as such the series provides an important service for the AI community.

We hope that the quality of the articles contained in this volume, written as they are by some of the finest researchers in the field, will contribute to an increased understanding of the significant advances that AI brings to the scientific world.

June 1999

Michael Wooldridge
Manuela Veloso

Acknowledgements

We would like to extend our deepest thanks to the area editors who solicited the articles contained in this book:

Jim Blythe	(USA)
Paolo Ciancarini	(Italy)
Michael Fisher	(UK)
Werner Nutt	(Germany)
Simon Parsons	(UK)
Paolo Petta	(Austria)

In addition, thanks to all the authors for preparing and contributing their manuscripts.

Contents

Behavioural Virtual Agents

Ruth Aylett

Centre for Virtual Environments, University of Salford, Salford, M5 4WT, UK

R.S.Aylett@iti.salford.ac.uk

Abstract. We discuss the application of behavioural architectures, in the robotic sense, to virtual agents. 'Virtual Teletubbies' are used as an example of the issues involved. we conclude that the use of such architectures has implications for the whole style in which a virtual world is modelled.

1. Introduction

A substantial amount of work is currently being carried on which brings together AI or ALIFE inspired work on agents with the advanced 3D interactive environments known sometimes as Virtual Reality, but herein as Virtual Environments or VEs. This may involve populating urban models with crowds [Musse & Thalmann 97] or traffic [Wright et al 98], the investigation of virtual humans [Thalmann & Thalmann 98] or virtual actors [Shawver 97, Wavish & Connah 97], the creation of virtual non-humans [Terzopoulos et al 94] or, at the more abstract level, the attempt to produce more adequate representations within VE tools for modelling behaviour and intelligence [VRML Consortium 98].

The very variety of this work means that there is as yet no consensus about what constitutes an appropriate architecture, or how one might choose such a thing out of a repertoire of alternatives. However one field in which an equivalent discussion is much more mature is that of robotics, where architectures needed to support autonomy have been investigated since the mid 1970s at least.

Of course it is important to note the differences between the real and the virtual environment. In robot domains, an agent-centred approach is inescapable - the environment is outside the control of the robot and only a portion of it can be perceived through the robot's sensors, quite apart from the problems of noise and ambiguity. Thus a robot's actions can only be determined by the processing within it of the available sensor data. A 'god-like' perspective only exists in a few systems where the whole environment is observed by an overhead camera.

However, in a virtual environment, this constraint does not exist - the environment is part of the overall system and all the data used to construct it is potentially available for use in agent behaviour. A 'god-like' perspective is in some sense the natural one (certainly for the system designer) and agents can be manipulated 'externally' as just another component of the environment, as for example in the use of animation. Nevertheless, as discussed in [Petta & Trappl 97], the omniscient approach to virtual agents in fact turns out to be very inefficient. The problem is that if virtual agents are to behave in a way that is convincing to the user and sustains the feeling of presence in a virtual world, they ought to appear to have the same limitations as agents in the real world. They ought to seem to collect information as it becomes available to them and to interact with objects - noticing, avoiding and manipulating - in a plausible manner. Omniscient agent management soon runs into combinatorial problems when it must keep track of what each agent is supposed to know and perceive. Far simpler to equip each agent with virtual sensors [Thalmann et al 97] and use these to autonomously drive their 'physical' manifestation as virtual effectors. Thus most groups who are interested in virtual agents follow an autonomous approach and the architectural approaches adopted in order to support autonomy in robotics seem an appropriate area for study.

1.1 Hierarchical and behavioural architectures

Two basic paradigms exist in robotic, that is, real-world agent architectures. One involves converting sensor data into more and more abstract world models, using the most abstract, symbolic model as a basis for symbolic decision making, and then converting the decisions back down into some primitive form to drive the agent. This is very problematic for real-world agents because of the time and effort required to construct and ascend the model-hierarchy [Brooks 95].

For virtual agents, since the elements of the more abstract world models are available 'for free' from the data-structures making up the virtual environment, 'sensing' is usually modelled at a much higher level than the bit streams typically returned by robot sensors (though see [Terzopoulos et al 94] for a low-level virtual sensing approach). Thus it is much easier to produce the type of knowledge needed by agents working at a cognitive level, where the focus is human-agent interaction at the symbolic level, sometimes using natural language. The STEVE agent [Johnson et al. 98], which acts as a mentor for trainees in maintenance for gas turbines in US navy ships, is a good example here.

This type of cognitively oriented agent may be thought of as one end of a spectrum which at its other end includes virtual agents whose main function is to interact with their environment in a physically competent and believable manner with little or no cognitive abilities or verbal communication. Here, a more appropriate paradigm may be the alternative robot approach to the hierarchical one just described.

This is an architecture in which tightly coupled mappings between sensors and actuators - possibly competing - are managed by a conflict resolution mechanism so as to produce an 'emergent' overall behaviour. These architectures are known as 'behavioural' and the best-known of them is the subsumption architecture of [Brooks 86]. In these architectures, complex behaviour is generated not by a complex decision-making process but by the interaction of competing responses to the complexity of the environment. No model of the environment is needed as sensor input is used directly. Their advantages include robustness and low processing requirements: *something* should always happen, and behaviours are very simple pieces of coding. This approach seems highly relevant to a virtual agent whose focus is physical interaction with its virtual environment. It may also be that the behaviour produced by this approach is more 'interesting' and 'believable' [Reilly 97] for the user as it supports bottom-up interactional complexity and emergent overall behaviour, rather than a top-down rigidly scripted interaction.

In the work described here, a novel behavioural architecture developed at University of Salford - the Behavioural Synthesis Architecture (BSA) [Barnes 96, Barnes et al. 97] for work in cooperating robots was reapplied to virtual agents in order to examine what issues this raised.

2. Virtual Teletubbies

The domain chosen was that of the UK TV children's characters, the Teletubbies (four of them, called Dipsy, Tinky-Winky, Laa-laa, and Po). These characters are owned by Ragdoll Ltd. who produce the TV programme in which they appear for the BBC. As agents, Teletubbies are both behaviourally and graphically tractable: they have a limited repertoire of identifiable behaviours, rounded two-colour bodies, simple limbs and single facial expressions (Figure 1)The environment in which they live is bounded, and park-like with the exception of a dome living area (Figure 2), and involves a small number of other devices - for example, a vacuum cleaner (the Noo-noo), a windmill, and a motor scooter (ridden by Po). These characteristics make the Teletubbies an appropriate starting point for this project..

Figure 1. A Teletubby

2.1 Overall Requirements

The requirements for the system were derived from the TV programme since an aim was to faithfully reproduce the 'look and feel'. A major difference however is that a TV programme is necessarily linear, with a beginning, middle and end, following a story (albeit a simple one). A VE is much more open, with the user's avatar having the freedom to wander and interact. Although work such as that in the OZ project [Bates 92] has investigated VEs as interactive drama, it was decided to concentrate initially on producing authentic behaviour which would interest the user without forming part of an overall 'story'. The following behaviours were seen as requirements:

Basic wandering by Teletubbies, with contour-following and obstacle avoidance
Ability to 'notice' objects in the environment, including each other
Ability to head for dome and consume Teletubby toast or custard when hungry
Ability to head for windmill when it rotates
Teletubby group behaviours such as hugging

Figure 2. Dome, landscape and Teletubbies

In addition, the Noo-noo (vacuum cleaner) can be thought of as a fifth Teletubby with behaviours required to notice 'mess' and clear it up while the windmill and the toaster (for making Teletubby toast) can also be thought of as agents with limited capabilities.

3.   The Behavioural Synthesis Architecture

The architecture used to develop the Virtual Teletubbies was the Behavioural Synthesis Architecture which we now briefly describe. Its components consist of *behaviour patterns*, *behaviour packets* and *behaviour scripts*, each of which is described below.

A behaviour pattern corresponds to what was described in the previous section as 'a behaviour' and is represented by a pair of functions. One function maps incoming sensor stimulus to actuator response, while the other maps the same sensor stimulus to utility,

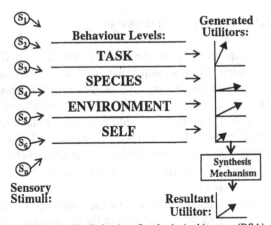

Figure 3: The Behaviour Synthesis Architecture (BSA)

which is a measure of how important the response is for that stimulus. A synthesis mechanism then combines all active patterns as weighted by their utilities to produce an emergent response for that actuator as shown in Figure 3.

This architecture differs from subsumption [Brooks 86] since in that case, the stimulus-response functions were combined into a network such that only one function had complete control of the actuators at any given moment and emergent behaviour was produced by time-slicing. In the BSA all active patterns contribute to emergent behaviour continuously via the synthesis mechanism.

For conceptual convenience, behaviour patterns in the BSA were divided into four categories. These were:

SELF: behaviours to do with self-preservation, like recharging a low battery

SPECIES: behaviours concerned with interaction between robots

ENVIRONMENT: behaviours such as obstacle avoidance, concerned with moving around the environment

UNIVERSE: Behaviour such as navigating to a particular beacon concerned with overall task achievement.

A known problem with behavioural architectures is that interactions between behaviour patterns may produce undesirable effects. For example, patterns designed to produce obstacle avoidance might not be very useful for a Teletubby that was trying to sit on a chair. To overcome this problem, the BSA provides a mechanism for grouping sets of mutually active behaviour patterns into structures known as *behaviour packets*. Each packet consists of a sensory pre-condition (for example, the Teletubby 'notices' a particular object), the names of behaviour patterns to be set *active*, and a sensory post-condition at which the packet ends, forming a triplet:

{sensor precondition(s), active behaviour patterns, sensor post condition(s)}.

The effect of a packet is to set the active flag on all the patterns it references as soon as the sensory precondition is met, and to unset the active flag, deactivating the patterns, when its sensory post-condition is met. Behaviour packets are very small structures, typically some tens of bytes at most, since they reference behaviour patterns actually held elsewhere in the robot. Sensor preconditions and post conditions are a combination of a particular sensor and either an initiating or terminating condition.

All that is then required is a way of switching between behaviour packets according to the context, and this is supplied by a *Behaviour Script*. This is a collection of packets, originally chained together sequentially, reflecting its origin in robot task-based environments. However there is no reason in principle why all packets should not be available for activation at any given time rather like rules in a production system or indeed why more complex schemes for packet activation should not be tried.

4.0   Applying the BSA to Virtual Teletubbies

An implementation was carried out using Division's DVS v4 on a Silicon Graphics O2 under IRIS 6.3. The computational capacity was only just enough in spite of efforts to keep the amount of rendering down by controlling the polygon count. Modelling was carried out by first using the MEDIT modelling tool and importing into DVS. The Teletubby world is a hilly landscape containing a dome and surrounded by a bounding hedge as seen in Figure 2. A Teletubby is modelled in the usual way as a wire frame as seen in Figure 4. The only unusual feature is the attachment of two sensors at waist level - one directed downwards to support contour - following and one pointing ahead for object avoidance, as seen in Figure 5.

The forward sensor is a ray-tracing sensor carrying out five sweeps a second. In addition, the equivalent of a ring of sensors is modelled using a bounding box which can be tested for intersection with bounding boxes round other objects. For Teletubbies, the bounding box extended 5 metres in each direction, while other agents have boxes proportional to their size. When these boxes collide with each other, the agents involved 'know' that they are in proximity to another agent, and release information to each other about their identity. This is not, of course, what happens for real-world agents who must derive all information by processing incoming sensor data. However the alternative appeared to be a complex model of the Teletubby visual system which was seen as infeasible.

In fact the bounding box should desirably be a bounding sphere, but the version of DVS used would not allow this. Neither the hedge surrounding the Teletubby world, nor the dome, which is classified as 'ground' possess bounding boxes, so only the forward facing sweeping sensor is capable of registering these.

An object hierarchy was created in order to produce a general agent architecture which could be reimplemented in a straightforward way in other

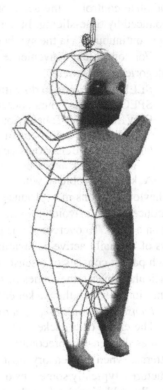

Figure 4. Teletubby wireframe

VEs. The root object in this hierarchy has as descendents graphical object and module. Graphical object in turn has a large number of subclasses: sensor (the bounding box already referred to); ray tester (the sweeping sensors already mentioned); the avatar, representing the user, and last but not least the agent class used for Teletubbies and other agents. The agent class has attached to it properties and attributes, with property itself a subclass of the root object. Among these are the agent name, its hunger and thirst levels and a reference to an instance of the module subclass of the root object mentioned above. This module instance has as a property a create routine which produces a particular Teletubby within the VE in an initial default posture together with associated limbs. The module instance also contains the update routine used to implement the behavioural architecture. Figure 6 shows part of the agent hierarchy. Note that the use of an update routine makes this overall architecture very general purpose. Here it has been used to implement the BSA, but it is equally useful for any other kind of mechanisms controlling agent behaviour in a VE - for example a neural net or a set of fuzzy rules could also be invoked like this.

The update routine may differ between Teletubbies to reflect the character-based variation in their behaviour. For example, Tinky Winky is bigger and heavier and can exert more force, so that he moves uphill faster but also has a longer reaction time to outside stimuli. Po, on the other hand, is more active, and therefore needs more sleep and displays a higher level of hunger.

4.1 Gravity and BSA improvements

This use of the module subclass of the root object is however only one of those possible since it also supports other types of external functionality. One instance of the module subclass, the environment module, was used to create a small physics model for the world.

Figure 5. Teletubby sensors

A consequence of applying a behavioural architecture is to focus attention on the interaction between agent and environment. Design decisions have to be made about how functionality should be divided between the two. While it is possible to install all the functionality into the agent, this runs against the philosophy of behavioural architectures which are concerned with complexity arising from *interaction*. Thus it seems sensible to give the world physical properties apart from the basic one of shape with which the agent can interact.

A separate gravity model was seen as a way of isolating the agent from the physical properties of the world in which they act, so that staying on the ground is a property of the world and of the agent's interaction with it rather than hard-coded into the agent. In this case, gravity is modelled in a simple way through the equation:

$$f = m * a$$

where f is force, m is mass and a is acceleration. Teletubbies output force rather than position so that this system makes Teletubbies move faster as they go downhill and prevents Teletubbies - and the user avatar - from flying. A result is that if the avatar - or a Teletubby - tries to leave the ground, they are pulled back, executing a jump. Note that jumping is thus an emergent behaviour which does not need to be explicitly programmed into an agent. As a refinement, bounce was inserted into the system so that a large jump upwards produces some subsequent bouncing action after gravity has been exerted.

Behaviour patterns and packets were implemented as described above in section 3, using the virtual sensor data as stimuli and the Teletubby graphical representations as actuators. As mentioned above, advantage was taken of the extra information available within the VE as against a real-world domain so that where a robot

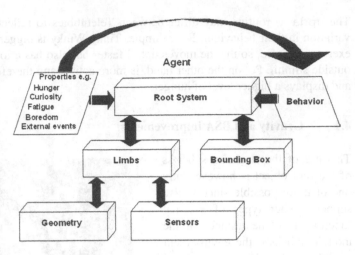

Figure 6. Part of the AGENT hierarchy

might just get an infra-red reading from a nearby object, a Teletubby gets information about what the object is.

At the behaviour script level, there is a basic difference between a task-directed robot and a Teletubby. A robot has a single set of goals to accomplish, so that a single script which chains behaviour packets into a sequence reflecting the sub-task structure is appropriate. A Teletubby, on the other hand, has much more open behaviour derived from a set of drives - curiosity, hunger, fatigue and boredom - and external events, such as the windmill turning, which require a set of behaviour scripts running for an unlimited time and constructed dynamically by interaction with the environment, including other Teletubbies. Thus a more sophisticated scheme was adopted at the behaviour script level than that which had been implemented for the BSA in robots.

In order to achieve this, four queues were constructed, one for each of the conceptual categories SELF, SPECIES, ENVIRONMENT and UNIVERSE referred to in section 3. The entries in this queue consist of groups containing one or more behaviour packets, effectively sub-scripts, each with an attached priority. The subscript with the highest priority is then selected for packet execution. For example, an agent property is hunger, which is increased over time. A very hungry Teletubby should ignore any other stimuli and execute a script which takes him or her to the Dome at once to feed up on custard or toast.

By relating priority to level of drive, and by linking level of drive to both internal state and external sensory data, it is possible to switch between sub-scripts in a plausible manner. Thus if a Teletubby has a high hunger level, the subscript for satisfying hunger will have a high priority which will stay high - allowing a consistent chunk of behaviour - until custard or toast is consumed, reducing hunger. At this point, an incoming stimulus might provoke curiosity-satisfying behaviour within the dome, or if no sub-script is activated, the default script, running at the ENVIRONMENT level, a single packet containing behaviour patterns for wandering in the environment, avoiding obstacles, will become active. This will be replaced by other sub-scripts as the sensory precondition of another set of packets is met. For example, sensing the presence of another Teletubby may trigger behaviour at the SPECIES level, while the windmill rotating triggers behaviour at the UNIVERSE level by drawing all Teletubbies to its vicinity.

5.   Results and Conclusion

The overall architecture was found to be straightforward to extend, by for example adding new properties to agents or modules. The BSA was found to be a convenient way to specify agent behaviour at a number of levels, from the lowest one of stimulus-response and stimulus-utility behaviour patterns to the highest one of behaviour scripts. This latter was a powerful idea which it was easy to develop for the larger behavioural repertoire it is possible to give virtual as distinct from real agents. Note that a script (or sub-script) merely enables a set of behaviour patterns so that while it has a high-level effect on what kind of thing a Teletubby does, it does not prescribe their actual activity at any given moment.

A concern was that the relatively impoverished nature of the virtual environment compared with the real world might make emergent behaviour rather predictable. This was not found to be true of basic movement patterns, though further evaluation is necessary of the 'interestingness' and 'believability' of the resulting Teletubby behaviour. All of the behavioural requirements listed in section 2 were met with the exception of hugging and other group behaviours, which need more thought. Hugging raises two important issues. The first is that realistic behaviour may require particular underlying 'physical' structures in the agent. A wire frame Teletubby constructed out of polygons as at present cannot produce the physical hugging action in any strightforward way. A more principled articulation of a Teletubby body seems to be required.

Secondly, if behaviour is to be sensor-driven, then one must determine what sensors are actually needed to produce hugging. It appears that some modelling of touch (haptic feedback) may be needed to prevent Teletubbies failing to make contact with each other or crushing each other in a hug. Of course, as always, these problems can be solved by graphical short-cuts (via animation), but again this seems to run counter to the philosophy of behavioural architectures.

Just as with behavioural architectures in real-world agents, a certain amount of ad hoc tweaking was found to be necessary in order to produce the desired emergent behaviour. In the case of the BSA, this involves adjustments to the utility function component of a behaviour pattern, since this determines how much of that pattern appears in the resultant under particular conditions. Thus, for example, the forward translate velocity was initially too great a component of emergent behaviour compared to obstacle avoidance, with the result that Teletubbies tended to run into the user avatar. Initial reduction of the translate utility left Teletubbies rotating gently without much forward progress. Mechanisms for learning the appropriate utilities are clearly required.

A certain number of implementation problems were encountered. The utility used for conversion from MEDIT to DVS produced results which often needed hand-editing. It had been hoped to use built-in physics from DVS rather than developing a new version as discussed above. Unfortunately the VC Physics routines appeared not to have been implemented in the version (v4) of DVS used. A number of bugs in this software also caused problems, from difficulties with the 'levels of detail' facility to problems with textures that gave the Teletubbies 'bleeding' faces at one point.

Finally, processing limitations were evident as more sophisticated models were used. While modern hardware and graphics technology leave some processing power over for intelligent agents, this is far from limitless. In the current version, the Teletubby models do not have a walking motion. A new model with articulated joints, using an animation in which walking is initiated at a rate proportional to the force generated by the BSA, has been developed. However its integration into the VE produced an unacceptable jerkiness on the O2 platform as too much processing power was abstracted from the renderer. Transfer to a more powerful platform is clearly needed.

This project could be extended in a number of directions. We have already discussed the requirement for a more sophisticated Teletubby model and the need for a allowing the utilities attached to behaviour patterns to be learned. Apart from including a wider range of agent behaviour, the introduction of an interactive fiction element would be interesting. The development of a user interface for the agent development framework, which would allow it to be applied without a great deal of programming is also an obvious next step. Finally, extending the physics model, possibly via a qualitative approach [Weld & de Kleer 90] to reduce the computational cost, might allow more extensive emergence of interesting behaviours.

References

Barnes, D.P. (1996) A behaviour synthesis architecture for cooperant mobile robots. Advanced Robotics and Intelligent Machines, eds J.O.Gray & D.G.Caldwell, IEE Control Engineering Series 51.295-314 1996

Barnes, D.P; Ghanea-Hercock, R.A; Aylett, R.S. & Coddington, A.M. (1997) `Many hands make light work? An investigation into behaviourally controlled coooperant autonomous mobile robots'. Proceedings, Autonomous Agents '97, ACM Press, pp 413-20, 1997

Bates, J. (1992) Virtual Reality, Art and Entertainment. Presence: The Journal of Teleoperators and Virtual Environments 1(1), pp133-38

Brooks, R. (1986) A Robust Layered Control System for a Mobile Robot, IEEE Journal of Robotics and Automation RA-2(1) pp14-23

Brooks, R. (1995) Intelligence without Reason. In: Steels, L. & Brooks, R. (eds) The Artificial Life Route to Artificial Intelligence, pp25-81, LEA, 1995

Goldberg,A.(1997) "Improv: A system for real-time animation of behavior-based interactive synthetic actors". In R. Trappl and P. Petta, editors, Creating Personalities for Synthetic Actors, pages 58-73. Springer-Verlag, 1997

Grand, S. & Cliff, D.(1998) "Creatures: Entertainment software agents with artificial life". Autonomous Agents and Multi-Agent Systems, 1(1):39--57, 1998.

Musse, S.R. & Thalmann, D. (1997) "A Model of Human Crowd Behavior", Computer Animation and Simulation '97, Eurographics workshop, Budapest,Springer Verlag, Wien, 1997, pp.39-51.

Petta, P. & Trappl, R. (1997) "Why to create Personalities for Synthetic Actors" In R. Trappl and P. Petta, editors, Creating Personalities for Synthetic Actors, pages 1-8. SpringerVerlag, 1997

Johnson, W.Lewis; Rickel, J; Stiles, R. & Munro, A. (1998) "Integrating pedagogical agents into virtual environments". Prescence, (5)2, 1998

Reilly, W.Scott.Neal. (1997) "A Methodology for Building Believable Social Agents". Proceedings, 1st

International Conference on Autonomous Agents, Marina Del Rey, CA, USA, ACM Press, pp 114-121

Shawver, D. (1997)"Virtual Actors and Avatars in a Flexible, User-Determined-Scenario Environment," Proceedings of the Virtual Reality Annual International Symposium, Albuquerque, NM, 1-5 March 1997

Terzopoulos, D; Tu, X. & Grzeszczuk, R. (1994) "Artificial Fishes with Autonomous Locomotion, Perception, Behavior and Learning, in a Physical World", Proceedings of the Artificial Life IV Workshop, Pattie Maes and Rod Brooks (editors), MIT Press, 1994.

Thalmann, D; Noser, H. & Huang, Z. (1997) "Autonomous virtual actors based on virtual sensors." In R. Trappl and P. Petta, editors, Creating Personalities for Synthetic Actors, pages 25-42. SpringerVerlag, 1997.

Thalmann, N.M. & Thalmann, D. (1998) "The Virtual Humans Story", IEEE Annals of the History of Computing, Vol. 20, No.2, 1998, pp.50-51.

VRML Consortium (1998) "Living Worlds"- Making VRML 2.0 Applications Interpersonal and Interoperable. Draft 2" URL: : http://www.vrml.org/WorkingGroups/living-worlds/

Wavish, P. & Connah, D. (1997) "Virtual Actors that can Perform Scripts and Improvise Roles". Proceedings, 1st International Conference on Autonomous Agents, pp 317-22, ACM Press, Feb 1997

Weld, D. S. and De Kleer, J., 1990. Readings in Qualitative Reasoning about Physical Systems. Morgan Kaufmann.

Wright,S; Fernado, T; Ward, N. & Cohn, A. (1998) "A Framework for Supporting Intelligent Traffic within the Leeds driving Simulator". Proceedings, Workshop on Intelligent Virtual Environments, 13th European Conference on AI, Brighton, August 1998

Logic-Based Knowledge Representation*

Franz Baader

Theoretical Computer Science, RWTH Aachen, 52074 Aachen, Germany
baader@informatik.rwth-aachen.de

Abstract. After a short analysis of the requirements that a knowledge representation language must satisfy, we introduce Description Logics, Modal Logics, and Nonmonotonic Logics as formalisms for representing terminological knowledge, time-dependent or subjective knowledge, and incomplete knowledge respectively. At the end of each section, we briefly comment on the connection to Logic Programming.

1 Introduction

This section is concerned with the question under which conditions one may rightfully claim to have *represented knowledge* about an application domain, and not just *stored data* occurring in this domain.[1] In the early days of Artificial Intelligence and Knowledge Representation, there was a heated discussion on whether logic can at all be used as a formalism for Knowledge Representation (see e.g. [135, 91, 92]). One aspect of the requirements on knowledge representation formalisms that can be derived from the considerations in this section is very well satisfied by logical formalisms. We shall see, however, that some other aspects are not treated satisfactorily, at least not by classical first-order predicate logic. The main purpose of this article is to demonstrate that these deficiencies can be overcome with the help of other logic-based formalisms, namely Description Logics, Modal Logics, and Nonmonotonic Logics. More recently, it has been argued (see e.g. [110, 23]) that Logic Programming can serve as a convenient and universal formalism for Knowledge Representation. However, as indicated by their name, Logic Programming languages are *programming* languages, and thus not necessarily appropriate as *representation* languages.

In a nut-shell (and somewhat exaggerated), the difference between knowledge-based programming (which processes knowledge) and classical programming (which processes data) can be formulated as follows. In classical programming, one designs specialized programs that are tailored to a specific application problem. The knowledge about the problem description and the application domain is implicitly represented in the structure of the program, and must thus be acquired by the programmer. In knowledge-based programming, the knowledge about the

---

* This is an extended and updated version of an article that has appeared (in German) in the journal KI, 3/96:8-16, 1996.

[1] The division between knowledge and data is, of course, not strict, and this article will not give a definitive answer to the problem of distinguishing between both.

application domain is represented explicitly (in an appropriate representation formalism); ideally, the processing can be done with the help of general (i.e., application-independent) problem solving methods. Thus, the knowledge can be acquired and represented by an application domain expert, who need not be well-acquainted with details of the implementation. As a simple example, let us consider the task of finding out whether two nodes in a directed graph (which may represent the hierarchical organization of a company) are connected (whether one employee is the boss of another one). A first solution, which is very far away from being knowledge-based, might be a program that encodes the structure of the specific graph in its control structure. A second, more reasonable, solution might explicitly represent the graph in an appropriate data structure (which list the nodes that are directly connected), and then code the meaning of "connected" in a program that is independent of the specific graph. This program must be able to compute the connected nodes from the given information about the directly connected nodes. Finally, an even more knowledge-based solution could be one in which the knowledge about the meaning of "connected" is also represented in an explicit way, for example, by the following Horn clauses:

$$\text{directly-connected}(x,y) \rightarrow \text{connected}(x,y),$$
$$\text{directly-connected}(x,z) \wedge \text{connected}(z,y) \rightarrow \text{connected}(x,y).$$

A general problem solving component, which is able to handle such clauses (e.g., the interpreter of a Logic Programming language), could now use these formulae together with the explicit information on the directly connected nodes to infer the connected nodes.

A knowledge representation (KR) formalism should allow for the symbolic representation of all the knowledge relevant in a given application domain. From what we have said so far about the use of knowledge in knowledge-based programming, we can derive two requirements that such a formalism must satisfy. On the one hand, it must be equipped with a *declarative semantics*, that is, the meaning of the entries in a knowledge base (KB) must be defined independently of the programs that operate on the KB (no purely procedural semantics). Otherwise, the knowledge cannot be acquired by a domain expert without detailed knowledge of the implementation of these programs. Usually, such a declarative semantics is given by mapping the symbolic expressions into (an abstraction of) the relevant segment of the "world." In addition, one needs a notion of "truth," which makes it possible to determine which of the symbolic statements hold in the current "world."

On the other hand, one needs an *"intelligent" retrieval mechanism*, which is able to realize the above-mentioned general problem solving component. This mechanism should allow to retrieve knowledge that is only implicitly present in the KB, that is, it should be able to deduce implicitly represented knowledge from the explicit knowledge. In our above example, the information that two nodes are connected is implicit knowledge, which must be deduced from the explicit knowledge (i.e., the information about directly connected nodes and the Horn clauses specifying the meaning of "connected") with the help of an appropriate inference engine. The behaviour of this deductive component should depend only on the semantics of the representation language, and not on the syntactic form of the entries in the KB, i.e., semantically equivalent entries should lead to the same results. If we use first-order predicate logic as semantics for the Horn clauses in our above example, then the usual Prolog interpreters do not fulfill this requirement. According to the semantics, the order of the clauses and of the conjuncts is irrelevant. Any Prolog programmer will know, however, that such a re-ordering may drastically change the behaviour of the program.

Another requirement that is usually imposed on KR formalisms is that of allowing for a *structured representation* of the knowledge. One aspect of a structured representation is that semantically related information (for example, all the knowledge about knowledge representation based on Description Logics) should also syntactically be grouped together. This requirement is, on the one hand, justified by cognitive adequacy.[2] On the other hand, there are purely pragmatic reasons, since a structured representation allows for faster retrieval.

Critics of a logic-based approach to KR often (implicitly) equate logic with first-order predicate logic. If we consider in how far *first-order predicate logic* satisfies the requirements introduced above, it shows in fact some strong deficits. The Tarskian semantics of predicate logic is the prototype of a declarative semantics; however, it does not allow for an adequate treatment of incomplete and contradictory knowledge, or of subjective and time-dependent knowledge. Later on, we shall see that this deficit can be overcome by considering Nonmonotonic Logics and Modal Logics. The usual syntax of first-order predicate logic does not support a structured representation of knowledge. Since all the relevant inference problems are undecidable, it is also not possible to provide for semantically adequate inference procedures. In the following section, we shall describe so-called Description Logics,[3] which are an attempt to overcome both of the last-mentioned problems by using a non-standard syntax and by restricting the expressive power.

According to what was said until now, Logic Programming languages qualify as representation languages only if they are equipped with an appropriate declarative semantics. This is not the case for Prolog, as illustrated by the example. It should be noted that I do not claim that it is not possible to solve a specific representation problem with the help of a Prolog program: since Prolog is computationally complete, this is always possible. However, this is a programming approach in which the knowledge is not encoded independently of the way in which it is processed. Exactly because of Prolog being computationally complete, all the responsibility (e.g., for termination of the inference process) lies in the hands of programmer, and cannot automatically be guaranteed. In a KR system, the intelligent retrieval mechanisms should (ideally) be able to handle all the knowledge that is represented in a syntactically correct way, which means that one must restrict oneself to a sublanguage (such as Datalog) if one wants to

---

[2] In the human brain, correlated information is also not stored in unrelated parts.
[3] Other names used in the literature are "terminological logics," "concept languages," and "KL-ONE-like KR languages."

use a Logic Programming approach for KR. Overviews on the topic of extended Logic Programs with declarative semantics and their application to representing knowledge can be found in [53, 134, 23, 4].

2 Description Logics

The attempt to provide for a structured representation of information was one of the main motivations for introducing early KR formalisms such as Semantic Networks and Frames. Description Logics[4] are logic-based formalisms that are based on the same ideas as Semantic Networks and Frames, but avoid the formal deficiencies that made the use of these precursor formalisms as KR formalisms problematic.

Precursors. *Frames* have been introduced by Minsky [135] as record-like data structures for representing prototypical situations and objects. The key idea was to collect all the information necessary for treating a situation in one place (the frame for this situation). In [135], Minsky combined his introduction of the frame idea with a general rejection of logic as a KR formalism. Hayes [91, 92] criticized that Frames lack a formal semantics, and showed that with an appropriate formalization (of their monotonic, non-procedural aspects), Frames can be seen as a syntactic variant of first-order predicate logic.

Semantic Networks, which we shall consider in somewhat more detail, have been developed by Quillian [155] for representing the semantics of natural language (this explains their name). They allow to represent concepts and objects as nodes in a graph (see Figure 1). Such a graph has two different types of edges: property edges assign properties (like colour) to concepts (e.g., frog) and objects (e.g., Kermit), whereas IS-A-edges introduce hierarchical relationships among concepts and instance relationships between objects and concepts.

Properties are inherited along IS-A-edges. For example, tree frogs, and thus also Kermit, inherit the colour green from frogs. In many systems, inheritance is only by default, that is, grass frogs do not inherit the property green, since this would be in contradiction with the explicit property edge saying that grass frogs are brown. The missing formal *semantics of Semantic Networks* was criticized by Woods [176] and Brachman [31]. The meaning of a given Semantic Network was left to the intuition of the users and the programmers who implemented the programs processing the networks. Consequently, identical networks could lead to very different results, depending on which of the systems was used to process it. As an illustration of this problem, we point out the possible ambiguities in the interpretation of property edges. In Figure 1, the property edge "colour" from "Frog" to "Green" may, on the one hand, mean that green is the only possible colour for frogs (value restriction). On the other hand, it could mean that any frog has at least the colour green, but may have other colours too (it might be

---

[4] Although there is no overview article that covers all aspects of this research area, [177, 15, 62] can serve as a starting point.

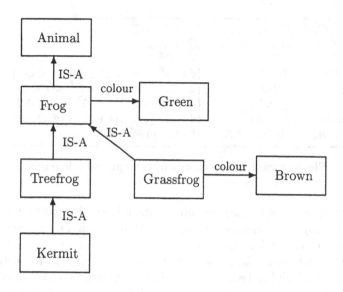

Fig. 1. A semantic network.

green with red stripes). A partial reconstruction of the semantics of Semantic Networks within first-order predicate logic was presented in [167].

Description Logics (DL) make the quantifier that is implicitly present in property edges (universal in the reading as value restrictions, and existential for the other option) explicit (see below).

Systems and applications. Description Logics are descended from so-called "structured inheritance networks" [31, 32], which were first realized in the system KL-ONE [34]. Their main idea is to start with atomic *concepts* (unary predicates) and *roles* (binary predicates), and use a (rather small) set of epistemologically adequate constructors to build complex concepts and roles. This idea has been further developed both from the theoretical and the practical point of view. In particular, there is a great variety of successor systems (e.g., BACK [143, 149, 96], CLASSIC [29, 33], CRACK [36], DLP [148], FACT [98], FLEX [152], K-REP [127, 128], KRIS [14], LOOM [122, 121], SB-ONE [106]), which have been used in different application domains such as natural language processing [154], configuration of technical systems [178, 42, 158, 133], software information systems [50], optimizing queries to databases [41, 25, 24], or planning [107].

Syntax and semantics. Figure 2 introduces syntax and semantics of some of the concept constructors employed in systems or investigated in the literature. Most of the systems do not provide for all of these constructors, and vice versa, they may use additional constructors not introduced here. An extensive list of (most of) the constructors considered until now can be found in [9]. The first column of the figure shows the (Lisp-like) concrete syntax that is used in most

(and $C_1 \ldots C_n$)	$C_1 \sqcap \ldots \sqcap C_n$	$C_1^{\mathcal{I}} \cap \ldots \cap C_n^{\mathcal{I}}$
(or $C_1 \ldots C_n$)	$C_1 \sqcup \ldots \sqcup C_n$	$C_1^{\mathcal{I}} \cup \ldots \cup C_n^{\mathcal{I}}$
(not C)	$\neg C$	$\Delta^{\mathcal{I}} \setminus C^{\mathcal{I}}$
(some $R\ C$)	$\exists R.C$	$\{d \in \Delta^{\mathcal{I}} \mid \exists e: (d,e) \in R^{\mathcal{I}} \wedge e \in C^{\mathcal{I}}\}$
(all $R\ C$)	$\forall R.C$	$\{d \in \Delta^{\mathcal{I}} \mid \forall e: (d,e) \in R^{\mathcal{I}} \Rightarrow e \in C^{\mathcal{I}}\}$
(atleast $n\ R$)	$(\geq n\,R)$	$\{d \in \Delta^{\mathcal{I}} \mid \mathrm{card}(\{e \in \Delta^{\mathcal{I}} \mid (d,e) \in R^{\mathcal{I}}\}) \geq n\}$
(atmost $n\ R$)	$(\leq n\,R)$	$\{d \in \Delta^{\mathcal{I}} \mid \mathrm{card}(\{e \in \Delta^{\mathcal{I}} \mid (d,e) \in R^{\mathcal{I}}\}) \leq n\}$
(and $R_1 \ldots R_n$)	$R_1 \sqcap \ldots \sqcap R_n$	$R_1^{\mathcal{I}} \cap \ldots \cap R_n^{\mathcal{I}}$

Fig. 2. Syntax and semantics of concept and role terms.

of the systems, whereas the second column introduces the abstract syntax that is usually employed in theoretical work on Description Logics. Starting with atomic concepts and roles, one can use these constructors to build complex *concept terms* and (in the last row) *role terms*. Using the abstract syntax, the concept "Frog," which has been introduced in the Semantic Network of Figure 1, can be described by the concept term Animal $\sqcap$ $\forall$colour.Green, where Animal and Green are atomic concepts (concept names), and colour is an atomic role (role name). The universal quantifier makes clear that we have interpreted the property edge as a value restriction.

In order to define the semantics of concept terms, one considers interpretations $\mathcal{I}$, which consist of a non-empty set $\Delta^{\mathcal{I}}$ (the domain of the interpretation) and an interpretation function that assigns to every atomic concept A a set $A^{\mathcal{I}} \subseteq \Delta^{\mathcal{I}}$ and to every atomic role R a binary relation $R^{\mathcal{I}} \subseteq \Delta^{\mathcal{I}} \times \Delta^{\mathcal{I}}$. The third column in Figure 2 shows how this interpretation function is extended to concept and role terms. An alternative way of defining the semantics of concept and role terms is to give a translation into formulae of first-order predicate logic: concept terms are translated into formulae with one free variable and role terms into formulae with two free variables. The exact definition of this translation is an easy consequence of the third column of Figure 2. For example, the above concept term for the concept "Frog" yields the following formula with free variable x:

$$\texttt{Animal(x)} \wedge \forall \texttt{y:(colour(x,y)} \rightarrow \texttt{Green(y))}.$$

Concept definitions can be used to assign names (abbreviations) to large terms. For example, the definition Frog $\doteq$ Animal $\sqcap$ $\forall$colour.Green assigns the name Frog to the term Animal$\sqcap$$\forall$colour.Green, which can then be used as an abbreviation for this term when constructing new concept terms.

A *terminology* (TBox) consists of a finite set of concept and role definitions of the form $A \doteq C$ and $P \doteq R$, where A is a concept name, P is a role name, C is a concept term, and R is a role term. Usually, one imposes the additional requirement that the definitions are unique (i.e., any name may occur at most once as a left-hand side of a definition) and acyclic (i.e., the definition of a name must not, directly or indirectly, refer to this name). As a consequence, definitions can be seen as macros, which can simply be expanded (see [141], Section 3.2.5, and [142]). An interpretation $\mathcal{I}$ is a model of a TBox iff it satisfies all the definitions $A \doteq C$ and $P \doteq R$ contained in the TBox, i.e., if $A^{\mathcal{I}} = C^{\mathcal{I}}$ and $P^{\mathcal{I}} = R^{\mathcal{I}}$ holds for these definitions.

In addition to this terminological component, the knowledge base of a DL system also has an *assertional component*, in which one can introduce individuals (by giving them names), and assert properties of these individuals. If a, b are names for individuals, C is a concept term, and R a role term, then $C(a)$ and $R(a, b)$ are *assertions*. A finite set of such assertions is called an *ABox*. An interpretation $\mathcal{I}$ (which also assigns elements $a^{\mathcal{I}} \in \Delta^{\mathcal{I}}$ to individual names a) is a model of these assertions iff $a^{\mathcal{I}} \in C^{\mathcal{I}}$ and $(a^{\mathcal{I}}, b^{\mathcal{I}}) \in R^{\mathcal{I}}$. For example, Frog(KERMIT) is a concept assertion and colour(KERMIT, Colour07) is a role assertion. A *knowledge base* (KB) consist of a TBox $\mathcal{T}$ and an ABox $\mathcal{A}$.

Inference problems. As mentioned in the introduction, one is not just interested in retrieving the knowledge that is explicitly stored in such a KB: one should also like to have access to the knowledge represented implicitly. To make this possible, one must be able to draw inferences from the explicit knowledge. As examples of two typical inference problems in Description Logics, we shall consider the subsumption and the instance problem. *Subsumption* is concerned with the question whether one concept is a subconcept of another one. Formally, we define for given concept terms C and D and a TBox $\mathcal{T}$: C is subsumed by D w.r.t. $\mathcal{T}$ ($C \sqsubseteq_{\mathcal{T}} D$) iff $C^{\mathcal{I}} \subseteq D^{\mathcal{I}}$ holds in all models $\mathcal{I}$ of $\mathcal{T}$. DL systems usually offer the computation of the subsumption hierarchy of the concepts defined in a TBox as a system service (classification). When defining the *instance problem*, one considers a TBox $\mathcal{T}$ and an ABox $\mathcal{A}$. The individual a is an instance of the concept term C w.r.t. $\mathcal{T}$ and $\mathcal{A}$ iff $a^{\mathcal{I}} \in C^{\mathcal{I}}$ holds in all interpretations $\mathcal{I}$ that are models of both $\mathcal{T}$ and $\mathcal{A}$. For example, if the TBox contains the above definition of the concept Frog, and the ABox contains the above assertions for KERMIT, then COLOUR07 is an instance of Green with respect to this TBox and ABox.

Inference algorithms. Many DL systems (for example, BACK, CLASSIC, K-REP, LOOM) employ inference procedures that only partially satisfy the requirement that the result should depend only on the semantics of the representation language, and not on the syntactic form of the entries in the KB. These systems use so-called *structural algorithms* (see, e.g., [141], Chapter 4), which are based on a point of view derived from Semantic Networks: the knowledge base is viewed as a directed graph. Structural subsumption algorithms usually proceed in two phases: first, the graphs corresponding to the concepts to be tested for subsumption are normalized, and then one tries to detect similarities in the normalized graphs. They have the advantage that they are usually very efficient (polynomial). An important disadvantage is that they are only sound, but *not complete* for reasonably expressive representation languages. If an incomplete subsumption algorithm answers a subsumption query with "yes," then this answer is correct (soundness). If it answers with "no," then this does not mean anything: because of the incompleteness, the subsumption relationship might nevertheless hold. Thus, the behaviour of the algorithm does not depend only on the semantics, but also on other factors that are not transparent to the user. As a way to overcome this problem without giving up the efficiency of the structural subsumption approach, the use of non-standard semantics has been proposed. In [146], a four-valued semantics characterizing the behaviour of a structural subsumption algorithm is introduced. The system CLASSIC [29, 33] employs an "almost" complete structural subsumption algorithm [30]. Its only incompleteness stems from the treatment of individuals inside concept terms, which can, however, again be characterized with the help of a non-standard semantics.

Since 1988, a new type of algorithms, so-called *tableau-based algorithms*, for reasoning in description logics has been developed. Here, the logical point of view is not only used to define the semantics, but also for the design of algorithms, that is, the inference problems are considered as deduction problems in logics. In principle, these algorithms are methods for generating finite models. They can be seen as specializations of the tableau calculus for first-order predicate logic [26, 170]. The non-standard syntax of DL and the restricted expressiveness of these logics allows to design terminating procedures, i.e., for many description languages one obtains decision procedures for the relevant inference problems (see [15] for an introductory exposition of tableau-based inference methods in DL). The first tableau-based subsumption algorithm was developed in [166] for the language $\mathcal{ALC}$, which allows for the first five constructors of Figure 2. Since then, this approach for designing subsumption algorithms was extended to the instance problem [93, 15] and to various description languages extending $\mathcal{ALC}$ (see, e.g., [95, 94, 20, 21, 8] for languages with number restrictions; [6] for transitive closure of roles and [159, 99, 101] for transitive roles; [12, 89, 87, 22] for constructs that allow to refer to concrete domains such as numbers; and [10, 40, 8] for the treatment of general axioms of the form $C \doteq D$, where C, D may both be complex concept terms).

Undecidability and complexity results. Other important research contributions for DL are concerned with the decidability and the complexity of the subsumption problem in different DL languages. It has turned out that the languages used in early DL systems were too expressive, which led to undecidability of the subsumption problem [165, 147]. More recent undecidability results for extensions of $\mathcal{ALC}$ can be found in [13, 89, 20, 21, 87, 22].

The first complexity results [115, 139] showed that, even for very small languages, there cannot exist subsumption algorithms that are both complete and polynomial. In the meantime, the worst-case complexity of the subsumption problem in a large class of DL languages, the so-called $\mathcal{AL}$-family, has (almost completely) been determined [59, 58, 57]. With the exception of a few polynomially decidable languages, the complexity results range between NP or coNP and PSPACE. Whereas these results are given with respect to an empty TBox (i.e., they consider subsumption of concept terms with respect to all interpretations), Nebel [142] has shown that the expansion of TBox definitions may lead to an exponential blow-up, which may result in a larger complexity (coNP instead of polynomial) for certain languages. In the presence of cyclic TBox definitions, so-called terminological cycles, the subsumption problem becomes PSPACE-complete even for these small languages [140, 5, 7, 112]. The use of general inclusion axioms (in $\mathcal{ALC}$) even causes the subsumption problem to become ExpTime-complete [163]. It has also been shown that for certain languages the instance problem can be harder than the subsumption problem [160, 61].

Optimizations. Considering these complexity results, one may ask whether incomplete, but polynomial algorithms should be preferred over the complete ones, which are necessarily of high worst-case complexity. First experiences [11, 36, 98] with implemented systems using complete algorithms show, however, that on realistic KBs the run time is comparable to that of CLASSIC and LOOM (i.e., mature systems using incomplete algorithms). These positive results depend on the use of sophisticated optimization techniques. Whereas [11] concentrated mostly on reducing the number of subsumption tests during classification, more recent work in this direction is concerned with optimizing the subsumption algorithm itself [83, 97, 98, 82, 100, 104].

Connections with other logical formalisms. Before we turn to the connection between DL and Logic Programming, we should like to mention several interesting connections between DL and more traditional areas of logics.

Schild [161] was the first to observe that the language $\mathcal{ALC}$ is a syntactic variant of the propositional multi-modal logic $\mathbf{K}_n$ (see next section), and that the extension of $\mathcal{ALC}$ by transitive closure of roles [6] corresponds to propositional dynamic logic (PDL) [67, 145]. In particular, the algorithms used in modal logics for deciding satisfiability are very similar to the tableau-based algorithms newly developed for DL languages. This connection between DL and modal logics has been used to transfer techniques and results from modal logics and propositional dynamic logic to DL [162, 163, 77–79, 47]. Instead of using tableau-based algorithms, decidability of certain propositional modal logics (and thus of the corresponding DL), can also be shown by establishing the finite model property (see, e.g., [68], Section 1.14) of the logic (i.e., showing that a formula/concept is satisfiable iff it is satisfiable in a finite interpretation) or by employing tree automata (see, e.g, [174]). It should be noted, however, that some of the very expressive DL languages considered in this context (e.g., the language $\mathcal{CIQ}$ introduced in [79]) no longer satisfy the finite model property. For these languages, reasoning with respect to finite models (which is, for example, of interest for database applications) differs from reasoning with respect to all models [43].

Given the translation of DL into first-order predicate logic mentioned above, one might ask whether general first-order theorem provers can be employed for reasoning in DL. In general, this approach will only yield semidecision procedures for DL inference problems such as subsumption. By employing appropriate translation techniques and resolution strategies, general purpose resolution provers can, however, be used to obtain decision procedures for subsumption in the language $\mathcal{ALC}$ [65, 103, 164].

Decidability of the inference problems for $\mathcal{ALC}$ can also be obtained as a consequence of the known decidability result for the two variable fragment of first-order predicate logic. The language L_2 consists of all formulae of first-order predicate logic that can be built with the help of predicate symbols (including equality) and constant symbols (but without function symbols) using only the variables x, y. Decidability of L_2 has been shown in [137]. More precisely, satisfiability of L_2-formulae is a NEXPTIME-complete problem [85]. It is easy to see that, by appropriately re-using variable names, any concept term of the language $\mathcal{ALC}$ can be translated into an L_2-formula with one free variable. A direct translation of the concept term $\forall R.(\exists R.A)$ yields the formula $\forall y{:}(R(x,y) \rightarrow (\exists z{:}(R(y,z) \wedge A(z))))$. Since the subformula $\exists z{:}(R(y,z) \wedge A(z))$ does not contain x, this variable can be re-used: renaming the bound variable z into x yields the equivalent formula $\forall y{:}(R(x,y) \rightarrow (\exists x{:}(R(y,x) \wedge A(x))))$, which uses only two variables (see [28] for details). This connection between $\mathcal{ALC}$ and L_2 shows that any extension of $\mathcal{ALC}$ by constructors that can be expressed with the help of only two variables yields a decidable DL. Number restrictions and composition of roles are examples of constructors that cannot be expressed within L_2. Number restrictions can, however, be expressed in C_2, the extension of L_2 by counting quantifiers, which has recently been shown to be decidable [86, 144].

Another distinguishing features of the formulae obtained by translating $\mathcal{ALC}$-concept terms into first-order predicate logic is that quantifiers are used only in a very restricted way: the quantified variables are always "guarded" by role expression. For example, in the formula $\forall y{:}(R(x,y) \rightarrow C(y))$, which is obtained as translation of the concept term $\forall R.C$, the quantified variable y is guarded by $R(x,y)$. For this reason, the formulae obtained as translations of $\mathcal{ALC}$-concept terms belong to the so-called *guarded fragment* GF of first-order predicate logic [2], which has the following inductive definition:

- Every atomic formula belongs to GF.
- GF is closed under the Boolean connectives.
- If $\boldsymbol{x}, \boldsymbol{y}$ are tuples of variables, R is a predicate symbol, and ψ is a formula of GF such that every free variable in ψ occurs in $\boldsymbol{x}, \boldsymbol{y}$, then the formulae
  - $\forall \boldsymbol{y}{:}(R(\boldsymbol{x}, \boldsymbol{y}) \rightarrow \psi)$
  - $\exists \boldsymbol{y}{:}(R(\boldsymbol{x}, \boldsymbol{y}) \wedge \psi)$

  also belong to GF.

It should be noted that there is no restriction to unary and binary predicate symbols, and that the free variables of the formula ψ in the third item above are not restricted to the quantified variables $\boldsymbol{y}$. Thus, GF is considerably more expressive than the fragment obtained by translating $\mathcal{ALC}$-concept terms into first-order predicate logic. In [2] it is shown that GF nevertheless has the finite model property, which implies that satisfiability of formulae in GF is decidable. More precisely, the satisfiability problem for GF is complete for double exponential time [84]. Decidability of GF can also be shown with the help of resolution methods [48].

Connection with Logic Programming Since Logic Programming languages are computationally complete and DL languages are usually decidable, one may say that DL languages have less expressive power. If we consider Logic Programming languages as representation languages rather than as programming languages, then one observes that several of the DL constructors cannot be expressed. In fact, disjunction and existential restrictions allow for incompletely specified knowledge. For example, the term

$$(\exists \mathtt{pet}.(\mathtt{Dog} \sqcup \mathtt{Cat}))(\mathtt{BILL})$$

leaves it open which ABox individual is Bill's pet, and whether it is a cat or a dog. Such an "under-specification" is not possible with the Horn clauses of traditional Logic Programming languages. To overcome this deficit, extensions of Logic Programming languages by disjunction and classical negation (in contrast to "negation as failure") have been introduced [76, 151, 119, 23, 35]. However, these extensions treat only some aspects of these constructors: for example, the "classical negation" in these approaches only represents the aspect that a set and its complement are disjoint; the fact that the union of a set with its complement is the whole universe is not taken into account. The integration of Description Logics with a rule calculus that is able to express Horn rules has been investigated in [90]. Other work in this direction can, for example, be found in [117, 116].

3 Modal Logics

This is an area of logics that has been investigated for quite a while, and for which a great variety of methods and results are available. In the following, we give a very short introduction, which emphasizes the connection between Description Logics and Modal Logics. For more detailed introductions and overviews of the area we refer the reader to [44, 102, 88, 68].

The propositional multi-modal logic $\mathbf{K}_n$ extends propositional logic by n pairs of unary operators, which are called box and diamond operators. The **K** stands for the basic modal logic on which most modal logics are build (see below), and "multi-modal" means that one considers more than one pair of box and diamond operators. Depending on the intended application, these operators may have different intuitive meanings. For example, if we want to represent time-dependent knowledge, then we can use the diamond operator ⟨*future*⟩ and the box operator [*future*], where the intended meaning of a formula ⟨*future*⟩ϕ is "Sometime in the future, ϕ holds," whereas [*future*]ϕ is meant to express "Always in the future, ϕ holds." If we want to represent knowledge about the beliefs of intelligent agents, then we can use the operators ⟨*robi1*⟩ and [*robi1*], where [*robi1*]ϕ should be interpreted as "Robot 1 believes that ϕ holds," and ⟨*robi1*⟩ϕ as "Robot 1 believes that ϕ is possible." The different meanings of the operators are taken into account by using additional axioms or by imposing additional restrictions on the semantic structures (see below).

Syntax and semantics. First, we consider the base logic $\mathbf{K}_n$ in a bit more detail. *Formulae* of this logic are built from atomic propositions p and n different modal parameters m using the Boolean connectives $\wedge, \vee, \neg$[5] and the modal operators $[m]$ and $\langle m \rangle$. For example,

$$[robi1]\langle future \rangle (p \wedge \langle robi2 \rangle \neg p)$$

is a formula of $\mathbf{K}_n$, which could be interpreted as saying "Robot 1 believes that, sometime in the future, p will hold, while at the same time Robot 2 will believe that $\neg p$ is possible." Here *robi1*, *robi2*, and *future* are modal parameters, and p is an atomic proposition.

In order to define the semantics of $\mathbf{K}_n$, we consider so-called *Kripke structures* $\mathcal{K} = (\mathcal{W}, \mathcal{R})$, which consist of a set of possible worlds $\mathcal{W}$ and a set $\mathcal{R}$ of transition relations. Each possible world $I \in \mathcal{W}$ corresponds to an interpretation of propositional logic, i.e., it assigns a truth value $p^I \in \{0,1\}$ to every atomic proposition p. The set $\mathcal{R}$ contains for every modal parameter m a transition relation $R_m \subseteq \mathcal{W} \times \mathcal{W}$. Validity of a $\mathbf{K}_n$-formula ϕ in the world I of a Kripke structure $\mathcal{K}$ is defined by induction on the structure of $\mathbf{K}_n$-formulae:

- $\mathcal{K}, I \models p$ iff $p^I = 1$ (for atomic propositions p).
- $\mathcal{K}, I \models \phi \wedge \psi$ iff $\mathcal{K}, I \models \phi$ and $\mathcal{K}, I \models \psi$. (The semantics of the other Boolean operators is also defined in the usual way.)
- $\mathcal{K}, I \models [m]\phi$ iff $\mathcal{K}, J \models \phi$ holds for *all* J such that $(I, J) \in R_m$.
- $\mathcal{K}, I \models \langle m \rangle \phi$ iff $\mathcal{K}, J \models \phi$ holds for *some* J with $(I, J) \in R_m$.

The $\mathbf{K}_n$-formula ϕ is *valid* iff $\mathcal{K}, I \models \phi$ holds for all Kripke structures $\mathcal{K}$ and all worlds I in $\mathcal{K}$.

Connection with Description Logics. This definition of the semantics for $\mathbf{K}_n$ looks very similar to the semantics for DL languages. Concept terms C of $\mathcal{ALC}$ can directly be translated into formulae ϕ_C of $\mathbf{K}_n$ by interpreting concept names as atomic propositions and role names as modal parameters. The Boolean connectives of $\mathcal{ALC}$ are simply replaced by the corresponding Boolean connectives of $\mathbf{K}_n$. Universal role restrictions (value restrictions) are replaced by the corresponding box operator, and existential role restrictions are replaced by the corresponding diamond operator. For example, the concept term $\forall R.A \sqcap \exists S.\neg A$ yields the $\mathbf{K}_n$-formula $[R]A \wedge \langle S \rangle \neg A$.

There is an obvious 1–1 correspondence between Kripke structures $\mathcal{K}$ and interpretations $\mathcal{I}$ of $\mathcal{ALC}$: the domain $\Delta^{\mathcal{I}}$ of $\mathcal{I}$ corresponds to the set of possible worlds $\mathcal{W}$, the interpretation $S^{\mathcal{I}}$ of the role name S corresponds to the transition relation R_S, and the interpretation $A^{\mathcal{I}}$ of the concept name A corresponds to the set of worlds in which A has truth value 1. It is easy to show (by induction on the structure of concept terms) that this correspondence also holds for complex

---

[5] Additional Boolean connectives like implication can, as usual, be introduced as abbreviations.

concept terms C: if $\mathcal{I}$ is an interpretation of $\mathcal{ALC}$ and $\mathcal{K}$ is the corresponding Kripke structure, then $C^{\mathcal{I}} = \{I \mid \mathcal{K}, I \models \phi_C\}$.

In particular, this implies that $C \sqsubseteq_{\emptyset} D$ iff $\phi_C \to \phi_D$ is valid. This shows that decision procedures for validity in $\mathbf{K}_n$ can be used to decide the subsumption problem in $\mathcal{ALC}$. One should note, however, that this observation does not yield decision procedures for ABox reasoning, or for reasoning in DL languages with number restrictions. More recent work on modal logics with "graded modalities" [66, 64, 172] (which correspond to number restrictions) and "nominals" [72] (which correspond to ABox individuals) did not focus on decidability issues. The extension of results from propositional modal and dynamic logic to logics allowing for number restrictions and individuals was addressed in [77, 46, 79].

Axiomatizations. If one wants to assign the modal operators with a specific meaning (like "knowledge of an intelligent agent" or "in the future"), then using the basic modal logic $\mathbf{K}_n$ is not sufficient since it does not model the specific properties that modal operators with this interpretation should satisfy. In order to describe these properties, one can use an axiomatic approach. Figure 3

All propositional tautologies	**Taut**	
$[m](\phi \to \psi) \to ([m]\phi \to [m]\psi)$	**K**	
$[m]\phi \to \phi$	**T**	axiom schemata
$[m]\phi \to [m][m]\phi$	**4**	
$\neg[m]\phi \to [m]\neg[m]\phi$	**5**	
$\phi \to \psi$ and ϕ yield ψ	**modus ponens**	inference rules
ϕ yields $[m]\phi$	**necessitation**	

Fig. 3. Axiom schemata and inference rules for modal logics.

introduces some axiom schemata and the corresponding inference rules modus ponens and necessitation. These are axiom schemata rather than axioms since ϕ and ψ may be substituted by arbitrary modal formulae.

The basic modal logic $\mathbf{K}_n$ is characterized by the axiom schemata **Taut** and **K** in the following sense: a formula ϕ of $\mathbf{K}_n$ is valid (i.e., holds in all worlds of all Kripke structures) iff it can be derived from instances of **Taut** and **K** using modus ponens and necessitation (see [88] for a proof). The other three schemata describe possible properties of modal operators that express "knowledge of intelligent agents," i.e., in this interpretation $[m]\phi$ should be read as "agent m knows ϕ." Thus, **T** can intuitively be read as "An intelligent agent does not have incorrect knowledge," or more precisely: "If agent m knows ϕ in a situation, then ϕ holds in this situation." This property distinguishes knowledge from belief: an agent may very well believe in incorrect facts, but it cannot know them. The axiom schema **4** describes positive introspection, i.e., "An intelligent agent knows what it knows," whereas axiom schema **5** describes negative introspection, i.e., "An intelligent agent knows what it does not know." While **T** and **4** are generally accepted as reasonable axioms for knowledge, **5** is disputable: negative introspection implies that the agent can asses its own competence in the sense that it knows when its own knowledge is not sufficient to solve a certain task. Consequently, there are two different modal logics that model knowledge of intelligent agents. The logic **S4** dispenses with negative introspection, i.e., it uses only the schemata **Taut, K, T, 4**, whereas **S5** additionally allows for **5**.

Properties of transition relations. As an alternative to this axiomatic approach for defining **S4** and **S5**, one can also characterize these logics in a semantic way by restricting the admissible transition relations in Kripke structures [88]. The logic **S4** corresponds to the restriction to *reflexive and transitive* transition relations, i.e., the formula ϕ holds in all worlds of all Kripke structures with reflexive and transitive transition relations iff it can be derived from instances of **Taut, K, T** and **4** using modus ponens and necessitation. Analogously, **S5** corresponds to the restriction to transition relations that are *equivalence relations*.

These correspondences can be used to design tableau algorithms for **S4** and **S5** by integrating the special properties of the transition relations into the rules of the tableau calculus. It should be noted that a naive integration of a tableau rule for transitivity would lead to a nonterminating procedure. This problem can, however, be overcome by testing for cyclic computations. This yields a PSPACE-algorithm for **S4**. For a single **S5**-modality, the satisfiability problem is "only" NP-complete, whereas the problem becomes PSPACE-complete if more than one such modality is available (see [88] for detailed proofs of these and other complexity results).

The properties of modal operators that model time-dependent knowledge have also been investigated in detail (see, e.g., [63, 171] for overview articles on this topic).

Integration with Description Logics. In order to represent time-dependent and subjective knowledge in Description Logics, one can integrate modal operators into DL languages. Because of the above mentioned close connection between DL and modal logics, such an integrations appeared to be rather simple. It has turned out, however, that it is more complex than expected, both from the semantic and the algorithmic point of view [113, 19, 18, 162, 175]. It should be noted that some of these combined languages [18, 175] are first-order modal logics rather than propositional modal logics.

Connection with Logic Programming. We close this section by mentioning some work that is concerned with the connection between modal logics and logic programming. Gelfond [73] extends Disjunctive Logic Programs to Epistemic Logic Programs by introducing modal operators **K** and **M**: for a literal L, the expression **K**L should be read as "L is known" and **M**L should be read as "L may be assumed." Giordano and Martelli [81] use modal logic to obtain a uniform representation of different approaches for structuring Logic Programs with the help of blocks and modules. In [49, 138, 1, 70], modal or temporal Logic Programming languages are introduced.

4 Nonmonotonic Logics

This research area has also created a huge number of approaches and results, which we cannot describe in detail here. The following is a brief introduction into the existing approaches and the problems treated by these approaches. Overviews of this research area can, for example, be found in [71, 38]. In addition, there are several monographs on the topic [37, 120, 126, 3]. An annotated collection of influential papers in the area can be found in [80].

Motivation. Knowledge representation languages based on classical logics (e.g., first-order predicate logic) are monotonic in the following sense: if a statement ϕ can be derived from a knowledge base, then ϕ can also be derived from any larger knowledge base. This property has the advantage that inferences once drawn need not be revised when additional information comes in. However, this leads to the disadvantage that adding information contradicting one of the drawn inferences leads to an inconsistency, and thus makes the knowledge base useless. In many applications, the knowledge about the world (the application domain) is represented in an incomplete way. Nevertheless, one wants to draw *plausible* conclusions from the available knowledge, that is, inferences that are not justified by reasoning in classical logic, but are plausible considering the available knowledge. In this situation, newly acquired information may show that some of these plausible conclusions were wrong. This should not lead to inconsistency of the knowledge base, but rather to a withdrawal of some of the plausible conclusions.

Let us start with three simple examples that illustrate the situations in which nonmonotonic inference methods are desirable. *Default rules* apply to most individuals (resp. typical or normal individuals), but not to all. As an example, we may consider property edges in Semantic Networks. In the network of Figure 1 we had the default rule "Frogs are *normally* green." This rule should be applied whenever there is no information contradicting it. As long as we only know that Kermit is a frog, we deduce that Kermit is green. The rule is not applied to grass frogs, of which it is known that they are not green (since they are brown).

The *Closed World Assumption (CWA)* [156] assumes by default that the available information is complete. If an assertion cannot be derived (using classical inference methods) from the knowledge base, then CWA deduces its negation. This assumption is, for example, employed in relational databases and in Logic Programming languages with "Negation as Failure" [45, 168]. As an example, we may consider train connections in a timetable: if a connection is not contained in the timetable, we conclude that it does not exist. If we learn later on that there is such a connection (which was not contained in the timetable), then we must withdraw this conclusion.

The *Frame problem* [130, 39] comes from the domain of modelling actions. In this context, it is important to describe which properties are changed and which remain unchanged by an application of the action. Usually, the application of an action changes very few aspects of the world. For example, by sending a manuscript of this article to a publisher, I have changed its location, but (hopefully) not its content. The so-called "frame axioms" describe which properties remain unchanged by the application of an action. Since there usually is a very large number of these axioms, one should try to avoid having to state them explicitly. A possible solution to this problem is to employ a nonmonotonic inference rule, which says that (normally) all aspects of the world that are not explicitly changed by the action remain invariant under its application.

Four approaches to nonmonotonic reasoning. In the literature, a great variety of different approaches to nonmonotonic reasoning has been introduced, of which none seems to be "the best" approach. A very positive development is the fact that recently several results clarifying the connection between different approaches have been obtained (see, e.g., [105, 108, 109, 118, 111]). In the following, we briefly introduce the four most important types of approaches.

Consistency-based approaches, of which Reiter's Default Logic [157] is a typical example, consider nonmonotonic rules of the form "A normally implies B." Such a rule can be applied (i.e., B is inserted into the knowledge base), if A holds, and inserting B does not destroy consistency of the knowledge base. As an example, we may again use the default rule "Frogs are normally green." Let us first assume that the knowledge base contains the information: "Grass frogs are brown. An individual cannot be both brown and green. Grass frogs are frogs. Kermit is a frog. Scooter is a grass frog." In this case, the default rule can be applied to Kermit, but not to Scooter. The major problem that a consistency-based approach must solve is the question of how to resolve conflicts between different rules: applying default rules in different order may lead to different results. To illustrate this problem, let us assume that the strict information "Grass frogs are brown" is replaced by the defeasible information "Grass frogs are normally brown," whereas all the other information remains the same. Now, both default rules are applicable to Scooter. As soon as one of them is applied, the other one is no longer applicable. Thus, one must decide which of the possible results should be preferred, or, if the conflict cannot be resolved due to priorities among rules, how much information can still be deduced from such an unresolved situation. For example, the conclusions concerning Kermit should not be influenced by the conflict for Scooter.

A *modal nonmonotonic logic* was, for example, proposed by McDermott and Doyle [132, 131]. This logic allows for a diamond operator, which is written as M, where $M\phi$ should intuitively be read as "ϕ is consistent." The default rule "Frogs are normally green" can then be written as the implication Frog $\wedge$ MGreen $\rightarrow$ Green. In order to treat this implication correctly, the logic needs an additional inference rule, which is able to derive formulae of the form $M\phi$ according to their intended semantics. In principle, this inference rule allows us to deduce $M\phi$, if $\neg\phi$ cannot be deduced. This is not as simple as it may sound since we are faced with the following cyclic dependency: which formulae of the form $\neg\phi$ are deducible already depends on the inference rule to be defined. Doyle and McDermott solve this problem by introducing an appropriated fixed-point semantics. Another representative of the class of modal nonmonotonic logics is the well-known autoepistemic logic [136].

In classical predicate logic, the notion of logical consequence is defined with respect to *all models* of a set of formulae. *Preferential semantics* [169] takes as logical consequences all the formulae that hold in *all preferred models*. The preferred models are usually defined as the minimal models with respect to a given *preference relation* on interpretations. To illustrate this idea, we consider a simple example from propositional logic. If we assume that there are only two propositional variables p, q, then we have four different interpretations: $I_{\neg p, \neg q}$, in which p and q are false, $I_{p, \neg q}$, in which p is true and q is false, $I_{\neg p, q}$, in which p is false and q is true, and $I_{p,q}$, in which p and q are true. Assume that the preference relation $<$ is given by

$$I_{\neg p, \neg q} < I_{p,q}, \quad I_{\neg p, \neg q} < I_{\neg p, q}, \quad I_{p,q} < I_{p, \neg q}, \quad \text{and} \quad I_{\neg p, q} < I_{p, \neg q},$$

where the smaller interpretation is preferred over the larger one. The empty set of formulae $\emptyset$ has all interpretations as model, which means that $I_{\neg p, \neg q}$ is the only minimal model. In particular, $\neg p$ is a consequence of $\emptyset$ with respect to this preferential semantics. The set $\{q\}$ excludes the two interpretations $I_{p, \neg q}$ and $I_{\neg p, \neg q}$. The remaining models, $I_{p,q}, I_{\neg p, q}$ are incomparable w.r.t. $<$, and are thus both minimal models. Since $\neg p$ does not hold in both, it can no longer be deduced. This shows that preferential semantics yields a nonmonotonic formalism. An important example for preferential semantics for the case of predicate logic is *circumscription* [129]. Here, the goal is to minimize the extension of a given predicate P, i.e., an interpretation $\mathcal{I}$ is preferred over an interpretation $\mathcal{J}$, if $P^{\mathcal{I}} \subset P^{\mathcal{J}}$ holds. Default rules like "Frogs are normally green" can then be expressed with the help of an "abnormality predicate," which is minimized:

$$\text{Frog}(x) \wedge \neg\text{Ab}(x) \rightarrow \text{Green}(x).$$

Exceptions to this rule can now be introduced by implications like $\text{Brown}(x) \rightarrow \text{Ab}(x)$. The fact that Ab is minimized makes sure that the default rule is applied to an individual unless it is a known exception.

Properties that a "reasonable" *nonmonotonic inference relation* $\vdash\!\!\!\sim$ should satisfy were, on the one hand, introduced for the purpose of comparing and evaluating different approaches to nonmonotonic reasoning [69, 124]. On the other hand, these properties can also be interpreted as inference rules (like modus ponens), which can be used to generate new nonmonotonic consequences [114]. Figure 4 gives several examples of such reasonable properties. It has also turned out that there is a close connection between preferential semantics and inferences relations satisfying certain properties [123, 111].

$$\phi \mathrel{|\!\sim} \phi \qquad\qquad\qquad\qquad\qquad\qquad\qquad\qquad \textbf{Reflexivity}$$

If $\phi \mathrel{|\!\sim} \psi$ and ϕ equivalent to ϕ' then $\phi' \mathrel{|\!\sim} \psi$ **Left equivalence**

If $\phi \mathrel{|\!\sim} \psi$ and ψ implies ψ' then $\phi \mathrel{|\!\sim} \psi'$ **Right weakening**

If $\phi \wedge \phi' \mathrel{|\!\sim} \psi$ and $\phi \mathrel{|\!\sim} \phi'$ then $\phi \mathrel{|\!\sim} \psi$ **Cut**

If $\phi \mathrel{|\!\sim} \phi'$ and $\phi \mathrel{|\!\sim} \psi$ then $\phi \wedge \phi' \mathrel{|\!\sim} \psi$ **Cautious monotony**

Fig. 4. Properties of nonmonotonic inference relations.

Connection with Logic Programming A similar approach for evaluating and comparing the semantics for Logic Programs was used in [51, 52]. As mentioned above, the "Closed World Assumption" in Logic Programs, and the corresponding treatment of negation as "Negation as Failure," leads to a nonmonotonic behaviour of Logic Programs. Thus, it is not surprising that there is a close connection between approaches for defining declarative semantics for (extended) logic programs (e.g., [74, 75, 27, 173]) and formalisms for nonmonotonic reasoning. In principle, these semantics depend on a preference relation between models. Their development was strongly influenced by the semantics for autoepistemic logic and for default logic. A first overview of these connections is given in [150]. More recent work in this direction can be found in the proceedings of the conferences "Non-Monotonic Extensions of Logic Programming" [55, 56] and "Logic Programming and Nonmonotonic Reasoning" [125, 54].

Connection with Description Logics The integration of default rules into Description Logics was investigated in [153, 16, 17]. In [60], an epistemic operator **K** is added to the DL $\mathcal{ALC}$. This operator is similar to the modal operators employed in modal nonmonotonic logic, and it can, for example, be used to impose a "local" closed world assumption.

References

1. M. Abadi and Z. Manna. Temporal logic programming. *Journal of Symbolic Computation*, 8:277–295, 1989.
2. H. Andréka, J. van Benthem, and I. Németi. Modal languages and bounded fragments of predicate logic. Research Report ML-96-03, ILLC, Amsterdam, 1996.
3. G. Antoniou. *Nonmonotonic Reasoning*. MIT Press, Cambridge, Mass., 1997.
4. K. R. Apt and R. N. Bol. Logic programming and negation: A survey. *Journal of Logic Programming*, 19–20:9–71, 1994.
5. F. Baader. Terminological cycles in KL-ONE-based knowledge representation languages. In T. Dietterich and W. Swartout, editors, *Proceedings of the 8th National Conference on Artificial Intelligence*, pages 621–626, Boston, Mass., 1990. AAAI Press / MIT Press.
6. F. Baader. Augmenting concept languages by transitive closure of roles: An alternative to terminological cycles. In J. Mylopoulos and R. Reiter, editors,

Proceedings of the 12th International Joint Conference on Artificial Intelligence, pages 446–451, Sydney, Australia, 1991. Morgan Kaufmann, San Francisco.

7. F. Baader. Using automata theory for characterizing the semantics of terminological cycles. *Annals of Mathematics and Artificial Intelligence*, 18(2–4):175–219, 1996.

8. F. Baader, M. Buchheit, and B. Hollunder. Cardinality restrictions on concepts. *Artificial Intelligence*, 88(1–2):195–213, 1996.

9. F. Baader, H.-J. Bürckert, J. Heinsohn, J. Müller, B. Hollunder, B. Nebel, W. Nutt, and H.-J. Profitlich. Terminological knowledge representation: A proposal for a terminological logic. DFKI Technical Memo TM-90-04, Deutsches Forschungszentrum für Künstliche Intelligenz, Kaiserslautern, 1990.

10. F. Baader, H.-J. Bürckert, B. Hollunder, W. Nutt, and J. Siekmann. Concept logics. In J. W. Lloyd, editor, *Proceedings of the Symposium on Computational Logic*, pages 177–201, Brussels, 1990. Springer–Verlag.

11. F. Baader, E. Franconi, B. Hollunder, B. Nebel, and H.-J. Profitlich. An empirical analysis of optimization techniques for terminological systems. *Journal of Applied Intelligence*, 4:109–132, 1994.

12. F. Baader and P. Hanschke. A scheme for integrating concrete domains into concept languages. In J. Mylopoulos and R. Reiter, editors, *Proceedings of the 12th International Joint Conference on Artificial Intelligence*, pages 452–457, Sydney, Australia, 1991. Morgan Kaufmann, San Francisco.

13. F. Baader and P. Hanschke. Extensions of concept languages for a mechanical engineering application. In *Proceedings of the 16th German AI-Conference, GWAI-92*, volume 671 of *Lecture Notes in Computer Science*, pages 132–143, Bonn (Germany), 1993. Springer–Verlag.

14. F. Baader and B. Hollunder. *KRIS*: *K*nowledge *R*epresentation and *I*nference *S*ystem. *SIGART Bulletin*, 2(3):8–14, 1991.

15. F. Baader and B. Hollunder. A terminological knowledge representation system with complete inference algorithms. In M. Richter and H. Boley, editors, *Proceedings of the First International Workshop on Processing Declarative Knowledge (PDK-91)*, volume 567 of *Lecture Notes in Computer Science*, pages 67–85, Kaiserslautern (Germany), 1991. Springer–Verlag.

16. F. Baader and B. Hollunder. Embedding defaults into terminological representation systems. *J. Automated Reasoning*, 14:149–180, 1995.

17. F. Baader and B. Hollunder. Priorities on defaults with prerequisites, and their application in treating specificity in terminological default logic. *J. Automated Reasoning*, 15:41–68, 1995.

18. F. Baader and A. Laux. Terminological logics with modal operators. In C. Mellish, editor, *Proceedings of the 14th International Joint Conference on Artificial Intelligence*, pages 808–814, Montréal, Canada, 1995. Morgan Kaufmann, San Francisco.

19. F. Baader and H.-J. Ohlbach. A multi-dimensional terminological knowledge representation language. *Journal of Applied Non-Classical Logics*, 5(2):153–197, 1995.

20. F. Baader and U. Sattler. Description logics with symbolic number restrictions. In W. Wahlster, editor, *Proceedings of the Twelfth European Conference on Artificial Intelligence (ECAI-96)*, pages 283–287. John Wiley & Sons Ltd, 1996.

21. F. Baader and U. Sattler. Number restrictions on complex roles in description logics. In L. C. Aiello, J. Doyle, and S. Shapiro, editors, *Proceedings of the Fifth*

International Conference on the Principles of Knowledge Representation and Reasoning (KR-96), pages 328–339, Cambridge, Mass., 1996. Morgan Kaufmann, San Francisco.

22. F. Baader and U. Sattler. Description logics with concrete domains and aggregation. In H. Prade, editor, *Proceedings of the 13th European Conference on Artificial Intelligence (ECAI-98)*, pages 336–340. John Wiley & Sons Ltd, 1998.

23. C. Baral and M. Gelfond. Logic programming and knowledge representation. *Journal of Logic Programming*, 19–20:73–148, 1994.

24. S. Bergamaschi and D. Beneventano. Incoherence and subsumption for recursive views and queries in object-oriented data models. *Data and Knowledge Engineering*, 21(3):217–252, 1997.

25. S. Bergamaschi, C. Sartori, D. Beneventano, and M. Vincini. ODB-tools: a description logics based tool for schema validation and semantic query optimization in object oriented databases. In M. Lenzerini, editor, *Proceedings of the 5th Congress of the Italian Association for Artificial Intelligence: Advances in Artificial Intelligence (AI*IA-97)*, volume 1321 of *Lecture Notes in Artificial Intelligence*, pages 435–438. Springer–Verlag, 1997.

26. E. W. Beth. *The Foundations of Mathematics*. North-Holland, Amsterdam, 1959.

27. N. Bidoit and C. Froidevaux. Negation by default and unstratified logic programs. *Theoretical Computer Science*, 78:85–112, 1991.

28. A. Borgida. On the relative expressiveness of description logics and predicate logics. *Journal of Artificial Intelligence*, 82(1–2):353–367, 1996.

29. A. Borgida, R. J. Brachman, D. L. McGuinness, and L. A. Resnick. CLASSIC: A structural data model for objects. In *Proceedings of the 1989 ACM SIGMOD International Conference on Management of Data*, pages 59–67, Portland, Oreg., 1989.

30. A. Borgida and P. Patel-Schneider. A semantics and complete algorithm for subsumption in the CLASSIC description logic. *Journal of Artificial Intelligence Research*, 1:277–308, 1994.

31. R. J. Brachman. What's in a concept: Structural foundations for semantic networks. *International Journal of Man-Machine Studies*, 9:127–152, 1977.

32. R. J. Brachman. Structured inheritance networks. In W. A. Woods and R. J. Brachman, editors, *Research in Natural Language Understanding*, Quarterly Progress Report No. 1, BBN Report No. 3742, pages 36–78. Bolt, Beranek and Newman Inc., Cambridge, Mass., 1978.

33. R. J. Brachman, D. L. McGuinness, P. F. Patel-Schneider, L. A. Resnick, and A. Borgida. Living with CLASSIC: When and how to use a KL-ONE-like language. In J. Sowa, editor, *Principles of Semantic Networks*, pages 401–456. Morgan Kaufmann, San Francisco, 1991.

34. R. J. Brachman and J. G. Schmolze. An overview of the KL-ONE knowledge representation system. *Cognitive Science*, 9(2):171–216, 1985.

35. S. Brass and J. Dix. Disjunctive semantics based upon partial and bottom-up evaluation. In L. Sterling, editor, *Proceedings of the 12th International Conference on Logic Programming*, pages 199–213. MIT Press, 1995.

36. P. Bresciani, E. Franconi, and S. Tessaris. Implementing and testing expressive description logics: A preliminary report. In *Proceedings of the International Symposium on Knowledge Retrieval, Use, and Storage for Efficiency, KRUSE-95*, Santa Cruz, USA, 1995.

37. G. Brewka. *Nonmonotonic Reasoning*. Cambridge University Press, Cambridge, UK, 1991.

38. G. Brewka, J. Dix, and K. Konolige. *Nonmonotonic Reasoning: An Overview.* CSLI Publications, Center for the Study of Language and Information, Stanford, Cal., 1997.

39. F. M. Brown, editor. *The Frame Problem in Artificial Intelligence: Proceedings of the 1987 Workshop.* Morgan Kaufman, 1987.

40. M. Buchheit, F. M. Donini, and A. Schaerf. Decidable reasoning in terminological knowledge representation systems. *Journal of Artificial Intelligence Research*, 1:109–138, 1993.

41. M. Buchheit, M. Jeusfeld, W. Nutt, and M. Staudt. Subsumption of queries to object-oriented databases. *Information Systems*, 19(1):33–54, 1994.

42. M. Buchheit, R. Klein, and W. Nutt. Configuration as model construction: The constructive problem solving approach. In *Proceedings of the Third International Conference on Artificial Intelligence in Design, AID'94*, Lausanne, Switzerland, 1994.

43. D. Calvanese. Finite model reasoning in description logics. In L. C. Aiello, J. Doyle, and S. Shapiro, editors, *Proceedings of the Fifth International Conference on the Principles of Knowledge Representation and Reasoning (KR-96)*, pages 292–303, Cambridge, Mass., 1996. Morgan Kaufmann, San Francisco.

44. B. F. Chellas. *Modal Logic: An Introduction.* Cambridge University Press, Cambridge, UK, 1980.

45. K. Clark. Negation as Failure. In *Logic and Data Bases*, pages 293–322. Plenum Press, New York, 1978.

46. G. De Giacomo. *Decidability of Class-Based Knowledge Representation Formalisms.* PhD thesis, Università degli Studi di Roma "La Sapienza", Italy, 1995.

47. G. De Giacomo. Eliminating "converse" from converse PDL. *Journal of Logic, Language, and Information*, 5:193–208, 1996.

48. H. de Nivelle. A resolution decision procedure for the guarded fragment. In C. Kirchner and H. Kirchner, editors, *Proceedings of the 15th International Conference on Automated Deduction (CADE-15)*, volume 1421 of *Lecture Notes in Artificial Intelligence*, pages 191–204, Lindau, Germany, 1998. Springer-Verlag.

49. L. Fariñas del Cerro. Molog: A system that extends Prolog with modal logic. *New Generation Computing*, 4:35–50, 1986.

50. P. Devanbu, R. J. Brachman, P. G. Selfridge, and B. W. Ballard. LaSSIE: A knowledge-based software information system. *Communications of the ACM*, 34(5):34–49, 1991.

51. J. Dix. A classification-theory of semantics of normal logic programs: I. Strong properties. *Fundamenta Informaticae*, XXII(3):227–255, 1995.

52. J. Dix. A classification-theory of semantics of normal logic programs: II. Weak properties. *Fundamenta Informaticae*, XXII(3):257–288, 1995.

53. J. Dix. Semantics of logic programs: Their intuitions and formal properties. An overview. In A. Fuhrmann and H. Rott, editors, *Logic, Action and Information – Essays on Logic in Philosophy and Artificial Intelligence*, pages 241–327. DeGruyter, 1995.

54. J. Dix, U. Furbach, and A. Nerode, editors. *Logic Programming and Nonmonotonic Reasoning, Fourth International Conference*, volume 1265 of *Lecture Notes in Artificial Intelligence*. Springer-Verlag, 1997.

55. J. Dix, L. Pereira, and T. Przymusinski, editors. *Non-Monotonic Extensions of Logic Programming, Proceedings*, volume 927 of *Lecture Notes in Artificial Intelligence*. Springer-Verlag, 1995.

56. J. Dix, L. Pereira, and T. Przymusinski, editors. *Non-Monotonic Extensions of Logic Programming, Proceedings*, volume 1216 of *Lecture Notes in Artificial Intelligence*. Springer–Verlag, 1997.

57. F. M. Donini, B. Hollunder, M. Lenzerini, A. M. Spaccamela, D. Nardi, and W. Nutt. The complexity of existential quantification in concept languages. *Journal of Artificial Intelligence*, 53:309–327, 1992.

58. F. M. Donini, M. Lenzerini, D. Nardi, and W. Nutt. The complexity of concept languages. In J. Allen, R. Fikes, and E. Sandewall, editors, *Proceedings of the 2nd International Conference on Principles of Knowledge Representation and Reasoning (KR-91)*, pages 151–162, Cambridge, Mass., 1991. Morgan Kaufmann, San Francisco.

59. F. M. Donini, M. Lenzerini, D. Nardi, and W. Nutt. Tractable concept languages. In J. Mylopoulos and R. Reiter, editors, *Proceedings of the 12th International Joint Conference on Artificial Intelligence*, pages 458–463, Sydney, Australia, 1991. Morgan Kaufmann, San Francisco.

60. F. M. Donini, M. Lenzerini, D. Nardi, W. Nutt, and A. Schaerf. Adding epistemic operators to concept languages. In B. Nebel, Ch. Rich, and W. Swartout, editors, *Proceedings of the 3rd International Conference on Principles of Knowledge Representation and Reasoning (KR-92)*, pages 342–356, Cambridge, Mass., 1992. Morgan Kaufmann, San Francisco.

61. F. M. Donini, M. Lenzerini, D. Nardi, and A. Schaerf. Deduction in concept languages: From subsumption to instance checking. *Journal of Logic and Computation*, 4(4):423–452, 1994.

62. F. M. Donini, M. Lenzerini, D. Nardi, and A. Schaerf. Reasoning in description logics. In G. Brewka, editor, *Principles of Knowledge Representation*, pages 191–236. CSLI Publications, Stanford (CA), USA, 1996.

63. W. A. Emerson. Temporal and modal logic. In J. van Leeuwen, editor, *Handbook of Theoretical Computer Science, Vol. B*. Elsevier, Amsterdam, The Netherlands, 1990.

64. M. Fattorosi-Barnaba and F. de Caro. Graded modalities I. *Studia Logica*, 44:197–221, 1985.

65. C. Fernmüller, A. Leitsch, T. Tammet, and N. Zamov. *Resolution Methods for the Decision Problem*, volume 679 of *Lecture Notes in Artificial Intelligence*. Springer–Verlag, 1993.

66. K. Fine. In so many possible worlds. *Notre Dame Journal of Formal Logics*, 13:516–520, 1972.

67. M. J. Fischer and R. E. Ladner. Propositional modal logic of programs. In *Ninth Annual ACM Symposium on Theory of Computing*, pages 286–294, New York, N.Y., 1977. ACM.

68. M. Fitting. Basic modal logic. In D. M. Gabbay, C. J. Hogger, and J. A. Robinson, editors, *Handbook of Logic in Artificial Intelligence and Logic Programming, Vol. 1*. Oxford University Press, Oxford, UK, 1993.

69. D. M. Gabbay. Theoretical foundations for non-monotonic reasoning in expert systems. In K. R. Apt, editor, *Proceedings of the NATO Advance Study Institute on Logics and Models of Concurrent Systems*, La Colle-sur-Loup, France, 1985. Springer–Verlag.

70. D. M. Gabbay. Modal and temporal logic programming. In A. Galton, editor, *Temporal Logics and Their Applications*. Academic Press, London, UK, 1987.

71. D. M. Gabbay, C. J. Hogger, and J. A. Robinson, editors. *Handbook of Logic in Artificial Intelligence and Logic Programming, Vol. 3: Nonmonotonic Reasoning and Uncertain Reasoning*. Oxford University Press, Oxford, UK, 1994.

72. G. Gargov and V. Goranko. Modal logic with names. *J. Philosophical Logic*, 22:607–636, 1993.

73. M. Gelfond. Logic programming and reasoning with incomplete information. *Annals of Mathematics and Artificial Intelligence*, 12(1–2):89–116, 1994.

74. M. Gelfond and V. Lifschitz. The stable semantics for logic programs. In R. Kowalski and K. Bowen, editors, *Proceedings of the 5th International Symposium on Logic Programming*, pages 1070–1080, Cambridge, MA., 1988. MIT Press.

75. M. Gelfond and V. Lifschitz. Logic programs with classical negation. In D. Warren and P. Szeredi, editors, *Proceedings of the 7th International Conference on Logic Programming*, pages 579–597, Cambridge, MA, 1990. MIT Press.

76. M. Gelfond and V. Lifschitz. Classical negation in logic programs and disjunctive databases. *New Generation Computing*, 9:365–385, 1991.

77. G. De Giacomo and M. Lenzerini. Boosting the correspondence between description logics and propositional dynamic logics. In *Proceedings of the Twelfth National Conference on Artificial Intelligence (AAAI-94)*, pages 205–212. AAAI-Press/The MIT-Press, 1994.

78. G. De Giacomo and M. Lenzerini. Concept languages with number restrictions and fixpoints, and its relationship with mu-calculus. In A. G. Cohn, editor, *Proceedings of the Eleventh European Conference on Artificial Intelligence (ECAI-94)*, pages 411–415. John Wiley and Sons, 1994.

79. G. De Giacomo and M. Lenzerini. TBox and ABox reasoning in expressive description logics. In L. C. Aiello, J. Doyle, and S. Shapiro, editors, *Proceedings of the Fifth International Conference on the Principles of Knowledge Representation and Reasoning (KR-96)*, pages 316–327, Cambridge, Mass., 1996. Morgan Kaufmann, San Francisco.

80. M. L. Ginsberg, editor. *Readings in Nonmonotonic Reasoning*. Morgan Kaufmann, San Francisco, 1987.

81. L. Giordano and A. Martelli. Structuring logic programs: A modal approach. *Journal of Logic Programming*, 21(2):59–94, 1994.

82. E. Giunchiglia, F. Giunchiglia, R. Sebastiani, and A. Tacchell. More evaluation of decision procedures for modal logics. In A. Cohn, L. Schubert, and S. Shapiro, editors, *Proceedings of the Sixth International Conference on Principles of Knowledge Representation and Reasoning (KR-98)*, pages 626–635, Trento, Italy, 1998. Morgan Kaufmann, San Francisco.

83. F. Giunchiglia and R. Sebastiani. A SAT-based decision procedure for $\mathcal{ALC}$. In L. C. Aiello, J. Doyle, and S. Shapiro, editors, *Proceedings of the Fifth International Conference on the Principles of Knowledge Representation and Reasoning (KR-96)*, pages 304–314, Cambridge, Mass., 1996. Morgan Kaufmann, San Francisco.

84. E. Grädel. On the restraining power of guards. *J. Symbolic Logic*, 1998. To appear.

85. E. Grädel, P. G. Kolaitis, and M. Y. Vardi. On the decision problem for two-variable first-order logic. *The Bulletin of Symbolic Logic*, 3(1):53–69, 1997.

86. E. Grädel, M. Otto, and E. Rosen. Two-variable logic with counting is decidable. In G. Winskel, editor, *Proceedings of the Twelfth Annual IEEE Symposium on Logic in Computer Science (LICS-97)*, pages 306–317, Warsaw, Poland, 1997. IEEE Computer Society Press.

87. V. Haarslev, C. Lutz, and R. Möller. Foundations of spatioterminological reasoning with description logics. In A. Cohn, L. Schubert, and S. Shapiro, editors, *Proceedings of the Sixth International Conference on Principles of Knowledge*

Representation and Reasoning (KR-98), pages 112–123, Trento, Italy, 1998. Morgan Kaufmann, San Francisco.

88. J. Y. Halpern and Y. Moses. A guide to completeness and complexity for modal logic of knowledge and belief. *Journal of Artificial Intelligence*, 54:319–379, 1992.

89. P. Hanschke. Specifying role interaction in concept languages. In B. Nebel, Ch. Rich, and W. Swartout, editors, *Proceedings of the 3rd International Conference on Principles of Knowledge Representation and Reasoning (KR-92)*, pages 318–329, Cambridge, Mass., 1992. Morgan Kaufmann, San Francisco.

90. P. Hanschke. *A Declarative Integration of Terminological, Constraint-based, Data-driven, and Goal-directed Reasoning*, volume 122 of *DISKI*. Infix, Sankt Augustin, Germany, 1996.

91. P. J. Hayes. In defence of logic. In *Proceedings of the 5th International Joint Conference on Artificial Intelligence, IJCAI'77*, pages 559–565, Cambridge, Mass., 1977.

92. P. J. Hayes. The logic of frames. In D. Mentzing, editor, *Frame Conceptions and Text Understanding*. Walter de Gruyter and Co., Berlin, Germany, 1979.

93. B. Hollunder. Hybrid inferences in KL-ONE-based knowledge representation systems. In *14th German Workshop on Artificial Intelligence*, volume 251 of *Informatik-Fachberichte*, pages 38–47, Ebingerfeld, Germany, 1990. Springer–Verlag.

94. B. Hollunder and F. Baader. Qualifying number restrictions in concept languages. In J. Allen, R. Fikes, and E. Sandewall, editors, *Proceedings of the 2nd International Conference on Principles of Knowledge Representation and Reasoning*, pages 335–346, Cambridge, Mass., 1991. Morgan Kaufmann, San Francisco.

95. B. Hollunder, W. Nutt, and M. Schmidt-Schauß. Subsumption algorithms for concept description languages. In L. C. Aiello, editor, *Proceedings of the 9th European Conference on Artificial Intelligence (ECAI-90)*, pages 348–353, Stockholm, Sweden, 1990. Pitman Publishing, London.

96. T. Hoppe, C. Kindermann, J. Quantz, A. Schmiedel, and M. Fischer. BACK V5: tutorial and manual. KIT Report 100, Technical University of Berlin, Berlin, Germany, 1993.

97. I. Horrocks. *Optimizing Tableaux Decision Procedures for Description Logics*. Ph.D. thesis, University of Manchester, Manchester, UK, 1997.

98. I. Horrocks. Using an expressive Description Logic: FaCT or fiction? In A. Cohn, L. Schubert, and S. Shapiro, editors, *Proceedings of the Sixth International Conference on Principles of Knowledge Representation and Reasoning (KR-98)*, pages 636–647, Trento, Italy, 1998. Morgan Kaufmann, San Francisco.

99. I. Horrocks and G. Gough. Description logics with transitive roles. In *Proceedings of the 1997 International Workshop on Description Logics (DL-97)*, pages 25–28, Gif sur Yvette, France, 1997. LRI, Université Paris-Sud.

100. I. Horrocks and P. F. Patel-Schneider. Optimising propositional modal satisfiability for description logic subsumption. In J. Calmet and J. Plaza, editors, *Proceedings of the International Conference on Artificial Intelligence and Symbolic Computation (AISC-98)*, volume 1476 of *Lecture Notes in Artificial Intelligence*, pages 234–246. Springer–Verlag, 1998.

101. I. Horrocks and U. Sattler. A description logic with transitive and converse roles and role hierarchies. In *Proceedings of the 1998 International Workshop on Description Logics (DL-98)*, pages 72–81, Povo - Trento, Italy, 1998. ITC-irst Report 9805-03.

102. G. E. Hughes and M. J. Cresswell. *A Companion to Modal Logic*. Methuen & Co., London, 1984.

103. U. Hustadt and R. A. Schmidt. On evaluating decision procedures for modal logics. In M. Pollack, editor, *Proceedings of the Fifteenth International Joint Conference on Artificial Intelligence (IJCAI'97)*, volume 1, pages 202–207. Morgan Kaufmann, 1997.

104. U. Hustadt and R. A. Schmidt. Simplification and backjumping in modal tableau. In H. Swart, editor, *Proceedings of TABLEAUX'98*, volume 1397 of *Lecture Notes in Computer Science*, pages 187–201. Springer–Verlag, 1998.

105. T. Imielinski. Results on translating defaults to circumscription. *Journal of Artificial Intelligence*, 32(1):131–146, 1987.

106. A. Kobsa. First experiences with the SB-ONE knowledge representation workbench in natural language applications. *SIGART Bulletin*, 2(3):70–76, 1991.

107. J. Koehler. An application of terminological logics to case-based reasoning. In J. Doyle, E. Sandewall, and P. Torasso, editors, *Proceedings of the Fourth International Conference on Principles of Knowledge Representation and Reasoning (KR-94)*, pages 351–362, Bonn, Germany, 1994. Morgan Kaufmann, San Francisco.

108. K. Konolige. On the relation between default and autoepistemic logic. *Journal of Artificial Intelligence*, 35(3):343–382, 1988.

109. K. Konolige. On the relation between circumscription and autoepistemic logic. In N. S. Sridharan, editor, *Proceedings of the 11th International Joint Conference on Artificial Intelligence, IJCAI-89*, pages 1213–1218, Detroit, MI, 1989. Morgan Kaufmann, San Francisco.

110. R. A. Kowalski. Logic for knowledge representation. In M. Joseph and R. Shyamasundar, editors, *Proceedings of the Fourth Conference on Foundations of Software Technology and Theoretical Computer Science*, pages 1–12, 1984.

111. S. Kraus, D. Lehmann, and M. Magidor. Nonmonotonic reasoning, preferential models and cumulative logics. *Journal of Artificial Intelligence*, 44(1–2):167–207, 1990.

112. R. Küsters. Characterizing the semantics of terminological cycles in $\mathcal{ALN}$ using finite automata. In A. Cohn, L. Schubert, and S. Shapiro, editors, *Proceedings of the Sixth International Conference on Principles of Knowledge Representation and Reasoning (KR-98)*, pages 499–510, Trento, Italy, 1998. Morgan Kaufmann, San Francisco.

113. A. Laux. Beliefs in multi-agent worlds: A terminological logics approach. In A. G. Cohn, editor, *Proceedings of the Eleventh European Conference on Artificial Intelligence (ECAI-94)*. John Wiley and Sons, 1994.

114. D. Lehmann. What a conditional knowledge base entails. In R. J. Brachman, editor, *Proceedings of the 1st International Conference on Principles of Knowledge Representation and Reasoning*, pages 212–222, Toronto, Ont., 1989.

115. H. J. Levesque and R. J. Brachman. Expressiveness and tractability in knowledge representation and reasoning. *Computational Intelligence*, 3:78–93, 1987.

116. A. Levy and M.-C. Rousset. Verification of knowledge bases based on containment checking. *Journal of Artificial Intelligence*, 101:227–256, 1998.

117. A. Levy and M.C. Rousset. CARIN: A representation language combining Horn rules and description logics. In W. Wahlster, editor, *Proceedings of the Twelfth European Conference on Artificial Intelligence (ECAI-96)*, pages 323–327. John Wiley & Sons Ltd, 1996.

118. V. Lifschitz. Between circumscription and autoepistemic logic. In R. J. Brachman, editor, *Proceedings of the 1st International Conference on Principles of Knowledge Representation and Reasoning*, pages 235–244, Toronto, Ont., 1989.

119. J. Lobo, J. Minker, and A. Rajasekar. *Foundations of Disjunctive Logic Programming.* MIT-Press, 1992.
120. W. Lukaszewicz. *Non-Monotonic Reasoning.* Ellis Horwood Series in Artificial Intelligence, 1991.
121. R. MacGregor. Inside the LOOM classifier. *SIGART Bulletin,* 2(3):88–92, 1991.
122. R. MacGregor and R. Bates. The LOOM knowledge representation language. Technical Report ISI/RS-87-188, University of Southern California, 1987.
123. D. Makinson. General theory of cumulative inference. In M. Reinfrank, J. de Kleer, M. L. Ginsberg, and E. Sandewall, editors, *Proceedings of the 2nd International Workshop on Non-monotonic Reasoning,* volume 346 of *Lecture Notes in Artificial Intelligence,* pages 1–18, Grassau, Germany, 1989. Springer-Verlag.
124. D. Makinson. General patterns in nonmonotonic reasoning. In D. M. Gabbay, C. J. Hogger, and J. A. Robinson, editors, *Handbook of Logic in Artificial Intelligence and Logic Programming, Vol. 3: Nonmonotonic and Uncertain Reasoning,* pages 35–110. Oxford University Press, Oxford, UK, 1994.
125. V. Marek, A. Nerode, and M. Truszczynski, editors. *Logic Programming and Nonmonotonic Reasoning, Third International Conference,* volume 928 of *Lecture Notes in Artificial Intelligence.* Springer-Verlag, 1995.
126. V. M. Marek and M. Truszczyński. *Nonmonotonic Logics; Context-Dependent Reasoning.* Springer-Verlag, Berlin-Heidelberg-New York, 1993.
127. E. Mays, C. Apté, J. Griesmer, and J. Kastner. Experience with K-Rep: An object-centered knowledge representation language. In *Proceedings of IEEE CAIA-88,* pages 62–67, 1988.
128. E. Mays, R. Dionne, and R. Weida. K-Rep system overview. *SIGART Bulletin,* 2(3):93–97, 1991.
129. J. McCarthy. Circumscription – A form of non-monotonic reasoning. *Journal of Artificial Intelligence,* 13(1–2):27–39, 1980.
130. J. McCarthy and P. J. Hayes. Some philosophical problems from the standpoint of AI. *Machine Intelligence,* 4:463–502, 1969. Reprinted in *Readings in Knowledge Representation,* R. J. Brachman and H. J. Levesque (editors), Morgan Kaufman, 1985.
131. D. McDermott. Nonmonotonic logic II: Nonmonotonic modal theories. *Journal of the ACM,* 29(1):33–57, 1982.
132. D. McDermott and J. Doyle. Non-monotonic logic I. *Journal of Artificial Intelligence,* 13(1–2):41–72, 1980.
133. D. L. McGuinness, L. Alperin Resnick, and C. Isbell. Description Logic in practice: A CLASSIC application. In *Proceedings of the 14th International Joint Conference on Artificial Intelligence, IJCAI'95,* pages 2045–2046, Montréal, Canada, 1995. Morgan Kaufmann, San Francisco. Video Presentation.
134. J. Minker. An overview of nonmonotonic reasoning and logic programming. *Journal of Logic Programming,* 17:95–126, 1993.
135. M. Minsky. A framework for representing knowledge. In P. Winston, editor, *The Psychology of Computer Vision.* McGraw-Hill, New York, 1975.
136. R. C. Moore. Semantical considerations on nonmonotonic logic. *Journal of Artificial Intelligence,* 25(1):75–94, 1985.
137. M. Mortimer. On languages with two variables. *Zeitschr. f. math. Logik und Grundlagen d. Math.,* 21:135–140, 1975.
138. B. C. Moszkowski. *Executing Temporal Logic Programs.* Cambridge University Press, Cambridge, UK, 1986.
139. B. Nebel. Computational complexity of terminological reasoning in BACK. *Journal of Artificial Intelligence,* 34(3):371–383, 1988.

140. B. Nebel. Terminological cycles: Semantics and computational properties. In J. Sowa, editor, *Principles of Semantic Networks*, pages 331–362. Morgan Kaufmann, San Francisco, 1989.

141. B. Nebel. *Reasoning and Revision in Hybrid Representation Systems*, volume 422 of *Lecture Notes in Computer Science*. Springer–Verlag, 1990.

142. B. Nebel. Terminological reasoning is inherently intractable. *Journal of Artificial Intelligence*, 43(2):235–249, 1990.

143. B. Nebel and K. von Luck. Hybrid reasoning in BACK. In Z. W. Ras and L. Saitta, editors, *Methodologies for Intelligent Systems*, volume 3, pages 260–269. North-Holland, 1988.

144. L. Pacholski, W. Szwast, and L. Tendera. Complexity of two-variable logic with counting. In G. Winskel, editor, *Proceedings of the Twelfth Annual IEEE Symposium on Logic in Computer Science (LICS-97)*, pages 318–327, Warsaw, Poland, 1997. IEEE Computer Society Press.

145. R. Parikh. Propositional dynamic logics of programs: A survey. In E. Engeler, editor, *Proceedings of the Workshop on Logic of Programs*, volume 125 of *LNCS*, pages 102–144, Zürich, Switzerland, 1979. Springer–Verlag.

146. P. F. Patel-Schneider. A four-valued semantics for terminological logics. *Journal of Artificial Intelligence*, 38(3):319–351, 1989.

147. P. F. Patel-Schneider. Undecidability of subsumption in NIKL. *Journal of Artificial Intelligence*, 39(2):263–272, 1989.

148. P. F. Patel-Schneider. DLP system description. In *Proceedings of the 1998 International Workshop on Description Logic (DL-98)*, pages 87–89, Trento, Italy, 1998. ITC-irst Report 9805-03.

149. C. Peltason. The BACK system – an overview. *SIGART Bulletin*, 2(3):114–119, 1991.

150. T. Przymusinski. Non-monotonic formalisms and logic programming. In *Proceedings of the 6th International Conference on Logic Programming*, pages 655–674, Cambridge, MA, 1989. MIT Press.

151. T. Przymusinski. Stable semantics for disjunctive programs. *New Generation Computing*, 9:401–424, 1991.

152. J. Quantz, G. Dunker, and V. Royer. Flexible inference strategies for DL systems. In *Proceedings of the 1994 International Workshop on Description Logic (DL-94)*, pages 27–30, Bonn, Germany, 1994. DFKI Document D-94-10, DFKI, Saarbrücken (Germany).

153. J. Quantz and V. Royer. A preference semantics for defaults in terminological logics. In B. Nebel, Ch. Rich, and W. Swartout, editors, *Proceedings of the 3rd International Conference on Principles of Knowledge Representation and Reasoning (KR-92)*, pages 294–305, Cambridge, Mass., 1992. Morgan Kaufmann, San Francisco.

154. J. Quantz and B. Schmitz. Knowledge-based disambiguation for machine translation. *Minds and Machines*, 4:39–57, 1994.

155. M. Quillian. Semantic memory. In M. Minsky, editor, *Semantic Information Processing*, pages 216–270. MIT Press, Cambridge, Mass., 1968.

156. R. Reiter. On closed world data bases. In *Logic and Data Bases*, pages 55–76. Plenum Press, New York, 1978.

157. Raymond Reiter. A logic for default reasoning. *Journal of Artificial Intelligence*, 13:81–132, 1980.

158. N. Rychtyckyj. DLMS: An evaluation of KL-ONE in the automobile industry. In L. C. Aiello, J. Doyle, and S. Shapiro, editors, *Proceedings of the Fifth International Conference on Principles of Knowledge Representation and Reasoning*

(KR-96), pages 588–596, Cambridge, Mass., 1996. Morgan Kaufmann, San Francisco.

159. U. Sattler. A concept language extended with different kinds of transitive roles. In G. Görz and S. Hölldobler, editors, *20. Deutsche Jahrestagung für Künstliche Intelligenz, KI'97*, volume 1137 of *Lecture Notes in Artificial Intelligence*. Springer-Verlag, 1996.

160. A. Schaerf. On the complexity of the instance checking problem in concept languages with existential quantification. *Journal of Intelligent Information Systems*, 2:265–278, 1993.

161. K. Schild. A correspondence theory for terminological logics: Preliminary report. In J. Mylopoulos and R. Reiter, editors, *Proceedings of the 12th International Joint Conference on Artificial Intelligence*, pages 466–471, Sydney, Australia, 1991. Morgan Kaufmann, San Francisco.

162. K. Schild. Combining terminological logics with tense logic. In M. Filgueiras and L. Damas, editors, *Progress in Artificial Intelligence – 6th Portuguese Conference on Artificial Intelligence, EPIA'93*, Lecture Notes in Artificial Intelligence, pages 105–120, Porto, Portugal, 1993. Springer-Verlag.

163. K. Schild. Terminological cycles and the propositional μ-calculus. In J. Doyle, E. Sandewall, and P. Torasso, editors, *Proceedings of the Fourth International Conference on Principles of Knowledge Representation and Reasoning (KR'94)*, pages 509–520, Bonn, Germany, 1994. Morgan Kaufmann, San Francisco.

164. R. A. Schmidt. Resolution is a decision procedure for many propositional modal logics. In M. Kracht, M. de Rijke, H. Wansing, and M. Zakharyaschev, editors, *Advances in Modal Logic*, volume 87 of *CSLI Lecture Notes*, pages 189–208. CSLI Publications, Stanford, Cal., 1998.

165. M. Schmidt-Schauß. Subsumption in KL-ONE is undecidable. In R. J. Brachman, editor, *Proceedings of the 1st International Conference on Principles of Knowledge Representation and Reasoning*, pages 421–431, Toronto, Ont., 1989. Morgan Kaufmann, San Francisco.

166. M. Schmidt-Schauß and G. Smolka. Attributive concept descriptions with complements. *Journal of Artificial Intelligence*, 47:1–26, 1991.

167. L. K. Schubert, R. G. Goebel, and N. J. Cercone. The structure and organization of a semantic net for comprehension and inference. In N. V. Findler, editor, *Associative Networks: Representation and Use of Knowledge by Computers*, pages 121–175. Academic Press, 1979.

168. J. C. Shepherdson. Negation as failure: A comparison of Clark's completed database and Reiter's closed world assumption. *J. Logic Programming*, 1(15):51–79, 1984.

169. Y. Shoham. A semantical approach to nonmonotonic logics. In *IEEE Symposium on Logic in Computer Science*, pages 275–279, Ithaca, N.Y., 1987.

170. R. M. Smullyan. *First-Order Logic*, volume 43 of *Ergebnisse der Mathematik und ihrer Grenzgebiete*. Springer-Verlag, Berlin, Heidelberg, New York, 1968.

171. C. Stirling. Modal and temporal logic. In S. Abramsky, D. M. Gabbay, and T. S. E. Maibaum, editors, *Handbook of Logic in Computer Science, Vol. 2*. Oxford University Press, Oxford, UK, 1993.

172. W. van der Hoek and M. de Rijke. Counting objects. *J. Logic and Computation*, 5(3):325–345, 1995.

173. A. van Gelder, K. A. Ross, and J. S. Schlipf. The well-founded semantics for general logic programs. *Journal of the ACM*, 38:620–650, 1991.

174. M. Y. Vardi and P. Wolper. Automata-theoretic techniques for modal logic of programs. *Journal of Computer and System Sciences*, 32:183–221, 1986.

175. F. Wolter and M. Zakharyaschev. Satisfiability problems in description logics with modal operators. In A. Cohn, L. Schubert, and S. Shapiro, editors, *Proceedings of the Sixth International Conference on Principles of Knowledge Representation and Reasoning (KR-98)*, pages 512–523, Trento, Italy, 1998. Morgan Kaufmann, San Francisco.

176. W. A. Woods. What's in a link: foundations for semantic networks. In D. G. Bobrow and A. M. Collins, editors, *Representation and Understanding: Studies in Cognitive Science*, pages 35–82. Academic Press, London, 1975.

177. W. A. Woods and J. G. Schmolze. The KL-ONE family. *Computers and Mathematics with Applications*, 23(2–5):133–177, 1992.

178. J. R. Wright, E. S. Weixelbaum, K. Brown, G. T. Vesonder, S. R. Palmer, J. I. Berman, and H. H. Moore. A knowledge-based configurator that supports sales, engineering, and manufacturing at AT&T network systems. *AI Magazine*, 14(3):69–80, 1993.

A Taxonomy of Theorem-Proving Strategies

Maria Paola Bonacina *

Department of Computer Science
The University of Iowa
Iowa City, IA 52242-1419, USA
E-mail: bonacina@cs.uiowa.edu

Abstract. This article presents a taxonomy of strategies for fully-automated general-purpose first-order theorem proving. It covers forward-reasoning ordering-based strategies and backward-reasoning subgoal-reduction strategies, which do not appear together often. Unlike traditional presentations that emphasize logical inferences, this classification strives to give equal weight to the inference and search components of theorem proving, which are equally important in practice. For this purpose, a formal notion of search plan is given and shown to apply to all classes of strategies. For each class, the form of derivation is specified, and it is shown how inference system and search plan cooperate to generate it.

1 Introduction

The objective of fully-automated theorem proving is to have computer programs that, given a collection of assumptions H and a conjecture φ, determine whether φ is a logical consequence of H (in symbols, whether $H \models \varphi$). Assumptions and conjecture need to be written in some language; let Θ be a first-order signature, providing symbols for variables, constants, functions and predicates; for now, let $\mathcal{L}_\Theta$ denote ambiguously a Θ-language of sentences, or clauses, or equations, depending on the problem, and $\mathcal{P}(\mathcal{L}_\Theta)$ its powerset. The theorem-proving approach to the problem is to try to show that there is a *proof* of φ from H (in symbols, $H \vdash \varphi$, or, refutationally, that there is a proof of a contradiction from $H \cup \{\neg\varphi\}$, i.e., $H \cup \{\neg\varphi\} \vdash \bot$), or disprove φ by exhibiting a *model* of $H \cup \{\neg\varphi\}$. A proof is a sequence[1] of statements in $\mathcal{L}_\Theta$ logically connected by applications of *inference rules*, that is, rules in the form:

$$f: \frac{\psi_1 \dots \psi_n}{\psi}$$

which says that the inference rule named f, if given premises in the form $\psi_1 \dots \psi_n$, infers a consequence in the form ψ. For example, *binary clausal resolution* is defined as

---

* Supported in part by the National Science Foundation with grant CCR-97-01508.
[1] Proofs are read sequentially also when they are presented as trees or graphs.

$$\frac{L_1 \vee D, L_2 \vee C}{(C \vee D)\sigma} \quad L_1\sigma = \neg L_2\sigma \quad (\sigma \text{ most general unifier})$$

where L_1 and L_2 are literals and C and D are disjunctions of literals. As another example, the *T-rule for conjunction* in analytic tableaux[2] with signed formulae is defined as

$$\frac{TA \wedge B}{TA, \, TB}$$

where A and B are sentences and T is the sign for true.

In order to make sure that once a proof has been obtained, it really means that $H \models \varphi$, one needs to check that the inference rules are *sound*: the generic inference rule f above is sound if for all interpretations $\mathcal{I}$ of Θ, that is, for all ways to give meaning to the predicates, functions and constants in Θ, if $\mathcal{I}$ satisfies $\{\psi_1 \ldots \psi_n\}$, then $\mathcal{I}$ satisfies ψ. Symmetrically, one wishes that whenever $H \models \varphi$, the inference rules are sufficiently strong to ensure that there is a proof of φ from H: a set of inference rules – or *inference system* – with this property is said to be *complete*. Since most inference systems for mechanical theorem proving work refutationally rather than directly, the requirement is that whenever $H \models \varphi$, there is a proof of $\perp$ from $H \cup \{\neg\varphi\}$, or the system is *refutationally complete*.

The availability of a sound and complete inference system guarantees the existence of a proof. It remains the problem of how to compute one. The initial state of a proof attempt contains H and $\neg\varphi$, and the application of an inference rule to this state produces a new state. Thus, the problem can be seen in the terms, familiar to Artificial Intelligence, of a *search problem*, with the inference rules as *transformation rules*, or *production rules*, *states* containing partial proofs, *successful states* containing complete proofs, and a *search plan* – or *computation rule* in terminology influenced by logic programming – controlling the search.

Let *States* denote, ambiguously, for now, the set of all possible states. Given a set of inference rules I, a search plan Σ is made of at least three components:

- A *rule-selecting function* $\zeta: States^* \to I$, which selects the next rule to be applied based on the history of the search so far;
- A *premise-selecting function* $\xi: States^* \to \mathcal{P}(\mathcal{L}_\Theta)$, which selects the elements of the current state the inference rule should be applied to;
- A *termination-detecting function* $\omega: States \to Bool$, which returns *true* if the given state is successful, *false* otherwise.

If the current state is not successful, ζ selects rule f and ξ selects premises $\psi_1 \ldots \psi_n$, the next step will consist of inferring ψ from $\psi_1 \ldots \psi_n$. The sequence of states thus generated forms the *derivation* by I controlled by Σ from the given input. A derivation is *successful* if it terminates in a successful state.

---

[2] Analytic tableaux are a form of semantic tableaux: see [126] for an introduction.

It is important to appreciate that given an initial state with H and $\neg\varphi$, there are many derivations that an inference system I can generate from the initial state. In this sense, an inference system is *non-deterministic*. If I is coupled with a search plan Σ, there is one and only one derivation generated by I and Σ from the initial state. The combination of inference system and search plan forms a deterministic procedure called a *theorem-proving strategy*. While the inference system is required to be sound and refutationally complete, a search plan is expected to be *fair*: if there are proofs, or, equivalently, if there are successful states in the search space, one will be generated eventually.

In summary, a *theorem-proving problem* has the form $S = H \cup \{\neg\varphi\}$, where φ is called the *target theorem* and $\neg\varphi$ is called the *goal*; a *theorem-proving strategy* C is specified by an inference system and a search plan, $C = \langle I, \Sigma \rangle$. If I is refutationally complete, whenever $H \models \varphi$, there exist proofs $H \cup \{\neg\varphi\} \vdash_I \bot$, and if Σ is fair, the unique derivation driven by Σ will generate one of these proofs.

There are many ways to classify theorem-proving strategies. From a proof-theoretical point of view, one may question whether the strategy is *analytic* (i.e., it only generates formulae that are subformulae of $H \supset \varphi$) or *generative* (i.e., not analytic). From the point of view of the language and its expressive power, one may be interested in whether the strategy works with equations, clauses, or sentences. From the point of view of the logic and its applicability, one may consider whether the strategy works for propositional logic, Horn logic, or first-order logic. The point of view of this taxonomy is to give a classification of strategies based on *how they search*.

A classification key for this purpose is to observe whether the strategy works from the assumptions – called *forward reasoning*, *forward chaining* or *bottom-up* reasoning – or from the goal – called *backward reasoning*, *backward chaining* or *top-down* reasoning. Since finding a proof generally requires some combination of the two, *forward-reasoning strategies* are strategies that work primarily, not exclusively, by forward reasoning, and *backward-reasoning strategies* are defined dually. This criterion alone, however, may not be sufficient. First, different strategies may not have the same notion of what is the goal: for instance, in resolution, $\neg\varphi$ is the goal, but in analytic tableaux one may consider the whole $\neg(H \supset \varphi)$ as the goal. Second, the same feature of a strategy can be used for either type of reasoning. For instance, in a strategy with set of support, one can get a backward-reasoning behaviour by putting in the set of support the goal clauses (i.e., those originated from the transformation of the goal into clausal form), and a forward-reasoning behaviour by putting in the set of support clauses originated from the transformation of the assumptions. Therefore, the distinction between forward and backward reasoning will be used in the following, but it will not be the only key.

The primary key will be to distinguish between those strategies that work on a set of objects (e.g., clauses) and develop implicitly many proof attempts, and those strategies that work on one object at a time (e.g., a goal clause, or a tableau) and develop one proof attempt at a time, backtracking when the current proof attempt cannot be completed into a proof. The strategies of the first type, on the other hand, never backtrack, because whatever they do may further one of the proof attempts. While other names may be chosen to emphasize other features, strategies in the first group will be called here *ordering-based strategies*, to emphasize that exactly because they work with a set of objects, they can use a *well-founded ordering* to order them, and possibly *delete* objects that are greater than and entailed by others. Thus, these strategies work by generating objects, *expanding* the set, and deleting objects, *contracting* the set. Since the set typically grow very large, they may employ *indexing techniques* to retrieve objects, and *eager-contraction* search plans to control the growth. Ordering-based strategies with an eager-contraction search plan are called *contraction-based strategies*. The strategies resulting from the merging of the resolution-paramodulation paradigm with the term-rewriting and Knuth-Bendix paradigm, as well as strategies based on generating instances instead of resolvents, belong to this class[3]. Theorem provers based on these strategies include Otter [97], RRL [76], Reveal [3], SNARK [134], EQP [98], Barcelona [104], CLIN-S [47], SPASS [142], Gandalf [137], OSHL [114], and daTac [138].

The strategies of the second type will be called *subgoal-reduction strategies*, because if one considers the single object they work on as the goal, each step consists in reducing the goal to subgoals. Since they do not generate a set of objects, subgoal-reduction strategies do not use an ordering to sort it, neither can they use an object to delete another one. Because they need backtracking, a typical choice of search plan is *depth-first search with iterative deepening*. Tableaux-based strategies, model elimination, linear resolution, and problem reduction format methods belong to this class. Theorem provers implementing these strategies include Setheo [87, 64], METEOR [4], Protein [17], TAP [23, 22] and Tatzelwurm [29]. More provers of both types can be found in the system descriptions in the CADE proceedings [123, 92, 135, 77, 41, 101, 100] and in [136].

Note that the notion of goal in "subgoal-reduction" does not necessarily coincide with the notion of goal based on the interpretation of the problem. For instance, model elimination can start with any input clause as the first goal, although it is natural to start with a goal clause. This, together with the above observation about strategies with set of support, which are ordering-based strategies, shows that it is not necessarily the case that ordering-based strategies do forward reasoning, and subgoal-reduction strategies do backward reasoning. However, most ordering-based strategies are forward-reasoning strategies, and most subgoal-reduction strategies are backward-reasoning strategies. Similarly, it is not necessarily the case that subgoal-reduction strategies work with tableaux and ordering-based strategies work with clauses, although this is true for many strategies. For instance, linear resolution strategies are subgoal-reduction strategies that work with clauses, and the disjunctive positive model elimination with subsumption of [16] is an example of an ordering-based strategy that works with

---

[3] E.g., a strategy that features only resolution is an ordering-based strategy with an empty ordering.

tableaux. Thus, the essential criterion to separate the strategies is the nature of the search. Table 1 summarizes these points.

	Ordering-based	Subgoal-reduction
data	set of objects	one goal-object at a time
proof attempts built	many implicitly	one at a time
backtracking	No	Yes
contraction	Yes	No

Table 1. Two main classes of strategies

The following sections cover first ordering-based strategies and their subclasses, and then subgoal-reduction strategies and their subclasses.

1.1 Remarks and further reading

Classical books in theorem proving are Chang and Lee [45], Loveland [91] and Bibel [28], while recent books include [24, 85, 128]. Wos et al. [145] emphasize experimentation with theorem provers. Books in logic useful for theorem proving include Smullyan [126], Gallier [63], Ramsay [115], and Fitting [60], while a classical reference for search in AI is Pearl [106].

Collections of research articles in theorem proving and related topics include [122], which makes early classical papers (1957-1970) available, and [83, 40, 62], while [27] emphasizes applications. A major forum for the presentation of results in theorem proving is CADE – the International Conference on Automated Deduction: recent issues are [123, 92, 135, 77, 41, 101, 100].

The inference+search paradigm may be as old as theorem proving itself; Kowalski emphasized search in theorem proving in [81]. The formalization of the inference+search paradigm and the taxonomy of strategies in this paper organize, improve and extend elements appeared in [36, 37, 35, 38, 39, 32]. This paper considers only sequential strategies: an extension to parallel and distributed strategies, continuing the work begun in [35], will be a subject of future work.

2 Ordering-based strategies

Since most ordering-based strategies work with clauses, in this section $\mathcal{L}_\Theta$ is the language of clauses on signature Θ and $\bot$ is the empty clause $\Box$. If $H \cup \{\neg\varphi\}$ is not already in clausal form, each element in $H \cup \{\neg\varphi\}$ is transformed into a set of clauses, whose union S is the clausal form of the theorem-proving problem (e.g., [45] for this transformation). The goal $\neg\varphi$ is considered as an additional assumption, and most ordering-based strategies do not distinguish the clauses coming from $\neg\varphi$ from those coming from H.

2.1 Inference systems for ordering-based strategies

Inference rules for ordering-based strategies operate on *sets*:

$$f\colon \frac{S}{S'}$$

where S and S' are sets of clauses. For instance, binary resolution is written

$$\frac{S \cup \{L_1 \vee D, L_2 \vee C\}}{S \cup \{L_1 \vee D, L_2 \vee C, (C \vee D)\sigma\}} \quad L_1\sigma = \neg L_2\sigma \quad (\sigma \text{ most general unifier})$$

Exactly because generated data are kept, it is possible to use them to establish that other generated data are not needed. What is not needed is determined by a *well-founded ordering* on clauses $\succ$: intuitively, if a clause φ is entailed by one or more smaller clauses, φ can be deleted. Thus, ordering-based strategies have two types of inference rules:

– *Expansion inference rules*, that generate and add clauses:

$$f\colon \frac{S}{S'} \; S \subset S'$$

where the condition $S \subset S'$ tells that something has been added, and implies $S \prec_{mul} S'$, where $\succ_{mul}$ is the multiset extension of $\succ$.
– *Contraction inference rules*, that delete clauses or replace them by smaller ones:

$$f\colon \frac{S}{S'} \; S \nsubseteq S'$$

where the condition $S \nsubseteq S'$ tells that something has been deleted; furthermore, $S' \prec_{mul} S$ needs to hold.

With this formulation of inference rules, the *soundness* requirement is written $Th(S') \subseteq Th(S)$, where $Th(S) = \{\varphi \mid S \models \varphi\}$, which means that whatever is added is a logical consequence of what was given. Since there are inference rules that delete elements, one needs also the dual property of *monotonicity*: $Th(S) \subseteq Th(S')$, which means that all theorems are preserved.

The ordering $\succ$ is fundamental for these strategies. In addition to being well-founded, it needs to be *monotonic* with respect to the term structure (i.e., $s \succ t$ implies $c[s] \succ c[t]$ for all terms s, t, c) and *stable* with respect to substitutions (i.e., $s \succ t$ implies $s\sigma \succ t\sigma$ for all substitutions σ). An ordering with these three properties is a *reduction ordering*. A *simplification ordering* has monotonicity, stability and the *subterm property* (i.e., a term is greater than any of its proper subterms), which together imply well-foundedness [52]. *Complete simplification orderings* – introduced in [69] – are also total on ground terms. Since complete simplification orderings are used most frequently, let $\succ$ be such an ordering. Once an ordering on terms and literals is given, it can be extended to equations and clauses in standard ways based on the multiset extension (e.g., [70, 12]).

In addition to *resolution*[4] [118], *paramodulation* (on clauses) [116, 70], and *superposition* (on rewrite rules [79] or equations [69, 10]) are expansion inference rules. Contraction rules include *tautology deletion*, *purity deletion* [50, 38], *subsumption* [118], *clausal simplification* (also called *unit simplification* or *unit deletion*, because a unit clause simplifies another clause), *functional subsumption* [69], and *simplification* [143, 79, 69, 10, 119]:

$$\frac{S \cup \{p \simeq q, L \vee D\}}{S \cup \{p \simeq q, L[q\sigma]_u \vee D\}} \quad L|u = p\sigma \ \wedge \ L \succ L[q\sigma]_u$$

where $L|u$ denotes the subterm of L at position u and $L[q\sigma]_u$ denotes the literal obtained by replacing $L|u$ by $q\sigma$.

In order to describe unambiguously how a strategy generates a derivation, inference rules can be characterized as functions $f: \mathcal{P}(\mathcal{L}_\Theta) \to \mathcal{P}(\mathcal{L}_\Theta) \times \mathcal{P}(\mathcal{L}_\Theta)$, which take as argument a set of premises, and return a pair of sets, a set of generated clauses and a set of clauses to be deleted[5]. If f does not apply to a set X, $f(X) = (\emptyset, \emptyset)$. Let π_1 and π_2 be the projection functions $\pi_1(x, y) = x$ and $\pi_2(x, y) = y$; then expansion and contraction rules (with respect to $\succ$) can be described in this form as follows:

– An inference rule f is an *expansion inference rule* if for all X, $\pi_2(f(X)) = \emptyset$.
– An inference rule f is a *contraction inference rule* if either $\pi_1(f(X)) = \pi_2(f(X)) = \emptyset$, or $\pi_2(f(X)) \neq \emptyset$ and $X - \pi_2(f(X)) \cup \pi_1(f(X)) \prec_{mul} X$.

Most inference rules generate and/or delete one clause at each application, so that $\pi_1(f(X))$ and $\pi_2(f(X))$ are singletons. In the following the same notation is used ambiguously to denote both the set and the single element it contains. The condition $X \models \pi_1(f(X))$ implies soundness, while $X - \pi_2(f(X)) \cup \pi_1(f(X)) \models \pi_2(f(X))$ implies monotonicity.

Contraction does more than deleting existing clauses. By deleting existing clauses, it also prevents the strategy from using those clauses to generate others. In order to understand better this deeper effect of contraction, the notion of *redundancy*, whereby clauses deleted by contraction are redundant, was developed (e.g., [119, 127, 12, 36]). The advantages of working with a notion of redundancy are several. First, not only clauses deleted by contraction are redundant, but also clauses that can be generated only by redundant clauses. Second, redundancy can be generalized from clauses to inferences, observing that an inference step that uses a redundant clause without deleting it is redundant. Third, restrictions to expansion inference rules such as *ordered inference rules* (e.g., [70, 12, 105]), *critical pair criteria* (e.g., [9, 73]), and *basic inferences* (e.g., [14]), can be explained as preventing the expansion rules from generating redundant clauses. Thus, the design of contraction rules to delete redundant clauses and the design of refinements of expansion rules to prevent the generation of redundant clauses are two sides of the same effort to contain redundancy.

---

[4] Here and in the rest of the paper resolution include factoring.
[5] In the notation, $\mathcal{P}(\ )$ means powerset, and if $X = \{\psi_1 \ldots \psi_n\}$ we may write $f(X)$ or $f(\psi_1, \ldots, \psi_n)$ instead of $f(\{\psi_1, \ldots, \psi_n\})$.

Redundancy depends on the well-founded ordering on clauses: like selecting different orderings may yield different contraction rules, selecting different orderings may yield different *redundancy criteria* [11]. A *redundancy criterion* is a mapping R on sets of clauses, such that $R(S)$ is the set of clauses that are redundant with respect to S according to R, and the following properties are satisfied: (1) $S - R(S) \models R(S)$, (2) if $S \subseteq S'$, then $R(S) \subseteq R(S')$, (3) if $(S' - S) \subseteq R(S')$, then $R(S') \subseteq R(S)$ [11].

A redundancy criterion R and a set of contraction rules I *correspond* if they are based on the same well-founded ordering $\succ$, and for all sets of clauses S:

- Whatever is deleted by I is redundant according to R: for all $f \in I$ and $X \in \mathcal{P}(S)$, $\pi_2(f(X)) \subseteq R(X - \pi_2(f(X)) \cup \pi_1(f(X)))$.
- If a clause in S is redundant with respect to S, I can delete it with no need to add other clauses (to make it redundant): for all $\varphi \in S \cap R(S - \{\varphi\})$, there exist $f \in I$ and $X \in \mathcal{P}(S)$, such that $\pi_1(f(X)) = \emptyset$ and $\pi_2(f(X)) = \{\varphi\}$.

Given an inference system I, I_E denotes the subset of expansion rules, and I_R denotes the subset of contraction rules, with R the corresponding redundancy criterion. The first property of redundancy criteria serves the purpose of implying that if $S \vdash_{I_R} S'$ then $Th(S) \subseteq Th(S')$, and it is equivalent in this respect to the condition $X - \pi_2(f(X)) \cup \pi_1(f(X)) \models \pi_2(f(X))$ formulated for all contraction rules in I_R. The second and third properties of redundancy criteria guarantee that $S \vdash_I S'$ implies $R(S) \subseteq R(S')$.

Redundancy control is fundamental for ordering-based strategies, exactly because they work by generating and keeping consequences. In first-order theorem proving, the search space of consequences that can be generated from a given $H \cup \{\neg\varphi\}$ is typically infinite: a strategy that searches this space by generating clauses without the possibility of deleting/avoiding redundant ones is not practical. In summary, ordering-based strategies need redundancy control, and at the same time they make it possible (e.g., one cannot use clauses to delete other clauses if clauses are not kept in the first place).

Remarks and further reading Much research on ordering-based strategies originated from works in *rewriting, orderings,* and *Knuth-Bendix completion*: a comprehensive treatment of this area can be found in [55], while theorem-proving oriented surveys include [111, 57, 108].

The essential role of orderings for these strategies can be appreciated by considering the history of *simplification, paramodulation* and *ordered resolution*. Simplification was introduced as *demodulation* in [144], but without a well-founded ordering to guarantee termination one had to impose a maximum number of rewriting steps. Paramodulation was introduced in [116], but the completeness proof required the functionally reflexive axioms and paramodulating into variables. The conjecture of [116] that these requirements are not necessary was proved in [107], but only postulating an ordering with a very rare property (order-isomorphism to ω), and finally in [70], with a complete simplification ordering as the fundamental ingredient. Ordered resolution is almost as old as resolution itself: the early research is summarized in [70], where prior references can be found. The main difference between the early formulations and the contemporary ones is the ordering on literals: the former treated clauses as lists, so that the ordering was arbitrary, whereas the latter use a complete simplification ordering. Further developments are treated in [13]; the references to previous work on *basic narrowing* and *basic paramodulation* can be found in [14].

While most ordering-based strategies work on clauses, the strategies that work with rewrite rules or equations in the *Boolean ring* [67] also belong to this class: their key characteristics include the uniqueness of normal forms in the Boolean ring representation, and simplification inferences that cannot be simulated by resolution and subsumption (see [102] for this comparison). These strategies began with the *N-strategy* of [67] and the *Gröbner basis method* of [74]. The strategy of [8] continued in the spirit of [74], while the N-strategy was extended to first-order logic with equality in [68], and to non-clausal input in [147]. Other developments can be found in [102], together with a comparison with clausal resolution methods continuing [56].

Other directions of growth for these inference systems have been *theory reasoning* and *constrained reasoning*. Theory resolution was pioneered in [131], while a recent overview of theory reasoning is available in Chapter 4 of [15]. In equational logic forms of theory reasoning may be obtained by replacing syntactic unification in the inference rules with semantic unification: two surveys of this large field are [72, 7]. Ordering-based strategies with constraints were studied in [78], where references to previous work can be found. A general treatment of constrained resolution was given in [42].

The RAMC method [44] and its successor EQMC [43] also work with constrained clauses. These methods combine searching for a refutation by generating consequences with searching for a model by generating *non-consequences*: if S were consistent, the fact that $S \not\models \psi$ means that there exists a model of S where ψ is false and $\neg\psi$ true, and therefore generating ψ is a step towards identifying such a model if it exists. The search for a refutation employs expansion rules, such as resolution, and contraction rules, such as subsumption, similar to other ordering-based strategies, while the search for a model employs dual *dis-inference rules* (e.g., dis-resolution, dis-subsumption), case analysis by splitting, generation of pure literals, and equational constraints to encode models.

2.2   Search plans for ordering-based strategies

Since ordering-based strategies work on sets of clauses, and multisets need to be used in order to apply the ordering, for these strategies *States* is the set of all multisets of $\mathcal{L}_\Theta$. The general notion of search plan given in Section 1 can be instantiated to a tuple $\Sigma = \langle \zeta, \xi_1, \xi_2, \omega \rangle$ where:

- $\xi_1 : States^* \to \mathcal{L}_\Theta$ selects a *primary premise* from the current state:
  $\xi_1((S_0 \ldots S_i)) = \psi_1 \in S_i$;
- $\zeta : States^* \times \mathcal{L}_\Theta \to I$ selects an inference rule, based on the history and the primary premise: $\zeta((S_0 \ldots S_i), \psi_1) = f^n \in I$;

- $\xi_2: States^* \times \mathcal{L}_\Theta \times I \to \mathcal{P}(\mathcal{L}_\Theta)$ selects one or more *secondary premises*, depending on the arity of the inference rule that ζ selected:
  $\xi_2((S_0 \ldots S_i), \psi_1, f^n) = \{\psi_2 \ldots \psi_n\} \subseteq S_i$;
- $\omega: States \to Bool$ returns *true* if and only if the given state contains the empty clause.

For example, if ξ_1 selects a clause ψ, and ζ selects a binary expansion rule, ξ_2 selects a second clause; if ζ selects simplification (normalization), ξ_2 selects the simplifier(s) to reduce ψ.

Concrete search plans may fit in this pattern in various ways. Consider the *given-clause algorithm* of Otter [97]: it works with a list of clauses to be selected, called **sos** for historical reasons (the Set of Support strategy of [143]), and a list of clauses already selected, called **usable**, because these clauses can be used for inferences. It selects a given clause from **sos**, makes all expansion inferences between the given clause and the clauses in **usable**, process and appends to **sos** the non-trivial normal forms of all clauses thus generated, moves the given clause from **sos** to **usable**, and repeats. Then ξ_1 is the mechanism that selects the given clause, ζ represents the order of the expansion rules in the code of the prover, and ξ_2 is the mechanism that selects the other premises from **usable**.

In the default configuration of Otter, the next given clause is the shortest clause in **sos**. Thus, ξ_1 performs a *best-first search*, with the length of the clause as heuristic evaluation function. Changing the heuristic evaluation function amounts to modifying the component ξ_1 of the search plan. For instance, Otter has a parameter, called *pick-given-ratio*, which allows one to to add some breadth-first search: if the value of *pick-given-ratio* is k, ξ_1 selects the oldest clause in **sos** (instead of the shortest) every k choices. The selection of suitable premises from **usable** is done by an *indexing technique* [133, 95, 46]. Then ξ_2 is the abstraction of the indexing technique, and choosing a different indexing technique amounts to changing the component ξ_2 of the search plan.

The equational prover EQP [98], which solved the Robbins conjecture [99], features search plans based on the given-clause algorithm, and search plans based on another algorithm, called the *pair algorithm*. This search plan works on an index of all possible pairs of equations in the database: it selects a pair from the index, performs all expansion inferences between the equations in the pair, if at least one of them belongs to **sos**, and repeats. Then there is no ξ_1, and ξ_2 is the mechanism that selects the next pair.

For the control of contraction, one needs to distinguish between *forward contraction*, which normalizes a newly generated clause with respect to the existing clauses, and *backward contraction*, which applies the normal form of a newly generated clause to reduce the existing clauses. For forward contraction, ξ_1 returns the newly generated clause, say ψ, ζ corresponds to the order of the contraction rules in the code of the prover, and ξ_2 to the indexing mechanism that selects the simplifers that match ψ. For backward contraction, ξ_2 corresponds to the indexing mechanism that selects the clauses matched by ψ.

It is possible to abstract from the relation between selection of the inference rule and selection of the premises, and use $\zeta: States^* \to I$ and $\xi: States^* \times I \to$

$\mathcal{P}(\mathcal{L}_\Theta)$, with the condition that $\xi((S_0\ldots S_i), f^n) = \{\psi_1\ldots\psi_n\}$ if and only if $\xi_1((S_0\ldots S_i)) = \psi_1$ and $\xi_2((S_0\ldots S_i), x_1, f^n) = \{\psi_2\ldots\psi_n\}$.

Given a theorem-proving problem S, an ordering-based strategy $\mathcal{C} = \langle I, \Sigma\rangle$, with $\Sigma = <\zeta, \xi, \omega>$, generates the *derivation*

$$S_0 \underset{\mathcal{C}}{\vdash} \ldots S_i \underset{\mathcal{C}}{\vdash} \ldots$$

where $S_0 = S$ and for all $i \geq 0$, if $\omega(S_i) = \textit{false}$, $\zeta((S_0\ldots S_i)) = f$, and $\xi((S_0\ldots S_i), f) = X$, then $S_{i+1} = S_i \cup \pi_1(f(X)) - \pi_2(f(X))$. An equivalent characterization can be given using ξ_1 and ξ_2.

Remarks and further reading Most theorem-proving search plans exist only in the code of theorem provers, with specifications in natural language in manuals or system descriptions. A definition of search plan was given by Kowalski in [81]: it was defined directly on the search space of resolution, and therefore did not account for the generation of the derivation. The definition given here allows to fit in concrete search plans; it is a refinement of the definition in [37], improved in [39, 32], which was the first one to account for the derivation in the context of general expansion and contraction.

The distinction between forward and backward subsumption was made when several authors working towards proving the completeness of resolution with subsumption discovered that unrestricted backward subsumption of variants can violate completeness: the solution was to perform forward subsumption before backward subsumption; Kowalski summarized this early work in the introduction of [81]. The problem was better understood later, when it was clarified that the difficulty is that the subsumption ordering is not well-founded. The solution is to label the clauses based on generation time and use a well-founded ordering given by the lexicographic combination of the proper subsumption ordering and a well-founded ordering on the labels of clauses, so that newly generated variants are forward-subsumed before they can back-subsume; Loveland presents problem and solution on pages 207–208 of [91]. An analysis and solutions of problems of the same nature with subsumption in distributed derivations can be found in [34]. McCune distinguishes between forward and backward subsumption, and forward and backward demodulation in the code of Otter [97] and EQP [98]; the distinction was generalized to any kind of contraction in [35].

2.3   Search spaces and proofs by ordering-based strategies

The *search space* of a theorem-proving problem S contains all the clauses that can be derived from S by using the inference system I: the *closure* of S with respect to I is the set $S_I^* = \bigcup_{k\geq 0} I^k(S)$, where $I(S) = S \cup \{\varphi|\ \varphi \in \pi_1(f(X)),\ f \in I,\ X \subseteq S\}$, $I^0(S) = S$, and for $k \geq 1$, $I^k(S) = I(I^{k-1}(S))$ for $k \geq 1$.

This search space can be modelled as a *search graph*, a hypergraph $G(S_I^*) = (V, E, l, h)$, where the vertices in V represent the clauses in the closure S_I^*, and the hyperarcs in E represent the inferences. The hypergraph is decorated by an *arc-labelling function* $h: E \to I$ from hyperarcs to inference rules, and an injective *vertex-labelling function* $l: V \to \mathcal{L}_\Theta/\doteq$ from vertices to equivalence classes of clauses, where $\doteq$ is equivalence up to variable renaming. Thus, all variants of a clause are associated to a unique vertex. For simplicity, $l(v)$ denotes a clause, meaning a representative of a class of variants.

If $f^n(\{\varphi_1 \dots \varphi_n\}) = (\{\psi_1 \dots \psi_m\}, \{\gamma_1 \dots \gamma_p\})$ for $f^n \in I$, E contains a hyperarc $e = (v_1 \dots v_k; w_1 \dots w_p; u_1 \dots u_m)$ where $h(e) = f^n$ and:

- $v_1 \dots v_k$ are the vertices labelled by those premises that are not deleted, i.e., $l(v_j) = \varphi_j$ and $\varphi_j \notin \{\gamma_1 \dots \gamma_p\}$, $\forall j$, $1 \le j \le k$, where $k = n - p$,
- $w_1 \dots w_p$ are the vertices labelled by the deleted clauses, i.e., $l(w_j) = \gamma_j$, $\forall j$, $1 \le j \le p$, and
- $u_1 \dots u_m$ are the vertices labelled by the generated clauses, i.e., $l(u_j) = \psi_j$, $\forall j$, $1 \le j \le m$.

Vertices and their labels can be used interchangeably, and without loss of generality one can consider hyperarcs in the form $(v_1 \dots v_n; w; u)$, where at most one clause is added or deleted. For instance, a *resolution* arc has the form $(v_1, v_2; u)$, where u is a resolvent of v_1 and v_2; a *simplification* arc has the form $(v; w; u)$, where v reduces w to u; and a *normalization* arc has the form $(v_1 \dots v_n; w; u)$, where u is a normal form of w with respect to the simplifiers $v_1 \dots v_n$. Contraction inferences that purely delete clauses are represented as replacement by *true*, where *true* is a dummy clause, such that $true \prec \varphi$ for all φ, and a special vertex $\top$ in $G(S_I^*)$ is labelled by *true*. The application of this representation to more inference rules and several examples of inference steps can be found in [39].

$G(S_I^*) = (V, E, l, h)$ represents the static structure of the search space. The dynamics of the search during a derivation is described by *marking functions* for vertices and arcs. A *marked search-graph* (V, E, l, h, s, c) is enriched with

- A *vertex-marking function* $s: V \to Z$ from vertices to integers, such that

$$ s(v) = \begin{cases} m & \text{if } m \text{ variants } (m > 0) \text{ of } l(v) \text{ are present,} \\ -1 & \text{if all variants of } l(v) \text{ have been deleted,} \\ 0 & \text{otherwise.} \end{cases} $$

- An *arc-marking function* $c: E \to Z^+$ from hyperarcs to non-negative integers, such that $c(e) = n$ if the inference of arc e has been executed n times.

The vertex-marking function represents the dynamic effect of contraction (if a clause is deleted, its marking becomes negative), while the arc-marking function represents the selections of steps done by the search plan.

It is then possible to represent the evolution of the search space during a derivation. First, a hyperarc $e = (v_1 \dots v_n; w; u) \in E$ is *enabled* if its premises are present: $s^k(v_j) > 0$ for $1 \le j \le n$ and $s^k(w) > 0$ ($s^k(w) > 1$ if $w \in \{v_1 \dots v_n\}$, e.g., for a variant subsumption arc $(v, v, \top)$).

A derivation induces a *succession of vertex-marking functions* $\{s_i\}_{i \ge 0}$ and a *succession of arc-marking functions* $\{c_i\}_{i \ge 0}$ initialized as follows: for all $v \in V$,

$s_0(v) = 0$, and for all $a \in E$, $c_0(a) = 0$. Then, $\forall i \geq 0$, if at stage i the strategy executes an enabled hyperarc $e = (v_1 \ldots v_n; w; u)$:

$$s_{i+1}(v) = \begin{cases} s_i(v) - 1 & \text{if } v = w \wedge s_i(v) > 1 \text{ (decrease marking of deleted clause)}, \\ -1 & \text{if } v = w \wedge s_i(v) = 1, \\ s_i(v) + 1 & \text{if } v = u \wedge s_i(v) \geq 0 \text{ (increase marking of generated clause)}, \\ 1 & \text{if } v = u \wedge s_i(v) = -1, \\ s_i(v) & \text{otherwise.} \end{cases}$$

$$c_{i+1}(a) = \begin{cases} c_i(a) + 1 & \text{if } a = e \text{ (increase marking of executed arc)}, \\ c_i(a) & \text{otherwise.} \end{cases}$$

The initialization $s_0(v) = 0$ for all vertices, including input clauses, assumes that also the steps of reading the input clauses are included in the derivation (e.g., modelled as expansion steps). Alternatively, one can start with $s_0(v) = 1$, if $\varphi = l(v)$ is in S_0, and $s_0(v) = 0$ otherwise.

Each state S_i has its associated search graph $G_i = (V, E, l, h, s_i, c_i)$, and S_i is exactly the multiset of clauses with positive marking in G_i. The subgraph containing only these clauses, $G_i^+ = (V^+, E^+, l, h, s_i, c_i)$, where $V^+ = \{v \mid v \in V, s_i(v) > 0\}$ and E^+ is the restriction of E to V^+, represents the *active part of the search space* at stage i. The subgraph of all the clauses with non-zero marking, $G_i^* = (V^*, E^*, l, h, s_i, c_i)$, where $V^* = \{v \mid v \in V, s_i(v) \neq 0\}$ and E^* is the restriction of E to V^*, represents the *generated search space* up to stage i. If the derivation halts at some stage k, G_k^* is the search space generated by the strategy during the entire derivation.

It is important to emphasize that neither G_k^* nor G_k^+ represent the *proof* computed by an ordering-based strategy. The notion of *ancestor-graph* of a clause clarifies this point. Given a search graph $G = (V, E, l, h)$, for all $v \in V$:

- If v has no incoming hyperarcs, the *ancestor-graph* of v is the graph made of v itself.
- If $e = (v_1 \ldots v_n; v_{n+1}; v)$ is a hyperarc in E and $t_1 \ldots t_{n+1}$ are ancestor-graphs of $v_1 \ldots v_{n+1}$, the graph with root v connected by e to the subgraphs $t_1 \ldots t_{n+1}$ is an *ancestor-graph* of v, denoted by the triple $(v; e; (t_1 \ldots t_{n+1}))$.

An ancestor-graph of v represents a sequence of inferences, or a *generation-path*, that generates its associated clause φ from the input clauses. If the strategy halts at stage k (i.e., $\square \in S_k$), *the computed proof is the ancestor-graph of $\square$ that has been traversed* to generate $\square$ during the derivation.

It is clear in this model why ordering-based strategies *generate many proof attempts*: at each stage i each ancestor-graph $(v; e; (t_1 \ldots t_{n+1}))$ in G_i^+ is a proof of $l(v)$ and an attempt at a proof of $\square$, because it may be possible to continue it into an ancestor-graph of $\square$. Of course, the strategy does not know which proof attempts (ancestor-graphs) can be extended into a proof (an ancestor-graph of $\square$). This is equivalent to saying that the strategy does not know which clauses in S_i are ancestors of $\square$. Also, the strategy works on S_i, not on G_i^+: hence the proof attempts are built *implicitly*.

After an empty clause has been generated, the prover engages in *proof reconstruction* to make the proof *explicit*. Proof reconstruction is the operation of extracting the ancestor-graph of □ from G_k^*. For instance, in Otter [97] and EQP [98], each clause is stored with its identifier and its "justification," that is, the name of the inference rule that generated it, and the identifiers of its parents. As soon as an empty clause is generated, the prover reconstructs the proof by listing first the empty clause, then its parents, then the parents of each parent and so on, until it reaches input clauses. Then, this list of clauses is printed with the input clauses first and the empty clause last.

The proof may include contraction steps and clauses deleted by contraction. Clauses deleted by forward contraction are not used as premises of other steps before deletion and therefore cannot occur in the proof. Clauses deleted by backward contraction may occur, because they may have been used as premises of other steps before being deleted. Therefore, provers such as Otter or EQP need to save the clauses deleted by backward contraction in a separate component of the database, which will be consulted only by the proof reconstruction algorithm.

Also, the proof is generally a graph, not a tree, because a clause may be used more than once in the proof, and all variants of a clause are associated to the same vertex. However, once the proof has been extracted, it is possible to transform it into a tree, by creating a distinct vertex (in the tree) for each occurrence of a clause in the proof. The resulting tree is a *deduction tree* [45], and since it is a deduction tree of □, it is a *refutation* of the initial set S.

Remarks and further reading A model of the search space of resolution as a search graph was given by Kowalski in [81]. The model given here appeared in [39]: it is compatible with the one in [81] for the representation of expansion inferences, it has been the first to model contraction inferences, and it has been extended to distributed search in [32]. A different representation of the search space is adopted by Plaisted and Zhu in [113] for other purposes. Comparisons of the model given here with those in [81] and [113] can be found in [39, 31].

2.4 Expansion-oriented and contraction-based strategies

Ordering-based strategies can be classified further based on usage of contraction and degree of goal-sensitivity, as shown in Figure 1.

Strategies that feature only expansion rules, and strategies that apply contraction rules only for forward contraction, are called *expansion-oriented strategies*[6]. If the strategy features contraction rules, it is convenient to separate the newly generated clauses from the others, because the former are subject to contraction, and the latter are not. Thus, the elements of *States* are pairs of sets $(S; N)$, where S is the set of clauses that may be used as premises of expansion or as simplifiers, whereas N is the set of *raw clauses*, or the newly generated clauses that need to be normalized before being inserted in S. If

---

[6] The names expansion-oriented and contraction-based appeared in [35].

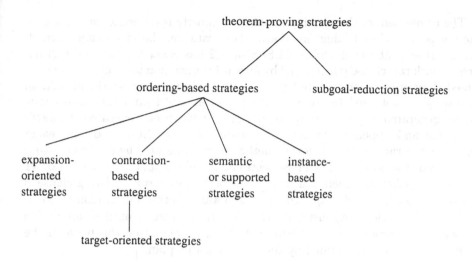

theorem-proving strategies

ordering-based strategies   subgoal-reduction strategies

expansion-oriented strategies   contraction-based strategies   semantic or supported strategies   instance-based strategies

target-oriented strategies

Fig. 1. Classes of ordering-based strategies

$\zeta((S_0; N_0) \ldots (S_i; N_i)) = f \in I_E$, then $\xi((S_0; N_0) \ldots (S_i; N_i), f) = X \subseteq S_i$, because clauses in N are not eligible to be premises for expansion until they are normalized and moved to S. If $\zeta((S_0; N_0) \ldots (S_i; N_i)) = f \in I_R$, then $\xi((S_0; N_0) \ldots (S_i; N_i), f) = X \subseteq S_i \cup N_i$, because contraction applies clauses in S to reduce clauses in N; and $\omega((S_i; N_i)) = true$ if $\square \in S_i \cup N_i$.

Given a theorem-proving problem S, an expansion-oriented strategy $\mathcal{C} = \langle I, \Sigma \rangle$, with $\Sigma = < \zeta, \xi, \omega >$, generates the *derivation*

$$(S_0; N_0) \underset{C}{\vdash} \ldots (S_i; N_i) \underset{C}{\vdash} \ldots$$

where $S_0 = S$, $N_0 = \emptyset$, and $\forall i \geq 0$, if $\omega((S_i; N_i)) = false$, $\zeta((S_0; N_0) \ldots (S_i; N_i)) = f$, and $\xi((S_0; N_0) \ldots (S_i; N_i), f) = X$, then

$$(S_{i+1}; N_{i+1}) = \begin{cases} (S_i; N_i \cup \pi_1(f(X))) & \text{if } f \in I_E, \\ (S_i \cup \pi_1(f(X)); N_i - \pi_2(f(X))) & \text{if } f \in I_R \text{ and } \pi_1(f(X)) \text{ is the} \\ & \quad S_i\text{-normal form of } \pi_2(f(X)), \\ (S_i; N_i \cup \pi_1(f(X)) - \pi_2(f(X))) & \text{otherwise.} \end{cases}$$

While expansion-oriented strategies allow a limited amount of contraction, at the other extreme there are *contraction-based strategies*, which not only allow both forward and backward contraction, but require contraction to be *eager*: A derivation $S_0 \vdash_{\mathcal{C}} \ldots S_i \vdash_{\mathcal{C}} \ldots$ has *eager contraction*, if for all $i \geq 0$ and $\varphi \in S_i$, if there are $f \in I_R$ and $X \subseteq S_i$, such that $\pi_2(f(X)) = \{\varphi\}$, then there exists an $l \geq i$ such that $S_l \vdash S_{l+1}$ deletes φ, and $\forall j, i \leq j \leq l$, $S_j \vdash S_{j+1}$ is not an expansion inference, unless the derivation succeeds sooner.
A search plan Σ is an *eager-contraction search plan*, if all derivations controlled by Σ have eager contraction. A strategy $\mathcal{C}$ is *contraction-based*, if its inference system includes contraction rules and its search plan is eager-contraction.

The component of the search plan which is mostly responsible for eager contraction is the rule-selecting function ζ. For instance, the given-clause search
plan of Otter that was described in Section 2.2 has eager forward contraction,
because each raw clause ψ is reduced by forward contraction to its normal form ψ'
immediately after generation, but it does not have eager backward-contraction,
because ψ' is not used to contract other clauses, until after all clauses that
can be generated by the current given clause have been generated, forward-
contracted and appended to sos. The search plans of EQP also have eager
backward-contraction: regardless of whether ψ was generated by the given-clause
algorithm or the pair algorithm (see Section 2.2), ψ' is applied to contract other
clauses right after its generation. If ψ' backward-simplifies an existing clause φ
to a new form φ', also φ' is applied to do backward contraction as soon as possible. Thus, the cycle of expansion inferences does not restart until all applicable
backward contraction has been performed. It may happen that this prevents the
generation of clauses generated by the Otter's search plan.

Remarks and further reading Early forward-reasoning strategies were typically expansion-oriented (e.g., based primarily on expansion by resolution). The
merging of the resolution-paramodulation paradigm with the term-rewriting and
Knuth-Bendix paradigm has led to contraction-based strategies. Most ordering-
based provers developed in recent years (e.g., Otter [97], RRL [76], Reveal [3],
SNARK [134], EQP [98], SPASS [142], Barcelona [104], and daTac [138]) are
based on contraction-based strategies, and also thanks to them succeeded in
solving challenge problems (e.g., [3, 2, 75, 134, 99, 138]).

2.5 Target-oriented strategies

The question of how to make contraction-based strategies more goal-sensitive
has long been a challenge to the automated deduction community. The situation of equational reasoning has been peculiar in this respect: the problem of
goal-sensitivity was ignored for a long time, because the strategies based on
the term-rewriting and Knuth-Bendix paradigm were regarded as completion
procedures to generate confluent (or saturated) rewrite systems, rather than
theorem-proving strategies. This view is not practical, because most theories
have infinite saturated systems, so that it is impossible to compile first the theory into a saturated system and then use the latter as a decision procedure for
the theory. Furthermore, since completion procedures do not have a goal, the
issue of goal-sensitivity for theorem-proving applications was not considered.
Nonetheless, working with a simpler logic has some advantages in this respect,
and some progress was made.

   In the purely equational case, H is a set of equations E, and φ has the
form $\forall \bar{x}\ s \simeq t$, so that $\neg\varphi$ has the form $\hat{s} \neq \hat{t}$, where the hat denotes that
all variables have been replaced by Skolem constants. Since the negation of the
target theorem is the only negative clause, it is trivial for the strategy to
identify it. Furthermore, the negation of the target theorem is ground, so that

unification involving a target term reduces to matching, and inferences on the target are simpler than general inferences. Therefore, it is possible to characterize contraction-based strategies for equational theories as *target-oriented strategies*. *States* is the set of pairs in the form $(E; \varphi)$, where E is the *presentation* and φ is the *target theorem*, which may be a ground equality $\hat{s} \simeq \hat{t}$ (e.g., in strategies based on *Unfailing Knuth-Bendix completion* and some of its extensions [69, 10, 36]), or a disjunction of ground equalities (e.g., in the extension of UKB of [3], called *Inequality Ordered Saturation* or *IOS-strategy* in [36]), or a disjunction of equalities with existentially quantified variables (e.g., in the *S-strategy* of [69]).

Accordingly, one can distinguish inference rules that apply to the presentation (forward reasoning) and inference rules that apply to the target (backward reasoning):

Presentation inference rules:
- *Expansion inference rules*: f: $\dfrac{(E; \varphi)}{(E'; \varphi)}$ where $E \subset E'$ and $E \prec_{mul} E'$.
- *Contraction inference rules*: f: $\dfrac{(E; \varphi)}{(E'; \varphi)}$ where $E \not\subseteq E'$ and $E' \prec_{mul} E$.

− *Target inference rules*:
- *Expansion inference rules*: f: $\dfrac{(E; \varphi)}{(E; \varphi')}$ where φ implies φ'.
- *Contraction inference rules*: f: $\dfrac{(E; \varphi)}{(E; \varphi')}$ where φ does not imply φ'.

An example of target contraction inference rule is simplification of the target, where the old target alone obviously does not imply its reduced form. An example of target expansion inference rule is the *ordered saturation* of the IOS-strategy:

$$\frac{(E \cup \{l \simeq r\}; N \cup \{\hat{s} \simeq \hat{t}\}) \qquad \hat{s}|u = l\sigma \quad \hat{s}[r\sigma]_u \to_S^* \hat{s}' \quad \hat{t} \to_S^* \hat{t}'}{(E \cup \{l \simeq r\}; N \cup \{\hat{s} \simeq \hat{t}, \hat{s}' \simeq \hat{t}'\}) \quad \{\hat{s}', \hat{t}'\} \not\preceq_{mul} \{\hat{g}, \hat{d}\} \quad \forall \hat{g} \simeq \hat{d} \in N \cup \{\hat{s} \simeq \hat{t}\}}$$

where E is a set (meaning a conjunction) of equations, N is a set (meaning a disjunction) of ground equalities, and clearly the old target logically implies the new one. Ordered saturation applies if $\hat{s} \prec \hat{s}[r\sigma]_u$, since if $\hat{s} \succ \hat{s}[r\sigma]_u$ held, simplification would apply. The target equality $\hat{s}' \simeq \hat{t}'$ might have a shorter proof than the other target equalities: the strategy keeps multiple target equalities to broaden the chance of reaching a proof as soon as possible.

The characterization of expansion and contraction of Section 2.1 applies to these rules as well: it is sufficient to negate the target and move it into the main set (e.g., if the disjunction of ground equalities that form the target of the IOS-strategy is negated and moved to the main set, it becomes a conjunction, or a set, of ground inequalities).

Since the negation of the target is not added to the presentation, success is not marked by the generation of the empty clause, but by the reduction of the target to *true*, as in the *target deletion* rule of the IOS-strategy:

$$\frac{(E; N \cup \{\hat{s} \simeq \hat{s}\})}{(E; true)}$$

If the target were negated and added to E, $\hat{s} \neq \hat{s}$ would generate an empty clause by resolving with $x = x$ (e.g., as done by the *unit conflict* in Otter, which needs $x = x$ in the input [97]), or because the theorem prover detects that the two sides of the inequality are equal (e.g., as done by the *unit conflict* in EQP which does not need $x = x$ in the input [98]). Accordingly, $\omega((E_i; \varphi_i)) = true$ if and only if φ_i is *true*.

Given a theorem-proving problem $(E_0; \varphi_0)$, a target-oriented strategy $C = \langle I, \Sigma \rangle$, with $\Sigma = \langle \zeta, \xi, \omega \rangle$, generates the *derivation*

$$(E_0; \varphi_0) \underset{C}{\vdash} \ldots (E_i; \varphi_i) \underset{C}{\vdash} \ldots$$

such that $\forall i \geq 0$, if $\omega((E_i, \varphi_i)) = false$, $\zeta((E_0; \varphi_0) \ldots (E_i; \varphi_i)) = f$, and $\xi((E_0; \varphi_0) \ldots (E_i; \varphi_i), f) = X$, then

$$(E_{i+1}; \varphi_{i+1}) = \begin{cases} (E_i; \varphi') & \text{if } \varphi_i \in X, \pi_1(f(X)) = \{\varphi'\} \\ & \text{and } \pi_2(f(X)) = \{\varphi_i\}, \\ (E_i \cup \pi_1(f(X)) - \pi_2(f(X)); \varphi_i) & \text{otherwise.} \end{cases}$$

A target-oriented strategy does not need monotonicity, but only *relevance*: if $(E; \varphi) \vdash_C (E'; \varphi')$, then $\varphi' \in Th(E')$ if and only if $\varphi \in Th(E)$.

Remarks and further reading Equational contraction-based strategies have been called rewriting-based, Knuth-Bendix-based, or completion-based. Their full characterization as target-oriented strategies was given in [36]. These strategies may take advantage of target-oriented heuristics, such as those of [3,1,51]. For instance, the combination of target inference rules, target-oriented heuristics, and inference rules for *cancellation* [71] in the IOS-strategy made possible to obtain results – the proofs of the Moufang identities [3] – that do not seem to have been reproduced by other theorem provers.

2.6 Semantic and supported strategies

In resolution-based theorem proving, the question of adding some backward reasoning to forward-reasoning strategies has been intertwined with the issue of limiting the generative power of expansion inference rules. In addition to restrictions based on redundancy criteria, restrictions that take knowledge about the problem into account have been investigated.

Since knowledge about the problem is semantic knowledge, *semantic resolution* [124] controls resolution by an interpretation $\mathcal{I}$: the given set of clauses S is partitioned into the subset T of all clauses in S that are satisfied by $\mathcal{I}$ and its complement $S - T$. Resolution is restricted in such a way that the consistent subset T is not expanded; only resolution steps with at most one premise from T are allowed: a clause in either T or $S - T$, called *nucleus*, resolves with one or more clauses in $S - T$, called *electrons*, until a resolvent that is false in $\mathcal{I}$, and therefore belongs to $S - T$, is generated. Semantic resolution may also assume an ordering on predicate symbols, and then require that the literal resolved upon in an electron contains the greatest predicate symbol in the electron.

If the interpretation $\mathcal{I}$ is defined based on sign, one obtains *hyperresolution* [117]: in *positive* hyperresolution, $\mathcal{I}$ contains all the negative literals, T contains the non-positive clauses, $S - T$ contains the positive clauses, and the electrons are positive clauses (from $S - T$) that resolve away all the negative literals in the nucleus (from T) to generate a positive hyperresolvent. Dually, in *negative* hyperresolution, $\mathcal{I}$ contains all the positive literals, T contains the non-negative clauses, $S-T$ contains the negative clauses, and the electrons are negative clauses (from $S - T$) that resolve away all the positive literals in the nucleus (from T) to generate a negative hyperresolvent. Hyperresolution can be more restrictive than semantic resolution with other interpretations, because hyperresolution excludes steps where both nucleus and electron are in $S - T$ (e.g., two negative clauses cannot resolve).

The intention of orienting the strategy towards backward-reasoning is more explicit in *resolution with set of support* [143]: a *set of support* (SOS) is a subset of S such that $S - SOS$ is consistent; only resolution steps with at most one premise from $S - SOS$ are allowed and all resolvents are added to SOS. The *set-of-support strategy* of [143] prescribed to put in SOS the goal clauses (those obtained from the transformation into clausal form of the negation of the target theorem), while $S-SOS$ contains the input assumptions, which form a consistent set, barring errors. Thus, the effect of working with a set of support is that most of the work done by the strategy is backward reasoning from the goal clauses.

Resolution with set of support fits in the paradigm of semantic resolution, with $T = S - SOS$ as the consistent subset and $SOS = S-T$ as its complement. Accordingly, the inferences allowed by the strategy, i.e., those with the electrons in SOS, are called *supported inferences*. However, resolution with set of support is less restrictive than semantic resolution, because it has the same condition on the choice of the premises (at most one from T), but it does not require that only resolvents that are false in $\mathcal{I}$ are generated. For instance, if SOS initially contains the positive clauses, resolution with set of support will generate and add to SOS also non-positive clauses, whereas positive hyperresolution will generate only positive clauses. Resolution with set of support can be seen as semantic resolution assuming an ad-hoc interpretation that makes all clauses in T true, and the clauses in SOS and all their descendants false.

Positive resolution [117] is binary resolution where one of the premises must be a positive clause (one where all literals are positive). Dually, *negative resolution* requires that a premise is a negative clause (one where all literals are negative). These strategies are considered sometime supported strategies where SOS contains the positive or negative clauses, respectively. Actually, positive resolution is more restrictive than resolution with set of support where SOS originally contains the positive clauses, because the former only allows steps with a positive premise, whereas the latter also allows resolutions between generated non-positive premises, as long as at least one of them is in SOS. On the other hand, positive hyperresolution is more restrictive than positive resolution, because the latter does not guarantee that only positive resolvents are generated. In essence, positive resolution and negative resolution are not semantic strategies, because they do not assume an interpretation with the provision that only clauses false in the interpretation are derived.

Since these *semantic* (or *supported*) strategies work by generating and keeping clauses, it is natural to enhance them with contraction rules (e.g., tautology deletion, subsumption, clausal simplification). For instance this combination is available in Otter [97]. In order to preserve completeness, however, it is necessary to apply contraction rules that replace clauses by other clauses, such as clausal simplification, in a way that respects the partition based on the interpretation: reduced forms of SOS-clauses stay in SOS, whereas reduced forms of T-clauses can stay in T only if they are true in the interpretation, and move to SOS otherwise [38].

A derivation by these strategies can be described as follows: *States* is a set of pairs $(T; SOS)$, ξ_1 selects the nucleus, ξ_2 selects the electrons from SOS, and $\omega((T; SOS)) = true$ if SOS contains $\square$. Given a theorem-proving problem S, and an interpretation $\mathcal{I}$, let $T_0 = \{\psi \mid \psi \in S, \mathcal{I} \models \psi\}$ and $SOS_0 = S - T_0$. The *derivation* generated by a semantic (or supported) strategy $\mathcal{C} = \langle I, \Sigma \rangle$, with $\Sigma = < \zeta, \xi, \omega >$, is the sequence

$$(T_0; SOS_0) \vdash_C \ldots (T_i; SOS_i) \vdash_C \ldots$$

such that $\forall i \geq 0$, if $\omega((T_i, SOS_i)) = false$, $\zeta((T_0; SOS_0) \ldots (T_i; SOS_i)) = f$, and $\xi((T_0; SOS_0) \ldots (T_i; SOS_i), f) = X$, then

$$(T_{i+1}; SOS_{i+1}) = \begin{cases} (T_i; SOS_i \cup \pi_1(f(X))) & \text{if } f \in I_E; \\ (T_i; SOS_i \cup \pi_1(f(X)) - \pi_2(f(X))) & \text{if } f \in I_R \text{ and} \\ & \quad \pi_2(f(X)) \in SOS_i; \\ (T_i \cup \pi_1(f(X)) - \pi_2(f(X)); SOS_i) & \text{if } f \in I_R \text{ and } X \subseteq T_i; \\ (T_i - \pi_2(f(X)); SOS_i \cup \pi_1(f(X))) & \text{if } f \in I_R, \pi_2(f(X)) \in T_i, \\ & \quad X - \pi_2(f(X)) \subseteq SOS_i, \\ & \quad \text{and } \mathcal{I} \not\models \pi_1(f(X)); \\ (T_i \cup \pi_1(f(X)) - \pi_2(f(X)); SOS_i) & \text{if } f \in I_R, \pi_2(f(X)) \in T_i, \\ & \quad X - \pi_2(f(X)) \subseteq SOS_i, \\ & \quad \text{and } \mathcal{I} \models \pi_1(f(X)). \end{cases}$$

The general definitions of semantic resolution and resolution with set of support imply neither backward reasoning nor forward reasoning. The type of reasoning produced by the strategy depends on the interpretation and the form of the problem. For instance, if the assumptions are non-negative clauses and the goal clauses are negative clauses, positive hyperresolution is a forward-reasoning strategy and negative hyperresolution is a backward-reasoning strategy compatible with the set-of-support strategy of [143]; this is the case in Horn logic. In general, the partition of S into T and SOS based on the distinction between assumptions and goal clauses may not agree with the partition based on sign (e.g., the goal clauses may not be negative clauses), so that hyperresolution and the set-of-support strategy are not always compatible.

In essence, if the set of support contains assumptions, supported inferences are forward inferences, and the semantic strategy is a forward strategy; if the set of support contains goal clauses, supported inferences are backward inferences, and the semantic strategy is a backward strategy. For instance in Otter or EQP [98], the sos list can be seen as SOS and the usable list as T. If one puts in sos only the goal clauses, the resulting strategy is a backward-reasoning strategy (i.e., the set-of-support strategy of [143]). By putting more input clauses in sos, one increases the forward character of the resulting strategy: for example, if the formulation of the problem includes fundamental axioms, special assumptions and the goal clauses, one can put the axioms in usable and the rest in sos. If all input clauses are in sos, the outcome is a pure forward-reasoning strategy. The latter is often the best choice for purely equational problems: based on this experience, the auto mode of Otter (the mechanism for automated choice of the strategy) places all input clauses in sos if equality is the only predicate in the input. Table 2 summarizes the considerations made so far on the issue of forward and backward reasoning.

	Forward reasoning	Backward reasoning
Expansion-oriented	all inferences	
Contraction-based	all inferences	
Target-oriented	inferences on the presentation	inferences on the target
Supported	if SOS contains assumptions	if SOS contains goals

Table 2. Classification of ordering-based strategies in terms of forward and backward reasoning

Semantic strategies can be enriched with controlled forms of *lemmatization*, where lemmas are the product of selected unsupported inferences [38]. If the set of support contains assumptions, lemmatization adds backward reasoning to a forward strategy; if the set of support contains goal clauses, lemmatization adds forward reasoning to a backward strategy. Thus, lemmatization is a general technique to combine forward and backward reasoning.

Remarks and further reading Much work has been done on trying to combine restrictions of resolution. The semantic resolution of [124] is compatible with assuming an ordering on predicate symbols, and establishing that the literal resolved upon in an electron contains the greatest predicate symbol in the electron. In propositional logic, an ordering on predicate symbols is also an ordering on literals; in first-order logic the two are different. Thus, semantic or supported strategies for ordered resolution have been investigated. The combination of semantic resolution with the early formulations of ordered resolution (with clauses treated as lists, hence an arbitrary ordering on literals) was not complete: this early work is presented in Section 6.6 of [45], which we refer to for references. With ordered resolution based on a complete simplification ordering on literals, the *positive ordered strategy* (positive ordered resolution and paramodulation) and *positive unit strategy* (for Horn logic) were proved complete in [70]. The *maximal-literal unit strategy* of [54] combines the unit restriction for Horn logic with the ordering. Many refinements of resolution are revisited in [13], including *positive ordered resolution, ordered resolution with maximal selection* (similar to positive ordered hyperresolution), and *ordered resolution with set of support*. Hyperresolution and the positive ordered strategy are used to design model-building methods in [58, 59].

2.7 Instance-based strategies

The principle of instance-based strategies is to implement directly the Herbrand Theorem (e.g., [45]): prove the unsatisfiability of S by generating sets of ground instances of its clauses, and applying an algorithm for propositional satisfiability to detect that one such set is unsatisfiable. Different methods differ in how they generate instances and test ground unsatisfiability.

The method of [84] interleaves instance generation by *hyperlinking* and unsatisfiability test by the *Davis-Putnam algorithm* [50]. A *hyperlink* involves a clause $N_1 \lor \ldots N_k$, called *nucleus*, and clauses $E_1, \ldots E_k$, called *electrons*, to generate an instance of the nucleus:

$$\frac{S \cup \{N_1 \lor \ldots N_k, E_1, \ldots E_k\}}{S \cup \{N_1 \lor \ldots N_k, E_1, \ldots E_k, (N_1 \lor \ldots N_k)\sigma\}} \quad \begin{array}{l} \forall i, 1 \leq i \leq k, \exists L_i \in E_i \\ N_i \sigma = \neg L_i \sigma \quad (\sigma \ mgu) \end{array}$$

Variants of a same clause may be used in a hyperlink, and all literals of the nucleus are linked, since the purpose is not to generate a resolvent, but to instantiate the nucleus as much as possible. Contraction is limited to unit subsumption and clausal simplification, because unrestricted subsumption would delete all instances and defeat the purpose of the strategy. In this regard, instance-based strategies are expansion-oriented strategies (see Section 2.4), with state $(S; N)$, where N contains the generated instances. After all hyperlinks in S_i have been considered, and contraction has been applied, all clauses in $S_i \cup N_i$ are made ground, by replacing all variables by a constant, and the Davis-Putnam algorithm is applied to the resulting ground set: if it is unsatisfiable, the procedure halts successfully; otherwise, the next phase of hyperlinking starts on $S_{i+1} = S_i \cup N_i$.

The Davis-Putnam algorithm [50] decides satisfiability of a set of ground clauses by trying all possible interpretations by case analysis (implemented as *splitting*) [45]. The case analysis is enhanced with *tautology deletion, purity deletion* and *unit propagation* (equivalent to unit resolution and unit subsumption), and these operations can be made very efficient by using fast data structures (e.g., [149]).

Remarks and further reading The idea of instance-based strategies dates back to the first implementations of Herbrand theorem, and has regained popularity as the efficiency of propositional methods has improved: a summary of the early work can be found in Section 7 of [84]. Hyperlinking has been applied also to model generation [48]; it can be augmented with interpretations to produce semantic strategies [47], and combined with orderings, and forms of paramodulation and simplification, to handle equality (e.g., [114]).

While instance-based strategies may be considered radically different than other ordering-based strategies, because they generate instances instead of resolvents, from the point of view of this classification they belong to the same class, because they work on a set of objects (clauses), build many proof attempts (the ground sets), do not backtrack, and feature some contraction. The analysis in [113] emphasizes the difference between generating resolvents and generating instances, and compares instance-based strategies, other ordering-based strategies and subgoal-reduction strategies in terms of measures of *duplication* in the total search space. Intuitively, a strength of instance-based strategies is that they do not duplicate literals by combining the literals of the parents in each resolvent.

The Davis-Putnam algorithm is the basis for efficient theorem provers or model finders for ground problems, with extensions for finding small finite models of first-order inputs[7]. Two such systems are SATO [146, 148] and MACE [96], while FINDER is related to Davis-Putnam but better understood in terms of tableaux [125], and SEM combines Davis-Putnam with other techniques [150].

3 Subgoal-reduction strategies

Supported strategies may be more goal-sensitive than general ordering-based strategies, but they belong to the same category, because they work by generating and keeping clauses, so that their *States* are multisets of clauses like for general ordering-based strategies. *Subgoal-reduction strategies* single out a goal object and work by reducing the goal to subgoals: one can distinguish classes of subgoal-reduction strategies as in Figure 2.

The rest of this section covers first linear and linear-input clausal strategies, and then tableau-based strategies.

3.1 Linear clausal strategies

Ordering-based strategies generate a portion of the search space (e.g., G_k^* if the derivation succeeded at stage k), and then extract the generated proof (the ancestor-graph of $\square$ contained in G_k^*). The idea of *linear strategies* is to restrict the search to search only for ancestor-graphs of $\square$ in a certain form, with the advantage of keeping in memory only the current proof attempt.

Linear resolution (e.g., [82, 90]) starts with a set of clauses $S = T \cup \{\varphi_0\}$, where clause φ_0 has been selected as the *top clause*. At each step i of the derivation, the strategy generates clause φ_{i+1} by resolving the *center clause* φ_i with a *side clause*, either a clause in T (an *input clause*), or a clause φ_j such that $j < i$

---

[7] Finite/infinite model means model with finite/infinite domain.

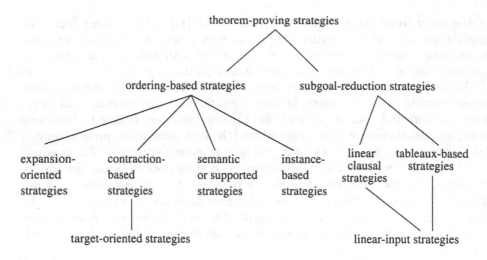

Fig. 2. Classes of strategies

(an *ancestor clause*). The strategy succeeds at stage k if φ_k is the empty clause, and the $\varphi_0 \ldots \varphi_k$ together with the side clauses form a comb-like ancestor-graph of $\Box$. Such an ancestor-graph is a *linear deduction tree*, and furthermore a *linear refutation*, because it is a deduction tree of $\Box$. Linear resolution is refutationally complete, in the sense that if $S = T \cup \{\varphi_0\}$ is unsatisfiable and T is consistent, there exists a linear refutation of S with φ_0 as the top clause. In other words, there exists in the search space a comb-like ancestor-graph of $\Box$ made of resolution steps with φ_0 as top clause and side clauses defined as above. It is sufficient to consider the center clauses as goals to see that linear resolution is a subgoal-reduction strategy: the most recently generated center clause is the current goal, each step consists in reducing the current goal to a subgoal, and the previous center clauses are ancestors of the current goal.

Refutational completeness guarantees the existence of a linear refutation, but the strategy needs to search for one. An ordering-based strategy is not looking for a proof of a specific form, and therefore it accumulates whatever it generates that is not redundant. A linear strategy, on the other hand, is looking for a linear refutation, and if it emerges that the deduction tree built so far cannot become a linear refutation, it needs to *backtrack*, that is, undo the last step and try a different continuation of the deduction tree. Therefore, search plans for linear strategies work by backtracking.

The set of *States* for these strategies contains triples $(T; \varphi; A)$, where φ is the current center clause, and A is the set of its ancestors. The search plan $\Sigma = \langle \zeta, \xi_1, \xi_2, \omega \rangle$ operates as follows:

- Since the primary premise is the current goal, the task of $\xi_1 : States^* \to \mathcal{L}_\Theta$ is to select a literal in the current goal:
  $\xi_1((T; \varphi_0; A_0) \ldots (T; \varphi_i; A_i)) = L \in \varphi_i;$

- $\zeta: States^* \times \mathcal{L}_\Theta \to I \cup \{backtrack\}$ accounts for the selection of the inference rule, and the decision to backtrack;
- $\xi_2: States^* \times \mathcal{L}_\Theta \times I \to \mathcal{L}_\Theta$ chooses the secondary premise among clauses in T or ancestors of the current goal:
  $\xi_2((T; \varphi_0; A_0) \ldots (T; \varphi_i; A_i), L, f) = \psi \in T \cup A_i;$
- $\omega((T; \varphi; A)) = true$ if and only if $\varphi = \square$.

Note how the definition of search plan for subgoal-reduction strategies fits in the same $\langle \zeta, \xi_1, \xi_2, \omega \rangle$ template used for ordering-based strategies.

Given a theorem-proving problem $S = T \cup \{\varphi_0\}$, a linear strategy $\mathcal{C} = \langle I, \Sigma \rangle$, with $\Sigma = < \zeta, \xi_1, \xi_2, \omega >$, generates the *derivation*

$$(T_0; \varphi_0; A_0) \underset{\mathcal{C}}{\vdash} \ldots (T_i; \varphi_i; A_i) \underset{\mathcal{C}}{\vdash} \ldots$$

such that $T_0 = T$, $A_0 = \emptyset$, and for all $i \geq 0$, if $\omega((T_i; \varphi_i; A_i)) = false$, $\xi_1((T_0; \varphi_0; A_0) \ldots (T_i; \varphi_i; A_i)) = L$, then

$$(T_{i+1}; \varphi_{i+1}; A_{i+1}) = \begin{cases} (T_i; \pi_1(f(\varphi_i, \psi)); A_i \cup \{\varphi_i\}) \\ \text{if } \zeta((T_0; \varphi_0; A_0) \ldots (T_i; \varphi_i; A_i), L) = f \in I \\ \text{and } \xi_2((T_0; \varphi_0; A_0) \ldots (T_i; \varphi_i; A_i), L, f) = \psi \\ \\ (T_{i-1}; \varphi_{i-1}; A_{i-1}) \\ \text{if } \zeta((T_0; \varphi_0; A_0) \ldots (T_i; \varphi_i; A_i), L) = backtrack. \end{cases}$$

A characterization of inference rules other than the one in Section 2.1 is not necessary: the differences are that there is *no contraction* $(\pi_2(f(X)) = \emptyset)$, and the generated clause $(\pi_1(f(X)))$ is *not added to a set*, but used to *replace* its predecessor. The depth-first search of the subgoal-reduction strategy is captured by the form of the derivation itself, where the current goal is the most recently generated goal. Depth-first search with backtracking, however, is not fair, so that *depth-first search with backtracking and iterative deepening (DFID)* [80, 130] is used instead.

Linear resolution can be regarded as a refinement of resolution with set of support: the center clauses form the set of support, and the only needed resolution steps between clauses in SOS are the resolutions with ancestors. Linear resolution is obviously compatible with the set-of-support strategy of [143], if one chooses as top clause a goal clause. In such a case, linear resolution performs backward reasoning. However, like resolution with set of support performs forward or backward reasoning depending on what one puts in the set of support, a linear strategy may perform forward or backward reasoning depending on the choice of the top clause. Selecting a goal clause is natural and common, although not necessary. Any input clause φ_0 can be chosen as top clause as long as $T = S - \{\varphi_0\}$ is consistent.

Remarks and further reading Many authors contributed to linear resolution: see Section 7.1 of [45] for a summary and the relevant references. Other independently developed subgoal-reduction strategies include the *problem reduction format strategies* of [109], which also yield semantic strategies [103].

3.2 Linear-input clausal strategies

Linear resolution requires to keep the ancestors around; this is not necessary in *linear input strategies*, where all side clauses are input clauses. This class includes *linear input resolution*, which is complete for Horn logic, and *model elimination*, which is complete for first-order logic.

Inference rules *Model elimination* [89] proves that $S = T \cup \{\varphi_0\}$ is unsatisfiable by showing that no model of T satisfies φ_0 as follows. It works on *chains*, that can be seen as clauses made of plain literals, called *B-literals*, and framed literals, called *A-literals*. A chain encodes a stage of model construction: the A-literals are those that are true in the current candidate model, whereas the B-literals are those that still need to be considered. A model elimination strategy picks an input clause φ_0 to be the initial chain, and $T = S - \{\varphi_0\}$ contains all other input clauses. If T contains $L_1 \vee D$, φ_0 is $L_2 \vee C$, and the literals L_1 and L_2 have opposite sign and unify, the *ME-extension* rule applies:

$$\frac{(T \cup \{L_1 \vee D\}; L_2 \vee C)}{(T \cup \{L_1 \vee D\}; (D \vee [L_2] \vee C)\sigma)} \quad L_1\sigma = \neg L_2\sigma \quad (\sigma \text{ most general unifier})$$

With this step, the procedure tries to build a T-model that makes $L_2\sigma$ true; since $L_1\sigma = \neg L_2\sigma$, such a model makes $L_1\sigma$ false. Therefore, in order to satisfy $(L_1 \vee D)\sigma$ it is necessary to satisfy $D\sigma$ by more ME-extension steps. Should this fail, it will be necessary to remove $L_2\sigma$ from the candidate model and try to satisfy $C\sigma$. The literals in $D\sigma$ are *subgoals* of $L_2\sigma$, because in order to satisfy $L_2\sigma$, the procedure needs to satisfy $D\sigma$, or, dually, in order to refute $L_2\sigma$ (and exclude it from the candidate model), the procedure needs to refute $D\sigma$.

If satisfying a subgoal would make the current candidate model inconsistent, the subgoal is eliminated by the *ME-reduction* rule:

$$\frac{(T; L \vee D \vee [L'] \vee C)}{(T; (D \vee [L'] \vee C)\sigma)} \quad L\sigma = \neg L'\sigma$$

If $L\sigma = \neg L'\sigma$ and L' is already in the model, L cannot be part of it.

If the candidate model that makes an A-literal true fails to satisfy its subgoals (i.e., it is not a T-model), the A-literal must be removed from the candidate model. This is detected by the *ME-contraction* rule when all literals on the left of an A-literal have been eliminated:

$$\frac{(T; [L] \vee C)}{(T; C)}$$

This means that L has been refuted (no T-model includes it), or, equivalently, $\neg L$ has been proved. The inference system is completed by *factoring* on B-literals. If the current chain becomes empty, it means that no T-model satisfies φ_0, or $T \cup \{\varphi_0\}$ is unsatisfiable.

Because it works on one chain at a time, and has a natural notion of subgoaling, model elimination fits in the template of subgoal-reduction strategies with the current chain as the current goal. Furthermore, model elimination may also be presented as a refinement of linear resolution (e.g., [90, 82, 45]): the succession of chains corresponds to the succession of center clauses. ME-extension inferences can be interpreted as input-resolution inferences, modified by saving the literal resolved upon in the goal as an A-literal in the successor goal. ME-reduction inferences can be interpreted as what replaces ancestor-resolution inferences. In this interpretation, the mechanism of saving literals resolved upon as A-literals is the refinement that makes ancestor-resolution inferences unnecessary: the A-literals are precisely the ancestor literals that is necessary to keep to complete the refutation.

Search plans Since each step involves either the current goal and an input clause or the current goal only, the set of *States* for these strategies contains pairs $(T; \varphi)$, where φ is the current goal, and the component A of the ancestors is no longer needed. The search plan $\Sigma = \langle \zeta, \xi_1, \xi_2, \omega \rangle$ works as for linear strategies, except that ξ_2 selects the secondary premise from T only: $\xi_2((T; \varphi_0) \ldots (T; \varphi_i), L, f) = \psi \in T$.

In the first formulation of model elimination, ξ_1 selected literals in right to left order [89]. The typical choice for ξ_1 became left to right order (implicitly assumed in the above presentation of the inference rules), in *Prolog Technology Theorem Proving* [130, 132], when it was discovered that model-elimination strategies can be implemented efficiently on top of a Prolog engine, such as the *Warren Abstract Machine* [140]. Since the set T of "axioms" – from a theorem proving point of view – or "program rules" – from a logic programming point of view – is static, it can be compiled at compile-time, and the strategy works on a stack of goals, operating at each step on the current goal, on top of the stack. In logic programming terminology, ξ_1 corresponds to the *AND computation rule*, and ξ_2 to the *OR computation rule*.

Given a theorem-proving problem $S = T \cup \{\varphi_0\}$, a linear input strategy $C = \langle I, \Sigma \rangle$, with $\Sigma = \langle \zeta, \xi_1, \xi_2, \omega \rangle$, generates the *derivation*

$$(T_0; \varphi_0) \underset{C}{\vdash} \ldots (T_i; \varphi_i) \underset{C}{\vdash} \ldots$$

such that $T_0 = T$, and $\forall i \geq 0$, if $\omega((T; \varphi_i)) = false$, $\xi_1((T_0; \varphi_0) \ldots (T_i; \varphi_i)) = L$, then

$$(T_{i+1}; \varphi_{i+1}) = \begin{cases} (T_i; \pi_1(f(\varphi_i, \psi))) & \text{if } \zeta((T_0; \varphi_0) \ldots (T_i; \varphi_i), L) = f^2 \in I \\ & \text{and } \xi_2((T_0; \varphi_0) \ldots (T_i; \varphi_i), L, f^2) = \psi; \\ (T_i; \pi_1(f(\varphi_i))) & \text{if } \zeta((T_0; \varphi_0) \ldots (T_i; \varphi_i), L) = f^1 \in I; \\ (T_{i-1}; \varphi_{i-1}) & \text{if } \zeta((T_0; \varphi_0) \ldots (T_i; \varphi_i), L) = backtrack. \end{cases}$$

The three cases cover, respectively, inferences involving the goal and an input clause, inferences on the goal only, and backtracking.

If the search plan is depth-first search with iterative deepening, ζ maintains the information of what is the depth bound of the current round of iterative deepening, say k, and associates to each goal φ_i a depth bound n_i $(0 \leq n_i \leq k_i)$, meaning that $k - n_i$ steps were used to reduce φ_0 to φ_i, and n_i more steps are allowed to try to reduce φ_i to $\square$. If $n_i = 0$, ζ orders to backtrack, because no more steps are available for φ_i. If at stage $j - 1$ the search space down to depth k has been exhausted, ζ resets the depth bound to $k + m$, for some $m > 0$, and starts the next round of iterative deepening in state $(T_j; \varphi_j)$, where $T_j = T$ and $\varphi_j = \varphi_0$, with $n_j = k + m$.

In addition to strategies for theorem proving and logic programming, strategies for functional programming and term rewriting can be seen as linear-input subgoal-reduction strategies. For instance, in term rewriting, T is a set of rewrite rules, φ_0 is the input term to be normalized, ξ_1 selects the subterm to be rewritten, and ξ_2 selects the rewrite rule to be applied. A main difference is that in term rewriting or functional programming there is only reduction, not search, and therefore no need for backtracking.

Refinements Subgoal-reduction strategies concentrate only on the current goal, and have no memory of previously solved goals. If the same subgoals, or instances thereof, are generated at different stages, the strategy solves them independently, repeating the same steps. While ordering-based strategies may run out of memory if they keep too many clauses, so that their set of clauses becomes too large, subgoal-reduction strategies may run out of memory if they repeat too many subgoals, so that their stack of goals becomes too large. Ordering-based strategies use contraction rules and restrictions to expansion rules to try to avoid the space explosion. Subgoal-reduction strategies try to avoid repetitions by using *pruning rules* and *lemmatization*.

Pruning rules affect backtracking, and therefore are part of the search plan. *Identical ancestor pruning* causes the procedure to backtrack if the current goal has the form $L \vee D \vee [L] \vee C$: if L has been inserted already in the candidate model, or, dually, if the procedure is trying already to refute L, it is useless to do it again.

Lemmatization is an extension of the inference system: when ME-contraction removes $[L]$, it means that no model of T satisfies L, hence $T \models \neg L$, and $\neg L$ can be added to T as a *lemma*. This holds, however, only if all subgoals of L were eliminated without recurring to ME-reduction by ancestors of L (i.e., A-literals on the right of $[L]$). If an ME-reduction step with ancestor $[A]$ was used, the lemma being proved is $\neg L \vee \neg A$ (no model of T satisfies $L \wedge A$, hence $T \models \neg L \vee \neg A$). If a subgoal of L was eliminated by factoring[8] with a B-literal B (on the right of $[L]$), the lemma being proved is $\neg L \vee B$ (no model of T satisfies $L \wedge \neg B$, hence $T \models \neg L \vee B$).

For reasons of efficiency, lemmatization may be restricted to the generation of unit lemmas, which are advantageous because a step with a unit lemma reduces the length of the goal. In Horn logic, all lemmas are unit lemmas, because ME-reduction is not necessary. Therefore, unit lemmatization can be replaced by *caching*, including *success caching*, where solutions are stored in a fast cache,

---

[8] In a typical ME-derivation ME-reduction applies more frequently than factoring.

rather than being turned into lemmas, and *failure caching*, which saves the information that a goal failed in order to avoid trying to solve it again (e.g., [110, 6]). Caching has the same logical justification as lemmatization, but it is different operationally: lemmas are used as premises for the regular inference mechanism of the subgoal-reduction strategy; the information stored in the cache is used to solve/fail a subgoal literal L without further inferences, based on the fact that the cache contains a more general subgoal L' that was solved or failed already.

Since it assumes that all lemmas are unit lemmas, caching is not consistent with inference systems for first-order logic, which need ME-reduction and factoring. It is not correct to solve a subgoal literal L by matching it with a cached solution $L'\rho$ of L', if the generation of this solution involved eliminating subgoals of L' by ME-reduction or factoring, because in such a case not $\neg L'\rho$ but some non-unit lemma $(\neg L' \vee \neg A_1 \ldots \vee \neg A_n)\rho$ was proved.

Both lemmatization and caching are enhancements of strategies that are already complete. Since cache retrieval replaces the regular inference mechanism, it is necessary to cache *all the solutions* in order to retain completeness. Also, caching is *incomplete* in the presence of identical ancestor pruning, because if identical ancestor pruning was used to prune the search of solutions of L', there is no guarantee that all solutions of L are instances of the cached solutions of L' [6]. Lemmatization obviously does not affect completeness.

In a strategy with lemmatization the T component is no longer static, because lemmas are added to T. Since clauses are generated and kept, it becomes possible to apply forms of contraction such as *lemma subsumption* or *cache subsumption* (e.g., [6, 129, 38]). Similar to linear resolution, model elimination does backward or forward reasoning depending on whether φ_0 is a goal clause or not. Assume the natural choice of picking as φ_0 a goal clause: then lemmatization adds forward reasoning to a backward-reasoning subgoal-reduction strategy. If the subgoal-reduction mechanism is interpreted as eliminating models, dually lemmatization can be interpreted as generating models, since a lemma is a logical consequence of T. Systems such as SATCHMO [93] and MGTP [66] use Prolog technology theorem proving as a basis for model generation.

Remarks and further reading Lemmatization was introduced with model elimination in [89]. At the time of its first implementation [61], unrestricted lemmatization generated more lemmas than the procedure could handle efficiently. This led to investigate weaker forms of lemmatization, such as *C-reduction* [121]. After the inception ([130, 132] and the MESON strategy in [91]) and maturation (e.g., [4, 19]) of Prolog technology theorem proving, lemmatization has been reintroduced, as in the METEOR theorem prover [5]. The analysis in [113] discusses how lemmaizing and caching may reduce from exponential to quadratic, or, at best, linear, certain measures of duplication in the search spaces of model elimination for problems in propositional Horn logic. A general treatment of lemmatization in supported strategies, covering lemmatization in model elimination as a special case, was given in [38]: it includes a formalization of caching and depth-dependent caching in iterative deepening strategies, and a discussion of contraction and caching as ways of reducing redundancy. Improvements of depth-first search with iterative deepening are proposed in [65].

The research on linear input resolution contributed to the invention of Prolog and logic programming: a theory-oriented introduction that emphasizes the connections with automated deduction can be found in [88]. A main conceptual difference is that in theorem proving one is interested in a refutation, whereas in logic programming one is interested in all the answer substitutions. This affects termination: in a theorem-proving problem, if the search space contains linear refutations, depth-first search with iterative deepening is guaranteed to find one and halt; in a logic programming problem, depth-first search with iterative deepening will reach all solutions eventually, but may still fail to terminate if the search space is infinite, because it deepens forever to look for more solutions. *Subsumption-based techniques* to enhance termination in Prolog were studied in [30]. *Linear Completion* is a linear strategy for logic programming with rewrite systems (e.g., [53, 33]). The effect of *simplification* on the termination of these programs was studied in [33], whose Linear Completion strategy also features a form of lemmatization (answer rules are added to the program to act as simplifiers). Section 8 in [33] contains comparisons with the subsumption-based techniques of [30], and the earlier work on Linear Completion. The relation between model elimination and computing answers in logic programming is investigated in [20]. Techniques similar to caching, called *memoing, tabling,* or *OLDT-resolution,* have been developed independently in logic programming to add a bottom-up component (logically, lemmas from the program) to top-down evaluations. Symmetrically, *magic sets* add a top-down component (logically, lemmas from the goal) to bottom-up evaluations in deductive databases. A survey of these areas was presented in [141], where more references can be found.

3.3 Tableaux-based strategies

While ordering-based strategies build implicitly many proof attempts, linear strategies build a proof attempt at a time, and backtrack to try another one. However, in clausal linear strategies the proof attempt is still implicit, because the strategy works on a stack of clauses and reconstructs at the end the produced linear refutation. *Tableau-based strategies* are subgoal-reduction strategies that inherit from natural deduction methods (e.g., analytic tableaux [126]) the property of working explicitly on the proof attempt. The inference system of the strategy is used to build a *tableau*: in essence, a tableau is a survey of the possible interpretations of S, with each branch representing an interpretation. If a branch contains a contradiction, the branch is *closed*, because it cannot be a viable interpretation. The purpose of the strategy is to develop the tableau to close all its branches, and show that S is unsatisfiable; the resulting *closed* tableau is the proof. The refutational completeness of the inference system guarantees the existence of a closed tableau if S is unsatisfiable. The search plan tries one tableau at a time: during the search an open tableau is a proof attempt, and if the current tableau cannot be closed, the search plan backtracks to try a different tableau. A fair search plan guarantees that a closed tableau will be generated if one exists. In propositional logic complete tableaux are finite, so that if the strategy terminates with a complete open tableaux its open branches represent models of S. In first-order logic the process of completing a tableau is infinite in general, but in some cases it is possible to extract a finite model from an open tableau.

Inference rules In *model elimination tableaux* [87, 86], the tableaux are built by using the inference rules of model elimination. A tableau is a tree with nodes labelled by literals. Given S, the strategy selects a clause $\varphi_0 = L_1 \vee \ldots \vee L_n$ to form the initial tableau $\mathcal{X}_0$, while $T = S - \{\varphi_0\}$ contains the remaining input clauses. $\mathcal{X}_0$ is a tree with no label at the root and n leaves labelled by the literals $L_1 \ldots L_n$, so that the branches represent all the ways of satisfying φ_0. If T contains a clause $F_1 \vee \ldots \vee F_k$ such that $F_1\sigma = \neg L_1\sigma$, ME-extension expands node L_1 with children $F_1 \ldots F_k$, closes node F_1 and applies σ to all literals in the resulting tableau. ME-reduction closes a leaf L if it has an ancestor L' such that $L\sigma = \neg L'\sigma$, and applies the unifier to all literals in the tableau. Factoring is also called *merging*, or *forward merging*, in tableaux terminology [139]: it closes a leaf L if there is an open node L' (e.g., sibling of an ancestor of L) such that $L\sigma = L'\sigma$, and applies σ to the tableau. When all the children of a node are closed, the node itself is closed (this corresponds to ME-contraction), and a tableau is closed when all its nodes are. Roughly speaking, open leaves in a tableau correspond to B-literals in a chain, while open internal nodes correspond to A-literals. A structural difference between the two is that ME-reduction and ME-contraction on chains remove literals, whereas in a tableau nodes are closed but not removed. The precise correspondence between model elimination operating on chains and model elimination operating on tableaux can be found in [18].

Assuming that $\mathcal{L}_\Theta$ is the language of clauses and tableaux on signature Θ, the characterization of inference rules as functions $f: \mathcal{P}(\mathcal{L}_\Theta) \to \mathcal{P}(\mathcal{L}_\Theta) \times \mathcal{P}(\mathcal{L}_\Theta)$ still holds. For instance, ME-extension takes a tableau and a clause and generates a tableau, while the other rules take a tableau and produce another tableau. Putting clauses and tableaux in $\mathcal{L}_\Theta$ is acceptable, considering that clauses and literals are terms, hence trees, and tableaux are trees. The rules in a basic subgoal-reduction strategy are expansion rules (regardless of whether the strategy works on clauses, or chains or tableaux), and what they generate is used to *replace* the previous goal, rather than being *added* to a set as in ordering-based strategies.

Search plans The elements of *States* have the form $(T; \mathcal{X})$, where $\mathcal{X}$ is the current tableau. The search plan $\Sigma = \langle \zeta, \xi_1, \xi_2, \omega \rangle$ works similarly to those for clausal linear-input strategies: ξ_1 selects an open leaf in the current tableau (i.e., if $open(\mathcal{X})$ denotes the open leaves in $\mathcal{X}$, $\xi_1((T_0; \mathcal{X}_0) \ldots (T_i; \mathcal{X}_i)) = L \in open(\mathcal{X}_i)$); ζ selects the inference rule and decides backtracking; ξ_2 selects a premise from T if needed; and $\omega((T; \mathcal{X})) = true$ if $\mathcal{X}$ is closed. Chains induce to think of left-to-right or right-to-left as the natural choices for ξ_1. Working with tableaux, on the other hand, ξ_1 can be any rule to visit a tree. The rule corresponding to selecting the leftmost literal in a chain is to select the leftmost open node in a tableau.

Given a theorem-proving problem $S = T \cup \{\varphi_0\}$, a tableau-based strategy $\mathcal{C} = \langle I, \Sigma \rangle$, with $\Sigma = \langle \zeta, \xi_1, \xi_2, \omega \rangle$, generates the *derivation*

$$(T_0; \mathcal{X}_0) \underset{C}{\vdash} \ldots (T_i; \mathcal{X}_i) \underset{C}{\vdash} \ldots$$

such that $T_0 = T$, $\mathcal{X}_0$ is the tableau for φ_0, and $\forall i \geq 0$, if $\omega((T; \mathcal{X}_i)) = false$, $\xi_1((T_0; \mathcal{X}_0) \ldots (T_i; \mathcal{X}_i)) = L$, then

$$(T_{i+1}; \mathcal{X}_{i+1}) = \begin{cases} (T_i; f(\mathcal{X}_i, \psi)) & \text{if } \zeta((T_0; \mathcal{X}_0) \ldots (T_i; \mathcal{X}_i), L) = f^2 \in I \\ & \text{and } \xi_2((T_0; \mathcal{X}_0) \ldots (T_i; \mathcal{X}_i), L, f) = \psi \\ (T_i; f(\mathcal{X}_i)) & \text{if } \zeta((T_0; \mathcal{X}_0) \ldots (T_i; \mathcal{X}_i), L) = f^1 \in I \\ (T_{i-1}; \mathcal{X}_{i-1}) & \text{if } \zeta((T_0; \mathcal{X}_0) \ldots (T_i; \mathcal{X}_i), L) = backtrack. \end{cases}$$

Refinements The refinements of Section 3.2 apply also in the context of tableaux. Identical ancestor pruning is replaced by *equal predecessor fail*, or *regularity*: if a node is identical to one of its ancestors, the tableau is said to be *irregular*; if the strategy generates an irregular tableau, it discards it and backtracks.

When all the children of a node L are closed, L itself is closed, and a lemma $\neg L$ is proved. Since closed nodes are not removed, it is not necessary to add $\neg L$ to T: the information about the lemma is encoded in the tableau. Lemmatization in tableaux [87, 86] is also known as *regressive merging* or *backward merging* [139], because in the context of tableaux, and from an operational point of view, it has the appearance of the dual operation of merging. Applying a merging step consists in closing an open leaf L that unifies with another open leaf L'. Since L' is an open leaf, the strategy has not selected it yet, and this gives an idea of merging forward (collapsing a node on a node that will be selected). Applying a lemma consists in closing an open leaf L that unifies with a closed node L' (i.e., a lemma $\neg L'$). Since L' is closed, it has been selected already, and this gives an idea of merging backward (collapsing a node on an already selected node).

If the problem is first-order, not all lemmas are unit lemmas: if nodes below L were closed by ME-reduction steps with ancestors of L (e.g., $A_1 \ldots A_n$), the lemma attached to the closing of L is a non-unit lemma (e.g., $\neg L \vee \neg A_1 \ldots \vee \neg A_n$). Non-unit lemmatization can be implemented as *folding-up* [86, 139], which is a way of encoding the non-unit lemma in the tableau. Symmetrically, *folding-down* implements merging [64].

If lemmas are not generated explicitly, it may be more complicated to use them for contraction (e.g., subsumption) within T. The tableau-based prover Setheo [87, 64] uses subsumption, tautology deletion and purity deletion during the pre-processing of the input. If the Delta pre-processor [120] is invoked, the subgoal-reduction phase in Setheo is preceded by a phase where *UR-resolution* (Unit-Resulting resolution: unit electrons resolve against all but one literal in the nucleus to produce a unit resolvent [94]) and other restricted forms of resolution are applied to expand the set T, and the contraction rules are applied throughout this phase. The principle that makes expansion by resolution useful is essentially the same that makes lemmatization useful: it makes T more powerful for the subgoal-reduction phase, and it provides an integration of *forward reasoning* (hence *contraction*) and *backward reasoning* (hence *goal-sensitivity*). A difference is that unit lemmas are often less general than UR-resolvents, exactly because they are generated during the subgoal-reduction phase. On some problems unit lemmas are advantageous, because intuitively in terms of search they are "closer" to the solution. On other problems, unit-resolvents are more useful: exactly because they are more general, they are more powerful for unit subsumption and the subgoal-reduction inferences themselves. Another feature of Setheo are *anti-lemmas*, which is basically a form of depth-dependent failure caching.

A different approach to enhancing tableau-based methods with contraction is *tableau subsumption* [86, 16], which is based on defining a subsumption ordering among tableaux, and using tableaux to subsume others, similar to clausal subsumption. There are two main difficulties with defining a practical notion of tableau subsumption [16]. First, comparing entire tableaux seems inefficient. Thus, one would like to compare only open leaves (e.g., $\mathcal{X}_1$ subsumes $\mathcal{X}_2$ if $open(\mathcal{X}_1)$ subsumes $open(\mathcal{X}_2)$). However, a subsumption rule that compares only leaves destroys completeness, because completeness requires remembering ancestors for ME-reduction. Roughly speaking, for $\mathcal{X}_1$ to subsume $\mathcal{X}_2$, it is also necessary that all ancestors of open leaves in $\mathcal{X}_2$ appear as ancestors of open leaves in $\mathcal{X}_1$. Therefore, one would like a notion of tableau subsumption that preserves completeness without imposing to compare entire tableaux. The approach of [16] consists in defining a complete restriction of model elimination, called *disjunctive positive model elimination (DPME)*, which is a refinement of the *positive model elimination* of [112]: in DPME the only ancestors needed for ME-reduction are *disjunctive positive ancestors*, that is, positive ancestors coming from non-Horn clauses.

Then, a subsumption relation among tableaux is defined based on open leaves and disjunctive positive ancestors only. The potential downside of this approach is that the advantage of tableau subsumption may be outweighted by the disadvantage of restricting ME-reduction to disjunctive positive ancestors. In practice, ME-reduction is very important to keep the stack of goals from growing too large. The solution of the Mission prover [16], where disjunctive positive model elimination with tableau subsumption is implemented, is to use unrestricted ME-reduction, while considering only disjunctive positive ancestors in tableau subsumption.

The second issue is that in order to apply tableau subsumption the strategy needs to generate and save tableaux. In other words, one needs to abandon the subgoal-reduction framework, where only one tableau is kept in memory, and adopt the style of ordering-based strategies, envisioning a strategy that generates all possible tableaux, and applies forward and backward subsumption among tableaux [16]. Such a strategy is an ordering-based strategy that works with a set of tableaux, instead of a set of clauses. It is quite natural, however, to translate tableaux into clauses, and define such a strategy to work on clauses of A-literals and B-literals.

A less radical option is to maintain the subgoal-reduction framework, but save the predecessors of the current tableau, and use them for forward tableau-subsumption. The result is a linear tableau-based strategy with derivations in the form $(T_0; \mathcal{X}_0; A_0) \vdash_C \ldots (T_i; \mathcal{X}_i; A_i) \vdash_C \ldots$, where A_i contains the predecessor tableaux $\mathcal{X}_0 \ldots \mathcal{X}_{i-1}$. If a newly generated tableau is forward-subsumed by one of its predecessors, the strategy backtracks.

Table 3 summarizes some refinements of subgoal-reduction strategies (the distinction between clausal and tableaux model elimination in the table is mostly one of terminology, since almost everything that can be done in one can be done in the other).

	Combination of forward and backward reasoning	Contraction	Pruning
Model elimination	lemmatization C-reduction success caching	lemma subsumption cache subsumption	identical ancestor pruning failure caching
Prolog Datalog	tabling/memoing magic sets		cut
Tableaux	regressive merging folding up UR-resolution hyperlinking	tableau subsumption subsumption tautology deletion purity deletion	irregularity anti-lemmas

Table 3. Refinements of subgoal-reduction strategies

Remarks and further reading General treatments of tableaux-based strategies and their relations with other strategies can be found in [26, 49].

Equality has long been a weak point of subgoal-reduction strategies, because for reasoning with equalities it is natural to generate and keep equations, and use them to rewrite other equations. In [21], approaches to equip analytic tableaux to handle equality include adding expansion rules for equality, or using forms of E-unification. Exactly because forward-reasoning with equalities is not a native feature of tableaux, in this context equality reasoning is considered as a form of *theory reasoning*, to be handled by a specialized component of the theorem prover: a general treatment of this topic can be found in [15]. E-Setheo is a version of Setheo with equality, continuing in the spirit of [120] of combining forward-reasoning and subgoal-reduction.

In addition to Setheo and Mission, other model-elimination tableau provers include Protein [17] and KoMeT [25], while provers based on analytic tableaux include TAP [23, 22] and Tatzelwurm [29]. Protein extends Prolog technology theorem proving with *theory reasoning*; KoMeT has lemmatization together with lemma subsumption, depth-dependent failure caching and some theory reasoning; Tatzelwurm enhances tableau-based strategies with UR-resolution and instance generation by hyperlinking [84].

4 Discussion

An advantage of subgoal-reduction strategies is that at each stage of the derivation, they need to keep in memory only the current proof attempt (e.g., the current goal and its ancestors, or the current tableau), whereas ordering-based strategies need to keep in memory all generated clauses not deleted by contraction (e.g., G_i^+ at stage i). Thus, if we call *active search space* what is held in memory, subgoal-reduction strategies tends to have a smaller active search space than ordering-based strategies. It is a fallacy, on the other hand, to conclude that the search space generated by subgoal-reduction strategies is also small. This fallacy is due to a confusion of active search space and *generated search space*. Because the subgoal-reduction strategy searches by backtracking, its generated search space is equal to the union of all the partial proofs it has attempted. Thus, the generated search space may be large, even if the active search space is small.

Another misconception is to say that ordering-based strategies search for a clause – the empty clause – whereas tableau-based strategies search for a proof. All theorem-proving strategies search for a proof. The difference is that ordering-based strategies build their proof attempts implicitly, and when an empty clause is generated, extract the completed proof from the generated search space (e.g., G_k^*). On the other hand, tableau-based strategies generate explicitly one proof attempt at a time, backtrack to modify it, and succeed when it is completed. A related error is to blame ordering-based strategies for generating huge proofs: this is based on mistaking the generated search space for the computed proof. Table 4 clarifies these points.

	Ordering-based	Subgoal-reduction
Generated search space	all generated clauses	all tried tableaux
Active search space	all kept clauses	the current tableau
Generated proof	the ancestor-graph of □	the closed tableau

Table 4. Two main classes of strategies (revisited)

If small active search space is an advantage of subgoal-reduction strategies, a main advantage of ordering-based strategies is contraction, which not only deletes existing redundant clauses, but also prevents their descendants in the search space from being generated. The study in [39] analyzes this behavior in term of *bounded search spaces* defined over the infinite search spaces of theorem-proving problems, and shows that in a contraction-based derivation the bounded search spaces are monotonically decreasing. In summary, the generated search space is typically large and the computed proof represents a small portion of it for both classes of strategies. The difference is in how the search proceeds, as reflected by small active search space on one hand, and monotonically decreasing bounded search spaces on the other.

References

1. Siva Anantharaman and Nirina Andrianarivelo. Heuristical criteria in refutational theorem proving. In Alfonso Miola, editor, *Proceedings of the 1st DISCO*, volume 429 of *LNCS*, pages 184–193. Springer Verlag, 1990.
2. Siva Anantharaman and Maria Paola Bonacina. An application of automated equational reasoning to many-valued logic. In Stéphane Kaplan and Mitsuhiro Okada, editors, *Proceedings of CTRS-90*, volume 516 of *LNCS*, pages 156–161. Springer Verlag, 1990.
3. Siva Anantharaman and Jieh Hsiang. Automated proofs of the Moufang identities in alternative rings. *Journal of Automated Reasoning*, 6(1):76–109, 1990.
4. Owen L. Astrachan and Don W. Loveland. METEORs: High performance theorem provers using model elimination. Pages 31–60 in [40].
5. Owen L. Astrachan and Don W. Loveland. The use of lemmas in the model elimination procedure. *Journal of Automated Reasoning*, 19(1):117–141, 1997.
6. Owen L. Astrachan and Mark E. Stickel. Caching and lemmaizing in model elimination theorem provers. Pages 224–238 in [77].
7. Franz Baader and Jörg H. Siekmann. Unification theory. In Vol. 2 of [62].
8. Leo Bachmair and Nachum Dershowitz. Inference rules for rewrite-based first-order theorem proving. In *Proceedings of LICS-87*, pages 331–337. IEEE Computer Society Press, 1987.
9. Leo Bachmair and Nachum Dershowitz. Critical pair criteria for completion. *Journal of Symbolic Computation*, 6(1):1–18, 1988.
10. Leo Bachmair, Nachum Dershowitz, and David A. Plaisted. Completion without failure. In Hassam Aït-Kaci and Maurice Nivat, editors, *Resolution of Equations in Algebraic Structures*, volume II: Rewriting Techniques, pages 1–30. Academic Press, 1989.
11. Leo Bachmair and Harald Ganzinger. Non-clausal resolution and superposition with selection and redundancy criteria. In Andrei Voronkov, editor, *Proceedings of LPAR-92*, volume 624 of *LNAI*, pages 273–284. Springer Verlag, 1992.
12. Leo Bachmair and Harald Ganzinger. Rewrite-based equational theorem proving with selection and simplification. *Journal of Logic and Computation*, 4(3):217–247, 1994.
13. Leo Bachmair and Harald Ganzinger. A theory of resolution. Technical Report MPI-I-97-2-005, Max Planck Institut für Informatik, 1997. To appear in J. Alan Robinson and Andrei Voronkov, eds., *Handbook of Automated Reasoning*.
14. Leo Bachmair, Harald Ganzinger, Christopher Lynch, and Wayne Snyder. Basic paramodulation. *Information and Computation*, 121(2):172–192, 1995.
15. Peter Baumgartner. *Theory Reasoning in Connection Calculi*, volume 1527 of *LNAI*. Springer, 1998.

16. Peter Baumgartner and Stefan Brüning. A disjunctive positive refinement of model elimination and its application to subsumption deletion. *Journal of Automated Reasoning*, 19:205–262, 1997.

17. Peter Baumgartner and Ulrich Furbach. PROTEIN: a PROver with a Theory Extension INterface. Pages 769–773 in [41].

18. Peter Baumgartner and Ulrich Furbach. Consolution as a framework for comparing calculi. *Journal of Symbolic Computation*, 16(5), 1993.

19. Peter Baumgartner and Ulrich Furbach. Model elimination without contrapositives and its application to PTTP. *Journal of Automated Reasoning*, 13:339–359, 1994.

20. Peter Baumgartner, Ulrich Furbach, and Frieder Stolzenburg. Model elimination, logic programming and computing answers. *Artificial Intelligence*, 90(1–2):135–176, 1997.

21. Bernhard Beckert. Semantic tableaux with equality. *Journal of Logic and Computation*, 7(1):39–58, 1997.

22. Bernhard Beckert, Reiner Hähnle, P. Ocl, and M. Sulzmann. The tableau-based theorem prover 3^{TAP}, version 4.0. Pages 303–307 in [101].

23. Bernhard Beckert and Joachim Posegga. leanTAP: lean tableau-based theorem proving. Pages 793–797 in [41].

24. Wolfgang Bibel. *Deduction: Automated Logic*. Academic Press, 1993.

25. Wolfgang Bibel, Stefan Brüning, Uwe Egly, and T. Rath. KoMeT. Pages 783–788 in [41].

26. Wolfgang Bibel and E. Eder. Methods and calculi for deduction. Pages 68–183 in Vol. 1 of [62].

27. Wolfgang Bibel and P. H. Schmitt, Eds. *Automated Deduction – A Basis for Applications*. Kluwer, 1998.

28. Wolgang Bibel. *Automated Theorem Proving*. Friedr. Vieweg & Sohn, 2nd edition, 1987.

29. Carsten Bierwald and Thomas Käufl. Tableau prover Tatzelwurm: hyper-links and UR-resolution. In Maria Paola Bonacina and Ulrich Furbach, editors, *Proceedings of the 1st FTP*, number 97-50 in Technical Reports of RISC, pages 22–28. Johannes Kepler Universität, 1997.

30. Roland N. Bol, Krzysztof R. Apt, and J. W. Klop. An analysis of loop checking mechanisms in logic programming. *Theoretical Computer Science*, 86:35–79, 1991.

31. Maria Paola Bonacina. A note on the analysis of theorem-proving strategies. AAR Newsletter, No. 36, pages 2–8, April 1997. Full version available as Technical Report, Department of Computer Science, University of Iowa, May 1996.

32. Maria Paola Bonacina. Analysis of distributed-search contraction-based strategies. In Jürgen Dix, Luis Fariñas del Cerro, and Ulrich Furbach, editors, *Proceedings of the 6th JELIA*, volume 1489 of *LNAI*, pages 107–121. Springer, 1998. Full version available as Tech. Rep., Dept. of Comp. Sci., Univ. of Iowa, April 1998.

33. Maria Paola Bonacina and Jieh Hsiang. On rewrite programs: semantics and relationship with Prolog. *Journal of Logic Programming*, 14(1 & 2):155–180, 1992.

34. Maria Paola Bonacina and Jieh Hsiang. On subsumption in distributed derivations. *Journal of Automated Reasoning*, 12:225–240, 1994.

35. Maria Paola Bonacina and Jieh Hsiang. Parallelization of deduction strategies: an analytical study. *Journal of Automated Reasoning*, 13:1–33, 1994.

36. Maria Paola Bonacina and Jieh Hsiang. Towards a foundation of completion procedures as semidecision procedures. *Theoretical Computer Science*, 146:199–242, 1995.

37. Maria Paola Bonacina and Jieh Hsiang. A category-theoretic treatment of automated theorem proving. *Journal of Information Science and Engineering*, 12(1):101–125, 1996.

38. Maria Paola Bonacina and Jieh Hsiang. On semantic resolution with lemmaizing and contraction and a formal treatment of caching. *New Generation Computing*, 16(2):163–200, 1998.

39. Maria Paola Bonacina and Jieh Hsiang. On the modelling of search in theorem proving – towards a theory of strategy analysis. *Information and Computation*, 147:171–208, 1998.

40. Robert S. Boyer, Ed. *Automated Reasoning – Essays in Honor of Woody Bledsoe*. Kluwer, 1991.

41. Alan Bundy, Ed. *Proceedings of the 12th CADE*, volume 814 of *LNAI*. Springer, 1994.

42. H.-J. Bürckert. *A Resolution Principle for a Logic with Restricted Quantifiers*, volume 568 of *LNAI*. Springer Verlag, 1991.

43. Ricardo Caferra and Nicolas Peltier. Model building in the cross-roads of consequence and non-consequence relations. In Maria Paola Bonacina and Ulrich Furbach, editors, *Proceedings of the 1st FTP*, number 97-50 in Technical Reports of RISC, pages 40–44. Johannes Kepler Universität, 1997.

44. Ricardo Caferra and N. Zabel. A method for simultaneous search for refutations and models by equational constraint solving. *Journal of Symbolic Computation*, 13:613–641, 1992.

45. Chin-Liang Chang and Richard Char-Tung Lee. *Symbolic Logic and Mechanical Theorem Proving*. Academic Press, 1973.

46. Jim Christian. Flatterms, discrimination nets and fast term rewriting. *Journal of Automated Reasoning*, 10:95–113, 1993.

47. Heng Chu and David A. Plaisted. CLINS-S: a semantically guided first-order theorem prover. In [136].

48. Heng Chu and David A. Plaisted. Model finding in semantically guided instance-based theorem proving. *Fundamenta Informaticae*, 21(3):221–235, 1994.

49. M. D'Agostino, Dov M. Gabbay, Reiner Hähnle, and Joachim Posegga, Eds. *Handbook of Tableau Methods*. Kluwer, 1998.

50. Martin Davis and Hilary Putnam. A computing procedure for quantification theory. *Journal of the ACM*, 7:201–215, 1960.

51. Jörg Denzinger and M. Fuchs. Goal-oriented equational theorem proving using team-work. In *Proceedings of the 18th KI*, volume 861 of *LNAI*, pages 343–354. Springer, 1994.

52. Nachum Dershowitz. Orderings for term-rewriting systems. *Theoretical Computer Science*, 17:279–301, 1982.

53. Nachum Dershowitz. Computing with rewrite systems. *Information and Control*, 65:122–157, 1985.

54. Nachum Dershowitz. Canonical sets of Horn clauses. In J. Leach Albert, B. Monien, and Mario Rodríguez Artalejo, editors, *Proceedings of the 18th ICALP*, volume 510 of *LNCS*, pages 267–278. Springer Verlag, 1991.

55. Nachum Dershowitz and Jean-Pierre Jouannaud. Rewrite systems. In Jan van Leeuwen, editor, *Handbook of Theoretical Computer Science*, volume B, pages 243–320. Elsevier, 1990.

56. Roland Dietrich. Relating resolution and algebraic completion for Horn logic. Pages 62–78 in [123].

57. Norbert Eisinger and Hans Jürgen Ohlbach. Deduction systems based on resolution. Pages 184–273 in Vol. 1 of [62].

58. Christian Fermüller and Alexander Leitsch. Hyperresolution and automated model-building. *Journal of Logic and Computation*, 6(2):173–203, 1996.
59. Christian Fermüller and Alexander Leitsch. Decision procedures and model-building in equational clause logic. *Journal of the IGPL*, 6(1):17–41, 1998.
60. Melvin Fitting. *First-order Logic and Automated Theorem Proving*. Springer, 1990.
61. S. Fleisig, Don W. Loveland, A. Smiley, and D. Yarmush. An implementation of the model elimination proof procedure. *Journal of the ACM*, 21:124–139, 1974.
62. Dov M. Gabbay, Christopher J. Hogger, and J. Alan Robinson, Eds. *Handbook of Logic in Artificial Intelligence and Logic Programming (Vol. 1 & 2)*. Oxford University Press, 1993.
63. Jean Gallier. *Logic for Computer Science – Foundations of Automatic Theorem Proving*. Harper & Row, 1986.
64. Chr. Goller, Reinhold Letz, K. Mayr, and Johann Schumann. SETHEO v3.2: recent developments. Pages 778–782 in [41].
65. John Harrison. Optimizing proof search in model elimination. Pages 313–327 in [101].
66. Ryuzo Hasegawa, Miyuki Koshimura, and Hiroshi Fujita. MGTP: a parallel theorem prover based on lazy model generation. Pages 776–780 in [77].
67. Jieh Hsiang. Refutational theorem proving using term rewriting systems. *Artificial Intelligence*, 25:255–300, 1985.
68. Jieh Hsiang. Rewrite method for theorem proving in first order theories with equality. *Journal of Symbolic Computation*, 3:133–151, 1987.
69. Jieh Hsiang and Michaël Rusinowitch. On word problems in equational theories. In Th. Ottman, editor, *Proceedings of the 14th ICALP*, volume 267 of *LNCS*, pages 54–71. Springer Verlag, 1987.
70. Jieh Hsiang and Michaël Rusinowitch. Proving refutational completeness of theorem proving strategies: the transfinite semantic tree method. *Journal of the ACM*, 38(3):559–587, 1991.
71. Jieh Hsiang, Michaël Rusinowitch, and Ko Sakai. Complete inference rules for the cancellation laws. In *Proceedings of the 10th IJCAI*, pages 990–992, 1987.
72. Jean-Pierre Jouannaud and Claude Kirchner. Solving equations in abstract algebras: a rule-based survey of unification. Pages 257–321 in [83].
73. Deepak Kapur, Dave Musser, and Paliath Narendran. Only prime superposition need be considered in the Knuth-Bendix completion procedure. *Journal of Symbolic Computation*, 6:19–36, 1988.
74. Deepak Kapur and Paliath Narendran. An equational approach to theorem proving in first order predicate calculus. In *Proceedings of the 9th IJCAI*, pages 1146–1153, 1985.
75. Deepak Kapur and Hantao Zhang. A case study of the completion procedure: proving ring commutativity problems. Pages 360–394 in [83].
76. Deepak Kapur and Hantao Zhang. An overview of RRL: rewrite rule laboratory. In Nachum Dershowitz, editor, *Proceedings of the 3rd RTA*, volume 355 of *LNCS*, pages 513–529. Springer Verlag, 1989.
77. Deepak Kapur, Ed. *Proceedings of the 11th CADE*, volume 607 of *LNAI*. Springer, 1992.
78. Claude Kirchner, Hélène Kirchner, and Michaël Rusinowitch. Deduction with symbolic constraints. *Revue Française d'Intelligence Artificielle*, 4(3):9–52, 1990.
79. Donald E. Knuth and Peter B. Bendix. Simple word problems in universal algebras. In J. Leech, editor, *Proceedings of the Conf. on Computational Problems in Abstract Algebras*, pages 263–298. Pergamon Press, 1970.

80. R. E. Korf. Depth-first iterative deepening: an optimal admissible tree search. *Artificial Intelligence*, 27(1):97–109, 1985.

81. Robert Kowalski. Search strategies for theorem proving. In B. Meltzer and D. Michie, editors, *Machine Intelligence*, volume 5, pages 181–201. Edinburgh University Press, 1969.

82. Robert Kowalski and D. Kuehner. Linear resolution with selection function. *Artificial Intelligence*, 2:227–260, 1971.

83. Jean-Louis Lassez and Gordon Plotkin, Eds. *Computational Logic – Essays in Honor of Alan Robinson*. The MIT Press, 1991.

84. Shie-Jue Lee and David A. Plaisted. Eliminating duplication with the hyperlinking strategy. *Journal of Automated Reasoning*, 9:25–42, 1992.

85. Alexander Leitsch. *The Resolution Calculus*. Springer, 1997.

86. Reinhold Letz, K. Mayr, and Chr. Goller. Controlled integration of the cut rule into connection tableau calculi. *Journal of Automated Reasoning*, 13(3):297–338, 1994.

87. Reinhold Letz, Johann Schumann, S. Bayerl, and Wolfgang Bibel. SETHEO: a high performance theorem prover. *Journal of Automated Reasoning*, 8(2):183–212, 1992.

88. John W. Lloyd. *Foundations of Logic Programming*. Springer Verlag, 2nd edition, 1987.

89. Don W. Loveland. A simplified format for the model elimination procedure. *Journal of the ACM*, 16(3):349–363, 1969.

90. Don W. Loveland. A unifying view of some linear Herbrand procedures. *Journal of the ACM*, 19(2):366–384, 1972.

91. Don W. Loveland. *Automated Theorem Proving: A Logical Basis*. North-Holland, 1978.

92. Ewing Lusk and Ross Overbeek, Eds. *Proceedings of the 9th CADE*, volume 310 of *LNCS*. Springer Verlag, 1988.

93. Rainer Manthey and François Bry. SATCHMO: a theorem prover implemented in Prolog. Pages 415–434 in [92].

94. J. McCharen, Ross Overbeek, and Larry Wos. Complexity and related enhancements for automated theorem proving programs. *Computers and Mathematics with Applications*, 2(1):1–16, 1976.

95. William W. McCune. Experiments with discrimination tree indexing and path indexing for term retrieval. *Journal of Automated Reasoning*, 9(2):147–167, 1992.

96. William W. McCune. A Davis-Putnam program and its application to finite first-order model search: quasigroup existence problems. Unpublished manuscript, May 1994.

97. William W. McCune. Otter 3.0 reference manual and guide. Technical Report 94/6, MCS Division, Argonne National Laboratory, 1994.

98. William W. McCune. 33 Basic test problems: a practical evaluation of some paramodulation strategies. In Robert Veroff, editor, *Automated Reasoning and its Applications: Essays in Honor of Larry Wos*, pages 71–114. MIT Press, 1997.

99. William W. McCune. Solution of the Robbins problem. *Journal of Automated Reasoning*, 19(3):263–276, 1997.

100. William W. McCune, Ed. *Proceedings of the 14th CADE*, volume 1249 of *LNAI*. Springer, 1997.

101. Michael McRobbie and John Slaney, Eds. *Proceedings of the 13th CADE*, volume 1104 of *LNAI*. Springer, 1996.

102. Jürgen Müller and Rolf Socher-Ambrosius. Topics in completion theorem proving. Technical Report SEKI SR-88-13, Fachbereich Informatik, Univ. Kaiserslautern, 1988.

103. Xumin Nie and David A. Plaisted. A complete semantic back chaining proof system. Pages 16–27 in [135].

104. Robert Niewenhuis, José Miguel Rivero, and Miguel Angel Vallejo. The Barcelona prover. In [136].

105. Robert Niewenhuis and A. Rubio. Theorem proving with ordering and equality constrained clauses. *Journal of Symbolic Computation*, 19(4):321–351, 1995.

106. Judea Pearl. *Heuristics - Intelligent Search Strategies for Computer Problem Solving*. Addison Wesley, 1984.

107. Gerald E. Peterson. A technique for establishing completeness results in theorem proving with equality. *SIAM Journal of Computing*, 12(1):82–100, 1983.

108. David A. Plaisted. Equational reasoning and term rewriting systems. Pages 273–364 in Vol. 1 of [62].

109. David A. Plaisted. A simplified problem reduction format. *Artificial Intelligence*, 18:227–261, 1982.

110. David A. Plaisted. Non-Horn clause logic programming without contrapositives. *Journal of Automated Reasoning*, 4(3):287–325, 1988.

111. David A. Plaisted. Mechanical theorem proving. In Ranan B. Banerji, editor, *Formal Techniques in Artificial Intelligence*. Elsevier, 1990.

112. David A. Plaisted. A sequent-style model elimination strategy and a positive refinement. *Journal of Automated Reasoning*, 6(4):389–402, 1990.

113. David A. Plaisted and Yunshan Zhu. *The Efficiency of Theorem Proving Strategies*. Friedr. Vieweg & Sohns, 1997.

114. David A. Plaisted and Yunshan Zhu. Ordered semantic hyper linking. In *Proceedings of AAAI-97*, 1997.

115. Allan Ramsay. *Formal Methods in Artificial Intelligence*. Cambridge University Press, 1988.

116. G. Robinson and Larry Wos. Paramodulation and theorem-proving in first-order theories with equality. In D. Michie and R. Meltzer, editors, *Machine Intelligence*, volume IV, pages 135–150. Edinburgh Univ. Press, 1969.

117. J. Alan Robinson. Automatic deduction with hyper-resolution. *International Journal of Computer Mathematics*, 1:227–234, 1965.

118. J. Alan Robinson. A machine oriented logic based on the resolution principle. *Journal of the ACM*, 12(1):23–41, 1965.

119. Michaël Rusinowitch. Theorem-proving with resolution and superposition. *Journal of Symbolic Computation*, 11(1 & 2):21–50, 1991.

120. Johann Schumann. Delta: a bottom-up pre-processor for top-down theorem provers. Pages 774–777 in [41].

121. Robert E. Shostak. Refutation graphs. *Artificial Intelligence*, 7:51–64, 1976.

122. Jörg H. Siekmann and Graham Wrightson, Eds. *Automation of reasoning - Classical Papers on Computational Logic*. Springer Verlag, 1983.

123. Jörg H. Siekmann, Ed. *Proceedings of the 8th CADE*, volume 230 of *LNCS*. Springer, 1986.

124. James R. Slagle. Automatic theorem proving with renamable and semantic resolution. *Journal of the ACM*, 14(4):687–697, 1967.

125. John Slaney. FINDER: finite domain enumerator. Pages 798–801 in [41].

126. Raymond M. Smullyan. *First-Order Logic*. Dover, 1995. (Republication of the work first published as "Band 43" Series *Ergebnisse der Mathematik und ihrer Grenzgebiete*, Springer Verlag, 1968).

127. Rolf Socher-Ambrosius. How to avoid the derivation of redundant clauses in reasoning systems. *Journal of Automated Reasoning*, 9(1):77–98, 1992.
128. Rolf Socher-Ambrosius and Patricia Johann. *Deduction systems*. Springer, 1997.
129. Mark E. Stickel. PTTP and linked inference. Pages 283–296 in [40].
130. Mark E. Stickel. A Prolog technology theorem prover. *New Generation Computing*, 2(4):371–383, 1984.
131. Mark E. Stickel. Automated deduction by theory resolution. *Journal of Automated Reasoning*, 1:333–355, 1985.
132. Mark E. Stickel. A Prolog technology theorem prover: implementation by an extended Prolog compiler. *Journal of Automated Reasoning*, 4:353–380, 1988.
133. Mark E. Stickel. The path-indexing method for indexing terms. Technical Report 473, SRI International, 1989.
134. Mark E. Stickel, Richard Waldinger, Michael Lowry, Thomas Pressburger, and Ian Underwood. Deductive composition of astronomical software from subroutine libraries. Pages 341–355 in [41].
135. Mark E. Stickel, Ed. *Proceedings of the 10th CADE*, volume 449 of *LNAI*. Springer, 1990.
136. Geoff Sutcliffe and Christian Suttner, Eds. The CADE-13 ATP system competition. *Journal of Automated Reasoning*, 18(2), 1997.
137. Tanel Tammet. Gandalf. Pages 199–204 in [136].
138. Laurent Vigneron. Automated deduction techniques for studying rough algebras. *Fundamenta Informaticae*, 33:85–103, 1998.
139. Kevin Wallace and Graham Wrightson. Regressive merging in model elimination tableau-based theorem provers. *Journal of the IGPL*, 3(6):921–937, 1995.
140. David H. D. Warren. An abstract Prolog instruction set. Technical Report 309, SRI International, 1983.
141. David S. Warren. Memoing for logic programs. *Communications of the ACM*, 35(3):94–111, 1992.
142. Christoph Weidenbach, B. Gaede, and G. Rock. SPASS & FLOTTER, version 0.42. Pages 141–145 in [101].
143. Larry Wos, D. Carson, and G. Robinson. Efficiency and completeness of the set of support strategy in theorem proving. *Journal of the ACM*, 12:536–541, 1965.
144. Larry Wos, G. Robinson, D. Carson, and L. Shalla. The concept of demodulation in theorem proving. *Journal of the ACM*, 14(4):698–709, 1967.
145. Lary Wos, Ross Overbeek, Ewing Lusk, and J. Boyle. *Automated Reasoning: Introduction and Applications*. McGraw-Hill, 2nd edition, 1992.
146. Hantao Zhang. SATO: an efficient propositional prover. Pages 272–275 in [100].
147. Hantao Zhang. A new method for the boolean ring based theorem proving. *Journal of Symbolic Computation*, 17(2):189–211, 1994.
148. Hantao Zhang, Maria Paola Bonacina, and Jieh Hsiang. PSATO: a distributed propositional prover and its application to quasigroup problems. *Journal of Symbolic Computation*, 21:543–560, 1996.
149. Hantao Zhang and Mark E. Stickel. Implementing the Davis-Putnam algorithm by tries. Technical Report 94-12, Department of Computer Science, University of Iowa, 1994.
150. Jian Zhang and Hantao Zhang. Generating models by SEM. Pages 308–312 in [101].

An Overview of Planning Under Uncertainty

Jim Blythe
Information Sciences Institute
University of Southern California
4676 Admiralty Way
Marina del Rey, CA 90292 USA
blythe@isi.edu

Abstract. The recent advances in computer speed and algorithms for probabilistic inference have led to a resurgence of work on planning under uncertainty. The aim is to design AI planners for environments where there may be incomplete or faulty information, where actions may not always have the same results and where there may be tradeoffs between the different possible outcomes of a plan. Addressing uncertainty in AI planning algorithms will greatly increase the range of potential applications but there is plenty of work to be done before we see practical decision-theoretic planning systems. This article outlines some of the challenges that need to be overcome and surveys some of the recent work in the area.

Introduction

AI planning algorithms are concerned with finding a course of action to be carried out by some agent to achieve its goals. In problems where actions can lead to a number of different possible outcomes, or where the benefits of executing a plan must be weighed against the costs, the framework of decision theory can be used to compare alternative plans.

For a long time the planning community has maintained an interest in decision-theoretic planning, with Feldman and Sproull's work being one of the earliest in this area [23]. After a period where attention was focussed on efficient algorithms for planning under quite restrictive assumptions, the past five years have seen a resurgence in work on planning under uncertainty and decision-theoretic planning. There are several reasons for this. The recent advances in Bayesian inference have made it feasible to compute (or approximate) the expected utility of a plan under conditions of uncertainty. The success of Markovian approaches in areas such as speech recognition and the closely-related reinforcement learning techniques have encouraged work in planning using Markov decision processes. Faster computers have made it feasible to build decision-theoretic planners, which in general have more complicated search spaces than their classical counterparts.

In this chapter, which also appeared as [6], I provide a brief overview of some of the recent work in decision-theoretic planning. I highlight some of the advances made and some technical problems that still lie ahead. In the next section I describe the problem addressed by decision-theoretic planning systems. The following two sections describe work based on classical planning algorithms and based on solving Markov decision processes respectively.

Goals of decision-theoretic planning

A planning problem in AI is usually specified as follows: Given a description of the current state of some system, a set of actions that can be performed on the system and a description of a goal set of states for the system, find a sequence of actions that can be performed to transform the system into one of the goal states. In the text-book example of the blocks world, the system consists of a set of named blocks, each of which may be on the ground or on top of another block. The possible actions move a block from one location to another and the goal is a particular configuration of blocks, for example a tower.

When planning programs are used to provide courses of action in real-world settings, such as medical treatments, high-level robot control or disaster relief, they must take into account the fact that actions may have several different outcomes, some of which may be more desirable than others. They must balance the potential of some plan achieving a goal state against the risk of producing an undesirable state and against the cost of performing the plan.

Decision theory [41] provides an attractive framework for weighing the strengths and weaknesses of a particular course of action, with roots in probability theory and utility theory. Given a probability distribution over the possible outcomes of an action in any state, and a reasonable preference function over outcomes, we can define a utility function on outcomes such that whenever the agent would prefer one plan over another, the preferred plan has higher expected utility. The task of the planner then seems straightforward — to find the plan with the maximum expected utility (MEU).

Unfortunately, decision theory says nothing about the task of constructing a plan with high expected utility. Therefore AI planning and decision theory would appear to be complementary and there has been interest in merging the two approaches for a considerable time [23]. However there are hard problems to overcome. It is usually not feasible to search the entire space of plans to find the MEU plan. Indeed, computing the expected utility of a single plan can be prohibitively expensive because the number of possible outcomes can grow very large. In order to avoid specifying the value of each possible outcome we need to find compact specifications of utilities as well as actions, and consider the interaction between them. The recent increase in research in decision-theoretic planning follows the recent success of work in reasoning under uncertainty, and draws on compact representations such as those of belief nets [16].

Extending classical planners

Since the early systems GPS [44] and STRIPS [24], most AI planners that have been designed make essentially the same assumptions about the world in which they operate. From the point of view of decision-theoretic planing, three assumptions of note are:

- the goal of the planner is a logical description of a world state,
- the actions taken by the planner are the only sources of change in the world, and
- each action can be described by the conditions under which it can be applied and its effects on the world. These effects are described by a set of facts which are either to be added to or deleted from the world state in which the action is applied.

The last is known as the "STRIPS assumption". I refer to planners that share these assumptions as the "classical planners". They include Prodigy [56], UCPOP [48], Graphplan [1] and the hierarchical task network planner Nonlin [55][1].

Here I describe work that relaxes one or more of these assumptions in a classical planner. First, we can relax the assumption that actions are deterministic by specifying a set of possible outcomes, rather than the single outcome in the deterministic case. Consider the planning problem of moving my kitchen china from an old apartment to a new one. The goal is to move the china unbroken, specified as (at china new-apartment) ∧ ¬ (broken china). Figure 1 shows three increasingly detailed descriptions of the drive-china action which can achieve this goal. The first is deterministic and could be used in a plan that achieves the goal with certainty: (put-in china), (drive-china old-apartment new-apartment), using the extra operators in Figure 2. The second drive-china operator has two alternative sets of effects, modeling two different world states that can arise if the operator is applied. The numbers on the arcs are the probabilities of each state of affairs. Under this model, the two-step plan will only achieve the goal with probability 0.7.

In the third formulation of drive-china, different sets of outcomes are possible based on the conditions that hold when the operator is applied and the arcs now show conditional probabilities. The two-step plan still has a probability of 0.7 of succeeding. The three-step plan (pack china) (put-in china) (drive-china ...) succeeds with probability 0.95.

Second, we can relax the assumption that goals are logical descriptions of world states, so that a plan either succeeds or fails. We can attach utilities to different world states representing degrees of desirability. For example suppose the state in which all my china is moved unbroken has a utility of 10, while one in which half of my china is moved and none is broken has a utility of 6, any state in which china is broken has a utility of -100 and any other state has a utility of 0. If the pack operator can only pack half of the china, the two-step plan has an expected utility of -23 while the three-step plan has an expected utility of 1. In this case the plan to pack some of the china is slightly better than doing nothing, which has a utility of 0, while the plan to simply move the china without packing it is much worse.

Challenges for classically-based decision-theoretic planning

In the next four sections I describe four different approaches for planning under uncertainty that can be viewed as extending a classical planning approach. These are SNLP-based planners, DRIPS, Weaver and Maxplan, although the last of these is arguably not a classical planner. Organizing the article around specific research programs makes it easier to keep in mind the specific assumptions behind each one, at the cost of making it harder to follow how they address some of the issues and challenges that must be faced in creating decision-theoretic planners. In this section I briefly describe some of those issues, as a way of forming a road-map for understanding the different approaches.

---

[1] Although compound operators in hierarchical task network planners are more complex, the primitive operators (that exclusively fill complete plans) have this form.

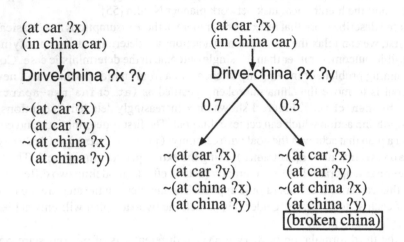

Deterministic effects   Non-deterministic effects

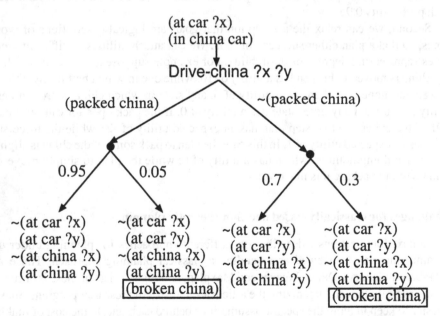

Non-deterministic effects with conditional probabilities

Fig. 1. Three versions of the operator drive-china

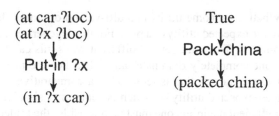

Fig. 2. Other operators in the moving-house example.

Action representation As the china-moving example shows, in order to represent uncertain actions one has to represent several alternative outcomes and their probabilities, conditional on the state. Providing a richer representation of action inevitably makes the planning problem harder, and planners must use a representation that expresses the different outcomes as concisely as possible while still being fully expressive. The representation of the final **drive-china** operator is not very concise, for example, because the four possible outcomes are described explicitly, even though the two branches only differ in their probabilities and each outcome only differs in whether the china is broken. When different state variables are affected independently by an action it is possible for the number of outcomes to grow exponentially in the number of variables.

Plan utility Several systems based on classical planning ignore outcome utility beyond the binary measure of goal achievement, although exceptions are DRIPS [33] and Pyrrhus [62]. In planners based on Markov decision processes, discussed later in this article, a numeric reward function is specified for an action in a state. While this is adequate from a purely decision-theoretic point of view, a more structured representation of utility is needed to make planning tractable, one where the utility of a state is built up from smaller building blocks so that it is less tedious to specify and also the utility of abstract states can be estimated. This problem has been approached in both frameworks.

Some planners relax the binary measure of goal achievement to allow partial satisfaction of goals. In the china-moving example the full goal is to move all the china unbroken, but we might attach partial credit for moving some of it unbroken. Given a conjunctive set of goals, sometimes the utility from solving a subset can be specified as the sum of some utility for each goal. Care must be taken with this approach, for example in the china-moving example the top-level goals are (at china new-apartment) and (not (broken china)), but a planner that achieves the first goal without the second should not receive half the credit. Sometimes the utility of an outcome can be made more modular by summing the cost of each operator independently [50], with the same caution.

Haddawy and Hanks describe an approach that further assumes a deadline by which a goal should ideally be achieved, with a separate penalty function that offsets the utility for the goal when it is achieved after the deadline. They propose a representation that encompasses most of these approaches independently of any planner in [29].

Plan evaluation Whether outcome utility is multi-valued or simply binary, one must compute or estimate the expected utility of a plan. For the degenerate case, this is simply the probability of success. There are several different ways this can be approached as we shall see, and none completely dominates any other. For the problem of deciding which partial plan to expand, all that is required is a comparative value — deciding which plan has higher expected utility — which is sometimes simpler than finding the absolute value. For efficient planning, one must also consider the tradeoff between time spent estimating plan value and time spent expanding a plan whose value is poorer than estimated.

Observability and conditional planning Most of these systems distinguish between observable and non-observable domain variables. A classical STRIPS plan essentially assumes no observability since the plan is a sequence of actions executed "blind". In normal Markov decision processes, the output is a policy, a mapping from state to action which assumes that every state variable can be observed without error, although some work that relaxes this assumption is described later. In the Buridan planner [38] actions can have sensing results as well as effects in the world, and noisy sensors can be modeled.

In an uncertain world, high-utility plans created in advance may need to have some actions that are conditional on future observations. Most of the planners discussed are capable of handling this, employing a variety of techniques. Note that planning agents must be able to make observations of their domain during execution in order to use conditional plans.

Tractability Perhaps the largest question mark hanging over the planners described here is their tractability. Few have been applied in large, high-dimensional domains although exceptions are DRIPS [32] and Weaver [5]. In addition it is rare that the planners are directly compared with each other although MAXPLAN is an exception [42]. This is partly because as we shall see the planners have concentrated on different aspects of the planning problem.

The tractability of the planners is affected by the kind of planning algorithm used: SNLP, Prodigy, refinement planning, HTN planning and compilation to satisfiability have all been used. It is also affected by the use of search control, which has been studied in several of the planners.

SNLP based planners

The classical planner SNLP maintains a plan as a partially-ordered set of actions, along with ordering constraints between steps, bindings for variables in steps and explicit data structures, called "causal links", that represent what the step is supposed to accomplish in the plan [57]. A causal link records the subgoal being achieved, the "consumer" step, that has this subgoal as a precondition, and the "provider" step, that has the subgoal as an effect. For example, the arrow between drive-china and goal in Figure 3 is a causal link for the subgoal (at china new-apartment with drive-china as provider and goal as consumer. goal is a dummy step added to the plan to represent the

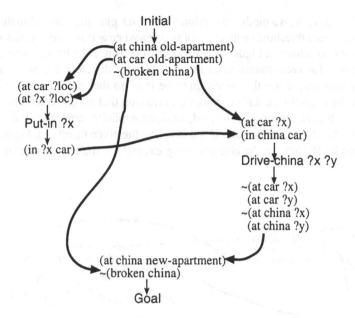

Fig. 3. A plan to move china, as found by SNLP. The bold arrows represent causal links in the plan.

top-level goals. Similarly `initial` is a dummy step representing the initial state. The SNLP algorithm follows the loop shown in Figure 4. It repeatedly picks an unsupported condition in the plan, adds a causal link supporting it from some step that achieves the condition, and removes any threats to the link by forcing any step that negates the condition to take place either before or after both linked steps. By considering all possible choices for causal links and threat orderings, SNLP is complete, ie it will find a plan if one exists. For more details see [57].

1. If the current plan has no unsupported conditions, return it.
2. Pick an unsupported condition P for some step U and add a causal link to the plan that supports it, achieving the condition with either an existing or a new step, A. (On backtracking, try all possible links.)
3. Resolve any *threats* to the new link. A threat comes from any step T in the plan that can take place between A and U and can negate P. Resolve the threat by ordering T either before A or after U if possible (on backtracking, try both orderings). If this is not possible, fail and backtrack.

Fig. 4. An outline of the SNLP algorithm

Buridan Buridan [38] is a modified version of the SNLP planning algorithm that can create plans that meet a threshold probability of success when actions are non-deterministic, as are the last two actions in Figure 1. Buridan differs from SNLP by allowing more than one causal link for each condition in the plan. Under different execution scenarios, different actions may cause the condition to be true, so the links combine to increase support for the condition. SNLP's termination criterion that all conditions have exactly one link is no longer appropriate. Instead, Buridan explicitly computes the probability of success of the plan and terminates if this is above the given threshold. Figure 5 shows a plan found by Buridan in the china-moving example if the third model of action is used.

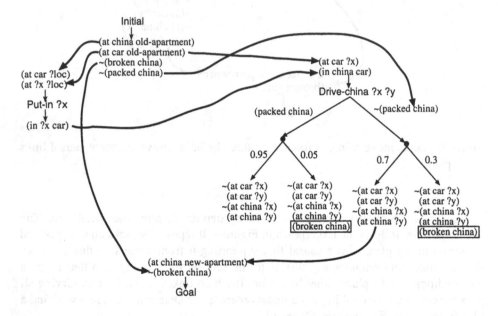

Fig. 5. A plan to move china, found by Buridan

This plan succeeds with probability 0.7, because with probability 0.3 executing `drive-china` can lead to the china being broken. This step is therefore a threat to the link for (`broken china`) from `Initial` to *Goal*. In addition to SNLP's re-orderings to remove threats, Buridan can *confront* a threat by decreasing the probability of an outcome in which the threatened condition is negated. In this case, that is done by adding a link from the outcome with probability 0.95 that does not add (`broken china`), and planning for its trigger, (`packed china`). Buridan can then find the plan [`pack-china`, `put-in china`, `drive-china`], that succeeds with probability 0.95.

So far we haven't discussed how a planner finds the probability that a plan succeeds. There are a number of possible strategies, based on forward projection or on analyzing the dependencies among state descriptors. Empirical experiments show no clear winner [38].

Step	State	Features	Parent	Prob
Pack-china	S_{pack}^1	packed	I	0.5
Pack-china	S_{pack}^2	¬ packed	I	0.5
Put-in-china	S_{put}^1	packed, in-car	S_{pack}^1	0.5
Put-in-china	S_{put}^2	¬ packed, in-car	S_{pack}^2	0.5
Drive-china	S_d^{11}	packed, ¬ broken	S_{put}^1	0.475
Drive-china	S_d^{12}	packed, broken	S_{put}^1	0.025
Drive-china	S_d^{21}	¬ packed, ¬ broken	S_{put}^2	0.35
Drive-china	S_d^{22}	¬ packed, broken	S_{put}^2	0.15

Fig. 6. Using forward projection to evaluate the plan for the china-moving problem.

Forward projection begins with the set of possible initial states and simulates executing the plan one step at a time, maintaining the set of possible states and their probabilities after each step is completed. When the simulation is finished, summing the probability of each state in which the goals are satisfied gives the plan's probability of succeeding. The table at the top of Figure 6 shows the sets of states that are built as the three-step plan is evaluated by forward projection. To make the example more interesting we assume that the **pack-china** action succeeds with probability 0.5, and otherwise has no effect. It therefore leads to two states in the forward projection, which are propagated through the **put-in-china** step and lead to four possible states after the **drive-china** action. The probability of success, 0.825, is found by summing the probabilities of states S_d^{11} and S_d^{21}.

In general, the number of states considered can clearly grow exponentially with the length of the plan. Many of the states created might differ only on features that are irrelevant to the plan. This observation suggests other plan evaluation strategies that exploit the structure of the plan. One such strategy is to evaluate the plan using a belief net [47]. The STRIPS representation for action, in which the preconditions contain sufficient information to completely determine the outcomes of the action, is a special case of the Markov assumption and this is preserved in the action representation used here [59]. One can use this observation to create a belief net that can be queried to determine the probability of success of the plan. There are many ways to do this — one example is shown in Figure 7. Its nodes are random variables representing either the value of state descriptors at a point in time or the outcomes of actions taken in the plan. The final action **goal** is included, with two possible values: **true** or **false**. The probability that this has value **true** is equal to the plan's probability of success.

Conditional planning CNLP was the first SNLP-based planner to represent conditional plans [49]. Each step in the plan has a set of *context labels* associated with it that denote the conditions under which the step will be executed. For example, Figure 8 shows a conditional plan for moving the china in which the agent loads the china in the car and then listens to the weather report before deciding whether to take the route over the mountain or around the mountain. The operator `get-weather-report` has two possible outcomes, each producing one of the observation labels ok or bad. Each of

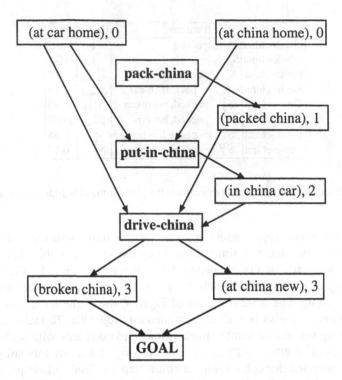

Fig. 7. Using a belief net to evaluate the plan for the china-moving problem. The nodes with bold text represent actions in the plan, while the others represent fluent values at a given point in time.

the two driving operators is marked with one of the labels as its context. Thus they must be executed after `get-weather-report`, and `drive-china-over-mountain`, for example, will only be executed if the label ok was produced. If any subsequent actions had no context labels, they would be executed on both "branches" of the conditional plan. Contexts are not as direct a representation as putting an explicit branch in a plan, but they can easily represent plans that branch and then re-merge as well as partially-ordered branching plans.

C-Buridan refines the approach of CNLP by keeping observations distinct from effects and allowing different outcomes of a sensing action to have the same observation label, thus modeling partial observability [22]. In C-Buridan, new contexts are added in response to threats between actions that can be put in separate branches of a conditional plan. Obviously, the ability to create conditional plans can make the planning problem even less tractable. Most conditional planners do not require a plan to be produced for every contingency (although Cassandra is an exception [51]). Onder and Pollack have studied how to choose which contingencies to plan for, both to improve efficiency and based on the observation that some contingencies can safely be left for re-planning at execution time [45].

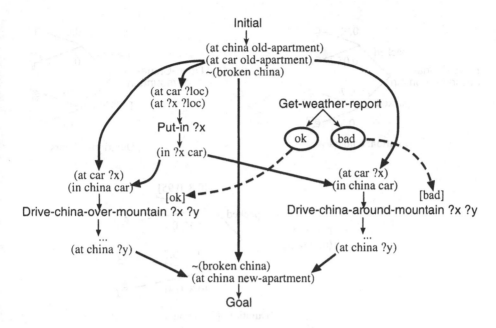

Fig. 8. A conditional plan represented using context labels attached to actions.

DRIPS: searching for optimal plans with a refinement planner

The planners described above search for plans that exceed a given minimum expected utility. In order to find the plan with maximum expected utility, however, one must somehow evaluate all possible plans to select the best one. In DRIPS, ranges of utility values are computed for partial plans, encompassing the best and worst expected utilities of all possible completions of the partial plan [33]. If the lowest value in some partial plan's range exceeds the highest value in another's the partial plan with the lower range can be dropped from consideration without expanding all the complete plans below it, an approach that can lead to significant savings. The dropped plan is said to be *dominated* by the other plan, an idea also explored by Wellman [59].

DRIPS accomplishes this by *skeletal refinement planning* based on an abstraction hierarchy of operators [25]. In this approach, a partial plan is a sequence of operators, one or more of which may be an abstraction of a number of ground operators. Planning proceeds by repeatedly choosing a more specific version of an operator in the plan until there are no abstract operators left. The planner begins with one of a set of skeletal plans containing highly abstract operators chosen from a library. Figure 9 shows some example ground and abstract operators from the china-moving example, extended with a richer model of the utilities of outcomes.

Figure 10 shows an abstraction/decomposition network that describes all possible specializations of a skeletal plan to move the china. Solid lines denote decomposition of an operator and dashed lines denote possible choices for an abstract operator. The skeletal plan encodes four potential plans: one can choose whether to pack the china and one can independently choose which route to take.

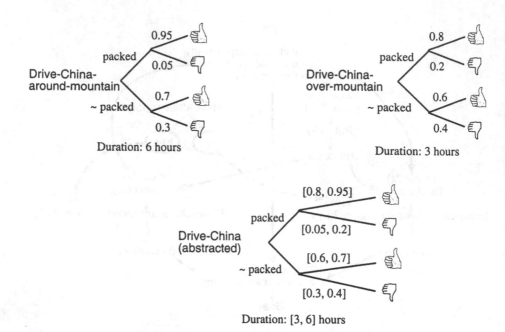

Fig. 9. Ground and abstract operators from the china-moving example that could be used by the refinement planner DRIPS. The thumbs-up symbol denotes an outcome in which the china is moved successfully and the thumbs-down icon denotes an outcome in which the china is broken.

Suppose DRIPS begins refining this plan by choosing between **pack-and-load** and **load** to refine the **load-up-china** operator. The planner will normally add both refinements to a queue of partial plans, but first it computes ranges of expected utility for each one. To do this, it explicitly considers each set of possible outcomes, or *chronicle*, for each plan, as shown in Table 1. Each plan has two possible chronicles, either the china gets broken or it does not. For each chronicle, DRIPS computes ranges for the duration, utility and probabilities based on the ranges or values found in the actions in the plan. A series of simple linear programming problems are solved to compute ranges for the expected utility of each abstract plan. In this case the ranges are [-17.6 0.7] for plan A and [-37 -23] for plan B. Therefore DRIPS will not add plan B to the list of plans to refine, since no refinement can do better than any refinement of plan A. DRIPS determined this without exploring the refinements of plan B, an ability that can lead to large computational savings in more complicated domains.

The use of skeletal refinement planning in DRIPS trades planning power for simplicity and the ability to compute utility ranges for partial plans. In some complex domains it may be burdensome to represent the range of possible plans as skeletal plans that can be refined in this way. On the other hand, this form allows utility ranges to be computed for partial plans based on the ranges computed for abstract actions. It is not clear how to compute utility ranges for, say, partial Buridan plans, because they include

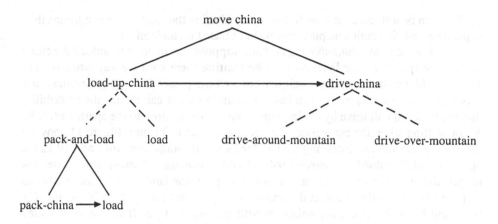

Fig. 10. Ground and abstract operators from the china-moving example that could be used by the refinement planner DRIPS. Solid lines represent compound decompositions and dotted lines represent alternative decompositions.

Plan A: pack and load china

Chronicle	Duration	Utility	prob
not broken	[3 6]	[3 6]	[0.8 0.95]
broken	[3 6]	-100	[0.05 0.2]

Plan B: load china, don't pack

Chronicle	Duration	Utility	prob
not broken	[3 6]	[5 10]	[0.6 0.7]
broken	[3 6]	-100	[0.3 0.4]

Table 1. A summary of the possible outcomes for each refinement of the skeletal plan found by refining the **load-china** abstract action.

no commitment for the action or actions used to achieve an open condition.

Some interesting work has been done on search control within the DRIPS framework. DRIPS has two choice-points: which abstract plan to specialize and which abstract action in a plan to specialize. The plan with current highest upper bound on expected utility must be expanded in order to provably find the optimal plan, so choosing such a plan to expand gives a search heuristic similar to A* [31, 28]. The representation of utilities in DRIPS allows for goal deadlines and goals of maintenance, following [29]. The system has been applied in challenging medical domains with favorable results [32].

Weaver: efficiently handling exogenous events

Weaver [5] is a probabilistic planner based on Prodigy [56]. Like C-Buridan, it has no representation of utilities. It has no explicit model of observability, but assumes the world is completely observable at plan execution time. However it has an explicit representation for uncertain exogenous events, in other words for events that take place outside the volition of the planning agent and that can be modeled as occurring with some conditional probability given the world state. External events often play a significant role in real domains, and should be considered by a decision-theoretic planner since

(1) they can be influenced at least indirectly by altering the world state conditions they depend on and (2) contingent plans can be built based on their effects.

For example in the china-moving domain, suppose that in order to unload the china at the new apartment, the landlord must be waiting there with the key when the car arrives. Initially the landlord is waiting, but as time passes he may get restless and leave, in which case he may return later. A planning agent can reduce the probability that the landlord will leave by calling him when the car is close to the apartment. If he is not waiting when the car arrives, the agent can search for him. Figure 11 shows a set of exogenous events modeling the landlord's whereabouts over time, as well as the operators **call-landlord** and **search-for-landlord**. Assuming a discrete-time model, the **landlord-moves** events mean that if at any time point the landlord is at the apartment and has not been called, he is at the apartment at the next time point with probability 0.95, and his whereabouts are unknown with probability 0.05. If he has been called the probability of his leaving drops to 0.02. If his whereabouts are unknown, he may reappear at the apartment with probability 0.01.

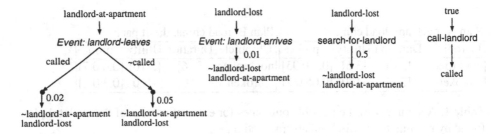

Fig. 11. Two exogenous events modeling the landlord's whereabouts and operators to call and search for the landlord.

In theory the use of exogenous events does not increase the representational power of the planner, since the effects of these events can be modeled by effects of the actions in the domain. For example, the drive-china actions could include effects describing the landlord's whereabouts, as could the pack-china operator if it takes a significant amount of time. In practice, modeling exogenous events in this way can be extremely inefficient, because their effects are duplicated in every operator in the domain, and conversely each operator may have to model many events.

Weaver evaluates plans efficiently when there are exogenous events using a three-step process. First a plan is built and partially evaluated ignoring exogenous events. In the china-moving domain, the same three-step plan that is found by Buridan will be found: **pack-china, put-in china, drive-china**. Second, the goal structure for this plan is used to determine the *relevant* exogenous events, which are those whose effects can alter the domain features required by the plan or can influence other relevant events. Third, the plan is improved by either adding steps to reduce the probability of an undesirable effect or by adding a conditional branch. The plan improvement operations are similar to those of C-Buridan [22], but using the Prodigy planner [56]. The main difference is that the exogenous events that affect the plan evaluation are also considered as well as the actions in the plan [2]. In the china-moving example, a possible improvement is to add a conditional branch to search for the landlord if he is not at the apartment when the car arrives.

The belief net fragment on the left in Figure 12 shows an evaluation structure for the plan before improvement, after the relevant events governing the movement of the landlord have been added. It is possible to make this evaluation more efficient by taking advantage of the fact that the exogenous events model a Markov process. Rather than explicitly modeling the events' effects at each time step, independent Markov chains are produced that describe parts of the world state's evolution over time — in this case, the landlord's whereabouts. The Markov chains are used to compute links in the belief net on the right in Figure 12. Such a belief net can be much more efficiently evaluated, especially when some actions have long durations compared with those of the exogenous events. Weaver uses a sound algorithm to create these streamlined belief nets automatically [4].

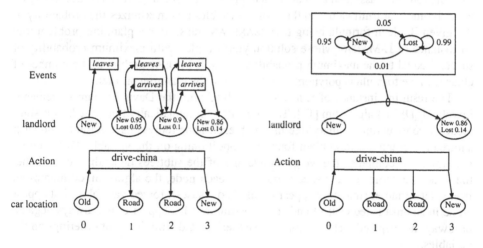

Fig. 12. Two time-slice bayes nets that can be used to evaluate the plan under exogenous events. The numbers along the x-axis represent time points while nodes for fluents, actions and events are grouped along the y-axis. In the fragment on the left, exogenous events are represented directly while on the right, their effects are compiled into Markov chains that are used to compute probabilities over the time intervals of interest.

Search heuristics for planning under uncertainty have also been studied in Weaver. When steps are added to a plan to increase the number of chronicles in which it succeeds, a useful strategy is to seek steps that succeed in cases that are complementary to those in which the original plan succeeds. This can be done using a local analysis of the possible steps, producing search heuristics that improve performance both in Weaver and in Buridan [3]. Weaver also makes use of analogy between different branches of a conditional plan [7]. These performance improvements allow it to be applied to problems requiring several rounds of improvement in plans some tens of steps in length [5]. This is encouraging in the search for tractable planning under uncertainty, but leaves plenty of room for further improvement.

MAXPLAN: probabilistic plan compilation

One way to improve the efficiency of planning under uncertainty may come from inspiration from recently developed classical planning algorithms, such as SATPLAN [35] which compiles a planning problem into a logical satisfiability problem. After this step, standard algorithms can be used to solve the problem.

MAXPLAN [42] is a probabilistic planner that is similar in spirit to SATPLAN. Littman, Goldsmith and Mundhenk show that, under reasonable conditions, probabilistic planning is NP^{PP}-complete and introduce an NP^{PP}-complete decision problem E-MAJSAT [39]. MAXPLAN compiles a probabilistic planning problem into an instance of E-MAJSAT and solves it. Just as Graphplan and SATPLAN are more efficient than classical planners in some domains, so MAXPLAN should have an advantage in some domains, as preliminary experiments indicate.

An instance of E-MAJSAT is a satisfiability problem, a Boolean formula whose variables are divided into two types, *choice* variables and *chance* variables. The chance variables are each assigned an independent probability of being true. The task is to find an assignment of truth values to the choice variables that maximizes the probability of the given Boolean formula being true. MAXPLAN transforms a planning problem into an instance of E-MAJSAT whose solution yields a plan with maximum probability of success, equal to the maximum probability of the E-MAJSAT problem. The number of clauses in the formula is polynomial in the size of the planning problem.

The resulting instance of E-MAJSAT is solved with the Davis-Putnam-Logemann-Loveland (DPLL) algorithm [17]. This algorithm systematically finds the best assignment by constructing a binary tree in which each node represents a variable and each subtree represents a subproblem found by conditioning on the variable. DPLL either maximizes or computes the weighted average of the subtrees depending on whether the node is a choice or a chance variable. At each node, the algorithm eliminates all irrelevant variables (that only appear in satisfied clauses), forced variables (that appear alone in an unsatisfied clause) and "pure" variables (that appear either always negated or always not negated). The authors have experimented with different orderings on the variables.

Graphplan [1] is Another classical planner that uses a plan compilation step, and is perhaps the best known. Probabilistic planning based on Graphplan has also been explored [53, 58].

Pointers to other work

There is a growing literature on extending classical planning approaches to plan under uncertainty. I apologize to those whose work I omit here for reasons of space.

Goldman and Boddy [27] explore the idea of relaxing the assumption that the outcomes of different actions in a plan are probabilistically independent, using a *knowledge-based model construction* approach [60]. This assumption is made in all the planners discussed above, although the causal influences used by Goldman and Boddy bear similarities to the external events of Weaver.

XFRM [43] produces plans using a rich language that can express do-while loops and include arbitrary LISP code. The system selects a plan from a user-defined library and applies transformations to improve its performance. Because of the rich plan representation it is hard to evaluate plans analytically, and instead XFRM relies on possible execution scenarios called *projections* to compare plans and find potential problems.

Cypress [61] is a framework for probabilistic planning built around three components: SIPE-2 is a hierarchical task network (HTN) planner, PRS-CL is a reactive plan execution system and GISTER-CL is an uncertain reasoning system. Cypress is broader than the planners described here in that it allows planning and execution to be done concurrently. The HTN planning style, where domain operators describe a problem decomposition rather than specify a set of subgoals, is successful in applications of classical planning. It typically offers a reduced search space at the cost of requiring more information to be specified as part of the domain knowledge.

Summary

Almost every approach that has been used to solve classical planning problems has been adapted for decision-theoretic planning. This section described decision-theoretic planners based on SNLP, skeletal refinement planning, Prodigy and compilation to satisfiability. This has necessarily been only a small sample of the work being done in this area, but a representative one.

Each described system concentrates on a different aspect of planning under uncertainty and while each has been successful, their relatively narrow focus has made meaningful comparison difficult. Future work should lead to broader systems that would allow us to compare alternative strategies directly.

Broadening the coverage of each of these planners raises a number of interesting research questions. For example, is it possible to exploit utility ranges to search for optimal plans in SNLP or Prodigy? How should plan compilation approaches deal with structured utility models? These approaches also have the potential to handle exogenous events gracefully although this has not yet been explored.

Solving Markov decision processes

In this section I review approaches to planning under uncertainty based on Markov decision processes (MDPs). My aim is to give the flavour of MDP approaches, the problems they engender and solutions being currently explored, and compare these approaches with those of the previous section. For a more thorough survey of MDP-based approaches, see [11]. After a brief description of MDP algorithms I show how at a broad level the two approaches are solving the same problem, and describe four approaches to exploiting structured representations of state, action and utility within the MDP framework.

Overview of Markov Decision Processes

This description of Markov decision processes follows [40] and [10]. A Markov decision process M is a tuple $M = <S, A, \Phi, R>$ where

- S is a finite set of states of the system.
- A is a finite set of actions.
- $\Phi : A \times S \to \Pi(S)$ is the *state transition function*, mapping an action and a state to a probability distribution over S for the possible resulting state. The probability of reaching state s' by performing action a in state s is written $\Phi(a, s, s')$.
- $R : S \times A \to \mathcal{R}$ is the *reward function*. $R(s, a)$ is the reward the system receives if it takes action a in state s.

A *policy* for an MDP is a mapping $\pi : S \to A$ that selects an action for each state. Given a policy, we can define its finite-horizon value function $V_n^\pi : S \to \mathcal{R}$, where $V_n^\pi(s)$ is the expected value of applying the policy π for n steps starting in state s. This is defined inductively with $V_0^\pi(s) = R(s, \pi(s))$ and

$$V_m^\pi(s) = R(s, \pi(s)) + \sum_{u \in S} \Phi(\pi(s), s, u) V_{m-1}^\pi(u)$$

Over an infinite horizon, a discounted model is frequently used to ensure policies have a bounded expected value. For some β chosen so that $\beta < 1$, the value of any reward from the transition after the next is discounted by a factor of β and the one after that by a factor of β^2, and so on. Thus if $V^\pi(s)$ is the discounted expected value in state s following policy π forever, we must have

$$V^\pi(s) = R(s, \pi(s)) + \beta \sum_{u \in S} \Phi(\pi(s), s, u) V^\pi(u)$$

This yields a set of linear equations in the values of $V^\pi()$.

A solution to an MDP is a policy that maximizes its expected value. For the discounted infinite-horizon case with any given discount factor β, there is a policy V^* that is optimal regardless of the starting state [34], that satisfies the following equation:

$$V^*(s) = \max_a \{ R(s, a) + \beta \sum_{u \in S} \Phi(a, s, u) V^*(u) \}$$

Two popular methods for solving this equation and finding an optimal policy for an MDP are *value iteration* and *policy iteration* [52].

In policy iteration, the current policy is repeatedly improved by finding some action in each state that has a higher value than the action chosen by the current policy for that state. The policy is initially chosen at random, and the process terminates when no improvement can be found. The algorithm is shown in Table 2. This process converges to an optimal policy [52].

In value iteration, optimal policies are produced for successively longer finite horizons, until they converge. It is relatively simple to find an optimal policy over n steps $\pi_n^*(.)$, with value function $V_n^*(.)$, using the recurrence relation:

$$\pi_n^*(s) = \operatorname{argmax}_a \{ R(s, a) + \beta \sum_{u \in S} \Phi(a, s, u) V_{n-1}^*(u) \}$$

with starting condition $V_0^*(s) = 0 \forall s \in S$, where V_m^* is derived from the policy π_m^* as described above. Table 3 shows the value iteration algorithm, which takes an MDP,

Policy-Iteration($S, \mathcal{A}, \Phi, R, \beta$):
1. For each $s \in S$, $\pi(s) = \text{RandomElement}(\mathcal{A})$
2. Compute $V^\pi(.)$
3. For each $s \in S$ {
4.   Find some action a such that
        $R(s, a) + \beta \sum_{u \in S} \Phi(a, s, u) V^\pi(u) > V^\pi(s)$
5.   Set $\pi'(s) = a$ if such an a exists,
6   otherwise set $\pi'(s) = \pi(s)$.
   }
7. If $\pi'(s) \neq \pi(s)$ for some $s \in S$ goto 2.
8. Return π

Table 2. The policy iteration algorithm

a discount value β and a parameter c and produces successive finite-horizon optimal policies, terminating when the maximum change in values between the current and previous value functions is below ϵ. It can also be shown that the algorithm converges to the optimal policy for the discounted infinite case in a number of steps that is polynomial in $|S|$, $|\mathcal{A}|$, $\log \max_{s,a} |R(s, a)|$ and $1/(1 - \beta)$.

Value-Iteration($S, \mathcal{A}, \Phi, R, \beta, \epsilon$):
1. for each $s \in S$, $V_0(s) = 0$
2. $t = 0$
3. $t = t + 1$
4. for each $s \in S$ {
5.   for each $a \in A$
6. $Q_t(s, a) = R(s, a) + \beta \sum_{u \in S} \Phi(a, s, u) V_{t-1}(u)$
7. $\pi_t(s) = \text{argmax}_a Q_t(s, a)$
8. $V_t(s) = Q_t(s, \pi_t(s))$
   }
9. if ($\max_s |V_t(s) - V_{t-1}(s)| \geq \epsilon$) goto 3
10. return π_t

Table 3. The value iteration algorithm

Planning under uncertainty with MDPs

Solving a Markov decision process is essentially the same problem as planning under uncertainty discussed in the first part of this article, with some minor differences. The standard algorithms for MDPs find a policy, which chooses an action for every possible state of the underlying system, while methods based on classical planners expect a set of possible initial states as input to the problem, and find a sequence of actions (possible branching) based on them. The difference is partly because the MDP solution methods emphasized the use of dynamic programming while AI planning methods emphasized the use of structured representations for the state space and for actions. However the improvements to policy and value iteration discussed below exploit structured representations.

Another difference is in the specification of goals. Markov decision processes attach a reward to an action in a state, while classical planning takes a logical description of a set of states as a goal. Some of the planners described in the last section attach utilities to goals, however, and again as the MDP algorithms described below make use of structure their objective functions become more goal-like.

The standard MDP algorithms seek a policy with maximum expected utility. Half of the planners of the last section do this while half seek a plan that passes a threshold probability of success. Again this is a minor difference, because given a thresholding planner one could produce an optimizing planner by repeatedly increasing the threshold until no plan is found. Conversely one could terminate policy iteration when a threshold value is reached.

Policy iteration and value iteration can find optimal policies in polynomial time in the size of the state space of the MDP. However, this state space is usually exponentially large in the inputs to a planning problem, which includes a set of literals whose cross product describes the state space. Attempts to build on these and other techniques for solving MDPs have concentrated on ways to gain leverage from the structure of the planning problem to reduce the computation time required.

Partitioning the state space and factored state representations.

Dean et al. used policy iteration in a restricted state space called an *envelope* [20]. A subset of the states is selected, and each transition in the MDP that leaves the subset is replaced with a transition to a new state OUT with zero reward. No transitions leave the OUT state. They developed an algorithm that alternated between solving the restricted-space MDP with policy iteration and expanding the envelope by including the n most likely elements of the state space to be reached by the optimal policy that were not in the envelope. The algorithm converges to an optimal policy considerably more quickly than standard policy iteration on the whole state space, but as the authors point out [19], it makes some assumptions that limit its applicability, including a sparse MDP in which each state has only a small number of outward transitions. Tash and Russell extend the idea of an envelope with an initial estimate of distance-to-goal for each state and a model that takes the time of computation into account [54].

Abstractions and hierarchical approaches

While the envelope extension method ignores portions of the state space, other techniques have considered abstractions of the state space that try to group together sets of states that behave similarly under the chosen actions of the optimal policy. Boutilier and Dearden [12] assume a representation for actions that is similar to that of Buridan [37] described earlier and a state utility function that is described in terms of domain literals. They then pick a subset of the literals that accounts for the greatest variation in the state utility and use the action representation to find literals that can directly or indirectly affect the chosen set, using a technique similar to the one developed by Knoblock for building abstraction hierarchies for classical planners [36]. This subset of literals then forms the basis for an abstract MDP by projection of the original states. Since the state space size is exponential in the set of literals, this reduction can lead to considerable time savings over the original MDP. Boutilier and Dearden prove bounds on the difference in value of the abstract policy compared with an optimal policy in the original MDP.

Dean and Lin refine this idea by splitting the MDP into subsets and allowing a different abstraction of the states to be considered in each one [21]. This approach can provide a better approximation because typically different literals may be relevant in different parts of the state space. However there is an added cost to re-combining the separate pieces unless they happen to decompose very cleanly. Dean and Lin assume the partition of the state space is given by some external oracle.

Factored action and state representations

While the last approaches exploited structure in the state utility description it is also possible to exploit it in the action description. Boutilier et al. extend *modified policy iteration* to propose a technique called *structured policy iteration* that makes use of a structured action representation in the form of 2-stage Bayesian networks [13]. The representation of the policy and utility functions are also structured, using decision trees. In standard policy iteration, the value of the candidate policy is computed on each iteration by solving a system of $|S|$ linear equations (step 2 in Table 2), which is computationally prohibitive for large real-world planning problems. Modified policy iteration replaces this step with an iterative approximation of the value function V_π by a series of value functions $V^0, V^1, \ldots$ given by

$$V^i(s) = R(s) + \beta \sum_{u \in S} \Phi(\pi(s), s, u) V^{i-1}(u)$$

Stopping criteria are given in [52].

In structured policy iteration, the value function is again built in a series of approximations, but in each one it is represented as a decision tree over the domain literals. Similarly the policy is built up as a decision tree. On each iteration, new literals might be added to these trees as a result of examining the literals mentioned in the action specification Φ and utility function R. In this way the algorithm avoids explicitly enumerating the state space.

Using classical planning ideas to help approximate MDPs

Structured policy iteration makes use of a factored action representation that is similar to actions in classical planning. It is also possible to make use of causal links and the planning graphs used in Graphplan [1]. In [9], Boutilier, Brafman and Geib decompose the reward function of the MDP into components and produce policies for them separately. They then make a causal link analysis of each policy to produce partially ordered action sets from them using UCPOP. The flexibility in the partial order makes it easier to merge the component policies into a policy for the original reward function, again much as an SNLP based planner such as UCPOP might merge subplans for individual goals. In [8], a reachability analysis inspired by Graphplan is used to restrict the states considered for policy creation given an initial state.

Givan and Dean [26] show that STRIPS-style goal regression computes an approximate minimized form of the finite state automaton corresponding to the problem. In [18] the authors show how to use model minimization techniques to solve MDPs.

Partial observability

Similar work has been done with *partially-observable Markov decision processes* or POMDPs, in which the assumption of complete observability is relaxed. In a POMDP there is a set of observation labels $\mathcal{O}$ and a set of conditional probabilities $P(o|a, s), o \in \mathcal{O}, a \in \mathcal{A}, s \in S$, such that if the system makes a transition to state s with action a it receives the observation label o with probability $P(o|a, s)$. Cassandra et al. introduce the *witness algorithm* for solving POMDPs [15]. A standard technique for finding an optimal policy for a POMDP is to construct the MDP whose states are the belief states of the original POMDP, ie each state is a probability distribution over states in the POMDP, with beliefs maintained based on the observation labels using Bayes' rule. A form of value iteration can be performed in this space making use of the fact that each finite-horizon policy will be convex and piecewise-linear. The witness algorithm includes an improved technique for updating the basis of the convex value function on each iteration. Parr and Russell use a smooth approximation of the value function that can be updated with gradient descent [46]. Brafman introduces a grid-based method in [14]. Although work on POMDPs is promising, it is still preliminary and can only be used to solve small POMDP problems [14].

Conclusions

After introducing decision-theoretic planning, this paper discussed four different approaches based on extending classical planning algorithms. The approaches all use different planning styles, and attack different aspects of the decision-theoretic planning problem. Approaches based on algorithms for solving Markov decision processes were briefly discussed, emphasizing extensions that make use of factored action representations, causal links, abstraction and other ideas from classical planning. There are interesting directions still to be explored that come from the interplay between the two approaches. Surprisingly, in improving MDP approaches little attention has been paid to the DRIPS style of planning, although it is the only classically-inspired planner mentioned here that aims to solve the same problem as an MDP: maximizing expected utility. Using dominance to eliminate portions of the state or action space may prove fruitful in MDP approaches. Similarly, few classical planning algorithms make use of local improvement search or dynamic programming, although some algorithms for SAT-compilation planning perform local improvements.

A blind spot shared by both approaches is the reliance on complete, detailed domain models. In many real domains, specifying full probability distributions for all actions and the initial state would be at best tedious, and typically impossible. There has been relatively little work in this area, but see a recent workshop on interactive decision-theoretic systems [30].

It should also be noted that most of the systems described here either concentrate on parts of the decision-theoretic planning task or represent individual techniques that will need to be used in combination to achieve significant results. Scaling up in this way is one of the largest challenges ahead. The techniques developed so far have been shown to be practical in some domains (*e.g* [5, 32]) but many simple domains still lie beyond our current capabilities. Still, the wealth of ideas being proposed show that this is an exciting time to be working in decision-theoretic planning.

References

1. Avrim Blum and Merrick Furst. Fast planning through planning graph analysis. *Artificial Intelligence*, 90:281–300, 1997.
2. Jim Blythe. Planning with external events. In Ramon Lopez de Mantaras and David Poole, editors, *Proc. Tenth Conference on Uncertainty in Artificial Intelligence*, pages 94–101, Seattle, WA, July 1994. Morgan Kaufmann. Available as http://www.cs.cmu.edu/jblythe/papers/uai94.ps.
3. Jim Blythe. The footprint principle for heuristics for probabilistic planners. In Malik Ghallab and Alfredo Milani, editors, *New Directions in AI Planning*, pages 173–185, Assissi, Italy, September 1995. IOS Press.
4. Jim Blythe. Decompositions of markov chains for reasoning about external change in planners. In Brian Drabble, editor, *Proc. Third International Conference on Artificial Intelligence Planning Systems*, pages 27–34, University of Edinburgh, May 1996. AAAI Press. Available as Pointer.
5. Jim Blythe. *Planning Under Uncertainty in Dynamic Domains*. PhD thesis, Carnegie Mellon University Computer Science Department, May 1998.
6. Jim Blythe. Decision-theoretic planning. *AI Magazine*, 20(2), Summer 1999.
7. Jim Blythe and Manuela Veloso. Using analogy in conditional planners. In *Proc. Fourteenth National Conference on Artificial Intelligence*. AAAI Press, 1997.
8. Craig Boutilier, Ronen Brafman, and Christopher Geib. Structured reachability analysis for markov decision processes. In *Proc. Fourteenth Conference on Uncertainty in Artificial Intelligence*, Madison, Wisconsin, August 1998. Morgan Kaufmann.
9. Craig Boutilier, Ronen I. Brafman, and Christopher Geib. Prioritized goal decomposition of markov decision processes: Toward a synthesis of classical and decision theoretic planning. In *Proc. 15th International Joint Conference on Artificial Intelligence*, Nagoya, Japan, August 1997. Morgan Kaufmann.
10. Craig Boutilier, Thomas Dean, and Steve Hanks. Planning under uncertainty: structural assumptions and computational leverage. In Malik Ghallab and Alfredo Milani, editors, *New Directions in AI Planning*, pages 157–172, Assissi, Italy, September 1995. IOS Press.
11. Craig Boutilier, Thomas Dean, and Steve Hanks. Planning under uncertainty: structural assumptions and computational leverage. *Journal of Artificial Intelligence Research*, in press, 1998.
12. Craig Boutilier and Richard Dearden. Using abstractions for decision-theoretic planning with time constraints. In *Proc. Twelfth National Conference on Artificial Intelligence*, pages 1016–1022. AAAI Press, 1994.

13. Craig Boutilier, Richard Dearden, and Moises Goldszmidt. Exploiting structure in policy construction. In *Proc. 14th International Joint Conference on Artificial Intelligence*, pages 1104–1111, Montréal, Quebec, August 1995. Morgan Kaufmann.
14. Ronen Brafman. A heuristic variable grid solution method of pomdps. In *Proc. Fourteenth National Conference on Artificial Intelligence*, pages 727–733. AAAI Press, 1997.
15. Anthony R. Cassandra, Leslie Pack Kaelbling, and Michael L. Littman. Acting optimally in partially observable stochastic domains. In *Proc. Twelfth National Conference on Artificial Intelligence*, pages 1023–1028. AAAI Press, 1994.
16. Bruce D'Ambrosio. Inference in bayesian networks. *AI Magazine*, 20(2), Summer 1999.
17. M. Davis, G. Logemann, and D. Loveland. A machine program for theorem proving. *Communications of the ACM*, 5:394–397, 1962.
18. Thomas Dean and Robert Givan. Model minimization in markov decision processes. In *Proc. Fourteenth National Conference on Artificial Intelligence*, pages 106–111. AAAI Press, 1997.
19. Thomas Dean, Leslie Kaelbling, Jak Kirman, and Ann Nicholson. Planning under time constraints in stochastic domains. *Artificial Intelligence*, 76(1-2):35–74, 1995.
20. Thomas Dean, Leslie Pack Kaelbling, Jak Kirman, and Ann Nicholson. Planning with deadlines in stochastic domains. In *National Conference on Artificial Intelligence*, National Conference on Artificial Intelligence, 1993.
21. Thomas Dean and Shieu-Hong Lin. Decomposition techniques for planning in stochastic domains. In *Proc. 14th International Joint Conference on Artificial Intelligence*, pages 1121–1127, Montréal, Quebec, August 1995. Morgan Kaufmann.
22. Denise Draper, Steve Hanks, and Daniel Weld. Probabilistic planning with information gathering and contingent execution. In Kristian Hammond, editor, *Proc. Second International Conference on Artificial Intelligence Planning Systems*, pages 31–37, University of Chicago, Illinois, June 1994. AAAI Press.
23. Jerome A. Feldman and Robert F. Sproull. Decision theory and artificial intelligence ii: The hungy monkey. *Cognitive Science*, 1:158–192, 1977.
24. Richard E. Fikes and Nil J. Nilsson. Strips: A new approach to the application of theorem proving to problem solving. *Artificial Intelligence*, 2:189–208, 1971.
25. Peter E. Friedland and Yumi Iwasaki. The concept and implementation of skeletal plans. *Journal of Automated Reasoning*, 1(2):161–208, 1985.
26. Robert Givan and Thomas Dean. Model minimization, regression, and propositional strips planning. In *Proc. 15th International Joint Conference on Artificial Intelligence*, Nagoya, Japan, August 1997. Morgan Kaufmann.
27. Robert P. Goldman and Mark S. Boddy. Epsilon-safe planning. In Ramon Lopez de Mantaras and David Poole, editors, *Proc. Tenth Conference on Uncertainty in Artificial Intelligence*, pages 253–261, Seattle, WA, July 1994. Morgan Kaufmann.
28. Richard Goodwin and Reid Simmons. Search control of plan generation in decision-theoretic planning. In Manuela Veloso Reid Simmons and Steve Smith, editors, *Proc. Fourth International Conference on Artificial Intelligence Planning Systems*, pages 94–101, Carnegie Mellon University, Pittsburgh, PA, June 1998. AAAI Press.
29. P. Haddawy and S. Hanks. Utility models for goal-directed decision-theoretic planners. *Computational Intelligence*, 14(3):392–429, 1998.
30. P. Haddawy and S. Hanks, editors. *Working notes of the AAAI Spring Symposium on Interactive and Mixed-Initiative Decision-Theoretic Systems*, Stanford, 1998. AAAI Press.
31. Peter Haddawy, AnHai Doan, and Richard Goodwin. Efficient decision-theoretic planning: Techniques and empirical analysis. In Philippe Besnard and Steve Hanks, editors, *Proc. Eleventh Conference on Uncertainty in Artificial Intelligence*, pages 229–326, Montreal, Quebec, August 1995. Morgan Kaufmann.

32. Peter Haddawy, AnHai Doan, and C. E. Kahn. Decision-theoretic refinement planning in medical decision making: Management of acute deep venous thrombosis. *Medical Decision Making*, 16(4):315–325, Oct/Dec 1996.

33. Peter Haddawy and M. Suwandi. Decision-theoretic refinement planning using inheritance abstraction. In Kristian Hammond, editor, *Proc. Second International Conference on Artificial Intelligence Planning Systems*, University of Chicago, Illinois, June 1994. AAAI Press.

34. Ronald A. Howard. *Dynamic Programming and Markov Processes*. MIT Press, 1960.

35. Henry A. Kautz and Bart Selman. Pushing the envelope: Planning, propositional logic, and stochastic search. In *Proc. Thirteenth National Conference on Artificial Intelligence*. AAAI Press, 1996.

36. Craig Alan Knoblock. *Automatically Generating Abstractions for Problem Solving*. PhD thesis, Carnegie Mellon University, 1991.

37. Nicholas Kushmerick, Steve Hanks, and Daniel Weld. An algorithm for probabilistic least-commitment planning. In *Proc. Twelfth National Conference on Artificial Intelligence*, pages 1073–1078. AAAI Press, 1994.

38. Nicholas Kushmerick, Steve Hanks, and Daniel Weld. An algorithm for probabilistic planning. *Artificial Intelligence*, 76:239 – 286, 1995.

39. Michael L. Littman, Judy Goldsmith, and Martin Mundhenk. The computational complexity of probabilistic planning. *Journal of Artificial Intelligence Research*, 9:1–36, 1998.

40. Michael Lederman Littman. *Algorithms for Sequential Decision Making*. PhD thesis, Department of Computer Science, Brown University, March 1996.

41. R. D. Luce and H. Raiffa. *Games and Decisions: Introduction and Critical Survey*. Wiley, 1957.

42. Stephen M. Majercik and Michael L. Littman. Maxplan: A new approach to probabilistic planning. In Manuela Veloso Reid Simmons and Steve Smith, editors, *Proc. Fourth International Conference on Artificial Intelligence Planning Systems*, pages 86–93, Carnegie Mellon University, Pittsburgh, PA, June 1998. AAAI Press.

43. Drew McDermott. Transformational planning of reactive behavior. Technical Report YALEU/CSD/RR/941, Yale University, December 1992.

44. Allen Newell and Herbert A. Simon. Gps: a program that simulates human thought. In E. A. Feigenbaum and J. Feldman, editors, *Computers and Thought*, pages 279–293, New York, 1963. McGraw-Hill.

45. Nilufer Onder and Martha Pollack. Contingency selection in plan generation. In *European Conference on Planning*, Toulouse, France, September 1997.

46. Ron Parr and Stuart Russell. Approximating optimal policies for partially observable stochastic domains. In *Proc. 14th International Joint Conference on Artificial Intelligence*, Montréal, Quebec, August 1995. Morgan Kaufmann.

47. Judea Pearl. *Probabilistic Reasoning in Intelligent Systems*. Morgan Kaufmann, 1988.

48. J Scott Penberthy and Daniel S. Weld. Ucpop: A sound, complete, partial order planner for adl. In *Third International Conference on Principles of Knowledge Representation and Reasoning*, pages 103–114, Cambridge, MA, October 1992.

49. Mark A Peot and David E Smith. Conditional nonlinear planning. In Jim Hendler, editor, *Proc. First International Conference on Artificial Intelligence Planning Systems*, pages 189–197, College Park, Maryland, June 1992. Morgan Kaufmann.

50. M. Alicia Pérez and Jaime Carbonell. Control knowledge to improve plan quality. In Kristian Hammond, editor, *Proc. Second International Conference on Artificial Intelligence Planning Systems*, pages 323–328, University of Chicago, Illinois, June 1994. AAAI Press.

51. Louise Pryor and Greg Collins. Planning for contingencies: A decision-based approach. *Journal of Artificial Intelligence Research*, 4:287–339, 1996.

52. Martin Puterman. *Markov Decision Processes: Discrete Stochastic Dynamic Programming.* John Wiley & Sons, 1994.
53. David E. Smith and Daniel Weld. Conformant graphplan. In *Proc. Fifteenth National Conference on Artificial Intelligence*, pages 889–896. AAAI Press, 1998.
54. Jonathan King Tash and Stuart Russell. Control strategies for a stochastic planner. In *Proc. Twelfth National Conference on Artificial Intelligence*, pages 1079–1085. AAAI Press, 1994.
55. Austin Tate. Generating project networks. In *International Joint Conference on Artificial Intelligence*, 1977.
56. Manuela Veloso, Jaime Carbonell, Alicia Pérez, Daniel Borrajo, Eugene Fink, and Jim Blythe. Integrating planning and learning: The prodigy architecture. *Journal of Experimental and Theoretical AI*, 7:81–120, 1995.
57. Daniel Weld. A gentle introduction to least-commitment planning. *AI Magazine*, 1994.
58. Daniel Weld, Corin Anderson, and David E. Smith. Extending graphplan to handle uncertainty and sensing actions. In *Proc. Fifteenth National Conference on Artificial Intelligence*, pages 897–904. AAAI Press, 1998.
59. Michael P. Wellman. *Formulation of Tradeoffs in Planning Under Uncertainty.* Pitman, 1990.
60. Michal P. Wellman, John S. Breese, and Robert P. Goldman. From knowledge bases to decision models. *Knowledge Engineering Review*, 7(1):35–53, 1992.
61. David E. Wilkins, Karen L. Myers, John D. Lowrance, and Leonard P. Wesley. Planning and reacting in uncertain and dynamic environments. *Journal of Experimental and Theoretical AI*, to appear, 1995.
62. Mike Williamson and Steve Hanks. Optimal planning with a a goal-directed utility model. In Kristian Hammond, editor, *Proc. Second International Conference on Artificial Intelligence Planning Systems*, pages 176–181, University of Chicago, Illinois, June 1994. AAAI Press.

Knowledge Representation for Stochastic Decision Processes

Craig Boutilier

Dept. of Computer Science, University of British Columbia,
Vancouver, BC V6T 1Z4, CANADA
cebly@cs.ubc.ca

Abstract. Reasoning about stochastic dynamical systems and planning under uncertainty has come to play a fundamental role in AI research and applications. The representation of such systems, in particular, of actions with stochastic effects, has accordingly been given increasing attention in recent years. In this article, we survey a number of techniques for representing stochastic processes and actions with stochastic effects using dynamic Bayesian networks and influence diagrams, and briefly describe how these support effective inference for tasks such as monitoring, forecasting, explanation and decision making. We also compare these techniques to several action representations adopted in the classical reasoning about action and planning communities, describing how traditional problems such as the frame and ramification problems are dealt with in stochastic settings, and how these solutions compare to recent approaches to this problem in the classical (deterministic) literature. We argue that while stochastic dynamics introduce certain complications when it comes to such issues, for the most part, intuitions underlying classical models can be extended to the stochastic setting.

1   Introduction

Within artificial intelligence, increasing attention has been paid to the problems of the monitoring, forecasting and control of complex stochastic processes. While classical planning has historically been the prime focus of those in AI interested in controlling dynamical systems, researchers have come to realize that many (or most) realistic problems cannot be adequately modeled using the assumptions of classical planning. Specifically, one is generally forced to consider actions with nondeterministic or stochastic effects, processes in which exogenous events occur, incomplete or uncertain knowledge of the system state, imprecise observations of the system state, problems with ill-defined goals or multiple, possibly conflicting objectives, and on-going (possibly nonterminating) processes with indefinite horizon.

Stochastic and decision theoretic planning [17, 19, 5] attempts to incorporate many of the above considerations into planning systems. As such, this area of research requires that attention be paid to the natural and effective representation of actions with stochastic effects. In addition, related tasks such as forecasting (or temporal projection), monitoring and smoothing (or temporal "explanation") of stochastic dynamical systems require appropriate representations of stochastic processes and actions.

Of course, representing and reasoning about action has been a central problem in artificial intelligence from its inception. Since the earliest attempts to formalize this problem, the straightforward encoding of actions and their effects has been fraught with difficulties, including the frame, qualification and ramification problems. Representations such as the situation calculus [41], STRIPS [20], and the $\mathcal{A}$-family of languages [22, 23], as well as various methodologies for using these systems (e.g., [33, 58, 3, 52, 31, 23, 62]) have been proposed for dealing with such issues. However, such problems are exacerbated by considerations of uncertainty and the concomitant complications.

To represent stochastic actions and systems, a number of researchers have adapted a tool used for the representation of probability distributions, namely *Bayesian networks* (BNs) [43], to the problem of action representation. BNs provide a formal, graphical way of decomposing a probability distribution by exploiting probabilistic independence relationships. BNs can also be augmented to represent *actions*, for instance, using the methods of *influence diagrams* (IDs) [56, 43], or representations such as *two-stage* or *dynamic* BNs (DBNs) [16]. The use of DBNs has not only provided a natural and concise means of representing stochastic dynamical systems, but has also given rise to a number of computationally effective techniques for inference tasks such as monitoring, prediction and decision making.

One goal of this paper is to provide an introduction to the use of BNs, IDs, and DBNs in the representation of stochastic actions and dynamical systems. We will focus on the independence assumptions embodied in such representations and how these gives rise in many instances to tractable inference and decision making procedures. We will also review some recent advances aimed at extending the expressive power and conciseness of DBN representations. A second goal of this paper is to illustrate the close relationship between DBN representations of stochastic actions and classical representations such as the STRIPS, the situation calculus and the $\mathcal{A}$ family of languages. In particular, recent methods for expressing conditional probability distributions in DBNs and IDs using decision trees, decision graphs and Horn rules can be viewed as solving certain aspects of the frame and ramification problems in similar ways to classical approaches. Furthermore, dealing with (say) the frame problem in this way has been demonstrated to provide computational advantages in probabilistic inference and planning.

In Section 2 we describe (deterministic, nondeterministic and stochastic) transition systems, providing the semantic models underlying all of the action languages we discuss. We begin with a description of Markov chains. We then describe Markov decision processes as a vehicle for introducing explicit actions with which a decision maker or planner can control the dynamical system, and briefly elaborate on the role of exogenous events. We introduce observations as a means for the decision maker to gain information about the true state of the system and describe a variety of control problems that have been addressed under the guise of "planning" within AI. Finally, we describe several variations on the control problem and describe related inference tasks for partially observable systems.

In Section 3 we introduce DBNs and IDs as a means of representing complex stochastic systems whose state is determined by a set of random variables (or features or propositions). We first describe Bayes networks as representations of probability distributions and the independence assumptions embodied therein. We then describe DBNs as a means of representing both processes and actions, and finally describe *decision-oriented DBNs*, a special form of ID, as a means of representing action *choices*. We will also emphasize the use of structured (as opposed to tabular) representations of the conditional probability distributions in DBNs using decision trees, decision graphs and Horn rules. Finally, we briefly point to several types of inference tasks commonly considered in stochastic processes and how the DBN representation can be exploited for efficient inference.

In Section 4 we compare the representation of actions afforded by DBNs and decision-oriented DBNs with those considered in the classical (or logical) reasoning about action community. We focus primarily on the relative size of the representations, and the effort required to specify an action, and specifically consider the frame and ramification problems. We compare DBNs primarily to situation calculus representations and specifically the method proposed by Reiter [52] for dealing with the frame problem. We also briefly discuss other approaches such as the $\mathcal{A}$ family of languages [22, 23].

We conclude in Section 5 by considering future directions in which DBN representations must be extended to more concisely and effectively represent dynamical systems and decision problems, and how the techniques developed for DBN representations can be exploited in deterministic and nondeterministic settings.

2 Transition Systems and Stochastic Processes

The basic model we use for stochastic processes in that of *transition systems*. We assume that system to be monitored, or possibly controlled, can be in one of a number of distinct *states*. The system state intuitively describes all aspects of the system that are relevant to accurate prediction and monitoring of the system.[1] The state changes over time, possibly in response to the occurrence of certain *exogenous events* or *actions* on the part of the decision maker or system controller. We are interested in predicting or controlling these *state transitions* over time.

In what follows, we assume a finite set of states $\mathcal{S}$, though much of what follows applies to countably infinite or continuous state spaces (see [14, 40, 50]). A *discrete-time stochastic transition system* consists of a state space and a set of probability distributions governing possible *state transitions*—how the *next state* of the system depends on past states. Again, extensions to continuous time are

---

[1] Formally, we might think of a state as a system description that renders the process Markovian [40] (see below).

not problematic, but we do not consider continuous time systems in detail here. We note that transitions may be influenced by actions taken by the decision maker—this will be discussed in detail in Section 2.2. In the following, will also define deterministic and nondeterministic transition systems.

2.1 Markov Processes

Formally, a discrete time transition systems evolves in *stages*, where the occurrence of an event or action (possibly a "no-op") marks the transition from stage t to stage $t+1$. In this section, we assume that the events or actions that drive the evolution of the process are determined (in a sense to be made clear), thus we do not consider the possibility of a decision maker varying its strategy for choosing actions over time. We typically equate stage and state transitions, though the state "transition" corresponding to a stage transitions may keep the system in the same state. We will often loosely refer to the stage of the process as "time." We model (potential) uncertainty about the system's state at stage t using a random variable S^t, taking values from $\mathcal{S}$, to denote this state. An assumption of "forward causality" requires that the variable S^t does not depend *directly* on the value of future variable S^k ($k > t$). Roughly, it requires that we *model* our system such that the past history "directly" determines the current state, or probability distribution over possible current states, whereas knowledge of future states can influence our estimate of the current state only indirectly by providing evidence as to what the current state may have been so as to lead to these future states. Given this modeling assumption, we specify transition systems slightly differently in the deterministic, nondeterministic and stochastic cases.

A *deterministic transition system* is one in which knowledge of the past allows a unique prediction of the state at time t. Using $Value(S^t|X)$ to denote the value of the variable S^t given information X, for any $k > t$, we require a *transition function*

$$Value(S^t|S^0, S^1, \cdots S^{t-1})$$

In other words, S^t can be viewed as a function from $S^0, \cdots S^{t-1}$ into $\mathcal{S}$. It is easy to verify that knowledge of S^0 enables exact prediction of the evolution of the system.

A *nondeterministic transition system* is one in which knowledge of the past allows one to predict a set of *possible* states at time t. In other words, S^t can be viewed as a function from $S^0, \cdots S^{t-1}$ into the powerset of $\mathcal{S}$. Let $Poss(S^t|X)$ denote the set of states variable S^t could take as values given information X. We then require a transition function of the form

$$Poss(S^t|S^0, S^1, \cdots S^{t-1})$$

A *stochastic transition system* is one in which the uncertainty about the system state can be quantified probabilistically. The assumption of forward causality is realized through transition functions of the form

$$Pr(S^t|S^0, S^1, \cdots S^{t-1})$$

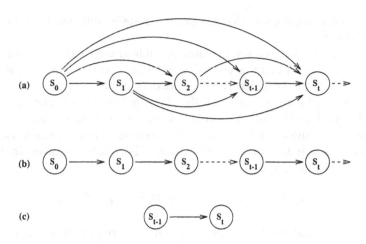

Fig. 1. (a) A general stochastic process; (b) a Markov chain; (c) and a stationary Markov chain

Figure 1(a) shows a graphical perspective on a discrete-time, stochastic dynamical system. The nodes are random variables denoting the state at a particular time, and the arcs indicate the direct probabilistic dependence of states on previous states. To describe this system completely we must also supply the conditional distributions $Pr(S^t|S^0, S^1, \cdots S^{t-1})$ for all times t.[2]

In most research in planning and control, it is assumed that the state contains enough information to predict the next state. In other words, any information about the *history* of the system relevant to predicting its future value is captured explicitly in the state itself. Formally this assumption, the *Markov assumption*, says that knowledge of the present state renders information about the past irrelevant to making predictions about the future. In a stochastic system, this is formalized as:

$$Pr(S^{t+1}|S^t, S^{t-1}, \ldots, S^0) = Pr(S^{t+1}|S^t)$$

In deterministic and nondeterministic systems the requirement is similar, referring to prediction of the next state or set of possible next states, rather than the distribution over next states. In other words, the current state uniquely determines the next state, or set of possibilities, without reference to past history. Markovian models can be represented graphically using a structure like that in

---

[2] Note that the assumption of forward causality for nondeterministic and stochastic systems does *not* render the current state independent of future states, given full knowledge of the past. It is not generally the case, e.g., that $Pr(S^t|S^0, S^1, \cdots S^{t-1}) = Pr(S^t|S^0, S^1, \cdots S^{t-1}, S^t)$, since knowledge of one state can provide evidence relevant to the assessment of the previous state. With deterministic systems, of course, since the past uniquely identifies the current state, no information about the future enhances our ability to predict the current state.

Figure 1(b) reflecting the fact that the present state is sufficient to predict future state evolution.[3]

Finally, it is common to assume that possible transitions (or as we will see, the effects of a random event or action) depend only on the prevailing state, and not the *stage* or time at which the event occurs. If the next state distribution (in a stochastic system), given a specific state, is the same regardless of stage, the model is said to be *stationary* and can be represented schematically using just two stages as shown in Figure 1(c). The relation between one state and its possible successors is that same at every stage. Formally, we insist that, for all times t, t' and states s_i, s_j:

$$Pr(S^{t+1} = s_i | S^t = s_j) = Pr(S^{t'+1} = s_i | S^{t'} = s_j)$$

For deterministic and nondeterministic systems, the requirement can be phrased analogously.

In this paper we generally restrict our attention to discrete-time, finite-state, stochastic dynamical systems with the Markov property, commonly called *Markov chains*. Furthermore, most of our discussion is restricted to stationary chains.

The dynamics of stationary Markov chains can be represented much more compactly than those of arbitrary transition systems. For each state, one must specify a function determining possible next states. Let $N = |\mathcal{S}|$ be the size of the state space. In a deterministic system, since the successor state is unique, a table of size $O(N)$ will suffice, listing the next state for each state of the system. In stochastic and nondeterministic systems, a *transition matrix* P of size $N \times N$ can be used. In the stochastic case, matrix P consists of probabilities p_{ij}, where $p_{ij} = Pr(S^{t+1} = s_j | S^t = s_i)$. In the nondeterministic case, a boolean matrix can be used to indicate the presence of possible transitions: $p_{ij} = 1$ if $s_j \in Poss(S^{t+1} | S^t = s_j)$ and 0 otherwise.[4]

Thus far we have discussed only the dynamics of transition systems. To complete the model we must provide a some information about the initial state. This can be in the form of probability distribution over initial states, a specific initial state, or a set of possible initial states. A distribution can be represented as a real-valued vector P^0 of size N (one probability entry for each state), while a set

---

[3] It is worth mentioning that the Markov property applies to the particular *model* and not to the system itself. Indeed, any non-Markovian model of a system (of finite order, i.e., whose dynamics depend on at most the k previous states for some k) can be converted to an equivalent though larger Markov model. In control theory, this is called conversion to *state form* [40].

[4] A stationary Markov process can also be represented using *state-transition diagram*, with nodes representing states and arcs denoting possible transitions. In a stochastic system, these arcs are directed from s_i to s_j only if $p_{ij} > 0$, and are labeled with this probability. The size of such a diagram is at least $O(N)$ and at most $O(N^2)$, depending on the number of arcs. This is a useful representation when the transition graph is relatively sparse, for example when most states have immediate transitions only to few "neighbors."

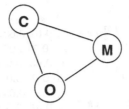

Fig. 2. Map of the robot's environment

of possible states can be represented using a similar boolean vector. Given an initial distribution over states P^0, the probability distribution over states after t stages can be computed using the transition matrix in a stochastic system or the transition table in a deterministic system. Given a set of possible initial states, the set of possibles states at stage t can be computed in either a deterministic or nondeterministic system.[5] Finally, given a specific initial state, one can compute the unique state at time t in a deterministic system, the set of possible states at time t in a nondeterministic system, and the distribution over states at time t in a stochastic system.

Example 1. To illustrate, consider the following simple Markov process. Imagine a robot that move between three possible locations, shown in Figure 2, in a clockwise fashion. The robot's ability to move is error prone, so with probability 0.1 at any time the robot will remain in it current location, and with probability 0.9 move to the (clockwise) adjacent location. There may also be coffee made and available in the coffee room. If there is coffee made, there is a 0.3 chance that someone will finish the coffee. If there is no coffee made, there is a 0.5 chance that someone will make coffee—unless the robot is in the coffee room, in which case people assume the robot will make the coffee and no coffee will be made (recall, the robot is simply moving clockwise).

This process can be viewed as a simple six state Markov process, with each state corresponding to one of the three locations and the status of the coffee (we use CR to denote "coffee ready"). The transition probabilities reflecting the story above are illustrated in stochastic state transition diagram in Figure 3(a), while the corresponding stochastic matrix is shown in Figure 3(b). We could envision a nondeterministic transition system in which all transitions with nonzero probability in the story above are deemed possible (but without quantification by probabilities). The corresponding nondeterministic diagram is obtained by deleting the arc labels (probabilities), while the appropriate nondeterministic transition matrix is obtained from the stochastic matrix by replacing all positive entries by 1. A deterministic version of the story might state that the robot always moves clockwise successfully and that the coffee always disappears when

---

[5] The set of possible states can be computed in a stochastic system as well, but a distribution cannot.

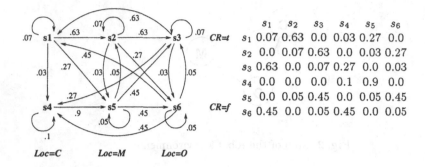

		s_1	s_2	s_3	s_4	s_5	s_6
CR=t	s_1	0.07	0.63	0.0	0.03	0.27	0.0
	s_2	0.0	0.07	0.63	0.0	0.03	0.27
	s_3	0.63	0.0	0.07	0.27	0.0	0.03
	s_4	0.0	0.0	0.0	0.1	0.9	0.0
CR=f	s_5	0.0	0.05	0.45	0.0	0.05	0.45
	s_6	0.45	0.0	0.05	0.45	0.0	0.05

Fig. 3. The state transition diagram and transition matrix for a moving robot.

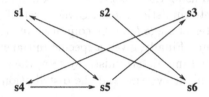

Fig. 4. Deterministic state transition diagram for a moving robot.

it is ready and is always made when it isn't ready, again, unless the robot is in the coffee room. The deterministic state transition diagram is shown in Figure 4. Notice that only one arc leaves any state (and that the corresponding matrix would have a single entry of 1 per row).

These diagrams and matrices represent the dynamics of the process. To fully specify a Markov chain, we must also specify an initial state, a set of possible initial states, or an initial state distribution.

2.2 Actions

We have said little about what *drives* the evolution of a deterministic, nondeterministic or stochastic process, what actually induces such a transition system to change state. In the example above, it is clear that the system state is being changed by the actions of various agents—the robot changing its location, and the status of coffee being changed by the resident coffee drinkers. We could also imagine situations in which state change is caused by events that one doesn't generally view as being under the control of an agent—the weather, for instance (though one could think of nature as an agent).

As an external observer, we can view all of these changes as being induced by the occurrence of *events*. However, if we adopt the perspective of the robot, or some other decision maker that can affect the state of the system, we want to distinguish the *actions* available to us, from other *exogenous events* over which we have no control. As decision makers, we must be able to reason about the various *choices* we have, set against the background of exogenous events beyond our control, in order to predict their consequences and therefore choose good actions that further our own interests to the greatest extent possible.

Adopting the perspective of a decision maker, we view the system as a *Markov decision process* (MDP) [4, 26, 50, 2, 59] instead of a Markov chain. Formally, the dynamics of an MDP is described by a set of system states $\mathcal{S}$, a set of actions $\mathcal{A}$, and a family of transition distributions Pr corresponding to the changes induced by these actions.[6]

Formally, for each $s \in \mathcal{S}$ and time t, we assume a subset of actions $\mathcal{A}_s^t \subseteq \mathcal{A}$, the *feasible action set* at s, is available to the decision maker. For any action $a \in \mathcal{A}_s^t$, we must specify the distribution over possible next states: $Pr(S^{t+1} = s_j | S^t = s, A^t = a)$, where A^t is a random variable denoting the action chosen at stage t. We make two assumptions that simplify the presentation and specification of MDPs, and which are often adopted in practice. First, we assume that all actions can be executed (or attempted) in all system states.[7] Thus, all feasible sets are identical. Second, we assume that these transition distributions are stationary. Therefore, we need only specify, for each $a \in \mathcal{A}$ and $s_i, s_j \in \mathcal{S}$,

$$p_{ij}^a = Pr(S^{t+1} = s_j | S^t = s_i, A^t = a)$$

where this relationship holds for all times t. Though we haven't mentioned it, we have also made the Markov assumption with respect to actions: the probability of moving to any state given knowledge of the current state and action is independent of any other facts about the history of the process.

In stationary decision processes, the effects of any action a can be represented by a *transition matrix* P^a of size $N \times N$, consisting of entries p_{ij}^a defined above (recall that $N = |\mathcal{S}|$), with the complete specification of the dynamics of an MDP requiring a set of $|\mathcal{A}|$ such matrices. In *nondeterministic decision processes*, actions have nondeterministic effects, and each action is specified using a nondeterministic transition matrix. Finally, deterministic transition systems with purely deterministic actions are specified using a transition table for each action.

It is sometimes profitable to view transition systems with actions as stochastic, nondeterministic or deterministic finite-state automata, where possible tran-

---

[6] The full specification of an MDP also requires some notion of observability of the system state and an objective function. We discuss these in subsequent sections.

[7] In fact, AI planning practice commonly assigns *preconditions* to actions defining the states in which they can meaningfully be executed. We take the view that any action can be executed (or "attempted") in any state. If the action has no effect when executed in some state, or its execution leads to disastrous effects, these can be noted in the action's transition matrix. Action preconditions are a often computational convenience rather than a representational necessity: they can make the planning process more efficient by identifying states in which the planner should not even consider selecting the action. Preconditions can be represented in MDPs by relaxing our assumption that feasible actions sets are the same at all states.

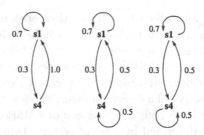

Fig. 5. State transition diagram for making coffee.

sitions from one state to another are labeled by the action inducing that transition (and by the probability of transition in a stochastic setting). We can also view each action individually as corresponding to a transition diagram as in the case of a Markov chain.

Example 2. The transition diagram and matrix shown in Figure 3 correspond to the transitions induced by the action *Clk* (moving clockwise). The transition diagram for a second action, that of the robot making coffee, is shown in Figure 5. This action causes coffee to become ready with probability one of the robot is in the coffee room, but has no impact on the system state otherwise (apart from the impact of passersby on coffee status).

2.3 Exogenous Events

Our specification of actions above intuitively "combines" the effects of the robot's actions and the impact of various *exogenous events* (specifically, the actions of the resident coffee drinkers).[8] The next state distributions for the robot's actions are the key factor in predicting, monitoring and controlling the trajectory taken by the system. However, we often most naturally think of these transitions as dictated by two separate factors: the effect of the robot's action (e.g., moving clockwise) and the effect of an exogenous event (e.g., a passerby taking coffee). More generally, we can view the overall transition distribution for a specific action in a stochastic system as comprising the effects of the agent's chosen action and those of several exogenous events beyond the agent's control, each of which may occur with a certain probability. When the effects of actions are decomposed in this fashion, we refer to the action model as an *explicit event model.*

Intuitively, such an explicit event model requires four types of information. First one specifies the effects of an action under the assumption that no exogenous events will occur—in other words, we isolate the effect of an action on the

---

[8] Recall that we are taking the point of view of the robot as a decision maker; thus, the actions of other agents, as they are beyond its control, are viewed as exogenous events by the robot.

	s_1	s_2	s_3	s_4	s_5	s_6
s_1	0.1	0.9	0.0	0.0	0.0	0.0
s_2	0.0	0.1	0.9	0.0	0.0	0.0
s_3	0.9	0.0	0.1	0.0	0.0	0.0
s_4	0.0	0.0	0.0	0.1	0.9	0.0
s_5	0.0	0.0	0.0	0.0	0.1	0.9
s_6	0.0	0.0	0.0	0.9	0.0	0.1

	s_1	s_2	s_3	s_4	s_5	s_6
s_1	0.0	0.0	0.0	1.0	0.0	0.0
s_2	0.0	0.0	0.0	0.0	1.0	0.0
s_3	0.0	0.0	0.0	0.0	0.0	1.0
s_4	0.0	0.0	0.0	1.0	0.0	0.0
s_5	0.0	0.0	0.0	0.0	1.0	0.0
s_6	0.0	0.0	0.0	0.0	0.0	1.0

	s_1	s_2	s_3	s_4	s_5	s_6
s_1	1.0	0.0	0.0	0.0	0.0	0.0
s_2	0.0	1.0	0.0	0.0	0.0	0.0
s_3	0.0	0.0	1.0	0.0	0.0	0.0
s_4	1.0	0.0	0.0	0.0	0.0	0.0
s_5	0.0	1.0	0.0	0.0	0.0	0.0
s_6	0.0	0.0	1.0	0.0	0.0	0.0

Fig. 6. The decomposed transition matrices for: (a) moving clockwise; (b) making coffee; and (c) taking coffee.

system state from the impact of exogenous events. In our description of the robot scenario, for example, this isolation was made apparent: the robot moving clockwise affects the state with respect to location and nothing else. The transition matrix for clockwise moves, ignoring the effects of exogenous events, is shown in Figure 6(a).

Second one specifies the effects of each exogenous event in isolation. Our scenario above can be understood in terms of two exogenous events: a passerby making coffee and a passerby taking coffee. Exogenous events, just like actions, are specified using transition matrices. The matrices for the make and take coffee events (assumed to be deterministic for simplicity) are shown in Figures 6(b) and (c).[9]

Third, we must specify the conditions under which these exogenous events might occur, and since they don't occur with certainty, the probability with which they occur. We can capture this with an *occurrence vector* for each exogenous event, a vector of size N, where the ith entry corresponds to the probability that the event will occur in state s_i.[10] Note the implicit assumption that these occurrence probabilities are stationary and Markovian. The occurrence of the make coffee event, given the story above, can be captured using the vector

$$\langle 0\ 0\ 0\ 0\ 0.5\ 0.5 \rangle$$

(i.e., someone will make coffee with probability 0.5 if there is no coffee made and the robot is not in the coffee room), while the occurrence vector for taking coffee is

$$\langle 0.3\ 0.3\ 0.3\ 0\ 0\ 0 \rangle$$

The final component of the specification is a *combination rule*. Given the first three components, we know for any action a taken by the decision maker at state s, the probability that any event e will occur and the distributions over next states induced by a and the events e of interest. A combination rule tells us the combined transition probabilities as a (simple, ideally) function of the above components.

---

[9] To keep the example manageable, we assume that taking coffee implies that no coffee remains (e.g., as if only one cup can be made at a time). Realistically, we should model this problem by encoding in the state the amount of coffee remaining.

[10] The probability of different events may be correlated with one another, and may depend on the chosen action (possibly at particular states). If this is the case, then it is necessary to specify occurrence probabilities for subsets of events, possibly conditioned on the choice of action. We will treat event occurrence probabilities as independent for ease of exposition.

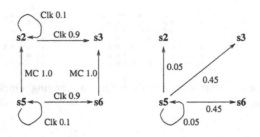

Fig. 7. Commutativity of clockwise movement and coffee making at state s_5; and resulting combined distribution (assuming coffee making occurs with probability 0.5).

Sometimes straightforward combination rules are appropriate and obvious. For example, suppose that in state s_5 the robot moves from the mailroom to the office at the same time someone makes coffee. Intuitively, this action and event do not conflict. If we think of the action and event in an interleaved fashion (i.e., as if one occurs before the other), this lack of conflict can be made precise. Specifically, at s_5, the action and event *commute*: the resulting state distribution obtained by first considering the action occurrence and then the event occurrence (applied to state s_5) is identical to that obtained by considering the event followed by the action (see Figure 7). In either case, the combined transition leads to s_2 with probability 0.1 and s_6 with probability 0.9. Since the event occurs with probability 0.5 (and the event of taking coffee occurs with probability 0, since there is no coffee in state s_5), the combined distribution for the clockwise action at state s_5 is as given in the transition matrix earlier (and shown in Figure 7).

We say that an explicit event model is *commutative* if, for any initial state s and any pair of events (including an agent's own action) e_1 and e_2, the distribution that results from applying event sequence $e_1; e_2$ to s is identical to that obtained from the sequence $e_2; e_1$. Furthermore the probability of an exogenous event occurrence must be unaltered by the transitions caused by other events. Under an interleaving semantics, the combined transition distribution for any action a is computed by considering the probability of any subset of events and applying that subset of events and the action a (in any order) to the state of interest. Formally, we can construct an action transition matrix from the various components of the explicit event model; thus the "natural" specification can be converted to the form usually used by decision making and prediction algorithms. We can form the combined transition matrix $Pr(s, a, t)$ for any action a, given the matrix $\widehat{Pr}_a(s, t)$ for a (which assumes no event occurrences), the matrices $Pr_e(s, t)$ for events e, and the occurrence vector $Pr_e(s)$ for each event e. We define the *effective transition matrix* for event e as follows:

$$\widehat{Pr}_e(s, t) = Pr_e(s)Pr_e(s, t) + \begin{cases} 1 - Pr_e(s) & : \quad s = t \\ 0 & : \quad s \neq t \end{cases}$$

This denotes the event transition probabilities with the probability of event occurrence factored in. If we let E, E' denote the diagonal matrices with entries $E_{ii} = Pr_e(s_i)$ and $E'_{ii} = 1 - Pr_e(s_i)$, then $\widehat{Pr_e}(s,t) = EPr_e + E'$. Under the assumptions above, the implicit event matrix $Pr(s,a,t)$ for action a is then given by $Pr = Pr_a \widehat{Pr_{e_1}} \cdots \widehat{Pr_{e_n}}$ for any ordering of the n possible events.

Unfortunately, this commutative property does not always hold. Even in our domain, the make coffee event and clockwise action do not commute at all states. For instance, at s_4, when the robot is in the coffee room, the probability of coffee making is 0, while at s_5 the probability of this event is 0.5. Suppose that the exogenous event and clockwise action occur at s_4. If we assume that the robot moves *before* the event occurs, then the probability of the event occurring is 0.45 (there is a 0.9 probability of the robot moving and a 0.5 probability of the event occurring if the move is successful). But if the robot moves *after* the event probability is "generated," then nobody will make coffee.

To specify an appropriate interleaving semantics for actions and events in general, one could specify the probability with which events or actions occur in any specific order. For instance, one might assume that each event occurs at a time—within the discrete (possibly nonuniform) time unit—according to some continuous distribution (e.g., an exponential distribution with a given rate). With this information, the probability of any particular ordering of transitions, given that certain events occur, can be computed, as can the resulting distribution over possible next states. The action transition matrix shown in the previous section for the clockwise action assumes that all exogenous events (making or taking coffee) occur *before* the robot's action takes effect.

The picture is more complicated if the actions and events can occur truly simultaneously over some interval—in this case the resulting transition need not be a composition of the individual transitions. As an example, if the robot lifts the side of a table on which a glass of water is situated, the water will spill; similarly if an exogenous event (say a distinct agent) causes the other side to be raised. But if the action and event occur simultaneously, the result is qualitatively different (the water is not spilled). Thus, the interleaving semantics described above is not always appropriate.

As we can see, simple combination rules usually require one to make certain assumptions about how one has modeled the domain; in general, combination rules may be arbitrarily complicated, obviating any advantage gained by specifying exogenous event and action transitions separately. But in many circumstances, appropriate modeling using explicit event models may be profitable.

We note that the above discussion can easily be generalized to handle nondeterministic or deterministic models. In the former case, we might assume that events have nondeterministic effects and that we represent for each state the set of events that must occur and those that might occur. In the deterministic case, event occurrences and event transitions are both deterministic.

2.4 Observations

Although the effects of an action can depend on any aspect of the prevailing state, the choice of action can depend only on what the agent can *observe* about the current state and remember regarding prior observations. We model the agent's observational or sensing capabilities by introducing a finite set of *observations* $\mathcal{Z} = \{z_1, \ldots, z_H\}$. The agent receives an observation from this set at each stage prior to choosing its action at that stage. We can model this observation as a random variable Z^t whose value is taken from $\mathcal{Z}$. We denote by p_{ijz}^a the probability

$$Pr(Z^t = z_h | S^{t-1} = s_i, A^{t-1} = a, S^t = s_j)$$

the probability that the agent observes z_h at stage t given that it performs a in state s_i and ends up in state s_j. As usual, we assume that observational distributions are Markovian and stationary. In many circumstances, we assume this distribution depends only on the current state and action, but not the resulting state; or on the resulting state and action, but not the current state.

This model is very general, allowing one to represent a wide variety of assumptions about the agent's sensory capabilities and the various types of actions that provide information about the system.

At one extreme are *fully observable MDPs* (FOMDPs), in which the agent knows exactly what state it is in at each stage t. We model this case by letting $\mathcal{O} = \mathcal{S}$ and $Pr(o_h | s_i, a_k, s_j) = 1$ iff $o_h = s_j$. In the example above, this means the robot always knows its exact location and the status of the coffee, even if it is not in the coffee room when someone takes or makes coffee.

At the other extreme we might consider *non-observable* systems (NOMDPs) in which the agent receives *no* information about the system's state during execution. We can model this case by letting $\mathcal{O} = \{o\}$. Here the same observation is reported at each stage, revealing no information about the state, hence $Pr(s_j | s_i, a_k, o) = Pr(s_j | s_i, a_k)$. In such *open-loop systems*, the agent receives no useful feedback about the results of its actions. In a stochastic setting, this means the agent has noisy effectors and *no* sensors.

The general model can also capture intermediate cases in which the agent receives incomplete or noisy information about the system state (i.e., *partially observable* MDPs, or POMDPs). For example, the robot may be able to determine its location exactly, but may not be able to determine coffee status unless it is in the coffee room. Furthermore, its "coffee" sensor might occasionally report inaccurately, leading to an incorrect belief as to whether there is coffee ready.

Example 3. Suppose the robot has a "check coffee" action which does not change the system state but generates an observation that is influenced by the presence of coffee, provided the robot is in the coffee room at the time the action is performed. If the robot is not in the coffee room, the sensor always reports "no coffee ." A noisy "check coffee" sensor can be described by a probability distribution like the one shown in Figure 8. Note that we can view these error probabilities as the probability of "false positives" (0.05) and "false negatives" (0.08).

We note that assumptions about observability are unimportant in deterministic transition systems (e.g., classical planning models): if the initial state is known an agent can predict its exact state after any sequence of actions without requiring

	$Pr(Obs = coffee)$	$Pr(Obs = nocoffee)$
$Loc(C), C$	0.92	0.08
$Loc(C), \overline{C}$	0.05	0.95
$\overline{Loc(C)}, C$	0.00	1.00
$\overline{Loc(C)}, \overline{C}$	0.00	1.00

Fig. 8. Observation probabilities for checking coffee status.

feedback. In a nondeterministic system, we might model sensors as providing information about the set of states considered possible given that sensor reading.

Finally, though we have described observation models in the context of Markov decision processes, it makes perfect sense to consider observation models of an agent that is simply monitoring the system in question, but not performing actions that influence the system's trajectory. In such a case, we have a model of the system dynamics given by the initial state distribution and the transition distributions, and a model of the agent's sensory capabilities given by a single observation model much like that described above, but without dependence on chosen actions. Such *hidden Markov models* [51] provide suitable foundations for monitoring and prediction tasks for systems that are not under the influence of the agent making the observations.

2.5 Reasoning and Planning Tasks

We have described the basics of stochastic (and nondeterministic and deterministic) transition systems, described various types of observability and control models. Given the specification of a dynamical system along these lines, one can identify a number of interesting reasoning and control tasks.

We begin by considering Markov processes without control. Without the ability to perform actions that influence the system, our tasks are restricted to pure inference tasks such as predicting the future evolution of the system. If we are simply given the specification of a Markov chain, we can envision a number of inference tasks designed to answer interesting questions about the system. For instance, we may be interested in determining the most likely trajectory the system can take, the distribution over possible states at stage t, prediction of the next state given partial information about previous states the system has passed through, determining the probability with which the system will pass through a specific state (or class of states) before time t, and so on. Markov chains have been studied in great depth (see, e.g., [34]). Most of these questions, *mutatis mutandis*, are well-formed in nondeterministic and deterministic systems as well. However, they are generally trivial in the deterministic case.

Problems become more interesting when the system is partially observable. With a hidden Markov model [51], we have available at any time t only a sequence of observations from which we generally want to answer questions about the true state of the system, or predict future states. An important task is *state estimation*: given a sequence of observations, what is the most likely current state of the system, or what is the distribution over possible current states. This is also referred to as *monitoring* and is a fundamental problem in control theory [2] (for instance, this is what Kalman filters [29] are designed to do, at least for specific transition and observation models). We might want to predict or *forecast* possible system trajectories, or systems states at specific future points, given our current observation stream. Finally, since previous state estimates may need to be revised in light of new observations, the task of *smoothing* or explanation attempts to do just that. These tasks are fundamental in control theory [14, 40] and time series analysis [64], for instance. For a detailed discussion of these tasks from an AI perspective, see Dean and Wellman [17].

When actions are added, the most studied reasoning task is that of control: what actions should be taken at any point in time in order to best meet stated objectives (e.g., reach a goal with high probability or with least cost, or maximize some more general objective function). Generally speaking, an agent can choose its actions on the basis of its *observable history* and not on the actual sequence of system states it has passed through. However, if the process is deterministic and the initial state is known, or if the process is fully observable, then the agent has access to the true state of the system at any point in time and can act on this basis. We can identify a number of different planning and control tasks that differ according to the observability assumptions made, assumptions about the system dynamics, and the structure of the objective function. We refer to [5] for a detailed discussion of different classes of control tasks, but summarize several important classes below.

Probably the most familiar task in AI circles is classical planning, whereby the transition system is deterministic, the initial state is known, and the objective is to reach one of a set of goal states (often as quickly as possible) [1]. Note that observability assumptions play no role here since the true state of the system is predictable without observations. Closely related to the classical model is *conformant planning*. Suppose that actions are deterministic, but one is given a set of possible initial states and the process is nonobservable. A conformant plan is one that will achieve the goal no matter which initial state one is in [60]. Conformant planning can also be formulated in nonobservable, nondeterministic settings without requiring imprecise knowledge of the initial state. In both classical and conformant planning, the agent can base its choice of action only on it knowledge of the (set of) initial state(s) and its previous actions; no observations are available to refine its plan.

Conditional planning is generally defined in a classical setting (i.e., with goals and deterministic actions), but where incomplete knowledge of the system state can be partially resolved with observations [63, 45]. These observations generally supply information of the form that the system is in one of a set of possible states.[11] Conditional planning can also be applied in nondeterministic settings. In either case, one can view a conditional plan as a mapping from the agent's

---

[11] This is a purely semantic picture; conditional planning is usually formulated with observations that inform about the truth of specific propositions.

sequence of previous observations and actions into its current action choice.

In the stochastic setting, the most widely studied model is that of fully observable MDPs [4, 26, 50], a model popular in operations research and quickly gaining favor in AI circles. In FOMDPs, actions are stochastic, but the system is fully observable. Objective functions usually involve maximizing reward (or minimizing cost) accumulated over some finite horizon, or discounted or average reward over an infinite horizon. As such FOMDPs can be used to model control problems of indeterminate horizon, or the control of ongoing processes. Goals can be viewed as a special case of reward functions that associate reward only with goal states. Because of the Markov property and full observability, *policies* need only account for the current state of the system (and possibly the time), but not on the history of the process (since the current state allows as accurate prediction of the future as any amount of history); therefore we can think of policies as mappings from states into actions. Such policies provide a form of conditional plan, where the action choice branches on the current (observed) system state. FOMDPs are generally solved using some form of stochastic dynamic programming.

Most general are partially observable MDPs [2, 59], in which imprecise observations of the system state are provided and actions must be chosen on the basis of observable history (since the true state is generally unknown at any point in time). POMDPs allow an agent to choose actions that will provide information about the current state, thus providing a natural semantic framework for modeling information-gathering actions. As with MDPs, the objective is generally to maximize accumulated reward over some horizon (with goal-oriented problems being a special case). A key result in the understanding of POMDPs is the fact that a *belief state* (i.e., a distribution over the possible current states of the system) is sufficient to summarize past history [2]; thus, policies can be viewed as mappings from belief states to actions. In principle, this means that the corresponding belief state MDP is fully observable (since one can easily update the belief state after an action and observation). Perhaps the most fundamental result in the solution of POMDPs is the fact that the value function for such a (finite horizon) belief state MDP has a special form allowing it to be represented and manipulated finitely [59].

Work on *probabilistic planning* provides a middle ground between MDPs and classical planning [36, 18]. In this work, actions are assumed to be stochastic, but the objective is to achieve a goal with probability above some threshold. Both nonobservable and partially observable models have been explored.

3   Bayesian Network Action Representations

The semantic viewpoint taken thus far offers a useful conceptual framework for thinking about dynamical systems, be they deterministic, nondeterministic or stochastic. For many applications, transition systems provide a practical computational model for inference and decision making problems. For instance, algorithms for MDPs are typically implemented using operations on matrices and vectors that correspond to the direct specification of the transition system in question.

Unfortunately, such approaches become impractical as state spaces become larger and more complex. In particular, most AI planning problems are described in terms of a set of *features* that are sufficient to describe the state of the dynamic system of interest. Even in the earlier examples, the state was decomposed into features such as the robot's location and the status of coffee. Because state spaces grown exponentially with the number of features of interest, it is generally impractical to manipulate explicit transition matrices and vectors. Furthermore, specification of such explicit transition systems in often impractical and unnatural.

An alternative view, one that has been predominant in AI since the earliest days of planning and reasoning about action, is to adopt *factored representations* of actions: one specifies transitions in terms of changes to particular state features rather than directly as state transitions. This often offers considerable representational economy. For instance, in the STRIPS action representation [20] the state transitions induced by actions are represented implicitly by describing only the effects of actions on features that *change* value when the action is executed. Factored representations can be very compact when individual actions affect relatively few features, or when their effects exhibit certain regularities. This compactness can often be exploited by reasoning and decision making algorithms. Furthermore, such factored representations offer a natural way to conceptualize and specify actions.

In this section, we describe a representation for actions that is especially suited to complex stochastic systems, namely, dynamic Bayesian networks. For the remainder of the section, we focus on stochastic systems, though we will draw parallels to similar ideas for deterministic and nondeterministic representations in Section 4.

3.1 Bayesian Networks

We first introduce *Bayesian networks* (BNs) for representing arbitrary probability distributions, ignoring details specific to dynamical systems. A Bayesian network [43] is a representational framework for compactly representing a probability distribution in factored form. Specifically, assume that some number of random variables $X_1, \cdots X_n$ describes a domain of interest. For ease of exposition throughout this subsection, we assume that these variables are boolean, taking on values $\top$ (true) and $\bot$ (false). We generally write x_i to denote the event $X_i = \top$ and $\neg x_i$ or $\overline{x_i}$ to denote $X_i = \bot$.[12]

Generally, specifying a joint distribution over variables $X_1, \cdots X_n$ requires that one specify the probability of every state of affairs or possible world, that

---

[12] The boolean assumption has no impact on the formal details to follow, only the presentation. Generally, random variables with finite domains can be treated in precisely the same way. BNs can also handle continuous-valued variables, for examples, through the use of Gaussian networks [38, 55] or mixture models, though the developments presented below must be generalized in certain details.

is, over each of the 2^n truth assignments to these variables. A BN allows one to represent a joint distribution over $X_1, \cdots X_n$ in a (typically) compact fashion by exploiting certain probabilistic independencies among these variables.

More precisely, a BN is a representation of a joint probability distribution over $X_1, \cdots X_n$, consisting of a directed acyclic graph (DAG), D, and a set of *conditional probability distributions* (CPDs) L. The nodes of the DAG correspond to the random variables $X_1, \ldots, X_n$, and the arcs of the DAG represent direct dependencies between the variables. If there is a directed arc from X_i to X_j, we call X_i a *parent* of X_j, and X_j a *child* of X_i. We use the notation Π_{X_i} to denote the set of parents of node X_i. The DAG D *directly* encodes the following set of independence statements: each variable X_i is independent of its nondescendants, given its parents in D. Other independence statements, involving arbitrary sets of variables, follow from these local assertions. These can be read from the structure of the BN using a graph-theoretic path criterion called *d-separation* that can be tested in polynomial time (see [43] for details).

The independence assumptions allow one to specify the probability of any event in a factored form:

$$Pr(X_1, \ldots, X_n) = \prod_{i=1}^{n} Pr(X_i \mid \Pi_{X_i}) \tag{1}$$

Note that to completely specify a distribution of this form, we need only to specify the CPDs that appear in the factored representation of P. This is precisely the second component of the Bayesian network, namely the set of CPDs L. This set of CPDs dictates the conditional probability $P(X_i \mid \Pi_{X_i})$ for all variables X_i. We can also think of a CPD as representing a family of probability distributions: for each instantiation v of Π_{X_i}, we must specify a distribution over X_i denoting $P(X_i \mid v)$. The specification of a joint distribution in this factored form requires $O(2^k n)$ parameters, where k is the maximum number of parents of any variable, in contrast to the $O(2^n)$ parameters required to specify the joint in explicit form. Furthermore, a number of exact and approximate inference algorithms have been developed that exploit the BN structure to permit fast inference [43].

An example BN, adapted from [43], is shown in Figure 9(a). Here we see the probability of an alarm sounding, S, depends directly on the occurrence of a burglary, B, or an earthquake, E, and whether the alarm was armed, A; we also see that a neighbor calling to report the alarm, C, depends (directly) only on whether it has sounded. The CPD for S is shown in tabular form in Figure 9(a): for each instantiation of its parents, A, B and E, the probability of S occurring (i.e., $Pr(s)$ or $Pr(S = \mathsf{T})$) is shown (since S is boolean, $Pr(\bar{s}) = 1 - Pr(s)$ and is omitted).

Note that the tabular representation of the CPD for S in the example above contains considerable redundancy: there are only four distinct parameters occurring among the eight CPD entries. For instance, if the alarm is unarmed its probability of sounding is 0, regardless of the occurrence of a burglary or earthquake. This suggests that one might simply express this as a single logical rule rather than a set of four CPD entries. Another way to think of this is as follows.

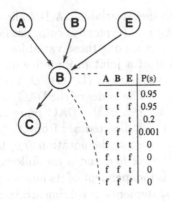
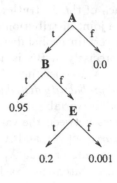

A	B	E	P(s)
t	t	t	0.95
t	t	f	0.95
t	f	t	0.2
t	f	f	0.001
f	t	t	0
f	t	f	0
f	f	t	0
f	f	f	0

Fig. 9. (a) An example of a Bayesian network with standard representation of the CPD $P(S \mid A, B, E)$. (b) A more compact representation of the same CPD using a tree.

The CPD is a function mapping assignments of truth values (in the boolean case) to parents into probability distributions over the target variable. This function in this example takes on only four distinct values and is thus amenable to a more compact function representation.

Extensions of BNs that exploit these regularities in CPDs have been proposed recently. For instance, Poole [46] has shown how probabilistic logic programs can be viewed as BNs with Horn clause representations for rules. Roughly, we might express the CPD above with the four stochastic rules:[13]

$$a \wedge b \rightarrow s(0.95) \tag{2}$$

$$a \wedge \neg b \wedge e \rightarrow s(0.2) \tag{3}$$

$$a \wedge \neg b \wedge \neg e \rightarrow s(0.001) \tag{4}$$

$$\neg a \rightarrow s(0.0) \tag{5}$$

Other proposals for exploiting the regularity in CPDs have been described under the guise of *similarity networks* [25] and the related *multinets* [21], and irrelevance [57]. A general treatment of this phenomenon, dubbed *context-specific independence*, has been explored in [9], where it is observed that general function representations for CPDs can be exploited for ease of specification and knowledge acquisition, inference and decision making, and learning. One function representation explored in depth is that of *decision trees*: a decision tree representation of the example CPD is shown in Figure 9(b). Notice that each branch of the tree corresponds to one of the stochastic Horn rules described above.

---

[13] This is merely intended to give the spirit of Poole's proposal; in fact, he requires the use of new atoms in the rules whose truth is probabilistic, while the rules themselves are deterministic. Conceptually, the intent and effect are similar.

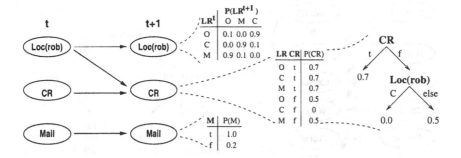

Fig. 10. A DBN for Markov process over a small set of variables.

3.2 Dynamic Bayesian Networks

Often dynamical systems are described in terms of state variables whose values evolve over time.[14] For instance, the Markov chain in Example 2.1 can naturally be viewed in terms of the evolution of two state variables, the robot's location and the status of coffee. Unfortunately, the size of the state space of a Markov process grows exponentially with the number of state variables of interest. However, just as BNs often allow one to represent arbitrary distributions naturally and compactly, so too can they be used to ease the representational burden for dynamic processes.

Recall that the dynamics of a Markov chain are determined by its transition distributions and its initial state distribution. A *factored Markov chain*, that is, a Markov chain whose state space is determined by the values of some number of fluents, can be represented using BNs to represent transition distributions and the initial state distribution. Suppose that the process is captured by n state variables or fluents, $X_1, \cdots X_n$. A T-stage Markov chain can be represented using a BN over $n(T+1)$ variables of the form X_i^t, $1 \le i \le n$, $0 \le t \le T$. The Markov assumption allows us factor this distribution into $T+1$ components, an initial distribution over variables X_i^0 and a set of transition distributions relating variables X_i^{t-1} and X_i^t (for all $1 \le t \le T$).

The initial distribution can be represented using a BN over variables X_i, as described in the previous section. We focus here on the special form of the transition distributions. If we assume the Markov chain is stationary, then a single BN can be used to *schematically* represent the transition probabilities: the probabilistic relationship between variables X_i^{t-1} and X_i^t (taken over all i) is unchanging for different values of t. Figures 10 and 11 illustrate *dynamic Bayesian networks* (DBNs) [16], showing how variables at one time are related stochastically to variables at the previous time (and to one another).

---

[14] These variables are often referred to as *fluents* in the AI literature [41]. In classical planning, these are the atomic propositions used to describe the domain.

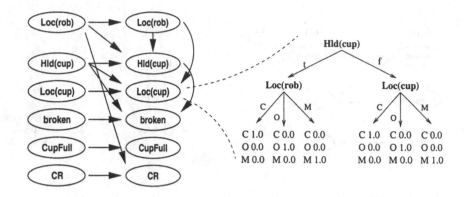

Fig. 11. A DBN for Markov process over a larger set of variables.

In a DBN, the set of variables is partitioned into those corresponding to state variables at a given time (or stage) t and those corresponding to state variables at time $t + 1$. Directed arcs indicate probabilistic dependencies between those variables in the Markov chain. *Diachronic arcs* are those directed from time t variables to time $t + 1$ variables, while *synchronic arcs* are directed between variables at time $t + 1$ (as long as the directed graph remains acyclic). Given any state at time t (i.e., any instantiation of the variables at time t), the network induces a unique distribution over states at $t + 1$. The quantification of the network at the $t + 1$ nodes describes how the state of any particular variable changes as a function of certain other state variables. The lack of a direct arc (or more generally a directed path if there are arcs among the $t + 1$ variables) from a variable X_t to another variable Y_{t+1} means that knowledge of X_t is irrelevant to the prediction of the (immediate) evolution of variable Y in the Markov process.

To fully represent a Markov chain over T stages, one can "string" together T copies of this schematic network. In representing the transition probabilities, only the variables at time slice $t + 1$ in the network are quantified with CPDs, since the distribution over the stage t variables is given by the $t + 1$ variables in the "preceding" copy. The one exception is the quantification of the variables at stage 0, which must be given explicitly. We will use the term DBN to refer both to the two-stage schematic BN that represents a transition matrix and to the (true) BN obtained by stringing some number of these together and providing joint distribution information over the stage 0 variables.

Example 4. Figure 10 shows the Markov chain induced by the robot moving clockwise repeatedly. This DBN corresponds to the Markov chain described in Example 2.1, with one additional state variable M: is mail waiting for pickup in the mail room—which becomes true with probability 0.2 at any stage if it was false, and stay true with probability 1.0 if it was true. This DBN illustrates how compact this representation can be in the best of circumstances, as many of the links between one stage and the next can be omitted. The graphical representation makes explicit the fact that the action *Clk* can affect only the state variable *Loc(robot)* and (via an exogenous event) *CR*. Furthermore, the dynamics of *Loc(robot)* (and the other variables) can be described using only knowledge of the state of their parent variables; for instance, the distribution over *Loc(robot)* at $t + 1$ depends only on the value of *Loc(robot)* at the previous stage (e.g., if $Loc^t = O$, then $Loc(robot)^{t+1} = C$ with probability 0.9 and $Loc(robot)^{t+1} = O$ with probability 0.1).[15] Finally, the effects on the relevant variables are independent. For any instantiation of the variables at time t, the distribution over next states can be computed by multiplying the conditional probabilities of relevant variables.

The ability to omit arcs from the graph based on the locality and independence of action effects has a strong effect on the number of parameters that must be supplied to complete the model. Although the full transition matrix the Markov chain in the example above would be of size would be of size $12^2 = 144$, the transition model in Figure 10 requires only 25 parameters.[16] While this example can be represented in an especially concise way, generally the change in one variable can depend on several others, requiring a number of diachronic arcs directed toward one variable at "time slice" $t + 1$; in addition, certain changes in variables may be correlated (captured by synchronic arcs within the slice $t + 1$). Still, DBNs offer considerable economy in these circumstances on many occasions.

Example 5. The more complex DBN in Figure 11 is obtained by considering a system with additional state variables (but where the Markov chain is still induced by the robot consistently moving clockwise, and the occurrence of exogenous events such as coffee being made and taken). Variables in the example include the location of the robot, the location of objects it might hold (e.g., coffee cup), whether coffee is ready, whether the cup is broken, whether the cup is full of coffee, and so on. We can easily envision a number of additional variables, which we omit to keep the diagram small (such as whether it is holding mail, whether mail is present, etc.). In this example we see the presence of synchronic arcs, indicating *correlations* among the changes in distinct variables. For instance, the CPD for *Loc(cup)* shows its correlation with *Loc(robot)* when *holding(cup)* is true; that is, the cup is where the robot is when the robot holds the cup, so if the robot moves, so too does the cup. We also assume that, if the robot is holding the cup, that it can slip with probability 0.5 when it enters the mail room, and that if the cup slips, it breaks with probability 0.75. This explains the dependence of *broken* at $t + 1$ on both *holding(cup)* at time t and *holding(cup)* at time $t + 1$.

---

[15] In the CPD for $Loc(robot)^{t+1}$, we superscript variables with the appropriate time. For the other CPDs, and in the remaining examples, we suppress these superscripts when context makes clear the time to which the variable refers.

[16] More precisely, exploiting the fact that probabilities sum to one, we can represent the full transition matrix with 132 parameters and the DBN with 14.

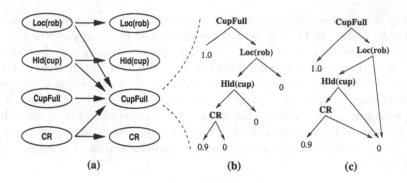

Fig. 12. A fragment of the DBN for action *pourCof* (a), and structured CPD representations (b,c).

We note that structured representations of CPDs can be exploited in the representation of Markov chains by DBNs. For example, rules or decision trees, as discussed in Section 3.1, can often provide a compact representation of a CPD. The decision tree shown in Figure 10 illustrates the "rule-like" structure inherent in the changes of the variable *CR* (is coffee ready); the tree in Figure 11 exploits similar context-specific independence. As we see below when representing actions, this type of structure is quite common. Note also the use of the else branch, which is often helpful when dealing with multi-valued (nonboolean) variables.

3.3 Factored Action Representations

Just as we extended Markov chains to account for different actions, we must extend the DBN representation to account for the fact that the state transitions are influenced by the agent's choice of action. As in Section 2, we will postpone discussion of observations until actions are introduced, and we consider implicit event models before explicit event models.

Implicit Event Models One way to model the dynamics of a Markov decision process MDP is to represent each action by a separate DBN. The DBNs in Figures 10 and 11 can be seen as a representation of the robot action *Clk* (albeit each referring to somewhat different models of the system). The network fragment in Figure 12(a) illustrates the interesting aspects of the DBN for the *pourCof* (pour coffee) action. Intuitively, this action causes the coffee cup to become full (with near certainty) if the robot is holding the cup, if it is in the right location, and if coffee is ready; otherwise the coffee cup stays empty (unless it was already full). The action also has an affect on the *CR* variable if robot is in the right location. Note that if the robot is not in the coffee room, *pourCof* is effectively a no-op.

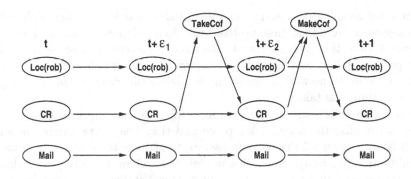

Fig. 13. An simplified explicit event model for *Clk*.

Once again we see that the CPDs have considerable structure. The type of structure illustrated here is common in action representation—typically for an action to have a certain effect, a number of specific conditions must hold. For this reason, logical rule representations, decision trees and other compact function representations offer considerable advantages. A decision tree representation (with "else" branches to summarize groups of cases involving multivalued variables like *Loc*) of the CPD for *cupFull* is shown in Figure 12(b). It can be represented more compactly still using a decision graph (Figure 12(c)).[17]

Decision tree and decision graph representations are used to represent actions in fully observable MDPs in [7] and are described in detail in [10]. These reflect context-specific independence in the transition distributions. Rule-based representations have been used directly by Poole [47, 48] in the context of decision processes and can often be more compact than trees [49].

Explicit Event Models Explicit event models can also be represented using DBNs in a somewhat different form. Again, as in our discussion in Section 2.3, the form that explicit event models take depends crucially on the assumptions one makes about the interplay between the effects of the action itself and exogenous events. However, under certain assumptions even explicit event models can be rather concise, and are often quite natural.

To illustrate, Figure 13 shows the deliver coffee action represented as a DBN with exogenous events explicitly represented. The first "slice" of the network shows the effects of the action *Clk* without the presence of exogenous events. The subsequent slices describe the effects of the exogenous events of taking coffee and making coffee, respectively, assuming that they must occur in that order (if they occur at all). Notice the presence of the extra random variables representing the *occurrence* of the events in question. The CPDs for these nodes (not shown) reflect the occurrence probabilities for the events under various conditions, while

---

[17] Decision graphs are especially useful to prevent duplication of repeating substructures, e.g., those induced by disjunction.

the directed arcs from the event variables to state variables indicate the effects of these events. Note that these probabilities do not depend on all state variables in general; thus, this DBN represents the occurrence vectors (see Section 2.3) in a compact form. In contrast, we do not explicitly represent the action occurrence as a variable in the network, since we are modeling the effect on the system *given* that the action was taken.[18]

This example reflects—for illustration only—the assumptions that that the events occur after the action takes place and that events are ordered as shown (recall from Section 2.3 that certain assumptions have to be made to construct a combination function). Under this model, the system actually passes through two intermediate (though not necessarily distinct) states as it passes from stage t to stage $t+1$; we use subscripts ε_1 and ε_2 to suggest this process. Of course, as described earlier, not all actions and events can be combined in such a decomposable way; more complex combination functions can also be modeled using DBNs (for one example, see [12]).

3.4 Decision-Oriented Dynamic Bayesian Networks

One difficulty with the DBN approach to action description is that each action is represented separately, offering no opportunity to exploit patterns across actions. For instance, the fact that the robot's location persists under all actions except movement actions means that the persistence relationship between $Loc(robot)^t$ and $Loc(robot)^{t+1}$ is duplicated in the DBN for all actions (other than the movement actions). In addition, correlations among action effects are duplicated across actions as well. For instance, the fact that the location of the cup is identical to the robot's location if the robot is holding the cup must be duplicated in all actions that affect the robot's location.

To circumvent this difficulty, we can introduce the choice of action as a "random variable" in the network, conditioning the distribution of state variable transitions on the value of this variable. Unlike state variables (or event variables in explicit event models), we do not generally require a distribution over this action variable—the intent is simply to model schematically the conditional state transition distributions *given* any particular choice of action. This is because the choice of action will be dictated by the decision maker once a policy is determined. For this reason, using the terminology of influence diagrams [27, 56], we call these nodes *decision nodes* and depict them in our network diagrams with boxes. Such a variable can take as its value any action available to the agent. As such, we call such a network a *decision-oriented DBN* (DDBN).[19]

---

[18] In Section 3.4 we will see representations that model the choice of action explicitly as a variable in the network.

[19] We use the terminology DDBN instead of influence diagram because influence diagrams are more general in two respects. First, they do not require that the structure between time slices be identical, or even contain the same variables; they have generally been used to hand-craft decision scenarios, though the more schematic use of influence diagrams has been discussed in depth by Tatman and Shachter [61].

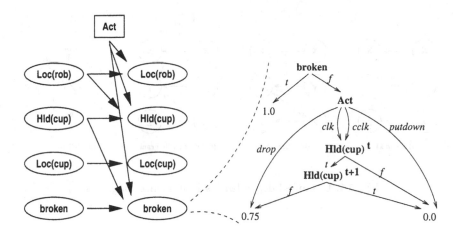

Fig. 14. (a) A DDBN for a restricted process; and (b) a structured CPD.

An example of a DBN with an explicit decision node is illustrated in Figure 14(a). In this restricted example, we might imagine the decision node can take one of four possible values, *Clk*, *CClk*, *putDown*, or *drop*. The fact that the cup remains broken at $t+1$ if it was broken previously, independent of the action choice, is represented once in the CPD for *broken*. Furthermore, the fact that the cup is in the same location as the robot if the robot is holding the cup and persists under any other course of action is also represented only once: we do not need to repeat arcs across multiple DBNs for distinct actions.

Notice that the CPDs for variables grow rather large due to their dependence on the decision node and the fact that the decision node can take on a large number of values. Fortunately, since it is generally the case that, for any specific variable, that many actions do not influence it, the CPD will contain many regularities. For instance, location is unaffected by dropping or putting down the cup. Furthermore, the effects of certain actions on a variable will often be identical (especially when dealing with correlations). For example, the cup will break with a fixed probability whether the cup slips while moving or it is dropped intentionally. These regularities can be captured by using decision trees or decision graphs. For instance, the CPD for *broken* in the DDBN can be represented very compactly as a decision graph, as illustrated in Figure 14(b). Here, instead of 32 CPD entries required by the tabular form (given four parents, one of which—the action node—has four values), we have three CPD entries (together with four interior nodes and ten arcs in the graph).

The ability to use decision trees and graphs is important in DDBNs. One difficulty with this straightforward use of decision nodes (which is the standard

---

Second, influence diagrams model the informational dependency required for policy construction in partially observable domains, as well as reward and value functions.

138

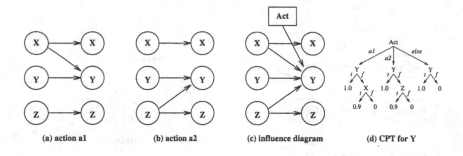

(a) action a1 (b) action a2 (c) influence diagram (d) CPT for Y

Fig. 15. Unwanted dependencies in influence diagrams.

representation in the influence diagram literature) is that adding candidate actions can cause an explosion in the network's dependency structure. For example, consider the two action networks shown in Figure 15(a) and (b). Action $a1$ makes Y true with probability 0.9 if X is true (having no effect otherwise), while $a2$ makes Y true if Z is true.

Combining these actions in a single network in the obvious way produces the DDBN shown in Figure 15(c). Notice that Y now has four parent nodes, inheriting the union of all its parents in the individual networks (plus the action node), requiring a CPT with 16 entries for actions $a1$ and $a2$ together with 8 additional entries for *each* action that does not affect Y. The individual networks reflect the fact that Y depends on X only when $a1$ is performed and on Z only when $a2$ is performed. This fact is lost in the naively constructed DDBN. However, structured CPTs can be used to recapture this independence and compactness of representation: the tree of Figure 15(d) captures the distribution much more concisely, requiring only 8 entries (and would need only three entries and four interior nodes if represented as a decision graph). This structured representation also allows us to concisely express that Y persists under all other actions. In large domains, we expect variables to generally be unaffected by a substantial number of (perhaps most) actions, thus requiring representations such as this for IDs.

While we provide no distributional information over the action choice, it is not hard to see that a DBN with an explicit decision node can be used to the represent the Markov chain induced by a particular policy in a very natural way. Specifically, by adding arcs from state variables at time t to the decision node, the value of the decision node (i.e., the choice of action at that point) can be dictated by the prevailing state.[20]

---

[20] More generally, once can represent a randomized policy by specifying a distribution over possible actions conditioned on the state.

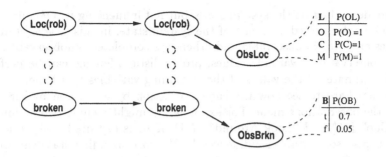

Fig. 16. Sensor models in DDBNs.

3.5 Observations

In one sense, no special machinery is needed to model observations in DBNs. Generally, one specifies the dynamics of the process in terms of state variables and assumes that observations of various state variables at different times will be made, from which one reasons using standard probabilistic inference techniques to predict the future evolution of the process, explain past behavior, or make decisions. Of course, generally inference methods are often tailored to exploit the special structure of a DBN (or DDBN), as we discuss in the next section.

In another sense, taking the HMM point of view, we often think of, and model, observations of the system as distinct from the underlying dynamic process. For this reason, one often specifies *sensor* models that describe how the state of a specific sensor is influenced—generally stochastically— by the true, underlying system state. A number of sensor values at each point in time then provide information about the true system trajectory. As an example, consider Figure 16, which shows two "sensor" variables that provide information about the robot's location and whether or not the coffee cup is broken. The values taken by these sensor variables are probabilistically determined by the corresponding state variables. In the case of location, the sensor is perfect: each location determines with probability 1 a unique observation value (which, for convenience, we label with the location name). The broken cup sensor is noisy, having a 0.3 chance of returning a false negative reading (i.e., failing to detect a broken cup), and a 0.05 false positive rate (reporting that an intact cup is broken). Of course, in general, sensor value need not correspond in a one to one fashion with values of the underlying variable, nor do sensor variables need stand in such close correspondence with state variables: an ensemble of sensors may provide information about one state variable, and a number of state variables may influence the value of a sensor.

We see how DBNs provide a factored view of HMMs: we have a process whose dynamics is specified by transition probabilities together with an observational process that determines sensor values as a function of the underlying state. When viewed this way, observational variables are often seen to "dangle" in the network diagram, depending on the system state, but not influencing it. Of course, these variables can be viewed as a part of the system state: in this case, certain state variables are directly observable and others are completely unobservable. Given a set of observational variable values, probabilistic inference can be performed to fill in estimates of the values of the remaining variables over time.

It is not hard to see how the choice of action by a decision maker can influence the observations made. For example, we might include two actions, "Inspect Cup" (*IC*) and "Look Around" (*LA*): if *IC* is executed, the value of the broken cup sensor variable is influenced by the corresponding state variable, but otherwise, a "null" value is returned; similarly, the location sensor provides an information-laden value only if the action *LA* is executed.

3.6   Reasoning and Planning with DBNs

All of the inference and control tasks described in Section 2.5 have counterparts in DBNs. The advantage of DBNs for representing Markov chains and Markov decision processes is the fact that processes with very large state spaces—exponential in the number of state variables—can often be represented concisely. However, inference in general BNs is intractable unless special structure exists. Since DBNs are typically very large by BN standards, one must hope that the special structure, specifically the independence between variables implied by the Markov property can be exploited. A number of researchers have developed algorithms that do just this.

DBNs were first described by Dean and Kanazawa [16], who devised a method for performing temporal projection (i.e., prediction or forecasting) given certain evidence. Efficient schemes for both forecasting and smoothing were developed by Kjaerulff [35] that exploit the special structure of DBNs. Other inference schemes developed specifically for DBNs include work on monitoring and sensor validation [42], inference via simulation [30, 15] and approximate monitoring [13]. The use of tree-structured representations of CPDs in DBNs to exploit context-specific independence in inference is considered in [15].

The use of decision nodes in DBNs is a central component of influence diagrams [27, 56]; their use in the schematic, repeated fashion typical of DBNs is first considered by Tatman and Shachter [61] who apply influence diagram evaluation techniques to (essentially) DDBNs and model MDPs in this way. The use of DBNs to represent actions in MDPs is pursued further by Boutilier, Dearden and Goldszmidt [7], who investigate the use of tree-structured CPDs in dynamic programming approaches to policy construction (see also [6] for an approximation algorithm). The application of tree-structured DBNs to the solution of POMDPs is pursued in [11]. Poole [47, 48] has investigated the use of rule-based representations of CPDs in DBNs for MDPs.

4   The Frame and Related Problems

The DBN and DDBN representations offer a natural and often concise method of specifying Markov processes and actions in stochastic settings. These techniques have been developed in large part independently of work in classical planning and reasoning about action. It is thus natural to ask whether problems that have been central in classical reasoning about action and planning, in particular, the frame and ramification problems, have analogues in stochastic settings, and if so, how they are dealt with in the DDBN framework. Our aim in this section is to show that, in fact, the frame and ramification problems do arise in the DDBN framework, and that the (implicit) solutions to these problems are based on intuitions similar to those adopted in more classical models, such as STRIPS and the situation calculus.

We will focus primarily on the frame problem in the situation calculus, but will also draw some connections to STRIPS and the $\mathcal{A}$-family of languages. We begin by reviewing the situation calculus and the frame problem. We then show how the frame problem arises in DBN and DDBN representation of actions and how the "solution" to the frame problem in DDBNs is similar to the solution proposed by Reiter [52]. We also describe the ramification problem, describe the connections to correlations in DDBNs and make some remarks on how ramifications might be compiled directly into DDBNs automatically.

4.1 The Situation Calculus and the Frame Problem

The situation calculus (SC) was among the first logical formalisms for representing (deterministic) actions adopted in AI [41] and continues to be the focus of much research [33, 58, 3, 52, 31]. We adopt a somewhat simplified version of SC here. SC is a sorted first-order language with two classes of domain objects, *states* and *actions*, a function symbol *do* mapping state-action pairs into states, and a set of unary predicate symbols, or *fluents* corresponding to the propositions of the underlying problem, that take state arguments.[21] We write $do(a, s)$ to denote the *successor state* of state s when action a is performed, and write $F(s)$ to denote that fluent F is true in state s.

SC can be used to describe the effects of actions quite compactly, in a way that exploits regularities in the effects actions have on particular propositions. A typical *effect axiom* is:

$$CR(s) \land holding(cup, s) \land Loc(robot, C, s)$$
$$\supset cupFull(do(pourCof, s)) \land \neg CR(do(pourCof, s)) \qquad (6)$$

which states that *cupFull* holds and *CR* (coffee ready) doesn't in the state that results from performing the action of pouring coffee if coffee was ready, the robot was holding the cup, and the robot is in the coffee room.[22] Because of the Markovian assumption in our semantics, we assume that the only state term

---

[21] The restriction to unary predicates means that the underlying domain is described using propositions rather than predicates itself. We adopt this merely for simplicity of exposition—rarely is the assumption made in practice. In our examples we use domain objects as well.

[22] We assume universal quantification over the state variable s throughout.

occurring in the antecedent is a unique state variable (e.g., s) and that each state term in the consequent has the form $do(a, s)$ for some action term a.

Note that Axiom (6) describes a property of a large number of state transitions quite concisely; however, it does not uniquely determine the transitions induced by the action $pourCof$. First, while it describes the effect of $pourCof$ on the fluents $cupFull$ and CR (under some conditions), it fails to describe its effect on other fluents. For example, to completely specify the transition function for $pourCof$, one must also assert the effect it has on other fluents in the domain (such as $holding(cup)$ or $broken$). Unfortunately, there are a typically a great many fluents that are completely unaffected by any given action, and that we do not consider part of the natural specification of an action's effects. Intuitively, we would like the user to specify how the action influences affected fluents, and assume that other fluents persist. We call this the problem of *persistence of unaffected fluents* (PUF). A second difficulty is that while Axiom (6) describes the effect of $pourCof$ on $cupFull$ and CR under the condition $CR(s) \wedge holding(cup, s) \wedge Loc(robot, C, s)$, it fails to specify what happens to those fluents when this condition is false. Once again, it is usually taken to be desirable not to force the user to have to say a fluent is unaffected in other circumstances, leaving it as a tacit assumption. We call this the problem of *persistence of affected fluents* (PAF).

The *frame problem* [41] is that of easing the user from the burden of having to specify conditions under which an action does not affect a fluent: PUF and PAF are two instances of this problem. One possible solution is to provide a means to automatically derive explicit *frame axioms* given the user's specification. For example, given the input

$$CR(s) \wedge Loc(robot, C, s) \wedge holding(cup, s)$$
$$\supset cupFull(do(pourCof, s)) \wedge \neg CR(do(pourCof, s)) \tag{7}$$
$$CR(s) \wedge Loc(robot, C, s) \wedge \neg holding(cup, s) \supset \neg CR(do(pourCof, s)) \tag{8}$$

one could, under the assumption that this describes *all* effects of $pourCof$, generate axioms such as

$$(\neg CR(s) \vee \neg Loc(robot, C, s)) \wedge cupFull(s) \supset cupFull(do(pourCof, s)) \tag{9}$$
$$(\neg CR(s) \vee \neg Loc(robot, C, s)) \wedge \neg cupFull(s) \supset \neg cupFull(do(pourCof, s)) \tag{10}$$
$$broken(s) \supset broken(do(pourCof, s)) \tag{11}$$
$$\neg broken(s) \supset \neg broken(do(pourCof, s)) \tag{12}$$

Axioms (9) and (10) deal with the PAF problem, while axioms (11) and (12) handle PUF. Letting $\mathbf{P}$ denote the set of fluents characterizing the domain, in general, we require $2|\mathbf{P}|$ such frame axioms, describing the lack of effect of a on each fluent in $\mathbf{P}$; or $2|\mathbf{P}||\mathcal{A}|$ such axioms for the entire set of action $\mathcal{A}$.

Other approaches deal not just with the specification problem, but also with the sheer number of axioms required. One example is the solution proposed by Reiter [52], extending the work of Pednault [44] and Schubert [54]. The aim is to directly encode the "assumption" that all conditions under which an action affects a fluent have been listed. This is accomplished by building a disjunction of all the conditions under which an action A affects a fluent F, asserting the F changes as dictated when these conditions hold, and that it retains its value otherwise (see [52] for further details).

If we assert one such axiom for each fluent F, it is not hard to see that we uniquely determine a (deterministic) transition function for action A over the state space. In our example, these *closure axioms* for action *pourCof* include:

$$cupFull(do(pourCof, s)) \equiv$$
$$[(CR(s) \wedge Loc(robot, C, s) \wedge holding(cup, s)) \vee cupFull(s)] \tag{13}$$
$$broken(do(pourCof, s)) \equiv broken(s) \tag{14}$$

We require $|\mathbf{P}|$ axioms to characterize an action in this way. While it allows a user to avoid *specifying* frame axioms, this is not a substantial saving with respect to number of axioms required in a knowledge base over the use of explicit frame axioms, for we require $|\mathcal{A}|$ such axiom sets (one per action). However, as we see below, Reiter's method avoids the repetition of these axioms in multiple action settings. The size of the axioms is also of interest. Imagine some (presumably small) number f of fluents is affected by a, that the average action condition has c conjuncts, and that affected fluents appear in an average of e effect axioms. Then we can expect the f closure axioms for affected fluents to be roughly of size ce, while the remaining $|\mathbf{P}| - f$ axioms are of constant size.

While specifying *individual* actions this way does not reduce the size of our axioms substantially, Reiter's solution is designed with multiple actions in mind. Reiter exploits the fact that, since they are terms in SC, one can quantify over actions. His procedure will (under reasonable conditions) produce one axiom of the form

$$\forall s, a \ \ F(do(a, s)) \equiv \gamma_F^+(a, s) \vee (F(s) \wedge \neg \gamma_F^-(a, s))$$

for each fluent F. Here $\gamma_F^+(a, s)$ denotes the disjunction of the formulae $a = A \wedge \gamma_{F,A}^+(s)$ for each specific action A which affects fluent F positively, where $\gamma_{F,A}^+(s)$ describes the conditions under which A has that positive effect on F (similar remarks apply to $\gamma_F^-(a, s)$). Thus, we see instead of having $|\mathcal{A}||\mathbf{P}|$ axioms, we have only $|\mathbf{P}|$ axioms, and the axiom for fluent F contains only reference to actions that influence it. If each fluent is affected by n actions (presumably n is much smaller than $|\mathcal{A}|$), each action condition has c conjuncts, and each affected fluents appear in e effect axioms for any action, then we expect this specification of the transition system to be of size $|\mathbf{P}|nce$. In our example, assuming the drop action causes the cup to become empty, the axiom for fluent *cupFull* is:

$$\forall s \ \ cupFull(do(a, s)) \equiv [(a = pourCof \wedge CR(s) \wedge Loc(robot, C, s)$$
$$\wedge holding(cup, s)) \vee (\neg(a = drop \wedge holding(cup, s)) \wedge cupFull(s))] \tag{15}$$

Notice that actions like *putDown* and *Clk* that have no influence (positive or negative) on *cupFull* are not mentioned.

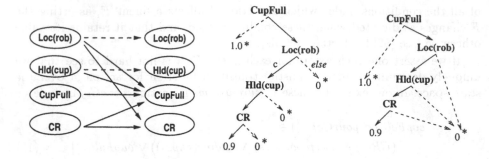

Fig. 17. (a) The DBN for *pourCof* with (b) decision tree and (c) decision graph representations of the *cupFull* CDP.

4.2 The Frame Problem in DBNs and DDBNs

The DBN and DDBN models of transition systems described in Section 3 assume that someone has explicitly provided the required network (DDBN) or networks (DBNs). These representations make explicit the fact that certain variable values are influenced, under certain actions, by others. They also require that one explicitly list the dependence of *persisting fluents* on their previous values. In Figure 17 we have redrawn the DBN for the *pourCof* with persistence relations noted as follows: first, dashed arcs in the figure describe persistence relations among fluents unaffected by the action (e.g., *Loc(robot)*); second, the starred entries in the CPD for node *cupFull* denote the persistence of affected fluent *cupFull* under the condition $\neg CR \vee \neg holding(cup) \vee \neg Loc(robot, C)$. The fact that a user must specify these persistence relationships explicitly is the counterpart of the PUF and PAF problems in the situation calculus. Therefore, we can take the *frame problem for DBNs* to be the need to make these relationships explicit.

As described above, there are two possible perspectives on what constitutes a solution to this problem: relieving the user of this burden, and minimizing the size of the representation of such persistence. The first type of solution is not especially hard to deal with in DBNs. A rather simple idea is to have the user specify only the unbroken arcs in the network and only those unhighlighted probabilities in the CPTs. It is a simple matter to then automatically add persistence relationships.

The size of the DBN for an action (whether or not persistence relations are generated automatically) is then comparable to that of Reiter's solution (with one substantial proviso). Again, assume that f fluents are affected by a, and that the average fluent is influenced by c preaction fluents. The CPDs for each of the f affected fluents will be of size 2^c, whereas the remaining $|\mathbf{P}| - f$ CPTs are of constant size. The important factor in the comparison to the Reiter's solution is the difference in the affected fluent representation, with this method requiring a representation of size roughly $f \cdot 2^k$, while SC requires a representation of size fce. Here k is the number of *relevant* preaction fluents for a typical affected fluent

F, those that are part of *some* condition that influences the action's effect on F (i.e., the number of parents of F in the DBN). Note that $k \leq ce$. The exponential term for the DBN formulation is due to the fact that CPTs require a distribution for the affected fluent for *each assignment to its parents*. For instance, since *CR*, *holding(cup)*, *Loc(robot)* and *cupFull* all impact the effect of *pourCof* on *cupFull*, we must specify this effect for all 24 assignments to these four variables (recall that *Loc(robot)* can take three values).

Axiom (7), and more significantly the closure Axiom (13), are much more compact, requiring only that the single positive effect condition be specified, with persistence under other circumstances being verified automatically. Unstructured (tabular) CPDs in DBNs fail to capture the regularities in the action effects that fall out naturally in SC. However, as pointed out in Section 3, recent work on structured representations of CPDs, such as logical rules, trees and graphs, allow one to more compactly represent CPDs to exploit such regularities. Examples of representations that capture this regularity are the decision tree and decision graph shown in Figures 17(b) and 17(c), corresponding to the original CPD for variable *cupFull*. The broken arrows indicate the persistence relationships that can be added automatically when left unspecified by the user.

In general, it will be hard to compare the relative sizes of different representations, and the logic-based method of Reiter, since this depends crucially on exact logical form of the action conditions involved. For instance, decision trees can be used to represent certain logical distinctions very compactly, but others can require trees of size exponentially greater than a corresponding set of logical formulae. However, one can also use graphs, logical formulae and other representations for CPTs—each has particular advantages and disadvantages with respect to size and speed of inference [9].

Similar problems plague DDBNs, when we consider the size of the representation of *all* actions in a transition system. Having a separate network for each action will require a representation of size $|\mathcal{A}|(2(|\mathbf{P}| - f) + f \cdot 2^k)$ (where f is the expected number of fluents affected by an action, k the number of conditions relevant to each affected fluent). The usual way to represent a transition system is to use an action node and condition each post-action variable on the action variable (we assume every variable can be influenced by some action).

As discussed in Section 3.4, since (most or) every fluent is affected by some action, the action node becomes a parent of each post-action node, increasing the size of each CPT by a factor of $|\mathcal{A}|$ (as if we had a separate network for each action). Indeed, this representation causes even greater difficulty because any preaction variable that influences a post-action variable under *any* action must be a parent. Since the size of the representation is exponential in the number of parents, this will virtually always be a substantially less compact representation than that required by a set of $|\mathcal{A}|$ action networks. In general, it will have size $|\mathcal{A}||\mathbf{P}|2^m$, where m is the expected number of fluents that are relevant to a post-action node under *any* action (typically much larger than k above).

Again, as discussed in Section 3.4, decision tree and decision graph representations can alleviate this problem substantially. In particular, using decision graphs with the action variable at or near the top of the graph (as in Figures 14 and 15), often keeps the size of the representation very compact. In addition, one can leave persistence relations unspecified if desired and have them filled in automatically.

The Ramification Problem Ramifications or *domain constraints* are synchronic constraints on possible state configurations (as opposed to diachronic constraints that relate features of one state to features of its successor). When representing multiple actions, domain constraints allows compact specification of regular effects that are independent of the action being performed. For instance, if the location of the cup is always the same as the location of the robot when the robot holds the cup, a statement to this effect relieves one from explicitly stating that every action a that changes the location of the robot also changes the location the cup (or anything else it is holding). We would like this effect (or ramification) of the robot moving clockwise, counterclockwise, running, etc., to be *derived* from the effect these actions on the robot's location itself.

In SC, domain constraints can easily be expressed; for instance:

$$\forall s \; holding(x, s)) \supset loc(x, s) = loc(robot, s) \tag{16}$$

The ramification problem has to do with the interaction of such constraints with possible solutions to the frame problem. Solutions have been proposed by Lin and Reiter [39] for SC, while others have proposed solutions to the ramification problem within other formalisms [32, 23, 62].

Domain constraints in DDBNs correspond to certain types of correlation among action effects, denoted as an arc between two post-action variables, representing the dependency between two fluents in a single state. Note that the constraints imposed by the limited language of DBNs, plus the restriction on the acyclicity of the underlying graphs limits some of the problems of including ramifications. In particular we only have to worry about modifying the specification of an action whenever a synchronic fluent becomes a new parent. Still the problem is similar to the case of SC: how to specify such domain constraints independently of a particular action, and then impose these relationships on the action network(s) in such a way that automatically derived persistence relationships account for these ramifications directly.

To illustrate, we might imagine that a ramification of the type mentioned above is encoded in a nontemporal, action-independent BN as shown in Figure 18. The left subtree of the CPD for $loc(cup)$ describes the ramification (the cup's location is identical to the robot's location). Intuitively, this ramification should override any persistence relation pertaining to the cup's location. It is a simple matter to automatically "graft" these conditions into a CPD for $Loc(cup)$ in any DBN. The right subtree is unspecified, since the domain constraint only holds when the robot is holding the cup: in this case, whatever effect an action has on $Loc(cup)$ remains intact. We should note, however, that undoubtedly complications can arise in any attempt to formalize such a procedure. For instance, if a ramification "conflicts" with an action's effect, an inconsistency will arise.

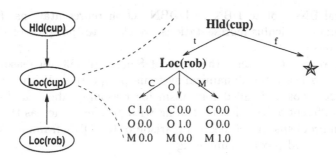

Fig. 18. A BN encoding an action-independent ramification.

To date, no detailed study of the ramification problem in DBNs and DDBNs has been undertaken.

4.3 Other Action Formalisms

Though we do not describe these in depth, we mention here several other action formalisms that exhibit some (often close) relationship with the DBN representation of stochastic actions.

The classic STRIPS representation has been extended to capture stochastic effects [24, 37]. Intuitively, a probabilistic STRIPS operator is much like a STRIPS operator with multiple change lists, each change associated with a certain probability of occurrence, thus fixing the probability of certain state transitions. It is similar to the DBN action representation in certain respects, but differs in that the effects of an action on different variables must be combined into single change lists (note that the DBN representation describes effects in a distributed fashion, with distinct CPDs for each distribution). Because of this, DBNs can often be much more compact that probabilistic STRIPS operators. The two formalisms are compared in great detail in [5].

The $\mathcal{A}$-family of languages [22, 23] provide another natural means for specifying actions, allowing one to deal with ramifications, noninertial fluents (which in some cases can be viewed as exogenously influenced variables) and nondeterminism to some extent. The semantics of these languages is based on a notion of minimal change, and much like STRIPS representations, do not require the specification of closure or frame axioms. Much like we have done here, the semantics is described in terms of transition systems (specifically, nondeterministic transition systems).

Thielscher [62] describes a classical formalism for reasoning about action that relies crucially on causal notions. Much of this work is influenced by the causal interpretation of the probabilistic dependencies in BNs. As such, this work can be seen to bridge the gap between classical theories and the BN framework for reasoning about action. Unfortunately, Thielscher compares his work only to atemporal BNs, not to DBN or DDBN action representations. In this one respect, situation calculus representations are closer to the spirit of DBN action representations.

Finally, we point out that the work of Sandewall [53] on reasoning about action takes to heart the dynamical systems perspective. Within this model, Sandewall develops a detailed formalism for reasoning about action, and for comparing different approaches to dealing with problems such as the frame and ramification problems. A detailed comparison of the DBN framework to Sandewall's model should prove illuminating.

5 Concluding Remarks

In this paper we have taken a close look at representational issues in encoding actions in stochastic domains using dynamic Bayesian networks. We have surveyed some of the relevant techniques for representing both Markov chains and Markov decision processes in which actions have stochastic effects on state variables, and where exogenous events can occur that either drive the dynamic process or modify the effects of actions. We have also shown how the frame and ramification problems arise within the DBN context, and how the implicit solutions that emerge within the DBN framework parallel solutions developed within the classical reasoning about action community. Within DBNs we can solve the frame problem in both senses of the term "solution"—we can relieve the user from the burden of explicitly specifying persistence relationships, and we can encode (automatically generated) frame "axioms" rather efficiently.

This comparison has laid bare some issues that deserve further research. First, we have not discussed nondeterministic actions in great detail. Several proposals for dealing with nondeterministic action effects have been proposed, with the key difficulty arising through the interaction of nondeterminism with persistence [32, 23]. However, additional difficulties arise when one considers correlations among action effects [8]. DBNs (and more generally BNs) have been designed to deal with stochastic effects (and hence correlations); as such, principles and concepts from DBN action representations should provide insight into the development of classical, nondeterministic action formalisms.

Another issue that deserves further study is that of ramifications in DBNs: how can one encode action-independent state constraints and automatically compile these into DBN action specifications. This issue has received little attention in the representation of stochastic systems. Insights from the classical reasoning about action community (e.g., [32, 23, 62, 39]) should be brought to bear on DBN representations.

A key issue that has been all but ignored in the BN community is that of first-order or relational representations. While some efforts have been made to add expressiveness to BN representations along these lines (e.g., [28]), the state of the art is sorely lacking, and no attention has been paid to issues relating to dynamics and actions. Thus, while more expressive than classical representations with respect to representing uncertainty, DBNs are less expressive with respect to relational properties and quantification. This important restriction must be lifted for DBNs to be used as natural and compact representations of many dynamical systems.

Finally, we note that BNs and DBNs are designed to facilitate efficient inference. The use of DBNs in inference is very flexible—standard BN algorithms can be used to answer queries with respect to temporal projection and explanation, for action sequences of arbitrary (finite) length, and can be used for plan generation [7, 61]. It remains to be seen to what extent classical action representations support efficient inference and plan generation.

Acknowledgements

Portions of the review in this article are derived from the research reported in the following two articles: C. Boutilier and M. Goldszmidt, "The Frame Problem and Bayesian Network Action Representations," in *Proc. Eleventh Biennial Canadian Conference on Artificial Intelligence*, LNAI 1081, pp.69–83, Springer-Verlag, Berlin, 1996; and C. Boutilier, T. Dean, S. Hanks, "Decision Theoretic Planning: Structural Assumptions and Computational Leverage" (unpublished manuscript). Thanks to Moisés Goldszmidt, Tom Dean and Steve Hanks for their helpful collaboration and conversation, and their influence on the present article. This work was supported by NSERC Research Grant OGP0121843 and NCE IRIS-III Program "Dealing with Actions: Foundations for Intelligent Systems."

References

1. James Allen, James Hendler, and Austin Tate, editors. *Readings in Planning*. Morgan-Kaufmann, San Mateo, 1990.
2. K. J. Astrom. Optimal control of Markov decision processes with incomplete state estimation. *J. Math. Anal. Appl.*, 10:174–205, 1965.
3. Andrew B. Baker. Nonmonotonic reasoning in the framework of the situation calculus. *Artificial Intelligence*, 49:5–23, 1991.
4. Richard E. Bellman. *Dynamic Programming*. Princeton University Press, Princeton, 1957.
5. Craig Boutilier, Thomas Dean, and Steve Hanks. Decision theoretic planning: Structural assumptions and computational leverage. *Journal of Artificial Intelligence Research*, 1998. To appear.
6. Craig Boutilier and Richard Dearden. Approximating value trees in structured dynamic programming. In *Proceedings of the Thirteenth International Conference on Machine Learning*, pages 54–62, Bari, Italy, 1996.
7. Craig Boutilier, Richard Dearden, and Moisés Goldszmidt. Exploiting structure in policy construction. In *Proceedings of the Fourteenth International Joint Conference on Artificial Intelligence*, pages 1104–1111, Montreal, 1995.
8. Craig Boutilier and Nir Friedman. Nondeterministic actions and the frame problem. In *AAAI Spring Symposium on Extending Theories of Action: Formal Theory and Practical Applications*, pages 39–44, Stanford, 1995.

9. Craig Boutilier, Nir Friedman, Moisés Goldszmidt, and Daphne Koller. Context-specific independence in Bayesian networks. In *Proceedings of the Twelfth Conference on Uncertainty in Artificial Intelligence*, pages 115–123, Portland, OR, 1996.

10. Craig Boutilier and Moisés Goldszmidt. The frame problem and Bayesian network action representations. In *Proceedings of the Eleventh Biennial Canadian Conference on Artificial Intelligence*, pages 69–83, Toronto, 1996.

11. Craig Boutilier and David Poole. Computing optimal policies for partially observable decision processes using compact representations. In *Proceedings of the Thirteenth National Conference on Artificial Intelligence*, pages 1168–1175, Portland, OR, 1996.

12. Craig Boutilier and Martin L. Puterman. Process-oriented planning and average-reward optimality. In *Proceedings of the Fourteenth International Joint Conference on Artificial Intelligence*, pages 1096–1103, Montreal, 1995.

13. Xavier Boyen and Daphne Koller. Tractable inference for complex stochastic processes. In *Proceedings of the Fourteenth Conference on Uncertainty in Artificial Intelligence*, pages 33–42, Madison, WI, 1998.

14. Peter E. Caines. *Linear stochastic systems*. Wiley, New York, 1988.

15. Adrian Y. W. Cheuk and Craig Boutilier. Structured arc reversal and simulation of dynamic probabilistic networks. In *Proceedings of the Thirteenth Conference on Uncertainty in Artificial Intelligence*, pages 72–79, Providence, RI, 1997.

16. Thomas Dean and Keiji Kanazawa. A model for reasoning about persistence and causation. *Computational Intelligence*, 5(3):142–150, 1989.

17. Thomas Dean and Michael Wellman. *Planning and Control*. Morgan Kaufmann, San Mateo, 1991.

18. Denise Draper, Steve Hanks, and Daniel Weld. A probabilistic model of action for least-commitment planning with information gathering. In *Proceedings of the Tenth Conference on Uncertainty in Artificial Intelligence*, pages 178–186, Seattle, 1994.

19. Steve Hanks (ed.). Decision theoretic planning: Proceedings of the aaai spring symposium. Technical Report SS-94-06, AAAI Press, Menlo Park, 1994.

20. Richard E. Fikes and Nils J. Nilsson. STRIPS: A new approach to the application of theorem proving to problem solving. *Artificial Intelligence*, 2:189–208, 1971.

21. Dan Geiger and David Heckerman. Advances in probabilistic reasoning. In *Proceedings of the Seventh Conference on Uncertainty in Artificial Intelligence*, pages 118–126, Los Angeles, 1991.

22. Michael Gelfond and Vladimir Lifschitz. Representing actions in extended logic programming. In K. Apt, editor, *Proceedings of the Tenth Conference on Logic Programming*, pages 559–573, 1992.

23. Enrico Giunchiglia, G. Neelakantan Kartha, and Vladimir Lifschitz. Representing action: Indeterminacy and ramifications. *Artificial Intelligence*, 95:409–438, 1997.

24. Steve Hanks and Drew V. McDermott. Modeling a dynamic and uncertain world i: Symbolic and probabilistic reasoning about change. *Artificial Intelligence*, 1994.

25. David Heckerman. *Probabilistic Similarity Networks*. PhD thesis, Stanford University, Stanford, 1990.

26. Ronald A. Howard. *Dynamic Programming and Markov Processes*. MIT Press, Cambridge, 1960.

27. Ronald A. Howard and James E. Matheson, editors. *Readings on the Principles and Applications of Decision Analysis*. Strategic Decision Group, Menlo Park, CA, 1984.

28. Manfred Jaeger. Relational Bayesian networks. In *Proceedings of the Thirteenth Conference on Uncertainty in Artificial Intelligence*, pages 266–273, Providence, RI, 1997.

29. R. E. Kalman. A new approach to linear filtering and prediction problems. *Journal of Basic Engineering*, 82:35–45, 1960.

30. Keiji Kanazawa, Daphne Koller, and Stuart Russell. Stochastic simulation algorithms for dynamic probabilistic networks. In *Proceedings of the Eleventh Conference on Uncertainty in Artificial Intelligence*, pages 346–351, Montreal, 1995.

31. G. Neelakantan Kartha. Two counterexamples related to Baker's approach to the frame problem. *Artificial Intelligence*, 69:379–392, 1994.

32. G. Neelakantan Kartha and Vladimir Lifschitz. Actions with indirect effects (preliminary report). In *Proceedings of the Fifth International Conference on Principles of Knowledge Representation and Reasoning*, pages 341–350, Bonn, 1994.

33. Henry A. Kautz. The logic of persistence. In *Proceedings of the Fifth National Conference on Artificial Intelligence*, pages 401–405, Philadelphia, 1986.

34. John G. Kemeny and J. Laurie Snell. *Finite Markov Chains*. Van Nostrand, Princeton, NJ, 1960.

35. Uffe Kjaerulff. A computational scheme for reasoning in dynamic probabilistic networks. In *Proceedings of the Eighth Conference on Uncertainty in AI*, pages 121–129, Stanford, 1992.

36. Nicholas Kushmerick, Steve Hanks, and Daniel Weld. An algorithm for probabilistic least-commitment planning. In *Proceedings of the Twelfth National Conference on Artificial Intelligence*, pages 1073–1078, Seattle, 1994.

37. Nicholas Kushmerick, Steve Hanks, and Daniel Weld. An algorithm for probabilistic planning. *Artificial Intelligence*, 76:239–286, 1995.

38. S. L. Lauritzen. Propagation of probabilities, means and variances in mixed graphical association models. *Journal of the American Statistical Association*, 87:1098–1108, 1992.

39. Fangzhen Lin and Ray Reiter. State constraints revisited. *Journal of Logic and Computation*, 4(5):655–678, 1994.

40. D. G. Luenberger. *Introduction to Dynamic Systems: Theory, Models and Applications*. Wiley, New York, 1979.

41. John McCarthy and P.J. Hayes. Some philosophical problems from the standpoint of artificial intelligence. *Machine Intelligence*, 4:463–502, 1969.

42. A. E. Nicholson and J. M. Brady. Sensor validation using dynamic belief networks. In *Proceedings of the Eighth Conference on Uncertainty in AI*, pages 207–214, Stanford, 1992.

43. Judea Pearl. *Probabilistic Reasoning in Intelligent Systems: Networks of Plausible Inference*. Morgan Kaufmann, San Mateo, 1988.

44. Edwin Pednault. ADL: Exploring the middle ground between STRIPS and the situation calculus. In *Proceedings of the First International Conference on Principles of Knowledge Representation and Reasoning*, pages 324–332, Toronto, 1989.

45. Mark A. Peot and David E. Smith. Conditional nonlinear planning. In *Proceedings of the First International Conference on AI Planning Systems*, pages 189–197, College Park, MD, 1992.

46. David Poole. Probabilistic Horn abduction and Bayesian networks. *Artificial Intelligence*, 64(1):81–129, 1993.

47. David Poole. Exploiting the rule structure for decision making within the independent choice logic. In *Proceedings of the Eleventh Conference on Uncertainty in Artificial Intelligence*, pages 454–463, Montreal, 1995.

48. David Poole. The independent choice logic for modelling multiple agents under uncertainty. *Artificial Intelligence*, 94(1–2):7–56, 1997.

49. David Poole. Probabilistic partial evaluation: Exploiting rule structure in probabilistic inference. In *Proceedings of the Fifteenth International Joint Conference on Artificial Intelligence*, pages 1284–1291, Nagoya, 1997.

50. Martin L. Puterman. *Markov Decision Processes: Discrete Stochastic Dynamic Programming*. Wiley, New York, 1994.

51. Lawrence R. Rabiner. A tutorial on hidden Markov models and selected applications in speech recognition. *Proceedings of the IEEE*, 77(2):257–286, 1989.

52. Raymond Reiter. The frame problem in the situation calculus: A simple solution (sometimes) and a completeness result for goal regression. In V. Lifschitz, editor, *Artificial Intelligence and Mathematical Theory of Computation (Papers in Honor of John McCarthy)*, pages 359–380. Academic Press, San Diego, 1991.

53. Erik Sandewall. *Features and Fluents*. Oxford University Press, Oxford, 1995.

54. Lenhart K. Schubert. Monotonic solution of the frame problem in the situation calculus: An efficient method for worlds with fully specified actions. In H. E. Kyburg, R. P. Loui, and G. N. Carlson, editors, *Knowledge Representation and Defeasible Reasoning*, pages 23–67. Kluwer, Boston, 1990.

55. R. D. Shachter and C. R. Kenley. Gaussian influence diagrams. *Management Science*, 35(5):527–550, 1989.

56. Ross D. Shachter. Evaluating influence diagrams. *Operations Research*, 33(6):871–882, 1986.

57. Solomon E. Shimony. The role of relevance in explanation I: Irrelevance as statistical independence. *International Journal of Approximate Reasoning*, 8(4):281–324, 1993.

58. Yoav Shoham. *Reasoning About Change: Time and Causation from the Standpoint of Artificial Intelligence*. MIT Press, Cambridge, 1988.

59. Richard D. Smallwood and Edward J. Sondik. The optimal control of partially observable Markov processes over a finite horizon. *Operations Research*, 21:1071–1088, 1973.

60. David E. Smith and Daniel S. Weld. Conformant graphplan. In *Proceedings of the Fifteenth National Conference on Artificial Intelligence*, pages 889–896, Madison, 1998.

61. Joseph A. Tatman and Ross D. Shachter. Dynamic programming and influence diagrams. *IEEE Transactions on Systems, Man and Cybernetics*, 20(2):365–379, 1990.

62. Michael Thielscher. Ramification and causality. *Artificial Intelligence*, 89:317–364, 1997.

63. D. Warren. Generating Conditional Plans and Programs. In *Proceedings of AISB Summer Conference*, pages 344–354, University of Edinburgh, 1976.

64. M. West and J. Harrison. *Bayesian Forecasting and Dynamic Models*. Springer-Verlag, New York, 1989.

A Survey of Automated Deduction *

Alan Bundy

Division of Informatics
The University of Edinburgh
Edinburgh EH1 2QL

Abstract. We survey research in the automation of deductive inference, from its beginnings in the early history of computing to the present day. We identify and describe the major areas of research interest and their applications. The area is characterised by its wide variety of proof methods, forms of automated deduction and applications.

1 A Potted History of Early Automated Deduction

Deduction is the branch of reasoning formalised by and studied in mathematical logic. The automation of deduction has a long and distinguished history in Artificial Intelligence. For instance, four of the 19 papers in one of the earliest and seminal AI texts, Feigenbaum and Feldman's "Computers and Thought", described implementations of deductive reasoning. These four were:

- a description of a theorem prover for propositional logic, called the Logic Theory Machine, written by Newell, Shaw and Simon, [75];
- two papers on Gelernter's Geometry Machine, a theorem prover for Euclidean Geometry, [32, 31];
- a description of Slagle's symbolic integrator, Saint. [91].

As can be seen from these examples, most of the early applications of automated deduction were to proving mathematical theorems. The promise offered to Artificial Intelligence, however, was the automation of commonsense reasoning. This dream is described by McCarthy in his description of the Advice Taker, [68], which proposes an application of automated deduction to what we would now call question answering. The earliest implemented applications of automated deduction to commonsense reasoning were to robot plan formation, for instance, the QA series of planners, [38], culminating in STRIPS, [30].

The automation of commonsense reasoning was seen to be at the heart of the Artificial Intelligence programme. Sensors, such as television cameras, microphones, keyboards, touch sensors, *etc*, would gather information about the world. This would be used to update a world model. Automated reasoning would then be used to draw inferences from this world model, filling in gaps, answering

---

* I would like to thank Richard Boulton, Michael Fisher, Ian Frank, Predrag Janičić, Andrew Ireland and Helen Lowe for feedback on an earlier version of this survey. I would also like to thank Carole Douglas for help in its preparation.

queries and planning actions. These actions would then be realised by actuators, such as robot arms, speakers, computer screens, mobile vehicles, *etc.*

Automated deduction seemed a very good candidate for the automation of commonsense reasoning. Results from Mathematical Logic suggested that automatic deductive reasoners for first-order, predicate logic could be built that were not only *sound*, *i.e.* only made correct deductions, but were also *complete*, *i.e.* were capable of deducing anything that was true. A theorem of Herbrand's, [43], suggested how a sound and complete automatic deduction procedure could be built. Variable-free instances of predicate logic formulae should be systematically and exhaustively generated then tested for contradiction. Many of the early implementations were based on Herbrand's theorem, *e.g.* [33, 26].

The culmination of this line of work was Robinson's *resolution* method, [89]. Robinson's key idea was *unification*: an algorithm for finding the most general common instance of two or more logical formulae, if it exists. Unification also generates a substitution, of terms for variables, called a *unifier*. This unifier instantiates the input formulae to their common instance. Using unification, the generation and testing phases of Herbrand's procedure could be merged; contradiction testing was carried out on partially instantiated formulae and guided their further instantiation. Resolution could also be viewed as a process of inferring new formulae from old by matching (using unification) and combining together old formulae. Resolution proved to be much more efficient than earlier techniques and automated deduction researchers switched their attention to it. Many ingenious ways were found to refine resolution, *i.e.* to reduce the generation of new formulae without loss of completeness, thus improving the efficiency of proof search.

Unfortunately, despite this progress in improving efficiency, automatic deduction in the late 1960s and early 1970s was unable to solve hard problems. To prove a mathematical theorem the axioms of the mathematical theory and the negation of the theorem to be proved were first put into a normal form, called *clausal form*. Resolution was then applied exhaustively to the resulting set of *clauses* in the search for a contradiction (the *empty clause*). For non-trivial theorems a very large number of intermediate clauses needed to be generated before the empty clause was found. This generation process exceeded the storage capacity of early computers and the timescales involved were sometimes potentially astronomical. This phenomenon was called *the combinatorial explosion*.

Work on automated deduction was subject to a lot of criticism in the early 1970s. The combinatorial explosion was thought to exclude resolution and similar techniques as viable candidates for the automation of reasoning. Various rival techniques were proposed, for instance, the "procedural representation of knowledge" as embodied in the Micro-Planner AI programming language, [95]. However, on close analysis these alternatives could be seen as offering very similar functionality and performance as existing automated deduction techniques, [41]. The combinatorial explosion could not be solved by either refinements of resolution or by more *ad hoc* techniques. The solution was seen to lie with the development of *heuristics*, *i.e.* rules of thumb for pruning inference steps (with possible loss of completeness) or for guiding search through the space of inference steps, (see §9).

Another, and more significant, AI criticism of automated deduction was that reasoning is not restricted to deductive inference steps and is not restricted to first-order predicate logic. The reaction to that criticism has been to broaden the coverage of automated reasoning to include a variety of logics, *e.g.* sorted, probabilistic, default, temporal and other modal, *etc.* Some of these logics include non-deductive inference steps, *e.g.* default logics, [14]. This survey, however, will be restricted to deductive inference.

2 Automated Deduction Today

Despite these early criticisms, automated deduction today is in a healthy state. The combination of much faster computers and more efficient coding techniques has enabled resolution theorem provers to prove non-trivial theorems — even open conjectures. A recent notable success has been the proof by the Argonne prover, EQP[2], that Robbins Algebras are boolean algebras, [69]. This was a famous and long standing open conjecture and its automated proof made the front pages of national newspapers all over the world.

Automated deduction has also found significant application in formal methods of system development. Using formal methods computer programs and electronic circuits can be described as logical formulae, as can specifications of their intended behaviour. Questions about such systems can then be posed as automated deduction problems. For instance, automated deduction can be used to ask whether a system meets its specification, to synthesise a system from a specification or to transform an inefficient system into an equivalent but more efficient one. As commercial pressures force hardware and software producers to provide guarantees of the security and safety of their products, automated deduction is playing an increasingly important role. The CAV conference proceedings give examples of such practical applications, *e.g.* [1].

Automated deduction can be viewed as a form of computation. This has inspired two paradigms for programming language design. These are: logic programming, which is based on the application of resolution to programs expressed as sets of predicate logic clauses (see §11 and [59]); and functional programming, which is based on the application of term rewriting to programs expressed as sets of equations in higher-order logic, [81]. Term rewriting is a rule of inference in which one subterm of a formulae is replaced by an equivalent subterm (see §4). The best known logic programming language is Prolog, [23], although there are now many variants, *e.g.* a higher-order, constructive version called λProlog, [71] and the various constraint logic programming languages, [51]. Functional programming has been implemented in many languages, *e.g.* Lisp, ML, Miranda, Haskell. There are also hybrid logical and functional languages, *e.g.* LogLisp, Mercury.

---

[2] A variant of Otter.

Resolution is no longer the dominant automated deduction technique. Formal methods, as well as AI, has forced the field to broaden its coverage. The representation of hardware and software has required the use of higher-order, richly typed, constructive, inductive, modal and linear logics (see §6 and 7). It also puts a strong emphasis on equational reasoning, *e.g.* using term rewriting (see §4). Attempts to emulate commonsense reasoning have required the exploration of default, probabilistic, temporal and other modal logics (see §10). Some of the search problems raised by these logics have defeated total automation, so there has been a lot of interest in interactive theorem proving, in which the burden of finding a proof is divided between the computer and a human user (see §8). Interactive provers usually use more 'human-oriented' presentations of logic, such as sequent calculus, natural deduction or semantic tableaux, rather than the 'machine-oriented' resolution.

The number and size of international conferences to serve the automated deduction community has steadily grown. The Conferences on Automated Deduction (CADEs), which started as a small workshop series in 1974, have now grown into an annual, international series with over a hundred of participants. There are also more specialist conferences devoted to: term rewriting (RTA), semantic tableaux (Tableaux), first-order theorem proving (FTP), higher-order theorem proving (TPHOLs), user interfaces (UITP) and formal verification (CAV). The Journal of Automated Reasoning, which specialises in automated deduction research, was founded in 1985 and is now up to volume 21[3]. The international Association for Automated Reasoning produces a regular newsletter, which is circulated to most automated deduction researchers. Automated deduction research is also reported in many journals and conference proceedings for AI, formal methods and logic and functional programming.

3   Resolution Theorem Proving

In the late 60s and early 70s most work in automated deduction went into finding resolution refinements. Variants of resolution with exotic names: hyper-resolution, model elimination, semantic resolution, RUE, *etc*, abounded, [61, 104]. There was also a technique called paramodulation for equational reasoning, which can be viewed as a generalisation of term rewriting, [88]. Most of this refinement activity has now died down. The major exception is work on superposition, [5], which seeks to apply work on orderings from termination research[4] to refine resolution.

Most work on resolution now focuses on efficient implementation methods. The goal is to enable resolution-based provers to generate millions of intermediate clauses in a brute force search for a proof, running for hours or days.[5]. Clever indexing techniques are used to enable required clauses to be retrieved quickly from a database containing millions of candidates, [77]. Parallelism is exploited

---

[3] As of August 1998.

[4] The use of orderings to prove the termination of rewriting is discussed in §4.

[5] Even, in extreme cases, years, [92].

to divide the task between many processors, [65]. Technology for precompiling unification and sharing storage is borrowed back from logic programming — so called, Prolog technology theorem proving, [94]. Algorithms are refined for detecting and removing redundant clauses.

Resolution-based provers are currently evaluated on empirical grounds. Comparisons between provers are mostly based on success rates and run times on standard corpora of problems. The main corpus is the TPTP (Thousands of Problems for Theorem Provers) library, [96]. This is also used as the basis for an annual competition between provers run in conjunction with the CADE conferences, [97]. There is also a lot of interest in tackling open conjectures in mathematics. Conjectures best suited to this approach are combinatorial problems in new areas of mathematics, where human intuitions are less well developed, [105]. The Robbins Algebra conjecture is a good example. Brute force search through all the various possibilities is often an appropriate approach to such problems — and machines are much better suited to brute force solutions than humans.

Resolution is a refutation-based procedure; it proves a conjecture when it derives a contradiction in the form of the empty clause. When the conjecture is false the search for a contradiction may terminate with failure or the search may continue unsuccessfully forever. In the case of terminating failure a counterexample can be constructed from the finite search space. This potential can be exploited to build models of formulae from unsuccessful attempts to find proofs of their negations. There has been a lot of interest in exploiting this potential recently; several model constructing programs have been built and successful applications developed, [92]. There is even a category in the CADE theorem prover competition for such model constructing programs.

4 Term Rewriting

A common pattern of reasoning in mathematics is to replace a subterm in an expression by an equivalent subterm. Some proofs consist of a chain of such replacements in which one expression is gradually transformed into another. For instance, when the conjecture is an equation the left-hand side may be transformed into the right-hand side. This transformation procedure is formalised in automated deduction as *term rewriting* using *rewrite rules*, [46]. A rewrite rule is an equation that has been oriented in one direction: conventionally left to right. To *rewrite* an expression, first a subterm of the expression is identified for replacement. Then a rewrite rule is selected whose left-hand side matches this subterm using a one-side unification. The rewrite rule is instantiated so that its left-hand side is identical to the subterm. The subterm is then replaced with the instantiated right-hand side of the rule.

Of course, this procedure is incomplete in general, *i.e.* when a conjecture can be proved using some of the rewrite rules in both orientations, but not with a single orientation. Sometimes, however, rewriting *is* complete, for instance, if a set of rewrite rules can be shown to be *confluent*. A set of rewrite rules is confluent if, whenever an expression can be rewritten into two distinct expressions then these two can both be further rewritten into a third common expression. A simple inductive proof shows that whenever there is a proof using a confluent set of rewrite rules as equations in both orientations then there is a rewriting proof.

If, in addition, the set of rewrite rules is terminating then rewriting constitutes a decision procedure, *i.e.* it is terminate with either a proof or a refutation of an equational conjecture . A set of rewrite rules is terminating if there are no infinite chains of rewriting using them. To prove an equation, for instance, each side of the equation is rewritten until no more rewriting is possible, which will happen after a finite number of steps. This final rewritten expression is called a *normal form*. The equation is true if and only if the two normal forms are identical. Confluence also ensures that these normal forms are unique, so there is no need to search.

In 1970 a breakthrough occurred in term rewriting with the discovery by Knuth and Bendix of a procedure for testing a set of rewrite rules for confluence, [56]. The Knuth-Bendix test compares the left-hand sides of rewrite rules to see whether they could give rise to a choice of rewriting. So called *critical pairs* are constructed and then tested to see if they rewrite to an identical normal form. If all critical pairs rewrite to identical normal forms then the set of rewrite rules is confluent. Moreover, Knuth and Bendix proposed a procedure to transform a non-confluent set of rules into a confluent one. If a critical pair generates two non-identical (but necessarily equal) normal forms then these are formed into the left- and right-hand side of a rewrite rule and added to the set of rewrite rules. This new set may, in turn, generate new critical pairs (using the new rule) and this whole process may not terminate. But if it does, then the final set of rewrite rules will be confluent. The invention of this procedure triggered a huge activity in term rewriting, which is now a major sub-area of automated deduction with its own conference series (RTA).

This has also spurred a renewed interest in proving termination of sets of rewrite rules. Termination proving is equivalent to the halting problem, so only partial solutions are possible. However, current techniques are capable of proving the termination of many of the sets of rewrite rules that arise in practice, *cf* [102], for instance. These techniques can also be automated, so that theorem provers can establish the termination of rewrite rule sets before applying them. All the techniques use a measure which maps expressions into a well-founded set. A *well-founded set* is an ordered set of objects in which there are no infinite descending chains. For each rewrite rule the measure of its left-hand side is shown to be greater than that of its right-hand side under this order. The ordering must also be shown to be preserved by the rewriting process, *i.e.* by substitution and replacement of subterms. Then each rewriting strictly reduces the measure of the rewritten expression. Since there are no infinite descending chains of measures this reduction cannot continue indefinitely, so rewriting must terminate.

Simple measures use the natural numbers as the well-founded set. More sophisticated measures use polynomials over natural numbers or combine previous measures using pairs and multi-sets (*aka* bags). One of the most interesting developments is the use of *term orderings*, in which the expressions themselves form the well-founded set, with the order being defined by a set of syntactic inference rules. The best known of these term orderings is *recursive path ordering* (rpo), [27].

As mentioned above, term rewriting can be viewed as a special case of paramodulation. Paramodulation extends rewriting in three ways. Firstly, equations can potentially be used in both orientations. Secondly, two-way unification rather than one-way matching is used to instantiate the replaced subterms as well as the equations. Thirdly, the equations are disjoined with other formulae to form a full clause. This relationship between paramodulation and rewriting has inspired new developments in both areas.

Rewriting has been extended towards paramodulation in two directions. Firstly, conditions have been added to rewrite rules. Usually these conditions must be established before the rule is applied. Secondly, two-way unification can be used to instantiate variables in the subterm. This form of rewriting is called *narrowing*, [29, 40]. It is useful for proving existential theorems, with the existential variables in the conjecture being represented by free variables and instantiated during the narrowing proof.

Paramodulation has been refined by using term orderings from termination theory to restrict its application without loss of completeness, [4]. This has in turn inspired the work on superposition mentioned in §3, in which similar ideas are applied to resolution.

Most applications of term rewriting apply the rewrite rules *exhaustively*, *i.e.* until the expression being rewritten is in normal form. Recently, there has been interest in *selective* rewriting, in which restrictions are imposed on rewriting. The best known of these selective rewriting techniques is *rippling*, [17, 8]. Meta-level annotations are inserted into the expressions to be rewritten and into the rewrite rules. The effect of these annotations is to prevent some subexpressions from being rewritten and to impose restrictions on the way in which other sub-expressions can be rewritten. The motive behind these restrictions is to direct the rewriting to produce an expression which matches some hypothesis. The main application is to the step cases of inductive proofs, in which the induction conclusion is directed towards a match with the induction hypothesis. It has also been used: to find closed forms to sums, [99]; to solve limit theorems, [107]; and to prove equalities, [49].

5 Built-In Unification

Robinson's original unification was based only on the syntactic structure of the formulae to be unified. So if two formulae had instances which were equal, but not syntactically identical, then Robinson's algorithm would declare then nonunifiable. In 1972, Plotkin built the associativity axiom into the unification algorithm, [85]. Associative unification finds a substitution which instantiates the input formulae to instances which are equal modulo associativity, but not necessarily identical. When using associative unification the associative axiom need not be used explicitly in the proof, *i.e.* it is completely built-into the unification algorithm.

This work initiated a major sub-area of automated deduction in which different combinations of axioms are hardwired into the unification algorithm, *e.g.* associativity, commutativity, idempotency, distributivity, *etc* and combinations of these. Built-in unification is especially valuable where an axiom causes problems if included in a set of clauses or rewrite rules. For instance, the commutative law causes non-termination when used as a rewrite rule, but commutative unification is quite efficient. So rewriting using commutative unification is an attractive solution. Many functions are both associative and commutative, so building both of these into unification (AC-unification) has received a lot of attention. A good survey of built-in unification algorithms can be found in [52].

Given unifiable formulae, Robinson's unification algorithm generates a unique, most-general unifier. "Most-general" means that any other unifier is an instance of it. Built-in unification problems are not all so well behaved. For some there is more than one unifier – sometimes infinitely many. Nor does a most-general unifier always exist. Some unification problems are even undecidable. Unification problems can be classified along these various dimensions: unique/finite/infinite number of unifiers; existence of most-general unifiers; decidable/undecidable.

Unification algorithms are nowadays presented as a set of transformation rules, which rewrite input formulae into substitutions, [52]. Such presentations facilitate proofs that the algorithms are both sound and complete and inform calculations of their complexity. They also enable general-purpose unification algorithms to be designed, *i.e.* algorithms which take a set of axioms to be built-in as an additional input. The work on general-purpose unification algorithms derives from work on term rewriting (see §4), since the axioms must usually be represented as a confluent rewrite rule set.

One of the major achievements of built-in unification was Huet's higher-order unification algorithm, [48, 52], which builds-in the α, β and optionally the η rules of λcalculus. This algorithm makes automated higher-order theorem proving possible. Higher-order unification is a badly behaved problem: there can be infinitely many unifiers and the problem is undecidable. Research into higher-order unification is active in at least two directions: the extension of the algorithm to new kinds of higher-order logic, such as constructive type theory; and the search for decidable, but still useful, sub-cases of the problem, which are, therefore, better behaved. For instance, if the input formulae are restricted to, so called, *higher-order patterns* then unique, most-general unifiers exist, [72].

Unification finds the most-general common instance of two formulae. The dual problem, *anti-unification*, finds the least-general common generalisation, *i.e.* a formula which has both of the input formulae as instances. Plotkin invented anti-unification in 1969, [84], but interest in it has recently revived in the area of machine learning, where it is used to find the general form of two or more examples of some concept. For instance, in *Inductive Logic Programming*, [73], it is used to learn a general logic program from instances of it.

6 Higher-Order Logic and Type Theory

Many problems in both mathematics and formal methods are more naturally represented in a higher-order logic than in first-order. For instance, functional programming languages are usually based on typed λ-calculus, which is a higher-order logic, [7]. So the reasoning about functional programs is naturally done in higher-order logic. Reasoning about limited resources can be done in linear logic, [34], which models resources with assumptions and places restrictions on the number of times they can be used in proofs. Similarly, mathematics uses second and higher-order functions, such as summation, differentiation, integration, etc, which are more naturally reasoned about in a higher-order framework.

First-order automatic deduction techniques are readily adapted to higher-order deduction by replacing first-order unification with higher-order unification. This is not quite as straightforward as it sounds. For instance, the potentially infinite branching of higher-order unification needs to be factored into the search space, e.g. by allowing backtracking to return alternative unifiers. Three examples of higher-order theorem provers are TPS [2], HOL [37] and PVS [79].

Some applications of theorem proving require even richer logics. For instance, automated deduction can be used to synthesise programs (and circuits) meeting a specification of their intended behaviour. A conjecture is posed that for any inputs an output exists obeying some specified relationship with the input. For instance, if a sorting program is required the output might be specified as an ordered permutation of the input. The required program can be extracted from a proof of the conjecture; different proofs yielding different programs. However, this synthesis can fail to yield a program if the conjecture is proved in a "pure existence" proof, namely a proof which shows the existence of an output without showing how it can be constructed from the inputs. This problem can be avoided by proving the conjecture in a *constructive* logic, *i.e.* one from which pure existence proofs are excluded.

Formal methods proof obligations (see §2) are also best conducted in a logic with a rich type structure, *i.e.* one in which the various data-structures (*e.g.* integers, reals, arrays, lists, trees, etc) and the arities of the procedures (*e.g.* lists to integers) are represented as types. Rich type structures, higher-order logic and constructive proofs are combined in *constructive type theories*, [67]. There are now a number of theorem provers based on constructive type theories, *e.g.* Coq [28], NUPRL [24], LEGO [64], ALF, [3]. Due to the difficulty of automating interesting proofs in some of these logics, most of these theorem provers are interactive (see §8).

A wide variety of different logics have been developed for formal methods. These include many different: constructive type theories, temporal logics for reasoning about changing behaviour over time, process algebras for reasoning about concurrent programs, dynamic logics for reasoning about imperative programs, *etc*. Building theorem provers for each of these logics is a massive challenge, especially since the logic design is itself often a variable in the research programme, so that the theorem prover is under constant modification. One answer to this is to build generic theorem provers, which take a specification of the logic as an input. the theorem prover is then easily reconfigured. One of the most popular of these is Paulson's Isabelle, [80]. Constructive type theories also turn out to be well suited as meta-logics for the specification of the input logic. They also have technical advantages, like providing a generic unification algorithm. Generic theorem provers taking this approach are usually called *logical frameworks*, [47].

7 Inductive Theorem Proving

In mathematics, formal methods and common-sense reasoning we often want to reason about repetition. Repetition might arise from: recursively defined mathematical objects, data-structures or procedures; iteration in programs; feedback loops in circuits; behaviour over time; or general object descriptions with a parameter. This repetition is often unbounded. To reason about unbounded repetition it is usually essential to use a rule of mathematical induction. Such rules are used to reduce a universally quantified conjecture into some number of base and step cases. In the base cases the conjecture is proved for some initial values, *e.g.* the number 0. In the step cases the theorem is assumed for a generic value, *e.g.* n and, using this assumption, proved for some subsequent value, *e.g.* $n + 1$. In this way the conjecture is incrementally proved for an infinite succession of values.

Logical theories which include induction rules are subject to some negative theoretical results which cause problems for automation.

1. They are usually *incomplete*, *i.e.* they contain true but unprovable formulae, [35]. This manifests itself in requiring an unlimited number of distinct induction rules.
2. They do not admit *cut elimination*, which means that arbitrary intermediate formulae may need to be proved and then used to prove the current conjecture, [60]. This manifests itself in requiring the generalisation of conjectures and/or the introduction of intermediate lemmas. In contrast, resolution generates any necessary intermediate formulae as a side effect.

Both of these negative results introduce potentially infinite branching points into the search space. At any stage: an unbounded number of induction rules can be specially constructed and applied; the current subgoal can be generalised in an unbounded number of ways; or any formula can be introduced as an intermediate lemma. Special heuristics are required to control these branching points. Some use the failure of initial, restricted proof attempts to introduce patches which extend the search space. Failures in rippling (see §4) have proved especially fruitful in suggesting such proof patches, [50].

Two main approaches have been developed for automating inductive proof: explicit and implicit. In explicit induction additional inductive rules of inference are added to the logic and used in the search for a proof, [101]. Since there are potentially infinitely many induction rules, it is usual to have a method for dynamically creating new rules customised to the current conjecture, [100]. It is also necessary to have a *cut rule* for generalising conjectures and creating intermediate lemmas. Explicit induction theorem provers include: Nqthm [13], INKA [9], RRL [54] and Oyster/CLaM [16].

A conjecture is an inductive consequence of a theory if and only if it is consistent to add it to that theory. Implicit induction is based on this theorem. This method is also called *inductionless induction* or *inductive completion*. Consistency is usually tested by trying to express the extended theory as a confluent and terminating set of rewrite rules and then rewriting the conjecture to normal form, [55]. Although explicit and implicit induction sound very different, close analysis of the rewriting process in implicit induction reveals proof steps which are very similar to the base and step cases of explicit induction. In fact, implicit induction can be viewed as a form of explicit induction using a term order, such as recursive path order, as the induction order, [87]. Implicit induction provers include: RRL [54] (which uses both implicit and explicit induction) and SPIKE [12].

8 Interactive Theorem Proving

The state of the art of automated deduction is that theorem proving programs will often fail to prove non-trivial theorems. One solution to this is to develop *interactive* theorem provers, where the task is divided between the computer and a human user. The role of the user can vary from specifying each proof step to setting some global parameters for an otherwise automated run. Usually, the human role is to make the difficult proof guidance decisions while the computer takes care of the book-keeping and the routine steps. All proof systems lie on a continuum between fully automatic and fully interactive; most 'automatic' systems have some facility for user interaction and most 'interactive' systems have some degree of automation. So although this is a survey of *automated* deduction, interaction must be discussed.

Many interactive provers provide some kind of macro facility so that users can apply multiple proof steps with one command. Of these, the best developed macro facility is called *tactics*, [36]. A tactic is a computer program which directs a theorem prover to apply some rules of inference. A primitive tactic applies one rule of inference. Tactics are composed together, using *tacticals*, into sequences, conditional cases, iterations, *etc.* They are typically used for: simplifying expressions by putting them into normal form; applying decision procedures; and following other common patterns of reasoning. Tactics are organised hierarchically with big tactics defined in terms of smaller ones and ultimately in terms of rules of inference. There are many tactic-based provers, *e.g.* HOL [37], Nuprl [24], Isabelle [80].

In order to be able to guide an interactive prover it is vital for a human user to interpret the structure of the emerging proof. One way to achieve this is for the interactive prover to, use a logic which presents proofs in a 'natural' format, such as Gentzen's sequent calculus, natural deduction or semantic tableaux. Resolution, with its clausal form and powerful single inference rule is usually considered too 'machine-oriented' for interactive provers[6].

Interactive provers frequently have elaborate graphical user interfaces to try to present emerging proofs and the operations on them in a congenial and accessible way. For instance, some systems present the overall structure of a proof as a tree in which the nodes represent formulae and the branches represent proof steps connecting them. These trees can be organised hierarchically, with nodes representing big tactics unpacking into sub-trees representing their smaller subtactics. This can be used to show the overall structure of the proof succinctly with the detail being revealed on demand. Menus, buttons, mouse clicks, *etc* can be used to present the various options to the user in a user-friendly way. For instance, the "proof by pointing" style selects rules of inference by clicking the mouse on appropriate parts of the conjecture. As well as guiding the proof, the user may need access to libraries of theories, conjectures, definitions, previous lemmas, *etc*. They may want to: store and recover partial proofs; reset global options; load or delete definitions, lemmas, heuristics, *etc*. Providing all the functionality that users may want, while orienting them in the partial proof and not overwhelming them with too much information is a very hard and unsolved problem. The annual workshops on User Interfaces for Theorem Provers (UITP) is a good source of research in this area, [6].

9 Meta-Reasoning and Proof Methods

Human mathematicians do not find proofs by combining low level rules of inference. They adopt a higher-level of abstraction combining common patterns of proof using meta-reasoning. To emulate their success it is necessary to automate such higher-level reasoning. Tactics are one route to do this by providing powerful, high-level reasoning steps for the prover. They are used to encode proof methods in a meta-language, like ML [81].

One common pattern of reasoning in proofs is the application of a decision procedure to solve a decidable subproblem. Popular decision procedures are available for:

Propositional logic: There has been a lot of recent interest in using tautology checkers to verify digital electronic circuits which can be modelled as propositional formulae. Very efficient tautology checkers have been built, of which the best known are based on Ordered Binary Decision Diagrams (OBDDs), [15]. However, tautology checking is an NP-complete problem so, failing a favourable solution to $P = NP$, even the most efficient tautology checkers are exponential in the worse case.

Presburger arithmetic: The additive fragments of integer and real number arithmetic is decidable, [86]. Sub-goals in this fragment often occur when reasoning about iteration in program verification. Various more efficient variants of Presburger's original algorithm have been developed, [25, 45], although

---
[6] Although, the logic programming work has shown that resolution proofs can be quite 'natural'.

they are all super-exponential in the worse case. Much work has limited to the quantifier-free sub-case, since this is all that is required for verification proofs and has much lower complexity, [10].

Euclidian geometry: Decision procedures for decidable subsets of geometry can be obtained by translating geometric problems into algebraic ones and then using algebraic decision procedures such as those for Presburger arithmetic, [106, 22]. These are available for a range of geometries.

There are also techniques for combining together decision procedures for disjoint decidable theories, [74, 90].

Many decision procedures are embedded in computer algebra systems. There is a lot of interest in interfacing theorem provers to computer algebra systems to be able to access these procedures. There is also interest in the other direction in using theorem provers to verify decision procedures or for checking their preconditions. A special issue of JAR addresses both of these interactions, [53].

Many proof methods of use in automated deduction systems are for non-decidable fragments of theories. Even though these are not decision procedures, they can have a high heuristic success rate and so be of practical use. One such family of useful, heuristic methods are for difference reduction, *i.e.* they identify differences between two formulae to be shown equal and then systematically reduce these differences. One of the best known such methods is *rippling* (see §4).

Meta-reasoning is used to reason about (object-level) logic theories in a meta-theory. The domain of discourse of the meta-theory is the formulae and proof methods of the object-level theory. For instance, meta-reasoning might be used to analyse the current goal, choose an appropriate method of proof and apply it. This lifts the search space from the object-theory to the meta-theory, which is often better behaved, *i.e.* has a smaller search space. One example of meta-reasoning is *reflection*, in which theorems in a meta-theory are related, via reflection rules, to theorems in an object-theory, and *vice versa*, [103]. Another example is *proof planning*, in which meta-reasoning is used to build a global outline of a proof, which is then used to guide the detailed proof, [18]. A third example is *analogy*, in which an old proof is used as a plan to guide the proof of a new theorem, [78]. Fourthly, many decision procedures reason at the meta-level. Meta-reasoning can also be used to explain the high-level structure of proofs, *e.g.* to the user of an interactive prover, [62].

10   Commonsense Reasoning

The everyday reasoning of humans involves knowledge, belief, time, uncertainty and guessing based on sparse information. A variety of 'non-classical' logics have been developed to capture these 'commonsense' aspects of reasoning. Modal logics contain special operators for representing beliefs of agents and time, [21]. Uncertainty logics associate degrees of certainty with logical formulae, [82]. Default logics have rules which infer *defeasible* steps, in that conclusions which can be assumed but later withdrawn in the face of contradictory evidence, [14]. Commonsense reasoning can be automated by building automatic theorem provers for these logics.

¿From an automated proof viewpoint most of these non-classical logics are much worse behaved than classical, first-order, predicate logic, *i.e.* they generate an even bigger combinatorial explosion. A common approach to solving this problem is to restrict the logic to reduce the amount of search. For instance, lots of work on modal logics is restricted to the propositional fragment, *i.e.* to propositional logic with modal operators. Many of these propositional, modal logics are decidable with relatively efficient decision procedures, [39].

Another popular approach to automating reasoning in non-classical logics is to *reify* them into classical logics. This is done by formalising the semantics of the non-classical logic in a classical logic, [98, 76]. For instance, the semantics of modal logics is expressed in a system of linked 'possible worlds'. To formalise this semantics each predicate of the classical logic is given an additional argument which specifies a possible world in which it is asserted. Universal and existential quantification over these possible worlds then represents the modal operators. Links between the possible worlds are expressed as relations between them, which can often be embedded into the unification algorithm. In this way modal reasoning can be automated (for instance) via a conventional resolution prover.

11 Logic Programming & Deductive Databases

Prolog gives a procedural interpretation to a fragment of first order, predicate logic. It applies resolution to *Horn clauses*, which are disjunctions of negated propositions and at most one unnegated proposition. This fragment has a natural procedural interpretation, [59], but if two unnegated propositions are included in a clause this interpretation begins to break down. There is significant interest in trying to give a procedural interpretation to more expressive logics. This is most readily done, not in classical predicate logic, but in constructive logics. One of the best developed examples is Miller's λProlog logic programming language, [71], which is based on a higher-order, constructive logic. Other researchers have given a logic programming interpretation to constructive type theory [83], linear logic and temporal logic..

Since logic programs are logical formulae they seem especially well suited to the application of formal methods. Unfortunately, practical logic programming languages, like Prolog, often contain non-logical features for the sake of efficiency, practicality and in order to support meta-programming. Prolog, for instance, has: an unsound unification algorithm[7]; predicates for asserting and retracting clauses; predicates for syntactic analysis; and the 'cut' for cutting out part of the search space. Research is directed at developing semantics of logic programming languages which capture some of the non-logical features, [11]. These semantics

---

[7] Missing the 'occurs check'.

are then used to reason about the operation of logic programs. For instance, we might want to transform Prolog programs into programs with the same run time behaviour (except, perhaps for their speed) and not just into programs which are logically equivalent but, for instance, explore the search space in a different order.

There is also research at developing logic programming languages with a more declarative semantics. The challenge is to provide comparable power and efficiency to Prolog within a purely logical language. For instance, meta-programming facilities can be provided with an explicit and cleanly separated meta-level. One of the best known attempts to do this is the Gödel logic programming language, [44].

One method for improving the efficiency of logic programs is *partial evaluation*, [57]. Suppose a program is to be run successively on similar input. The computation performed on each run might have large parts in common, leading to redundancy if it is re-performed each time. This can be prevented by performing the common computation once and saving it in the form of a transformed version of the original program. This can be implemented by running the original program on a generalised form of the inputs which captures their similarities and using the result as the transformed program.

Running logic programs on generalised or abstract data can also be used as an analysis technique called *abstract interpretation*. The abstraction might, for instance, throw away all details of the data except for its type or its mode[8]. Running a logic program on this abstract data can be used to infer its type or mode signature, [70].

One of the most successful extensions to logic programming is to combine it with constraint reasoning, called *constraint logic programming*, [51]. Formulae are divided between those to be treated by logic programming and those to be treated as constraints. The latter are typically equations, inequalities, *etc.* The constraints are solved by a decision procedure, *e.g.* an equation or inequality solver or optimiser, such as the Simplex algorithm. Constraint logic programming has found many industrial applications. It enables the smooth combination of qualitative and quantitative methods of problem solving. It allows traditional operational research methods to be augmented with symbolic reasoning techniques.

Logic programming languages provide a form of default reasoning by interpreting the failure to prove a goal as evidence for its negation, so called *negation as failure*. There is research to relate this technique to other forms of default reasoning, *e.g.* non-monotonic logics, circumscription, *etc.* There is also interest in relating this default technique to the use of integrity constraints in databases, [58].

In fact, logic programs can be seen as a logical extension of relational databases, in which rules can be used to derive new data not explicitly stored in the original database. Datalog is the best known of the logic programming languages

---

[8] The mode of a logic program specifies which arguments can be input, output or either.

adapted for use as extended databases, [20]. It is purely relational, *i.e.* it differs from Prolog, say, by having no functions, but extends relational databases with the use of rules.

12 Conclusion

Automated deduction has grown into a broad field in which a wide variety of proof methods is used on a wide variety of logics and applied to a wide variety of applications. Proof methods range from interactive to automatic — and include every stage in-between. Both machine-oriented methods, such as decision procedures and resolution, and human-oriented methods, such as natural deduction and rewriting, are used and mixed. The logics range from classical first-order to constructive type theory and take in temporal, other modal, default, uncertainty, *etc* on the way. All these are applied to: proof obligations in formal methods; the design and implementation of programming languages; commonsense reasoning in artificial intelligence; relational databases; knowledge-based systems; *etc.* The system descriptions in the CADE proceedings contain a good record of the rich variety of implemented automated deduction provers.

Automated deduction techniques are being integrated with other techniques into practical systems. For instance, the Amphion system, [63], uses a theorem prover for synthesising programs to control space probes from a library of subroutines. The theorem prover is hidden from the user and a graphical front-end enables people unfamiliar with automatic deduction or logic to use it. Hybrid approaches are being developed. For instance, the Stanford temporal prover, [66] combines automatic deduction with model checking.

Throughout its development automated deduction has drawn on and fed back to work in mathematics and especially logic. Most of the logics have come from mathematical or philosophical logic. However, some logics, such as default and uncertainty logics, arose from automated deduction and then attracted mathematical interest. The interests of automated deduction have also refocussed mathematical interest, *cf.* the rising mathematical interest in constructive logics because of their computational applications. Mathematicians have also been interested to solve some of the mathematical problems that arise from automated deduction. These problems include: finding termination proofs; proving soundness, completeness and complexity results for proof methods; inventing new decision procedures.

There is no end to the variety of problems, methods and applications thrown up by automated deduction. The amount of work being conducted is greater than ever in its history, but the number of open research problems has grown, not diminished. We are entering an exciting phase of research as new application areas are coming into maturity and exciting new research directions are being identified.

References

1. Rajeev Alur and Thomas A. Henzinger, editors. *Proceedings of the 1996 Conference on Computer-Aided Verification*, number 1102 in LNCS, New Brunswick, New Jersey, U. S. A., 1996. Springer-Verlag.
2. P. B. Andrews, M. Bishop, I. Sunil, D. Nesmith, F. Pfenning, and H. Xi. TPS: A theorem proving system for classical type theory. *Journal of Automated Reasoning*, 16(3):321–353, 1996.
3. L. Augustsson, T. Coquand, and B. Nordström. A short description of another logical framework. In *Proceedings of the First Workshop on Logical Frameworks, Antibes*, pages 39–42, 1990.
4. L. Bachmair and H. Ganzinger. On restrictions of ordered paramodulation with simplification. In M. E. Stickel, editor, *Proc. 10th Int. Conf. on Automated Deduction, Kaiserslautern*, volume 449, pages 427–441. Springer-Verlag, 1990.
5. L. Bachmair and H. Ganzinger. Rewrite-based equational theorem proving with selection and simplification. *Journal of Logic and Computation*, 4(3):217–247, 1994. Revised version of Research Report MPI-I-91-208, 1991.
6. R. Backhouse, editor. *2nd International Workshop on User Interfaces for Theorem Provers*, 1998.
7. H. P. Barendregt. *The Lambda Calculus*. Elsevier, 1985.
8. David Basin and Toby Walsh. A calculus for and termination of rippling. *Journal of Automated Reasoning*, 16(1–2):147–180, 1996.
9. S. Biundo, B. Hummel, D. Hutter, and C. Walther. The Karlsruhe induction theorem proving system. In Joerg Siekmann, editor, *8th International Conference on Automated Deduction*, pages 672–674. Springer-Verlag, 1986. Springer Lecture Notes in Computer Science No. 230.
10. W. W. Bledsoe. The Sup-Inf method in Presburger arithmetic. Memo ATP-18, Department of Mathematics, University of Texas at Austin, USA, Dec 1974.
11. E. Borger and D. Rosenzweig. A mathematical definition of full Prolog. *Science of Computer Programming*, 24:249–286, 1994.
12. A. Bouhoula, E. Kounalis, and M. Rusinowitch. SPIKE: an automatic theorem prover. In *Proceedings of LPAR '92*, number 624 in LNAI. Springer-Verlag, July 1992.
13. R. S. Boyer and J S. Moore. *A Computational Logic Handbook*. Academic Press, 1988. Perspectives in Computing, Vol 23.
14. R. Brachman, H. Levesque, and Reiter. R, editors. *Artificial Intelligence*, volume 49. Elsevier, 1991.
15. R. E. Bryant. Symbolic boolean manipulation with ordered binary-decision diagrams. *ACM Computing Surveys*, 24(3):293–318, September 1992.
16. A. Bundy, F. van Harmelen, C. Horn, and A. Smaill. The Oyster-Clam system. In M. E. Stickel, editor, *10th International Conference on Automated Deduction*, pages 647–648. Springer-Verlag, 1990. Lecture Notes in Artificial Intelligence No. 449. Also available from Edinburgh as DAI Research Paper 507.
17. A. Bundy, A. Stevens, F. van Harmelen, A. Ireland, and A. Smaill. Rippling: A heuristic for guiding inductive proofs. *Artificial Intelligence*, 62:185–253, 1993. Also available from Edinburgh as DAI Research Paper No. 567.
18. Alan Bundy. A science of reasoning. In J.-L. Lassez and G. Plotkin, editors, *Computational Logic: Essays in Honor of Alan Robinson*, pages 178–198. MIT Press, 1991. Also available from Edinburgh as DAI Research Paper 445.

19. Alan Bundy, editor. *12th International Conference on Automated Deduction*, Lecture Notes in Artificial Intelligence, Vol. 814, Nancy, France, 1994. Springer-Verlag.

20. Stefano Ceri, Georg Gottlob, and Leitzia Tanca. *Logic Programming and Databases*. Surveys in Computer Science. Springer-Verlag, Berlin, 1990.

21. B.F. Chellas. *Modal Logic: An Introduction*. Cambridge University Press, 1980.

22. S-C Chou. *Mechanical Geometry Theorem Proving*. Reidel Pub. Co., Dordrecht, 1988.

23. W. F. Clocksin and C. S. Mellish. *Programming in Prolog*. Springer Verlag, 1981.

24. R. L. Constable, S. F. Allen, H. M. Bromley, et al. *Implementing Mathematics with the Nuprl Proof Development System*. Prentice Hall, 1986.

25. D. C. Cooper. Theorem proving in arithmetic without multiplication. In B. Meltzer and D. Michie, editors, *Machine Intelligence 7*, pages 91–99. Edinburgh University Press, 1972.

26. M. Davis and H. Putnam. A computing procedure for quantification theory. *J. Association for Computing Machinery*, 7:201–215, 1960.

27. Nachum Dershowitz. Orderings for term rewriting systems. *Journal of Theoretical Computer Science*, 17(3):279–301, 1982.

28. G. Dowek, A. Felty, H. Herbelin, G. Huet, C. Paulin, and B. Werner. The Coq proof assistant user's guide, version 5.6. Technical Report 134, INRIA, 1991.

29. M.J. Fay. First-order unification in an equational theory. In *Procs. of the Fourth Workshop on Automated Deduction*, pages 161–167. Academic Press, 1979.

30. R. E. Fikes, , and N. J. Nilsson. STRIPS: A new approach to the application of theorem proving to problem solving. *Artificial Intelligence*, 2:189–208, 1971.

31. H. Gelernter. Empirical explorations of the geometry theorem-proving machine. In E. Feigenbaum and J. Feldman, editors, *Computers and Thought*, pages 153–163. McGraw Hill, 1963.

32. H. Gelernter. Realization of a geometry theorem-proving machine. In E. Feigenbaum and J. Feldman, editors, *Computers and Thought*, pages 134–152. McGraw Hill, 1963.

33. P. C. Gilmore. A proof method for quantificational theory. *IBM J Res. Dev.*, 4:28–35, 1960.

34. J.-Y. Girard, Y. Lafont, and L. Regnier, editors. *Advances in Linear Logic*. Number 222 in London Mathematical Society Lecture Note Series. Cambridge University Press, Cambridge, 1995.

35. K. Gödel. Über formal unentscheidbare sätze der principia mathematica und verwandter systeme i. *Monatsh. Math. Phys.*, 38:173–198, 1931. English translation in [42].

36. M. J. Gordon, A. J. Milner, and C. P. Wadsworth. *Edinburgh LCF - A mechanised logic of computation*, volume 78 of *Lecture Notes in Computer Science*. Springer-Verlag, 1979.

37. M. J. Gordon. HOL: A proof generating system for higher-order logic. In G. Birtwistle and P. A. Subrahmanyam, editors, *VLSI Specification, Verification and Synthesis*. Kluwer, 1988.

38. Cordell Green. Application of theorem proving to problem solving. In *Proceedings of the 1st International Joint Conference on Artificial Intelligence*, pages 219–239, Washington, D. C., U. S. A., 1969.

39. J. Y. Halpern and Y. Moses. A guide to completeness and complexity for modal logics of knowledge and belief. *Artificial Intelligence*, 54:319–379, 1992.

40. M. Hanus. The integration of functions into logic programming: from theory to practice. *J. Logic Programming*, 19 & 20:583–628, 1994.
41. P Hayes. In defence of logic. In *Proceedings of IJCAI-77*, pages 559–565. International Joint Conference on Artificial Intelligence, 1977.
42. J van Heijenoort. *From Frege to Gödel: a source book in Mathematical Logic, 1879-1931*. Harvard University Press, Cambridge, Mass, 1967.
43. J. Herbrand. Researches in the theory of demonstration. In J van Heijenoort, editor, *From Frege to Goedel: a source book in Mathematical Logic, 1879-1931*, pages 525–581. Harvard University Press, Cambridge, Mass, 1930.
44. P. M. Hill and J. W. Lloyd. *The Gödel Programming Language*. MIT Press, 1994.
45. Louis Hodes. Solving problems by formula manipulation in logic and linear inequalities. In *Proceedings of the 2nd International Joint Conference on Artificial Intelligence*, pages 553–559, Imperial College, London, England, 1971. The British Computer Society.
46. G. Huet and D. C. Oppen. Equations and rewrite rules: A survey. In R. Book, editor, *Formal languages: Perspectives and open problems*. Academic Press, 1980. Presented at the conference on formal language theory, Santa Barbara, 1979. Available from SRI International as technical report CSL-111.
47. G. Huet and G. D. Plotkin. *Logical Frameworks*. CUP, 1991.
48. G. Huet. A unification algorithm for typed lambda calculus. *Theoretical Computer Science*, 1:27–57, 1975.
49. D. Hutter. Coloring terms to control equational reasoning. *Journal of Automated Reasoning*, 18(3):399–442, 1997.
50. A. Ireland and A. Bundy. Productive use of failure in inductive proof. *Journal of Automated Reasoning*, 16(1–2):79–111, 1996. Also available as DAI Research Paper No 716, Dept. of Artificial Intelligence, Edinburgh.
51. J. Jaffar and M. Maher. Constraint logic programming: A survey. *Journal of Logic Programming*, 19/20:503–581, 1994.
52. Jean-Pierre Jouannaud and Claude Kirchner. Solving equations in abstract algebras: A rule-based survey of unification. In Jean-Louis Lassez and Gordon Plotkin, editors, *Computational Logic*, chapter 8, pages 257–321. MIT Press, 1991.
53. D. Kapur and l. Wos, editors. *Journal of Automated Reasoning*, volume 21. Kluwer, 1998.
54. D. Kapur and H. Zhang. An overview of rewrite rule laboratory (RRL). *J. of Computer Mathematics with Applications*, 29(2):91–114, 1995.
55. D. Kapur, P. Narendran, and H. Zhang. Automating inductionless induction by test sets. *Journal of Symbolic Computation*, 11:83–111, 1991.
56. D. E. Knuth and P. B. Bendix. Simple word problems in universal algebra. In J. Leech, editor, *Computational problems in abstract algebra*, pages 263–297. Pergamon Press, 1970.
57. H. J. Komorowski. Partial evaluation as a means for inferencing data structures in an applicative language: A theory and implementation in the case of PROLOG. In *Proceedings of the ninth conference on the Principles of Programming Languages (POPL)*, pages 225–267, Albuquerque, New Mexico, 1982. ACM.
58. R. Kowalski, F. Sadri, and P. Soper. Integrity checking in deductive databases. In *Proc. 13th VLDB, Brighton*, pages 61–69. Morgan Kaufmann, 1987.
59. R. Kowalski. *Logic for Problem Solving*. Artificial Intelligence Series. North Holland, 1979.
60. G. Kreisel. Mathematical logic. In T. Saaty, editor, *Lectures on Modern Mathematics*, volume 3, pages 95–195. J. Wiley & Sons, 1965.

61. D. W. Loveland. *Automated theorem proving: A logical basis*, volume 6 of *Fundamental studies in Computer Science*. North Holland, 1978.

62. H. Lowe and D. Duncan. XBarnacle: Making theorem provers more accessible. In William McCune, editor, *14th International Conference on Automated Deduction*, pages 404–408. Springer-Verlag, 1997.

63. M. Lowry, A. Philpot, T. Pressburger, and I. Underwood. Amphion: Automatic programming for scientific subroutine libraries. In *Proc. 8th Intl. Symp. on Methodologies for Intelligent Systems*, Charlotte, North Carolina, October 1994.

64. Z. Luo and R. Pollack. Lego proof development system: User's manual. Report ECS-LFCS-92-211, Department of Computer Science, University of Edinburgh, May 1992.

65. E.L. Lusk, W.W. McCune, and J. Slaney. Roo: A parallel theorem prover. In Deepak Kapur, editor, *11th International Conference on Automated Deduction*, pages 731–734, Saratoga Springs, NY, USA, June 1992. Published as Springer Lecture Notes in Artificial Intelligence, No 607.

66. Z. et al Manna. Step: the stanford temporal prover. Technical Report STAN-CS-TR;94-1518, Stanford University, 1994.

67. P. Martin-Lof. *Notes on Constructive Mathematics*. Almqvist and Wiksell, Stockholm, 1970.

68. J. McCarthy. Programs with common sense. In *Mechanisation of Thought Processes (Proceedings of a symposium held at the National Physics Laboratory, London, Nov 1959)*, pages 77–84, London, 1959. HMSO.

69. W. McCune. Solution of the Robbins problem. *J. Automated Reasoning*, 19(3):263–276, 1997.

70. C. S. Mellish. Abstract interpretation of Prolog programs. In S. Abramsky and C. Hankin, editors, *Abstract Interpretation of Declarative Languages*, pages 181–197. Ellis Horwood, 1987.

71. D. Miller and G. Nadathur. An overview of λProlog. In R. Bowen, K. & Kowalski, editor, *Proceedings of the Fifth International Logic Programming Conference/ Fifth Symposium on Logic Programming*. MIT Press, 1988.

72. D. Miller. Unification of simply typed lambda-terms as logic programming. In P.K. Furukawa, editor, *Proc.1991 Joint Int. Conf. Logic Programming*, pages 253–281. MIT Press, 1991.

73. S.H. Muggleton. Inductive logic programming. *New Generation Computing*, 8(4):295–318, 1991.

74. G. Nelson and D. C. Oppen. Simplification by cooperating decision procedures. *ACM Transactions on Programming Languages and Systems*, 1(2):245–257, October 1979.

75. A. Newell, J. C. Shaw, and H. A. Simon. Empirical explorations with the Logic Theory Machine. In *Proc. West. Joint Comp. Conf.*, pages 218–239, 1957. Reproduced in Computers and Thought (eds Feigenbaum and Feldman), McGraw Hill, New York, pp 109-133, 1963.

76. H.J. Ohlbach. Semantics based translation methods for modal logics. *Journal of Logic and Computation*, 1(5):691–746, 1991.

77. R. A. Overbeek and E. L. Lusk. Logic data structures and control architecture for implementation of theorem proving programs. In W. Bibel and R. Kowalski, editors, *5th International Conference on Automated Deduction*. Springer Verlag, 1980. Lecture Notes in Computer Science No. 87.

78. S. Owen. *Analogy for Automated Reasoning*. Academic Press Ltd, 1990.

79. S. Owre, J. M. Rushby, and N. Shankar. PVS : An integrated approach to specification and verification. Tech report, SRI International, 1992.

80. L.C. Paulson. Natural deduction as higher order resolution. *Journal of Logic Programming*, 3:237–258, 1986.

81. L.C. Paulson. *ML for the Working Programmer*. Cambridge University Press, 1991.

82. J. Pearl. *Probabilistic Reasoning in Intelligent Systems: Networks of Plausible Inference*. Morgan Kaufmann, 1988.

83. F. Pfenning. Logic programming in the LF logical framework. In *Logical Frameworks*, pages 149 – 182. Cambridge University Press, 1991.

84. G. Plotkin. A note on inductive generalization. In D Michie and B Meltzer, editors, *Machine Intelligence 5*, pages 153–164. Edinburgh University Press, 1969.

85. G. Plotkin. Building-in equational theories. In D Michie and B Meltzer, editors, *Machine Intelligence 7*, pages 73–90. Edinburgh University Press, 1972.

86. Mojżesz Presburger. Über die Vollständigkeit eines gewissen Systems der Arithmetik ganzer Zahlen, in welchem die Addition als einzige Operation hervortritt. In *Sprawozdanie z I Kongresu metematyków slowiańskich, Warszawa 1929*, pages 92–101, 395. Warsaw, 1930. Annotated English version also available [93].

87. U. S. Reddy. Term rewriting induction. In *Proc. of Tenth International Conference on Automated Deduction*. Springer-Verlag, 1990.

88. G. Robinson and L. Wos. Paramodulation and theorem-proving in first-order theories with equality. In D. Michie, editor, *Machine Intelligence 4*, pages 103–33. Edinburgh University Press, 1969.

89. J. A. Robinson. A machine oriented logic based on the resolution principle. *J Assoc. Comput. Mach.*, 12:23–41, 1965.

90. R. E. Shostak. Deciding combinations of theories. *Journal of the ACM*, 31(1):1–12, January 1984. Also: *Proceedings of the 6th International Conference on Automated Deduction*, volume 138 of *Lecture Notes in Computer Science*, pages 209–222. Springer-Verlag, June 1982.

91. J. R. Slagle. A heuristic program that solves symbolic integration problems in freshman calculus. In E. A. Feigenbaum and J. Feldman, editors, *Computers and Thought*, pages 191–203. McGraw Hill, 1963.

92. J. Slaney. The crisis in finite mathematics: automated reasoning as cause and cure. In Bundy [19], pages 1–13.

93. Ryan Stansifer. Presburger's article on integer arithmetic: Remarks and translation. Technical Report TR 84-639, Department of Computer Science, Cornell University, September 1984.

94. M. E. Stickel. A Prolog technology theorem prover. *New Generation Computing*, 2(4):371–83, 1984.

95. G.J. Sussman, T. Winograd, and E. Charniak. Micro-planner reference manual. Technical Report 203a, MIT AI Lab, 1971.

96. G. Sutcliffe, C. Suttner, and T. Yemenis. The TPTP problem library. In Bundy [19], pages 252–266.

97. C. Suttner and G. Sutcliffe. The CADE-14 ATP system competition. *Journal of Automated Reasoning*, 21(1):99–134, 1998.

98. L. A. Wallen. *Automated Proof Search in Non-Classical Logics*. MIT Press, London, 1990.

99. T. Walsh, A. Nunes, and Alan Bundy. The use of proof plans to sum series. In D. Kapur, editor, *11th International Conference on Automated Deduction*, pages

325–339. Springer Verlag, 1992. Lecture Notes in Computer Science No. 607. Also available from Edinburgh as DAI Research Paper 563.

100. C. Walther. Combining induction axioms by machine. In *Proceedings of IJCAI-93*, pages 95–101. International Joint Conference on Artificial Intelligence, 1993.

101. C. Walther. Mathematical induction. In C. J. Hogger D. M. Gabbay and J. A. Robinson, editors, *Handbook of Logic in Artificial Intelligence and Logic Programming*, volume 12, pages 122–227. Oxford University Press, Oxford, 1994.

102. C. Walther. On proving termination of algorithms by machine. *Artificial Intelligence*, 71(1):101–157, 1994.

103. R. W. Weyhrauch. Prolegomena to a theory of mechanized formal reasoning. *Artificial Intelligence*, 13:133–170, 1980.

104. L. Wos, R. Overbeek, E. Lusk, and J. Boyle. *Automated Reasoning: Introduction and Applications*. Prentice-Hall, 1984.

105. L. Wos. Automated reasoning answers open questions. *Notices of the AMS*, 5(1):15–26, January 1993.

106. Wen-Tsün Wu. The Char-Set method and its applications to automated reasoning. In William McCune, editor, *14th International Conference on Automated Deduction*, pages 1–4. Springer-Verlag, 1997.

107. Tetsuya Yoshida, Alan Bundy, Ian Green, Toby Walsh, and David Basin. Coloured rippling: An extension of a theorem proving heuristic. In A. G. Cohn, editor, *In proceedings of ECAI-94*, pages 85–89. John Wiley, 1994.

The World Wide Web as a Place for Agents

P. Ciancarini[1] and Robert Tolksdorf[2] and F. Vitali[1]

[1] Dipartimento di Scienze dell'Informazione
Mura Anteo Zamboni, 7 - 40127 Bologna, Italy
University of Bologna - Italy
E-mail: {ciancarini,vitali}@cs.unibo.it
[2] Technische Universität Berlin, Fachbereich Informatik, FLP/KIT,
Sekr. FR 6-10, Franklinstr. 28/29, D-10587 Berlin, Germany,
mailto:tolk@cs.tu-berlin.de, http://www.cs.tu-berlin.de/~tolk/

Abstract. The Word Wide Web was born as an Internet service supporting a simple distributed hypertext management system. Since its start a number of technologies have been proposed to enhance its capabilities. In this paper we describe our concept of an *active Web*, namely how we design the software architecture of interactive cooperative applications based on the Word Wide Web. An active Web includes *agents* able to use the services offered by Word Wide Web clients and servers. In an active Web both users and agents can interoperate using a set of basic mechanisms for communication and synchronization. The active Web we describe here is based on coordination technology: we explore two alternative implementations, both based on Java enriched with alternative coordination kernels.

1 Introduction

The Word Wide Web is currently the de facto standard platform to access several Internet services, like FTP or USENET news. Given its pervasivity, it has the potential to become the most used infrastructure to build geographically distributed applications as well. In fact, several enterprises are turning to the Word Wide Web as the environment of choice for building innovative and sophisticated applications leveraging on the open standards, their diffusion, and the programmable nature of the environment. In fact, the Internet can be used as an effective and economical infrastructure for business support. For instance, there is a growing interest in groupware applications based on the WWW infrastructure. These applications are typically *multiagent*, meaning that they are highly concurrent, distributed, and based on mobile code (Munson und Dewan, 1997).

However, the Web in its current state does not provide enough support for applications based on agent-oriented programming, like groupware or workflow, which require multi-agent coordination and complex transactions. Most WWW applications are either server-centric (applications interfacing via CGI to a central mainframe-like server machine), client-centric (applications made mostly of applets providing services to users), or not integrated at all with the Web (applications whose user interface is implemented by applets or plug-ins using some proprietary protocol to connect to a proprietary server). All these approaches do not really satisfy the idea of an active Web based on some structured configuration of (autonomous) agents: they are either not really distributed, or not integrated with the Web.

The PageSpace architecture (Ciancarini et al., 1998) provides a design framework for overcoming these limitations, creating a new paradigm for Web-based applications that are composed of autonomous agents performing their duties regardless of their physical locations. The PageSpace architecture is based on the Linda coordination model (Carriero und Gelernter, 1992) and can be controlled with different coordination languages. In this paper we demonstrate the flexibility of the architecture by describing two different coordination languages and applications where the PageSpace architecture has been fruitfully used.

The paper is structured as follows: in section 2 we discuss the issues arising when one has to design distributed, interactive applications on the WWW. In section 3 we illustrate the PageSpace reference architecture, that can be used to design these applications. In section 3 we discuss a direct implementation in Java of the PageSpace reference architecture. In section 5 we discuss how we implemented a PageSpace-based application using Java enriched with some coordination primitives. In section 6 we discuss alternative research and commercial efforts to provide interactivity and coordination on the Web. Section 7 concludes the paper.

2 Designing active Web applications

The Word Wide Web was born as a simple and efficient distributed system for managing hypertext documents. The minimal set of components of such a system are servers, clients, and documents including hyperlinks. The interactions among these components are driven by the HTTP protocol and the CGI (Common Gateway Interface) mechanism. HTTP is a very simple TCP/IP based protocol used by clients in order to retrieve documents stored on a disk under the control of an HTTP server. Usually documents are stored in HTML format, a markup language with a typographical semantics used by browsers to display the document contents. However, documents can also be created on-the-fly by a server-side application. With CGI a client requests a document as the output of a process that is run on the server when the request comes in. This simple mechanism can be used in a "tricky" way in order to implement more complex forms of interaction among documents, clients, and servers (Bannan, 1997).

According to the original design the only activity that can be dynamically triggered in the Word Wide Web is associated to the CGI mechanism. Soon users asked for more interaction than just browsing documents and this brought to the development of a family of languages that can be embedded into an HTML document and executed by the user's browser. These languages are very different in their capabilities and target; in fact, some are scripting languages intended to interact heavily with the document itself (as in the case of JavaScript or ActiveX), some are complex and fully-fledged languages that have minimal interaction with the document (as in the case of Java).

Although these technologies allow us to "activate" the two key components of the WWW architecture, namely servers and clients, we still need techniques and protocols to control the coordination of such components.

2.1 The WWW as an agent world

Intuitively, an *active Web* is a system based on standard WWW clients and servers including some kind of agents performing some activities on Internet resources. The activities can take place at the client, at the server, at the middleware level, at the gateway with another active software system (eg. an external database, a decision support system or an expert system), or even at the user level.

An active Web includes several *agents*. In fact, each component of an active Web is as an autonomous agent in a world offering several services to agents: thus, an agent is not just capable of computations but can also interact (in possibly complex ways) with other agents.

The interaction among agents is usually accomplished using a client/server architecture (as in any RPC-based system, such as CORBA) (Lewis, 1995). However, sometimes the client-server architecture is not adequate: the interactions among the components may change in time and their client/server relationship needs to be reversed, or a designer may need to decouple the components, for instance to deal with an application distributed over a world-wide intranet including heterogeneous networks and machines.

A solution to these problems consists of designing the distributed application as made of spatially scattered agents acting autonomously: such a schema fits quite well into the so called *distributed objects model* (Adler, 1995, Orfali et al., 1996). When an application is composed of several agents, the control of their coordination is an important issue. In our approach we distinguish between agent computation and agent coordination.

Agent computation is what concerns the internal behavior of an agent. An agent performs actions which are either method invocations or message deliveries. Synchronization actions (eg. starting, blocking, unblocking, and terminating an activity) are the remaining mechanisms in object invocation.

Agent coordination is what concerns the relationship between an agent and its environment, namely synchronization, communication, and service provision and usage.

Coordination languages separate coordination from computation, not as independent or dual concepts, but as orthogonal ones: they are two dimensions both necessary to design agent worlds (Ciancarini, 1996).

A coordination language should thus combine two languages: one for coordination (the inter-agent actions) and one for computation (the intra-agent actions). The most famous example of a coordination model is Linda's Tuple Space

(Carriero und Gelernter, 1992, implemented on several hardware architectures and integrated with several programming languages.

Linda can be seen as a sort of assembly coordination language in two ways. First and foremost, it includes very simple coordination entities, active and passive tuples, which represent agents and messages, respectively; it includes a generic coordination medium, namely the Tuple Space, in which all tuples reside; it includes a small number of coordination primitives. Second, we say that Linda is a minimalist coordination assembly because it can be used to implement higher leve,l more complex coordination languages. For instance, we have used it to implement Shade, an extension of Java including a concept of transactions (Ciancarini und Rossi, 1998).

In fact, the Linda coordination model is quite minimalist to be immediately used to coordinate WWW components (Bjornson et al., 1997). What lacks is the definition of a *reference architecture*, including the basics of tuple space coordination but adding specific services for WWW agents. The interest for coordination architectures is rapidly rising in the industrial world: CORBA can be considered one of these architectures. Another one is Jini, by SunSoft. In the next section we describe PageSpace, that is an example of such an architecture.

3 The PageSpace

PageSpace is a reference architecture for multiagent applications built on top of the WWW (Ciancarini et al., 1998). PageSpace applications consist of several distributed agents which coordinate themselves to accomplish some cooperative task.

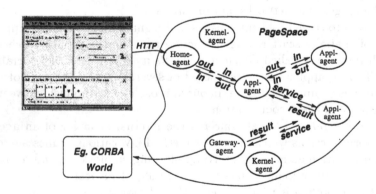

Fig. 1. The PageSpace reference architecture

In the PageSpace reference architecture, therefore, we distinguish several types of *agents*, as depicted in Fig. 1:

- *User interface agents* (also called *alpha agents*), implement application-specific user interfaces in general-purpose browsers. They are displayed in a browser according to the requests of the user. Depending on the complexity of the application and the capabilities of the browser, there may be different instantiations of user interface agents (in HTML, JavaScript, Java, etc.) that are displayed or executed on the browser.

- *Homeagents* (also called *beta agents*) are a persistent representation (avatar) of users in a PageSpace. Even if at any moment users can disconnect from the shared workspace, it is still necessary to collect, deliver, and possibly act on the messages and requests of the other agents. The homeagent receives all the messages bound to a user, and delivers them orderly to the user on request (ie. when the user is on-line). Evoluted homeagents can in some circumstances actively perform actions or provide answers on behalf of the user in her absence.

- *The coordination kernel* (or *gamma*) is the actual operating environment where agents live and communicate. In PageSpace we do not dictate the use of a specific coordination kernel. In fact, different coordination kernels may provide different mechanisms for creating and controlling the agents of an application. Thus, a designer should choose the coordination kernel most suitable to his application. In this paper we will describe two different coordination kernels we have used, both based on Java.

- *Application agents* (also called *delta agents*), are the agents that actually perform the working of the coordinated application. They are specific of one application, and can be started and interrupted according to the needs of the application. They live and communicate in the coordination kernel, offer and use each other's services, interact with the shared data, and realize useful computations within the PageSpace.

  Some application agents will not interact directly with a user in any way, and therefore will have no need for a user interface. They will just use or offer services to other agents. Other application agents, on the other hand, will have to be controlled and monitored by a user. In this case, they will provide on request an ad hoc user interface agent, in the form of an HTML document, a Java applet, etc., which will be delivered to the requesting user and will be displayed or executed on the user's machine.

- *Kernel agents* (also called *epsilon agents*), provide system services to the application agents. They perform management and control task on the agents active within the PageSpace environment. They deal with the activation, interruption, and mobility of the agents within the physical configuration of connected nodes. Ideally, there would be one kernel agent for each participating machine, providing access to the local workspace. Kernels maintain the illusion of a single shared PageSpace when it is actually distributed on several computers, and provide mobility of the agents on the different machines for load balancing and application grouping as needed.

- *Gateway agents* (also called *zeta agents)*, provide access to the external world for PageSpace applications. Applications needing to access other coordination kernels, network services, legacy applications, middleware platforms, etc., may do so by requesting services to the appropriate gateway agent. Each gateway agent is specialized for dealing with one type of external environment, and will translate and deliver externally the services requests of the application agents, and will deliver the corresponding response back to the appropriate agent.

We call "agents" the entities present in the PageSpace architecture since they are more complex than pure objects: the application agents are autonomous and possibly mobile, homeagents can include knowledge bases to work on behalf of a user, etc.

We foresee a user interface agent in each user browser, which is connected to a homeagent providing stable access to the PageSpace. A set of application agents implement the functionality of a distributed application, and a gateway agent provides access to a external environment, for instance, some OLE-based document-centered applications, like a spreadsheet, or some network service, like e-mail or news.

4 A prototypical implementation of PageSpace

In this section we describe one initial instance of the PageSpace reference architecture that has been implemented in Java for evaluation purposes. Since this prototypical implementation never had any other name, we will inappropriately use here the term "PageSpace" to refer to it, rather than to the reference architecture described in Ciancarini et al., 1998, as we do in the rest of the paper.

The user interacts with his homeagent via the user interface agent as shown in a Web browser. The homeagent is identified by a normal URL, such as `http:// pagespace.cs.tu-berlin.de/cgi-bin/beta`. A specific homeagent is identified by the URL plus a user name, such as `http://pagespace.cs.tu-berlin.de/ cgi-bin/beta/robert`.

After logging into the homeagent, the browser displays an user interface such as the one shown in Figure 2. The list on the top left contains all the messages received from all the application agents needing to communicate with the user. The control area on the top right offers the user a set of buttons to control the homeagent. Finally, by clicking on one of the messages in the list an appropriate application-specific user interface is shown in the display area on the bottom.

Specifically, the steps involved in using an application are the following ones:

1. The user selects an application from a list in the control area and instructs the homeagent to use it.

2. The homeagent retrieves additional data on the application via HTTP and the initial interface for that application (a static HTML document stored somewhere on some Web server). This interface is sent as a message for the user.

3. The user selects the correct item from the message queue and the corresponding interface is shown in the display area. A set of buttons there defines the set of possible interactions with the application.

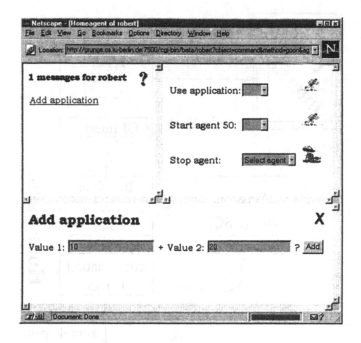

Fig. 2. A user interface agent

4. Selecting a button results in a request to the homeagent to use a specific method of the application agent. The homeagent issues a corresponding service request with the PageSpace coordination operations. The result of that interaction with an application agent is a string containing the new application interface generated by the agent, command, which is stored as a message for the user.
5. The user selects that message and is presented with the next interface, which includes the results of the previously-invoked operation.

Figure 3 shows the architecture of homeagents for the experimental prototype. It consists of three components that are implemented as different processes or threads: the interface for the interaction with the user which is visible as the generated user interface, the interface to the coordination kernel, and a repository where received messages are kept until they are deleted by the user

Applications in PageSpace are identified by a URL to a resource which contains a special application description. The use of a URL makes this approach wholly integrated with the Web. Paralelly to plain document-oriented Web, the agent-oriented PageSpace uses no central directory of applications.

Any application agent consists of three modules called Kernel, Service-Handler and Kernel-Connector. The Kernel is the "main-program" that loads and launches the module containing the provided services of the specific application, the Service-Handler. The Kernel-Connector provides the connection to

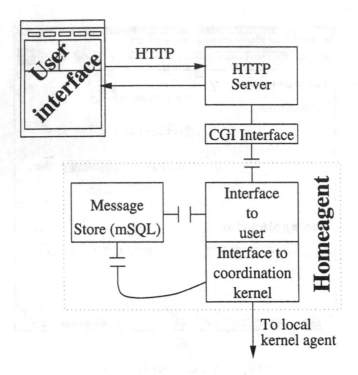

Fig. 3. The Architecture for the Homeagents

the Coordination Kernel of PageSpace by managing the connection to a Kernel agent and by propagating messages.

Kernel Agents are daemon processes that exist on specific machines and together spawn the Coordination Kernel, the virtual room for coordinating agents. Their functionality is central to the prototypical architecture of PageSpace. Kernel Agents contain the following modules:

- A *central control-unit* that invokes the kernel modules and executes them as Java threads. It constantly controls them by checking their states and taking appropriate action in the case of failures.
- A *server for homeagents* that is accessible via HTTP.
- The *Kernel-Connector* that establishes and manages the connections to other Kernel-Agents and implements the protocols for the distributed coordination kernel
- Some *Repositories* as the actual coordination technology used. They usually consist of a store of data items and methods to access them by coordination operations. In this prototypical PageSpace implementation, repositories for the coordination languages Laura (Tolksdorf, 1998) and Java/Linda are foreseen.
- The *Kernel-Connector* for the application and gateway Agents.

- The *Agent-Store* as a repository of application Agents that operate as threads within the Kernel-Agent. Application agents can be loaded by the Kernel and started as threads but do not necessarily have to. Gateway agents are always assumed to run external to the kernel.

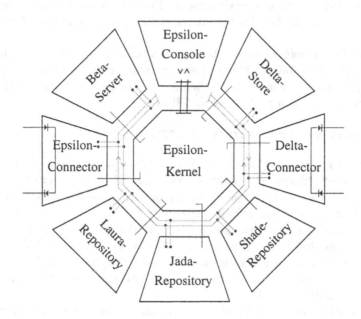

Fig. 4. The structure of the kernel agents

Figure 4 outlines the structure described. The initial prototype of PageSpace was implemented to evaluate our approach. Its implementation basis was Java 1.02 – with the RMI mechanism in Java 1.1 several technical details would change.

5 Building a PageSpace for cooperation: MUDWeb

In (Ciancarini und Rossi, 1997 we introduced Jada, a Java-Linda combination. Jada was a first experiment in combining Java with a coordination model. Here we describe JaCoPo, a combination of Java with a more expressive coordination model based on nested tuple spaces, as in Paradise.

JaCoPo is composed of a syntactic extension of the Java Language and a run-time environment. The syntactic extension enriches Java with a set of Linda-like coordination constructs. The run-time environment, implemented in Jada, supports multiple nested tuple spaces. The basic entity in a JaCoPo program is the *agent*. Each agent can access the available tuple spaces or create new ones.

Every agent has a *reference tuple space* that is used as the default shared space for the coordination operations that do not specify one.

A "move" operation is provided to allow an agent to change its reference tuple space at run-time, enabling what we call "migration by reference": although the agents do not move physically, their references for the outside world do, thus modifying the agent's environment. This is similar to what happens to Unix processes when they "move" across a file system changing their working directory.

In JaCoPo a *handle* identifies the root of a tuple space tree. Each tuple space tree is handled by a JaCoPoManager server named **root**. An agent can access a JaCoPoManager server using **Open**, then any *TupleSpace* managed by that server can be accessed using a path name as follows:

```
root # "ATupleSpace":"Subspace#1":"Subsubspace#2"
```

"ATupleSpace" is a subspace of root, "Subspace#1" is a subspace of "ATupleSpace", "Subsubspace#2" is a subspace of "Subspace#1".

All tuple space operations should specify a pathname. If no pathname is used, the operation refers to the default reference tuple space.

JaCoPo includes the basic *Linda-like* primitives: **Out**, **Read**, and **In**, either blocking or non-blocking. Moreover, it includes some set-oriented operations, like **rdall** and **inall**, whose result is a multiset of tuples stored in an array. For instance, the operation **rdall("message",?String:messages)** stores in array **messages** all strings found in the tuple space.

The JaCoPo runtime is based on two main classes, namely **JaCoPoManager**, which manages a tree of nested tuple spaces, and **JaCoPoObject**, which exploits the coordination services offered by a JaCoPoManager object.

5.1 MUDWeb

MUDWeb is a groupware platform we have designed and implemented using JaCoPo. We were inspired by MUD (Multi User Dungeon), a cooperative environment in which many people socialize and interact. MUDs can be used as enabling technologies for several groupware applications (Das et al., 1997, Rowley, 1997, Tarau et al., 1997, Doppke et al., 1998). A MUD platform usually offers the infrastructure of a role-playing game (hence the name) where human and robot players interact, visit dark and magical places, fight monsters or other players, and seek treasures. More generally, a MUD is an abstract platform that users can program to create shared virtual realities. Thus, a MUD is a very powerful abstraction to describe a general platform for cooperative work on the WWW, that provides a general framework for users to interact with each other and to manage items to be shared, such as documents and resources.

MUDWeb consists of a number of agents which coordinate themselves with respect to a set of services according to a number of protocols based on tuple exchanges. MUDWeb includes several "rooms" which correspond to tuple spaces including some default services.

A room is defined by a set of attributes: its name, some exits, some HTML code, some access rights, and some services. For instance, Fig. 5 shows the declaration of a room.

```
room JustARoom
access USER1, WIZARD
code "http://java/gaggi/nik/html/RoomCode.html"
service Counter "Services.CounterService"
    START\_VAL="1"
    HTML\_FILE="html/RoomCode.html"
exit OtherRoom1, OtherRoom2, Hall
data ("Tuple\_1", 1), ("Tuple\_2", 2, 2)
end
```

Fig. 5. A room in MudWeb

This room is named `JustARoom`. The clause `access` specifies that only users USER1 and WIZARD can enter the room. Clause `code` is mandatory, and describes the HTML code to be displayed when a user enters the room. Clause `service` specifies an agent named `Counter` being active in the room, offering service `Services.CounterService` (see below a description of the main available services). Clause `exit` specifies other rooms connected to this one, so that a user can "navigate" from room to room. Clause `data` specifies that this room contains two tuples.

The MudWeb architecture is implemented by a number of coordinated servers offering the basic abstraction of nested tuple spaces. Fig. 6 shows the software architecture of MUDWeb.

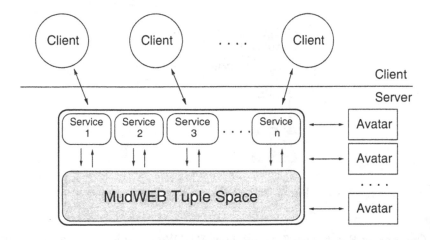

Fig. 6. A MUD-like active Web

Services are autonomous agents that wait for command tuples and perform services based on their content. Services are generally very small and specialized modules that react to a limited list of commands. The functionalities of an application are thus implemented by a score of services cooperating together. Clients are user interfaces using some role-specific HTML page or Java applet.

5.2 MUDWeb as a PageSpace

We have used JaCoPo as a coordination kernel, used by all agents to coordinate their activities. A MUDWeb server contains three kinds of agents: the *avatars*, the *services*, and the *mudshell*. The avatar is the persistent representation of a human user: it is a Homeagent controllable by the user through the Interface agent to be displayed within a browser. Actually an avatar can accept commands and return data in a variety of methods, including e-mail messages. Services are the Application agents in the shared space, that implement the actual computations of the distributed application. The Mudshell is the client of the MUDWeb application, and is the interface framework where the interaction with the user takes place: the MUDshell provides primitives for moving from one available shared space to another, and allow the user to interact with the services by providing a MUD-like text box for direct commands, and displaying the most common ones on appropriate buttons. Furthermore they allow avatars to display their interfaces just like the other services.

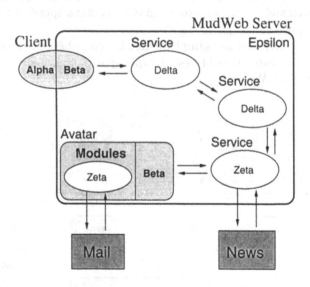

Fig. 7. MUDWeb as a PageSpace.

Comparing Fig. 6 with 7 we see how MUDWeb implements the PageSpace architecture.

The main innovation consists of how Homeagents are implemented. In MUD-Web a Homeagent is based on two different classes: the MudShell client and the Avatar. Both classes implement the MudPlayer interface, which define how people can interact with the architecture.

MUDWeb services are defined as agents operating in a room. Interestingly, some services are implemented as gateway agents. For instance, this is useful when a service has to input messages formed according to some special protocol like NNTP (news) and output their contents in some MUDWeb room. As another example, avatars exploit specific gateway agents to answer by e-mail to their users. An avatar can also emulate an HTTP server, because it has to be accessible by HTTP as well.

The design of a cooperative application based on MUDWeb consists of instantiating the classes of the framework showed in Fig. 8.

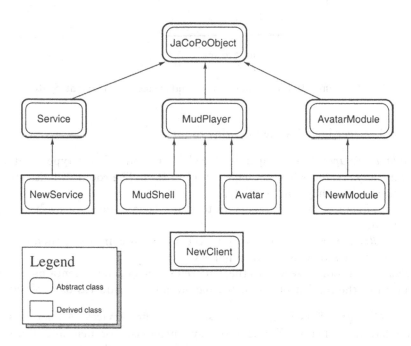

Fig. 8. The MUDWeb framework.

5.3 Conference management in MUDWeb

MUDWeb has been used to design and implement a workflow system supporting the management of a scientific conference. The system, named *ConfManager*, has the goal to simplify the management of the review of papers submitted to an international scientific conference.

The problem of managing the peer-review of papers submitted to a conference can be considered a case study in coordination. In fact, authors, reviewers, and program committee members can interact with the system using both synchronous (online WWW) and asynchronous (e-mail) communication interactions. Several activities can be automated, aiming at supporting the coordination protocols typical of a specific conference model.

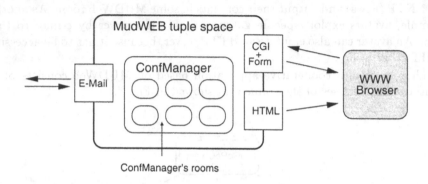

Fig. 9. Using MudWeb to design a Conference management System

ConfManager includes the following rooms:

- *SubmittedPaper* Every paper is stored in a room of this type, that is dynamically created when the paper is submitted. The room will also store the reviews when they will be ready.
- *ReviewRoom* is used by reviewers to store their reviews before they are finalized.
- *SelectRoom* is a room accessible to the program committee members only; it stores the scores assigned to papers.
- *Papers* is a room reserved to the conference organizers: it contains managing data like the full list of submitted papers and the address data of authors.

ConfManager offers in each room some specific services. All services come in two flavors, either synchronous or asynchronous. For instance, the service *Services.Announcer* accepts reviews coming by e-mail, checking that they refer to the paper stored in the same room. The service *Services.Submitter* is similar to the preceding one, but supports on line user interaction.

Asynchronous services rely upon *avatars*, which have to be programmed to perform the necessary tasks. The (server-side) avatar acts as an e-mail client of an e-mail server; it controls the user mailbox and processes the messages it contains.

Services for authors of papers A new room is added when a new paper is submitted, and an avatar is created for the author(s). Submission is either online or by email: in both cases the command **submit** is used. Fig. 10 shows the format of an e-mail submission.

```
submit
Title: The World Wide Web as a Place to Work in
Authors: P. Ciancarini and R. Tolksdorf and F. Vitali
URL: http://hostname/click\_here
In this paper we describe our concept of an active Web,
namely how we design the software architecture of interactive
cooperative applications based on the WWW.  END
```

Fig. 10. Submitting a paper.

The method `processMail()` parses and interprets the message. The message has to specify the values for the title, authors, and URL fields on different lines. Other lines (eg. the abstract) are considered plain text to be simply translated in HTML and inserted in the room associated to the paper.

Another service that can be invoked by an author is **status**, in order to know some information on the review status (see below).

Services for reviewers Each *SubmittedPaper* room, created to store a submitted paper, will also store the reviews to it. User input is handled by HTML forms and two CGI scripts. The CGI scripts generate a form and build a tuple, respectively. The tuple is temporarily stored in the same room containing the paper being reviewed until it is "confirmed"; after the confirmation the tuple is moved in the selection room.

A reviewer can work either on-line or by email. If the reviewer is working on-line he/she has to be in a paper's room. If the reviewer is using e-mail, he/she has to send a message **announce**, such as the one in Fig. 11.

```
announce
Paper: 1
Agent: reviewer1
```

Fig. 11. Announcing a review.

The message specifies an article id number and a username associated to the agent sending the message. A reviewer then fills in a form according to some evaluation grades. The filled form is sent to the reviewer avatar which transforms the message in a tuple to be stored in the paper room. Then the service **Services.Submitter** will be activated.

Services for PC members The service *Services.Selector* can be activated in the room *SelectRoom* and is implemented by the class **Services.Selector**.

This service is essentially a chat system to be used by PC members to talk and browse the stored dialogs.

6 Technology for Coordinating Web Applications

The PageSpace reference architecture is intended as a framework to help designers to deal with the coordination of distributed activities in Web based applications. It is interesting to compare our solution with alternative ones. One can distinguish different approaches studying where a Web application designer puts the main focus of activity in such applications, namely server-side, or client-side, or somewhere "in the middle", namely in the middleware.

In fact, the most conventional location of activity in Web based applications is at the servers side. This approach was taken very early in standard Web server technology by the introduction of the *Common Gateway Interface (CGI)*. According to CGI, some program can be executed upon the request of a URL, which dynamically generates an HTML page by performing some activity. The classical example for this approach is the generation of a report from some database contents, to be delivered to the requesting Web client in the form of an HTML page.

Mechanisms to preprocess additional tags within HTML pages appeared soon with early server software as *"server-side includes"*. For higher expressiveness, complete languages were made available. The Web* system is a good example of such server sided activity is Web* (Almasi et al., 1995). Such a system interfaces a Web server with a Tcl/Tk interpreter, which in turn can access objects via CORBA. As a variant, the OreO approach implemented processing of information by using proxies (Brooks et al., 1995).

Meanwhile, commercial vendors provided complete server-based solutions for interactive and collaborative applications on the Web, such as Lotus Domino, or the systems based on Microsofts' active server pages.

In conclusion, today systems with server-side activity in applications are the dominant technology for Web applications. However, they inherit all problems of centralized systems, for example with respect to single point of failures, or performance bottlenecks.

A different option for designers of Web applications is to put the main focus of activity at the client side. With the first browser generations, only *helper* applications could be activated at the client side. A helper is an autonomous program callable from the browser but offering a different user interface, usually displayed in a different window: a typical example is the helper to display PostScript documents. Systems like SHAREDweb (Kumar et al., 1994) used helpers to provide application services, rather than displaying special media types. The coordination of multiple helpers became an issue; for example, the WWWinda system (Gutfreund et al., 1994) used Linda-like coordination technology to coordinate a browser orchestrating multiple helpers to be synchronized for multimedia documents.

It became rapidly clear that it was desirable to integrate an execution environment *within* the browser. A variety of prototypical browsers was developed for various languages, such as Objective Caml (Rouaix, 1996), or Python, (see the Grail browser at `http://grail.cnri.reston.va.us/grail/tcl`), etc.

The dominance of Java and JavaScript, incorporated in the two major Internet browsers, has pretty much satisfied the "market" for client-side activity. However, despite the initial hopes, both are currently not widely used for distributed applications. Java can be used to design highly "intelligent terminals" to access special applications – an example is Internet banking software, such as Twister from Brokat (see www.brokat.de). Instead, JavaScript seems to be used only to enhance the user interface of Web pages, hardly ever more than "highlighting" parts of pages by exchanging displayed images when the mouse pointer moves across them.

HTTP as the communication protocol in the Web makes interactive applications very complicated to implement. This is mainly due to the connectionless, unidirectional paradigm embedded in HTTP. Activity could be coordinated by extensions to the communication protocol.

With the advent of plugins, this option has been used to establish communication channels between plugins and proprietary servers, that go beyond the limitations of HTTP. The HTTP-NG protocol currently developed by the World Wide Web Consortium will also contain extensions to allow coordination of activity at the server and the client side. Currently, however, HTTP provides the communication platform for the Web and it is unclear which browser generations will support more sophisticated protocols.

One could also understand HTTP as a pure transport protocol and stick to existing middleware environments to coordinate open systems for applications. First prototypes used CORBA (Rees et al., 1995) and DCE (Beitz et al., 1995) as the actual implementation basis for open applications.

Soon, commercial vendors have developed systems and specifications that allow for interaction of distributed components and objects via the Web. Examples are RMI from Sun within the Java standard, DCOM from Microsoft, and IIOP, an Internet integration of CORBA that can be found, for example in Netscapes Java libraries giving access to OMG compliant object brokers.

Today, there seems enough of such enabling technology implemented and available within Web technology. However, there is still no "killer application" in widespread use that turns Internet users into participants in a distributed world of active objects or agents. Our proposal, namely PageSpace, defines a design framework and offers some enabling tools to help designers of coordinative, agent-based Web applications.

7 Conclusions and Future Work

Our initial vision of PageSpace had to be refined in the course of designing and implementing the platform. During the project we made several observations on applying coordination technology to the Web. In fact, the issue of coordination in Web applications is still an open question which is not settled in a satisfactory manner. The Web can be the environment in which coordination technology could prove its strength and provide a convincing example of its usefulness of because it has the potential for the integration of an active, agent-based Web by a uniform notion of activity and coordination. Interestingly, the family of Linda-like coordination languages we have developed is only one possible flavor of coordination technology, and it stands in direct competition with other, more industrial technologies, like distributed, heterogeneous object-oriented platforms à la CORBA. In the field of Web applications, coordination technology has to compare with approaches that at moment have a much stronger industrial support and service resources. The implementation of coordination technology in the form of a programming language to control agents over the World Wide Web faces severe engineering problems with respect to the organization of shared coordination media to be used, their replication, the addressing of elements therein, and handling potentially high load demands.

At the moment we are exploring the interaction capabilities offered by Linda-like coordination models to mobile Java agents. Another issue we are exploring is security, that is especially important for e-commerce applications based on PageSpace (Ciancarini et al., 1997, Rodriguez et al., 1997). We also are studying how the advent of XML technology can be exploited for agent-based programming. More information on current activities in PageSpace can be found on the Web at http://www.cs.tu-berlin.de/~pagespc.

Acknowledgments. PageSpace has been supported by the EU as ESPRIT Open LTR project #20179. It is currently supported by the German DAAD and the Italian CNR within the VIGONI program. Several people contributed to the development of the ideas described in this paper; we thank here especially the students G. Busi and N. Gaggi of UniBologna, and A. Knoche of TU Berlin.

References

Adler, R. (1995). Distributed Coordination Models for Client/Server Computing. *IEEE Computer*, 28(4):14–22.

Almasi, G. et al. (1995). Web*: A Technology to Make Information Available on the Web. In *Proc. 4th IEEE Workshop on Enabling Technology: Infrastructure for Collaborative Enterprises*, pages 147–153, Berkley Springs, WV. IEEE Computer Society Press.

Bannan, J. (1997). *Intranet Document Management*. Addison-Wesley.

Beitz, A. et al. (1995). Integrating WWW and Middleware. In Debreceny, R. und Ellis, A., editors, *Proc. 1st Australian World Wide Web Conference*, Lismore, NSW. Norsearch Publishing.

Bjornson, R., Carriero, N., und Gelernter, D. (1997). From weaving threads to untangling the web: a view of coordination from Linda's perspective. In Garlan, D. und LeMetayer, D., editors, *Proc. 2nd Int. Conf. on Coordination Models and Languages*, volume 1282 of *Lecture Notes in Computer Science*, pages 1–17, Berlin, Germany. Springer-Verlag, Berlin.

Brooks, C., Mazer, M., Meeks, S., und Miller, J. (1995). Application-Specific Proxy Servers as HTTP Stream Transducers. In *Electronic Proc. 4th Int. World Wide Web Conference "The Web Revolution"*, Boston, MA.

Carriero, N. und Gelernter, D. (1992). Coordination Languages and Their Significance. *Communications of the ACM*, 35(2):97–107.

Ciancarini, P. (1996). Coordination Models and Languages as Software Integrators. *ACM Computing Surveys*, 28(2):300–302.

Ciancarini, P., Knoche, A., Rossi, D., Tolksdorf, R., und Vitali, F. (1997). Coordinating Java Agents for Financial Applications on the WWW. In *Proc. 2nd Int. Conf. on Practical Applications of Intelligent Agents and MultiAgent Technology (PAAM)*, pages 179–193, London, UK.

Ciancarini, P. und Rossi, D. (1997). Jada: Coordination and Communication for Java agents. In Vitek, J. und Tschudin, C., editors, *Mobile Object Systems: Towards the Programmable Internet*, volume 1222 of *Lecture Notes in Computer Science*, pages 213–228. Springer-Verlag, Berlin.

Ciancarini, P. und Rossi, D. (1998). Coordinating Java Agents Over the WWW. *World Wide Web*, 1(2):87–99.

Ciancarini, P., Tolksdorf, R., Vitali, F., Rossi, D., und Knoche, A. (1998). Coordinating Multiagent Applications on the WWW: a Reference Architecture. *IEEE Transactions on Software Engineering*, 24(5):362–375.

Das, T. et al. (1997). Developing Social Virtual Worlds using NetEffect. In *Proc. 6th IEEE Workshops on Enabling Technologies: Infrastructure for Collaborative Enterprises (WETICE)*, pages 148–154, Boston. IEEE Computer Society Press.

Doppke, J., Heimbigner, D., und Wolf, A. (1998). Software Process Modeling and Execution within Virtual Environments. *ACM Transactions on Software Engineering and Methodology*, 7(1):1–40.

Gutfreund, Y., Nicol, J., Sasnett, R., und Phuah, V. (1994). WWWinda: An Orchestration Service for WWW Browsers and Accessories. In *Proc. 2nd Int. World Wide Web Conference*, Chicago, IL.

Kumar, V., Glicksman, J., und Kramer, G. (1994). A SHAREd Web To Support Design Teams. In *Proc. 3rd IEEE Workshop on Enabling Technologies: Infrastructure for Collaborative Enterprises*, Morgantown, WV.

Lewis, T. (1995). Where is Client/Server Software Headed? *IEEE Computer*, 28(4):49–55.

Munson, J. und Dewan, P. (1997). Sync: a Java Framework for Mobile Collaborative Applications. *IEEE Computer*, 30(6):59–66.

Orfali, R., Harkey, D., und Edwards, J. (1996). *The Essential Distributed Objects Survival Guide*. Wiley.

Rees, O., Edwards, N., Madsen, M., Beasley, M., und McClenaghan, A. (1995). A Web of Distributed Objects. *World Wide Web Journal*, 1(1):75–88.

Rodriguez, J., Noriega, P., Sierra, C., und Padget, J. (1997). FM96.5 A Java-based Electronic Auction House. In *Proc. 2nd Int. Conf. on Practical Applications of Intelligent Agents and MultiAgent Technology (PAAM)*, pages 207–224, London, UK.

Rouaix, F. (1996). A Web navigator with applets in Caml. *Computer Networks and ISDN Systems*, 28(7-11):1365–1371.

Rowley, M. (1997). Distributing MOO-Based Shared Worlds. In *Proc. 6th IEEE Workshops on Enabling Technologies: Infrastructure for Collaborative Enterprises (WETICE)*, pages 155–160, Boston. IEEE Computer Society Press.

Tarau, P., Dahl, V., und DeBosschere, K. (1997). A Logic Programming Infrastructure for remote Execution, Mobile Code and Agents. In *Proc. 6th IEEE Workshops on Enabling Technologies: Infrastructure for Collaborative Enterprises (WETICE)*, pages 106–112, Boston. IEEE Computer Society Press.

Tolksdorf, R. (1998). Laura – A Service-Based Coordination Language. *Science of Computer Programming*, 31(2-3):359–382.

Lifelike Pedagogical Agents and Affective Computing: An Exploratory Synthesis

Clark Elliott[1], Jeff Rickel[2], and James Lester[3]

[1] Institute for Applied Artificial Intelligence,
School of Computer Science, Telecommunications, and Information Systems,
DePaul University, 243 South Wabash Ave., Chicago, IL 60604,
elliott@ils.nwu.edu,
WWW home page: http://condor.depaul.edu/~elliott/
[2] Information Sciences Institute and Computer Science Department,
University of Southern California,
rickel@isi.edu,
WWW home page: http://www.isi.edu/isd/VET/vet.html
[3] Multimedia Laboratory,
Department of Computer Science,
North Carolina State University,
lester@eos.ncsu.edu,
WWW home page: http://multimedia.ncsu.edu/imedia

1 Introduction

Lifelike pedagogical agents have been the subject of increasing attention in the agents and knowledge-based learning environment communities [2, 17, 19–21]. In parallel developments, recent years have witnessed great strides in work on cognitive models of emotion and affective reasoning [4, 18, 22]. As a result, the time is now ripe for exploring how affective reasoning can be incorporated into pedagogical agents to improve students' learning experiences.

This chapter investigates how these two converging research efforts may yield a new form of pedagogical agent that is sensitive to students' emotive state and can reason about affective aspects of problem-solving contexts. Initial forays have been taken into pedagogical emotion generation [1] and reasoning about learners' emotions [3], indicating the potential richness offered by affective learner-system interactions. These efforts suggest important new functionalities for learning environments. Rather than speculating in the abstract about how these new functionalities may come about, we explore them with the particulars of a specific computational model of emotion and specific lifelike pedagogical agents. We discuss preliminary conceptual work on integrating the Affective Reasoner, being developed at DePaul University, with two extant learning environments: the Soar Training Expert for Virtual Environments (Steve) being developed at the Information Sciences Institute (Figure 1), and the Design-A-Plant (Herman the Bug) system being developed at North Carolina State University (Figure 2). These types of integration are undertaken in an effort to create pedagogical agents with rich models of personality, context-sensitive emotional responsiveness, and affective user modeling.

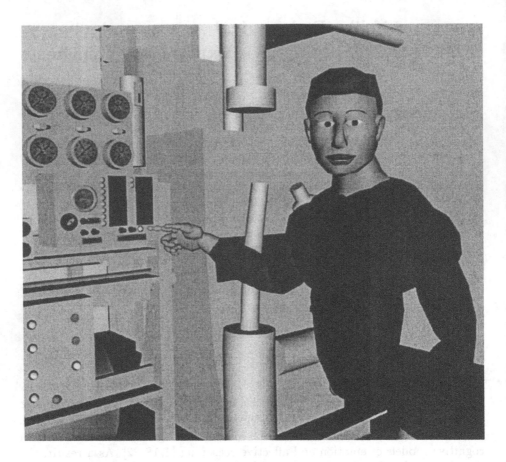

Fig. 1: The Steve Agent in the VET Learning Environment

In the following section we describe the motivations for our work, arguing that affective reasoning will make pedagogical agents better teachers. The remainder of the paper outlines the basic elements of the Affective Reasoning framework and how it might apply to Steve and Herman. We use Steve as a platform for discussing application of personality and emotional responsiveness in pedagogical agents, whereas we use Herman as a platform for discussing affective user modeling. However, this is only for convenience of exposition; each kind of emotion reasoning applies equally well to both systems.

2   Objectives

Good teachers are often good motivators. Motivation is a key ingredient in learning, and emotions play an important role in motivation. We therefore believe that pedagogical agents will be more effective teachers if they display and understand emotions. This could facilitate learning in several ways:

Fig. 2: The Herman Agent in the Design-A-Plant Learning Environment

1. A pedagogical agent should appear to care about students and their progress. This can foster in a student a feeling that she and the agent are "in things together," and can encourage the student to care about her own progress, and the agent's opinion of her.
2. A pedagogical agent should be sensitive to the student's emotions. For example, the agent must recognize a student's frustration so as to intervene with assistance and encouragement before the student loses interest.
3. A pedagogical agent should convey enthusiasm for the subject matter, in order to foster similar enthusiasm in the student. To achieve a credible appearance of enthusiasm in an agent, it is useful to model the emotions that underlie it.
4. A pedagogical agent with a rich and interesting personality may simply make learning more fun. A student that enjoys interacting with a pedagogical agent will have a more positive perception of the whole learning experience. A student that enjoys a learning environment will undoubtedly spend more time there, which is likely to increase learning.

We cannot, at this point, claim to elevate these much beyond the level of intuition, but they are highly commonsensical, and are also testable hypotheses (and c.f. [13]). With respect to the effectiveness of lifelike characters, a recent large-scale study on animated pedagogical agents has demonstrated the *persona effect*, which is that the presence of a lifelike character in an interactive learning environment can have a strong positive effect on students' perception of their learning experience [11]. Other studies have revealed similar findings [2, 9]. By directly comparing the effectiveness of pedagogical agents with and without various types of emotional capabilities, we can better understand the role of emotion in learning.

3 The Affective Reasoning Platform

What we refer to as "emotions" in this paper arise naturally in many human social situations as a byproduct of goal-driven behavior, principled (or unprincipled) behavior, simple preferences, and relationships with other agents. This includes many situations not normally thought of as emotional (e.g., becoming annoyed at someone, a mild form of anger in our theory), but explicitly excludes representation of any physical (i.e., bodily) properties of emotions.

At DePaul University, in our current research on the Affective Reasoner (AR), embodied in a large-scale Lisp-based implementation, we build agents capable of responding "emotionally" to other agents and interactive users, as a function of their concerns. Agents are given unique pseudo-personalities modeled as both a set of *appraisal frames* representing their individual goals (with respect to events that arise), *principles* (with respect to perceived intentional actions of agents), *preferences* (with respect to objects), *moods* (temporary changes to the appraisal mechanism), and as a set of about 440 differentially activated *channels* for the expression of emotions [4, 7]. Situations that arise in the agents' world may map to twenty-six different emotion types (e.g., *pride*, as approving of one's own intentional action), twenty-two of which were originally theoretically specified by Ortony, *et al.* [16]. Qualities, and intensity, of emotion instances in each category are partially determined by some subset of roughly twenty-two different *emotion intensity variables* [8].

To communicate with users the AR agents use various multimedia modes including facial expressions, speech, and even music. Agents have about 70 line-drawn facial expressions, which are morphed in real time, yielding about 3,000 different morphs. (A central assumption of our work is that social interaction based on emotion states *must* run in real time.) This is extensible since the morphs are efficiently computed on the client computer each time they are displayed. Agents can select facial expressions, speed of morph, size of the display, and color of the foreground and background. Agents, whose mouths move when they speak, communicate with users through minimally inflected text-to-speech software, which allows us to dynamically construct spoken sentences at run time.

With regard to music, to add qualitatively to their expression of emotions, agents have access to a large database of MIDI files, any portion which they can retrieve in less than a second, and in which they can index down to 1/1000th of a second. Each of these (mostly music) files are real performances (that is, are creations of human performers, not of computers playing sounds from scores). Speech recognition software, used with some AR applications, has allowed children as young as two years old to interact with AR application agents. In all cases, the agents respond in real time to input from the world around them: when spoken to, they speak back [6]. These particular agents have been shown quite effective at communicating a wide range of emotion, comparing favorably with a human actor [5].

4 Creating Virtual Affective States in Steve

The Soar Training Expert for Virtual Environments (Steve) [19] is a pedagogical agent for virtual environments (Figure 1). Steve's objective is to help students learn to perform physical, procedural tasks, such as operating or repairing complex equipment. Students are immersed in a 3D computer simulation of their work environment where they can improve their skills through practice on realistic tasks. Steve cohabits the virtual environment with them, continually monitoring the state of the environment and periodically controlling it through virtual motor actions. Steve appears in the environment as a full upper body, and he communicates to students via text-to-speech software. Steve helps students in various ways: he can demonstrate tasks, answer questions about the rationale behind task steps, and monitor students while they practice tasks, providing help when requested. He functions as part of a larger Virtual Environments for Training (VET) system being developed jointly by the USC Information Sciences Institute, the USC Behavioral Technology Laboratory, and Lockheed Martin.

The VET system includes two main components in addition to Steve. The first of these, the virtual reality software, handles the interface between students and the virtual world, updating the view on their head-mounted display as they move around and detecting their interactions with virtual objects. The second of these, a world simulator, maintains the state of the virtual world as agents (such as Steve) or students interact with it. When the student interacts with the virtual world, Steve gets a message from the virtual reality software describing the interaction, and he gets messages from the simulator describing the resulting changes in the world (in terms of attribute-value pairs). In this way, Steve is aware of both the student's action (e.g., pulling on the dipstick), and the result of that action (e.g., the dipstick is pulled out).

How can affective reasoning be integrated into Steve? We provide a tentative but concrete answer to this question by outlining some potential roles for affective reasoning in Steve and show how these map to elements of the existing Affective Reasoning framework. Throughout, we use examples from Steve's current domain, that of operating a high pressure air compressor. Although Steve is designed as a domain independent tutor, capable of providing instruction in a variety of different domains given the appropriate knowledge, this domain has served as a testbed for his early development.

4.1 Emotion Antecedents in Steve

As discussed above, in the AR scheme, emotions arise as a result of agents' appraisals of their world. Goal-based emotions, such as joy and distress, are generated when there is a match between some event, and the goal-based concerns of the agent. Similarly, principle-based emotions, such as admiration and reproach, are generated when there is a match between what is seen as an accountable act of some agent and the beliefs of an observing agent, with respect to right and wrong. Lastly, preference-based emotions, such as liking and disliking, are generated when there is a match between appealing or unappealing objects that the observing agent attends to, and the preferences of that agent.

In this architecture, one part of the pseudo-personality of an agent—that which stems from their emotional predisposition—is based on the way they see the world, and this in turn is partially determined by the goals, values, and likes they hold. In any particular context (such as that in which Steve operates), it is thus necessary to describe the personality of the automated agents in terms of the situations that arise, characterized as sets of goals, principles, and preferences in the content domain.

In Steve's virtual world such situations arise, and are formally represented, thereby allowing us to test for possible appraisals with respect to his personality. An "emotionally intelligent" Steve might, or might not, have emotion responses to these situations, depending upon his concerns. Similarly, Steve might have emotions based on the presumed state of the student, and about future and past events. Here we examine some basic mappings from situations to emotions.

Sample Goals for Steve Steve has a set of goals which help define his personality. These goals may match situations that arise in the simulation. In some cases, these matches represent achieved goals; in others, they represent thwarted goals. In this way, we model Steve's *desires* so that when the world takes on a new state, events represented by that state may combine with Steve's goals to determine how he "feels." Some goals are *serendipity* goals which can only be matched when achieved, some are *preservation* goals which can only be matched when thwarted, and still others are *bi-valenced* which can be matched either way. The following are simple examples of such goals for Steve.

- **Goal 1: I will give explanations about the subject domain and discuss interesting details about the domain with the student.** For example, we want Steve to be happy when he has a chance to give the student useful, albeit not necessarily critical, information about the underlying domain. By exhibiting happiness when he has a chance to share information about the subject domain, Steve manifests a rudimentary form of enthusiasm about the subject.
  Example situation: (a) Student is learning to start the compressor, (b) Student goes through pre-startup routine but neglects to open the cut-out valve, (c) Student attempts to start compressor, (d) Steve intervenes and says, "Before starting compressor, you must always open the cut-out valve. It is actually pretty interesting what can happen if you do not," and gives the explanation.

- **Goal 2: I will engage the student.** For example, we want Steve to be distressed, or anxious, when the student appears bored with the tasks at hand.
  Example situation: (a) Steve is giving an explanation about why the cut-out valve must be opened when starting the compressor, (b) Steve and the cut-out valve are not in the student's field of vision, i.e., the student is looking elsewhere. Steve frowns and in an irritated voice says, "Look over here."
- **Goal 3: The student will retain task knowledge.** For example, we want Steve to be upset with himself if the student does not retain critical knowledge; we want Steve to be happy if the student remembers important points. By caring about how well the student performs, Steve shows the student that he is interested in the student's progress.
  Example situation: (a)–(d) (from Goal 1), then later the student repeats the startup procedure, and either (e) student attempts to start the compressor without opening the cut-out valve, or (f) the student has not opened the cut-out valve and asks Steve if there is anything else to be done before starting the compressor, or (g) the student remembers to open the cut-out valve. Should (e) or (f) obtain, Steve's goal would be thwarted, and he would feel distressed; should (g) obtain, he would feel joy.
- **Goal 4: The student will be cautious.** For example, we want Steve to have an "Oh no!" distress, or fear, response to the situation when the student is careless and exposes both Steve, and herself, to danger.
  Example situation: (a)–(e) (from Goal 3), and (f) failing to open the cut-out valve is potentially dangerous.

Such goals alone might not fully determine Steve's response. Steve's emotions may also be affected by his *relationship* with the student, and the perceived appraisal of the situation by the student. Relationships are independent of the goals of the agent, but can combine with the goals to determine fortunes-of-others emotions that may arise. For example, suppose that Steve believes a student to be distressed about forgetting a particular task. If Steve is in a *friendship* relationship with the student he might feel *sorry-for* her. If he is in an *animosity* relationship with her (which could be useful for modeling competition), he might *gloat* over her misfortunes. In both cases the argument can be made that Steve is exhibiting not only care about what the student does, but also a rudimentary form of care about the student herself.

Fear and *hope* over prospective future events—these are emotions which are also based on an agent's goals—must be handled somewhat differently. Since these emotions may later be resolved (i.e., with satisfaction, fears-confirmed, relief, or disappointment), the internal representation of the matched situation must remain active. With a cautious Steve, for example, there might be both a recurring hope, and a recurring fear with respect to an accident happening to a student, subsequent to training. In this case each instance of student caution would raise the threshold which controls whether or not a *rumination* occurrence (implemented as a cyclic, self-generating, event) actually leads to an instance of *fear* on Steve's part. Similarly each instance of sloppiness, leading to a simulation accident (or potential accident), would lead to a reduced threshold for activation of *fear*. With identical structure, but in a contrasting manner, ruminations leading to *hope* that an accident will not occur would take the same form: the more the student exhibits caution, the more *hope* will tend to arise because of a lowered threshold for activation; the more the student exhibits sloppiness the less *hope* will tend to arise because of a raised threshold.

Example Principles for Steve. Like his goals, Steve's principles would also help to determine the make-up of his personality. Situations that arise in the simulated world can be appraised by Steve in terms of their effects as events (e.g., looking only at *what happened*) relevant to his goals, but can also, in some cases, be appraised as perceived accountable actions of some observed agent (e.g., by making a determination about who is to take credit, or blame, for the situation coming about). In still other cases one situation can be appraised as being simultaneously relevant to both an agent's goals and the agent's principles. The following examples illustrate this difference between principles and goals:

- **Principle 1: Student should attend to me when I am talking with them.** For example, we want Steve to show annoyance when the student is not paying attention.
  Example situation: (a) Steve is giving an explanation about why the cut-out valve must be opened when starting the compressor, and (b) Steve, and the cut-out valve, are not in the student's field of vision, i.e., the student is looking elsewhere]. Note that these constraints are the same as with the parallel goal above, but here Steve's concerns have a different focus. That Steve could be wrong about the student paying attention (e.g., when the student is visualizing the problem internally) is not something we worry about because people are often wrong in their perceptions as well; wrong or right, it should still be clear to the student that Steve *cares*.
- **Principle 2: Student should be cautious when it is appropriate to do so.** For example, we want Steve to express admiration for the quality of being careful with the expensive equipment, or reproach when a student is not cautious.
  Example situation: (a)–(d) (from goal 1), then later the student repeats the compressor start-up sequence and then either (e) fails to open the cut-out valve before attempting to start the compressor, or (f) remembers to open the cut-off valve. In contrast to the event-based emotion detailed above, here Steve's focus is on the blameworthiness of the student forgetting to open the valve, or the praiseworthiness of remembering.
- **Principle 3: I should be patient with the user.** For example, we want Steve to get angry with a student (serving to get her attention), but then feel shame or remorse about losing his temper with her (serving to assuage bad feeling).
  Example situation: As a result of Goal 4, and Principle 2 above, Steve gets angry at the student (where *anger* is the result of the student's blameworthy

action thwarting one of Steve's goals), yielding, (1) Steve gets angry, and (2) the anger is directed at the student.

- **Principle 4: I should tutor my students well enough that they make adequate progress on the domain tasks.** For example, we want Steve to feel shame, or remorse, when his students fail to show good progress.

  Example situation: (a) a student has established a benchmark time for successfully completing the pre-start procedure for the compressor although it is below competency level, (b) the student fails to improve on this time in three successive attempts.

Emotion Generation in Steve. Although it is not possible to cover the many details that will go into a rich, plausible, emotion model for Steve, the following touch on a few salient points not covered in the preceding examples. Because Steve's emotion states are based on antecedents, it is possible for him to give rich explanations for why he feels the way he does. These in themselves can be useful pedagogical tools: One emotion state may be the result of many different goals, principles, and a large collection of intensity values. The student might, for example, be motivated to ask Steve what makes him happy, or angry. The explanation can serve to inform the user that Steve cares about the student's progress, wants the user to learn safety rules, and so forth.

Agents such as Steve can have multiple, and even conflicting, goals and principles, just as people do (e.g., he might be simultaneously experiencing *hope* that the user will not have an accident subsequent to training, based on instances of caution, and *fear* that the user will have an accident, based on instances of sloppiness). In designing solutions to tutoring-interaction problems it is possible to come up with several, possibly conflicting, approaches. For example, Steve might take on different personalities for different students giving him such personality characteristics as sanguine, melancholy, supportive, competitive, warm, formal, etc., yielding a wide array of different types to use for instruction, engagement, humor, and the like. Moreover, by design, the emotion model supports having more than one agent at a time so it is possible to have more than one Steve agent simultaneously interacting with the student, yielding, e.g., "good cop / bad cop," a chorus of approval, or agents with interests in different, albeit equally important, aspects of the domain.

Although not likely to be stressed in the first pass of this work, interesting, yet cohesive, dynamic changes in the ways Steve appraises the world can be made, by using emotion theory. For example, a negative emotion might lead Steve to have "self-directed attributions of negative worth." This in turn can be expressed as a change in the thresholds for variables used in the match process, putting him in a bad mood, or making it easier for him to be saddened, and harder for him to feel happy. Such a technique would allow us to support a pedagogical model that includes Steve becoming "depressed" over a student's continual poor attention, which in turn is consistent with fostering the belief that Steve and the student are both in the learning process together.

4.2 Emotion Intensity in Steve

In generating emotions, it is critical to assign them intensities that is commensurate with the situation in which they will be expressed. The following examples illustrate the two most important (from a full set of twenty-two) variables used in AR emotion intensity calculations. (For a full exposition see [8].)

In general, there are two major variables that contribute to emotion intensity. There are correlates for both principle-based emotions (e.g., *pride*), and goal-based emotions (e.g., satisfaction). The first of these, *simulation-event* variables, measure those factors which are external to any particular agent and might simultaneously, and differentially, affect more than one agent at the same time. An example of this might be the *number of parts damaged* when a compressor overheats. For example, consider that Steve has the following goals:

- **High Level Goal: Do not allow students to damage the (virtual) equipment.**
- **(Steve) Goal 1: Teach the student to check the oil level before starting the compressor (inherits from High Level Goal).**

Example situation: (a) compressor overheats and parts are damaged, and (b) history does not show an instance of the student checking the oil level.

In this case, the number of compressor parts which are damaged might affect the modeled experience of failure on Steve's part. The greater the number of damaged parts, the greater the failure. Now consider that the student has the following goals and principles (see Affective User Modeling section, below):

- **(Student) Goal 1: Do not fail on any tasks that the tutor gives me to do.**
- **Principle 1: It is wrong to break the virtual equipment.**
- **Principle 2: Steve should teach me well enough that I do not end up breaking the equipment.**

Simultaneously, the number of compressor parts which are damaged might also affect a student, Sarah, with respect to the above goal: she might be disappointed that she damaged the compressor; she might be ashamed of having damaged the compressor; she might be angry at Steve for failing to teach her how to avoid damaging the compressor. In each case, the extent of damage to the compressor is likely to be directly proportional to the degree of intensity in the negatively valenced emotions.

By contrast, the *stable disposition* variables are those which determine the *importance* of a particular goal, or principle, to an agent. These values are internal, and changes in them do not affect any other agents. For example, one Steve might be very concerned about safety, and damage to the equipment, whereas another Steve might be more concerned with exposing the student to explanations. For Safety-Steve, the *importance* of the equipment being damaged might be quite high, whereas for Explanation-Steve the importance might be quite low (or even help him to achieve a goal through affording him a chance to give an explanation). Since these are internal variables, and help to give the agents their own dispositional personalities, changes in the importance values for one agent will not affect another.

5 Affective User Modeling

So far, we have considered how affective reasoning can be used to generate emotive communication in pedagogical agents. The complementary functionality required of agents is the ability to model students' emotive states. We now turn to affective student modeling and illustrate its operation with examples drawn from a second pedagogical agent, Herman the Bug [10], and the learning environment he inhabits, Design-A-Plant (Figure 2), developed at North Carolina State University's Multimedia Laboratory.

Design-A-Plant is a knowledge-based learning environment project to investigate interactive problem-solving with animated pedagogical agents within the design-centered learning paradigm. With Design-A-Plant, students learn about botanical anatomy and physiology by graphically assembling customized plants that can thrive in specified environmental conditions. The Design-A-Plant work focuses on several intertwined aspects of introducing lifelike pedagogical agents into learning environments: dynamically sequencing the explanatory behaviors of animated pedagogical agents [20], user modeling and artifact-based task modeling [12], focusing learners' problem-solving activities [14], and increasing the believability of animated pedagogical agents [13]. Design-A-Plant's agent, Herman, performs a variety of lifelike, entertaining actions as it supplies advice to students when they solve design problems.

5.1 Overview of Affective User Modeling Architecture

The general idea behind the model we are investigating is that AR agents have relatively reusable structures for appraising the world. The same structures that give them their own dispositions can be built and maintained for other agents as well. The vehicle for attempting to model some rudimentary form of the affective state of users is based on the following insights:

- AR agents have a dispositional component which determines how they appraise the world. This frame-based structure allows them to interpret situations that arise in ways that may give rise to emotion responses.
- Because agents have emotions about the fortunes of other agents, it is necessary for them to also maintain similar structures for these other agents. For example, if an agent's team wins he will be happy for himself, but might gloat over an agent rooting for the other team. To effect this the agent's own appraisal structure must result in an appraisal of an achieved goal from the situation, but the agent's own structure of the *presumed* goals of the second agent must result in an appraisal of a blocked goal from that same situation.
- Agents, who already keep these concerns-of-others structures, can maintain them for users as well.

A perfect structure of each individual user's goals, principles, and preferences, (e.g., a perfect affective user model, albeit begging the question of updating it correctly) would allow a great many correct inferences to be made about their emotion responses to the situations that arise while using the system. Since such a structure is not possible, it is necessary for us to use multiple types of inference in an attempt to approximate it using the following mechanisms:

1. *Inquiry:* Ask the user. In work with the AR, it appears to be true that users are *motivated* to express themselves to a computer agent who appears to have some understanding of how they feel.
2. *Stereotypes:* Use other known information to make assumptions about user *types.* Some users like to win, some like to have fun, some prefer to follow the rules, some are impatient. These qualities will tend to remain constant across tasks and domains.
3. *Context:* Use context information. For example, a user who has just repeatedly failed is likely to feel bad, whereas one who has been successful is likely to feel good.
4. *Affective Stereotypes:* Infer how *most users* would feel. The more user models extant, the stronger a prototype we have for a typical user.
5. *Self-Inspection:* If all else fails, infer what the agent would feel if it happened to him. Agents have affective "lives" too. One can always ask how they themselves would feel, and make the assumption that the user would feel that way too, i.e., the agent would filter the situation through its own appraisal mechanism and examine the resulting emotions which do, or do not, arise.

In general, our hypothesis is that we can be at least minimally effective at filling in missing information when working from a structure that specifies (a) what is *likely to be true* of the antecedents of user emotion, and (b) gives us a high-level understanding of different plausible affective user models, in a relatively comprehensive (albeit purely descriptive) model of human emotion. In other words, having a rigorously defined model of what user affect we are looking for helps us to map system events, and responses from the user to direct queries, effectively.

5.2 Examples of Student Goals and Principles

In this section we present a few brief examples of what we might want to model on behalf of the student, based on observations of seventh graders interacting with the Design-A-Plant software.

Example Student Goals

- **Goal 1: I want to do well on each task in the learning environment.**
This is reflected in wanting always to get the right answer by selecting the correct component (roots, stems, and leaves) for the current environment. Sample situation: (a) student, or tutoring sequence, selects component (e.g., [stem, root, leaves]). (b) *correct-value* is bound to the correct value for chosen

component (e.g., type of stem). (c) *selected-value* is bound to the student-selected value for the chosen component. (d) components match, or (e) components do not match.

Sample intensity variables:

1. *Importance to student:* This is *high* by default, but this can be modified to fit individual personalities.
2. *Effort*: This increases as the student spends more time trying to solve this particular set of tasks.
3. *Anxiety-Invincibility:* If the student has had a pattern of recent success, then invincibility is increased. If a student has had a pattern of recent failures, then anxiety is increased.
4. *Arousal:* The default is *normal*. This can be modified to fit individual student profiles, and context. Context heuristics can include rules like the following: (1) If the student is performing normally, then, all other things being equal, the student is aroused at the *normal* level. If the student is either having an above-average (for the student) success rate, or a below average success rate then *arousal* is increased proportionally. (2) If student responses show little wall-clock dead time then student engagement is assumed to be higher and higher engagement affects arousal similarly.

– **Goal 2: I want to be entertained.**
   The developers of Design-A-Plant believe there to be a very strong "immediate gratification" element in student interaction with the learning environments. In general there are good mechanisms for providing what is likely to be entertaining (based on the long history of computer games, and entertainment systems of varied types), and general ad hoc heuristics for measuring entertainment levels (e.g., by market share). What we do *not* have is a method for agents to assess this dynamically as the interaction is taking place.
   Affective user modeling can address this in two ways: (1) It may be provably true that interesting interactive agents are more entertaining than static, or impoverished, agents are, or systems that operate without interactive agents. Agents with rich affective lives of their own can be extremely interesting to interact with. (2) Through observation we have some clues as to what is entertaining. Having an agent that makes inferences about student state by tracking situations believed to be entertaining may help the overall timing of the system. For example, we might believe that events we have tagged as, *funny, visual, with audio appeal, exhibiting cartoon effects* may be entertaining. A learning environment may call on resources to effect its limited arsenal of entertaining actions at more appropriate times (e.g., to cheer up a student perceived to be distressed).

– **Goal 3: I want to learn the material.**
   Through built-in testing procedures it is possible to effect an *estimate* of the *student's* assessment of how well they learned the material.

Example Student Principles. Principles are less well defined at this stage, but here are some that are based on observation with students of Design-A-Plant. These are *sample* principles, and it is clear that different students will hold different subsets of these, and others, in practice.

- **Principle 1: It is good to work cautiously and avoid making any errors.**
  Students who hold this principle will feel (some form of) *shame* when they make a mistake, and will be *proud* of themselves if they complete a set of tasks relatively error-free. This can be important, because for students who hold this to be true, it is inappropriate to praise them for, e.g., getting seven out of ten correct. In other words, it might be better to agree that it was sloppy work, and then suggest that if the student slows down, it might be possible to get them all right—it is sometimes easier to help a student achieve their own standards than it is to get them to change those standards.
  The principle might be adopted, for example, for students who respond in a particular way to simple questions (e.g., Herman: "If someone works fast, and gets seven out of ten right, is this good or bad?"; Student: "Bad"; Herman, "O.K. – I'll remember that. Thanks!")
  The general idea is that while most everyone would agree that it is important to address the situation when a student is frustrated, this is not always easy to assess: seven out of ten for one student means frustration, while for another it means success.
- **Principle 2: It is right to have fun with the system.**
  Most students would fall in this category, rather than the one above. They would not like to see themselves get too serious about the system.
- **Principle 3: It is right to be successful solving problems.**
  Not only might students be happy over achieving the goals of problem solving, they might also be *proud* of themselves for performing an admirable action in doing so.
- **Principle 4: Long explanations (e.g., of photosynthesis) at inappropriate times (and possibly all times are inappropriate) are wrong and should not be inflicted on me.**
  Herman might benefit from knowing that giving long explanations might make the student angry, even though he might still give the explanation for other reasons. It might also be possible for Herman to discriminate between a typical student in a typical state, and one that is particularly unreceptive to a long explanation: it would not be wise to give a long explanation to a student already perceived to be in an angry or frustrated state.

Inference with Intensity Variables. Simulation events in the AR are a frame representation of the salient points of situations that arise in the course of interaction with the user. In learning environments these would take a theoretically equivalent form, regardless of the actual implementation. Agents maintain internal representations of what they believe to be true of the appraisal mechanisms (e.g.,the *dispositions*) of the students, and call on these for interpreting the supposed effect of simulation events on a student. For example, if an agent believes that student Sarah has a strong desire (e.g., the stable-disposition variable *importance* is high) to succeed on Task A, but that she does not care much about Task B, then the agent might feel *pity* for Sarah if she fails on Task A, or *happy-for* her if she succeeds, but would have no *fortunes-of-other* response for Sarah's relative success, or lack thereof, with Task B.

As part of the internal models that agents keep of other agents, including the student, they may update *mood variables* dynamically, which tend to affect the thresholds at which emotions arise. Therefore, if an agent believed Sarah to be feeling particularly *anxious*, he might, after all, feel *pity* for Sarah's failure on Task B, because failure on even a relatively unimportant (to her) task such as Task B might be perceived as surpassing the lowered threshold for activation of the distress emotion. Similarly, if the agent believed Sarah to be feeling particularly *invincible* (e.g., after a string of grand successes), he might not believe Sarah to be distressed about failure on the important (to her) Task A, and hence might not feel *pity* for her.

6 Concluding Remarks

This paper has provided a brief overview of how an affective reasoning framework can be introduced into lifelike pedagogical agents. Our objective has been to sketch a model of how an an agent might express emotions and evaluate the effects of these emotions on student learning. The required affective reasoning naturally decomposes into two areas: emotional responsiveness of the tutor itself, and affective user modeling. We have illustrated some of the issues involved in these two areas using two extant agents, Steve and Herman the Bug.

The next steps in integrating affective reasoning into lifelike pedagogical agents are suggested by the following research agenda. First, techniques must be created to perform comparisons of an agent's goals and principles against simulation events and student actions to identify appropriate triggering conditions for emotions. A promising starting place for this work is example goals and principles described in this paper. Second, mechanisms need to be created for converting these triggering conditions into appropriate emotional states. Conversion processes are likely to be complex and, therefore, non-trivial to design. Finally, mechanisms need to be created for expressing the internal emotive states of agents to user. We have seen some progress in the latter area [15] and will be pursuing the others activities in our future work.

7 Acknowledgments

We would like to thank Lewis Johnson and Gary Stelling for their valuable comments throughout the course of this work. The authors also gratefully acknowledge Charles Callaway for his assistance in preparing in the manuscript and Bradford Mott for comments on an earlier draft of this paper. Support for this work was provided by the Office of Naval Research under grant N00014-95-C-0179; an internal research and development grant from the USC Information Sciences Institute; the National Science Foundation under grants CDA-9720395 (Learning and Intelligent Systems Initiative) and IRI-9701503 (CAREER Award Program); the North Carolina State University IntelliMedia Initiative; and an industrial gift from Novell.

References

1. Sassine Abou-Jaoude and Claude Frasson. Emotion computing in competitve learning environments. In *Working Notes of the ITS '98 Workshop on Pedagogical Agents*, pages 33–39, San Antonio, Texas, 1998.
2. Elisabeth André, Thomas Rist, and Jochen Müller. Integrating reactive and scripted behaviors in a life-like presentation agent. In *Proceedings of the Second International Conference on Autonomous Agents*, pages 261–268. Minneapolis, 1998.
3. Angel de Vicente and Helen Pain. Motivation diagnosis in intelligent tutoring systems. In *Proceedings of the Fourth International Conference on Intelligent Tutoring Systems*, pages 86–95, San Antonio, Texas, 1998.
4. Clark Elliott. *The Affective Reasoner: A Process Model of Emotions in a Multi-agent System*. PhD thesis, Northwestern University, May 1992. The Institute for the Learning Sciences, Technical Report No. 32.
5. Clark Elliott. I picked up catapia and other stories: A multimodal approach to expressivity for "emotionally intelligent" agents. In *Proceedings of the First International Conference on Autonomous Agents*, pages 451–457, 1997.
6. Clark Elliott and Jack Brzezinski. Autonomous agents as synthetic characters. *AI Magazine*, 19(2), 1998.
7. Clark Elliott and Andrew Ortony. Point of view: Reasoning about the concerns of others. In *Proceedings of the Fourteenth Annual Conference of the Cognitive Science Society*, pages 809–814, Bloomington, IN, August 1992. Cognitive Science Society.
8. Clark Elliott and Greg Siegle. Variables influencing the intensity of simulated affective states. In *AAAI technical report SS-93-05 for the Spring Symposium on Reasoning about Mental States: Formal Theories and Applications*, pages 58–67. American Association for Artificial Intelligence, 1993. Stanford University, March 23-25, Palo Alto, CA.
9. Pentti Hietala and Timo Niemirepo. The competence of learning companion agents. *International Journal of Artificial Intelligence in Education*, 1998.
10. James Lester, Brian Stone, and Gary Stelling. Lifelike pedagogical agents for mixed-initiative problem solving in constructivist learning environments. *User Modeling and User-Adapted Interaction*, 1999. In press.
11. James C. Lester, Sharolyn A. Converse, Susan E. Kahler, S. Todd Barlow, Brian A. Stone, and Ravinder Bhogal. The persona effect: Affective impact of animated pedagogical agents. In *Proceedings of CHI'97 (Human Factors in Computing Systems)*, pages 359–366, Atlanta, 1997.
12. James C. Lester, Patrick J. FitzGerald, and Brian A. Stone. The pedagogical design studio: Exploiting artifact-based task models for constructivist learning. In *Proceedings of the Third International Conference on Intelligent User Interfaces*, pages 155–162, Orlando, Florida, 1997.

13. James C. Lester and Brian A. Stone. Increasing believability in animated pedagogical agents. In *Proceedings of the First International Conference on Autonomous Agents*, pages 16–21, Marina del Rey, CA, 1997. ACM Press.
14. James C. Lester, Brian A. Stone, Michael A. O'Leary, and Robert B. Stevenson. Focusing problem solving in design-centered learning environments. In *Proceedings of the Third International Conference on Intelligent Tutoring Systems*, pages 475–483, Montreal, 1996.
15. James C. Lester, Stuart G. Towns, and Patrick J. FitzGerald. Achieving affective impact: Visual emotive communication in lifelike pedagogical agents. *International Journal of Artificial Intelligence in Education*, 1999. In press.
16. Andrew Ortony, Gerald L. Clore, and Allan Collins. *The Cognitive Structure of Emotions*. Cambridge University Press, 1988.
17. Ana Paiva and Isabelle Machado. Vincent, an autonomous pedagogical agent for on-the-job training. In *Proceedings of the Fourth International Conference on Intelligent Tutoring Systems*, pages 584–593, San Antonio, Texas, 1998.
18. Rosalind W. Picard. *Affective Computing*. MIT Press, 1997.
19. Jeff Rickel and W. Lewis Johnson. Animated agents for procedural training in virtual reality: Perception, cognition, and motor control. *Applied Artificial Intelligence*, 1998. Forthcoming.
20. Brian A. Stone and James C. Lester. Dynamically sequencing an animated pedagogical agent. In *Proceedings of the Thirteenth National Conference on Artificial Intelligence*, pages 424–431, Portland, Oregon, 1996.
21. Stuart Towns, Charles Callaway, Jennifer Voerman, and James Lester. Coherent gestures, locomotion, and speech in life-like pedagogical agents. In *Proceedings of the Fourth International Conference on Intelligent User Interfaces*, pages 13–20, San Francisco, 1998.
22. Juan D. Velasquez. Modeling emotions and other motivations in synthetic agents. In *AAAI-97: Proceedings of the Fourteenth National Conference on Artificial Intelligence*, pages 10–15, 1997.

OBDD-based Universal Planning: Specifying and Solving Planning Problems for Synchronized Agents in Non-deterministic Domains

Rune M. Jensen and Manuela M. Veloso

Computer Science Department
Carnegie Mellon University
Pittsburgh, PA 15213
{runej,mmv}@cs.cmu.edu

Abstract. Recently model checking representation and search techniques were shown to be efficiently applicable to planning, in particular to non-deterministic planning. Such planning approaches use Ordered Binary Decision Diagrams (OBDDs) to encode a planning domain as a non-deterministic finite automaton (NFA) and then apply fast algorithms from model checking to search for a solution. OBDDs can effectively scale and can provide universal plans for complex planning domains. We are particularly interested in addressing the complexities arising in non-deterministic, multi-agent domains. In this chapter, we present UMOP,[1] a new universal OBDD-based planning framework for non-deterministic, multi-agent domains, which is also applicable to deterministic single-agent domains as a special case. We introduce a new planning domain description language, *NADL*,[2] to specify non-deterministic multi-agent domains. The language contributes the explicit definition of controllable agents and uncontrollable environment agents. We describe the syntax and semantics of *NADL* and show how to build an efficient OBDD-based representation of an *NADL* description. The UMOP planning system uses *NADL* and different OBDD-based universal planning algorithms. It includes the previously developed strong and strong cyclic planning algorithms [9, 10]. In addition, we introduce our new optimistic planning algorithm, which relaxes optimality guarantees and generates plausible universal plans in some domains where no strong or strong cyclic solution exist. We present empirical results from domains ranging from deterministic and single-agent with no environment actions to non-deterministic and multi-agent with complex environment actions. UMOP is shown to be a rich and efficient planning system.

1 Introduction

Classical planning is a broad area of research which involves the automatic generation of the appropriate choices of actions to traverse a state space to achieve

---

[1] UMOP stands for Universal Multi-agent OBDD-based Planner.
[2] *NADL* stands for Non-deterministic Agent Domain Language.

specific goal states. A variety of different algorithms have been developed to address the state-action representation and the search for action selection.

Traditionally these algorithms have been classified according to their search space representation as either state-space planners (e.g., PRODIGY, [41]) or plan-space planners (e.g., UCPOP, [35]).

A new research trend has been to develop new encodings of planning problems in order to adopt efficient algorithms from other research areas, leading to significant developments in planning algorithms, as surveyed in [43]. This class of planning algorithms includes GRAPHPLAN [3], which uses a flow-graph encoding to constrain the search and SATPLAN [29], which encodes the planning problem as a satisfiability problem and uses fast model satisfaction algorithms to find a solution.

Recently, another new planner MBP [8] was introduced that encodes a planning domain as a non-deterministic finite automaton (NFA) represented by an Ordered Binary Decision Diagram (OBDD) [5]. In contrast to the previous algorithms, MBP effectively extends to non-deterministic domains producing universal plans as robust solutions. Due to the scalability of the underlying model checking representation and search techniques, it can be shown to be a very efficient non-deterministic planner [9, 10].

One of our main research objectives is to develop planning systems suitable for planning in uncertain, single, or multi-agent environments [25, 42, 39]. The universal planning approach, as originally developed [38], is appealing for this type of environments. A universal plan is a set of state-action rules that aim at covering the possible multiple situations in the non-deterministic environment. A universal plan is executed by interleaving the selection of an action in the plan and observing the resulting effects in the world. Universal planning resembles the outcome of reinforcement learning [40], in that the state-action model captures the uncertainty of the world. Universal planning is a precursor approach,[3] where all planning is done prior to execution, building upon the assumption that a non-deterministic model can be acquired, and leading therefore to a sound and complete planning approach.

However, universal planning has been criticized (e.g., [22]), due to a potential exponential growth of the universal plan size with the number of propositions defining a domain state. An important contribution of MBP is thus the use of OBDDs to represent universal plans. In the worst case, this representation may also grow exponential with the number of domain propositions, but because OBDDs are very compact representations of boolean functions, this is often not the case for domains with a regular structure [9]. Therefore, OBDD-based planning seems to be a promising approach to universal planning.

MBP specifies a planning domain in the action description language $\mathcal{AR}$ [23] and translates it to a corresponding NFA, hence limited to planning problems with finite state spaces. The transition relation of the automaton is encoded as an OBDD, which allows for the use of model checking parallel breadth-first

---

[3] The term *precursor* originates from [13] in contrast to *recurrent* approaches which replan to recover from execution failures.

search. MBP includes two algorithms for universal planning. The *strong planning* algorithm tries to generate a plan that is guaranteed to achieve the goal for all of the possible outcomes of the non-deterministic actions. If no such strong solution exists, the algorithm fails. The *strong cyclic planning* algorithm returns a strong solution, if one exists, or otherwise tries to generate a plan that may contain loops but is guaranteed to achieve the goal, given that all cyclic executions eventually terminate. If no such strong cyclic solution exists, the strong cyclic planning algorithm fails.

In this chapter, we present our OBDD-based planning system, UMOP, which uses a new OBDD-based encoding, generates universal plans in multi-agent non-deterministic domains, and includes a new "optimistic" planning algorithm (UMOP stands for Universal Multi-agent OBDD-based Planner).

Our overall approach for designing an OBDD-based planner is similar to the approach developed in [9, 10]. Our main contribution is an efficient encoding of a new front end domain description language, *NADL* (*NADL* stands for Non-deterministic Agent Domain Language.). *NADL* has more resemblance with previous planning languages than the action description language $\mathcal{AR}$ currently used by MBP. It has powerful action descriptions that can perform arithmetic operations on numerical domain variables. Domains comprised of synchronized agents can be modelled by introducing concurrent actions based on a multi-agent decomposition of the domain.

In addition, *NADL* introduces a separate and explicit environment model defined as a set of *uncontrollable* agents, i.e., agents whose actions cannot be a part of the generated plan. *NADL* has been carefully designed to allow for efficient OBDD-encoding. Thus, in contrast to MBP, UMOP can generate a partitioned transition relation representation of the NFA, which is known from model checking to scale up well [6, 37]. Our empirical experiments suggest that this is also the case for UMOP.

UMOP includes the previously developed algorithms for OBDD-based universal planning. In addition, we introduce a new "optimistic" planning algorithm, which relaxes optimality guarantees and generates plausible universal plans in some domains where no strong or strong cyclic solution exists.

The chapter is organized as follows. Section 2 gives a brief overview of OBDDs and may be skipped by readers already familiar with the subject. Section 3 introduces *NADL*, shows how to encode a planning problem, and formally describes the syntax and semantics of this description language in terms of an NFA. We also discuss the properties of the language based on an example and argue for our design choices. Section 4 presents the OBDD representation of *NADL* domain descriptions. Section 5 describes the different algorithms that have been used for OBDD-based planning and introduces our optimistic planning algorithm. Section 6 presents empirical results in several planning domains, ranging from single-agent and deterministic ones to multi-agent and non-deterministic ones. We experiment with previously used domains and introduce two new ones, namely a power plant and a soccer domain, as non-deterministic multi-agent planning problems. Section 7 discusses previous approaches to planning in non-deterministic domains. Finally, Section 8 draws conclusions and discusses directions for future work.

2 Introduction to OBDDs

An Ordered Binary Decision Diagram [5] is a canonical representation of a boolean function with n linear ordered arguments $x_1, x_2, ..., x_n$.

An OBDD is a rooted, directed acyclic graph with one or two terminal nodes of out-degree zero labeled 1 or 0, and a set of variable nodes u of out-degree two. The two outgoing edges are given by the functions $high(u)$ and $low(u)$ (drawn as solid and dotted arrows). Each variable node is associated with a propositional variable in the boolean function the OBDD represents. The graph is ordered in the sense that all paths in the graph respect the ordering of the variables.

An OBDD representing the function $f(x_1, x_2) = x_1 \wedge x_2$ is shown in Figure 1. Given an assignment of the arguments x_1 and x_2, the value of f is determined by a path starting at the root node and iteratively following the high edge, if the associated variable is true, and the low edge, if the associated variable is false. The value of f is *True* if the label of the reached terminal node is 1; otherwise it is *False*.

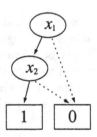

Fig. 1. An OBDD representing the function $f(x_1, x_2) = x_1 \wedge x_2$. High (true) and low (false) edges are drawn solid and dotted, respectively.

An OBBD graph is reduced so that no two distinct nodes u and v have the same variable name and low and high successors (Figure 2(a)), and no variable node u has identical low and high successors (Figure 2(b)).

The OBDD representation has two major advantages: First, it is an efficient representation of boolean functions because the number of nodes often is much smaller than the number of truth assignments of the variables. The number of nodes can grow exponential with the number of variables, but most commonly encountered functions have a reasonable representation [5]. Second, any operation on two OBDDs, corresponding to a boolean operation on the functions they represent, has a low complexity bounded by the product of their node counts. A disadvantage of OBDDs is that the size of an OBDD representing some function is very dependent on the ordering of the variables. To find an optimal variable

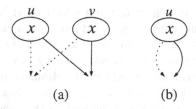

Fig. 2. Reductions of OBDDs. (a): nodes associated to the same variable with equal low and high successors will be converted to a single node. (b): nodes causing redundant tests on a variable, are eliminated.

ordering is a co-NP-complete problem in itself, but fortunately a good heuristic is to locate dependent variables near each other in the ordering [7].

OBDDs have been successfully applied to model checking. In model checking the behavior of a system is modelled by a finite state automaton with a transition relation represented as an OBDD. Desirable properties of the system is checked by analyzing the state space of the system by means of OBDD manipulations.

As introduced in [9, 10], a similar approach can be used for a non-deterministic planning problem. Given an NFA representation of the planning domain with the transition relation represented as an OBDD, the algorithms used to verify CTL properties in model checking [11, 34] can be used to find a universal plan solving the planning problem.

3 NADL

In this section, we first discuss the properties of *NADL* based on an informal definition of the language and a domain encoding example. We then describe the formal syntax and semantics of *NADL*.

An *NADL* domain description consists of: a definition of *state variables*, a description of *system* and *environment agents*, and a specification of an *initial* and *goal conditions*.

The set of state variable assignments defines the state space of the domain. An agent's description is a set of *actions*. The agents change the state of the world by performing actions, which are assumed to be executed synchronously and to have a fixed and equal duration. At each step, all of the agents perform exactly one action, and the resulting action tuple is a *joint action*. The system agents model the behavior of the agents controllable by the planner, while the environment agents model the uncontrollable world. A valid domain description requires that the system and environment agents constrain a disjoint set of variables.

An action has three parts: a set of *state variables*, a *precondition* formula, and an *effect* formula. Intuitively the action takes responsibility of constraining the values of the set of state variables in the next state. It further has exclusive access to these variables during execution. In order for the action to be applicable, the precondition formula must be satisfied in the current state. The effect of the action is defined by the effect formula which must be satisfied in the next state. To allow conditional effects, the effect expression can refer to both current and next state variables, which need to be a part of the set of variables of the action. All next state variables not constrained by any action in a joint action maintain their value. Furthermore only joint actions containing a set of actions with consistent effects and a disjoint set of state variable sets are allowed. System and environment agents must be independent in the sense that the two sets of variables, their actions constrain, are disjoint.

The initial and goal conditions are formulas that must be satisfied in the initial state and the final state, respectively.

There are two causes for non-determinism in *NADL* domains: (1) actions not restricting all their constrained variables to a specific value in the next state, and (2) the non-deterministic selection of environment actions.

A simple example of an *NADL* domain description is shown in Figure 3.[4] The domain describes a planning problem for Schoppers' (1987) robot-baby domain. The domain has two state variables: a numerical one, *pos*, with range $\{0, 1, 2, 3\}$ and a propositional one, *robot_works*. The robot is the only system agent and it has two actions *Lift-Block* and *Lower-Block*. The baby is the only environment agent and it has one action *Hit-Robot*. Because each agent must perform exactly one action at each step, there are two joint actions (*Lift-Block,Hit-Robot*) and (*Lower-Block,Hit-Robot*).

Initially the robot is assumed to hold a block at position 0, and its task is to lift it up to position 3. The *Lift-Block* (and *Lower-Block*) action has a conditional effect described by an if-then-else operator: if *robot_works* is true, *Lift-Block* increases the block position with one, otherwise the block position is unchanged.

Initially *robot_works* is assumed to be true, but it can be made false by the baby. The baby's action *Hit-Robot* is non-deterministic, as it only constrains *robot_works* by the effect expression $\neg robot\_works \Rightarrow \neg robot\_works'$. Thus, when *robot_works* is true in the current state, the effect expression of *Hit-Robot* does not apply, and *robot_works* can either be true or false in the next state. On the other hand, if *robot_works* is false in the current state, *Hit-Robot* keeps it false in the next state. The *Hit-Robot* models an uncontrollable environment, in this case a baby, by its effects on *robot_works*. In the example above, *robot_works* stays false when it, at some point, has become false, reflecting that the robot cannot spontaneously be fixed by a hit of the baby.

An NFA representing the domain is shown in Figure 4. The calculation of the next state value of *pos* in the *Lift-Block* action shows that numerical variables can be updated by an arithmetic expression on the current state variables. The update expression of *pos* and the use of the if-then-else operator further demonstrate the advantage of using explicit references to current state and next state variables in effect expressions. *NADL* does not restrict the representation

---

[4] Unquoted and quoted variables refer to the current and next state, respectively. Another notation like v_t and v_{t+1} could have been used. We have chosen the quote notation because it is the common notation in model checking.

```
variables
  nat(4) pos
  bool robot_works
system
  agt: Robot
    Lift-Block
      con: pos
      pre: pos < 3
      eff:  robot_works → pos' = pos + 1, pos' = pos
    Lower-Block
      con: pos
      pre: pos > 0
      eff:  robot_works → pos' = pos - 1, pos' = pos
environment
  agt: Baby
    Hit-Robot
      con: robot_works
      pre: true
      eff:  ¬robot_works ⇒ ¬robot_works'
initially
  pos = 0 ∧ robot_works
goal
  pos = 3
```

Fig. 3. An *NADL* domain description.

by enforcing a structure separating current state and next state expressions. The if-then-else operator has been added to support complex, conditional effects that often are efficiently and naturally represented as a set of nested if-then-else operators.

The explicit representation of constrained state variables enables any non-deterministic or deterministic effect of an action to be represented, as the constrained variables can be assigned to any value in the next state that satisfies the effect formula. It further turns out to have a clear intuitive meaning as the action takes the "responsibility" of specifying the values of the constrained variables in the next state.

Compared to the action description language $\mathcal{A}$ and $\mathcal{AR}$ [20, 23] that are the only prior languages used for OBDD-based planning [14, 9, 10, 8], *NADL* introduces an explicit environment model, a multi-agent decomposition and numerical state variables. It can further be shown that *NADL* can be used to model any domain that can be modelled with $\mathcal{AR}$ (see Appendix A).

The concurrent actions in *NADL* are assumed to be synchronously executed and to have fixed and equal duration. A general representation allowing partially overlapping actions and actions with different durations has been avoided, as it requires more complex temporal planning (see e.g., O-PLAN or PARCPLAN,

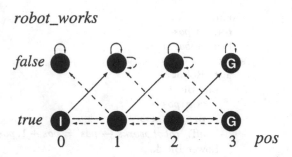

robot_works

Fig. 4. The NFA of the robot-baby domain (see Figure 3). There are two state variables: a propositional state variable *robot_works* and a numerical state variable *pos* with range $\{0, 1, 2, 3\}$. The (*Lift-Block, Hit-Robot*) and (*Lower-Block, Hit-Robot*) joint actions are drawn with solid and dashed arrows respectively. States marked with "I" and "G" are initial and goal states.

[12, 31]). Our joint action representation has more resemblance with $\mathcal{A}_c$ and $\mathcal{C}$ [2, 24], where sets of actions are performed at each time step. In contrast to these approaches, though, we model multi-agent domains.

An important issue to address when introducing concurrent actions is synergetic effects between simultaneously executing actions [33]. A common example of destructive synergetic effects is when two or more actions require exclusive use of a single resource or when two actions have inconsistent effects like $pos' = 3$ and $pos' = 2$. In *NADL* actions cannot be performed concurrently if: 1) they have inconsistent effects, or 2) they constrain an overlapping set of state variables. The first condition is due to the fact that state knowledge is expressed in a monotonic logic which cannot represent inconsistent knowledge. The second rule addresses the problem of sharing resources. Consider for example two agents trying to drink the same glass of water. If only the first rule defined interfering actions both agents, could simultaneously empty the glass, as the effect *glass_empty* of the two actions would be consistent. With the second rule added, these actions are interfering and cannot be performed concurrently.

The current version of *NADL* only avoids destructive synergetic effects. It does not include ways of representing constructive synergetic effects between simultaneous acting agents [33]. A constructive synergetic effect is illustrated in [2], where an agent spills soup from a bowl when trying to lift it up with one hand, but not when lifting it up with both hands. In $\mathcal{C}$ and $\mathcal{A}_c$ this kind of synergetic effects can be represented by explicitly stating the effect of a compound action. A similar approach could be used in *NADL*, but is currently not supported.

3.1 Syntax

Formally, an *NADL* description is a 7-tuple $D = (SV, S, E, Act, d, I, G)$, where:

- $SV = PVar \cup NVar$ is a finite set of state variables comprised of a finite set of propositional variables, $PVar$, and a finite set of numerical variables,

NVar.
- S is a finite, nonempty set of system agents.
- E is a finite set of environment agents.
- *Act* is a set of action descriptions (c, p, e) where c is the state variables constrained by the action, p is a precondition state formula in the set *SForm* and e is an effect formula in the set *Form*. Thus $(c, p, e) \in Act \subset 2^{SV} \times SForm \times Form$. The sets *SForm* and *Form* are defined below.
- $d : Agt \to 2^{Act}$ is a function mapping agents $(Agt = S \cup E)$ to their actions. Because an action is associated to one agent, d must satisfy the following conditions:

$$\bigcup_{\alpha \in Agt} d(\alpha) = Act$$

$$\forall \alpha_1, \alpha_2 \in Agt \,.\, d(\alpha_1) \cap d(\alpha_2) = \emptyset$$

- $I \in SForm$ is the initial condition.
- $G \in SForm$ is the goal condition.

For a valid domain description, we require that actions of system agents are independent of actions of environment agents:

$$\bigcup_{\substack{e \in E \\ a \in d(c)}} c(a) \;\cap\; \bigcup_{\substack{s \in S \\ a \in d(s)}} c(a) = \emptyset,$$

where $c(a)$ is the set of constrained variables of action a. The set of formulas *Form* are constructed from the following alphabet of symbols:

- A finite set of current state v and next state v' variables, where $v \in SV$.
- The natural numbers $\mathbf{N}$.
- The arithmetic operators $+, -, /, *$ and *mod*.
- The relation operators $>, <, \leq, \geq, =$ and $\neq$.
- The boolean operators $\neg, \vee, \wedge, \Rightarrow, \Leftrightarrow$ and $\to$.
- The special symbols *true*, *false*, parenthesis and comma.

The set of arithmetic expressions is constructed from the following rules:

1. Every numerical state variable $v \in NVar$ is an arithmetic expression.
2. A natural number is an arithmetic expression.
3. If e_1 and e_2 are arithmetic expressions and $\oplus$ is an arithmetic operator, then $e_1 \oplus e_2$ is an arithmetic expression.

Finally, the set of formulas *Form* is generated by the rules:

1. *true* and *false* are formulas.
2. Propositional state variables $v \in PVar$ are formulas.
3. If e_1 and e_2 are arithmetic expressions and $\mathcal{R}$ is a relation operator then $e_1 \; \mathcal{R} \; e_2$ is a formula.
4. If f_1, f_2 and f_3 are formulas, so are $(\neg f_1)$, $(f_1 \vee f_2)$, $(f_1 \wedge f_2)$, $(f_1 \Rightarrow f_2)$, $(f_1 \Leftrightarrow f_2)$ and $(f_1 \to f_2, f_3)$.

Parenthesis have their usual meaning and operators have their usual priority and associativity with the if-then-else operator "→" given lowest priority. $SForm \subset Form$ is a subset of the formulas only referring to current state variables. These formulas are called *state formulas*.

3.2 Semantics

All of the symbols in the alphabet of formulas have their usual meaning with the if-then-else operator $f_1 \rightarrow f_2, f_3$ being an abbreviation for $(f_1 \land f_2) \lor (\neg f_1 \land f_3)$. Each numerical state variable $v \in NVar$ has a finite range $rng(v) = \{0, 1, \cdots, t_v\}$, where $t_v > 0$.

The formal semantics of a domain description $D = (SV, S, E, Act, d, I, G)$ is given in terms of an NFA M:

Definition 1 NFA. A Non-deterministic Finite Automaton is a 3-tuple, $M = (Q, \Sigma, \delta)$, where Q is the set of states, Σ is a set of input values and $\delta : Q \times \Sigma \rightarrow 2^Q$ is a next state function.

In the following construction of M we express the next state function as a transition relation. Let $\mathcal{B}$ denote the set of boolean values $\{True, False\}$. Further, let the *characteristic function* A: $B \rightarrow \mathcal{B}$ associated to a set $A \subseteq B$ be defined by: $A(x) = (x \in A)$.[5] Given an NFA M we define its *transition relation* $T \subseteq Q \times \Sigma \times Q$ as a set of triples with characteristic function $T(s, i, s') = (s' \in \delta(s, i))$. The states Q of M equals the set of all possible variable assignments $Q = (PVar \rightarrow \mathcal{B}) \times (Nvar \rightarrow \mathbf{N})$. Σ of M is the set of joint actions of system agents represented as sets. That is, $\{a_1, a_2, \cdots, a_{|S|}\} \in \Sigma$ if and only if $(a_1, a_2, \cdots, a_{|S|}) \in \prod_{\alpha \in S} d(\alpha)$, where $|S|$ denotes the number of elements in S.

To define the transition relation $T : Q \times \Sigma \times Q \rightarrow \mathcal{B}$ of M we constrain a transition relation $t : Q \times J \times Q \rightarrow \mathcal{B}$ with the joint actions J of all agents as input by existential quantification to the input Σ.

$$T(s, i, s') = \exists j \in J . i \subset j \land t(s, j, s')$$

The transition relation t is a conjunction of three relations A, F and I. Given an action $a = (c, p, e)$ and a current state s, let $P_a(s)$ denote the value of the precondition formula p of a. Similarly, given an action $a = (c, p, e)$ and a current and next state s and s', let $E_a(s, s')$ denote the value of the effect formula e of a. $A : Q \times J \times Q \rightarrow \mathcal{B}$ is then defined by:

$$A(s, j, s') = \bigwedge_{a \in j} \left(P_a(s) \land E_a(s, s') \right)$$

A defines the constraints on the current state and next state of joint actions. A further ensures that actions with inconsistent effects cannot be performed concurrently as A reduces to false if any pair of actions in a joint action have

---

[5] Note: the characteristic function has the same name as the set.

inconsistent effects. Thus, A also states the first rule for avoiding interference between concurrent actions.

$F : Q \times J \times Q \to B$ is a frame relation ensuring that unconstrained variables maintain their value. Let $c(a)$ denote the set of constrained variables of action a. We then have:

$$F(s, j, s') = \bigwedge_{v \notin C} (v = v'),$$

where $C = \bigcup_{a \in j} c(a)$.

$I : J \to B$ ensures that concurrent actions constrain a non overlapping set of variables and thus states the second rule for avoiding interference between concurrent actions:

$$I(j) = \bigwedge_{(a_1, a_2) \in j^2} \left(c(a_1) \cap c(a_2) = \emptyset \right),$$

where j^2 denotes the set $\{(a_1, a_2) \mid (a_1, a_2) \in j \times j \wedge a_1 \neq a_2\}$. The transition relation t is thus given by:

$$t(s, j, s') = A(s, j, s') \wedge F(s, j, s') \wedge I(j)$$

4 OBDD Representation of NADL Descriptions

To build an OBDD $\tilde{T}$ representing the transition relation $T(s, i, s')$ of the NFA of a domain description $D = (SV, S, E, Act, d, I, G)$, we must define a set of boolean variables to represent the current state s, the joint action input i and the next state s'. As in Section 3.2 we first build a transition relation with the joint actions of both system and environment agents as input and then reduces this to a transition relation with only joint actions of system agents as input.

Joint action inputs are represented in the following way: assume action a is identified by a number p and can be performed by agent α. a is then defined to be the action of agent α, if the number expressed binary by a set of boolean variables A_α, used to represent the actions of α, is equal to p. Propositional state variables are represented by a single boolean variable, while numerical state variables are represented binary by a set of boolean variables.

Let A_{e_1} to $A_{e_{|E|}}$ and A_{s_1} to $A_{s_{|S|}}$ denote sets of boolean variables used to represent the joint action of system and environment agents. Further, let $x_{v_j}^k$ and $x'^k_{v_j}$ denote the k'th boolean variable used to represent state variable $v_j \in SV$ in the current and next state. An ordering of the boolean variables, known to be efficient from model checking, puts the input variables first followed by an interleaving of the boolean variables of current state and next state variables:

$$A_{e_1} \prec \cdots \prec A_{e_{|E|}} \prec A_{s_1} \prec \cdots \prec A_{s_{|S|}}$$
$$\prec x_{v_1}^1 \prec x'^1_{v_1} \prec \cdots \prec x_{v_1}^{m_1} \prec x'^{m_1}_{v_1}$$
$$\cdots$$
$$\prec x_{v_n}^1 \prec x'^1_{v_n} \prec \cdots \prec x_{v_n}^{m_n} \prec x'^{m_n}_{v_n}$$

where m_i is the number of boolean variables used to represent state variable v_i and n equals $|SV|$. The construction of an OBDD representation $\tilde{T}$ is quite similar to the construction of T in Section 3.2. An OBDD representing a logical expression is built in the standard way. Arithmetic expressions are represented as lists of OBDDs defining the corresponding binary number. They collapse to single OBDDs when related by arithmetic relations.

To build an OBDD $\tilde{A}$ defining the constraints of the joint actions we need to refer to the values of the boolean variables representing the actions. Let $i(\alpha)$ be the function that maps an agent α to the value of the boolean variables representing its action and let $b(a)$ be the identifier value of action a. Further let $\tilde{P}(a)$ and $\tilde{E}(a)$ denote OBDD representations of the precondition and effect formula of an action a. $\tilde{A}$ is then given by:

$$\tilde{A} = \bigwedge_{\substack{\alpha \in Agt \\ a \in d(\alpha)}} \left(i(\alpha) = b(a) \Rightarrow \tilde{P}(a) \wedge \tilde{E}(a) \right)$$

Note that logical operators now denote the corresponding OBDD operators. An OBDD representing the frame relation $\tilde{F}$ changes in a similar way:

$$\tilde{F} = \bigwedge_{v \in SV} \left(\left(\bigwedge_{\substack{\alpha \in Agt \\ a \in d(\alpha)}} (i(\alpha) = b(a) \Rightarrow v \notin c(a)) \right) \Rightarrow s'_v = s_v \right),$$

where $c(a)$ is the set of constrained variables of action a and $s_v = s'_v$ expresses that all current and next state boolean variables representing v are pairwise equal. The expression $v \notin c(a)$ evaluates to *True* or *False* and is represented by the OBDD for *True* or *False*.

The action interference constraint $\tilde{I}$ is given by:

$$\tilde{I} = \bigwedge_{\substack{(\alpha_1, \alpha_2) \in S^2 \\ (a_1, a_2) \in c(\alpha_1, \alpha_2)}} \left(i(\alpha_1) = b(a_1) \Rightarrow i(\alpha_2) \neq b(a_2) \right) \wedge$$

$$\bigwedge_{\substack{(\alpha_1, \alpha_2) \in E^2 \\ (a_1, a_2) \in c(\alpha_1, \alpha_2)}} \left(i(\alpha_1) = b(a_1) \Rightarrow i(\alpha_2) \neq b(a_2) \right),$$

where $c(\alpha_1, \alpha_2) = \{(a_1, a_2) \mid (a_1, a_2) \in d(\alpha_1) \times d(\alpha_2) \wedge c(a_1) \cap c(a_2) \neq \emptyset\}$.

Finally the OBDD representing the transition relation $\tilde{T}$ is the conjunction of $\tilde{A}$, $\tilde{F}$ and $\tilde{I}$ with action variables of the environment agents existentially quantified:

$$\tilde{T} = \exists A_{e_1}, \cdots, A_{e_{|E|}} \cdot \tilde{A} \wedge \tilde{F} \wedge \tilde{I}$$

Partitioning the transition relation

The algorithms we use for generating universal plans all consist of some sort of backward search from the states satisfying the goal condition to the states satisfying the initial condition (see Section 5). Empirical studies in model checking have shown that the most complex operation for this kind of algorithms normally is to find the preimage of a set of visited states V.

Definition 2 Preimage. Given an NFA $M = (Q, \Sigma, \delta)$ and a set of states $V \subseteq Q$, the *preimage* of V is the set of states $\{s \mid s \in Q \wedge \exists i \in \Sigma, s' \in \delta(s, i) . s' \in V\}$.

Note that states already belonging to V can also be a part of the preimage of V. Assume that the set of visited states are represented by an OBDD expression $\tilde{V}$ on next state variables and that we for iteration purposes, want to generate the preimage $\tilde{P}$ also expressed in next state variables. For a monolithic transition relation $\tilde{T}$ we then calculate:

$$\tilde{U} = (\exists \mathbf{x}' . \tilde{T} \wedge \tilde{V})[\mathbf{x}/\mathbf{x}']$$
$$\tilde{P} = \exists \mathbf{i}' . \tilde{U}$$

where $\mathbf{i}$, $\mathbf{x}$ and $\mathbf{x}'$ denote input, current state and next state variables, and $[\mathbf{x}'/\mathbf{x}]$ denotes the substitution of current state variables with next state variables. The set expressed by $\tilde{U}$ consists of state input pairs (s, i), for which the state s belongs to the preimage of V and the input i may cause a transition from s to a state in V. In the universal planning algorithms presented in the next section, the universal plans are constructed from elements in $\tilde{U}$.

The OBDD representing the transition relation $\tilde{T}$ and the set of visited states $\tilde{V}$ tend to be large, and a more efficient computation can be obtained by performing the existential quantification of next state variables early in the calculation [6, 37]. To do this the transition relation has to be split into a conjunction of partitions $T_1, T_2, ..., T_n$ allowing the modified calculation:

$$\tilde{U} = (\exists \mathbf{x}'_n . \tilde{T}_n \wedge \cdots (\exists \mathbf{x}'_2 . \tilde{T}_2 \wedge (\exists \mathbf{x}'_1 . \tilde{T}_1 \wedge \tilde{V})) \cdots)[\mathbf{x}/\mathbf{x}']$$
$$\tilde{P} = \exists \mathbf{i}' . \tilde{U}$$

That is, $\tilde{T}_1$ can refer to all variables, $\tilde{T}_2$ can refer to all variables except $\mathbf{x}'_1$, $\tilde{T}_3$ can refer to all variables except $\mathbf{x}'_1$ and $\mathbf{x}'_2$ and so on.

As shown in [37] the computation time used to calculate the preimage is a convex function of the number of partitions. The reason for this is that, for some number of partitions, a further subdivision of the partitions will not reduce the total complexity, because the complexity introduced by the larger number of OBDD operations is higher than the reduction of the complexity of each OBDD operation.

NADL has been carefully designed to allow a partitioned transition relation representation. The relations A, F and I all consist of a conjunction of subexpressions that normally only refer to a subset of next state variables. A partitioned transition relation that enables early variable quantification can be constructed by sorting the subexpressions according to which next state variables they refer to and combining them in partitions with near optimal sizes that satisfy the above requirements.

5 OBDD-based Universal Planning Algorithms

In this section we will describe two prior algorithms for OBDD-based universal planning and discuss which kind of domains they are suitable for. Based on this discussion we present a new algorithm called *optimistic planning* that seems to be suitable for some domains not covered by the prior algorithms.

The three universal planning algorithms discussed are all based on an iteration of preimage calculations. The iteration corresponds to a parallel backward breadth first search starting at the goal states and ending when all initial states are included in the set of visited states (see Figure 5). The main difference between the algorithms is the way the preimage is defined.

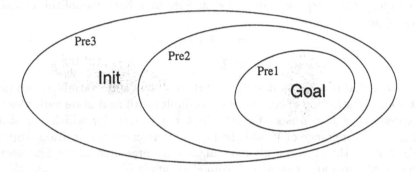

Fig. 5. The parallel backward breadth first search used by universal planning algorithms studied in this chapter.

5.1 Strong Planning

Strong Planning [10] uses a different preimage definition called strong preimage. For a state s belonging to the strong preimage of a set of states V, there exists at least one input i where all the transitions from s associated to i leads into V. When calculating the strong preimage of a set of visited states V, the set of state input pairs U represents the set of actions for each state in the preimage that, for any non-deterministic effect of the action, causes a transition into V. The universal plan returned by strong planning is the union of all these state-action rules. Strong planning is complete. If a strong plan exists for some planning problem the strong planning algorithm will return it, otherwise, it returns that no solution exists. Strong planning is also optimal due to the breadth first search. Thus, a strong plan with the fewest number of steps in the worst case is returned.

5.2 Strong Cyclic Planning

Strong cyclic planning [9] is a relaxed version of strong planning, as it also considers plans with infinite length. Strong cyclic planning finds a strong plan if it exists. Otherwise, if the algorithm at some point in the iteration is unable to find a strong preimage it adds an ordinary preimage (referred to as a weak preimage). It then tries to prune this preimage by removing all states that have transitions leading out of the preimage and the set of visited states V. If it succeeds, the remaining states in the preimage are added to V and it again tries to add strong preimages. If it fails, it adds a new, weak preimage and repeats the pruning process. A partial search of strong cyclic planning is shown in Figure 6. A strong cyclic plan only guarantees progress towards the goal in the strong

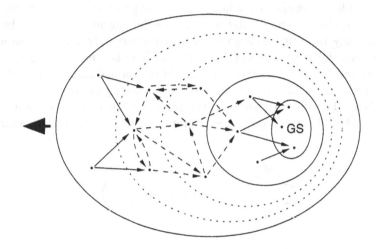

Fig. 6. Preimage calculations in strong cyclic planning. Dashed ellipses denote weak preimages while solid ellipses denote strong preimages. Only one action is assumed to exist in the domain. All the shown transitions are included in the universal plan. Dashed transitions are from "weak" parts of the plan while solid transitions are from "strong" parts of the plan.

parts. In the weak parts, cycles can occur. To keep the plan length finite, it must be assumed that a transition leading out of the weak parts eventually will be taken. The algorithm is complete as a strong solution will be returned if it exists. If no strong or strong cyclic solution exist the algorithm returns that no solution exists.

5.3 Strengths and Limitations

An important reason for studying universal planning is that universal planning algorithms can be made generally complete. Thus, if a plan exists for painting the floor, an agent executing a universal plan will always avoid to paint itself into the corner or reach any other unrecoverable dead-end. Strong planning and strong cyclic planning algorithms contribute by providing complete OBDD based algorithms for universal planning.

A limitation of strong and strong cyclic planning is their criteria for plan existence. If no strong or strong cyclic plan exist, these algorithms fail. The domains that strong and strong cyclic planning fail in are characterized by having unrecoverable dead-ends that cannot be guaranteed to be avoided.

Unfortunately, real world domains often have these kinds of dead-ends. Consider, for example, Schoppers' robot-baby domain described in Section 3. As depicted in Figure 4 no universal plan represented by a state-action set can guarantee the goal to be reached in a finite or infinite number of steps, as all relevant actions may lead to an unrecoverable dead-end.

A more interesting example is how to generate a universal plan for controlling, e.g., a power plant. Assume that actions can be executed that can bring the plant from any bad state to a good state. Unfortunately the environment can simultaneously fail subsystems of the plant which makes the resulting joint action non-deterministic, such that the plant may stay in a bad state or even change to an unrecoverable failed state (see Figure 7). No strong or strong cyclic solution can be found because an unrecoverable state can be reached from any initial state. An *NADL* description of a power plant domain is studied in Section 6.2.

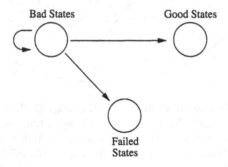

Fig. 7. Abstract description of the NFA of a power plant domain.

Another limitation of strong and strong cyclic planning is the inherent pessimism of these algorithms. Strong cyclic planning will always prefer to return a strong plan if it exists, even though a strong cyclic plan may exist with a shorter, best case plan length. Consider for example the domain described in Figure 8. The strong cyclic algorithm would return a strong plan only considering solid

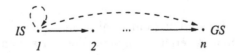

Fig. 8. The NFA of a domain with two actions (drawn as solid and dashed arrows) showing the price in best case plan length when preferring strong solutions. IS is the initial state while GS is the goal state.

actions. This plan would have a best and worst case length of n. But a strong cyclic plan considering both solid and dashed actions also exists and could be preferable because the best case length of 1 of the cyclic solution may have a much higher probability than the infinite worst case length.

By adding a unrecoverable dead-end for the dashed action and making solid actions non-deterministic (see Figure 9) strong cyclic planning now returns a strong cyclic plan considering only solid actions. But we might still be interested in a plan with best case performance even though the goal is not guaranteed to be achieved.

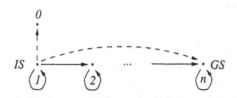

Fig. 9. The NFA of a domain with two actions (drawn as solid and dashed arrows) showing the price in best case plan length when preferring strong cyclic solutions. IS is the initial state while GS is the goal state.

5.4 Optimistic Planning

The analysis in the previous section shows that there exist domains and planning problems for which we may want to use a fully relaxed algorithm, that always includes the best case plan and returns a solution even if it includes dead-ends which cannot be guaranteed to be avoided. An algorithm similar to the strong planning algorithm, that adds an ordinary preimage in each iteration has these properties. Because state-action pairs that can have transitions to unrecoverable dead-ends are added to the universal plan, we call this algorithm *optimistic planning*. The algorithm is shown in Figure 10.

The optimistic planning algorithm is incomplete because it does not necessarily return a strong solution if it exists. Intuitively, optimistic planning only guarantees that there exists some effect of a plan action leading to the goal, where strong planning guarantees that all effects of plan actions lead to the goal.

The purpose of optimistic planning is not to substitute strong or strong cyclic planning. In domains where strong or strong cyclic plans can be found and goal achievement has the highest priority these algorithms should be used. On the other hand, in domains where goal achievement cannot be guaranteed or the shortest plan should be included in the universal plan, optimistic planning might be the better choice.

Consider again, as an example, the robot-baby domain described in Section 3. For this problem an optimistic solution makes the robot try to lift the block

```
procedure OptimisticPlanning(Init, Goal)
        VisitedStates := Goal
        UniversalPlan := ∅
    while (Init ⊄ VisitedStates)
            StateActions := Preimage(VisitedStates)
            PrunedStateActions := Prune(StateActions, VisitedStates)
            if StateActions ≠ ∅ then
                    UniversalPlan := UniversalPlan ∪ PrunedStateActions
                    VisitedStates := VisitedStates ∪ StatesOf(PrunedStateActions)
            else
                    return "No optimistic plan exists"
    return UniversalPlan
```

Fig. 10. The optimistic planning algorithm. All sets in this algorithm are represented by their characteristic function which is implemented as an OBDD. Preimage(*VisitedStates*) returns the set of state-action pairs U associated with the preimage of the visited states. Prune(*StateActions, VisitedStates*) removes the state-action pairs, where the state already is included in the set of visited states. StatesOf(*PrunedStateActions*) returns the set of states of the pruned state-action pairs.

as long as it is working. A similar optimistic plan is generated in the power plant domain. For all bad states the optimistic plan recommend an action that brings the plant to a good state in one step. This continues as long as the environment keeps the plant in a bad state. Because no strategy can be used to avoid the environment from bringing the block lifting robot and power plant to an unrecoverable dead-end, the optimistic solution is quite sensible.

For the domains shown in Figure 8 and 9 optimistic planning would return a universal plan with two state-action pairs: (1, *dotted*) and (n − 1, *solid*). For both domains this is a universal plan with the shortest best case length. Compared to the strong cyclic solution the price in the first domain is that the plan may have an infinite length, while the price in the second domain is that a dead-end may be reached.

6 Results

The UMOP planning system is implemented in C/C++ and uses the BUDDY package [32] for OBDD manipulations. The input to UMOP is an *NADL* description and a specification of which planning algorithm to use. The output is a universal plan or sequential plan depending on the planning algorithm. The current implementation of *NADL* only includes the arithmetic operators + and −, but an implementation of the remaining operators is straight forward and has only been omitted due to time limitations. UMOP generates an OBDD representation of the partitioned transition relation as described in Section 4, which is used to generate the universal plan. During planning the dynamic variable reordering facility of the BUDDY package can be used to speed up the OBDD operations. A universal plan is represented by an OBDD and defines for each domain state a set of joint actions that the system agents must execute synchronously in order to achieve the goal. The implemented planning algorithms are:

1. Classical deterministic planning (see description below).
2. Strong planning.
3. Strong cyclic planning.
4. Optimistic planning.

The backward search of the deterministic planning algorithm is similar to the optimistic planning algorithm. A sequential plan is generated from the universal plan by choosing an initial state and iteratively adding an action from the universal plan until a goal state is reached. The deterministic planning algorithm has been implemented to verify the performance of UMOP compared to other classical planners. It has not been our intention though, to develop a fast OBDD-based classical planning algorithm like [14] as our main interest is non-deterministic universal planning.

In the following four subsections we present results obtained with the UMOP planning system in nine different domains ranging from deterministic and single-agent with no environment actions to non-deterministic and multi-agent with complex environment actions.[6] A more detailed description of the experiments can be found in [26].

6.1   Deterministic Domains

A number of experiments have been carried out in deterministic domains in order to verify UMOP's performance and illustrate the generality of universal plans versus classical, sequential plans. In the next section, we compare run time results obtained with UMOP in some of the AIPS'98 competition domains to the results of the competition planners. We then generate a universal plan in a deterministic obstacle domain to show that a large number of classical sequential plans are contained in the universal plan.

AIPS'98 Competition Domains Five planners BLACKBOX, IPP, STAN, HSP and SGP participated in the competition. Only the first four of these planners competed in the three domains, we have studied. BLACKBOX is based on SAT-PLAN [29], while IPP and STAN are graphplan-based planners [3]. HSP uses a heuristic search approach based on a preprocessing of the domain. The AIPS'98

---

[6] All experiments were carried out on a 350 MHz Pentium PC with 1 GB RAM running Red Hat Linux 4.2.

planners were run on 233/400 MHz[7] Pentium PCs with 128 MB RAM equipped with Linux.

The Gripper Domain. The gripper domain consists of two rooms A and B, a robot with a left and right gripper and a number of balls that can be moved by the robot. The task is to move all the balls from room A to room B, with the robot initially in room A. The state variables of the *NADL* encoding of the domain are the position of the robot and the position of the balls. The position of the robot is either 0 (room A) or 1 (room B), while the position of a ball can be 0 (room A), 1 (room B), 2 (in left gripper) or 3 (in right gripper). For the AIPS'98 gripper problems the number of plan steps in an optimal plan grows linear with the problem number. Problem 1 contains 4 balls, and the number of balls grow with two for each problem. The result of the experiment is shown in Table 1 together with the results of the planners in the AIPS'98 competition. A graphical representation of the execution time in the table is shown in Figure 11. UMOP generates shortest plans due to its parallel breadth first search algorithm. As depicted in Figure 11, it avoids the exponential growth of the execution time that characterizes all of the competition planners except HSP. When using a partitioned transition relation UMOP is the only planner capable of generating optimal plans for all the problems. For this domain the transition relation of an *NADL* description can be divided into $n + 1$ basic partitions, where n is the number of balls. As discussed in Section 4, the optimal number of partitions is not necessarily the largest number of partitions. For the results in Table 1 each partition equaled a conjunction of 10 basic partitions. Compared to the monolithic transition relation representation the results obtained with the partitioned transition relation was significantly better on the larger problems. The memory usage for problem 20 with a partitioned transition relation was 87 MB, while it, for the monolithic transition relation, exceeded the limit of 128 MB at problem 17.

The Movie Domain. In the movie domain the task is to get chips, dip, pop, cheese and crackers, rewind a movie and set the counter to zero. The only interference between the subgoals is that the movie must be rewound, before the counter can be set to zero. The problems in the movie domain only differs by the number of objects of each type of food. The number of objects increases linear from 5 for problem 1 to 34 for problem 30.

Our *NADL* description of the movie domain represents each type of food as a numerical state variable with a range equal to the number of objects of that type of food. Table 2 shows the execution time for UMOP and the competition planners for the movie domain problems. In this experiment and the remaining

---

[7] Unfortunately no exact record has been kept on the machines and there is some disagreement about their clock frequency. According to Drew McDermott, who chaired the competition, they were 233 MHz Pentiums, but Derek Long (STAN) believes, they were at least 400 MHz Pentiums, as STAN performed worse on a 300 MHz Pentium than in the competition.

Problem	UMOP Part.			UMOP Mono.		STAN		HSP		IPP		BLACKBOX	
1	20	11	1	20	11	46	11	2007	13	50	15	113	11
2	150	17	1	130	17	1075	17	2150	21	380	23	7820	17
3	710	23	1	740	23	54693	23	2485	31	3270	31	-	-
4	1490	29	2	2230	29	3038381	29	3060	37	26680	39	-	-
5	3600	35	2	6040	35	-	-	3320	47	226460	47	-	-
6	7260	41	2	11840	41	-	-	3779	53	-	-	-	-
7	13750	47	2	24380	47	-	-	4797	63	-	-	-	-
8	23840	53	2	38400	53	-	-	5565	71	-	-	-	-
9	36220	59	3	68750	59	-	-	6675	79	-	-	-	-
10	56200	65	3	95140	65	-	-	7583	85	-	-	-	-
11	84930	71	3	145770	71	-	-	9060	93	-	-	-	-
12	127870	77	3	216110	77	-	-	10617	101	-	-	-	-
13	197170	83	3	315150	83	-	-	12499	109	-	-	-	-
14	290620	89	4	474560	89	-	-	15050	119	-	-	-	-
15	411720	95	4	668920	95	-	-	16886	125	-	-	-	-
16	549610	101	4	976690	101	-	-	20084	135	-	-	-	-
17	746920	107	4	-	-	-	-	23613	143	-	-	-	-
18	971420	113	4	-	-	-	-	26973	151	-	-	-	-
19	1361580	119	5	-	-	-	-	29851	157	-	-	-	-
20	1838110	125	5	-	-	-	-	33210	165	-	-	-	-

Table 1. Gripper domain results. Column one and two show the execution time in milliseconds and the plan length. UMOP Part. and UMOP Mono. show the execution time for UMOP using a partitioned and a monolithic transition relation respectively. For UMOP with partitioned transition relation the third column shows the number of partitions. (- -) means the planner failed. Only results for executions using less than 128 MB are shown for UMOP.

experiments UMOP used its default partitioning of the transition relation. For every problem all the planners find the optimal plan. Like the competition planners UMOP has a low computation time, but it is the only planner not showing any increase in computation time even though, the size of the state space of its encoding increases from 2^{24} to 2^{39}.

The Logistics Domain. The logistics domain consists of cities, trucks, airplanes and packages. The task is to move packages to specific locations. Problems differ by the number of packages, cities, airplanes and trucks. The logistics domain is hard and only problem 1,2,5,7 and 11 of the 30 problems were solved by any planner in the AIPS'98 competition (see Table 3). The *NADL* description of the logistics domain uses numerical state variables to represent locations of packages, where trucks and airplanes are treated as special locations. Even though, the state space for the small problems is moderate, UMOP fails to solve any of the problems in the domain. It succeeds to generate the transition relation but fails to finish the preimage calculations. The reason for this might be a bad representation or variable ordering. It might also be that no compact OBDD

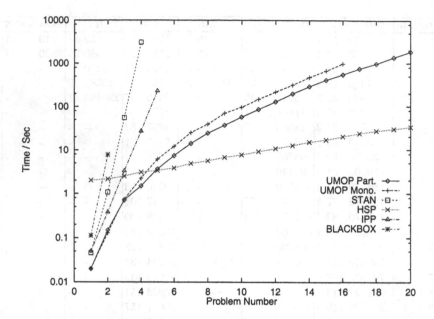

Fig. 11. Execution time for UMOP and the AIPS'98 competition planners for the gripper domain problems. UMOP Part. and UMOP Mono. show the execution time for UMOP using a partitioned and a monolithic transition relation respectively.

representation exists for this domain in the same way, that no compact OBDD representation exists for the integer multiplier [5]. More research is needed to decide this.

The Obstacle Domain The obstacle domain has been constructed to demonstrate the generality of universal plans. It consists of a 8×4 grid world, n obstacles and a robot agent. The position of the obstacles are not defined. The goal position of the robot is the upper right corner of the grid, and the task for the robot is to move from any position in the grid, different from the goal position, to the goal position. Because the initial location of obstacles is unknown, the universal plan must take any possible position of obstacles into account, which gives $2^{5(n+1)} - 2^{5n}$ initial states. For a specific initial state a sequential plan can be generated from the universal plan. Thus, $2^{5(n+1)} - 2^{5n}$ sequential plans are comprised in one universal plan. Note that a universal plan with n obstacles includes any universal plan with 1 to n obstacles, as obstacles can be placed at the same location. Note moreover, that the universal plans never covers all initial states, because obstacles can be placed at the goal position, and obstacles can block the way for the agent.

A universal plan for an obstacle domain with 5 obstacles was generated with UMOP in 420 seconds and contained 488296 OBDD nodes (13.3 MB). Sequential plans were extracted from the universal plan for a specific position of the obstacles, for which 16 step plans existed. Figure 12 shows the extraction time

Problem	UMOP		STAN		HSP		IPP		BLACKBOX	
1	14	7	19	7	2121	7	10	7	11	7
2	12	7	18	7	2104	7	10	7	12	7
3	14	7	19	7	2144	7	10	7	14	7
4	4	7	20	7	2188	7	10	7	16	7
5	14	7	21	7	2208	7	10	7	18	7
6	16	7	22	7	2617	7	10	7	20	7
7	14	7	22	7	2316	7	20	7	22	7
8	12	7	23	7	2315	7	20	7	24	7
9	14	7	25	7	2357	7	-	-	26	7
10	14	7	26	7	2511	7	10	7	29	7
11	14	7	27	7	2427	7	30	7	30	7
12	4	7	28	7	2456	7	30	7	32	7
13	16	7	29	7	3070	7	20	7	36	7
14	14	7	31	7	2573	7	30	7	35	7
15	16	7	32	7	2577	7	30	7	38	7
16	14	7	34	7	2699	7	10	7	39	7
17	16	7	35	7	2645	7	30	7	41	7
18	14	7	37	7	2686	7	10	7	43	7
19	16	7	39	7	2727	7	30	7	45	7
20	12	7	40	7	2787	7	20	7	47	7
21	16	7	42	7	2834	7	20	7	49	7
22	14	7	45	7	2834	7	20	7	51	7
23	16	7	48	7	2866	7	20	7	53	7
24	14	7	50	7	3341	7	20	7	55	7
25	16	7	52	7	2997	7	30	7	57	7
26	16	7	54	7	3013	7	40	7	58	7
27	16	7	57	7	3253	7	50	7	60	7
28	4	7	62	7	3049	7	40	7	63	7
29	18	7	64	7	3384	7	50	7	64	7
30	16	7	67	7	3127	7	40	7	66	7

Table 2. Movie domain results. For each planner column one and two show the run time in milliseconds and the plan length. (- -) means the planner failed. UMOP used far less than 128 MB for any problem in this domain.

Problem	STAN		HSP		IPP		BLACKBOX	
1	767	27	79682	43	900	26	2062	27
2	4319	32	97114	44	-	-	6436	32
5	364932	29	144413	26	2400	24	-	-
7	-	-	788914	112	-	-	-	-
11	12806	34	86195	30	6940	33	6544	32

Table 3. Logistics domain results. For each planner column one and two show the run time in milliseconds and the plan length. (- -) means the planner was unable to find a solution.

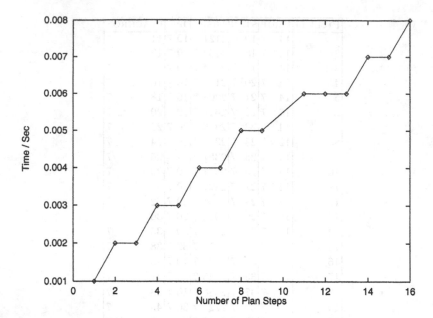

Fig. 12. Time for extracting sequential plans from a universal plan for the obstacle domain with 5 obstacles.

of sequential plans for an increasing number of steps in the plan. Even though the OBDD representing the universal plan is large, the extraction is very fast and only grows linear with the plan length. The set of actions associated with a state s in a universal plan p is extracted by computing the conjunction of the OBDD representation of s and p. As described in Section 2, this operation has an upper bound complexity of $O(|s||p|)$. For the universal plan in the obstacle domain with five obstacles this computation was fast (less than one millisecond) and would allow an executing agent to meet low reaction time constraints, but in the general case, it depends on the structure of the universal plan and might be more time consuming.

6.2 Non-deterministic Domains

In this section we first test UMOP's performance for some of the non-deterministic domains solved by MBP [9, 10]. Next, we present a version of the power plant domain briefly described in Section 5.2 and finally, we show results from a multi-agent soccer domain.

Domains Tested by MBP One of the domains introduced in [9, 10] is a non-deterministic transportation domain. The domain consists of a set of locations and a set of actions like drive-truck, drive-train and fly to move between the locations. Non-determinism is caused by non-deterministic actions (e.g., a truck may use the last fuel) and environmental changes (e.g., fog at airports). We defined the two domain examples from [9, 10] for strong and strong cyclic planning in *NADL* and ran UMOP using strong and strong cyclic planning. Both examples were solved in less than 0.05 seconds. Similar results were obtained with MBP. In [9] a general version of the hunter and prey domain [30] and a beam walk domain is also studied. Their generalization of the hunter and prey domain is not described in detail. Thus, we have not been able to make an *NADL* implementation of this domain.

The problem in the beam walk domain is for an agent to walk from one end of a beam to the other without falling down. If the agent falls, it has to walk back to the end of the beam and try again. The finite state machine of the domain is shown in Figure 13. The edges denotes the outcome of a walk action. When the agent is on the beam, the walk action can either move it one step further on the beam or make it fall to a location under the beam. We implemented a generator

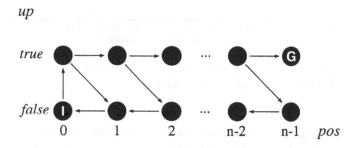

Fig. 13. The beam walk domain. The *NADL* encoding of the beam walk domain has one propositional state variable *up*, which is true if the agent is on the beam and a numerical state variable *pos*, which denotes the position of the agent either on the beam or on the ground. "I" and "G" are the intial state and goal state repspectively.

program for *NADL* descriptions of beam walk domains and produced domains with 4 to 4096 positions. Because the domain only contains two state variables, UMOP cannot exploit a partitioned transition relation for this domain, but have to use a monolithic representation. As shown in Figure 14 the execution time of UMOP was a little smaller than MBP. When discounting that we used a 75% faster machine MBP performs better in this domain. We do not believe this to be caused by an inefficient representation, as UMOP exploits the regularity of the domain in the same way as MBP. A more reasonable explanation is that UMOP uses a less efficient implementation of the strong cyclic planning algorithm.

A detailed comparison of UMOP and MBP is very interesting, as the two systems represent planning problems in a quite different way. Currently MBP is unable to use a partitioned transition relation representation, but it is still an open question if UMOP is able to solve larger problems than MBP due to this feature.

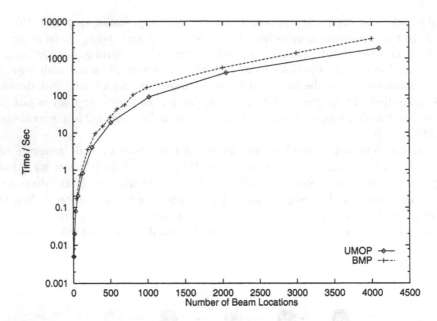

Fig. 14. Execution time of UMOP and MBP in the beam walk domain. The MBP data has been extracted with some loss of accuracy from [9].

The Power Plant Domain Until now we have concentrated on presenting results that show UMOP's performance compared to other planners. The purpose of the remaining experiments is to show universal planning results for domains, where the multi-agent and environment modelling features of *NADL* have been used.

The power plant domain demonstrates a multi-agent domain with an environment model and further exemplifies optimistic planning. It consists of reactors, heat exchangers, turbines and valves. A domain example is shown in Figure 15. In the power plant domain each controllable unit is associated with an agent such that all control actions can be executed simultaneously. The environment consists of a single agent that at any time can fail a number of heat exchanges and turbines and ensures that already failed units remain failed. A failed heat exchanger leaks radioactive water from the internal to the external water loop and must be closed by a block action b. For a failed turbine the stop action s must be carried out. The energy production from the reactor can be controlled by p to fit the demand f, but the reactor will always produce two energy units. To transport the energy from the reactor away from the plant at least one heat exchanger and one turbine must be working. Otherwise the plant is in an unrecoverable failed state, where the reactor will overheat.

The state space of the power plant can be divided into three disjoint sets: good, bad and failed states. In the good states the power plant satisfies its safety and activity requirements. In our example the safety requirements ensures that energy can be transported away from the plant and failed units are shut down:

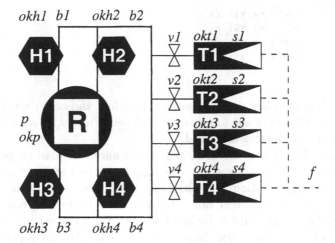

Fig. 15. A power plant domain example. The reactor R is surrounded by the four heat exchangers H1, H2, H3 and H4. The heat exchangers produces high pressure damp to the four electricity generating turbines T1, T2, T3 and T4. A failed heat exchanger must be closed by a block action *b*. For a failed turbine the stop action *s* must be carried out. The energy production of the reactor is *p* and can be controlled to fit the demand *f*. Each turbine can be closed of by a valve *v*.

```
% energy can be transported away from the plant
(okh1 \/ okh2 \/ okh3 \/ okh4) /\
(okt1 \/ okt2 \/ okt3 \/ okt4) /\

% heat exchangers blocked if failed
(~okh1 => b1) /\
(~okh2 => b2) /\
(~okh3 => b3) /\
(~okh4 => b4) /\

% turbines stopped if failed
(~okt1 => s1) /\
(~okt2 => s2) /\
(~okt3 => s3) /\
(~okt4 => s4)
```

The activity requirements state that the energy production equals the demand and that all valves to working turbines are open:

```
% power production equals demand
p = f /\

% turbine valve is open if turbine is ok
```

```
(okt1 => v1) /\
(okt2 => v2) /\
(okt3 => v3) /\
(okt4 => v4)
```

In a bad state the plant does not satisfy the safety and activity requirements, but on the other hand is not unrecoverably failed. Finally, in a failed state all heat exchangers or turbines are failed.

The universal planning task is to generate a universal plan to get from any bad state to some good state without ending in a failed state. Assuming that no units fail during execution, it is obvious that only one joint action is needed. Unfortunately, the environment can fail any number of units during execution, thus, as described in Section 5.2, for any bad state the resulting joint action may loop back to a bad state or cause the plant to end in a failed state. (see Figure 7). For this reason no strong or strong cyclic solution exists to the problem.

An optimistic solution simply ignores that joint actions can loop back to a bad state or lead to a failed state and finds a solution to the problem after one preimage calculation. Intuitively, the optimistic plan assumes that no units will fail during execution and always chooses joint actions that lead directly from a bad state to a good state. The optimistic plan is an optimal control strategy, because it always chooses the shortest way to a good state and no other strategy exists that can avoid looping back to a bad state or end in a failed state.

The size of the state space of the above power plant domain is 2^{24}. An optimistic solution was generated by UMOP in 0.92 seconds and contained 37619 OBDD nodes. As an example, a joint action was extracted from the plan for a bad state where H3 and H4 were failed and energy demand f was 2 energy units, while the energy production p was only 1 unit. The extraction time was 0.013 seconds and as expected the set of joint actions included a single joint action changing $b3$ and $b4$ to true and setting p to 2.

The Soccer Domain The purpose of the soccer domain is to demonstrate a multi-agent domain with a more elaborate environment model than the power plant domain. It consists of two teams of players that can move in a grid world and pass a ball to each other. At each time step a player either moves in one of the four major directions or passes the ball to another team player. The task is to generate a universal plan for one of the teams that can be applied, whenever the team possesses the ball in order to score a goal.

A simple *NADL* description of the soccer domain models the team possessing the ball as system agents that can move and pass the ball independent of each other. Thus, a player possessing the ball can always pass to any other team player. The opponent team is modelled as a set of environment agents that can move in the four major directions but have no actions for handling the ball. The goal of the universal plan is to have a player with the ball in front of the opponent goal without having any opponents in the goal area.

Clearly, it is impossible to generate a strong plan that covers all possible initial states. But a strong plan covering as many initial states as possible is useful, because it defines all the "scoring" states of the game and further provides a plan for scoring the goal no matter what actions, the opponent players choose.

We implemented an *NADL* generator for soccer domains with different field sizes and numbers of agents. The Multi-Agent graph in Figure 16 shows UMOP's execution time using the strong planning algorithm in soccer domains with 64 locations and one to six players on each team. The execution time seems to

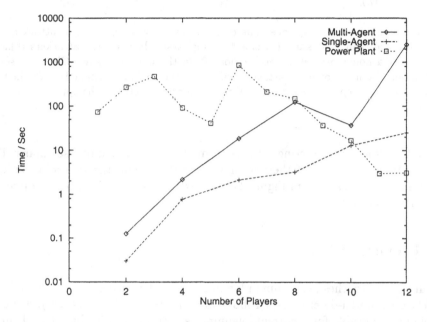

Fig. 16. Execution time of UMOP for generating strong universal plans in soccer domains with one to six players on each team. For the multi-agent experiment each player was associated with an agent, while only a single system and environment agent was used in the single-agent experiment. The power plant graph show execution time for a complex deterministic power plant domain using 1 to 12 system agents.

grow exponential with the number of players. This is not surprising as not only the state space but also the number of joint actions grow exponential with the number of agents. To investigate the complexity introduced by joint actions, we constructed a version of the soccer domain with only a single system and environment agent and ran UMOP again. The Single-Agent graph in Figure 16 shows a dramatic decrease in computation time. Its is not obvious though, that a parallelization of domain actions increases the computational load as this normally also reduces the number of preimage calculations, because a larger number of states is reached in each iteration. Indeed, in a deterministic version of the power plant domain we found the execution time to decrease (see the Power Plant graph in Figure 16), when more agents were added [26]. Again we mea-

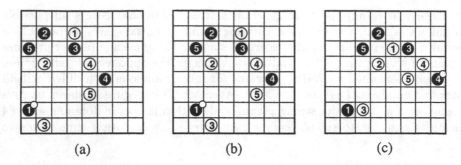

Fig. 17. Plan execution sequence. The three states show a hypothetical attack based on a universal plan. The state (a) is a "scoring" state, because the attackers (black) can extract a nonempty set of joint actions from the universal plan. Choosing some joint actions from the plan the attackers can enter the goal area (shaded) with the ball within two time steps (state (b) and (c)) no matter what actions, the opponent players choose.

sured the time for extracting actions from the generated universal plans. For the multi-agent version of the five player soccer domain the two joint actions achieving the goal shown in Figure 17 were extracted from the universal plan in less than 0.001 seconds.

7 Previous Work

Recurrent approaches performing planning in parallel with execution have been widely used in non-deterministic robotic domains (e.g., [21, 19, 44, 25]). A group of planners suitable for recurrent planning is action selectors based on heuristic search [30, 4]. The min-max LRTA* algorithm [30] can generate suboptimal plans in non-deterministic domains through a search and execution iteration. The search is based on a heuristic goal distance function, which must be provided for a specific problem. The ASP algorithm [4] uses a similar approach and further defines a heuristic function for STRIPS-like [18] action representations. In contrast to min-max LRTA*, ASP does not assume a non-deterministic environment, but is robust to non-determinism caused by action perturbations (i.e., that another action than the planned action is chosen with some probability).

In general recurrent approaches are incomplete, because acting on an incomplete plan can make the goal unachievable. Precursor approaches perform all decision making prior to execution and thus may be able to generate complete plans by taking all possible non-deterministic changes of the environment into account.

The precursor approaches include conditional [17, 36], probabilistic [16, 13] and universal planning [38, 9, 10, 27]. The CNLP [36] partial ordered, conditional planner handles non-determinism by constructing a conditional plan that accounts for each possible situation or contingency that could arise. At execution time it is determined which part of the plan to execute by performing sensing actions that are included in the plan to test for the appropriate conditions.

Probabilistic planners try to maximize the probability of goal satisfaction, given conditional actions with probabilistic effects. In [16] plans are represented as a set of Situated Control Rules (SCRs) [15] mapping situations to actions. The planning algorithm begins by adding SCRs corresponding to the most probable execution path that achieves the goal. It then continues adding SCRs for less probable paths, and may end with a complete plan taking all possible paths into account.

Universal plans differs from conditional and probabilistic plans by specifying appropriate actions for every possible state of the domain.[8] Like conditional and probabilistic plans universal plans require the world to be accessible in order to execute the universal plan.

Universal planning was introduced in [38] who used decision trees to represent plans. Recent approaches include [27, 9, 10]. In [27] universal plans are represented as a set of Situated Control Rules [15]. Their algorithm incrementally adds SCRs to a final plan in a way similar to [16]. The goal is a formula in temporal logic that must hold on any valid sequence of actions.

Reinforcement Learning (RL) [28] can also be regarded as a kind of universal planning. In RL the goal is represented by a reward function in a Markov Decision Process (MDP) model of the domain. In the precursor version of RL the MDP is assumed to be known and a control policy maximizing the expected reward is found prior to execution. The policy can either be represented explicitly in a table or implicitly by a function (e.g., a neural network). Because RL is a probabilistic approach, its domain representation is more complex than the domain representation used by a non-deterministic planner. Thus, we may expect non-deterministic planners to be able to handle domains with a larger state space than RL. On the other hand, RL may produce policies with a higher quality, than a universal plan generated by a non-deterministic planner.

All previous approaches to universal planning, except [9, 10], use an explicit representation of the universal plan (e.g., SCRs). Thus, in the general case exponential growth of the plan size with the number of propositions defining a domain state must be expected, as argued in [22].

The compact and implicit representation of universal plans obtained with OBDDs do not necessarily grow exponentially for regular domains as shown in [9]. Further, the OBDD-based representation of the NFA of a non-deterministic domain enables the application of efficient search algorithms from model checking, capable of handling very large state spaces.

---

[8] The plan solving an *NADL* problem will only be universal if the initial states equals all the states in the domain.

8 Conclusion and Future Work

In this chapter we have presented a new OBDD-based planning system called UMOP for planning in non-deterministic, multi-agent domains. An expressive domain description language called *NADL* has been developed and an efficient OBDD representation of its NFA semantics has been described. We have analyzed previous planning algorithms for OBDD-based planning and deepened the understanding of when these planning algorithms are appropriate. Finally, we have proposed a planning algorithm called optimistic planning for finding sensible solutions in some domains where no strong or strong cyclic solution exists. The results obtained with UMOP are encouraging, as UMOP has a good performance compared to some of the fastest classical planners known today.

Our research has drawn our attention to a number of open questions that we would like to address in the future. The most interesting of these is how well our encoding of planning problems scales compared to the encoding used by MBP. Currently MBP's encoding does not support a partitioned representation of the transition relation, but the encoding may have other properties that, despite the monolithic representation, makes it a better choice than UMOP's encoding. On the other hand, the two systems may also have an equal performance when both are using a monolithic representation (as in the beam walk example), which should give UMOP an advantage in domains where a partitioning of the transition relation can be defined. We are planning a joint work with Marco Roveri in the Fall of 1999 to address these issues.

Another interesting question is to investigate which kind of planning domains is suitable for OBDD-based planning. It was surprising for us that the logistics domain turned out to be so hard for UMOP. A thorough study of this domain may be the key for defining new approaches and might bring important new knowledge about the strengths and limitations of OBDD-based planning.

The current definition of *NADL* is powerful but should be extended to enable modelling of constructive synergetic effects as described in Section 3. Also, more experiments comparing multi-agent and single-agent domains should be carried out to investigate the complexity of *NADL*'s representation of concurrent actions.

Several planners, in particular PRODIGY [41], have shown that domain knowledge should be used by a planning system in order to scale up to real world problems. Also [1] show how the search tree of a forward chaining planner can be efficiently pruned by stating the goal as formula in temporal logic on the sequence of actions leading to the goal. In this way the goal can include knowledge about the domain (e.g., that towers in the blocks world must be built from bottom to top). A similar approach for reducing the complexity of OBDD-based planning seems promising, especially because techniques for testing temporal formulas already have been developed in model checking.

Other future challenges include introducing abstraction in OBDD-based planning and defining specialized planning algorithms for multi-agent domains (e.g., algorithms using the least number of agents for solving a problem).

Acknowledgements A special thanks to Paolo Traverso, Marco Roveri and the other members of the IRST group for introducing us to MBP and for many rewarding discussions on OBDD-based planning and model checking. We also wish to thank Randal E. Bryant, Edmund Clarke, Henrik R. Andersen, Jørn Lind-Nielsen and Lars Birkedal for advice on OBDD issues and formal representation.

This work was carried out while the first author was visiting Carnegie Mellon University from the Technical University of Denmark. The first author was sponsored in part by McKinsey & Company, Selmar Tranes Fond. The research is supported in addition by the Defense Advanced Research Projects Agency (DARPA) and the Air Force Research Laboratory (AFRL) under agreement number F30602-97-2-0250. The views and conclusions contained herein are those of the authors and should not be interpreted as necessarily representing the official policies or endorsements, either expressed or implied, of the Defense Advanced Research Projects Agency (DARPA), the Air Force Research Laboratory (AFRL) or the U.S. Government.

Appendix A. *NADL* Includes the $\mathcal{AR}$ Family

Theorem 3. *If A is a domain description for some $\mathcal{AR}$ language A, then there exists a domain description D in the NADL language with the same semantics as A*

Proof: let $M_a = (Q, \Sigma, \delta)$ denote the NFA (see Definition 1) equal to the semantics of A as defined in [23]. An *NADL* domain description D with semantics equal to M_a can obviously be constructed in the following way: let D be a single-agent domain, where all fluents are encoded as numerical variables and there is an action for each element in the alphabet Σ of M_a. Consider the action a associated to input $i \in \Sigma$. Let the set of constrained state variables of a equal all the state variables in D. The precondition of a is an expression that defines the set of states having an outgoing transition for input i. The effect condition of a is a conjunction of conditional effects $P_s \Rightarrow N_s$. There is one conditional effect for each state that has an outgoing transition for input i. P_s in the conditional effect associated with state s is the characteristic expression for s and N_s is a characteristic expression for the set of next states $\delta(s, i)$. $\square$

References

1. F. Bacchus and F. Kabanza. Using temporal logic to control search in a forward chaining planner. In M. Ghallab and A. Milani, editors, *New directions in AI planning*, pages 141–153. ISO Press, 1996.
2. C. Baral and M. Gelfond. Reasoning about effects of concurrent actions. *The Journal of Logic Programming*, pages 85–117, 1997.
3. A. Blum and M. L. Furst. Fast planning through planning graph analysis. In *Proceedings of the 14'th International Conference on Artificial Intelligence (IJCAI-95)*, pages 1636–1642. Morgan Kaufmann, 1995.

4. B. Bonet, G. Loerincs, and H. Geffner. A robust and fast action selection mechanism for planning. In *Proceedings of the 14'th National Conference on Artificial Intelligence (AAAI'97)*, pages 714–719. AAAI Press / The MIT Press, 1997.

5. R. E. Bryant. Graph-based algorithms for boolean function manipulation. *IEEE Transactions on Computers*, 8:677–691, 1986.

6. J.R. Burch, E.M. Clarke, and D.E. Long. Symbolic model checking with partitioned transition relations. In *International Conference on Very Large Scale Integration*, pages 49–58. North-Holland, 1991.

7. E. Carke, O. Grumberg, and D. Peled. *Model Checking*. MIT Press, 1999. In Press.

8. A. Cimatti, E. Giunchiglia, F. Giunchiglia, and P. Traverso. Planning via model checking: A decision procedure for $\mathcal{AR}$. In *Proceedings of the 4'th European Conference on Planning (ECP'97)*, Lecture Notes in Artificial Intelligence, pages 130–142. Springer-Verlag, 1997.

9. A. Cimatti, M. Roveri, and P. Traverso. Automatic OBDD-based generation of universal plans in non-deterministic domains. In *Proceedings of the 15'th National Conference on Artificial Intelligence (AAAI'98)*, pages 875–881. AAAI Press/The MIT Press, 1998.

10. A. Cimatti, M. Roveri, and P. Traverso. Strong planning in non-deterministic domains via model checking. In *Proceedings of the 4'th International Conference on Artificial Intelligence Planning System (AIPS'98)*, pages 36–43. AAAI Press, 1998.

11. E. M. Clarke, E. A. Emerson, and A. P. Sistla. Automatic verification of finite-state concurrent systems using temporal logic specifications. *ACM transactions on Programming Languages and Systems*, 8(2):244–263, 1986.

12. K. Currie and A. Tate. O-plan: the open planning architecture. *Artificial Intelligence*, 52:49–86, 1991.

13. T. Dean, L. P. Kaelbling, J. Kirman, and A. Nicholson. Planning under time constraints in stochastic domains. *Artificial Intelligence*, 76:35–74, 1995.

14. M. Di Manzo, E. Giunchiglia, and S. Ruffino. Planning via model checking in deterministic domains: Preliminary report. In *Proceedings of the 8'th International Conference on Artificial Intelligence: Methodology, Systems and Applications (AIMSA'98)*, pages 221–229. Springer-Verlag, 1998.

15. M. Drummond. Situated control rules. In *Proceedings of the 1'st International Conference on Principles of Knowledge Representation and Reasoning (KR'89)*, pages 103–113. Morgan Kaufmann, 1989.

16. M. Drummond and J. Bresina. Anytime synthetic projection: Maximizing the probability of goal satisfaction. In *Proceedings of the 8'th Conference on Artificial Intelligence*, pages 138–144. AAAI Press / The MIT Press, 1990.

17. O. Etzioni, S. Hanks, D. Weld, D. Draper, N. Lesh, and M. Williamson. An approach for planning with incomplete information. In *Proceedings of the 3'rd International Conference on Principles of Knowledge Representation and Reasoning*, 1992.

18. R. E. Fikes and N. J. Nilsson. STRIPS: A new approach to the application of theorem proving to problem solving. *Artificial Intelligence*, 2:189–208, 1971.

19. E. Gat. Integrating planning and reacting in a heterogeneous asynchronous architecture for controlling real-world mobile robots. In *Proceedings of the 10'th National Conference on Artificial Intelligence (AAAI'92)*, pages 809–815. MIT Press, 1992.

20. M. Gelfond and V. Liftschitz. Representing action and change by logic programs. *The Journal of Logic Programming*, 17:301–322, 1993.

21. M. P. Georgeff and A. L. Lansky. Reactive reasoning and planning. In *Proceedings of the 6'th National Conference on Artificial Intelligence (AAAI'87)*, pages 677–682, 1987.
22. M. L. Ginsberg. Universal planning: An (almost) universal bad idea. *AI Magazine*, 10(4):40–44, 1989.
23. E. Giunchiglia, G. N. Kartha, and Y. Lifschitz. Representing action: Indeterminacy and ramifications. *Aritificial Intelligence*, 95:409–438, 1997.
24. E. Giunchiglia and V. Lifschitz. An action language based on causal explanation: Preliminary report. In *Proceedings of the 15'th National Conference on Artificial Intelligence (AAAI'98)*, pages 623–630. AAAI Press/The MIT Press, 1998.
25. K. Z. Haigh and M. M. Veloso. Planning, execution and learning in a robotic agent. In *Proceedings of the 4'th International Conference on Artificial Intelligence Planning Systems (AIPS'98)*, pages 120–127. AAAI Press, 1998.
26. R. M. Jensen. OBDD-based universal planning in multi-agent, non-deterministic domains. Master's thesis, Technical University of Denmark, Department of Automation, 1999. IAU99F02.
27. F. Kabanza, M. Barbeau, and R. St-Denis. Planning control rules for reactive agents. *Artificial Intelligence*, 95:67–113, 1997.
28. L. P. Kaebling, M. L. Littman, and A. W. Moore. Reinforcement learning: a survey. *Journal of Artificial Intelligence Research*, 4:237–285, 1996.
29. H. Kautz and B. Selman. Pushing the envelope: Planning, propositional logic and stochastic search. In *Proceedings of the 13'th National Conference on Artificial Intelligence (AAAI'96)*, volume 2, pages 1194–1201. AAAI Press/MIT Press, 1996.
30. S. Koenig and R. G. Simmons. Real-time search in non-deterministic domains. In *Proceedings of the 14'th International Joint Conference on Artificial Intelligence (IJCAI-95)*, pages 1660–1667. Morgan Kaufmann, 1995.
31. J. Lever and B. Richards. *Parcplan*: a planning architecture with parallel actions and constraints. In *Lecture Notes in Artificial Intelligence*, pages 213–222. IS-MIS'94, Springer-Verlag, 1994.
32. J. Lind-Nielsen. BuDDy - A Binary Decision Diagram Package. Technical Report IT-TR: 1999-028, Institute of Information Technology, Technical University of Denmark, 1999. http://cs.it.dtu.dk/buddy.
33. A. R. Lingard and E. B. Richards. Planning parallel actions. *Artificial Intelligence*, 99:261–324, 1998.
34. K. L. McMillan. *Symbolic Model Checking*. Kluwer Academic Publ., 1993.
35. J. S. Penberthy and D. S. Weld. UCPOP: A sound, complete, partial order planner for ADL. In *Proceedings of the 3'rd International Conference on Principles of Knowledge Representation and Reasoning*, pages 103–114. Morgan Kaufmann, 1992.
36. M. Peot and D. Smith. Conditional nonlinear planning. In *Proceedings of the 1'st International Conference on Artificial Intelligence Planning Systems (AIPS'92)*, pages 189–197. Morgan Kaufmann, 1992.
37. R. K. Ranjan, A. Aziz, R. K. Brayton, B. Plessier, and C. Pixley. Efficient BDD algorithms for FSM synthesis and verification. In *IEEE/ACM Proceedings International Workshop on Logic Synthesis*, 1995.
38. M. J. Schoppers. Universal plans for reactive robots in unpredictable environments. In *Proceedings of the 10'th International Joint Conference on Artificial Intelligence (IJCAI-87)*, pages 1039–1046. Morgan Kaufmann, 1987.
39. P. Stone and M. M. Veloso. Towards collaborative and adversarial learning: A case study in robotic soccer. *International Journal of Human-Computer Studies (IJHCS)*, 1998.

40. R. S. Sutton and Barto A. G. *Reinforcement Learning: An Introduction.* MIT Press, 1998.
41. M. Veloso, J. Carbonell, A. Pérez, D. Borrajo, E. Fink, and J. Blythe. Integrating planning and learning: The PRODIGY architecture. *Journal of Experimental and Theoretical Artificial Intelligence,* 7(1), 1995.
42. M. M. Veloso, M. E. Pollack, and M. T. Cox. Rationale-based monitoring for planning in dynamic environments. In *Proceedings of the 4'th International Conference on Artificial Intelligence Planning Systems (AIPS'98),* pages 171–179. AAAI Press, 1998.
43. D. Weld. Recent advances in AI planning. *Artificial Intelligence Magazine,* 1999. (in press).
44. D. E. Wilkins, K. L. Myers, J. D. Lowrance, and L. P. Wesley. Planning and reacting in uncertain and dynamic environments. *Journal of Experimental and Theoretical Artificial Intelligence,* 6:197–227, 1994.

Combining Artificial Intelligence and Databases for Data Integration

Alon Y. Levy

Department of Computer Science and Engineering
University of Washington
Seattle, Washington 98195, USA.
alon@cs.washington.edu

Abstract

Data integration is a problem at the intersection of the fields of Artificial Intelligence and Database Systems. The goal of a data integration system is to provide a uniform interface to a multitude of data sources, whether they are within one enterprise or on the World-Wide Web. The key challenges in data integration arise because the data sources being integrated have been designed independently for autonomous applications, and their contents are related in subtle ways. As a result, a data integration system requires rich formalisms for describing contents of data sources and relating between contents of different sources. This paper discusses works aimed at applying techniques from Artificial Intelligence to the problem of data integration. In addition to employing Knowledge Representation techniques for describing contents of information sources, projects have also made use of Machine Learning techniques for extracting data from sources and planning techniques for query optimization. The paper also outlines future opportunities for applying AI techniques in the context of data integration.

1 Introduction

The fields of Artificial Intelligence and Database Systems have traditionally explored opposite ends of the expressivity spectrum of representation languages [Rei88, LB87]. In database systems, where the major concern is scalability to large amounts of data, the relational model has been prevalent. Under this model, assertions about the domain of discourse are limited to ground atomic facts, and to restricted forms of integrity constraints on the contents of the database relations. In Artificial Intelligence, the focus has been on modeling more complex domains with smaller quantities of data. An essential element in modeling such domains is the ability to represent partial information, such as disjunctions and existential statements, which are not possible in the relational database model.

Data integration is a classical example of a problem that requires techniques developed in both fields [GMPQ+97, HKWY97, LRO96a, FRV96, FW97, DG97a, Coh98b, AAB+98, BEM+98, ACPS96, LR98, LK98, CCM+98]. In a nutshell, the goal of a data integration system is to provide a *uniform* interface to a multitude of data sources. As an example, consider the task of providing information about movies from data sources on the World-Wide Web (WWW). There are numerous sources on the WWW concerning movies, such as the Internet Movie Database (providing comprehensive listings of movies, their casts, directors, genres, etc.), MovieLink (providing playing times of movies in US cities), and several sites providing reviews of selected movies. Suppose we want to find which movies directed by Woody Allen are playing tonight in Seattle, and their respective reviews. None of these data sources *in isolation* can answer this query. However, by combining data from multiple sources, we can answer queries like this one, and even more complex ones. To answer our query, we would first search the Internet Movie Database for the list of movies directed by Woody Allen, and then feed the result into the MovieLink database to check which ones are playing in Seattle. Finally, we would find reviews for the relevant movies using any of the movie review sites.

The most important advantage of a data integration system is that it enables users to focus on specifying *what* they want, rather than thinking about *how* to obtain the answers. As a result, it frees the users from the tedious tasks of finding the relevant data sources, interacting with each source in isolation using a particular interface, and combining data from multiple sources.

The main characteristics distinguishing data integration systems from distributed and parallel database systems is that the data sources underlying the system are *autonomous*. In particular, a data integration system provides access to *pre-existing* sources, which were created independently. Unlike multidatabase systems (see [LMR90] for a survey) a data integration system must deal with a large and constantly changing set of data sources. These characteristics raise the need for richer mechanisms for describing our data, and hence the opportunity to apply techniques from Knowledge Representation. In particular, a data integration system requires a flexible mechanism for describing contents of sources that may have overlapping contents, whose contents are described by complex constraints, and sources that may be incomplete or only partially complete. Languages originating from Knowledge Representation formalisms have shown to be useful in capturing such complex relationships between data sources.

In this paper I survey the application of AI techniques and their combination with database techniques in the context of data integration. Although the focus is on the application of Knowledge Representation techniques, I also discuss the application of Machine Learning techniques to the problem of extracting data out of sources, and of techniques for interleaving planning and execution for the purpose of query optimization in the more dynamic environment of data integration. Section 2 is a brief introduction to database systems terminology. Section 3 describes the novel challenges encountered in data integration systems, and provides a reference architecture for such a system. Section 4 considers the problem of modeling the contents of data sources, and 5 discusses the modeling of source (in)completeness. Section 6 describes the issues concerning the construction of wrapper programs, whose task is to extract structured data from data sources, and the application of Machine Learning techniques to this task. Section 7 describes the novel issues that arise for query optimization in the context of data integration systems, and the need for interleaving of planning and execution. Section 8 describes the problem of web-site management which is currently one of the significant applications of data integration, and in itself presents several important opportunities for future AI research. Section 9 contains concluding remarks.

Let me state at the outset that this paper is not meant to be a comprehensive survey of the work on data integration in the AI community. My goal is simply to highlight the main issues that arise, and to provide a flavor of the solutions. I apologize in advance for any omissions, of which I am sure there are many.

2 Schemas and Queries

Our discussion will use the terminology of relational databases. A *schema* is a set of relations. Columns of relations are called attributes, and their names are part of the schema (traditionally, the type of each attribute is also part of the schema but we will ignore typing here).

Queries can be specified in a variety of languages. For simplicity, we consider the language of conjunctive queries, and several variants on it. A conjunctive query has the form:

$$q(\bar{X}) :- e_1(\bar{X}_1), \ldots, e_n(\bar{X}_n),$$

where $e_1, \ldots, e_n$ are database relations, and $\bar{X}_1, \ldots, \bar{X}_n$ are tuples of variables or constants. The atom $q(\bar{X})$ is the head of the query, and the result of the query is a set of tuples, each giving a binding for every variable in $\bar{X}$. Interpreted predicates such as $<, \leq, \neq$ are sometimes used in the query. Queries with unions are expressed by multiple rules with the same head. A *view* refers to a named query.

3 Challenges in Data Integration

As described in the introduction, the task of a data integration system is to provide a uniform interface to a collection of data sources. The data sources can either be full-fledged database systems (of various flavors: relational, object-oriented, etc.), legacy systems, or structured files hidden behind some interface program. For the purposes of our discussion we model data sources as containing relations. In this paper (as in most of the research) we only consider data integration systems whose goal is to query the data, and not to perform updates on the sources.

Throughout the discussion it is instructive to keep in mind the distinction between different classes of data integration applications. For example, integration of arbitrary sources on the WWW is quite a different task from that of integrating multiple sources within a single enterprise (though it is unclear which one is harder!). In the latter case, the sources are not as autonomous as they are on the WWW, but the requirements imposed on a data integration system may be more stringent.

To understand the challenges involved in building data integration systems, we briefly compare the problems that arise in this context with those encountered in traditional database systems. Figure 1 illustrates the different stages in processing a query in a data integration system.

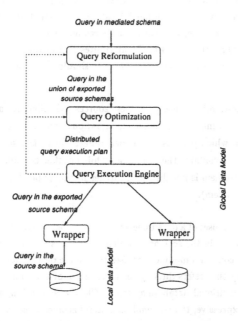

Figure 1: Prototypical architecture of a data integration system

Data modeling: in a traditional database application one begins by modeling the requirements of the application, and designing a database schema that appropriately supports the application. As noted earlier, a data integration application begins from a set of pre-existing data sources. Hence, the first step of the application designer is to develop a *mediated schema* that describes the data that exists in the sources, and exposes the aspects of this data that may be of interest to users. Note that the mediated schema does not necessarily contain all the relations and attributes modeled in each of the sources. Users pose queries in terms of the mediated schema, rather than directly in terms of the source schemas. As such, the mediated schema is a set of *virtual* relations, in the sense that they are not actually stored anywhere. For example, in the movie domain, the mediated schema may contain the relation MOVIEINFO(ID, TITLE, GENRE, COUNTRY, YEAR, DIRECTOR) describing the different properties of a movie, the relation MOVIEACTOR(ID, NAME), representing the cast of a movie, and MOVIEREVIEW(ID, REVIEW) representing reviews of movies.

Along with the mediated schema, the application designer needs to supply *descriptions* of the data sources. The descriptions specify the relationship between the relations in the mediated schema and those in the local schemas at the sources. The description of a data source specifies its contents (e.g., contains movies), attributes (e.g., genre, cast), constraints on its contents (e.g., contains only American movies), completeness and reliability, and finally, its query processing capabilities (e.g., can perform selections, or can answer arbitrary SQL queries).

The fact that data sources are pre-existing requires that we be able to handle the following characteristics in the language for describing the sources:

1. *Overlapping* and even *contradictory* data among different sources.

2. Semantic mismatches among sources: since each of the data sources has been designed by a different organization for different purposes, the data is modeled in different ways. For example, one source may store a relational database in which all the attributes of a particular movie are stored in one table, while another source may spread the attributes across several relations. Furthermore, the names of the attributes and of the tables will be different from one source to another, as will the choice of what should be a table and what should be an attribute.

3. Different naming conventions for data values: sources use different names or formats to refer to the same object. Simple examples include various conventions for specifying addresses or dates. Cases in which persons are named differently in the sources are harder to deal with (e.g., one source contains the full name, while another contains only the initials of the first name). This problem is not discussed further in this paper (see [Coh98b] for an elegant treatment of the problem).

Query reformulation: a user of a data integration system poses queries in terms of the mediated schema, rather than directly in the schema in which the data is stored. As a consequence, a data integration system must contain a module that uses the source descriptions in order to *reformulate* a user query into a query that refers directly to the schemas of the sources. Such a reformulation step does not exist in traditional database systems. Clearly, as the language for describing data sources becomes more expressive, the reformulation step becomes harder. Aside from wanting the reformulation to be semantically correct (i.e., the answers obtained from the sources will actually be correct answers to the query), an important goal of query reformulation is to ensure that we do not access irrelevant sources (i.e., sources that cannot contribute any answer or partial answer to the query). Data source modeling and query reformulation are discussed in Section 4.

Wrappers: the other layer of a data integration system that does not exist in a traditional system is the wrapper layer. Unlike a traditional query execution engine that communicates with a local storage manager to fetch the data, the query execution plan in a data integration system must obtain data from remote sources. A wrapper is a program which is specific to a data source, whose task is to translate data from the source to a form that is usable by the query processor of the system. For example, if the data source is a web site, the task of the wrapper is to translate the query to the source's interface, and when the answer is returned as an HTML document, it needs to extract a set of tuples from that document. Wrapper construction is described in Section 6.

Query optimization and execution: a traditional relational database system accepts a *declarative* SQL query. The query is first parsed and then passed to the *query optimizer*. The role of the optimizer is to produce an efficient *query execution plan*, which is an imperative program that specifies exactly how to evaluate the query. In particular, the plan specifies the *order* in which to perform the different operations in the query (join, selection, projection), a specific algorithm to use for each operation (e.g., sort-merge join, hash-join), and the scheduling of the different operators (in cases where parallelism is possible). Typically, the optimizer selects a query execution plan by searching a space of possible plans, and comparing their estimated cost. To evaluate the cost of a query execution plan the optimizer relies on extensive statistics about the underlying data, such as sizes of relations, sizes of domains and the selectivity of predicates. Finally, the query execution plan is passed to the query execution engine which evaluates the query.

The main differences between the traditional database context and that of data integration are the following:

- Since the sources are autonomous, the optimizer may have no statistics about the sources, or unreliable ones. Hence, the optimizer cannot compare between different plans, because their costs cannot be estimated.

- Since the data sources are not necessarily database systems, the sources may appear to have different processing capabilities. For example, one data source may be a web interface to a legacy information system, while another may be a program that scans data stored in a structured file (e.g., bibliography entries). Hence, the query optimizer needs to consider the possibility of exploiting the query processing capabilities of a data source. Note that query optimizers in distributed database systems also evaluate where parts of the query should be executed, but in a context where the different processors have identical capabilities.

- Finally, in a traditional system, the optimizer can reliably estimate the time to transfer data from the disc to main memory. But in a data integration system, data is often transferred over a wide-area network, and hence delays may occur for a multitude of reasons. Therefore, even a plan that appears to be the best based on cost estimates may turn out to be inefficient if there are unexpected delays in transferring data from one of the sources accessed early on in the plan.

Semistructured data: an issue that cuts across many layers of a data integration system is the problem of managing semistructured data. The term semistructured data has been used to refer to data that does not necessarily fit into a rigidly predefined schema, as is required in traditional database systems. This may arise because the data is very irregular (e.g., objects of the same type may have varying sets of attributes, attribute names are used in an irregular fashion), and hence can be described only by a schema that is relatively large. In other cases, the schema may be rapidly evolving, or not even declared at all (i.e., it may be implicit in the data). The database community has developed several methods to model and query for semistructured data (see [Bun97, Abi97] for recent surveys). Semistructured data is important for data integration systems for two reasons: first, in many cases, the data in the sources is semistructured; second, when integrating data from many sources, each with differing data models, it is convenient to consider a data model that is the least common denominator of these models. Data models for semistructured data, based on labeled directed graphs, tend to have this property. It should also be noted that XML, the emerging standard for data exchange over the WWW, has many features in common with semistructured data. An application of Description Logics to the the problem of reasoning about semistructured data is described in [CGL98].

4 Modeling Data Sources and Query Reformulation

As described in the previous section, one of the main differences between a data integration system and a traditional database system is that users pose queries in terms of a mediated schema. The data, however, is stored in the data sources, organized under local schemas. Hence, in order for the data integration system to answer queries, there must be some description of the relationship between the source relations and the mediated schema. The query processor of the integration system must be able to reformulate a query posed on the mediated schema into a query against the source schemas.

In principle, one could use arbitrary formulas in first-order logic to describe the data sources. But in such a case, sound and complete reformulation would practically impossible. Hence, several approaches have been explored in which restricted forms of first-order formulas have been used in source descriptions, and effective accompanying reformulation algorithms have been presented. These approaches include: *Global as view* (GAV) [GMPQ+97, PAGM96, ACPS96, HKWY97, FRV96, TRV98], *Local as view* (LAV) [LRO96b, KW96, DG97a, DG97b, FW97], and the use of Description Logics [AKS96, CL93, LRO96a, LR98].[1] Description Logics are covered in a different paper in this volume, and we do not elaborate on it any further here.

Global As View: This approach has its origins in multidatabase systems (e.g., Multibase [LR82]). In the GAV approach, for each relation R in the mediated schema, we write a query over the source relations specifying how to obtain R's tuples from the sources.

For example, suppose we have two sources DB_1 and DB_2 containing titles, directors and years of movies. We can describe the relationship between the sources and the mediated schema relation MOVIEYEAR as follows:

$$DB_1(id, title, director, year) \Rightarrow MovieYear(title, year)$$
$$DB_2(id, title, director, year) \Rightarrow MovieYear(title, year).$$

If we have a third source that shares movie identifiers with DB_1 and provides movie reviews, the following sentence describes how to obtain tuples for the MOVIEREVIEW relation:

---

[1]It should be noted that although Description Logics were used in [AKS96] to describe the data sources, the reformulation problem is viewed as a planning problem, and hence solved by a specialized planner.

$DB_1(id, title, director, year) \wedge DB_3(id, review) \Rightarrow MovieReview(title, director, review)$

In general, GAV descriptions are Horn rules that have a relation in the mediated schema in the consequent, and a conjunction of atoms over the source relations in the antecedent.

Query reformulation in GAV is relatively straightforward. Since the relations in the mediated schema are defined in terms of the source relations, we need only unfold the definitions of the mediated schema relations. For example, suppose our query is to find reviews for 1997 movies:

$q(title, review) : - MovieYear(title, 1997), MovieReview(title, review)$.

Unfolding the descriptions of MOVIEYEAR and MOVIEREVIEW will yield the following queries over the source relations: (the second of which will obviously be deemed redundant)

$q(title, review) : - DB_1(id, title, director, year), DB_3(id, review)$
$q(title, review) : - DB_1(id, title, director, year),$
$\qquad DB_2(title, director, year), DB_3(id, review)$

Local As View: The LAV approach is the opposite of GAV. Instead of writing rules whose consequents are relations in the mediated schema, the rules contain a conjunction of atoms over the mediated schema in the consequent, and an atom of the source relation in the antecedent. That is, for every data source S, we write a rule over the relations in the mediated schema that describes which tuples are found in S.

Suppose we have two sources: (1) V_1, containing titles, years and directors of American comedies produced after 1960, and (2) V_2 containing movie reviews. In LAV, we would describe these sources by the following sentences (variables that appear only on the right hand sides are assumed to be existentially quantified):

$S_1 : V_1(title, year, director) \Rightarrow Movie(title, year, director, genre) \wedge American(director) \wedge$
$\qquad year \geq 1960 \wedge genre = Comedy$.

$S_2 : V_2(title, review) \Rightarrow Movie(title, year, director, genre) \wedge year \geq 1990 \wedge Review(title, review)$.

Query reformulation in LAV is more tricky than in GAV, because it is not possible to simply unfold the definitions of the relations in the mediated schema. In fact, the reformulation problem here leads to a new inference problem, which can be explained intuitively as follows. Because of the form of the LAV descriptions, each of the sources can be viewed as containing an answer to a query over the mediated schema (the one expressed by the right hand side of the source description). Hence, sources represent materialized answers to queries over the virtual mediated schema. A user query is also posed over the mediated schema. The problem is therefore to find a way of answering the user query using only the answers to the queries describing the sources.

For example, suppose our query asks for reviews for comedies produced after 1950:

$q(title, review) : - Movie(title, year, director, Comedy), year \geq 1950, Review(title, review)$.

The reformulated query on the sources would be:

$q'(title, review) : - V_1(title, year, director), V_2(title, review)$.

The LAV reformulation problem is very closely related to the problem of answering queries using views, studied in the database literature [YL87, TSI96, LMSS95, CKPS95, RSU95, DG97b]. This problem has received significant attention because of its relevance to other database problems, such as query optimization [CKPS95], maintaining physical data independence [YL87, TSI96], and data warehouse design.

As it turns out, the query reformulation problem is in general NP-complete in the size of the source descriptions and user query even when the queries describing the sources and the user query are conjunctive and don't contain interpreted predicates [LMSS95]. However, in this and other important cases, reformulation is still polynomial in the number of data sources, and more importantly, answering queries is polynomial in the size of the data in the sources. Algorithms for query reformulation in LAV have been considered in [LRO96a, DG97a, FW97, LK98].

An interesting phenomenon in several variants of LAV descriptions is that the reformulated query may actually turn out to be a *recursive* query over the sources. The most interesting of these variants is the common case in which data sources can only be accessed with particular patterns.

Consider the following example, where the first source provides papers (for simplicity, identified by their title) published in AAAI, the second source records citations among papers, and the third source stores papers that have won significant awards. The superscripts in the source descriptions depict the access patterns that are available to the sources. The superscripts contain strings over the alphabet $\{b, f\}$. If a b appears in the i'th position, then the source requires a binding for the i'th attribute in order to produce provide answers. If an f appears in the i'th position, then the i'th attribute may be either bound or not. From the first source we can obtain all the AAAI papers (no bindings required); to obtain data from the second source the first we must provide a binding for a paper and then receive the set of papers that it cites; with the third source we can only query whether a *given* query won an award, but not ask for all the award winning papers.

$$AAAIdb^f(X) \Rightarrow AAAIPapers(X)$$
$$CitationDB^{bf}(X, Y) \Rightarrow Cites(X, Y)$$
$$AwardDB^b(X) \Rightarrow AwardPaper(X)$$

Suppose our query is to find all the award winning papers:

$$Q(X) : -AwardPaper(X)$$

As the following queries show, there is no finite number of conjunctive queries over the sources that is guaranteed to provide *all* the answers to the query. In each query, we can start from the AAAI database, follow citation chains of length n, and feed the results into the award database. Since we cannot limit the length of a citation chain we need to follow apriori (without examining the data), we cannot put a bound on the size of the reformulated query.

$$Q'(X) : -AAAIdb(X), AwardDB(X)$$
$$Q'(X) : -AAAIdb(V), CitationDB(V, X_1), \ldots, CitationDB(X_n, X), AwardDB(X).$$

However, if we consider recursive queries over the sources, we can obtain a finite concise query that provides all the answers, as follows (note that the newly invented relation *papers* is meant to represent the set of all papers reachable from the AAAI database):

$$papers(X) : -AAAIdb(X)$$
$$papers(X) : -papers(Y), CitationDB(Y, X)$$
$$Q'(X) : -papers(X), AwardDB(X).$$

Other cases in which recursion may be necessary are in the presence of functional dependencies on the mediated schema [DL97], when the user query is recursive [DG97a], and when the descriptions of the sources are enriched by description logics [BLR97].

Finally, it turns out that slight changes to the form of source descriptions in LAV can cause the problem of answering queries to become NP-hard in the size of the data in the sources [AD98]. Most of these cases arise when we discuss completeness information (Section 5), but even in our case, it may happen, for example in the case where the query contains the predicate $\neq$. This phenomenon hints at the fact that in some sense, LAV has a greater expressive power than GAV.

A Comparison of the Approaches: The main advantage of the GAV approach is that query reformulation is very simple, because it reduces to rule unfolding. However, adding sources to the data integration system is non-trivial. In particular, given a new source, we need to figure out all the ways in which it can be used in order obtain tuples for each of the relations in the mediated schema. Therefore, we need to consider the possible interaction of the new source with each of the existing sources, and this limits the ability of the GAV approach to scale to a large collection of sources.

In contrast, in the LAV approach each source is described in isolation. It is the system's task to figure out (at query time) how the sources interact and how their data can be combined to answer the query. The downside, however, is that query reformulation is harder, and sometimes requires recursive queries over the sources. An additional advantage of the LAV approach is that it is easier to specify rich constraints on the contents of a source (simply by specifying more conditions in the source descriptions). Specifying complex constraints on sources is essential if the data integration system is to distinguish between sources with closely related and overlapping data.

5 Modeling Source Completeness

The source descriptions we considered in the previous section only allowed us to express necessary conditions for finding a certain piece of data in a source but not sufficient conditions. For example, we were able to express that V_1 contains American comedies produced after 1960, but we could not state that the source contains *all* such movies.

Such source descriptions are adequate to capture incomplete sources, which at least in the case of sources on the WWW, covers many of the cases. However, there are situations in which we want to state that a source is complete, or at least partially complete. For example, the DB&LP Database[2] contains the complete set of papers published in most major database conferences; the Library of Congress web site contains the complete list of books published in the U.S. When modeling data sources within an enterprise, completeness assertions are even more common.

Knowledge of a data source's completeness can help a data integration system in several ways. Most importantly, since a *negative* answer from a complete source is meaningful, the data integration system can prune access to other sources. For example, if our query asks whether a certain person authored a paper in SIGMOD-98, we need only consult the DB&LP bibliography, and not other sources that may contain overlapping data.

Local completeness assertions were first considered in the context of the Internet Softbot project [EGW94]. In that work, the authors considered statements of the form:[3]

$LCW(V_1(title, director, year), American(director) \wedge year \geq 1960)$

---

[2]http://www.acm.org/sigmod/dblp/db/index.html
[3]LCW stands for Local Closed World [EGW94].

meaning that the movie source is complete with respect to films produced by American directors after 1960. These statements were shown to be a restricted form of more general non-monotonic reasoning formalisms.

The inference question that arises in the presence of such completeness statements is the *answer completeness problem:* given a user query Q, a reformulation Q' of Q over the data sources, and a set of source completeness statements, does Q' produce the complete answer for Q? For example, if the user asks for titles of recent American comedies, the source above would provide a complete answer, but if the user also asks for reviews of such movies then the answer may be incomplete if our review sources are incomplete.

In [EGW94] the authors describe several rules for inferring completeness statements for queries. In [Lev96] is it shown that this inference problem is closely related to the problem of deciding whether a database query is independent of an insertion or deletion update to the database. This relationship enables the transfer of several algorithms and complexity results to the answer completeness problem. Several other works have considered more expressive forms of local completeness statements ([Dus97, FW97]). Finally, Abiteboul and Duschka [AD98] show that in the presence of completeness assertions in LAV descriptions, the complexity of answering a query becomes NP-hard in the size of the data in the sources.

Using probabilistic information for data integration: a different approach to handling incompleteness and source overlap based on using probabilistic information is proposed in [FKL97]. To motivate the use of probabilistic information, consider a data integration system providing access to multiple bibliography data sources available online.[4] Figure 2 shows a set of classes (i.e., unary relations) and a set of attributes we may associate with papers in our domain. The schema contains a class CS-Paper denoting the set of publications in Computer Science. One partition of the CS-paper class is by publication type, i.e., the classes Journal, Conference and Book, which are assumed to be pairwise disjoint. A second partition is by a topic hierarchy. Note that whereas in the first case, the classes in the partition were pairwise disjoint, these classes in the second partition are obviously overlapping.

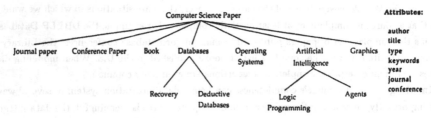

Figure 2: Mediated schema for publication domain.

The first kind of probabilistic information we would like to consider is a generalization of the completeness statements described above. Instead of specifying that a source is complete with respect to its content, we would want to express the probability of finding a certain data item in the source. For example, we would like to specify that the probability of finding an arbitrary paper on Deductive Databases in source S_1 is 0.8, which we can denote by $P(S_1 \mid DDB) = 0.8$. As a result, we are able to distinguish between sources that are relatively complete and those that are rather sparse.

---

[4]See http://glimpse.cs.arizona.edu/bib/ for a large class of such sources.

The second kind of information concerns overlap between classes in the mediated schema. With purely logical formalisms, we can only express three kinds of relationships between classes: (1) one class is a superset of the other; (2) two classes are disjoint; (3) there is *some* overlap between a pair of classes. In our example, since no pair of topics in Computer Science are completely disjoint, if we asked for papers about Database Systems, the data integration system cannot prune *any* source containing Computer Science papers. However, we would like to be able at least to order the access to the sources, depending on their potential relevance to the query. Hence, we need a mechanism for specifying the *degree* of overlap between the classes. For example, we would like to specify that $P(AI \mid DB) = 0.05$, denoting that the probability that a Database paper is also about AI is 0.05, and $P(DB \mid OS) = 0.2$, showing that the overlap between the fields of Databases and Operating Systems is much larger.[5]

Finally, we may want to represent information on the overlap between information sources. While it is possible to assume that the overlap between sources can be automatically derived from the first two kinds of information, in some particular cases we may have more specific overlap information. For example, one source may be known to be a subset of another.

The work in [FKL97] describes a method for describing these three kinds of probabilistic information, and algorithms that exploit this information to order the access to data sources. The key challenge in designing a formalism for specifying probabilistic information is that the size of the specification is exponential in the size of number of classes considered in the schema. For example, suppose we want to specify a probability distribution on the set of topics of Computer Science. That is, for every set of topics $\mathcal{A}$ we want to know the probability that a paper belongs to all the topics in $\mathcal{A}$. To do so, we need to specify 2^n numbers, where n is the number of topics. This presents two problems. First, from a modeling viewpoint, we do not want to specify such a large number of probabilities. Second, performing computations with such a large set of probabilities will be prohibitively expensive. Instead, we would like to specify only a small number of probabilities (e.g., intersections only between pairs or subset of the pairs of topics in Computer Science), and to efficiently compute the other probabilities that may be needed in the process of source selection. It is interesting to note that Bayesian Networks are inadequate for describing the overlap between classes in the mediated schema because the set of classes are highly related to each other (leading to a highly connected network). Instead, [FKL97] describes a tree-based representation of the probability distribution.

6 Extracting Data from Sources: Wrapper Construction

In a traditional database system tuples of the database relations are obtained by the query execution engine via an interface to the local storage manager. However, a data integration system must communicate with external sources in order to obtain data. External sources typically do not provide the data integration system with a stream of tuples in a standard format, but rather in a format native to the source. Hence, the integration system communicates with each source through a wrapper program, whose main task is to pose queries to the data source and convert the answer into a format that can be manipulated by the execution engine.

When the data source is a web-site, the answer to a query is usually an HTML document. The wrapper must then extract a set of answer tuples out of the resulting HTML page. The main difficulty in building wrappers is that the HTML page is usually designed for human viewing, rather than for programmatic manipulation data by programs. Hence, the data is often embedded

---

[5]The probabilities in this example are pure fiction.

in natural language text or hidden within graphical presentation primitives. Moreover, the form of the HTML pages changes frequently (even within one web-site), making it hard to write rules for extracting the data from the HTML file and to maintain these rules over time.

Several works have considered the problem of building tools for rapid creation of wrappers. One class of tools (e.g., [HGMN+98, GRVB98]) is based on developing specialized grammars for specifying how the data is laid out in an HTML page, and therefore how to extract the required data.

A second class of techniques for building wrappers is based on developing inductive learning techniques for automatically learning a wrapper. Using such algorithms, we provide the system with a set of HTML pages where the data in each page is labeled. The algorithm uses the labeled examples to automatically learn a grammar by which the data can be extracted from subsequent pages. Naturally, the more examples we give the system, the more accurate the resulting grammar can be, and the challenge is to discover wrapper languages that can be learned with a small number of examples.

The first formulation of wrapper construction as inductive learning was presented in [KDW97]. In that work, the authors identified HLRT, a class of wrappers which is efficiently learnable, yet expressive enough to handle numerous actual Internet information resources. HLRT is designed for resources that display their content in a tabular layout. HLRT wrappers scan their input for substrings that delimit the information to be extracted. For example, in the context of Internet sources, these delimiters can be HTML tags. HLRT corresponds essentially to a class of finite-state automata, so wrapper induction is similar to FSA induction (e.g., [Ang82]). Since FSAs run in linear time, HLRT satisfies the desire that wrappers be fast. However, since wrappers are used for parsing (rather than just classification), the learned FSA must have a specific state topology. Existing FSA induction algorithms do not make such guarantees, hence specialized algorithms for HLRT induction had to be developed.

Other works that have considered this approach to wrapper construction include [AK97] that exploits heuristics specific to the common uses of HTML in order to obtain faster learning, and [Coh98a] who describes an algorithm for learning wrappers that do not output their answers in tabular form, but rather in the form of nested tables. Finally, we note that the emergence of XML may lead web-site builders to export the data underlying their sites in a machine readable form, thereby greatly simplifying the construction of wrappers. However, it should be emphasized that XML does not solve the problems of semantic integration.

The work described [CDF+98] is a first step in bridging the gap between the approaches of Machine Learning and of Natural Language Processing to the problem of wrapper construction. Another important use of Machine Learning in the context of data integration has been to learn the mapping between the source schemas and the mediated schemas [PE95, DEW97].

7 Query Optimization and Execution

In a traditional database system, query optimization refers to the process of translating a declarative query (e.g., in SQL) into a query execution plan, i.e., a specific sequence of steps that the query execution engine should follow to evaluate the query. As we have discussed earlier, in the data integration context, some optimizations are done already at the query reformulation step: the query is reformulated as to not access any irrelevant or redundant data sources, and to pose the most specific query possible to each of the sources it does access.

By and large, the query optimization problem for data integration has received relatively little attention, compared to the problems of query reformulation and wrapper construction. As stated earlier, the challenges for query optimization arise because the sources have different processing capabilities, there are few statistics about the data sources, and data transfer rates over the network cannot always be anticipated in advance. The issue of describing the query processing capabilities of a data source and creating query execution plans that conform to these capabilities is considered in [LRO96b, PGGMU95, VP97, HKWY97]. Adapting query execution plan in the presence of network delays is considered in [UFA98].

The above characteristics of the data integration problem force us to reconsider the architecture of a query processor for data integration. Whereas a traditional system first decides on a query execution plan and then executes it, the absence of statistics and the need to adapt to network delays renders such a two-phase approach infeasible. Hence, an approach followed in recent work [Kno95, IFF+98] is to interleave optimization and execution of the query. Instead of creating a complete plan for the query in advance, the query optimizer may create a plan fragment, which answers only part of the query. Once this fragment has been executed, the optimizer may have additional information to use for planning for the subsequent parts of the query. The main challenge in this architecture is to find the effective points for interleaving the optimization and execution.

8 Web-Site Management

One of the prime forces driving many data integration applications is web-site construction and management. The first step that an enterprise needs to tackle when constructing a web-site is to build a coherent view of all the data that is available across the enterprise. Providing a uniform interface to all this data significantly simplifies the task of constructing the site. Furthermore, results of data integration queries in this context are not considered in isolation, but rather as entry points into complex webs of data (e.g., hyperlinks to information related to the answer).

The problem of building web-sites with complex structures that serve data from multiple sources has very recently received significant attention in the Database community. The theme underlying many of the works in this area is to represent the *content* and the *structure* (i.e., the set of pages, the data at each page and the links between the pages) of a web-site in a declarative fashion. The main advantage of this approach is the ability to easily *restructure* a web-site and to construct multiple versions of a web-site from the same underlying content (e.g., consider a company that creates an internal web-site for its employees and several external ones for its customers, suppliers, or other affiliate companies).

The realization that web-sites can be constructed (or at least, modeled) as richly connected pieces of data/knowledge, presents an important opportunity for future contributions of AI techniques. Before discussing such opportunities, I briefly describe the STRUDEL system [FFK+98], which was the first to introduce the idea of constructing web-sites using declarative representations.

The architecture of STRUDEL is shown in Figure 3. At the bottom level, STRUDEL uses a data integration system to accessed a set of data sources containing the data that will be served on the web-site. The data may be stored in databases, in structured files, or in existing web-sites. The data is represented throughout the system as a labeled directed graph, in the spirit of models proposed for semistructured data [Bun97, Abi97].

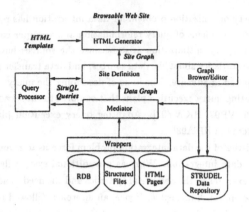

Figure 3: Architecture for Web-Site Management Systems

The main step in building a web-site is to write a declarative expression that represents the structure of the site. The expression is written in the STRUQL language, which is a language for querying and restructuring graphs. That is, STRUQL accepts a set of graphs as input, and outputs a graph. The result of applying this query to the underlying data, called the *site-graph,* is the logical representation of the web-site. The logical representation specifies the pages of the site, the data at each page, and the links between the pages, but *not* how to graphically render each paer. To create HTML pages the system applies a set of HTML templates to the nodes in the site graph. An HTML template is an HTML file where some constants are replaced by variable names that can be bound to different values.

STRUDEL is best illustrated by an example. Consider the construction of a simplified version of a researcher's homepage. The source of raw data is a Bibtex bibliography that contains the researcher's publications. In the data graph, we represent this data by a class PUBLICATIONS, as seen in Figure 4 (note that the data can easily be represented by a labeled graph).

```
object pub1 in Publications {
    title "Web-Sites With Common Sense"
    author "John McCarthy"
    author "Tim Berners-Lee"
    year    1998
    booktitle "AAAI 98"
    pub-type  "inproceedings"
    abs-file  "abstracts/bm98"
    ps-file   "proceedings/aaai98.ps"
    category  "Philosophical Foundations"
    category  "Knowledge Representation"
}
```

Figure 4: Fragment of data graph for homepage site

The structure of the homepage site is defined by the STRUQL expression in Figure 5. The site has four types of pages: a root page containing general information, an "All Titles" page containing the list of titles of the researcher's papers, a "category" page containing summaries of papers in a particular category, and a "Paper Presentation" page for each paper.

The first clause creates the RootPage and AllTitles pages and links them. Lines 7-9 create a page for each publication, and links the publication page to each of its attributes. Note that we copy all the attributes of a given publication using the arc variable L, which gets bound to attribute names, rather than objects. Lines 12-16 consider the category attribute of each publication and create the appropriate category pages with links to the appropriate publication pages. Finally, lines 19-21 link the "All Titles" page to the titles of all the papers and the papers' individual pages.

```
1    INPUT BIBTEX
2    // Create root page and abstracts page and link them
3    CREATE RootPage(), AllTitlesPage()
4    LINK   RootPage() -> "All Titles" -> AllTitlesPage()
5
6    // Create a presentation for every publication x
7    WHERE  Publications(X), X -> L -> V
8    CREATE PaperPresentation(X)
9    LINK   PaperPresentation(X) -> L -> V,
10
11   // Create a page  for every category
12     { WHERE  L = "category"
13       CREATE CategoryPage(V)
14       LINK   CategoryPage(V)  -> "Paper" -> PaperPresentation(X),
15              CategoryPage(V)  -> "Name" -> V
16
17       // Link root page to each category page
18              RootPage()  -> "CategoryPage"  -> CategoryPage(V) }
19     { WHERE L = "title"
20       LINK  AllTitlesPage() -> "title" -> V,
21             AllTitlesPage -> "More Details" -> PaperPresentation(X) }
22   OUTPUT HomePage
```

Figure 5: Site definition query for example homepage site

The main point to note about STRUDEL and its sibling systems (e.g., [AMM98, AM98, CDSS98, PF98, JB97, TN98]) is that the structure of the site is specified declaratively, and hence restructuring the site or creating multiple versions of the site amount to writing different site definition queries. Given that web-sites can be specified declaratively, one can start tackling higher-level issues in managing web-sites, as the following.

Reasoning about integrity constraints: as builders of web-sites, we would like to enforce constraints on the structure of our site (e.g., no dangling pointers, an employee's homepage should point to their department's homepage). Clearly, once we have created the web-site, we can go through it and check whether the constraints are satisfied, but in that case, we would have to repeat the check every time the web-site is updated. A more interesting approach is to look at the intensional definition of the structure of the web-site (i.e., the STRUQL query), and verify that a certain integrity constraint will hold for every web-site generated by the definition. This leads to a problem which is similar in spirit to that of knowledge base verification [LR96, SS97]. A first attempt to address this problem is described in [FFLS98].

Rule-based specification of web-sites: in the above approach, we specify the structure of the web-site, and then check whether the given integrity constraints are guaranteed to hold for every instantiation of the structure. A different approach is to specify the structure of the site at a higher level: to specify only the integrity constraints for the site. The system would then consider the constraints and would propose a structure for the web-site. This approach can be useful in cases where most of the structure is driven by constraints. For example, [LS98] considers the design of online stores and proposes a set of rules that, if followed, would improve the site design. The challenge we face is to build a system that receives the constraints as input, and outputs the *best* possible site structure.

Automatically restructuring web-sites: the short experience in building web-sites has already shown that it is a highly iterative process. Even after the web-site is up, designers will frequently want to restructure it after understanding the patterns with which users browse the site. Perkowitz and Etzioni [PE97] have proposed the notion of *adaptive* web-sites that restructure themselves automatically. Declarative representations of web-sites provide a basis on which to build adaptive web-sites. In particular, once we have a model of a web-site, we can analyze the user browsing patterns and propose ways to restructure the web-site.

9 Conclusions

As shown in this paper, AI techniques have had a significant impact on building data integration systems. Of particular note is the use of various Knowledge Representation techniques for modeling contents of data sources. Machine Learning algorithms offer the most promising methods for rapid construction of wrappers.

Furthermore, current problems being addressed by the data integration community can also benefit from AI techniques: the need for techniques for interleaving query optimization and execution, use of probabilistic reasoning for modeling domains of data integration, and the use of Machine Learning algorithms for automatically deriving source descriptions. The area of web-site management poses several important challenges for AI researchers.

As we embark on these and future challenges it is important to keep in mind a couple of principles. First, an AI technique applied in isolation to a data integration problem, but rather in the context of a larger system. Hence, for an AI technique to have significant impact on the practice of data integration, one must understand well the rest of the system and how to best tailor the technique to this setting. This principle applies especially in the consideration of Knowledge Representation techniques and in future applications of planning methods. Second, data integration research has matured to the point where significant progress must be validated empirically. Hence I believe that future contributions must be accompanied by significant performance studies.

Acknowledgements

I would like to thank Dana Florescu, Zack Ives, Nick Kushmerick, Werner Nutt, Rachel Pottinger and Dan Weld for their input in writing this paper.

References

[AAB+98]   Jos Luis Ambite, Naveen Ashish, Greg Barish, Craig A. Knoblock, Steven Minton, Pragnesh J. Modi, Ion Muslea, Andrew Philpot, and Sheila Tejada. ARIADNE: A system for constructing mediators for internet sources (system demonstration). In *Proc. of ACM SIGMOD Conf. on Management of Data*, Seattle, WA, 1998.

[Abi97]   Serge Abiteboul. Querying semi-structured data. In *Proc. of the Int. Conf. on Database Theory (ICDT)*, Delphi, Greece, 1997.

[ACPS96]   S. Adali, K. Candan, Y. Papakonstantinou, and V.S. Subrahmanian. Query caching and optimization in distributed mediator systems. In *Proc. of ACM SIGMOD Conf. on Management of Data*, Montreal, Canada, 1996.

[AD98]   S. Abiteboul and O. Duschka. Complexity of answering queries using materialized views. In *Proc. of the ACM SIGACT-SIGMOD-SIGART Symposium on Principles of Database Systems (PODS)*, Seattle, WA, 1998.

[AK97]   Naveen Ashish and Craig A. Knoblock. Wrapper generation for semi-structured internet sources. *SIGMOD Record*, 26(4):8-15, 1997.

[AKS96]   Yigal Arens, Craig A. Knoblock, and Wei-Min Shen. Query reformulation for dynamic information integration. *International Journal on Intelligent and Cooperative Information Systems*, (6) 2/3:99-130, June 1996.

[AM98]   Gustavo Arocena and Alberto Mendelzon. WebOQL: Restructuring documents, databases and webs. In *Proc. of Int. Conf. on Data Engineering (ICDE)*, Orlando, Florida, 1998.

[AMM98]   Paolo Atzeni, Giansalvatore Mecca, and Paolo Merialdo. Design and maintenance of data-intensive web sites. In *Proc. of the Conf. on Extending Database Technology (EDBT)*, Valencia, Spain, 1998.

[Ang82]   D. Angluin. Inference of reversible languages. *Journal of the ACM*, 29(3):741-65, 1982.

[BEM+98]   C. Beeri, G. Elber, T. Milo, Y. Sagiv, O.Shmueli, N.Tishby, Y.Kogan, D.Konopnicki, P. Mogilevski, and N.Slonim. Websuite-a tool suite for harnessing web data. In *Proceedings of the International Workshop on the Web and Databases*, Valencia, Spain, 1998.

[BLR97]   Catriel Beeri, Alon Y. Levy, and Marie-Christine Rousset. Rewriting queries using views in description logics. In *Proc. of the ACM SIGACT-SIGMOD-SIGART Symposium on Principles of Database Systems (PODS)*, Tucson, Arizona., 1997.

[Bun97]   Peter Buneman. Semistructured data. In Proc. of the ACM SIGACT-SIGMOD-SIGART Symposium on Principles of Database Systems (PODS), pages 117-121, Tucson, Arizona, 1997.

[CCM+98]   T. Catarci, S.K. Chang, M.Lenzerini, D. Nardi, and G. Santucci. Turning the web into a database: the WAG approach. In *Proceedings of HICSS*, 1998.

[CDF+98]   Mark Craven, Dan DiPasquo, Dayne Freitag, Andrew McCallum, Tom Mitchell, Kamal Nigam, and Sean Slattery. Learning to extract symbolic knowledge from the world-wide web. In *Proceedings of the AAAI Fifteenth National Conference on Artificial Intelligence*, 1998.

[CDSS98]   Sophie Cluet, Claude Delobel, Jerome Simeon, and Katarzyna Smaga. Your mediators need data conversion. In *Proc. of ACM SIGMOD Conf. on Management of Data*, Seattle, WA, 1998.

[CGL98]   Diego Calvanese, Giuseppe De Giacomo, and Maurizio Lenzerini. What can knowledge representation do for semi-structured data? In *Proceedings of the National Conference on Artificial Intelligence*, 1998.

[CKPS95]   Surajit Chaudhuri, Ravi Krishnamurthy, Spyros Potamianos, and Kyuseok Shim. Optimizing queries with materialized views. In *Proc. of Int. Conf. on Data Engineering (ICDE)*, Taipei, Taiwan, 1995.

[CL93]   T. Catarci and M. Lenzerini. Representing and using interschema knowledge in cooperative information systems. *Journal of Intelligent and Cooperative Information Systems*, 1993.

266

[Coh98a]   W. Cohen. A web-based information system that reasons with structured collections of text. In *Proc. Second Intl. Conf. Autonomous Agents*, pages 400–407, 1998.

[Coh98b]   William Cohen. Integration of heterogeneous databases without common domains using queries based on textual similarity. In *Proc. of ACM SIGMOD Conf. on Management of Data*, Seattle, WA, 1998.

[DEW97]   B. Doorenbos, O. Etzioni, and D. Weld. Scalable comparison-shopping agent for the world-wide web. In *Proceedings of the International Conference on Autonomous Agents*, February 1997.

[DG97a]   Oliver M. Duschka and Michael R. Genesereth. Answering recursive queries using views. In *Proc. of the ACM SIGACT-SIGMOD-SIGART Symposium on Principles of Database Systems (PODS)*, Tucson, Arizona., 1997.

[DG97b]   Oliver M. Duschka and Michael R. Genesereth. Query planning in infomaster. In *Proceedings of the ACM Symposium on Applied Computing*, San Jose, CA, 1997.

[DL97]   Oliver M. Duschka and Alon Y. Levy. Recursive plans for information gathering. In *Proceedings of the 15th International Joint Conference on Artificial Intelligence*, 1997.

[Dus97]   Oliver Duschka. Query optimization using local completeness. In *Proceedings of the AAAI Fourteenth National Conference on Artificial Intelligence*, 1997.

[EGW94]   Oren Etzioni, Keith Golden, and Daniel Weld. Tractable closed world reasoning with updates. In *Proceedings of the Conference on Principles of Knowledge Representation and Reasoning, KR-94.*, 1994. Extended version to appear in *Artificial Intelligence*.

[FFK+98]   Mary Fernandez, Daniela Florescu, Jaewoo Kang, Alon Levy, and Dan Suciu. Catching the boat with Strudel: Experiences with a web-site management system. In *Proc. of ACM SIGMOD Conf. on Management of Data*, Seattle, WA, 1998.

[FFLS98]   Mary Fernandez, Daniela Florescu, Alon Levy, and Dan Suciu. Reasoning about web-sites. In *Working notes of the AAAI-98 Workshop on Artificial Intelligence and Data Integration. American Association of Artificial Intelligence.*, 1998.

[FKL97]   Daniela Florescu, Daphne Koller, and Alon Levy. Using probabilistic information in data integration. In *Proc. of the Int. Conf. on Very Large Data Bases (VLDB)*, pages 216–225, Athens, Greece, 1997.

[FRV96]   Daniela Florescu, Louiqa Raschid, and Patrick Valduriez. A methodology for query reformulation in cis using semantic knowledge. *Int. Journal of Intelligent & Cooperative Information Systems, special issue on Formal Methods in Cooperative Information Systems*, 5(4), 1996.

[FW97]   M. Friedman and D. Weld. Efficient execution of information gathering plans. In *Proceedings of the International Joint Conference on Artificial Intelligence*, Nagoya, Japan, 1997.

[GMPQ+97]   H. Garcia-Molina, Y. Papakonstantinou, D. Quass, A. Rajaraman, Y. Sagiv, J. Ullman, and J. Widom. The TSIMMIS project: Integration of heterogeneous information sources. *Journal of Intelligent Information Systems*, 8(2):117–132, March 1997.

[GRVB98]   Jean-Robert Gruser, Louiqa Raschid, María Esther Vidal, and Laura Bright. Wrapper generation for web accessible data sources. In *Proceedings of the CoopIS*, 1998.

[HGMN+98]   Joachim Hammer, Hector Garcia-Molina, Svetlozar Nestorov, Ramana Yerneni, Markus M. Breunig, and Vasilis Vassalos. Template-based wrappers in the TSIMMIS system (system demonstration). In *Proc. of ACM SIGMOD Conf. on Management of Data*, Tucson, Arizona, 1998.

[HKWY97]   Laura Haas, Donald Kossmann, Edward Wimmers, and Jun Yang. Optimizing queries across diverse data sources. In *Proc. of the Int. Conf. on Very Large Data Bases (VLDB)*, Athens, Greece, 1997.

[IFF+98]   Zachary Ives, Daniela Florescu, Marc Friedman, Alon Levy, and Dan Weld. An adaptive query execution engine for data integration. submitted for publication, 1998.

[JB97]   R. Jakobovits and J. F. Brinkley. Managing medical research data with a web-interfacing repository manager. In *American Medical Informatics Association Fall Symposium*, pages 454–458, Nashville, Oct 1997.

[KDW97]   N. Kushmerick, R. Doorenbos, and D. Weld. Wrapper induction for information extraction. In *Proceedings of the 15th International Joint Conference on Artificial Intelligence*, 1997.

[Kno95]   Craig A. Knoblock. Planning executing, sensing and replanning for information gathering. In *Proceedings of the 14th International Joint Conference on Artificial Intelligence*, 1995.

[KW96]   Chung T. Kwok and Daniel S. Weld. Planning to gather information. In *Proceedings of the AAAI Thirteenth National Conference on Artificial Intelligence*, 1996.

[LB87]   Hector J. Levesque and Ronald J. Brachman. Expressiveness and tractability in knowledge representation and reasoning. *Computational Intelligence*, 3:78–93, 1987.

[Lev96]   Alon Y. Levy. Obtaining complete answers from incomplete databases. In *Proc. of the Int. Conf. on Very Large Data Bases (VLDB)*, Bombay, India, 1996.

[LK98]   E. Lambrecht and S. Kambhampati. Optimization strategies for information gathering plans. TR-98-018, Arizona State University Department of Computer Science, 1998.

[LMR90]   Witold Litwin, Leo Mark, and Nick Roussopoulos. Interoperability of multiple autonomous databases. *ACM Computing Surveys*, 22 (3):267–293, 1990.

[LMSS95]   Alon Y. Levy, Alberto O. Mendelzon, Yehoshua Sagiv, and Divesh Srivastava. Answering queries using views. In *Proc. of the ACM SIGACT-SIGMOD-SIGART Symposium on Principles of Database Systems (PODS)*, San Jose, CA, 1995.

[LR82]   T. Landers and R. Rosenberg. An overview of multibase. In *Proceedings of the Second International Symoposium on Distributed Databases*, pages 153–183. North Holland, Amsterdam, 1982.

[LR96]   Alon Y. Levy and Marie-Christine Rousset. Verification of knowledge bases using containment checking. In *In Proceedings of AAAI*, 1996.

[LR98]   Veronique Lattes and Marie-Christine Rousset. The use of the CARIN language and algorithms for information integration: the PICSEL project. In *Proceedings of the ECAI-98 Workshop on Intelligent Information Integration*, 1998.

[LRO96a]   Alon Y. Levy, Anand Rajaraman, and Joann J. Ordille. Query answering algorithms for information agents. In *Proceedings of AAAI*, 1996.

[LRO96b]   Alon Y. Levy, Anand Rajaraman, and Joann J. Ordille. Querying heterogeneous information sources using source descriptions. In *Proc. of the Int. Conf. on Very Large Data Bases (VLDB)*, Bombay, India, 1996.

[LS98]   Gerald Lohse and Peter Spiller. Electronic shopping. *Comm. of the ACM*, 41(7), July 1998.

[PAGM96]   Y. Papakonstantinou, S. Abiteboul, and H. Garcia-Molina. Object fusion in mediator systems. In *Proc. of the Int. Conf. on Very Large Data Bases (VLDB)*, Bombay, India, 1996.

[PE95]   Mike Perkowitz and Oren Etzioni. Category translation: Learning to understand information on the internet. In *Working Notes of the AAAI Spring Symposium on Information Gathering from Heterogeneous Distributed Environments*. American Association for Artificial Intelligence, 1995.

[PE97]   Mike Perkowitz and Oren Etzioni. Adaptive web sites: an AI challenge. In *Proceedings of the 15th International Joint Conference on Artificial Intelligence*, 1997.

[PF98]   P. Paolini and P. Fraternali. A conceptual model and a tool environment for developing more scalable, dynamic, and customizable web applications. In *Proc. of the Conf. on Extending Database Technology (EDBT)*, Valencia, Spain, 1998.

[PGGMU95] Yannis Papakonstantinou, Ashish Gupta, Hector Garcia-Molina, and Jeffrey Ullman. A query translation scheme for rapid implementation of wrappers. In *Proc. of the Int. Conf. on Deductive and Object-Oriented Databases (DOOD)*, 1995.

[Rei88]   Raymond Reiter. Towards a logical reconstruction of relational database theory. In John Mylopoulos and Michael Brodie, editors, *Readings in Artificial Intelligence and Databases*, pages 301–326. Morgan Kaufmann, Los Altos, CA, 1988.

[RSU95]   Anand Rajaraman, Yehoshua Sagiv, and Jeffrey D. Ullman. Answering queries using templates with binding patterns. In *Proc. of the ACM SIGACT-SIGMOD-SIGART Symposium on Principles of Database Systems (PODS)*, San Jose, CA, 1995.

[SS97]   James Schmolze and Wayne Snyder. Detecting redundant production rules. In *Proceedings of the National Conference on Artificial Intelligence*, 1997.

[TN98]   Motomichi Toyama and T. Nagafuji. Dynamic and structured presentation of database contents on the web. In *Proc. of the Conf. on Extending Database Technology (EDBT)*, Valencia, Spain, 1998.

[TRV98]   A. Tomasic, L. Raschid, and P. Valduriez. Scaling access to distributed heterogeneous data sources with Disco. IEEE Transactions On Knowledge and Data Engineering *(to appear)*, 1998.

[TSI96]   Odysseas G. Tsatalos, Marvin H. Solomon, and Yannis E. Ioannidis. The GMAP: A versatile tool for physical data independence. *VLDB Journal*, 5(2):101–118, 1996.

[UFA98]   Tolga Urhan, Michael J. Franklin, and Laurent Amsaleg. Cost based query scrambling for initial delays. In *Proc. of ACM SIGMOD Conf. on Management of Data*, pages 130–141, Seattle, WA, 1998.

[VP97]   Vasilis Vassalos and Yannis Papakonstantinou. Describing and using the query capabilities of heterogeneous sources. In *Proc. of the Int. Conf. on Very Large Data Bases (VLDB)*, Athens, Greece, 1997.

[YL87]   H. Z. Yang and P. A. Larson. Query transformation for PSJ-queries. In *Proc. of the Int. Conf. on Very Large Data Bases (VLDB)*, pages 245–254, Brighton, England, 1987.

"Underwater Love"
Building Tristão and Isolda's Personalities

Carlos Martinho and Ana Paiva

Instituto de Engenharia de Sistemas e Computadores,
Rua Alves Redol 9, 1000-029 Lisboa, Portugal,
{Carlos.Martinho|Ana.Paiva}@inesc.pt

Abstract. Believability is one of the key concerns when developing synthetic characters in intelligent virtual environments. To achieve believability, the virtual characters must behave consistently with their assumed or perceived personality.

This paper describes a model for the construction of believable emotional characters with synthetic personae in intelligent virtual environments. The model assumes that personality and emotions are essentially the same mechanism and allows the definition of the characters personality by a set of emotional reactions. The system designer defines a set of concepts, which structure is inspired by Ortony, Clore and Collins's theory of emotions, that will then automatically integrated in the IVE character cycle, inspired by Fridja's theory of emotions. Then, the system designer implements the final IVE specific characteristics around those concepts. The methodology was applied to a real time IVE, S3A, developed in the context of the last world exposition of the century, EXPO'98, which featured two pathematic dolphins, Tristão and Isolda, who lived in the synthetic estuary of the river Sado during the four months of the EXPO'98, and were displayed to more than one million visitors.

The project showed that the followed approach is a viable solution for the creation of the synthetic personae of believable emotional agents in intelligent virtual environments.

1 Introduction

The integration of user-independent components in virtual environments has grown to a point where it is almost impossible to consider building virtual worlds without them. Synthetic actors are presently one of the most investigated components of Intelligent Virtual Environments (IVE). The Jack system [2], STEVE [10], Virtual Theater [7], Cosmo and Herman [11], Oz [12], ALIVE [13] and Artificial Fishes [22], are but a few examples.

Naturally, developing intelligent virtual environments raised new concerns. One of the major concerns is the creation of *believable characters*, characters that give the illusion of life and allow the participants' *suspension of disbelief* [1]. Believability is crucial to bind the IVE participants with the synthetic characters inhabiting it. As stated in Ortony, Clore and Collins (OCC) cognitive theory of emotions [16], the participants are bound to virtual characters that display positive and negative reactions making sense when considering their perceived or assumed goals, beliefs and attitudes. In other words, to achieve believability, the behaviour of the synthetic character has to be consistent with the his or her *personality*.

Hence, the development of computational personality models may be a key factor in the achievement of believable characters. Models and techniques from parallel fields to artificial intelligence and artificial life are completing the world's personality model digital library [18]: drama and literary studies (e.g. [7]), neurology hypotheses (e.g. [3] and [6]), and psychology models (e.g. [15] and [19]), all strive to provide computational models for the definition of synthetic personalities.

This paper describes an implementational model for the definition of believable emotional characters with synthetic personae, which we call pathematic agents, in intelligent virtual environments. The model assumes that personality and emotions are essentially the same mechanism [15], and allows the definition of the characters personality by a set of emotional reactions. The system designer defines a set of concepts, which structure is inspired by OCC's theory of emotions, which are then automatically integrated in the IVE character cycle, inspired by Fridja's theory of emotions [5]. Then, the system designer implements the final IVE specific characteristics around those concepts.

The methodology was applied to a real time IVE, S3A, developed in the context of the last world exposition of the century, EXPO'98, which featured two pathematic dolphins, Tristão and Isolda, who lived in the virtual estuary of the river Sado during the four months of the EXPO'98, and were displayed to more than one million visitors.

The document is organized as follows. After a brief overview of the use of emotions and personality in the field of believable agents, followed by a description of the scenario for the implemented IVE, the three-modules architecture of the IVE is described. This description is followed by the explanation of the building process of Tristão and Isolda's personalities and its implementation in the mind module of the IVE. The integration of these concepts in the character cycle closes the paper body. Finally, the results are explained, and conclusions drawn.

2   Related Work

When developing intelligent virtual environments, one of the major concerns goes into the problem of achieving the believability of the autonomous agents represented in the virtual world. Thus, it is not surprising that the interest in believable characters (characters that give the illusion of life and allows the user's suspension of disbelief [1]), has grown enormously over the past few years. The idea of believability goes back to universal literature, being the turning point in animation (for example, Disney). To bind the participants to the virtual characters, the positive and negative reactions of the synthetic actors have to make sense when considering their perceived or assumed goals, beliefs and attitudes [16].

In general, we can find two main lines of research to address the problem of believability. The first one uses techniques from artificial life inspired in biological and neurological theories. One of its major sources of inspiration is the seminal work by Damásio [4]. Along with several hypotheses in the field of neurology, it encourages the use of Neural Nets and Reinforcement Learning as a base for simulation of the agents' behaviour. In such virtual environments, the agents acquire by themselves the capabilities to deal with the specific characteristics of the synthetic worlds. This learning process, done without the user supervision, is conducted in order for the agent to achieve its inner goals. By observation of the results of one generation of agents and using techniques such as genetic algorithms, it is then possible to create a new set of newborn agents better adapted to the world. Examples using such approach are Gridland [3], where the agents placed in a 2D world can acquire various learning and problem solving capabilities, according to the Society of Mind framework by Minsky, and Creatures from Cyberlife Technology [6], a commercial home-entertainment software. The main advantage of this neurological approach lies in the fact that the agents acquire their knowledge about the world by themselves, not relying on the intervention or the supervision of the user. One can just sit back and watch the agents (eventually) develop interesting and rational behaviour.

However, when the aim is to build agents with specific and predefined personalities, such approach is obviously not the most adequate. A more immediate one, based on empirical evidence, and following a development process where agents are designed and planned for their task, will be, almost certainly, a better alternative. This second approach follows an artistic perspective, where agents, like actors interpreting a well-defined role in a play, will act according to some configured behaviour, aiming to obtain a consistent exteriorisation of their personality. "Like human actors, the synthetic agents have prescribed roles, follow scripts, scenarios and direction, striving to breathe life into their characters - that is, to be in character" [8]. Following this second approach for creating believable synthetic agents, a set of projects revealing different strategies were developed during the past few years. At Carnegie Mellon University, in the group of J. Bates, the agents developed to inhabit the Edge of Intention virtual world (the woggles) had moods represented by a set of linear variables. Such variables were used to represent the physical, social and emotional dimentions of the synthetic characters. Taking this idea one step further, the group of B. Hayes-Roth based the agents' behaviour on personality traits. However, even having a great appeal in psychology, personality trait models remain a too generic way to define the characters' personalities. Indeed, as argued in [19], believable social agents can not be created from parameterised values of personality factors, since such values do not distinguish between psychological personality and artistic personality. To overcome this limitation, Reilly adopted, in the emotion system Em, a scaled down version of the cognition-based emotion model of Ortony, Clore and Collins [16]. The Em system was implemented atop of the Tok architecture [12] and allowed the fusion of emotions in the agent design. Another important work in the field is the Will architecture [15]. With Will, D. Moffat followed a similar path to B. Hayes-Roth's Virtual Theatre [7] using also personality traits to define the personality of the agents in very specific situations. However, in this particular case, the Big-5 psychology personality model was chosen instead of empirical variables adapted to the specific implemented situation. Two features of this work are also important. First, a two-stage emotional stimuli appraisal based on Fridja's theory of emotion [5] was used to develop emotions beyond the reaction process. Second, emotions are two views over the same concept differentiated by two dimensions: duration and focus [15].

Finally, although most of the research presented so far falls into the entertainment area of application, believable agents are a growing topic in other application areas such as Intelligent Learning Environments (ILEs) and Intelligent Interfaces. Some analysis of the persona effect has been performed using the pedagogical agent- Herman the Bug, revealing the enormous impact that a synthetic agent has on children's learning. In a similar way, other pedagogical agents such as Cosmo [11], STEVE [10] and Vincent [17] are good examples of using personality to convey tutoring agents' believability and building more engaging, effective and fun learning environments.

Believable Agents may well be the key for information cost structure reduction, the modelling force of XXIst century Graphical User Interfaces. In providing higher abstraction level over information, they will allow a better perceptual control over its complexity, enabling the manipulation of new thought structures.

3 Scenario

Lisbon held the last world exposition of the XXth century: EXPO'98. Its theme was "The Oceans a Heritage for the Future".

One of the greatest symbols of the oceans is the dolphins. However, dolphins could not be brought to the EXPO since they are far to sensitive mammals to support, without risking harm, the stressful conditions of the exposition. So, the only way to have dolphins represented at the exposition was to aim for the creation of synthetic ones. This goal, combined with the purpose of the Territory Pavilion to promote Portuguese scientific projects, lead to the development of S3A, an interactive application featuring two artificial dolphins. The S3A project team had to combine people from diverse fields of knowledge. From the Delphim project, a group of Biologists and Ethologists provided the necessary expertise to guarantee that the dolphins motion and behaviour was realistic. For the definition of the personality of the characters, their background, history and all the artistic aspects necessary to capture the visitor's attention, a team of designers and artists from the Territory Pavilion came into play. Finally, from INESC, where the application was developed, the team included people from computer graphics and artificial intelligence. This heterogeneous group of people worked together during four months to bring the dolphins to the EXPO, creating a project where a good balance between the artistic and realistic visual expression is a fact.

On the 20th of May 1998, the S3A became a reality in the EXPO. Tristão and Isolda (Figure 1) started their journey in the river Sado.

Fig. 1. Tristão and Isolda

The two dolphins: Tristão and Isolda.

Entering the S3A room of the Territory Pavilion, the visitor is driven to the beginning of Ages, "(...) to Atlantis, a place where humans and dolphins had a special way to communicate with each other. This communication was based on an apparatus that helped Humans to express their feelings to the dolphins. This strong relation between the two species was kept until the tragic disappearance of Atlantis. However, fragments of the apparatus, spread in the Atlantic waters, were collected over the years, and their analysis allowed the reconstruction of the communication device."

The visitor of the S3A room, aware of the story, can observe the reconstructed model of the apparatus, touch it and experience the communication with one dolphin: Isolda. The apparatus is a porcelain sculpture of a dolphin, equipped with four pressure-button sensors, laid in the middle of the exhibition room, in front of a wide screen, as show in Figure 2.

To communicate with Isolda and express her some emotions, the visitor can, at any time, approach the sculpture and touch one of the buttons. The four types of emotions that the visitor can express to Isolda are represented in the four sensors of Figure 2.

Isolda is a bottle-nose dolphin, quick and agile. She has faith in the human-kind and still has embedded in her genes the ability to sense the action of the apparatus. But Isolda is not alone in the scenario. In the waters of the Portuguese shore she met Tristão, a typical dolphin from the river Sado. Tristão is heavy,

Fig. 2. Interface and Sensors

shy and very suspicious of men activities, especially since fishermen from the Portuguese coast killed so many from his species throughout this century. He is insensible to the apparatus.

4 Architecture

To support the development of Tristão and Isolda, an architecture based on a theatrical metaphor was adopted. The developed system was instanced over a modular architectural framework composed by three functional units (or modules):

- The *dynamic script-writer* (or *mind module*) is responsible for the creation of the narrative. It manages all the agents at the narrative level and controls the emotional believability of the characters.
- The *theatrical company* (or *body module*), with its director and cast of actors, interprets the narrative and performs upon it. It manages the geometrical and audio-visual planning and controls the life-like believability of all characters.
- The *virtual stage manager* (or *world module*) controls all aspects related to audio-visual display of the character performance as well as handling the virtual camera and the stage special effects.

Figure 3 shows the overall architecture.

As represented in Figure 3, each agent is implemented by three distinct images: a mind image, a body image, and a world image. Each image is managed by its associated module. Hence, each module implements a specific part of *all* the agents.

Each image can communicate with all images of the same module but only with the image of the same agent in neighbour modules. For instance, the mind image of Tristão can communicate with the mind images of any agent of the IVE but can only communicate with Tristão's body image.

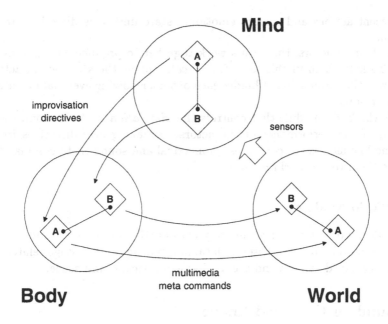

Fig. 3. Architecture Theatrical Metaphor

In the following subsections, we will present each module's architectural purpose.

4.1 Mind Module

The mind module dynamically generates the storyboard which involves taking all the critical decisions for the story. So, at each *narrative cycle* (a mind module run), it generates a new set of improvisation directives stating the behaviour of each synthetic actor of the story, based on the agents' definition and the sensored data stored since the last narrative cycle. The narrative emerges from the individual actor performances.

The improvisation directives are then passed to the body module.

4.2 Body Module

The improvisation directives received from the mind module are interpreted and performed by the body module *actors*.

The actors are bound to follow the script (defined by the directives) accurately but can improvise around it, as long as they convey to the viewer the actions specified by the improvisation directives (*directed improvisation paradigm*) and stay "in character". Since some actors perform their directives quicker than others, the improvisation paradigm is critical. Actors must act according to their most recent actions and current emotional state until new directives are given to them.

Like human actors, the agents work together to produce engaging perform- ances. To help them in this task, the *director* plans the sequence of actions in such a way that actors do not hinder each others, resolving eventual interruptions and exceptions.

It is the body module that controls the *simulation cycle*. It monitorises the progress of the performance of the actors, retrieving new directives from the mind module as needed, computes geometrical and sound meta-commands, and outputs them to the world module.

4.3 World Module

The world module translates the body commands into audio-visual output, in- forms the mind module of sensored data, and manages other stage related effects such as the world camera and the audio-visual background scene.

5 Building the Mind Images

To specify the mind image of a synthetic actor, a set of components must be defined.

This section presents the architecture of the mind module and the compon- ents used to specify the mind image of the agents. Using Tristão and Isolda as an example, we will present the steps leading to the creation of the agents for our IVE.

5.1 Mind Module Architecture

The mind module is implemented as a two-layer architecture:

- The *core layer* contains the default mechanisms and class templates sup- porting the basic functionality of the IVE.
- The *configuration layer* is the instantiation of the core layer classes and their extension to support the desired functionality of the IVE.

Therefore, to define the mind image of an agent we need to create a set of components in the configuration layer, using or extending the default templates provided by the core layer. The core layer will then automatically insert these components in the narrative cycle.

5.2 S3A Virtual World

The virtual estuary of the river Sado is implemented by a 3D area grid. Although no physical obstacle - except the plane pieces and some rocks on the bottom - really blocks the character vision, the level of pollution of the waters appreciably

decreases the vision distance. That fact justified the implementation of distinct
visibility areas. The fishes will have a hard time seeing predators coming. On
the other side, the dolphins sonar system allows them to overcome this perception restriction. Thus, some actions will be implemented without visibility
restrictions.

The décor is constituted by three pieces from the plane crash and three rocks
at the bottom of the sea. The virtual world of S3A is represented in Figure 4.

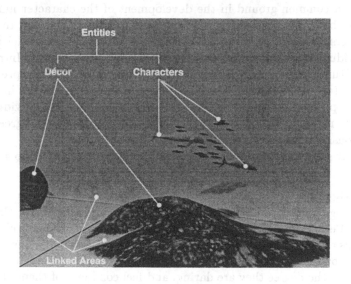

Fig. 4. S3A World Abstraction

The characters are organized in an underwater creature taxonomy. All entities
are underwater creatures of two types:

- The *predators*: Tristão and Isolda, the dolphins and main characters of S3A.
- The *preys*: the creatures that predators eat. Sardines, Surmullet, Dories and
  Mullets are the favorite dolphins' food. Preys enter and leave the virtual
  world almost randomly (the scene has to be kept interesting).

The prey template extends the character behaviour with the notion of swimming speed, food value and will-power (reflecting how easily a fish gives up
running away from a predator). Dolphins are more complex. They integrate the
notions of swimming speed but also the notions of stamina, resistance to fatigue,
breathing capacity, hunger resistance, curiosity and food preference. Each specie
implements different combination of the values according to ethological data.

The behaviour implementation is the same for both Tristão and Isolda and
maps the real world behaviour of bottle-nose dolphins. Only the personality

implementation of the characters provides them with different perceivable behaviour.

For aesthetic purposes, there are other fishes wandering around in the background. They are considered by the world module, not by the mind module, since they are irrelevant for the plot.

5.3 Personality

Aiming for a common ground in the development of the character images, two Human psychology models - Myers-Briggs and Big-Five - were used to establish the base personality of Tristão and Isolda. The Myers-Briggs model [21] rates each individual in a four-dimension bipolar space (Extroversion/Introversion, Sensing/iNtuition, Thinking/Feeling and Judgement/Perception) represented by four letters (e.g. ISTP) which dynamically interact to explain the individual's approach to problem solving. The Big-Five model [9] rates each individual in five major traits representing her personality: surgency/extroversion, agreeableness, conscientiousness, emotional stability and openness.

The next subsections present the personality definition of Tristão and Isolda.

Myers-Briggs

According to the Myers-Briggs model, Tristão is an instrumentor (ISTP) and Isolda is a Performer (ESFP), both from the Artisan temperament class.

Artisans are concrete in communicating and utilitarian in implementing goals. They are proud of themselves in the degree they are graceful in action, respect themselves in the degree they are daring, and feel confident of themselves in the degree they are adaptable. This is the "sensation seeking personality" trusting in spontaneity and hungering for impact on others. They are usually hedonic about the present. optimistic about the future, cynical about the past and their preferred time and place is here and now.

Tristão (instrumentor) is not only concrete in communication and utilitarian in getting things done, he is also directive and attentive in his social role. He does not approach strangers readily, but once in contact with them, he does not hesitate to tell them what to do.

Isolda (performer) is informative and expressive in her social interactions. She is not comfortable in telling others what to do, preferring to offer information rather than issue orders. Playful and fun-loving, her primary social interest lies in stimulating those around her, arousing their senses and her pleasureful emotions-charming them. Energetic and inhibited, she is able to lift other's spirit with her contagious manners and irrepressible joy of living.

Big-Five

Tristão and Isolda personalities are diametrically opposed according to the Big-Five model. This helps in the creation of interesting virtual interactions.

Tristão has high conscientiousness and emotional stability. He is cautious, rational, purposeful, orderly, controlled, imperturbable, moderate and tranquil.

Isolda has a high surgency/extroversion, agreeableness and openness. She is friendly, assertive, talkative, warmth, with a high sense of moral, tender and empathic.

5.4 Personality and Emotions

To implement the character personalities, a first good method would be to use directly the previous personality models to parametrize the characters, an approach used in the Virtual Theatre [20] and the Will Architecture [15]. But if personality theories are a good methodology at the design stage, they are not so useful at the implementation stage. Stating that Tristão is introverted is still a too abstract implementational argument: how does he express this introversion?

As stated in [15], the concept of personality and the concept of emotion are very close, although appearing very different:

- *Personality* is defined in terms of temporal consistency whislt emotions are defined in terms of temporal inconsistency.
- *Emotions* are focused on a particular event or object whilst personality is described in general terms.

Focus and duration can then be two dimensions identifiable at the cognitive level, over a *same* underlying mechanism. Pursuing this idea, personality emerges from emotion consistency and can be expressed as a set of typical emotional reactions to specific events.

This is the approach followed within our system. In the next sections, we present the core layer components allowing the implementation of this paradigm.

5.5 Behaviour Features

As stated previously, the personality models of the two characters do not provide enough information for the complete definition of the characters. To overcome this difficulty, a set of typical situations was sketched based on the personality models. The situations depicted real world behaviour, typical moods, and interactions of the dolphins, highlighting their personality quirks. Following a similar path to that of character animators', the principal aspects of each character's behaviour were sketched.

For instance, Tristão does not like the plane which lies at the bottom of the sea and does not dare to explore it. On the other side, Isolda is very courageous and daring, spending most of her time around the plane. Only Tristão's love for Isolda will help him in overcoming his fears (and she likes to provoke him a lot, swimming around him...).

From those sketches, the four relevant behaviour features of the dolphins were chosen: *pleased*, *displeased*, *passionate*, and *frighten*. They represent the important aspects characterizing each character's behaviour. In other words, each behaviour is (potentially) affected by each behaviour feature and, for example, dolphins will swim differently when pleased, displeased, passionate or frighten.

Four behaviour features may seam minimalist, but considering crossing them with the over ten behaviours (e.g. swimming, chasing, exploring), and considering the effect of the different intensities of each behaviour features (e.g. frighten ranges from slightly nervous to terrified), there is enough diversity for S3A. Note that, additionally, the four behaviour features allow a direct mapping between the four sensors and Isolda's behaviour features: when a visitor presses the pleased button, he is short-cutting the emotional appraisal and raising the pleased behaviour feature.

5.6   Interest Filters

Another important aspect of the agent development is the definition of the agent's concerns [5]. Characters are not interested in *all* that is happening in the world. The interest filters define which events[1] are relevant for the character. They are specified as a set of event patterns and represent the character's interests, major needs and preferences. Events not matching the filters will not be perceived by the character.

Preys in S3A have only one goal in life: to escape the dolphins. Hence, they are only interested in actions performed by the predators, all the actions performed by predators:

```
((subject    DPredator)
 (action     ANY)
 (object     ANY)
 (parameters ANY)
 (location    ANY))
```

Dolphins, however, are interested in all that is happening in the virtual world. Therefore, the dolphins' only filter is:

```
((subject    ANY)
 (action     ANY)
 (object     ANY)
 (parameters ANY)
 (location    ANY))
```

5.7   Agents' World Model

Characters may not perceive the virtual world as it "really" is. To model this feature, characters are provided with world models.

The character's world model represents the objects (and classes of objects) relevant for the characters. They are subsets of attributes associated with an object which are updated when the entity is perceived or during the reasoning

---

[1] Events in the world are defined as sentences with the following format: subject, action, object, parameters, location, time.

process. This indirection layer allows the characters to perceive things differently from what they really are and may lead sometimes to misinterpretations.

The preys' only concern is to know if one predator is nearby and, therefore, their world model is resumed to a boolean value.

Dolphins' world model traces their most recent friend (happy dolphins also play with fishes) and their current prey. Every other aspect is automatically perceived from the virtual world. The current prey model stores the relative velocity of the prey (Tristão gives up easily when the prey is fast and he is sad, but very hardly when he is angry) and its food value (sometimes, something better comes along).

Each dolphin also keeps the perceived happiness of the other dolphin. This value is appraised according to the other dolphin's perceived events. For instance, performing a loop is a good sign of great happiness (dolphins follow the simple assumption that the others act the same way they do).

5.8 Goal Graph

Characters act because they are motivated to do so. Characters rarely engage in random actions devoid of goal and purposes. Therefore, characters must have a structure of goals and interests that underline their behaviour. The goal graph, organized as the OCC theory [16] suggests, represents that structure.

Besides the goal/subgoal relationship, goals are also connected through four types of semantic links:

- *Necessary link:* if the goal fails, the linked goal also fails.
- *Sufficient link:* if the goal succeeds, the linked goal also succeeds.
- *Facilitative link:* if the goal succeeds, the likelihood of success of the linked goal increases.
- *Inhibitory link:* if the goal succeeds, the likelihood of success of the linked goal decreases.

Figure 5 shows the goal graphs of dolphins and preys.

All underwater creatures have the wander goal (GWander). This goal is activated when no other goal is active.

Dolphins must breathe from time to time (GBreathe). This replenishment goal is implemented in such a way that dolphins never die from lack of oxygen. When dolphins get tired, they slow down to rest (GRest). When they get hungry, they select a prey, chase it, and (eventually) catch it (GEat). From time to time, their curiosity must be satisfied by exploration (GExplore).

Preys, on their side, avoid predators when they are near (GRun). They barely do anything else.

5.9 Emotional Profile

Only dolphins are provided with emotions. Each character's emotional profile is defined by:

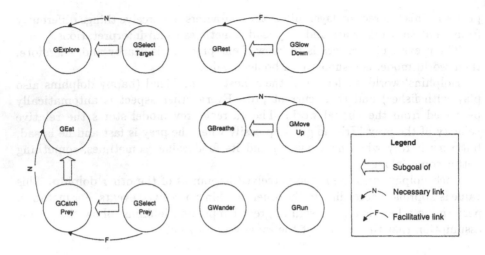

Fig. 5. Character Goal Graph

- The *emotional conditioning*: a set of values specifying the emotional resistance and the emotional memory of the character.
- The *emotional reactions*: a set of pattern matching components representing the character's persona.

Emotional Conditioning

The first step in defining Tristão and Isolda emotions is to set the *emotional threshold* (representing the character emotional resistance), and the *emotional decay-rate* (representing the character emotional memory) for each OCC base emotion class [16]. In S3A, the emotion thresholds and decay-rates were set for emotional categories (groups of emotion classes). Figure 6 shows the emotional threshold and decay-rates for Tristão and Isolda, according to their previously defined personalities.

The values are interpreted as follows. Tristão is quite indifferent to objects around him, except when they interfere directly with his goals (aspects-of-objects high threshold). He is very critic about his actions, much more than with Isolda's action (actions-of-agents lower threshold for self than for other), and his emotions tend to last long (low decay-rate).

Isolda, on the other side, is more emotionally unbalanced (higher standard deviation in Isolda's values). She has a shorter emotional memory (higher decay-rate) and is always interested in events and objects around her (low aspect-of-objects threshold). Additionally, she barely thinks about the consequences of the correctedness of her acts (high threshold for actions-of-agents-self).

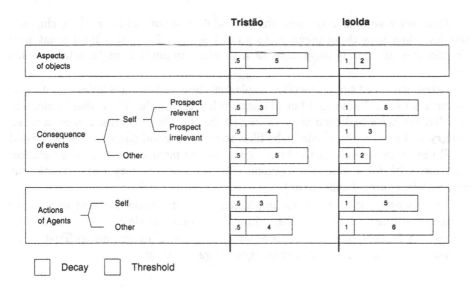

Fig. 6. Emotional Condition

Emotional Reactions

The next step is to instantiate each dolphin's emotional reactions. Emotional reactions are an automated mechanism based on the OCC classification of emotions [16] that launches emotions according to the objects and events perceived by the actors and their emotional characterization. Emotional reaction are of four types:

- *Attraction reactions* handle emotions related with *aspects of objects*, appraising the liking of entities with respect to the agent attitudes. They are triggered by the proximity of perceived relevant entities (agent or objects).
- *Event reactions* handle emotions related with consequences of prospect irrelevant events, appraising the pleasingness of the events. They are triggered by pattern matching on perceived events.
- *Prospect reactions* handle emotions related with consequences of prospect relevant events, appraising the pleasingness of the events with respect to the agents goals. They are triggered by pattern matching on perceived events.
- *Attribution reactions* handle emotions related with actions of agents, appraising the approval of the actions with respect to the agent standards of behaviour. They are triggered by pattern matching on perceived events.

Attraction reactions implement the love that dolphins share for each other, Tristão's hate for the plane pieces, Isolda's attraction towards them, Tristão's attraction for the hiding places behind the rocks, and both dolphins' irresistible attraction for the mysterious atlantean symbols painted on the plane.

Prospect reactions implement the playful manner of Isolda and how she only worries when something menaces to spoil her fun. They also implement how Tristão sees all that is happening as a possible impeachment in achieving his goals.

Attribution and event reactions implement how exploring is a daring thing to do for Tristão and a normal but pleasant thing for Isolda. They also implement how Tristão feels bad each time he must take the life of a creature, even when hungry and how, controversially, he likes to watch a good chase and is interested in all the tactical issues of the hunt. They also implement how Tristão valuates creatures with fun-loving temperament (playing was a rare event for Tristão: he had no friend until Isolda came).

Isolda's attribution reactions implement how she hates cowards and to see creatures eating but not sharing, while they could be doing more interesting things. Isolda does not care much about standards of behaviour as Tristão: he is much more likely to resent actions going against them.

Simple Emotional Reaction Example

The definition of all the dolphins' emotional reaction falls outside of the context of this paper (the complete description can be found in [14]). As a simple example of the emotional reaction process, we will describe Isolda's attraction and Tristão repulsion towards the plane, and give an overview of the reaction process.

The emotional reactions are defined as follows (all values fall in the interval $[-10, 10]$ but only *appeal* can be lower than 0):

```
([TRISTAO-RATT1] of RATTRACTION      ([ISOLDA-RATT2]  of RATTRACTION

(agent                  [TRISTAO])    (agent                  [ISOLDA])
(object                  DWRECK)      (object                  DWRECK)
(sense-of-reality             9)      (sense-of-reality             9)
(proximity                    9)      (proximity                    9)
(unexpectedness               1)      (unexpectedness               9)
(arousal                      5)      (arousal                      5)
(appeal                      -9)      (appeal                       7)
(familiarity                  5)      (familiarity                  3)
(liking                       0)      (liking                       9)
(strength-of-cognitive-unit 1))       (strength-of-cognitive-unit 1))
```

Those values have the following interpretation. The old pieces of the plane crash are very real to the dolphins (high *sense − of − reality*) and right there, in front of their eyes (high *proximity*). If Tristão is used to this image (low *unexpectedness*), since it is part of his home habitat, the same can not be said about the new comer Isolda (high *unexpectedness*): it is not everyday that she discovers the remains of an old plane crash.

The pieces are as much unappealing to Tristão that they are appealing to Isolda (*appeal* and *liking*[2]). Although Tristão swims around the plane pieces every day, its familiarity with it is only slightly above Isolda's, since he rarely goes near them anyway (*familiarity*). Finally, the plane is a strange artifact in the dolphins world (low *strength − of − cognitive − unit*).

Assuming that Tristão perceives that a plane piece is near him (perception of an object of the *DWreck* class, for instance *SOUTH − WRECK*, in the same location) and since *appeal* is negative, a *HATE* emotion is created with a *potential* intensity of 5.6[3].

```
([gen77]         of EHATE
(time            77)
(agent           [TRISTAO])
(potential       5.6)
(intensity       0.6)
(cause           SOUTH-WRECK)
(direction       SOUTH-WRECK))
```

Since Tristão's emotional threshold for *HATE* emotions is 5 (aspect-of-objects threshold), the emotion *intensity* is only $5.6 - 5 = 0.6$. Since Tristão's emotional decay-rate for *HATE* emotions is 0.5, the emotion will be forgotten in 2 narrative cycles.

5.10 Reasoning and Acting

The reasoning, action planning, and selection are implemented by two distinct set of production rules.

Reasoning Production Rules

Preys do not realize any kind of reasoning and the dolphins production rules only perform reasoning to update the dolphins' world model.

Action Production Rules

The action production rules are designed around the concept of resource. A *resource* is an abstraction over the availability of means to perform an action.

---

[2] *Appeal* and *liking* are two different variables: one can be appealed to something one does not like.

[3] The emotional potential P_{Em} is calculated as follows:

$$G_{Em} = \frac{(senseofreality + proximity + unexpectedness + arousal)}{4}$$

$$S_{Em} = \frac{(familiarity + liking + strengthofcognitiveunit)}{3}$$

$$P_{Em} = \frac{(G_{Em} + |appeal| + S_{Em})}{3}$$

In S3A, the dolphins have a resource for each part of their body: the head, the mouth, each one of the fins and the tail are the dolphins physical resources. Therefore, if the mouth is used to eat something then it can not be used for anything else in the same narrative cycle. Preys do not need resources.

The action production system in S3A was implemented as goal clustered exclusive rules which implement planning according to current behaviour features and resource availability. When a goal becomes active, the associated production rules become active. Production rules can have behaviour feature restrictions. In this case, all rules not verifying them are deactivated. Active production rules are organized by resource. For each resource, the rule for the highest priority goal is fired: the character acts.

The preys' production rule system is very simple. Preys flee when a predator is nearby, that is, they increase their speed to get away, preferably out of the virtual world. In any other case they wander randomly.

Dolphins implement a more complex behaviour. Besides "normal" dolphin behaviour (breathing when low on oxygen, eating when hungry, resting when tired, amongst others), the dolphins implement the following main emotional conditioning rules:

- Happy dolphins generally swim at high velocity and never stay in the same area for long. An happy dolphin rarely gives up his prey, and generally plays with it before eating it.
- Sometimes, very happy dolphins perform loops.
- Sad dolphins usually move slowly near the bottom of the sea. Sad dolphins tend to end the hunt quickly, but if the prey shows resistance, they also give up as quickly.
- Sometimes, very sad dolphins literally stop.
- Passionate dolphins like to provoke other dolphins and play with food. A passionate dolphin does not feel fatigue, but looses its appetite.
- Very passionate dolphins like to follow other dolphins very closely at high speed and swim around them.
- Scared dolphins swim in a chaotic way, at high velocity, trying to avoid décor elements or hiding behind them. Scared dolphins give up their preys.
- Very scared dolphins "attack" the world camera.

The action production rules are the same for both dolphins. So, Tristão and Isolda only behave differently because of their different emotional characterization.

6 Narrative Cycle

All the concepts described in the previous section are integrated in the narrative cycle by the core layer of the mind module.

A narrative cycle is a sequence of character cycles, performed one after the other. "Quicker" characters perform their cycle first and have better chances in concurrent resource competition (such as picking up an object), but all characters perceive (potentially) the same events.

Each character's cycle is decomposed in four sequential phases: *perception, reaction, reasoning,* and *action.* The character cycle is shown in Figure 7.

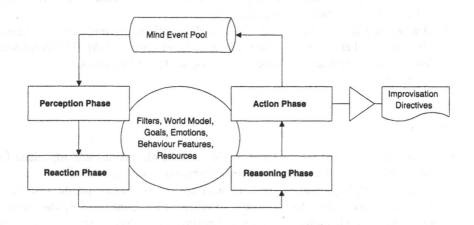

Fig. 7. Character Cycle Overview

The next subsections describe each phase of the character cycle.

6.1 Perception Phase

In the perception phase, the events of the world are filtered according to the characters' interests and location. Each character also updates its model of the world at this stage.

This is performed in three sequential steps:

1. *Visibility filtering:* the character only perceives the events happening in the area where he or she stands. All events and entities falling outside the character's location are discarded.
2. *Interest filtering:* the character only perceives events that are relevant for her concerns. All events not matching the character's interest filters (section 5.6) are discarded.
3. *World model update:* the character updates the immediate aspects of her world model (section 5.7) for each perceived entity.

6.2 Reaction Phase

In the reaction phase, the filtered events are appraised towards goal affectation and emotional reaction, and the agents' behaviour features are updated.

This is performed in three sequential steps:

1. *Goal update*: all the character's goals (section 5.8) are checked for activation, success or failure. The goals likelihood of success is also revised to reflect the current changes in the world model.
2. *Emotional reaction*: the character reacts emotionally to the perceived events, entities and goal changes. New emotions are created according to the character's emotional profile[4] (section 5.9).
3. *Behaviour features update*: the character's emotions are mapped the externally perceived emotions: the behaviour features (section 5.5). The behaviour feature intensities are updated according to the currently active emotions intensities[5].

6.3 Reasoning Phase

In the reasoning phase, the goal and world model's alterations are appraised for further world model affectation and secondary emotional appraisal.

This "thought" process is implemented by the reasoning production rules (section 5.10). According to the new behaviour feature intensities, the character's emotional conditioning (emotional thresholds and decay-rates) and interest filters are updated to reflect the mood of the character. For example, a dolphin in-love may only have eyes for the other dolphin, forgetting about everything surrounding him (or her).

New emotions can be generated in the reasoning phase but, since the behaviour features will not be updated before the next narrative cycle, they will not contribute for the current cycle action. This implements the difference between primary and secondary appraisal expressed in Fridja's theory of emotions [5].

6.4 Action Phase

In the action phase, the result of a run on the action production rules (section 5.10) - a set of parallel actions representing the character's performance in the current narrative cycle - is sent to the mind pool and to the body module as improvisation directives.

The action selection is based on the resource availability, the behaviour feature intensities, the active goals, the world model and the evaluation performed by all previous steps.

---

[4] Note that each character perceives her own actions and reacts to them (unless stated otherwise by the filters - e.g. preys). This is essential to allow appraising the approval of self-performed actions.

[5] For instance, in S3A, *pleased* is the "sum" of positive emotions, *displeased* is the "sum" of negative emotions, *passionate* is the "sum" of love emotions, and *frighten* is the "sum" of fear emotions. This mapping is defined when creating the behaviour features in the mind module configuration layer.

6.5 Complete Character Cycle

Figure 8 represents the complete character cycle. It shows the integration of the components described in section 5 within the cycle presented along the current section.

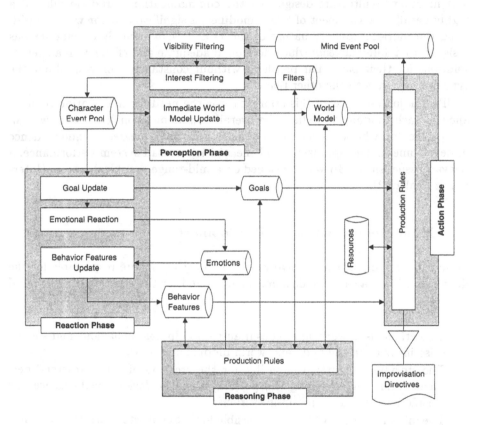

Fig. 8. Character Cycle

7 Results

S3A ran non-stop during the length of EXPO'98. The following aspects must be evaluated separately:

- The architecture impact on development.
- The mind module impact on development.
- The overall system performance.

- The life-like behaviour of the characters.
- The emotional behaviour of the characters.

7.1 Architecture Impact on Development

The modular architecture design and the communication paradigm allowed a highly parallel development of S3A's modules, a significant factor when considering the pluri-disciplinary nature of the IVE development. Each module was assigned to a different team which developed adequate and efficient area-specific solutions for their particular problems without constantly worrying about the synchronization with the other teams.

The major weakness of this approach was the need for information redundancy in each module, to reduce the overall communication load. This was an acceptable "drawback", since we were aiming for some degree of independence in development. The approach also benefited the overall system performance, a relevant issue, since S3A was developed on a mid-range graphical system (Intergraph Realizm2).

7.2 Mind Module Impact on Development

From the team of 15 persons involved in the project, 4 were responsible for the definition of Tristão and Isolda's personalities and for the creation of their mind images:

- Two ethologists, working as consultants on dolphins' behaviour and sounds (also involved in the body and world module creation).
- The storyboard writer, responsible for the creation of the characters' personae, who help sketching the possible scenario developments as well as Tristão and Isolda's typical interactions.
- The mind module developer, responsible for the character narrative personae implementation.

The total effort for the mind module implementation of Tristão and Isolda was 2 persons months, about 10% of the total project effort. Since the project was developed from scratch, these 10% include the core layer implementation and testing.

Although the methodology used to create the synthetic personality of the virtual actors presents a direction towards systematization, the model still uses a considerable amount of parameters which must be empirically tuned and adjusted to convey the desired effect on the IVE. The tuning process required almost as much effort as the core development.

However the specification process demonstrated to be intuitive, even to people from outside Computer Science.

7.3 Overall System Performance

The mind module light weight implementation confirmed the viability of its integration in a real time full 3D IVE with minimum performance degradation on a mid range graphical system.

The overwhelming weight of the geometrical calculation component of the system allowed the mind module implementation not to degrade S3A performance. The application run over the two processors of an Intergraph Realizm2 at 12 frames per seconds (average).

7.4 Life-Like Believability

The prime requisite of S3A was that the simulation had to be faithful to real life. Tristão and Isolda could not demonstrate unrealistic behaviour, even if, by exaggeration, the behaviour would allow a clearer emotional perception [1]. The challenge was to use the real world behaviour of the *tursiop truncatus* dolphins to convey to the viewer the inner human personalities attributed to them.

Statistical data confirmed the implemented behaviour: a simulation was performed analysing the goal selection over 400,000 narrative cycles (approximately 4 months of simulation time). At each simulation cycle, the goal tied to the selected action rule was accounted. Table 1 shows the results. These numbers, along with some preliminary results during the installation time of the system were a good "guaranty" that the life-like behaviour would be according to the designed personalities.

	Tristão	Isolda	Preys
GWander	35.3%	36.3%	98.1%
GBreathe+GMoveUp	7.1%	11.2%	-
GRest+GSlowDown	10.3%	0.1%	-
GSelectPrey	12.6%	8.7%	-
GCatchPrey	33.7%	15.1%	-
GExplore+GSelectTarget	1.0%	28.6%	-
GRun	-	-	1.9%

Table 1. Goal Selection Statistics

As Table 1 shows, both dolphins spend about $\frac{1}{3}$ of their time swimming around the virtual environment. Isolda spends more time breathing than Tristão. This was expectable considering her tireless nature. She will be generally swimming at high speeds (spending more oxygen) than her friend Tristão. Furthermore, the fact that Isolda almost never rests confirms that idea. Tristão will be spending most of its time swimming slowly around. Tristão is much more a hunter than Isolda and spends twice as much time pursuing his preys. This is not contradictory with the last statement. Tristão will be expected to swim slowly and then "attack" his prey very quickly, catch it and then return to his slow rhythm, which is consistent with his hunter trait. While Tristão is hunting, Isolda will be mostly exploring. Tristão exploration are mainly motivated by his love for Isolda.

After an initial two week evaluation period, the rational and life-like quality of the dolphins was confirmed by the biologists and ethologists, and also by the visitors. Hence, and after this test period, we concluded that S3A conveyed the life-like quality of dolphins successfully. The body module conveyed a realistic movement and the mind module conveyed a realistic behaviour according to the dolphins initial characterization based on real life parameters.

7.5 Emotional Believability

As for the life-like aspects of the synthetic dolphins life, the average level of dolphins' behaviour features was measured to convey an idea of the emotional behaviour of Tristão and Isolda. Table 2 shows the results.

	Tristão	Isolda
Pleased	3.7	4.7
Displeased	2.5	1.2
Passionate	3.4	3.4
Frighten	2.0	0.2

Table 2. Behaviour Feature Statistics

As Table 2 shows, dolphins are generally in a good mood, although Isolda is much more happier than Tristão (this is a logarithmic scale). Complementarily, and as expected, Tristão can get more upset than Isolda. Both can get really in-love, and note that, the two will be passionate mostly at the same time. Finally Isolda hardly worries about not achieving something. The same cannot be said about Tristão, which can get pretty frighten in those situations. Those statistics are very delicate to deal with, since what is really important is that the value of those behaviour features at a determined point of time will provoke some very particular behaviours. In this case, only direct observation confirmed the emotional personality exteriorisation of the dolphins.

After this first pre-testing the dolphins were submitted to the public for the first two weeks testing. If the life-like quality was immediately recognized by everyone, the emotions, however, were not always undoubtedly perceived.

This is pretty much what happens with real dolphins. Looking at a dolphin pool for a couple of minutes will not allow the visitor to understand the dolphins behaviour and personality. For a visitor to understand the personality of actors, he or she has to take some time to observe the dolphins' interaction with its surroundings and other characters or, at least, be briefed about the dolphins habits and behaviour. In the context of a world exposition pavilion with no guided tour and a high visitor throughput, this was rarely the case. The average

10,000 visitors spent an average of two minutes in the room. Thus, if ten persons supervising the exposition rooms of the pavilion perfectly understood the dolphin emotional behaviour in the first two weeks, the same can not be said about the average visitor who spent rarely more than a couple of minutes in the room.

Solutions and Improvements

To overcome all those problems, several alternatives were considered. A textual feedback of what was going on in the IVE could remove all the ambiguity of the visual feedback. As Figure 9 shows, if we associate a word with any of the dolphin physical movements stating their inner state, the ambiguity can be removed.

Fig. 9. Aspects of a Behaviour

Another solution was to use posters to explain some typical behaviour, but it was found out that the average visitor would not bother reading them.

Both solution were ruled out, mainly because of the multi-linguistic nature of EXPO'98. The solution had to be implementational. A set of high priority rules overrode the dolphin behaviour when sensor information was gathered. For instance, even if a dolphin had a highly need of oxygen, if a visitor pressed the pleased sensor, it would stop emerging and perform a typical pleased behaviour (e.g. a loop).

This was as far as we could go to convey immediate perceivable behaviour without ruining the realism of the simulation and without compromising the project philosophy. Note, that if no sensor is activated, the character behaviour remains unaltered. The behaviour interruption was not perceivable by the visitor since it is very hard for a new visitor to guess what are the designs of a swimming dolphin. The same was not the case of the supervising person or anyone that would have spend some time watching Tristão and Isolda.

8 Conclusions

S3A confirmed the adequacy of the mind conceptual abstraction for the development of pathematic agents. Although the aspect of emotional believability was not undoubtedly perceived by all visitors, due to the characteristics of EXPO'98, the architecture confirmed its suitability for implementing life-like believable characters with pre-defined personalities. The assumption that personality and emotions are essentially the same mechanism, the base for the mind module implementation, allowed the characters' personality to be specified by a set of emotional components based on the OCC cognitive theory of emotions. This methodology proved to be a good definition process. The four-phase character cycle (perceive-react-reason-act), inspired by Fridja's theory of emotions, was adequate to manage the emotional aspects of each character.

Indeed, S3A showed that the followed approach is a viable solution for the creation of the synthetic personae of believable emotional agents in intelligent virtual environments. The building process used to develop Tristão and Isolda's personality and behaviour proved to be intuitive and allowed a smooth integration of ethological data and the character persona definition in the S3A system.

Developing personality for believable agents may well be the key for information cost structure reduction, the modelling force of XXIst century Graphical User Interfaces. In providing higher abstraction level over information, they will allow a better perceptual control over its complexity, enabling the manipulation of new thought structures.

Acknowledgments
We would like to express a special thank you to all those who always believed in our work and to all the INESC S3A/RVLab team who made it happen. Thank you Alexandra Freitas, Ana Isabel Torres, Ana Paula Costa, André Silva, António Cerveira Pinto, João Pereira, Joaquim Antunes, José António Conde,

José António Proença, Manuel Eduardo dos Santos, Mário Rui Gomes, Tiago Sepúlveda and Vanda de Sousa, for making this IVE real. We hope everyone feels gratified.

References

1. Bates, J.: The Role of Emotion in Believable Agents. Technical Report CMU-CS-94-136, Carnegie Mellon University (1994).
2. Badler, N., Reich, B., Webber, B.: Towards Personalities for Animated Agents with Reactive and Planning Behaviours. in Creating Personality for Synthetic Actors, Trappl, R., Petta, P. (eds), Springer-Verlag (1997).
3. Cañamero, D.: Modelling Motivation and Emotions as a Basis for Intelligent Behavior. Proceedings of Autonomous Agents 97 Conference, Johnson, L., Hayes-Roth, B. (eds), ACM Press. (1997).
4. Damásio, A.: Descartes' Error. Publicações Europa-América (1994).
5. Fridja , N.: Emotions. Cambridge University Press (1987).
6. Grand, S., Cliff, D., Malhotra, A.: Creatures: Artificial Autonomous Software Agents for Home Entertainment. Proceedings of Autonomous Agents 97 Conference, Johnson, L., Hayes-Roth, B. (eds), ACM Press. (1997).
7. Hayes-Roth, B., Robert, van G.: Story-Making with Improvisational Puppets and Actors. Technical Report KSL-96-24, Stanford University (1995).
8. Hayes-Roth, B., van Gent, R., Huber, D.: Acting in Character. in Creating Personality for Synthetic Actors, Trappl, R., Petta, P. (eds), Springer-Verlag (1997).
9. International Personality Item Pool: Big-Five Factor Analysis Internet Site. http://www.ipip.com (1997).
10. Johnson, L., Rickel, J., Stiles, R., Munro, A.: Integrating Pedagogical Agents into Virtual Environments. to appear in Journal Presence (1998).
11. Lester, J., Towns, S., FitzGerald, P.: Achieving Affective Impact: Visual Emotive Communication in Lifelike Pedagogical Agents. To appear in International Journal of AIED special issue on ITS'98 (1999).
12. Loyall, A., Bates, J.: Real-time Control of Animated Broad Agents. Proceedings of the 15th Annual Conference of the Cognitive Science Society (1993).
13. Maes, P., Darrell, T., Blumberg, B., Pentland, A.: The ALIVE System: Wireless, Full Body Interaction with Autonomous Agents. in Multimedia Systems Vol.5, Rangan P. (ed), ACM/Springer (1995).
14. Martinho, C.: Emotions in Motion. MSc Thesis, Universidade Técnica de Lisboa, IST (1999).
15. Moffat, R.: Personality Parameters and Programs. in Creating Personality for Synthetic Actors, Trappl, R., Petta, P. (eds), Springer-Verlag (1997).
16. Ortony, A., Clore, G., Collins, A.: The Cognitive Structure of Emotions. Cambridge University Press (1988).
17. Paiva, A., Machado, I.: Vincent, an Autonomous Pedagogical Agent for On-the-Job training. Proceedings of ITS'98 Conference, Lecture Notes in Computer Science, Goettl, B., Halff, H., Redfield, C., Shule, V. (eds), Springler-Verlag (1998).
18. Petta, P., Trappl, R.: Personalities for Synthetic Actors: Current Issues and Some Perspectives. in Creating Personality for Synthetic Actors, Trappl, R., Petta, P. (eds), Springer-Verlag (1997).
19. Reilly, W.: Believable Social and Emotional Agents. PhD Thesis, Carnegie Mellon University (1996).

20. Rousseau, D., Moulin, B.: Personality in Computer Characters. Technical Report KSL 96-13, Stanford University (1996).
21. Team Technology: Myers-Briggs Internet Site. http://www.team-technology.com (1997).
22. Terzopoulos, D., Rabie, T., Grzeszczuk, R.: Perception and Learning in Artificial Animals. Proceeding of Artificial Life V Conference on the Synthesis and Simulation of Living Systems, (1996).

An Oz-Centric Review of Interactive Drama and Believable Agents

Michael Mateas

Computer Science Department, Carnegie Mellon University, 5000 Forbes Avenue,
Pittsburgh, PA 15217, USA
michaelm@cs.cmu.edu

Abstract. Believable agents are autonomous agents that exhibit rich personalities. Interactive dramas take place in virtual worlds inhabited by believable agents with whom an audience interacts. In the course of this interaction, the audience experiences a story. This paper presents the research philosophy behind the Oz Project, a research group at CMU that has spent the last ten years studying believable agents and interactive drama. The paper then surveys current work from an Oz perspective.

1 Introduction

This paper provides an overview of research in believable agents and interactive drama. Many of the original sources used in compiling this paper can be found on the web; the annotated bibliography provides URLs for these web resources.

This paper unabashedly surveys its topic with the bias of the Oz project at CMU. The reason for this is threefold. First, I am a member of this research group and have internalized much of their perspective; I won't pretend not to have a viewpoint. Second, there is not much work that is *directly* related to interactive drama and believable agents; using the Oz project as a center allows me to make sense of more peripheral work. Finally, Oz is the only group giving equal attention to both character (believable agents) and story (interactive drama); an Oz perspective allows me to present character and story as a unified whole.

For much of the content of this paper, I am indebted to the members of the Oz project: Joe Bates, Bryan Loyall, Scott Neal Reilly, Phoebe Sengers, and Peter Weyhrauch. Much of my understanding grew out of conversations with them.

The first item of business is to define the research goal for believable agents and interactive drama: building worlds with character and story.

1.1 Drama = Character + Story + Presentation

Artists building non-interactive dramas (e.g. movies, books) have commented on the importance of both character *and* story for authoring powerful, dramatic experiences.

For example, Lajos Egri, in the Art of Dramatic Writing [46] has this to say about premise (i.e. plot or story).

> No idea, and no situation, was ever strong enough to carry you through to its logical conclusion without a clear-cut premise.
>
> If you have no such premise, you may modify, elaborate, vary your original idea or situation, or even lead yourself into another situation, but you will not know where you are going. You will flounder, rack your brain to invent further situations to round out your play. You may find these situations - and you will still be without a play.

Later, in talking about character, he defines three dimensions every character must have: physiology, sociology and psychology. He has this to say about these three dimensions:

> Analyze any work of art which has withstood the ravages of time, and you will find that it has lived, and will live, because it possesses the three dimensions. Leave out one of the three, and although your plot may be exciting and you may make a fortune, your play will still not be a literary success.
>
> When you read drama criticisms in your daily papers, you encounter certain terminology time and again: dull, unconvincing, stock characters (badly drawn, that is), familiar situations, boring. They all refer to one flaw - the lack of tridimensional characters.

Figure 1 shows the high level architecture of the Oz project. This architecture arose out of a desire to treat character and story in interactive drama as *seriously* as do dramatic artists in traditional media.

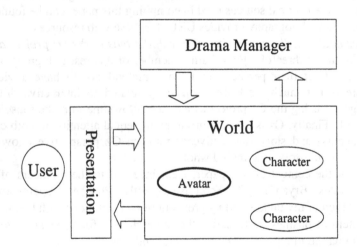

Fig. 1. Dramatic world architecture

A simulated world contains characters. These characters exhibit rich personalities, emotion, social behavior, motivations and goals.

The user interacts with this world through some presentation. This presentation may be an objective, third person perspective on the world, or it may introduce various kinds of dramatic filtering - effecting camera angles and point of view in graphical worlds, or changing the style of language used in textual worlds.

The drama manager can see everything happening in the world. It tries to guide the experience of the user in order to make a story happen. This may involve changing the physical world model, inducing characters to pursue a course of action, adding or deleting characters, etc.

1.2 Overview

The rest of the paper is divided into two main sections, Believable Agents (character) and Interactive Story, and a third, small section describing interactive video work.

In the believable agents section, I will first describe the Oz research philosophy. Then I will present work related to believable agents (artificial life, virtual humanoids, embodied characters, chatterbots, and behavioral animation) in light of this philosophy. Finally, I will discuss why believable agents is an important and interesting research area.

In the interactive drama section, I will first define the problem of interactive drama in terms of the inherent tension between the concepts of *interaction* and *drama*. After a brief description of the Oz drama manager, I will describe three design dimensions which help structure the design space of interactive drama systems.

In the final section, I'll describe the relationship between the virtual world approach to story and character vs. the interactive video approach.

2 Believable Agents Research: The Oz Philosophy

2.1. Taking Character Seriously

When attempting to marry a technical field like Computer Science with a cultural activity such as story telling, it is extremely easy to become sidetracked from the artistic goals and to begin pursuing purely technical research. This research, while it may be good science, does not lead you closer to building a new kind of cultural experience: engaging, compelling, and hopefully beautiful and profound. Effective techno-artistic research must continuously evaluate whether the technology is serving the artistic and expressive goals. The application of this principle to interactive characters implies that interactive character technology should follow from an understanding of what makes characters believable. And indeed, creators of non-interactive characters have written extensively on what makes a character believable.

Before continuing, it's a good idea to say something about this word *believable*. For many people, the phrase *believable agent* conjures up some notion of an agent that tells the truth, or an agent you can trust. But this is not what is meant at all. *Believable* is a term coming from the character arts. A believable character is one who seems lifelike, whose actions make sense, who allows you to suspend disbelief. This is not the same thing as realism. For example, Bugs Bunny is a believable character, but not a realistic character.

So believability is this good thing that we want characters to have. After examining the writings of several character artists including The Illusion of Life [70], Chuck Amuck [54], and The Art of Dramatic Writing [46], the Oz group defined a set of requirements for believability including the following:

- Personality - Rich personality should infuse everything that a character does, from they way they talk and move to the way they think. What makes characters interesting are their unique ways doing things. Personality is about the *unique* and *specific*, not the *general*.
- Emotion - Characters exhibit their own emotions and respond to the emotions of others in personality-specific ways.
- Self-motivation - Characters don't just react to the activity of others. They have their own internal drives and desires which they pursue whether or not others are interacting with them.
- Change - Characters grow and change with time, in a manner consistent with their personality.
- Social relationships - Characters engage in detailed interactions with others in a manner consistent with their relationship. In turn, these relationships change as a result of the interaction.
- Illusion of life - This is a collection of requirements such as: pursuing multiple, simultaneous goals and actions, having broad capabilities (e.g. movement, perception, memory, language), and reacting quickly to stimuli in the environment. Traditional character artists do not mention these requirements explicitly, because they often get them for free (from a human actor, or as a deep assumption in animation). But builders of interactive characters must concern themselves explicitly with building agent architectures that support these requirements.

Chapter 2 of Bryan Loyall's thesis [61] offers a more detailed analysis of the requirements for believability.

2.2 Classical vs. Behavioral AI

To begin thinking about how to meet the Illusion of Life believability requirement, let's explore the distinction between classical and behavioral AI. In order to make the distinction clear, the following discussion describes the *extreme* classical and behavioral positions. There is certainly work in AI which incorporates aspects of both approaches. Table 1 contrasts the properties of classical and behavioral AI systems.

Table 1. Contrasting properties of classical and behavioral AI systems

Classical AI	Behavioral AI
narrow/deep	broad/shallow
generality	fits an environment
disembodied	embodied and situated
semantic symbols	state dispersed and uninterpreted
sense-plan-act	reactive

Classical AI concerns itself with building mind, not complete agents. This research program consists of isolating various capabilities of mind (e.g. reasoning, memory, language use, etc.), and building theories and systems to implement a capability in isolation. While it is believed that these disembodied pieces of mind will be put together to form a complete "person", this integration is deferred to the future. Behavioral AI seeks to build complete agents (rather than minds or pieces of minds) that can operate in complex environments. This concern with the environment is one of the key distinguishing characteristics between classical and behavioral AI. Where classical AI attempts to build mental components that duplicate the capabilities of high-level human reasoning in abstract, simplified environments, behavioral AI attempts to build systems with the savvy of insects in complex environments. Behavioral systems have a *broad* range of *shallow* sensory, decision and action capabilities rather than a single, *narrow*, *deeply* modeled capability.

Classical AI seeks general solutions; *the* theory of language understanding, *the* theory of planning, etc. Behavioral AI starts with the assumption that there is a complex "fit" between an agent and its environment; there may not be generic solutions for all environments (just as many animals don't function well when removed from their environment).

Classical AI divorces mental capabilities from a body; the interface between mind and body is not commonly addressed. Behavioral AI assumes that having a body which is embedded in a concrete situation is essential for intelligence. Thus, behavioral people don't buy into the Cartesian split. For them, it is the body that defines many of the interaction patterns between the agent and its environment.

Because of AI's historical affinity with symbolic logic, many classic AI systems utilize semantic symbols - that is, pieces of composable syntax which make one-to-one reference to objects and relationships in the world. The state of the world within which the mind operates is represented by a constellation of such symbols. Behavioral AI, because of it's concern with environmental coupling, eschews complex symbolic representations; building representations of the environment and keeping them up-to-date is notoriously difficult (e.g. the frame and symbol grounding problems). Some researchers, such as Brooks [14], maintain the extreme position that *no* symbolic representations should be used (though all these systems employ state - one can get into nasty arguments about what, precisely, constitutes a symbol).

In classical AI, agents tend to operate according to the sense-plan-act cycle. During sensing, the symbolic representation of the state of the world is updated by making inferences from sense information. The agent then constructs a plan to accomplish its current goal in the symbolically represented world by composing a set of operators (primitive operations the agent can perform). Finally, the plan is executed. After the plan completes (or is interrupted because of some unplanned-for contingency), the cycle repeats. Rather than employing the sense-plan-act cycle, behavioral systems are reactive. They are composed of bundles of behaviors, each of which describes some simple action or sequence of actions. Each behavior is appropriate under some environmental and internal conditions. As these conditions constantly change, a complex pattern of behavioral activation occurs, resulting in the agent taking action.

In order to build characters that have the illusion of life, they will need to have broad capabilities to interact with complex environments. This has lead Oz to develop a research philosophy and technology with strong affinities to behavioral AI. The insect-like capability to continuously act in a complex and changing environment is more immediately useful for building lifelike characters than the brain-in-a-vat cogitation of classical AI. The discerning reader, however, may have noticed that Bugs Bunny (or Hamlet, or James Bond, or Charlie Chaplin's Tramp, ...) doesn't seem very similar to either a brain-in-a-vat or an insect. Thus, while behavioral AI begins to give us a handle on the illusion-of-life requirement, the other requirements for believability don't seem to be well served by either camp.

2.3 Research Goals: Believable Agents vs. AI

Both behavioral and classical AI share some high level research goals which are at odds with research in believable agents.

Table 2. Contrasting goals of believable agents and traditional AI research agendas

Believable Agents	AI
personality	competence
audience perception	objective measurement
specificity	generality
characters	realism

For believable agents, personality is king. A character may be smart or dumb, well adapted to its environment or poorly adapted. But regardless of how "smart" a character is at dealing with their environment, everything they do, they do in their own personal style. On the other hand, the focus in AI is on competence. For classical AI, this has often meant competence at complex reasoning and problem solving. For behavioral AI, this has often meant moving around in complex environments without getting stepped on, falling off a ledge, or stuck behind obstacles.

The success of a believable agent is determined by audience perception. If the audience finds the agent believable, the agent is a success. AI tries to measure success objectively. How many problems could the program solve? How long did the robot run around before it got into trouble? How similar is the system's solution to a human's solution? Such audience independent evaluations of research don't make sense for characters.

Believable agents stress specificity. Each character is crafted to create the personality the author has in mind. AI, like most sciences, tries to create general and universal knowledge. Even behavioral AI, while stressing the importance of an agent's fit to its environment, seeks general principles by which to describe agent/environment interactions. But for characters, that type of general knowledge doesn't make sense. To what general problem is Mickey Mouse, or Don Quixote, a solution?

Finally, believable agent research is about building characters. Characters are not reality, but rather an artistic abstraction of reality. Much AI research is motivated by realism. A classic AI researcher may claim that their program solves a problem the way human minds really solve the problem; a behavioral AI researcher may claim that their agent *is* a living creature, in that it captures the same environment/agent interactions as an animal.

So, though the need for reactive intelligence gives Oz some affinities with behavioral AI, believable agents are not a problem to which the wholesale import of some AI technology (such as behavioral AI) is the solution. Any technology used for building believable agents will be transformed in the process of making it serve the artistic creation of characters. Thus, believable agents research is not a subfield of AI. Rather it is a stance or viewpoint from which all of AI is reconstructed. Any technology, whether it comes from classical or behavioral AI, or from outside of AI entirely, is fair game for exploration within the Oz context as long as it opens up new expressive and artistic spaces.

2.4 Authoring

The desire to pursue the specific rather than the general is strongly connected with the desire to support the direct artistic creation of characters. In traditional media, such as writing, painting, or animation, artists exhibit fine control over their creations. Starting with an idea or vision in her head, the artist uses this fine control to create a representation of her vision in her chosen medium. Similarly, Oz wants to support the same level of artistic control in the creation of believable agents. This approach provides an interesting contrast with both traditional AI and Alife.

In Figure 2, AI, Alife and Hap (a language developed in the Oz project) are laid out along a spectrum of *explicitness*. Traditional AI lies on the high explicitness end of the spectrum. That is, such systems tend to explicitly encode (often in a human-readable form) high level features of the system. For example, suppose you wanted to build James Bond using the traditional AI mindset. First you would think about characters in the abstract. What general theory captures the notion of character? How might this general theory by parameterized (perhaps through infusions of "knowledge") to select specific characters? To inform the work, you might look at the dimensions of personality as described by various personality models in psychology (e.g. introvert-extrovert, thinking-feeling, intuitive-sensing, judging-perceiving). Once a generic architecture has been built, you could then define different characters by setting the right personality knobs. Though the position just described is a bit of an exaggeration, it is not dissimilar to the approach taken by the Virtual Theater Project [32] at Stanford. For example, in both their CyberCafe and Master/Servant work, they describe using explicit personality dimensions to specify characters. Thus you can actually look in a character's mind and find some symbol denoting whether the character is introverted, intuitive, etc.

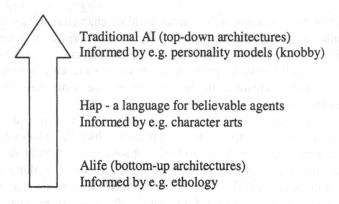

Traditional AI (top-down architectures)
Informed by e.g. personality models (knobby)

Hap - a language for believable agents
Informed by e.g. character arts

Alife (bottom-up architectures)
Informed by e.g. ethology

Fig. 2. Explicitness of representation

Alife lies at the low-explicitness end of the spectrum. A major methodological assumption in Alife work is that you want high-level features (such as introvertedness) to emerge from simple, low-level mechanisms. So how would you go about building James Bond as an Alifer? First, you would demure, saying that Alife technology is not at the stage yet to emerge such high-level behavior. So you might build something else, like a dog. To inform this work, you might look at models developed by biologists, such as ethological models of animal behavior. Then you would build a general architecture capturing an ethological theory of action selection (how animals decide what action to take). Finally, you would instill dog-specific behavior into your general architecture. This approach is not dissimilar to Bruce Blumberg's [30] approach at the Media Lab in building Silas the dog (though his group's current work seems more directly focused on building characters rather than building biologically motivated systems).

Hap, a language developed in the Oz project for writing believable agents, lies at a midpoint in the spectrum. Hap provides mechanisms that support writing behaviors for characters. A behavior is a chunk of activity; such behaviors can be high-level (a behavior for "having fun"), or low-level (a behavior for moving the character's body when they open a door). If you wanted to build James Bond in Hap, you would identify high-level goals (motivations) that make James Bond who he is. Then you would think of the multiple ways (behaviors) that James Bond might use to accomplish these high level goals. These multiple behaviors probably themselves have subgoals. Any given behavior is only appropriate under certain conditions (what's recently happened, how Bond is feeling, what's happening right now in the world, etc.); these conditions are captured within each behavior. At every level of description, James Bondness can be infused into the character. From how Bond thinks, to how Bond walks, the artist has the control to create the character consistent with their vision.

Both the traditional AI and Alife approaches make architectural commitments; there is some general architecture which characters have to be made to "fit." The traditional AI approach tries to capture high-level mental regularities (e.g. types of personalities). The problem is, how many of these personality knobs are needed to "tune in" a large number of characters? How many personality knobs need to be turned, and how many degrees of freedom does each knob need, in order to allow the creation of Bugs Bunny, Hamlet, The Terminator, Bambi? The differences between these characters seem to far outweigh any similarities. Or to put it another way, is Bugs Bunnyness captured in a few symbols which can be read inside the mind, or is his way-of-being smeared throughout his mind and body?

The Alife approach avoids the use of high level knobs to define personality. Instead, it depends on low-level mechanisms to cause the high-level behavior to emerge. Pragmatically, if you want to build human-like characters, the Alife approach is not understood well enough yet to emerge such high-level behavior. However, this might just be a matter of time. The Hap approach to behavior authoring would then be a useful stop-gap for building characters *today* (we're impatient and don't want to wait) until Alife has developed enough to support such characters. However, from an Oz perspective, there is another problem with Alife: the dependence on emergence. The notion of emergence is that you can't tell what kind of high-level behavior will emerge from low-level mechanisms without actually running the system. But Oz wants to build systems that give artists the control to express their artistic visions. An emergent system removes this control from the artist; the best they can do is make (principled) guesses about mechanism and see what kind of behavior emerges.

2.5 Oh, What a Tangled Web We Weave...

Figure 3 summarizes the above description of the Oz philosophy.

Taking the character arts seriously leads to requirements for believable agents. The "illusion of life" requirements, namely reactive, situated and embodied behavior, lead Oz to utilize techniques and ideas from behavioral AI. However, work in classic AI and Alife is not automatically rejected on ideological grounds; whatever enriches the space of characters will be *modified* and assimilated. Modification is key: even the behavioral AI ideas, while supporting the "illusion of life", need to be modified in order to support emotion, personality, self-motivation, etc. Believability is not a subfield of AI - it is a stance from which all of AI is transmuted. This is clearly seen in the conflict between believability research goals and traditional research goals. Believability leads Oz to reject the supremacy of the traditional research goals, to which both behavioral and classical AI subscribe. The character arts also point out the importance of artistic control over character creation (authoring). Artistic control opposes traditional research goals as well, particularly generality. Oz wants to build a new canvas and paint brush, not paint-by-number kits. Finally, believability leads to an affinity with robotics. The desire to build believable agents is at heart pragmatic; the agents must live and breath in engaging story worlds. Similarly, roboticists must build systems that act and move effectively in the real world. Thus believability and robotics both share the technical interests of embodied, situated action, as well as a certain pragmatic bent that leads one to pursue what works, regardless of ideological lines.

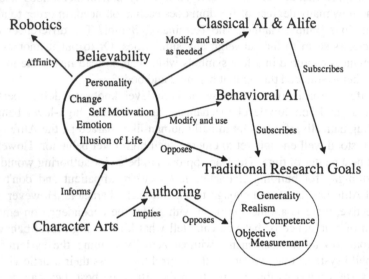

Fig. 3. The Oz research philosophy

3 Believable Agents Research: Related Areas

Now, with the Oz research philosophy in mind, I will explore related research areas. For each of these areas, I will point out similarities and differences with the Oz research program.

3.1 Artificial Life

The application of artificial life to believable agents is most evident in the design of virtual pets. One of the beauties of virtual pets is that, since they are animals, the audience expectation of the agent's behavior is set at a level the technology can reasonably meet. If the actions of the pet are sometimes confusing, they can be forgiven because we don't always know what animals are doing. Difficult natural language technologies can be avoided because animals don't have language competence. Virtual pets are often cute; cuteness can in itself evoke a strong response in an audience. Two examples of virtual pets are Dogz [6], and Creatures [1]. Dogz are virtual dogs that you can pet, play with using various toys, and teach tricks. Over time the user develops a relationship with the pet. Creatures is a world inhabited by small, cute creatures that autonomously explore the environment. The user is a caretaker; she can provide positive and negative feedback to the creatures, teach them to associate words with objects in the world, and move the creatures around the world. Without the user's intervention, the creatures don't live long.

How do virtual pets relate to Oz believable agents? Pets are one kind of believable agent; Oz wants to build all kinds of characters. Oz focuses on building specific, unique characters. Rather than building dogs, Oz wants to build Pluto, or Goofy. Users interact with virtual pets over extended periods of time; the user builds a relationship with the pet through repeated interaction. Oz believable agents are often designed to be part of a specific story world. Interactions with the character are intended to be intense, but bounded in duration and context by the story world. The notion of repeated interaction with long term characters is certainly an appealing one. It just becomes more difficult to pull off as the character becomes more sophisticated.

Artificial life approaches to building animal characters often rely on modeling of biologically plausible processes. For example, the creatures in Creatures [1] utilize a neural net for action selection, a model of bio-chemistry for modeling motivations and drives, an artificial genome (with crossover and mutation) for reproduction, and an artificial immune system. Blumberg's [30] Silas uses an action-selection mechanism motivated by ethology. The intuition behind utilizing such models is that biological systems already exhibit complicated behavior. If structurally similar computational processes are used, this may enable equally complex behavior in artificial systems. However, in Oz, the goal is an artistic abstraction of reality (*believable* agents), not biologically plausible behavior. By taking a programming language approach to the construction of character (the Hap believable agent language), Oz hopes to avoid premature commitment to an architecture that then limits the space of characters that can be created. Oz remains agnostic with respect to architectures and models. If biologically inspired models end up proving useful in opening up some new space of characters, then they will be used. But modeling for its own sake is eschewed in order to stay focused on the construction of characters.

Finally, artificial life focuses on the concept of emergence. As described in section 2.4, emergence is at odds with maintaining artistic control over believable agent construction.

3.2 Humanoids

Humanoids is the label I'm using for a body of work concerned with building systems that have physical properties (arms, legs, sensory systems) similar to humans. *Virtual humanoid* work is concerned with building realistic, animated humans that live in virtual worlds. Two examples of this work are the Jack [13] project at the University of Pennsylvania and the work done at MIRALab [24] (including the famous virtual Marilyn Monroe) at the University of Geneva. In both Jack and the projects in

MIRALab, the focus is on building general tools for the animation of human figures, including animating complicated tasks, providing automatic reach and grasp capabilities, and supporting collision detection. MIRALab is currently focusing on the animation of clothes, faces and hair as well as developing architectures to give virtual humanoids autonomy. Though virtual humanoid work started in the graphics and animation communities and was informed by that research agenda, as the humanoid figures have become more sophisticated there has been a natural progression into research concerned with giving these figures autonomous intelligence.

Virtual humanoid work differs from Oz believable agent work in its concern with generality and realism. General toolkits for realistic movement are certainly useful for designing avatars for virtual worlds and perhaps for building background characters (extras). Much of a character's personality, however, is reflected in the unique way a character moves. For building main characters, an author needs detailed control over a character's movement. Much of the autonomy work associated with virtual humanoids is concerned with providing humanoids with competent action (perhaps to accomplish tasks in virtual worlds) rather than with rich personality.

Japanese robotics researchers are building *physical* humanoids (e.g. JSK [21], Waseda Humanoid Project [33]). Examples of this work include a robot that can swing on a swingset [53], and a robot with a 3D face [51] that can recognize and produce facial expressions. Such work has focused primarily on the engineering necessary to build and control a complex, jointed humanoid. These robots are not yet capable of sophisticated, autonomous behavior. As such technology becomes more mature, it may open up the possibility of physical believable agents.

Finally, there is a small body of humanoid work concerned with growing intelligence through interaction with the world via a humanoid body ("grow a baby" projects). Cog [14], at the MIT AI Lab, is probably the best known example of this work. Cog is a robot that has been engineered to have sensory and movement capabilities similar to humans (though its torso is fixed to a pedestal). Cog started with simple motor and sensory reflexes. The hope is that as Cog interacts with the world, it will begin developing intellectual capabilities similar to a human. The guiding hypothesis is that much of human intelligence is the result of sensory-motor interactions with the environment as constrained by human bodies. Neo [44], at the University of Massachusetts, is a virtual baby living in a simulated world. Neo, like Cog, starts with simple sensory-motor reflexes. As Neo interacts with its world, it learns concepts through a hierarchical sequence of abstractions on streams of sensory-motor data. Both these projects are concerned with growing human-like intelligence (realism) as opposed to building characters.

All the humanoid work shares with Oz the desire to build broad agents which have bodies, sense the world, and take action. Capabilities developed by these projects, either for animating human movement, moving physical humanoid bodies, or physically grounding conceptual thought, may indeed prove useful for opening new levels of sophistication in believable agent behavior. The challenge will be to translate work that seeks to develop general solutions and realistic models into a framework which provides authorial control over the construction of characters.

3.3 Embodied Characters

Embodied character work is concerned with building physical characters. The physicality of such characters seems to evoke a strong, visceral effect in an audience. While I know of no formal studies of this effect, there is informal evidence.

For example, Tamagocchi [7], a toy from Bandai corporation, is wildly popular in Japan. It is about the size of a key chain, has a small LCD screen and three buttons. By pushing the buttons to administer positive and negative feedback, provide food and medicine, and clean up feces, the user nurtures a small bird-like creature that lives on the screen. If the creature is not taken care of, it dies. Stores can't keep Tamagocchi in stock; it is being sold for many times its retail price on the street. Office workers bring Tamagocchi to work and care for it throughout the day. Theft of Tamagocchi is on the rise, especially among teens for whom it is a valued status symbol.

It is unclear how much of this powerful effect is due to social conditions unique to Japan, such as the high cost of pet ownership. However, much of this effect may be due to Tamagocchi's physicality: the fact that it is a small, jewelry-like object (and in fact, teenage girls are wearing Tamagocchi on chains around their necks) that can be incorporated into daily life. Since the character itself is not that complex, the emotional intensity surrounding Tamagocchi may be related to its *ubiquitous* presence.

At Agents 97, Sony demoed a robot dog as an example of their OpenR standard for household entertainment robots [48]. The dog responds to colors, audible tones, and physical touch on its head. The most impressive feature of the dog was its fluid, lifelike movements. As an example, it can smoothly lay down, place its head on its paws, then get back up. In the demo group I was in, everyone responded to this action with "ahhhhh" (cuteness). In this case, I believe the strong response comes from the animal-like movement of a physical object.

Karl Wurst [23] at the University of Connecticut is building robotic puppets based on the woggles (characters built by the Oz project). While these puppets roll rather than hop (the original woggles hop), they are able to stretch and squish (woggle body language) and communicate with each other via IR sensing. It would be interesting to compare the audience response to these puppets with the response to the behaviorally similar screen-based woggles.

Providing a believable agent with a physical body is an interesting research direction to pursue. The combination of rich behavior, personality, and physicality could produce a powerful audience response.

3.4 Chatterbots

Chatterbots are programs that engage in conversation. The original chatterbot is Eliza [73], a program that uses sentence template matching to simulate the conversation of a non-directive therapist. Julia [22] is a chatterbot that connects to multi-user dungeons (MUD). Besides engaging in conversation, Julia has a simple memory that remembers what's been said to her and where she's been. She uses this information in her conversations (e.g. repeating what someone else said or providing directions). When she is not engaged in conversation, she wanders about the MUD exploring. Erin the bartender from Extempo [2] is a recent example of a chatterbot. Erin serves drinks and converses with customers (music is a favorite topic of conversation). She has an emotional state (influenced by what you say to her, whether you argue with her, etc.) and forms attitudes about customers. How she responds to any particular utterance is influenced by her current state.

There are several differences between chatterbots and believable agents. First, chatterbots primarily interact in language. Body movement and physical activity play a secondary role; if it is present at all, it is used to provide some background color during lulls in a conversation. The language interaction is primarily reactive; the chatterbot is responding to each utterance without its own goals for the conversation. In the absence of an utterance to respond to, the chatterbot may fall back on some small number of stock phrases that it uses to try and start a conversation. Second, many chatterbots are designed for entry into a restricted form of the Turing test (the Loebner Prize [10]). The goal is to fool a human for some short period of time into thinking that they are interacting with another human. Notice that the goal is not to communicate a personality, but rather to briefly fool a user into thinking that they are talking to some generic person during a context-free conversation. Finally, most chatterbots don't have a long-term motivational structure; they don't have goals, attitudes, fears and desires. The conversations they engage in don't go anywhere. A chatterbot's only goal is to engage in open-ended conversation.

In contrast, believable agents express their personalities through their movements and actions, not just through language. Believable agents are designed to strongly express a personality, not fool the viewer into thinking they are human. For example, when watching a play or film, viewers know that the characters are not "real," but that does not detract from being engaged by the character. Finally, believable agents have long-term motivational structures. Their behavior is designed within the context of a particular world. Within this context, the believable agent's behavior is conditioned by desires and attitudes. However, the lack of a long term motivational structure and the focus on language interaction allows chatterbots to function within open environments (such as chat rooms or MUDs) where they can serve as a social catalyst for the human participants.

3.5 Behavioral Animation

Behavioral animation has developed in the graphics community as an alternative to hand-animation. In more traditional computer animation, the animator builds a model of the character they wish to animate, defines parameters that move and deform parts of the model, and writes functions that smoothly interpolate the values of parameters given beginning and end values. Now, in order to make the figure do something, the animator must define a set of initial and final values of all the parameters (keyframes) and apply the interpolation functions to generate all the intermediate frames. Even after doing all the upfront work of building the model and defining the functions, the animator still needs to define keyframes in order to make the model move.

Behavioral animation seeks to eliminate the work involved in defining keyframes by pushing more work into the upfront creation of a model. Instead of just defining the geometry, the model also includes code that tells the model how to move in different situations. Given a state of the world, the model moves itself. Some behavioral animation work focuses on general strategies for realistic movement. In this respect, behavioral animation shares some common goals with virtual humanoid work. However, as more internal state is added to the behavioral routines, state which may represent emotions or social attitudes, behavioral animation begins converging on believable agents. Whereas believable agent research begins in AI (the building of minds), and then appropriates and modifies AI technology to the task of building characters (minds and bodies), behavioral animation research begins in graphics (the building of bodies), and adds behaviors to these bodies to build characters (bodies and minds).

A good example of the convergence between behavioral animation and believable agents is IMPROV [18], a system built by Perlin and Goldberg at NYU. As part of IMPROV, they have developed a scripting language for writing animation behaviors. Behaviors written in this language can be conditional on author-maintained internal state as well as external events. The main mechanism for creating non-deterministic characters is the tuning of probabilities. The author communicates the character's personality and mood by tuning probabilities for selecting one action over another. Both IMPROV and Oz share an author-centered point of view. However Hap (the Oz believable agent language) provides more support for expressing complex control relationships among behaviors. In addition, Em [66] provides support for maintaining complex emotional state (something that would have to be done manually using the IMPROV language). On the other hand, the procedural animation portion of the IMPROV scripting language provides more language support for animating control points on the model.

4 Why Study Believable Agents?

I've described the Oz philosophy regarding the believable agent research program and reviewed related research areas. The reader still may be left with a nagging question: why study believable agents at all? The most obvious answer is that believable agents are necessary if you want to build interactive story worlds. This is the primary motivation behind the Oz research program. There are other reasons to pursue this research, however.

Believable agents may greatly enhance learning in educational settings by providing engagement and motivation for the learner. Research in this area is being pursued by the IntelliMedia [20] project at North Carolina State University. They have built a constructivist learning environment in which children learn about the biology of plants by building a plant (selecting different kinds of roots, and leaves, etc.). A believable agent serves as a companion and guide for the student.

Believability will be important for building anthropomorphic interface agents. Research by Nass and Reeves [29] at Sanford University has shown that users interpret the actions of computer systems using the same social rules and conventions used to interpret the actions of people, whether or not the computer system is explicitly anthropomorphic. Since most systems aren't designed with this fact in mind, the resulting social behavior of the system (its personality) is accidental. As designers begin building systems with *designed* personalities, they will need techniques for communicating this personality to the user. This is precisely the research area of believable agents.

The three motivations given above are pragmatic reasons to pursue this research. There is also a more distant, idealistic, yet compelling reason for pursuing this research: the AI Dream. This Dream, to build companions such as Data on Startrek, has motivated many workers in the field of AI. Woody Bledsoe, a former president of AAAI, captured this dream nicely in his 1985 Presidential Address [41]. In describing the dream that motivated his career in AI, he opened:

Twenty-five years ago I had a dream, a *daydream*, if you will. A dream shared with many of you. I dreamed of a special kind of computer, which had eyes and ears and arms and legs, in addition to its "brain." ... my dream was filled with the wild excitement of seeing a machine act like a human being, at least in many ways.

Note that he did not talk about some disembodied mind; this is a complete creature. Later he states:

My dream computer person *liked* (emphasis added) to walk and play Ping-Pong, especially with me.

Clearly the AI dream is not just about rational competence, but about personality and emotion. As described above, believable agents research is not a subfield of AI, but rather a stance from which AI can be reinterpreted and transformed. The believable agents research program, by directly engaging the issue of building complete agents with rich personality and emotion, provides a new approach for pursuing the AI Dream.

5 Interactive Story

Drama consists of both characters and story. In *interactive* drama, believable agents are the characters. Now it's time to talk about story.

5.1 Interactive Story: an Oxymoron

Many observers have remarked that the concept of interactive story contains a contradiction. A story is an experience with temporal structure. Interaction is doing what you want, when you want (interaction as control; other models are possible).

Accounts of story structure often describe some form of dramatic arc (first introduced by Aristotle [40]). One form of the dramatic arc is shown in Figure 4. The vertical axis represents tension, or unresolved issues or questions. The horizontal axis represents time. At the beginning of the story, during the exposition, the tension rises slowly as the audience learns the background of the story. An inciting incident then sparks the story. Tension begins rising more rapidly after this incident. Eventually, the amount of tension, the number of unresolved questions, the intertwining between plot elements, reaches a critical state. During this crisis, the tension rises rapidly to the climax. During the climax, questions are answered and tensions resolved. After the climax, the tension falls rapidly as any remaining tensions are resolved. Finally, during the denouement, the world returns to some status quo. The experience of a story is thus structured; events don't happen in some willy-nilly fashion. The experience has a global shape. Interaction, on the other hand, is generally construed as the freedom to do anything at anytime. Story is predestination; interaction is freedom. Thus the conflict.

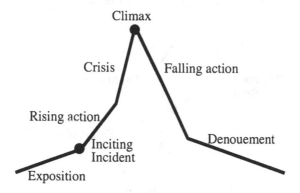

Fig. 4. Dramatic arc

Some have resolved the conflict by saying that interactive story is impossible. Others have redefined the notion of story to have less structure; whatever emerges from interaction is defined as story. Brenda Laurel, in her 1986 thesis [57], described a hypothetical expert system that causes a structured story to happen in the face of interaction. While the technology is different, the Oz drama manager takes this approach of simultaneously honoring story structure *and* interaction.

5.2 Oz Drama Manager

The Oz drama manager [74] controls a story at the level of plot points. Plot points are "important moments" in a story. In a typical hour and a half film, there may be 12-15 of them. Given a particular set of plot points, the space of all possible stories is the set of permutations of all possible plot points. The vast majority of these permutations will be garbage - unsatisfying stories which don't make sense. The author of the story has some particular ordering of the plot points in mind - this is the story she wants to tell. Rather than expressing this preferred sequence via structural constraints on the story world, the author writes an evaluation function that captures her sense of aesthetics for the story. This aesthetic is captured by some set of features the evaluation function looks for in a permutation. Conforming to the shape of some dramatic arc may be one feature in the function. Given a permutation of plot points, the evaluation function rates the permutation. Assuming the author has successfully captured her aesthetic, the original story should be ranked high by the function. So the authorial process is:

1. write some linear (non-interactive) story as a sequence of "important moments"
2. reverse-engineer your own thinking to figure out why you think that particular sequence is a "good" story
3. capture this aesthetic as a set of features (over sequences) in an evaluation function
4. make sure that you have (approximately) captured your aesthetic by comparing the output of the evaluation function with your own evaluation of a set of sequences (of course include the original story - the one your "really" want to tell)

With an evaluation function in hand, you can now do search.

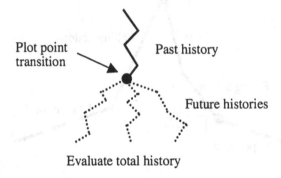

Fig. 5. Oz drama manager evaluates possible story histories

The drama manager watches the state of the world (including the user interaction). While the user is moving around and interacting with characters *within* some particular plot point, the system isn't doing anything but watching. Eventually, some sequence of activities in the world will be recognized as causing a plot transition. The drama manager springs into action. There exists some past history of plot points. At this point in time, the future histories consist of all possible sequences of remaining plot points. Sequences of events that result in a plot transition are abstracted as user moves. The drama manager has a set of operations it can perform to warp the world: these are the system moves. In a manner similar to game playing programs (such as chess programs), the manager examines every possible system move it could perform to warp the world, every possible user move the user could make to cause a plot transition, every possible system move from that new state of the world, etc. until it has played out the possible histories. The past history plus each possible history forms a set of total histories. The evaluation function can now evaluate each total history. The system then makes a system move (warping the world in some way) that maximizes the probability of generating a highly ranked total history. In this way, a story structure is imposed on the viewer's experience, while still allowing interaction.

5.3 Design Dimensions

Having briefly examined the Oz approach to interactive drama, I will now examine related work. The first comment to make is that there is less related work on interactive story than on believable agents. Believable agents work can be construed as the construction of little "people". Even though there is not much work directly concerned with believability, there is a body of work concerned in one way or another with building little people. Interactive story, by comparison, is relatively unexplored. Instead of describing the relationship between various research areas and the Oz approach, as was done for believable agents, I will describe three design dimensions. Each of these dimensions represents a spectrum of choices that can be made with respect to a design question. Various research projects in interactive story can be displayed along these dimensions.

While each dimension has a "low" end and a "high" end, this is not meant to imply that low is bad and high is good. Systems laying on different points along these dimensions have different properties; each is useful for generating different kinds of experiences. The dimensions merely indicate a space of potential to be explored.

Local vs. Global Control. A drama manager can take smaller or larger blocks of spatio-temporal structure into account when deciding how to control a story. By spatio-temporal structure I mean *action* as it unfolds in the space of the story world across the time of the story. To the extent that a drama manager only looks at the action that has immediately occurred in the area around the audience (user), the control is local. To the extent that the manager takes into account the entire history of the story across the entire space of the story world, the control is global.

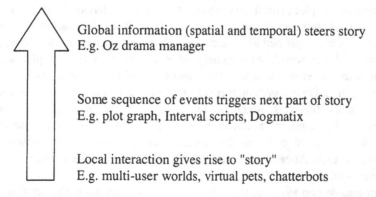

Global information (spatial and temporal) steers story
E.g. Oz drama manager

Some sequence of events triggers next part of story
E.g. plot graph, Interval scripts, Dogmatix

Local interaction gives rise to "story"
E.g. multi-user worlds, virtual pets, chatterbots

Fig. 6. Local vs. global control

At the extreme local end of the spectrum are systems in which interaction with characters is the only mechanism structuring experience. For example, when interacting with other people in a multi-user world, the structure of the experience arises out of these moment-to-moment interactions. As a shared history develops among users, this history will condition future interactions. Similarly, interaction with artificial characters such as virtual pets and chatterbots share such local structure. Such purely local control doesn't give rise to story in any strong sense of the word; an audience is not carried through some author-defined shaped experience in the course of their interaction with a system.

At an intermediate point on the spectrum are systems that control a story by taking into account some history across some physical space of the story world. Such systems can be characterized as *script-and-demon* systems. The script specifies a linear or branching sequence of events. These events can be guarded by demons that won't let the event happen unless some preconditions on the state of the world have been satisfied. Plot graphs [55], an early approach to drama in the Oz project, are one example of such a system. A plot graph lays out scenes in a directed acyclic graph (DAG). The arcs represent the must-precede relationship. Only after all preceding plot points have happened can the next plot point be entered. Associated with the arcs are hints and obstacles. These are ways that the drama manager can influence the world. Hints make it more likely that the user will move into the next scene; obstacles slow the user down. Demons recognize when a user has completed a scene. Another example, Pinhanez's Interval Scripts [68], represents the script by using a temporal calculus to record temporal relationships among intervals. Some of these intervals are connected to sensors (demons) that wait for events to occur in the world; others are connected to actuators that make events happen in the world. A constraint propagation mechanism is used to determine the state of each interval (now, past, future, or some mixed state). When a sensor has the value now, it begins looking for its associated event to happen in the world. When an actuator has the value now, it makes its associated event happen in the world. The final script-and-demon system I'll discuss is the plot control mechanism in Galyean's Dogmatix [49]. Galyean makes an analogy between the action selection problem in behavioral agents and the event selection problem in plot control. At each point in time, a behavioral agent must select one (or in general, some small subset) behavior from its pool of possible behaviors. This selection is accomplished as a function of the internal state of the agent and the external state of the world. Analogously, at each point in time a plot selection mechanism must select an event to make happen out of the set of all events it could make happen. In Galyean's system, this selection is a function of story state variables (history), sensors (demons watching for events in the world), and *temporal relationships*. The temporal relations hierarchy, before, xor, and must-happen place a partial order on the possible sequences of events chosen by the selection mechanism. At each point in time, the event that has the highest "fitness" is chosen for execution.

In script-and-demon systems, the complexity of the demons is the limiting factor. In order to take more and more global information into account, the firing conditions on the demons must become more and more complex. Perhaps because of this complexity, in practice demons tend to fire on relatively local sequences of events. And regardless of how complex a demon's firing condition becomes, it can only take the past into account. It can not look into the future to see what might happen in the story.

At the global end of the spectrum is the Oz drama manager. Whenever it detects a user move, it considers total story histories by concatenating the entire past history with projected future histories. These total histories are evaluated to determine which events to make happen in the world.

Granularity of story control. A drama manager can seek to control the story at different levels of detail. To the extent that a manager controls precisely the actions of characters (what they do and when they do it), the manager is controlling the story at a small grain size. To the extent that a manager controls the general direction of the story, but does not directly control the activities of particular actors, the manager is controlling the story at a large grain size.

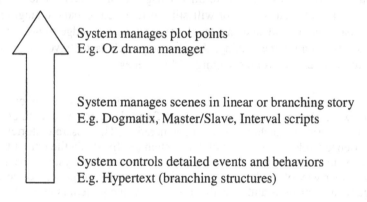

System manages plot points
E.g. Oz drama manager

System manages scenes in linear or branching story
E.g. Dogmatix, Master/Slave, Interval scripts

System controls detailed events and behaviors
E.g. Hypertext (branching structures)

Fig. 7. Granularity of control

At the extreme small-grain-size end of the spectrum, are systems that directly control the detailed events in the story and behaviors of the characters. In such systems, there isn't really a distinction between the drama manager and the world; the structure of the world *is* the drama manager. Hypertext stories are an example of such a system. The branching structure of the story precisely describes what happens and when it will happen. Within a node of the branching structure, there is no variation. The same fixed events happen at a given node every time it is visited. Some CD-ROM games also use this approach to story; each node in a branching structure completely describes what a user will experience.

At an intermediate point on the spectrum are systems that manage scenes. In such systems, the progression of scenes is fixed by a linear or branching structure. But what happens within a scene is not completely predetermined; within the scene, there is room for variation in response to user action or non-determinism on the part of the agents. Script-and-demon systems can be used to provide this granularity of control. Two examples are Galyean's event selection system and Pinhanez's interval scripts (described above). Hayes-Roth's master/servant scenario [52] is another example of scene level control. In this system, which is not interactive (the user doesn't play a character), a master and servant play out a power struggle which can end in the master and servant switching roles. The script issues directives to the characters. The characters engage in action as a function of these directives and their internal state. The script specifies the order in which directives are issued. Demons wait for certain conditions to be met in the world (e.g. "improvise until the master's demeanor is low") before allowing the script to continue.

At the large-grain-size end of the spectrum are systems that decide the order of plot points (which can be scenes); there is no linear or branching structure fixing the order of scenes. For example, the Oz drama manager repeatedly searches the space of scene orderings in order to decide what to do next to influence the story. "Good" orderings are captured *implicitly* in the evaluation function. Each time the user runs through the story, the ordering of scenes can be different.

A single story system may need multiple drama managers at different granularities of story control. A system like the Oz drama manager could select scene orderings. However, within a scene, story control will still be required to handle staging. One approach is to have the individual characters have enough knowledge to not only play their roles but also control the staging. Another approach is to have some sort of script-and-demon system control the staging within scenes.

Generation. A drama manager can be more or less generative while it controls a story. To the extent that a drama manager has a fixed description of a single story (linear) or set of stories (branching), it is not generative. The possible stories that a user can experience while interacting with the system are fixed. To the extent that the manager can create a new story each time a user experiences the system, the story is generative. Another way of thinking about this is capacity for surprise. To the extent that a manager can surprise its author with a novel story, the system is generative.

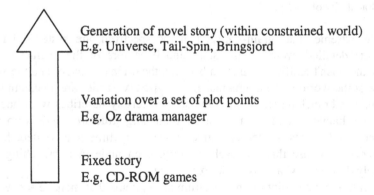

Generation of novel story (within constrained world)
E.g. Universe, Tail-Spin, Bringsjord

Variation over a set of plot points
E.g. Oz drama manager

Fixed story
E.g. CD-ROM games

Fig. 8. Degree of generation

At the fixed end of the spectrum lie systems like CD-ROM games. The story structure is completely fixed by a branching structure. Such games don't often bear replaying; after having played through the game, there is nothing new to experience.

A bit higher on the spectrum are systems that support variations on a theme. For example, the Oz drama manager can change the order of plot points, or not include plot points, each time the user experiences the story. Though the same story is not experienced each time, it will consist of some sequence of plot points from a fixed pool. The extent to which such a system seems generative will depend on the level of abstraction of the plot points and the complexity of the evaluation function.

Still higher on the spectrum are systems that generate novel stories. Unfortunately, the examples of such systems are not interactive; in general these systems generate a textual story that is read by the user. Universe [58] tells a serial soap-opera-like story. Characters are described by sets of attributes. Example attributes are interpersonal relationships (e.g. ex-spouse, div-mom), stereotypes (e.g. party-goer, egomaniac), and goals (e.g. become-famous, associate-right). A library of plot fragments (plans) serves as the raw material for composing stories. Each plot fragment describes the kinds of characters it requires (constraints on the traits), the goals the plot fragment can be used to satisfy, and the subgoals necessary to accomplish the plot fragment. Stories are told by composing these plot fragments. In addition, the system learns new plot fragments by generalizing old ones. Tail-spin [64] tells Aesop-fable-like stories. It does not use a library of plot fragments. Instead, stories are generated purely by trying to accomplish the (sometimes conflicting) goals of characters. Both these systems view story telling as a planning problem. Bringsjord's [28] work is a modern example of non-interactive story generation.

Generation raises the interesting riddle of authorial control. Good authors write good stories - that is, stories which audiences find engaging. If an author takes the trouble to write a good story, you probably want your system to tell that story. At what levels of abstraction can an author still exert authorial control? An author can say "tell this exact love story." Clearly they have control; its a fixed story where interaction basically means moving through at your own pace. An author might say "tell a love story generally similar to this one." Somehow you would have to capture the author's knowledge of what makes a story "similar to this one." This is the aesthetic as captured by the evaluation function in the Oz drama manager. An author might say "make up a love story that sounds like I made it up." What aspects of the author (knowledge, feelings, history) have to be captured in the system to maintain authorial control but allow this kind of flexibility? As you increase the generative power of a system, can you still capture the richness of a particular authorial point of view?

6 Clip-Based Work

A non-agent based approach to interactive drama is interactive digital video. The work of Davenport [19] is characteristic of this approach. I include this work in a separate section, rather than including it under character or story, since interactive video combines aspects of both.

The basic approach is to store and index some large number of video segments. As the user interacts with the system, the system must decide which segment is the appropriate one to play next. The system making this decision may be something very like a drama manager. However, interactive video can also be used primarily as a character, rather than a story technology. The Entertainment Technology Center [16] at Carnegie Mellon has built several prototypes of such systems. One of their systems, recently demoed at the ACM 50th Anniversary conference, allows the user to have conversation with Einstein. In this system, many shots of an actor playing Einstein are stored and indexed on disk. A user speaks to the system. A speech recognition system converts the user's utterance into text. Based on this text, the most appropriate clip is played. While the simplest version of such a lookup involves comparing the user's utterance against the video index using word-based indexing technology, one can easily imagine building some kind of personality model that maintains state based on the previous course of the conversation. This state could then be used to bias the selection of the video clip. The goal of these interactive interviews is to give the audience the feeling of actually talking with a famous personage.

For both character and story, a clip-based approach is based on selection rather than generation. An appropriate clip must be chosen from some set of clips. In a believable agent approach to character, the behavior is generated in real time. Though the library of behaviors for such an agent is fixed, the granularity is much smaller than a video clip. There is thus much more flexibility in composing these behaviors. In addition, the structures for representing internal state (such as emotion) and for representing behaviors are made out of the same "stuff" - computer code. This allows the state information and the behaviors to intermingle in complex ways. In interactive video, the code representing the character's state and the data representing the actions (video) are of different kinds. To achieve the same flexibility as the computational representation of behavior, there would have to be a video indexing scheme that captures the detailed action of each clip, as well as a means for changing clips during playback (speeding them up, slowing them down, changing whether the figure in the scene is looking left or right, etc.).

On the other hand, clip-based approaches can immediately take advantage of the skills of actors. Rather than having to generate a facial expression, a movement or an utterance with all the subtlety of a human actor, you can immediately use the skill of the human actor by filming her and including the clip in the database. Also, all the cinematic techniques developed over the last 100 years for creating engaging video sequences are at your disposal.

7 Conclusion

Believable agents and interactive drama are two relatively new research fields. Both research areas are combining insights and knowledge from the dramatic arts with computer technology. Bringing rich personalities and story structures to computing promises to open up new realms of human expression and experience.

References

Industry

1. Cyberlife (makers of Creatures): http://www.cyberlife.co.uk/
   Creatures are Alife pets that you raise from eggs. Their technology is distinctive in its level of biological modeling. A Creature has a neural net for action selection, artificial biochemistry (including hormonal effects on the neural net), an immune system, and a reproductive system (a genome encodes for creature traits).
2. Extempo Systems: http://www.extempo.com/
   Extempo Systems was founded by Barbara Hayes-Roth, leader of the Virtual Theater Project at Stanford. Extempo is creating architectures and authoring tools for the creation of improvisational characters. Their first demo is Erin the bartender, a character who serves drinks and chats with customers in a virtual bar.
3. Fujitsu Interactive (makers of Fin Fin): http://www.fujitsu-interactive.com/
   Fin Fin is a half-bird half-dolphin creature who lives in a world called Teo. Users interact with Fin Fin via a microphone, proximity sensor and mouse. Fin Fin is shy; a user has to slowly build up a relationship with Fin Fin over time. Fin Fin utilizes technology developed by the Oz group at Carnegie Mellon.
4. Motion Factory: http://www.motion-factory.com/
   Motion Factory is developing "Intelligent Digital Actor technology." Digital actors generate their own animation (motion) based on interactions with the environment. Motion Factory is an example of work converging on believable characters from the graphics community rather than the artificial intelligence community.
5. Persona Project at Microsoft Research:
   http://www.research.microsoft.com/research/ui/persona/home.htm
   The Persona project at Microsoft Research is developing the technologies required to produce conversational assistants-- lifelike animated characters that interact with a user in a natural spoken dialog. Their first prototype is Peedy, a character that responds to requests to play music. Gene Ball, a researcher in the Persona Project, organizes the conference Lifelike Computer Characters.
6. P.F. Magic (makers of Petz): http://www.pfmagic.com/
   Petz are autonomous pets that live on your screen.
7. Tamagocchi (from Bandai): http://www.virtualpet.com/vp/farm/lleg/lleg.htm
   Tamagocchi is a small, egg shaped plastic toy with an LCD screen and 3 buttons. Users must nurture a creature that lives on the screen by feeding it, giving it medicine, disciplining it, and cleaning up excrement. If the user is negligent in these tasks, the creature dies. This product is a craze in Japan. While Tamagocchi possesses neither sophisticated personality nor sophisticated behaviors, it is an example of the powerful effect (in terms of effect on users) of even a small amount of lifelike behavior.
8. Zoesis
   Zoesis was recently founded by Joseph Bates (head of the Oz project) and Oz project alumni. Its goal is to build interactive story experiences utilizing believable agents.

Groups Collecting and Disseminating Research

9. Contact Consortium: http://www.ccon.org/
   A group that promotes avatar spaces.

10. Loebner Prize: http://acm.org/~loebner/loebner-prize.htmlx
    The Loebner Prize contest, held each year, awards $2000.00 to the author of the program which does the best job passing a limited form of the Turing test.
11. Virtual Pet Home Page: http://www.virtualpet.com/vp/vpindex2.htm
    A page discussing research and commercial products related to virtual pets.

Academic Research Projects

12. Affective Reasoning Project (Depaul University): http://condor.depaul.edu/~elliott/ar.html
    Led by Clark Elliott. The goal of this project is to build agents that can reason about emotion. Currently they have systems that can detect emotion in human voice, express emotion through facial expressions and speech inflection, and "have" emotions (in the sense that emotions detected in the user trigger emotions in the agent).
13. Center for Human Modeling and Simulation (University of Pennsylvania)
    http://www.cis.upenn.edu/~hms/index.html
    Home of Jack, a graphical human simulation package. The research at the Center is focused around building behavior and physics-based simulations of human figures.
14. The Cog Shop (MIT AI Lab): http://www.ai.mit.edu/projects/cog/
    Led by Rodney Brooks, the father of subsumption architecture. Rodney has been arguing for over a decade that the road to intelligence consists of building situated, embodied, broad agents (in his case, robots) which employ no semantic representations. Cog is a humanoid robot. As Cog interacts with the world using a body similar to a human body, it is hoped that Cog will learn to think the way humans do.
15. The Cognition and Affect Project (University of Birmingham)
    http://www.cs.bham.ac.uk/~axs/cog_affect/COGAFF-PROJECT.html
    A project led by Aaron Sloman and Glyn Humphries. The goal of this project is to explore the design space of AI architectures in order to understand the relationship between what kinds of architectures are capable of what kinds of mental phenomena. They are interested in the whole range of human mental states; in particular they wish to discover whether emotions are an accident of evolution or fundamental to the design of any resource-limited intelligent agent.
16. Entertainment Technology Center (Carnegie Mellon University)
    Founded by Don Marinelli and Randy Pausch. They are charged with developing an entertainment technology program at CMU. Their current focus is Synthetic Interviews, an interactive video technology with which a user can have a conversation with some character.
17. Gesture and Narrative Language (MIT Media Lab)
    http://gn.www.media.mit.edu/groups/gn/
    Led by Justine Cassell. Using ideas from discourse theory and social cognition, this group designs agents which have discourse competence (e.g. knowing how to integrate gestures and speech to communicate, knowing how to take turns in a conversation, etc.).
18. IMPROV Project (NYU Media Research Lab): http://www.mrl.nyu.edu/improv/index.html
    This project is led by Ken Perlin and Athomas Goldberg . "The IMPROV Project at NYU's Media Research Lab is building the technologies to produce distributed 3D virtual environments in which human-directed avatars and computer-controlled agents interact with each other in real-time, through a combination of Procedural Animation and Behavioral Scripting techniques developed in-house." An example of convergence towards believable characters from the graphics side (vs. AI).
19. Interactive Cinema Group (MIT Media Lab): http://ic.www.media.mit.edu/
    A project at the Media Lab led by Glorianna Davenport. They study techniques for bringing interactivity to the traditional cinematic medium (with notable exceptions such as Tinsley Galyean's Dogmatic, which is set in a virtual world). In general, this involves breaking down a linear medium (such as video) into a database of clips, somehow annotating those clips,

and then intelligently choosing the right clips at the right time as a user interacts with the system. The video may be accompanied by other media such as email (e.g. Lee Morgenroth's Lurker).

20. IntelliMedia (North Carolina State University)
http://www.csc.ncsu.edu/eos/users/l/lester/www/imedia/
Led by James Lester. This group focuses on intelligent multimedia. Currently they are focusing on animated pedagogical agents.
21. Jouhou System Kougaku Laboratory (University of Tokyo)
http://www.jsk.t.u-tokyo.ac.jp/index.html
A robotics research lab, including remote-brained and humanoid robotics.
22. Julia (Carnegie Mellon University): http://www.fuzine.com/mlm/julia.html
The home page for Julia, a chatterbot that lives in TinyMUDS.
23. Karl Wurst (Robotics and Puppetry, University of Connecticut)
http://www-rfcc.cse.uconn.edu/www/KarlHome.html
Karl Wurst, in collaboration with the University of Connecticut's world-renowned Puppet Arts Program, is building robotic versions of the Woggles.
24. MIRALab (University of Geneva): http://miralabwww.unige.ch/
Led by Nadia Thalmann. This group works on virtual humanoids. Focus is on realistic modeling of human faces, movement, clothing, etc. Now starting to do work on autonomous systems.
25. Neo (University of Massachusetts)
http://eksl-www.cs.umass.edu/research/conceptual-systems/index.html
Led by Paul Cohen. This group is building a baby that interacts in a simulated world. The goal is for the baby to learn the conceptual structure of the world through physical interaction.
26. Oz Project (Carnegie Mellon University)
http://www.cs.cmu.edu/afs/cs.cmu.edu/project/oz/web/oz.html
Led by Joseph Bates, founder of Zooesis. The goal of the Oz project is to build interactive story worlds containing personality rich, believable characters. A drama manager ensures that the user experiences a high-quality story.
27. Phil Agre: http://dlis.gseis.ucla.edu/people/pagre/
An alumnus of the MIT AI Lab, Phil Agre developed Pengi, a system which played the video game Pengo. Pengi is an instance of "alternative AI": it employed reactive behaviors and deictic (context dependent) representations. He has written elegantly on why classical AI is inappropriate for building agents which engage in situated, embodied, routine activity.
28. Selmer Bringsjord: http://www.rpi.edu/~brings/
Primarily a philosopher of AI, Selmer also does research in story generation. His forthcoming book, *AI, Story Generation and Literary Creativity: The State of the Art* will describe BRUTUS, his latest story generation system.
29. Social Responses to Communication Technology (Stanford University)
http://www.stanford.edu/group/commdept/
A project led by Clifford Nass and Byron Reeves. They are studying the way people apply social rules and schemas to their interactions with technology.
30. Software Agents Group (MIT Media Lab)
http://agents.www.media.mit.edu/groups/agents/
Led by Patti Maes. The software agent group explores the use of autonomous agents in a wide variety of contexts. Much of their work tends to have an artificial life flavor (by which I mean that the work focuses on useful behavior emerging out of the interactions of many software agents). Agents as synthetic characters was explored by Bruce Blumberg in the ALIVE and Hamsterdam projects. The synthetic character work has how shifted to a new group being started by Bruce. He developed an ethologically motivated action selection mechanism to drive his synthetic characters.

31. Virtual Environments for Training (USC Information Sciences Institute)
http://www.isi.edu/isd/VET/vet.html
Led by W. Lewis Johnson. This group has built a pedagogic agent named Steve that trains humans in virtual worlds. Steve teaches people how to perform tasks, gives advice as it watches users perform tasks, and answers student's questions.

32. Virtual Theater Project (Stanford): http://www-ksl.stanford.edu/projects/cait/index.html
Led by Barbara Hayes-Roth, founder of Extempo. The metaphor informing their work is that of an improvisational actor. That is, they build actors who try to improvise behavior in different situations. An actor's improvisational choices may be influenced by an explicitly specified personality (a set of values along some dimensions of personality). They are also exploring how a human might exert high level control over one of these actors.

33. Waseda Humanoid Project (Waseda University)
http://www.shirai.info.waseda.ac.jp/humanoid/index.html
They are building a humanoid robot including sensing, recognition, expression and motion subsystems.

Articles and Books

34. Articles written by the OZ Project (CMU)
http://www.cs.cmu.edu/afs/cs.cmu.edu/project/oz/web/papers.html
On-line articles available about the OZ project. Articles include overall descriptions of the goals of the project, the action architecture, the emotion architecture, and natural language generation (for the text based worlds).

35. Articles written by the Software Agents Group (MIT Media Lab)
http://agents.www.media.mit.edu/groups/agents/publications/
On-line articles from the Software Agents Group. Articles relevant to believable agents are listed under "Modeling Synthetic Characters: Applications and Techniques." Articles include descriptions of ALIVE, action-selection architectures, and the role of artificial life in entertainment.

36. Articles written by the Virtual Theater Project (Stanford)
http://www-ksl.stanford.edu/projects/cait/publicity.html
On-line articles available about the Virtual Theater Project. Articles include descriptions of their approach to emotion, personality, and user control of improvisational puppets.

37. Special Issue on Situated Cognition: Cognitive Science 17 (1993)
The articles in this issue discuss the relationship between "alternative AI" (sometimes called behavioral AI, or situated action) and "classical AI." Simon and Vera wrote an article in which they argue that all of the specific work that falls under the rubric of situated action can *not* be construed as refutations of the physical symbol system hypothesis. Situated action is just a subset of symbolic AI which focuses on perception and motor control. The rest of the issue consists of articles written by various situated action proponents responding to Simon and Vera's article.

38. Agre, P.: The Dynamic Structure of Everyday Life. A.I. Memo 1085. Artificial Intelligence Lab, MIT (1988)
ftp://publications.ai.mit.edu/ai-publications/1000-1499/AITR-1085/AITR-1085.ps
Agre's Ph.D. thesis. Describes Pengi, a program that can play a video game called Pengo. Pengi is able to play the game without employing any traditional planning.

39. Agre, P., Chapman, D.: What are plans for? A.I. Memo 1050a. Artificial Intelligence Lab, MIT (1988)
ftp://publications.ai.mit.edu/ai-publications/1000-1499/AIM-1050A.ps
Argues for a view of plans as plans-for-communication (as opposed to the classic view of plans-as-programs).

40. Aristotle: The Poetics. Dover, Mineola, New York (1997) (first written 330 BC)
41. Bledsoe, W.: I Had a Dream: AAAI Presidential Address. AI Magazine (Spring 1986) 57-61
    Bledsoe describes the dream that brought him (and many AI researchers) into AI research in the first place: the dream of building computer companions.
42. Brooks, R.: Intelligence Without Reason. A.I. Memo 1293. Artificial Intelligence Lab, MIT (1991)
    ftp://publications.ai.mit.edu/ai-publications/1000-1499/AIM-1293.ps.Z
    Argues for a situated, embodied, semantic-symbol-free approach to achieving intelligence in artificial systems.
43. Brooks, R.: Elephants Don't Play Chess. Robotics and Autonomous Systems 6 (1990) 3-15
    Argues for a situated, embodied, semantic-symbol-free approach to achieving intelligence in artificial systems.
44. Cohen, P., Atkin, M., Oates, T., Beal C.: Neo: Learning Conceptual Knowledge by Sensorimotor Interaction with an Environment. Proceedings of the First International Conference on Autonomous Agents. Marina del Rey, CA, USA (1997) 170-177
    Describes a simulated baby who learns concepts by "physically" interacting with a simulated world. This work comes out of the Neo project.
45. Damasio, A.: Descartes' Error: Emotion, Reason and the Human Brain. Avon Books (1994)
    Describes recent research findings in neuropsychology which seem to indicate that emotion plays a fundamental role in human intelligence. Much of traditional cognitive psychology and artificial intelligence has assumed that emotion is not critical to understanding intelligence.
46. Egri, L.: The Art of Dramatic Writing: Its Basis in the Creative Interpretation of Human Motives. Simon and Schuster (1946)
    Describes how plays work via a theory which relates character, motive and story.
47. Elliott, C.: I Picked Up Catapia and Other Stories: A Multimodal Approach to Expressivity for "Emotionally Intelligent" Agents. Proceedings of the First International Conference on Autonomous Agents. Marina del Rey, CA, USA (1997) 451-457
    Describes an agent which communicates emotionally with people using speech recognition, text-to-speech conversion, real-time morphed schematic faces and music. This work comes out of the Affective Reasoning Project.
48. Fujita, M., Kageyama, K.: An Open Architecture for Robot Entertainment. Proceedings of the First International Conference on Autonomous Agents. Marina del Rey, CA, USA (1997) 435-442
    Describes a standard defined by Sony Corporation for household entertainment robots.
49. Galyean, T.: Narrative Guidance of Interactivity. Ph.D. thesis, MIT Media Lab, MIT (1995)
50. Grand, S., Cliff, D., Malhotra, A.: Creatures: Artificial Life Autonomous Software Agents for Home Entertainment. Proceedings of the First International Conference on Autonomous Agents. Marina del Rey, CA, USA (1997) 22-29
    Describes the architecture behind virtual pets which employ Alife technology (see Cyberlife).
51. Hara, F., Kobayashi, H.: A Face Robot Able to Recognize and Produce Facial Expression. Proceedings of the 1996 IEEE/RSJ International Conference on Intelligent Robots and Systems. Senri Life Science Center, Osaka, Japan (1996) 1600-1607.
    Describes a robot with a human-like face that can recognize and produce human facial expressions.
52. Hayes-Roth, B., van Gent, R., Huber, D.: Acting in Character. Proceedings of the AAAI Workshop on AI and Entertainment (1996)
    ftp://www-ksl.stanford.edu/pub/KSL_Reports/KSL-96-13.ps

Describes a system that portrays a role change between a master and a servant. The master and servant improvise within the constraints of a script.

53. Inaba, M., Nagasaka, K., Kanehiro, F., Kagami, S., Inoue, H.: Real-Time Vision-Based Control of Swing Motion by a Human-form Robot Using the Remote-Brained Approach. Proceedings of the 1996 IEEE/RSJ International Conference on Intelligent Robots and Systems, Senri Life Science Center, Osaka, Japan (1996) 15-22
Describes a humanoid robot that can swing on a swing using visual tracking for control.

54. Jones, C.: Chuck Amuck: The Life and Times of an Animated Cartoonist. Farrar, Straus and Giroux. (1989)
The autobiography of Chuck Jones, an animator at Warner Bros. Describes the Warner Bros. approach to creating characters and story.

55. Kelso, M., Weyhrauch, P., Bates, J.: Dramatic Presence. Presence: The Journal of Teleoperators and Virtual Environments Vol. 2 No. 1, MIT Press (1993)
http://www.cs.cmu.edu/afs/cs.cmu.edu/project/oz/web/papers/CMU-CS-92-195.ps
Describes a series of live experiments to test the effect of interactive freedom on the dramatic experience. Also includes a description of plot graphs.

56. Laurel B.: Computers as Theater. Addison-Wesley (1991)
Draws on Aristotle's theory of drama to define a new approach to designing *dramatic* human-computer interfaces.

57. Laurel, B.: Toward the Design of a Computer-Based Interactive Fantasy System. Ph.D. thesis, Drama department, Ohio State University (1986)
Describes a hypothetical drama manager that guides an interactive story experience.

58. Lebowitz, M.: Story Telling as Planning and Learning. Poetics 14 (1985) 483-502
Describes the use of plan-like plot-fragments in UNIVERSE, a system that writes soap opera-like stories.

59. Lebowitz, M.: Creating Characters in a Story-Telling Universe. Poetics 13 (1984) 171-194
Describes the representations of characters in UNIVERSE, a system that writes soap opera-like stories.

60. Lester, J., Stone, B.: Increasing Believability in Animated Pedagogical Agents. Proceedings of the First International Conference on Autonomous Agents. Marina del Rey, CA, USA (1997) 16-21
http://www.csc.ncsu.edu/eos/users/l/lester/Public/dap-aa-97.ps
Describes a competition-based behavior sequencing engine which produces life-like behavior while maintaining pedagogical appropriateness (e.g. don't distract a learner with some fancy behavior when they are problem solving). This work is part of the IntelliMedia project.

61. Loyall, A. B.: Believable Agents. Ph.D. thesis, Tech report CMU-CS-97-123, Carnegie Mellon University (1997)
Describes requirements for believability derived from the character arts. These requirements motivate the description of Hap, an agent language designed to facilitate writing believable agents. The thesis then describes several examples of agents written in Hap. Finally, a method for doing believable, embodied natural language generation in Hap is described. This work is part of the Oz Project.

62. Loyall, A. B., Bates, J.: Personality-Rich Believable Agents That Use Language. Proceedings of the First International Conference on Autonomous Agents. Marina del Rey, CA, USA (1997) 106-113
Describes the integration of embodied natural language generation into a behavioral agent architecture. This work is part of the Oz Project.

63. McCloud, S.: Understanding Comics: The Invisible Art. HarperCollins (1993)
Written in comic book form, this book describes the semiotics of comics.

64. Meehan, J.: The Metanovel. Ph.D. Dissertation, Yale University (1976)
Describes a system that generates Aesop fable-like stories. It generates stories by using planning to achieve the goals of characters.

65. Neal Reilly, W. S.: A Methodology for Building Believable Social Agents. Proceedings of the First International Conference on Autonomous Agents. Marina del Rey, CA, USA (1997) 114-121
Describes a methodology for building social behaviors on a character-by-character basis. The philosophy behind this approach is that generic taxonomies of social behavior and personality are *inappropriate* for building believable characters. This work is part of the OZ Project.

66. Neal Reilly, W. S.: Believable Social and Emotional Agents. Ph.D. thesis. Tech report CMU-CS-96-138, Carnegie Mellon University (1996)
http://www.cs.cmu.edu/afs/cs.cmu.edu/project/oz/web/papers/CMU-CS-96-138-1sided.ps
Describes a system that maintains emotional state and a methodology for incorporating emotion into the behaviors of believable agents. The thesis then describes a methodology for building believable social behaviors. This work is part of the Oz Project.

67. Perlin, K., Goldberg, A.: Improv: A system for Scripting Interactive Actors in Virtual Worlds. Proceedings of SIGRAPH 96. New Orleans, LA, USA (1996) 205-216
http://www.mrl.nyu.edu/improv/sig96-paper/
Describes the interactive character architecture of the Improv project. An animation engine manipulates the control points of a graphical model. A behavior engine allows the user to specify higher level scripts which control the characters motions. The scripts are written in an English-like scripting language.

68. Pinhanez, C.: Interval Scripts: a Design Paradigm for Story-Based Interactive Systems. Proceedings of CHI97. Atlanta, GA, USA (1997) 287-294
http://pinhanez.www.media.mit.edu/cgi-bin/tr_pagemaker
Describes a method whereby interaction can be scripted with a temporal calculus that represents the relationships between intervals. A constraint propagation mechanism is used to determine the temporal value of each interval. Intervals can be associated with sensors and effectors.

69. Rich, C., Sidner, C.: COLLAGEN: When Agents Collaborate with People. Proceedings of the First International Conference on Autonomous Agents. Marina del Rey, CA, USA (1997) 284-291
Describes a toolkit that supports the construction of agents who follow the rules of collaborative discourse. This work comes out of MERL.

70. Thomas, F., Johnston, O.: The Illusion of Life: Disney Animation. Hyperion (1981)
Written by two Disney animators, this book describes the history of animation at Disney and what techniques the animators developed to make their characters seem believable. This book has been highly influential in the OZ Project at CMU.

71. Thorison, K.: Communicative Humanoids: A Computational Model of Psychosocial Dialogue Skills. PhD Thesis. MIT Media Laboratory (1996)
http://kris.www.media.mit.edu/people/kris/abstr.html
Describes a system called Gandalf that models human dialog competence in order to communicate with a human using speech and gesture.

72. Wavish, P., Connah, D.: Virtual Actors that Can Perform Scripts and Improvise Roles. Proceedings of the First International Conference on Autonomous Agents. Marina del Rey, CA, USA (1997) 317-322
Describes a script based architecture developed at Phillips Research Labs for controlling virtual characters.

73. Weizenbaum, J.: ELIZA -- A computer program for the study of natural language communication between man and machine. Communications of the ACM 9(1) 1966 36-45
Original paper describing ELIZA, a template-based pattern-matching program that simulates the conversational patterns of a non-directive therapist.
74. Weyhrauch, P.: Guiding Interactive Drama. Ph.D. thesis, Tech report CMU-CS-97-109, Carnegie Mellon University (1997)
Describes the Oz drama manager, a search-based system for guiding an interactive story experience. This work is part of the Oz project.

Robots with the Best of Intentions

S. Parsons[1]   O. Pettersson[2]   A. Saffiotti[2]   M. Wooldridge[1]

[1] Department of Electronic Engineering
Queen Mary and Westfield College
University of London, London E1 4NS, U.K.
s.d.parsons, m.j.wooldridge@qmw.ac.uk

[2] Applied Autonomous Sensor Systems
Department of Technology and Science
Örebro University, S-70182 Örebro, Sweden
ola.pettersson, alessandro.saffiotti@ton.oru.se

Abstract. Intelligent mobile robots need the ability to integrate robust navigation facilities with higher level reasoning. This paper is an attempt at combining results and techniques from the areas of robot navigation and of intelligent agency. We propose to integrate an existing navigation system based on fuzzy logic with a deliberator based on the so-called BDI model. We discuss some of the subtleties involved in this integration, and illustrate it on a simulated example. Experiments on a real mobile robot are under way.

1   Introduction

Milou works in a food factory. He has to regularly go and fetch two food samples (potato crisps) from two production lines in two different rooms, A and B, and bring them to an electronic mouth in the quality control lab. Milou must now plan his next delivery. He decides to get the sample from A first, since room A is a little bit nearer than B. While going there, however, he finds the main door to that room closed. Milou knows that there is another door that he could use, but he considers the desirability of doing so. The alternative way to A is hard for Milou, since it goes through a narrow corridor which is usually cluttered with boxes. Besides, doors usually do not stay closed long. Hence, Milou decides to first go to B, and come back to A later on. He goes to room B, picks up the potato crisp and returns. The door to A is still closed, and this time Milou has no other choice than taking the difficult route. He does so, obtains the desired crisp, and finally rolls over to the lab and completes his task.

Performing the above task requires the ability to navigate robustly in real-world, unmodified environments. The robot Milou must be able to reliably find his way, keep track of his own position, avoid the obstacles in the cluttered corridor, and so on. However, this task also requires some higher level capabilities, like reasoning about alternative ways to perform a given task, and reconsidering the available options in face of new events. Our ability to develop intelligent mobile robots and to deploy them in real-world environments will critically depend on our ability to integrate these two aspects of the autonomous navigation problem.

Today's research on mobile robotics has produced a great deal of techniques for robust robot navigation in real environments in the presence of uncertainty. These techniques typically focus on the navigation problem, and do not engage in abstract reasoning processes of the type encountered in the above scenario. On the other hand, research in intelligent agency has resulted in a number of interesting theories for reasoning about actions and plans. Unfortunately, these theories are typically stated at a very abstract level, and ignore the oddities and uncertainties that arise from operating in a real, physical environment.

This paper is a preliminary attempt at integrating results and techniques from the areas of robot navigation and of intelligent agency. Our two main ingredients are: (i) a theory of intelligent agency based on the interplay between *beliefs, desires* and *intentions,* commonly referred to as 'BDI'; and (ii) a behaviour-based robot navigation system grounded in fuzzy logic, called 'Thinking Cap'. In what follows, we outline the characteristics of these ingredients that are relevant to this paper, and discuss how we can integrate them. We also show an illustrative example based on the above scenario.

2 The BDI Model

In the past few years there has been a lot of attention given to building formal models of autonomous software agents; pieces of software which operate to some extent independently of human intervention and which therefore may be considered to have their own goals, and the ability to determine how to achieve their goals. Many of these formal models are based on the use of mentalistic attitudes such as beliefs, desires and intentions. The beliefs of an agent model what it knows about the world, the desires of an agent model which states of the world the agent finds preferable, and the intentions of an agent model those states of the world that the agent actively tries to bring about.

The development of the BDI paradigm was to a great extent driven by Bratman's theory of (human) practical reasoning [1], in which *intentions* play a central role. Put crudely, since an agent cannot deliberate indefinitely about what courses of action to pursue, the idea is it should eventually *commit* to achieving certain states of affairs, and then devote resources to achieving them. These chosen states of affairs are intentions, and once adopted, they play a central role in future practical reasoning [2, 3].

A major issue in the design of agents that are based upon models of intention is that of when to *reconsider* intentions. An agent cannot simply maintain an intention, once adopted, without ever stopping to reconsider it. From time-to-time, it will be necessary to check, for example, whether the intention has been achieved, or whether it is believed to be no longer achievable [3]. In such situations, it is necessary for an agent to deliberate over its intentions, and, if necessary, to *change focus* by dropping existing intentions and adopting new ones.

In [15] we started the formal analysis of this problem. In particular we proposed a notion of optimality of deliberation, which can be glossed as "an agent is optimal if it always deliberates when deliberation will change its intentions and never deliberates when deliberation would not change its intentions", and showed that this can be used to develop a formal description of agents which are *bold* and *cautious* in the sense of Kinny and Georgeff [8]. The idea is that different types of environment require different types of strategies. In rapidly changing environments it makes sense for an agent to spend a lot of time deliberating in order to avoid spending time trying to achieve things which have become impossible. In more static environments there is much less call for agents to deliberate because once they have adopted an intention there is only a small chance that the world will change so as to make that intention impossible to achieve.

3 The 'Thinking Cap'

The 'Thinking Cap' (TC) is a system for autonomous robot navigation based on fuzzy logic which has been implemented and validated on several mobile platforms. A full description of the TC can be found in [11]. Parts of the TC were previously reported in [13, 12, 14]. The main ingredients of TC are:

- a library of *fuzzy behaviours* for indoor navigation, like obstacle avoidance, wall following, and door crossing;
- a *context-depending blending* mechanism that combines the recommendations from different behaviours into a tradeoff control;
- a set of *perceptual routines*, including sonar-based feature extraction, and detection of closed doors and blocked corridors;
- an approximate *map* of the environment, together with a positioning mechanism based on natural landmarks;
- a *navigation planner* that generates a behaviour combination strategy, called a B-plan, that achieves the given navigation goal; and
- a *monitor* that reinvokes the planner whenever the current B-plan is no more adequate to the current goal.

For the goals of this paper, we regard TC as a black box that provides a robust navigation service, and that accepts goals of the form '(goto X)'. There are however two peculiar characteristics of TC that are important here.

Firstly, navigation goals in TC are fuzzy: in '(goto X)', 'X' is a fuzzy location in the robot's map. (More precisely, a goal is formally defined in the TC framework as a fuzzy set of trajectories.) This means that a goal in TC can be more or less satisfied, as measured by a *degree of satisfaction*, a real number in the $[0, 1]$ interval. Typically, this degree depends on the distance between the robot and the desired location, but more complex goals may have more complex degrees of satisfaction.

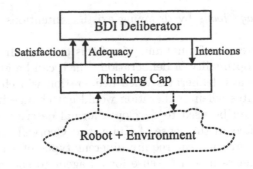

Fig. 1. Integration between a BDI deliberator and the Thinking Cap.

Secondly, the 'adequacy' of the current B-plan which is monitored by the TC is in fact a *degree of adequacy*, again measured by a number in $[0,1]$. This degree of adequacy is the result of the composition of three terms. (i) A degree of 'goodness', that takes into account the prior information available about the environment; for example, a B-plan that includes passing through a long and narrow corridor has a small degree of goodness. (ii) A degree of 'competence', that dynamically considers the truth of the preconditions of the B-plan in the current situation; for example, if a door that has to be crossed is found closed this degree drops to 0. And (iii) a degree of 'conflict', that measures the conflict between the behaviours which are currently executing in parallel. Both the degrees of satisfaction of the current goal and the degree of adequacy are recomputed by the TC at each control cycle (100 ms).

4 Integrating the BDI Model and the Thinking Cap

Our work is based on the premise that the BDI model and the Thinking Cap represent two ends of the spectrum as far as the mental abilities of an autonomous robot are concerned. The TC can construct plans to achieve a single high level intention (like "go to the lab"), but has little to say about when such a plan has either failed or should be reconsidered because it might now be impossible to carry out. In contrast, the BDI model (at least in so far as we have analysed it with respect to intention reconsideration) is only concerned with high level intentions and whether or not they should be reconsidered as its beliefs about the world themselves change.

A consequence of this premise is that it might be profitable to combine the TC with a BDI architecture of the kind proposed in [15]. Our first attempt to integrate these two different systems is to consider them as separated blocks with a minimal interface between them, as shown in Fig. 1.

The BDI deliberator generates high-level intentions of the type (goto X) and sends them to the TC. (In future versions, intentions may include manipulation

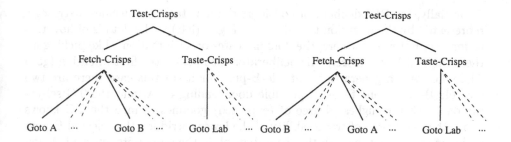

Fig. 2. Two intention trees for our example task.

or observation activities.) The TC receives these intentions and considers them as goals. For each goal, it generates a B-plan, and starts execution. It also monitors this execution, and switches to a new B-plan if the current one turns out to be inadequate. During execution, it constantly computes the current degrees of satisfaction and of adequacy, as mentioned above.

These degrees are sent back to the BDI deliberator. From the point of view of the deliberator, the degree of satisfaction measures how much the current intention has been achieved, and the degree of adequacy measures how much this intention is considered achievable. Differently from the standard BDI model, however, this information is not given by binary values, but by continuous measures. It is these indicators of the state of the world *vis à vis* the current intention which help the deliberator determine when it is appropriate to reconsider its intentions.

More precisely, the deliberator uses these values in two ways. Firstly, to decide *when* it is time to deliberate. Two of the possible causes that lead the deliberator to reconsider its intentions are: (i) an increase in the value of satisfaction; and (ii) a drop in the value of adequacy. Secondly, to actually *deliberate*, that is to reconsider its intentions in light of the new information. Deliberation may involve comparing the available options, and possibly adopting a new intention which is then sent to the TC. As we shall see below, considering degrees instead of binary values allows the deliberator to take more informed decisions.

5 Example

We report a simple experiment where we execute the potato crisp scenario in a simulated environment. We have used the Nomadic simulator, which includes simulation of the sensors and some moderate sensor and positioning noise. This experiment is meant to illustrate the concepts and mechanisms involved in our integrated approach to robot deliberation and navigation. The successive phases of the simulated run are shown in Figures 3 and 4. Fig. 5 shows the values of adequacy and of satisfaction of the currently executing intention at each moment of the run.

Initially, the BDI deliberator considers the new task and decides a strategy, represented by the intention tree shown in Fig. 2 (left). (The details of how this is done are not relevant here; the dots indicates other intentions, like picking up the crisp, which we ignore.) The deliberator then passes the first intention (goto A) to TC, which generates a suitable B-plan for it. In this case there are two possible B-plans, one for each possible door leading to A, and the TC selects the one with the highest degree of (expected) goodness. Since the TC knows about the low degree of traversability of the lower corridor,[1] the selected B-plan is the one that goes through the main door of A, the one on its left wall. Milou starts executing this B-plan from the lower left corner, as indicated by (1) in Fig. 3 (left).

When Milou arrives to this door (2), the sonars detect that the door is closed. Since one of the assumptions in the B-plan is that the door must be traversable, the degree of adequacy of this plan drops to 0 (Fig. 5 at about 20 s). The TC notices the problem, generates a new B-plan that goes through the second door, and starts executing it. However, this B-plan has a low degree of goodness because it includes passing through the cluttered corridor. This causes a drop of the adequacy level to a low 0.2. This is soon[2] noticed by the BDI deliberator, which reconsiders its options. Since the current intention turns out to be difficult (although not impossible) to achieve, and since there is an alternative way to perform the task (Fig. 2 right), the BDI deliberator decides to swich to this alternative way and to reverse the order of visiting the two production lines. Hence, it sends the new intention (goto B) to the TC (Fig. 5 at 30 s). The TC generates a new B-plan for this intention and swaps it in. Poor Milou then stops its travel to the lower corridor (point (3) in Fig. 3 left), turns around, heads to room B, and eventually reaches the fetch point in front of conveyer belt B.

The achievement of the intention (goto B) is reflected in the rise of the satisfaction level (Fig. 5 at 75 s). This is noticed by the BDI deliberator, which then sends the next intention to the TC: in our case, this is again the intention (goto A). Since the information about closed doors inside the TC is transient, the TC again generates a B-plan for this intention that goes through the main door. Milou finds its way from room B, but unfortunately it finds that the door is still closed (Fig. 3 right). As before, the TC generates an alternative B-plan going through the lower corridor and starts to execute it. This produces a drastic drop in the adequacy level, which is noticed by the BDI deliberator (Fig. 5 at 160 s). However, this time there is no alternative option, so the deliberator decides to keep with the current intention, even if it is difficult to achieve. The navigation functionalities of the TC allow Milou to safely, if slowly, get around the obstacles, and reach the fetch point in front of conveyer belt A.

The first two intentions are now fulfilled, and the BDI deliberator sends the

---

[1] Currently, this information is stored in the map; in the future, the robot may acquire this knowledge during exploration.

[2] We add some delay on the adequacy level in order to leave the TC the time to try and fix problems (like the closed door) before the deliberator does something.

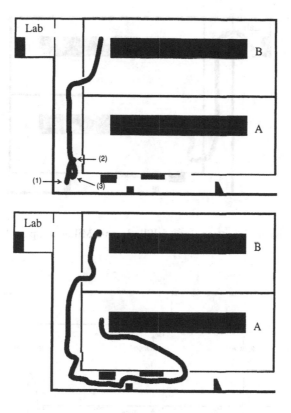

Fig. 3. Top: Milou has the intention **(goto A)**, but this turns out to be difficult to achieve, and adopts the new intention **(goto B)**. Bottom: Milou again has the intention **(goto A)**.

last one **(goto Lab)** to the TC. Again, the TC tries the main door first. This time we are lucky, since someone has actually opened this door, and Milou eventually finds its way to the lab, thus completing the mission (Fig. 4).

6 Discussion

The problem of how to integrate the execution of low-level navigation primitives to high-level reasoning processes is at the hart of autonomous robot navigation. Several proposals have already appeared in the literatures that use a BDI approach for this goal. For example, the Saphira architecture [9] uses a simplified version of PRS [4], a computational incarnation of the BDI model, at the higher level, and fuzzy navigation behaviours at the lower level. In that architecture, the PRS system arbitrates the on-off activation of individual fuzzy behaviours, which are seen as ground level intentions. A similar approach is taken in [7] and in [10], where PRS-like systems are used to arbitrate low-level processes.

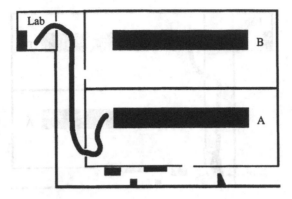

Fig. 4. Both previous intentions are fulfilled, and Milou adopts the intention (goto Lab).

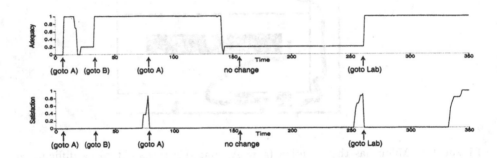

Fig. 5. Measures of adequacy (top) and satisfaction (bottom) sent by the TC to the deliberator during the run. The arrows indicate the deliberation points, and the new intentions generated.

Our proposal departs from these approaches in the way we partition the responsibilities between the Thinking Cap and the BDI deliberation system. We rely on the underlying navigation abilities of the TC to take care of fuzzy behaviour arbitration and blending in a sophisticated way. And we limit the role of the deliberation system to take care of higher level decisions about which overall navigation goal should be pursued next. This repartition allows us to make a better use of the respective powers of the TC and of the BDI level. By passing the adequate performance measures from the lower to the upper level we allow the latter to take more abstract, yet still fully informed decisions. We have shown that the use of measures instead of crisp values helps the higher level processes to generate the best possible intentions given the oddities and uncertainties that are inherent in real-world operation. We believe that a careful integration between these two levels in face of uncertainty is pivotal to our ability to deploy fully autonomous mobile robots.

The work presented above is still preliminary, and should be taken as a feasibility study more than a report of assessed results. Many variations of and extensions to the simple ideas presented here are possible, and their investigation is part of our current work. Firstly, the information passed by the TC to the BDI level can be much richer. For example, it may include the reasons why a B-plan has (partially) failed, the conditions that would increase its level of adequacy, or indications about the existence of alternative B-plans and their degrees of adequacy. Secondly, in our framework the BDI level does not have any way to recognise new opportunities that arise at the navigation level, like an open door that offers an unanticipated shortcut. Thirdly, and related to the previous point, we have not addressed the important issue of which information about the environment is available to the BDI level. Currently, no perceptual information is passed to this level by the TC, but this will clearly have to be changed in the future. Fourthly, more measures about the quality of execution could be communicated between the TC and the BDI deliberator, e.g., a measure of the current positional uncertainty. Finally, the choice of the strategy used to decide when the BDI should deliberate and when it should let the TC do its job depends on the characteristics of the environment, and it may itself be the result of another, higher level deliberation. Including this idea in our framework would lead to a "tower of meta-controllers" similar to the one suggested in [15].

In closing, we note that the example shown above has only been run in simulation — although the navigation system alone has been extensively validated on several real robots [13, 12, 11]. We are aware that the actual verification of the ideas sketched in this paper will only come from intensive testing in real and challenging environments. We are currently in the process of implementing our integrated system on a Nomad 200, and we hope to be able to show the first experimental results soon.

References

1. M. E. Bratman. *Intention, Plans, and Practical Reason.* Harvard University Press, Cambridge, MA, 1987.
2. M. E. Bratman, D. J. Israel, and M. E. Pollack. Plans and resource-bounded practical reasoning. *Computational Intelligence*, 4:349–355, 1988.
3. P. R. Cohen and H. J. Levesque. Intention is choice with commitment. *Artificial Intelligence*, 42:213–261, 1990.
4. M. P. Georgeff and F. F. Ingrand. Decision-making in an embedded reasoning system. In *Procs. of the AAAI Conf.*, pages 972–978, Detroit, MI, 1989.
5. M. P. Georgeff and F. F. Ingrand. Monitoring and control of spacecraft systems using procedural reasoning. In *Proceedings of the Space Operations Automation and Robotics Workshop*, 1989.
6. M. P. Georgeff and A. S. Rao. Profile of the Australian Artificial Intelligence Institute. *IEEE Expert*, 6, December:89–92, 1996.
7. F. F. Ingrand, R. Chatila, R. Alami, and F. Robert. PRS: a high level supervision and control language for autonomous mobile robots. In *Procs. of the Int. Conf. on Robotics and Automation*, Minneapolis, MN, 1996.

8. D. Kinny and M. Georgeff. Commitment and effectiveness of situated agents. In *Procs. of the Int. Joint Conf. on Artificial Intelligence*, pages 82–88, Sydney, Australia, 1991.

9. K. Konolige, K.L. Myers, E.H. Ruspini, and A. Saffiotti. The Saphira architecture: A design for autonomy. *Journal of Experimental and Theoretical Artificial Intelligence*, 9(1):215–235, 1997.

10. J. Lee, M. J. Huber, E. H. Durfee, and P. G. Kenny. UM-PRS: an implementation of the procedural reasoning system for multirobot applications. In *AIAA/NASA Conf. on Int. Robots in Field, Factory, Service and Space*. American Institute of Aeronautics and Astronautics, 1994.

11. A. Saffiotti. *Autonomous robot navigation: a fuzzy logic approach*. PhD thesis, Université Libre de Bruxelles, Brussels, Belgium, 1998.

12. A. Saffiotti, K. Konolige, and E. H. Ruspini. A multivalued-logic approach to integrating planning and control. *Artificial Intelligence*, 76(1-2):481–526, 1995.

13. A. Saffiotti, E. H. Ruspini, and K. Konolige. Blending reactivity and goal-directedness in a fuzzy controller. In *Proc. of the 2nd IEEE Int. Conf. on Fuzzy Systems*, pages 134–139, San Francisco, California, 1993. IEEE Press.

14. A. Saffiotti and L.P. Wesley. Perception-based self-localization using fuzzy locations. In M. van Lambalgen L. Dorst and F. Voorbraak, editors, *Reasoning with Uncertainty in Robotics — Proc. of the 1st Int. Workshop*, number 1093 in LNAI, pages 368–385. Springer, Berlin, DE, 1996.

15. M. Wooldridge and S. Parsons. Intention reconsideration reconsidered. In *Proc. of the 5th Int. Workshop on Agent Theories Architectures and Languages (ATAL)*, Paris, F, 1998.

Agent-Based Project Management

Charles Petrie[1], Sigrid Goldmann[2], and Andreas Raquet[2]

[1] Center for Design Research, Stanford University
Stanford, CA 94305-2232
petrie@stanford.edu
[2] AG Künstliche Intelligenz, Universität Kaiserslautern
Kaiserslautern, Germany
sigig, raquet@informatik.uni-kl.de

Abstract. Integrated project management means that design and construction planning are interleaved with plan execution, allowing both the design and plan to be changed as necessary. This requires that the right effects of change need to be propagated through the plan and design. When this is distributed among designers and planners, no one may have all of the information to perform such propagation and it is important to identify what effects should be propagated to whom, and when. We describe a set of dependencies among plan and design elements that allow such notification by a set of message-passing software agents. The result is to provide a novel level of computer support for complex projects.

1 Introduction

Today, traditional project management methods are not sufficient for managing the many tasks in the design and development process. They do not take into account all the sources of change, the task interactions, and the necessity for distributed planning. They do not provide proper **change notification**: notifying the right agents (people or software) of the effects at the right time in the process.

Process coordination is always most complex in domains that require artifact design and construction planning. This is particularly true when the artifacts are large and many people and software tools must be coordinated and managed.

When design changes cause plan and schedule changes, the problem is worse than simply modifying the design. Somehow, all the people assigned to the affected tasks, and no one else, should be notified of the change and how it affects them. This difficulty is reflected in the expense of coordinating projects and in the achievement of suboptimal results[2, 16].

1.1 Example Problems

The following few examples serve both to illustrate this difficulty and to suggest the kind of questions answered by this paper.

"Fast track" construction attempts allow the architect to finish or change the design after construction has started. These design changes frequently necessitate a change in the construction plan and or schedule. As a simple example, suppose that the design calls for concrete roof tiles. Then the wall plaster must be applied after the roof is built, or the heavy tiles will deform the walls causing the plaster to crack. But if it is decided later that lighter fiberglass tiles should be used instead, it is no longer necessary to wait to plaster the walls - the two tasks can be more concurrent and the plan schedule shortened. What kind of computer support could ensure that when the architect changes the material specification, the contractor will be notified of the possibility of shortening the schedule?

Suppose that we are designing and building a prototype of a new gyroscope for use in navigation equipment. Suppose further that one engineer decides that high resolution encoders is a better design than the rate sensors plus low resolution encoders in the current design. How can we ensure that the machinist who is designing the frame to hold the components will be notified of this change?

A hospital adds a new surgery wing. The architectural specifications for the width of the doors into the new wing were determined by the width of the hospital beds that had to be wheeled through them. During construction of the new surgery, someone in the hospital decided independently to buy new, much wider, beds. What kind of process mechanism could have avoided the subsequent remodeling of doors in the freshly built surgery?

Imagine building the international space station with hundreds or even thousands of companies and engineers and contractors of all sorts. How can the emerging mass of design decisions and changes be coordinated across organizations? How could this ever be "fast-tracked"?

The problem is not lack of connectivity. With the Internet, and intranets, combinations of email and groupware enabling everyone to reach everyone else with ease, one could make a case that the ability to task each other so easily is actually making the problem worse. The problem is that there insufficient structure supporting the distributed task interactions of modern enterprises, especially for project management.

1.2 What Is Missing

Today's distributed project management tool are still based upon a single-user model of planning and the change notification is still primitive- meaning that all change notifications must be pre-specified, usually by the users.

If one considers single-user project management tools, such as *MacProject* or *MS Project*, one can see immediately that they are completely inadequate. The model is that a single general contractor makes decisions and changes and then somehow notifies the people involved. Notifications to the general contractor that cause changes and the notification of the people affected by the change are simply not part of the computer support, though very much a part of any project. The only distributed support from such products is that emails may be sent when a task is assigned and completed.

AutoPlan{5} is in contrast a distributed project management tool that provides an electronic blackboard for change notification. This allows people to receive email when a pre-specified type of event occurs, such as assignment of a task. This definitely takes the computer support of Distributed Project Management (DPM) one step further, but it is still based upon a single-user model of planning and the change notification is still primitive. That is, the general contractor is still responsible for all changes and all of the change notification must be pre-specified, usually by the users.

In small or medium sized projects, a general contractor may track the hundreds of informal change orders with a cork bulletin board and notes. That we do not provide better support for such projects limits the complexity of the project to that which can be managed by a single person. As a result, plans are kept simple and rigid and many opportunities to improve the plan, or even to avoid mistakes, are missed.

But worse is the cumbersome formal change order process required on large engineering projects, which multiple levels of management approvals, with increased time and cost, in an attempt to catch most interactions. Usually, many more people are notified for a given design change than are actually necessary, burdening the whole design process.

The current lack of technology for coordinating design decisions and managing change over the life of a product creates higher costs, longer cycle times, and poorer quality than is currently possible. Occasionally, this lack of technology is even dangerous, whether one is maintaining an older passenger plane or decommissioning a nuclear weapon.

1.3 Distributed Integrated Project Management

As described in more detail in the white paper "Distributed Integrated Process Coordination"{9}, process coordination missing from various well-known computer support approaches to business integration, group collaboration, and project management. Process coordination means the runtime determination of who should be notified and what task should be performed next. Computer support for this means some automation of the notification and tracking of task properties as they are created or change.

Process coordination is more general than workflow in that it does not require that all tasks and ways of doing them be identified prior to process execution. For instance, anyone should be able to assign any tasks to anyone else at any time during process execution. And appropriate notifications associated with that task delegation, or subtask assignment, should be handled by the computer support system.

Process coordination is most complex in domains that require artifact design and construction planning, especially when the artifacts are large and many people and software tools must be coordinated and managed. *Distributed Integrated Project Management* (**DPIM**) is an extreme form of Process Coordination in which design, planning, scheduling, and execution are interleaved across distributed organizations and engineering disciplines as well as computer tools.

In particular, we want to be able to support *change that occurs from incomplete designs*, in order to support "fast tracking", as well as *contingencies and planning under uncertainty*. We also want to be able to support *design and planning that is distributed among people and software* that can best solve parts of the problem.

Computer support for DPIM necessarily involves a heterogeneous mix of software and people passing messages describing tasks and changes. The least commitment strategy, with respect to platform, of federating people and their software tools is to use an *agent communications language* (ACL) such as KQML{6} or FIPA{7} . This only supposes that each software module, possibly just an interface for a person, can exchange ASCII text messages according to standard Internet protocols such as socket connections with TCP/IP.

If the software systems are sufficiently homogeneous so that they can make a stronger commitment, they can directly exchange objects using a facilities such as Java RMI and CORBA. An standard ACL. using an agent[23] model, requires less of a commitment to transport mechanism and more of a commitment to message semantics and protocol. In any case, the choice of the interoperability infrastructure is necessary but not sufficient for coordination and management of distributed projects.

What is also necessary is that the human and software agents also agree upon a *model of coordination*. This is also consistent with the view of agents as software and humans that share a common protocol of messages in which some responses are legal and some are not[11].

Because the central problem of distributed interleaved planning is *change propagation*, we characterize our coordination model as a *logical set of dependencies* among the project elements that can be used to determine the effects of changes within the project. This paper defines a such set of dependencies that should be managed by a computer system in order to coordinate a distributed project.

1.4 Scope of this Paper

This paper does not address enterprise process models prior to runtime or organizational models such as VDT {1} and the Process Handbook and PIF{2}. We do not address specific buisiness integration approaches such as the commercial systems of SAP{3} and PeopleSoft{4}. All of these approaches are successful in their domains.

One key problem for change notification is agreement upon the technical terms and words used to describe different parts of the project. There are various schemes, proposals, and mechanisms for doing so, such as the ontologies in {14}, and so we do not address that important topic explicitly here.

However, managing the dependencies of the various aspects of a project, and understanding how changes should be propagated has been a generally neglected topic in the literature. Therefore, we address the latter rather than the former.

In this paper, we describe what the authors have learned in researching the topic of dependencies for distributed integrated project management while trying to extend a specific approach to the general problem. We address the use of dependencies for *change propagation* once a change to the plan, schedule, or design has been made. We do not address here the use of such dependencies for decision support prior to decision-making.

And while decision rationale is important for change propagation, we do not address specific forms of argumentation; i.e., reasons for or against particular courses of action. We focus on capturing facts and statements supporting decisions and the notification appropriate when they change.

We do not require that an *agent* be either "intelligent" or "autonomous"[23] but only require that they be able to exchange messages with one another and be able to act either by making decisions or acting upon the results of such decisions. This paper will not prescribe a precise agent protocol such as *contract nets*[15] but will define a set of dependencies with which a given protocol should be consistent. We have implemented such a protocol within the *ProcessLink* project{0}.

Finally, we do not require a totally decentralized model such as market-based agent systems{8}. The dependencies we propose are consistent with such models as we make no restrictions on how planning decisions are arrived at, but we do require at least one special facilitating agent be aware of the actions of all others to the degree that dependencies among the actions can be tracked. That is, at least one agent's knowledge is complete with respect to these dependencies.

2 Dependency Key Ideas

This paper uses "design" to mean generally the design of the target artifact. A "plan" is generally the determination of the tasks and subtasks required to build the artifact, including the durations and other task features, except for the start and end dates, which are assigned by the "schedule". "Execution" will generally refer to the execution of the plan, which will change the state of the developing artifact.

Thus, the architect designs a building, for which a general contractor develops an overall plan and schedule for constructing. As concrete is poured, the plan is executed and the building takes shape.

We note here briefly, and explain further later, that these simple notions can be endlessly complicated. For instance, design itself can be planned, and the execution of such plans results in a design. Then we plan to build the design (which is sometimes called, confusingly, the "execution" of the design.) Anyone who decides how much time should be alloted to developing a part of a design has done design planning to some extent. However, we refer to the simpler uses, defined at the beginning of this section, of design, planning, scheduling, and execution in the discussion of dependency requirements below.

2.1 Precedence Is Not Enough

Projects follow plans about tasks, their durations, and resources. These factors always implicitly depend upon the design of the artifact being constructed. As the design changes, these factors may change, because of *interactions between the design and the plan and schedule.*

One of the most important of these factors are the precedence relationships. These are usually functions of resources and other interactions of tasks. Yet such interactions are rarely captured. Traditional project management requires precedences to be input at the beginning of the plan. Therefore there can be no dynamic adjustment of the plan as factors that influence precedence change.

The roof tile and plastering example mentioned previously illustrates this. The two tasks of roofing and plastering are connected by the design feature of the weight of the roofing material. The precedence that the plastering task should follow the roofing task depends upon this weight. If this weight changes because of the design change, then the precedence ordering should be reconsidered.

This is an example of how a change in the design of the artifact may introduce an opportunity to improve the plan for constructing it. But this opportunity would be lost if precedence relationships are static and not tied to features of the design.

A key insight here is that the way to relate the artifact design and the plan is by including *artifact features and conditions in the plan.*

2.2 Plans are Designs Too

This suggests the next insight: that plans and schedules are also designs. Artifact designs can be characterized by design decisions about components and features. Plans and schedules are also designed artifacts with components and features.

A fundamental component of a plan is a *task.* Fundamental task features that need to be taken into account are *task inputs and outputs.* If one task outputs something that is an input for a second task, then at least there is a precedence relationship that the second task cannot end before the first. Thus, the *plan* design decision, which we will call a *planning decision,* was to have the second task follow the first, with a decision decision based upon a design rationale consisting of the task inputs and outputs.

The idea of design decisions gives us a way to think about *interactions between task planning, scheduling, and task execution.* If we can determine a general model for design change propagation, then we can apply it to planning and scheduling and interleave all three as is required.

And if this model allows concurrent design, then since planning and scheduling can be viewed as design, then the model should support distributed planning and scheduling as well.

3 The Redux Design Model

There is a general model of design change propagation: Redux[20]. Our approach is to extend it to planning and scheduling, identifying specialized extensions, and allowing for special conditions that may arise as a plan is executed.

The first cut of these extensions was the Procura design[10]. This has been furthered by the forthcoming diplom thesis of Raquet and discussions with the developers of ComMoKit[8].

3.1 Redux Overview

We begin this description with some general observations about Redux dependencies.

The basic Redux model is similar to that of gIbis[4]. However, whereas gIbis is a passive recording of issues, Redux computes the propagation of changes to the design. By adding simple notions of conflicts and rationales, very useful inferences can be derived as shown in [21].

In addition to simply documenting design rationale, Redux makes the design rationale active by tracking its validity in several respects and notifying designers when it changes.

We have found that even in small design projects, people lose their ability to maintain a comprehensive picture of the history and interplay of design decisions, constraints and rationales. Under these conditions the advice generated by Redux' soon becomes non-obvious and intuitive only in hindsight as Redux' reveals forgotten opportunities and hidden conflicts.

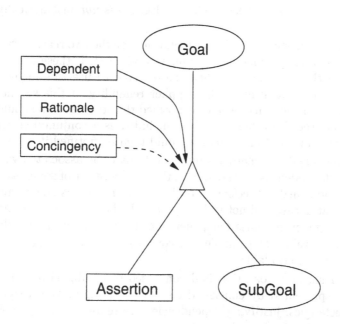

Fig. 1. Redux structures

Design Decisions The Redux model of design is a model based on a simple notion of design decisions that could be used in a distributed design project such as PACT[6]. First a *decision* must be about some *goal*: this can be any sort of design task, issue, or question. The purpose of the decision is to somehow address this goal. For example, a design goal might be "design a computer".

Further, a decision must include some result of one or both of two kinds: an *assignment* and/or a new goal that is a *subgoal* of the original goal. The assignment is some statement about the design such as "the computer will use a fast chip". The assignment may optionally be structured so that it has a *feature*, such as "part-of"; an object, such as "memory-1", and a value, such as "fast memory chip mcp-2", resulting in a complete assignment such as "part-of memory-1 fast memory chip mcp-2". A subgoal is some new design goal that is necessary to satisfy before the original goal can be satisfied, such as "design the memory controller".

This model does not assume the existence of a single root goal and allows design to be represented in general as an arbitrary set of goals to be achieved. But in general, a goal is satisfied when all of its subgoals are satisfied so it is easy and useful to represent a design problem as beginning with a single top-level root goal, such as "design the computer".

If *reasons* are provided for a decision, Redux uses them to generate a decision rationale. If one of these reasons subsequently becomes invalid, then the decision rationale may become invalid, if there are no other supporting valid reasons. If the rationale becomes invalid, the agent that made the decision is notified that the decision should be reconsidered. The decision is *not* automatically retracted in this case.

For example, a decision rationale might include the two reasons "this memory costs 2 cents" and "this memory supplier is reliable". If these are two separate reasons, and the cost changes, then the decision to use this memory still has a valid rationale consisting of the supplier reliability. If this second condition changes, the decision maker would be notified that the decision should be reconsidered. If desired, both facts could be included as a conjunction comprising a single reason and the decision maker would then be notified if either changes.

Dependents and *contingencies* may additionally be associated with a Redux decision. A dependent is an assignment that is the result of some other decision. It can also be called a "decision input". A contingency is some environmental condition that is assumed not to be the case. If the dependent becomes invalid, or the contingency becomes true, then the decision is automatically retracted and becomes invalid. An example of a contingency is a statement such as "this memory part is unavailable".

Figure 1 shows a goal, that is decomposed to a subgoal and a assignment. Goals are represented by ellipses, decisions by triangles and assignments and facts by rectangles. justifying dependencies are represented by a solid line, retracting dependencies by a dashed line.

Multiple design decisions conflict with each other via their assignments. A set of conflicting design assignments is expressed as a *constraint violation*, though Redux says nothing about how such violations are detected and does no constraint propagation. However, given a constraint violation, Redux will determine which among a set of possible decisions might be rejected in order to resolve the violation. If a decision is rejected, it is *retracted* and a reason for the *rejection* is noted.

If a decision is retracted, the decision become invalid. Redux can also maintain reasons for the retraction. A decision can be arbitrarily retracted, but in general it will be rejected, meaning that there are good reasons for having rejected the decision, such as "this kind of memory doesn't work with this cpu".

A decision may become invalid if retracted/rejected or if an dependent becomes invalid or if a contingency occurs. in this case, all of its assignments and subgoals may become invalid, if they are not supported additionally by some other decision.

3.2 Redux Notifications

The simple Redux model allows inferences to be drawn that are useful in the notification of participants. There is an implemented Redux agent in ProcessLink that does just this. The essential requirement is that all agents notify the Redux agent when decisions have been made, describing the decision as above. The agents should notify Redux of constraint violations, goal blocks, and general decision rejections as well. Finally, facts may be asserted and deleted as desired. Changes will be reported according to the Redux model.

If a decision becomes invalid, then its objective goal is no longer reduced. The *decision maker should be notified at least that progress has been lost in working on this goal*. If the goal was previously satisfied, then the decision maker will be notified that *the goal is no longer satisfied*. If this goal satisfaction previously contributed to the satisfaction of some supergoal, then the decision maker for the supergoal will be notified of the loss of satisfaction of that goal.

If a decision becomes invalid, some of its assertions and subgoals may become invalid. The invalidity of these assignments and goals will have further ramifications. If a goal becomes invalid, then any decision maker for that goal should be informed that *the goal is now redundant* and any decision reducing that goal is now suboptimal as a result.

If an invalid assignment was used as dependent to a decision, then that decision becomes invalid, with the same notifications as above. If the assignment was used as a rationale, then *the decision becomes suboptimal* and the decision maker is informed the decision should be reconsidered.

If some decision was previously rejected in part because of of an assignment that is now invalid, the decision maker will be informed that *this decision may now be optimal* and should be reconsidered. The same is true for any fact or constraint in the rejection reason that becomes invalid.[1]

If some decision maker has attempted to make decisions about a goal and each has been rejected or invalidated, and the decision maker cannot think of a new way to work on the goal, the decision maker may declare a *goal block*. All of the decision makers responsible for an assignment in any of the rejection

---

[1] This implements a version of Pareto optimality[9] tracking described in [21].

reasons or dependents for the previously defeated decisions will be notified of the impasse, as will the decision maker that created the blocked goal, if any.

3.3 Distributed Design Example

In order to show how the Redux model works with distributed design, we present a simplified version of work done recently with Toshiba.

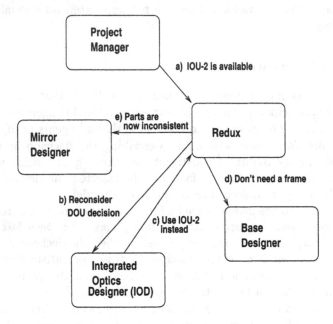

Fig. 2. Design Agents

Figure 2 represents a Redux agent working with four design agents in a project to design an optical device. There is an overall Project Manager that sets the top-level goals and resolves disputes, a Mirror Designer that designs the mirror systems, the Integrated Optical Designer (IOD) that chooses the optical detector mechanisms, and a Base Designer who designs the base that holds the whole array of components.

During the course of the design, the IOD has tried to use two varieties of an "integrated optical unit" (IOU) but ran into problems in both cases, in one case simply because inventory said the part was not available. The IOD ended up using a "discrete optical unit" (DOU) which necessitated the Base Designer building an extra frame to hold the discrete components.

Using Redux, the Product Manager can examine the rationale for the DOU decision and see that in one case, a particular part, an IOU-2, was not used because inventory said it was unavailable. However, the Product Manager knows that this was an arbitrary status based upon project priorities, and declares the part available in message **a)** to Redux.

Redux knows to notify the IOD to reconsider using IOU-2 instead of the DOU in message **b)** in the figure. The IOD makes this change in message **c)** and in messages **e)** and **d)**, Redux notifies the Mirror Designer that the mirror parts decision uses the DOU information that is no longer valid, and the Base Designer that the goal of designing a frame for the discrete DOU parts is also no longer valid.

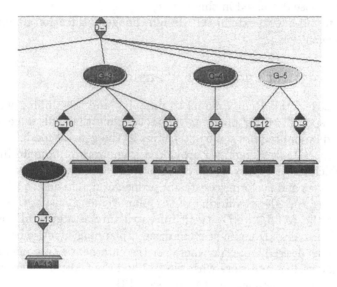

Fig. 3. Agent Applet Graph

Such a system is implemented and running using the JAT*Lite* agent infrastructure{10} and Java applets that display colored decision graphs such as in Figure 3 using the KQML messages and extensions documented at {13}. This system has the great advantage that the applets can be downloaded to any Java-compatible browser anywhere on the Internet and the outstanding messages for that agent read and processed.

In Figure 3, the decision to use a DOU is *D-10* and the decision to use IOU-2 is *D-6* and the goal to build the discrete component frame is *G-9*. Since the part unavailability was a contingency that prevented the use of that part in attempted decision *D-6*, and since Redux automatically constructs a decision rationale for further decisions *D-7* and *D-10* based upon *D-6*, Redux can send message **b)** to the owner of *D-6*, the IOD. The goal *G-9* was a subgoal of *D-10* and so was automatically invalidated when that decision was rejected. This caused *D-13* to be suboptimal and message **d)** was sent to that decision owner, the Base Designer. Further, an assignment of *D-10* was used as a dependent by a decision of the Mirror Designer in choosing parts, so Redux invalidates that decision and sends message **e)** that the mirror parts goal is no longer satisfied.

This particular scenario is detailed on the web at {11}. Engineers enter these decisions either directly using a desktop applet agent, or indirectly by using CAD tools that have been "wrapped" to become ProcessLink agents{10} or by using design documentation authoring tools that allow Redux annotation{12}. A detailed examination of Redux rationale maintenance in another application is available in [21], in which the Redux support for resolving conflicts and maintaining a design rationale using dependency-directed backtracking is emphasized (and not otherwise discussed in this paper).

Now we would like to extend this design change notification functionality to project management.

4 Planning Dependency Extensions

In order to extend this Redux model to planning and scheduling, we will posit other agents specialized for planning and scheduling that will make special requests of Redux and require some extensions to the general model.

In the ProcessLink system, we provide a framework of domain independent agents of which one is Redux, one is a Constraint Manager (CM) that manages constraint solvers and performs constraint propagaton, and on is a Plan Manager (PM) that performs global tracking of the plan elements, using the Redux and the CM, and the JAT¡I¿Lite¡/I¿ agent infrastructure as a general "bus" for the exchange of messages. Domain-specific design, planning, and scheduling agents may connect as desired from anywhere on the Internet. These agents can also make Redux decisions and work with the PM and the CM using the ProcessLink Electronic Project Language (EPL) protocol{13}.

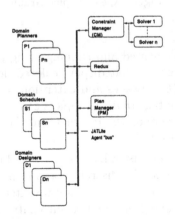

Fig. 4. The ProcessLink Framework

One simple extension is that Redux especially treats assignments that have a feature with the keyword *"assign-agent"*. Then the feature object is expected to be the name of a goal and the value is expected to be the name of an agent. Given the new validity of such an assignment, when the goal is valid, the agent is sent a message that *the goal has been assigned to that agent.* When either the goal or the assignment become invalid, the agent is advised of this change.

However, most planning and scheduling extensions will be handled by the PM either by using the decision model to establish the right dependencies to be maintained by Redux, and the CM, or maintaining the dependencies itself. In addition to the dependencies described below, the PM must provide common project management functions, including resource management and representation and scheduling. We do not address these problems here as they are well understood and may be handled by a number of algorithms by the PM or other planning and scheduling agents.

4.1 Interleaving Designs and Plans

The first way in which Redux dependencies can be used effectively is to ensure that the plan does not contain valid elements that are unnecessary. We can do this by using plan subgoal validity.

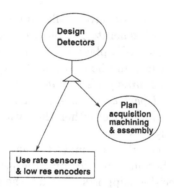

Fig. 5. Plan Subgoal of Design Goal

In Figure 5, the design decision to use rate sensors and low-resolution encoders directly generates a plan goal to acquire the encoders and sensors, and machine the base for them and assemble them. This goal will become invalid as soon as the design decision is rejected in favor of high resolution encoders. This behavior is what is desired. Any planning decisions made based on this plan goal will become suboptimal and the planner notified, though the decisions will not automatically be invalidated. There will be possibly many subgoals and decisions beneath this high-level plan goal that should be carefully handled given a change.

However, this simple model is flawed because the super goal of the plan goal is a design goal, not another plan goal. Apart from the strangeness of the naming conventions, this has two disadvantages. First, it necessarily puts the designer in the position of generating plan goals, and two, it is now not possible to use the Redux goal satisfaction mechanism to determine if either the design or the plan alone is complete, without a lot of awkwardness.

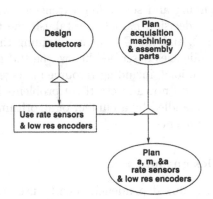

Fig. 6. Design Rationale for Plan

What is going on here is that we have conflated the goal dependency with the goal generation. We need not generate the plan goal directly as a subgoal. We can instead posit the existence of a planning agent that reviews the design and decides independently on when and how to plan the execution of the design. It is only necessary *that the planning goals should become invalid when the planned parts are no longer a valid part of the design.* The easiest way to do this is to make design assignments a part of either the rationale or the dependents of planning decisions as in Figure 6.

The most automatic alternative is to make the design assignment a dependent so if the design decision becomes invalid, and the assignment becomes invalid (no other valid design decision supports it), then the planning decision to plan for those components will become invalid.

However, notice that this scheme a) biases in favor of the designer, and b) automatically invalidates any plan subgoals. Another choice for representation is to use the design assignment as only a rationale. This also results in a notice to the planner, but does not invalidate any subgoals or change the plan in any way. The planner and the designer can then argue about whether the plan or the design takes precedence.

This general idea can be elaborated in many different ways but it allows Redux to be used to manage the satisfaction of different aspects of the work, such as design and construction planning and scheduling. It requires only the general idea of a Plan Manager (PM) agent that either reviews the design periodically or requests Redux to be notified when design decisions are initially made. The Plan Manager then decides what aspects of the design to plan when, recording these decisions in Redux, using decision rationales and dependents to connect to the design features. An example of this general idea is shown in Figure 7.

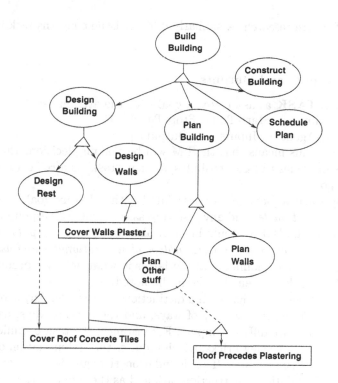

Fig. 7. Complex Planning

At some point in this example, the design for the building, done by the architect, results in the two assignments that are used as dependents by the plan decision that results in the explicit precedence statement that the end of the roof task should precede the beginning of the plastering task. This figure does not specify all of the preceding goals and decisions but only shows these as examples. This precedence statement would then be used as input to some scheduling decision. When the "Cover Roof Concrete Tiles" assignment becomes invalid, the precedence statement would become invalid (unless there were another valid decision supporting it) and the schedule would then be changed. Thus an action by the architect would result in a necessary plan change and a notification to a PM.

Various specific schemes are possible. Goldmann has described one in [10] and Raquet is developing a successor system with important variations[24]. These systems vary in the dimensions of exactly how the goals and decisions are generated by what agents when and how much information is cached. In fact, the situation is not quite as simple as suggested above as there are several important further considerations.

One consideration is that the last scheme of Figure 6 in which the planner is free to decide when to plan based upon a review of the design does not provide for any automatic notice as does the scheme of Figure 5. Reconciling these features is a topic of future research. A similarly difficult issue concerns task inputs and outputs.

4.2 Task Inputs and Outputs

First, define a **TASK** as associated a goal with the attributes:

| . Duration   . Start-Time . Stop-Time|
|. Assigned-Agent   . Inputs   . Outputs |

Notice that this means that the PM will be making decisions that result in assignments of values to task attributes, so that "task" is a reification in Redux of a Redux goal.

If we represent a plan task as associated with a Redux goal, then decision *dependents* and *rationales* and any resulting assignments correspond to the task inputs and outputs. But it should be clear also that *planned inputs and outputs for a task are distinct from the decision dependents, rationales and assignments.* The former is what is planned and the latter is what actually occurred. If the two are not equivalent, then this should be noted.

It should also be clear that such a distinction is desirable. Any arbitrary task may be accomplished in a variety of ways, and the various ways, described as decisions, may require different inputs. For instance, the task of building a wall may accomplished by using bricks, which requires that a foundation of sufficient strength be constructed first. This foundation strength is represented as the output of the foundation construction task and as the input to the wall building task.

But we may choose to build the wall using a crane and prefabricated lightweight wall sections. In this case, the needed input is the overhead clearance along the wall. Determining this clearance, or creating it, may then be another task. The clearance is then a new input for the task of building the wall.

Thus, one should use *planned* task inputs and outputs for planning purposes while realizing that the *actual* task inputs and outputs are those dependents and rationales used and assignments produced by decisions about these tasks. Planned and actual inputs must be compared by a PM.

If each input and output is described using a feature and object, the PM can register with Redux an interest in any changes in assignments that match that description. The PM can also register an interest in any decisions made about the goal in general, so that it can identify whether the assigned agent corresponded to the actual agent, for instance.

In the current implementation, this is done by having the PM send a "TRACE" message to Redux concerning the designated goal or feature and object.

For example,

```
( Trace :sender PM :receiver Redux :language ProcessLink
 :content (Goal | acquire-encoder &
           Variable | input acquire-encoder & ) )
```

is a request from the PM to Redux to track all changes in the Redux goal named "acquire-encoder" and also the variable (feature plus object) of the "input" of the task "acquire-encoder" corresponding to the Redux goal of the same name. Redux responds with an "UPDATE" message whenever the status of the goal "acquire-encoder" changes or whenever the status of any assignment of any value to "input acquire-encoder" changes.[2]

This alone is not sufficient in a distributed planning environment. The PM must take further steps to track planned inputs and outputs against these assignments. For example, the PM may have anticipated that one of the inputs to "acquire-encoder" was the design assignment named "encoder-weight". However, this planning task was handed off to a specialist who decomposed the task into subtasks eventually resulting in a low-level plan that never involved. How is the PM to know that something (the use of a planned input) never happened?

The PM could ask Redux for the exact description of the decisions used, but it can also just enforce the rule that whenever a planning decision is made, the actual dependents and rationales are explicitly recorded as assignments; e.g., "actual-input acquire-encoder encoder-weight". It is the responsibility of the PM to enforce this rule and compare the plan against execution.

4.3 Scheduling Extensions

Scheduling involves a large number of arithmetic constraints that must be checked and trigger notifications if they are violated. These are distinct from model dependencies tracked by Redux and are best done by a combination of the PM and the CM as described in [24].

The only special dependency that need be tracked is that when a plan or scheduling decision is made using some set of resource assumptions. These should be recorded as a rationale for the decision. That is, in the notification that a decision has been made, *the decision definition should include the resource as a part of the decision rationale.*

If the resources change, this may affect the optimality of the decision and the decision maker should be notified. If the decision maker is using a commercial tool, the the decision maker may request a new schedule from that tool.

There are some specific representation issues concerning scheduling however, especially with respect to reconciling start and stop times of abstract tasks with the start and stop times of their subtasks. One of the key issues will be to reduce suboptimal time "buffers" as more is known about the design and plan.

The lower-level abstract tasks may be performed by different agents with better knowledge. It may be that the planned inputs and outputs were not used, which will dramatically affect the possibilities for a tighter schedule. These possibilities should be communicated to the relevant agents.

Figure 8 shows a simplified example for several scheduling decisions. In this figure, we represent the actual construction tasks, such as "Construct Building", as squares to denote that they are specializations of goals. Each scheduling goal

---

[2] The ProcessLink "TRACE", "UPDATE", and "UNTRACE" performatives are not part of any standard ACL, but as they are fundamental, we have added them to our KQML performative set.

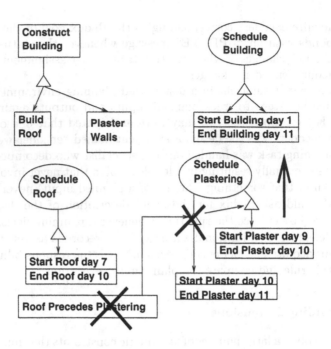

Fig. 8. Scheduling dependencies

is associated with such a task, as are the assignments of start and end times. Each scheduling decision may be performed by a separate scheduling agent with the best knowledge to perform that task.

The scheduling decision for the plastering task depends, in part, on the plan information that plastering has to take place after the roof has been built. This fact in turn depends on the design decision to use concrete tiles, as shown Figure 7. Because of this precedence relationship, plastering cannot start before day 10, when the roof is finished. Since the plastering is the last subtask of "Construct Building" to be done, this supertask's end date cannot be earlier than the plastering task's end date, day 11 (based on a task duration of 1 day, not shown).

Now suppose that the roof design is changed in a way that calls for the fiberglass tiles instead of the concrete ones, thereby making the precedence relationship between roof construction and plastering obsolete. The responsible agent will be notified that the scheduling decision for the plastering task is now suboptimal, and should be reconsidered. The task can be moved "to the left" in the schedule, i.e. be scheduled to be executed in parallel with roof construction.

Figure 8 shows that when the precedence assignment becomes invalid, and then the decision to start plastering after the roof is finished becomes invalid, a new scheduling decision is made for the plastering task. In turn, the scheduler of the whole building needs to be notified.

Such notification is a good example of **not** using the Redux decision model, which is essentially propositional because the notification depends upon the specific numeric values of the schedules. Notice, for instance, relating end times for tasks and supertasks is outside the scope of TRACE. The better approach is to use the more general constraint manager (CM)[22] that can ask Redux to track assignments of, say, feature *End-Time*, as well as explit assignments of feature *Sub-Task* (versus the implicit Redux subgoal relationship) and check more complicated constraints of whether the *End-Time* of any abstract task is either inconsistent or unnecessarily long.

4.4 Execution Extensions

In the same way that we connect plan goals with design decisions, we can connect "execution goals" with planning decisions. Then a execution decision with an assignment that the wall is built, perhaps with a certain height, records the completion of the action. Thus is the execution goal satisfied.

However, the result of such execution decisions will be assignments that reflect a change in the real world. For instance, one result might be "built-wall height 2m", recording that a wall was constructed with a height of 2m. This is very different from a planned wall height of 2m that can be changed at will.

Thus plan and design assignments should never be used as dependents in execution decisions. They can and should be used as rationales. When the design or plan changes, the agent that made the execution decision will be notified that their is an element of the construction that no longer corresponds to what is currently desired. However, such a decision can only be retracted manually, and only when a separate execution of wall demolition has been recorded.

Though it is out of the scope of this paper, planning agents must also consider how to represent time. The simplest way is to record that the wall was erected at a certain time and to generally reason explicitly about the time for which the wall actually exists and has designated properties, using constraints and the CM.

4.5 Demolition Costs

Upon being notified that some aspect of the construction, say a wall, is no longer desired, via a decision suboptimality message from Redux, and upon determining that the wall should actually be torn down, the PM can now inquire about what resources have been expended on the wall and what needs to be done to demolish it and the plan changed accordingly.

More abstractly, when any task is canceled, outputs created by this activity pose a similar problem. They may be undesired and may cause time and money to eliminate. A demolition task must be added to the plan.

Consider an activity that has built a number of computer parts which are no longer usable due to technology advance. As storage also causes costs, these parts must be removed, but they often cannot just be thrown away. Instead an activity must be planned to get rid of them. Such activities will cost resources.

This kind of costs is referred to as 'demolition costs'. Note that 'demolition' is used here in a very broad sense. It can just mean transfer to other companies. In software design, most produced artifacts are just specifications or code stored in electronic form. If no longer desired, they can just be deleted without note-worthy costs. Therefore, given an canceled task, *a general PM must inquire to domain-dependent agents about demolition costs and decide whether a new task of demolition must be planned.*

We make no commitment here as to whether the original task to build the wall remains as a part of the current plan. In Redux terms, the corresponding goals and assignments will be initially invalid but may be revalidated by a new decision that also includes the demolition as a follow-on activity. That is, there is a question of whether the new plan should say there had previously been a task to build a wall and it is now invalid or there is a valid and completed task to build the wall, followed by a subsequent task of demolition.

This suggests the more general topic of costs expended pursuing a task.

4.6 Sunk Costs

In a environment of interleaved planning and execution it is not sufficient only to react to changes. It is also necessary to prohibit certain changes. Activities that have already been executed can not be undone, used resources can often not be regained. Such resources are referred to as 'sunk costs'. They are 'sunk' into the process and cannot be regained. When the wall is constructed, some amount of time, money, and materials have been consumed and this must be taken into account.

If a project manager removes such an already conducted activity that used non-regain-able resources from a plan, he will automatically generate an inconsistency between plan and execution. To ensure correct resource tracking we must avoid such changes.

Time is a special case that can be dealt in a domain-independent way. Given a task that is either completed or to be canceled prior to completion, the time spent already on this task must be accounted for. One way to do this is by creating a new task in the plan that consumes the right amount of time and showing it as completed. This task should also consume the inputs and produce the outputs that model the work done. These facts can alternatively be represented by the PM - the important point is that *time and irretrievably consumed resources not depend upon the validity of the task.*

However not all resources 'sink' into the process. Resources like available space can be regained if undesired objects are removed, parts that have been assembled to a composite product can in some cases be regained by disassembling this product. Without domain knowledge it is not possible to determine whether a resource will 'sink' into the project or whether it will be regainable. So although a domain-independent PM can so model canceled tasks, *the PM will have to make requests of domain-dependent agents in order to ascertain actual resource consumption.*

4.7 Miscellaneous Issues

Redux only has two notions of authority: 1) only a decision maker has the authority to retract a decision, 2) except there is one overall "design manager" who can retract any decision. Perhaps a more extensive but flexible authorities and permissions agent to control who can make and retract decisions of various types will be needed such as is being developed for the *Enterprise*{14} project by Peter Jarvis. The current Redux model assumes that anyone can see all of the information, but this may not be a generally applicable principle.

There is also the topic of information goals discussed in [10]. In this implementation, such goal and information structures were explicitly cached as part of the entire planning trace. However, it is not clear that this need be done. Another implementation we are exploring allows agents to generate a separate project for acquiring the information needed to make a decision in the original project. This separate project goal and decision tree is finally collapsed to the assignments and facts used in this separate decision-making process. This collapsed set of assignments and facts can then be used as a rationale for a decision in the original project.

For instance, in deciding between hi res encoders and low res encoders, their may be an information project that results, after some work, in costs of various components from various suppliers. These can be used in the rationale for, say, the decision to use a hi res encoder.

This paper does not address all of the issues that planning agent alone needs to address, such as resource leveling and the difference between task inputs such as artifact parts, tools constructed especially for special tasks, and simple information, such as specifications.

Finally, we note that the *project management representation presented here can be recursively applied to design itself.* Often, before any design is done, there is some design planning and scheduling. E.g., before a new CDROM player is designed, one plans for the design of the "actuator" as that is a common part. And one schedules the actuator design on the Gantt chart shown to management. Thus is the design process planned and scheduled prior to design. Since the actual design will at least add information to such planning and scheduling activities, if not correct them, it is necessary to use a mechanism such as the one presented in this paper to manage the design.

Thus we now have as a minimum, interactions between the components of

- the artifact design plan and schedule,
- the artifact design,
- the artifact plan and schedule of construction, and
- artifact construction.

Each includes design decisions that also interact with each other, also managed by the Redux model. Notice also that the design is the execution of the design plan and schedule, just as the artifact construction is the execution of the artifact plan and schedule of construction.

5   Comparison to Other Systems

Redux, as the core of the ProcessLink multiagent design system is compared to some other mechanisms in [14]. It is a very different approach from, though not incompatible with, constraint-based systems such as Bowen. We are developing agent systems that integrate this mechanism[22].

Redux is also not the same sort of system as the Contract Net Protocol[7] although a round of such negotiation could be initiated by a Redux task assignment or a constraint violation notice. Finally, none of these types of systems deals with planning and scheduling.

Redux in its original form as a complete planner[19], together with these planning and scheduling extensions, are most similar to O-Plan[5, 25] in that both treat planning as an explicit processes which can be controlled via an agenda. Both also use constraint representations extensively[22, 26] for search, pruning and backtracking. However, Redux provides a richer model of the types of changes and their effects to be propagated, especially in characterizing design decisions and distinguishing between decision validity and optimality. And the ProcessLink system makes a stronger commitment to an agent architecture{10} and protocol{13}. However, O-Plan is open and the primitives seem to be largely consistent with Redux and it would be interesting to see if the two systems could work together in the future.

The Minerva[1] system also guarantees consistency among design decisions and coordinates design activities for VLSI design. The model includes design objectives similar to Redux goals as well as constraints. The model does not have the same change propagation mechanism as Redux, though the system intent is very similar.

Shared-DRIMS[18] is another similar design process system that distinguishes also between goals and constraints, as does O-Plan and Minerva, and provides a richer model of design rationale argumentation. However, DRIMS has no explicit characterization of design decisions and plans to accomplish goals are tied directly to goals prior to runtime. Also, though DRIMS rationales are more complex than in Redux, the latter better supports changes in the rationale factors.

Finally, the planning ontology of tasks used by any planning agent could be consistent with the PIF[15] standard, but as that standard is concerned only with processes prior to runtime, this standard is somewhat orthogonal to the runtime coordination representation described here. The same is true for other process models though DesignRoadmap[17] has a very similar process model.

6   Summary

We have presented here a novel approach for managing complex distributed projects using agents and a particular representation based upon a general model of design: Redux. We have shown how design, planning, scheduling, and construction can be interleaved and distributed but coordinated by using a central facilitating agent, but which is not a planner or scheduler itself. Indeed, the design, planning, and scheduling for the project may be distributed as required among human and software agents as appropriate.

This enables, in principle, the management of much more complex projects then are now possible. Alternatively, it enables distributed projects to be completed more quickly, or to start earlier with less complete information because there change notification is supported.

This model has been modified for various applications. For example in CoMoKit[8], invalid goals invalidate their decisions also. But the general model has proved useful and the first implementation of a Project Management system, Procura[10] was shown to work.

This paper is intended to assist other system builders with reusable principles in hopes that experimentation with this particular model of agent coordination will be accelerated.

7 Acknowledgments

Professor Mark R. Cutkosky of the Stanford Mechanical Engineering Department and and Professor Martin Fischer of the Stanford Civil Engineering Department have been of great assistance in developing and exploring these ideas. Stanford Center for Design Research work was funded by Navy contract SHARE N00014-92-J-1833 under the US DARPA RaDEO program. This paper is also available at http://cdr.stanford.edu/ProcessLink/papers/DPM/dpm.html as CDR Technical Report 19981118.

8 WWW URLs

{0} http://cdr.stanford.edu/ProcessLink/

{1} http://www-leland.stanford.edu/group/CIFE/VDT/

{2} http://ccs.mit.edu/pifintro.html

{3}http://www.sap.com/

{4} http://www.peoplesoft.com/

{5} http://www.digit.com/ap.html

{6} http://www.cs.umbc.edu/kqml/software/kats/kqml-sdd_ToC.html

{7} http://drogo.cselt.stet.it/fipa/

{8} http://www.sics.se/isl/coord/

{9} http://cdr.stanford.edu/ProcessLink/papers/white-dpm.html

{10} http://cdr.stanford.edu/ProcessLink/ABE/

{11} http://cdr.stanford.edu/ProcessLink/talks/wulkow/proj-27.html

{12}http://cdr.stanford.edu/ProcessLink/talks/wulkow/proj-22.html

{13} http://cdr.stanford.edu/ProcessLink/protocol/EPL-syntax.html

{14} http://www.aiai.ed.ac.uk/~entprise/

References

1. Jacome M. F. and S. W. Director, "Design Process Management for CAD Frameworks," In 29th ACM/IEEE Design Automation Conference, Washington D.C. IEEE Computer Society Press (1992).
2. Benda, M., internal survey of Boeing managers, 1998.
3. Bowen J. and Bahler D., "Task Coordination in Concurrent Engineering", *Enterprise Integration Modeling*, C. Petrie, ed., MIT Press, October, 1992.
4. Conklin, J. and M. Begeman, "gIBIS: A Hypertext Tool for Exploratory Policy Discussion," Proceedings of CSCW '88 (Computer Supported Cooperative Work), September 1988.
5. Currie, K.W. and Tate,A. (1991) "O-Plan: the Open Planning Architecture", Artificial Intelligence Vol 52, No. 1, pp. 49-86 Autumn 1991, Elsevier. http://www.aiai.ed.ac.uk/~oplan/oplan/oplan-doc.html
6. Cutkosky, M., et al., "PACT An Experiment in Integrating Concurrent Engineering Systems,", *IEEE Computer*, January, 1993.
7. Davis, R. and Smith R., "Negotiation as a Metaphor for Distributed Problem Solving," *AI Journal* 1983, 20(1): 63-109.
8. Dellen, B., Maurer, F., and Pews, G., " Knowledge-based techniques to increase the flexibility of workflow management," *Data & Knowledge Engineering*, North-Holland, 1997. See also http://wwwagr.informatik.uni-kl.de/~comokit/.
9. Feldman, Allan M., *Welfare Economics and Social Choice Theory*, Kluwer, Boston, 1980.
10. Goldmann, S., "Procura: A Project Management Model of Concurrent Planning and Design," *Proc. WETICE-96*, Stanford, CA., June, 1996. See also http://cdr.stanford.edu/ProcessLink/Procura/papers/procura.html.
11. Haddadi, A., *Communication and Cooperation in Agent-Systems: A Pragmatic Theory*, Springer Verlag, Lecture Notes in Computer Science, No. 1056, 1996 .
12. Kuokka, D. and L. Harada, "A Communication Infrastructure for Concurrent Engineering," *Journal of Artificial Intelligence for Engineering Design, Analysis and Manufacturing* (AIEDAM), **9**, 1995.
13. Labrou, Y. and Finin, T., "A Proposal for a new KQML Specification," U. of Mayland CS and EE Dept. TR CS-97-03, February 1997. Also http://www.cs.umbc.edu/kqml/.
14. Lander, S., "AI in Design: Issues in Multiagent Design Systems," *IEEE Expert*, April, 1997.
15. Lee, J., and Malone, T., "Partially Shared Views: A scheme for communicating between groups using different type hierarchies," *ACM Transactions on Information Systems*, 8(**1**), 1-26, 1990.
16. *McKinsey Quarterly*, No. 1, 1997.
17. Park, H., "Modeling of Collaborative Design Processes for Agent-Assisted Product Design", Dissertation, Center for Design Research, Stanford U., January, 1995.
18. Pea-Mora, F., *esign Rationale for Computer Supported Conflict Mitigation during the Design-Construction Process of Large-Scale Civil Engineering Systems*, Doctor of Science Thesis, MIT, September 1994.
19. Petrie, C., "Scheduling with REDUX: A Technology for Replanning," *Proc. Aerospace Applications of AI*, October, 1990, Dayton. Also Microelectronics and Computer Technology Corporation TR ACT-RA-340-90, November, 1990.
20. Petrie, C., "The Redux' Server," *Proc. Internat. Conf. on Intelligent and Cooperative Information Systems (ICICIS)*, Rotterdam, May, 1993.

21. Petrie, C., Webster, T., and Cutkosky, M., "Using Pareto Optimality to Coordinate Distributed Agents" *Artificial Intelligence for Engineering Design, Analysis and Manufacturing* (AIEDAM), **9**, 269-281, 1995.

22. Petrie, C., Jeon, H., and Cutkosky, M., "Combining Constraint Propagation and Backtracking for Distributed Engineering," *ECAI-96 Workshop on Non-Standard Constraint Processing*, Budapest, August, 1996, revised for *AAAI-97 Workshop on Constraints and Agents*, Providence, RI, July, 1997. See also http://cdr.stanford.edu/ProcessLink/papers/non-stan-const/non-stan-const.html.

23. Petrie, C., "Agent-Based Engineering, the Web, and Intelligence," *IEEE Expert*, December, 1996. See also http://cdr.stanford.edu/NextLink/Expert.html

24. Raquet, A., "Dynamic Project Management for distributed Processes," Diplom Thesis, Kaiserslautern, in progress.

25. Tate, A., Drabble, B. and Dalton, J. (1996) "The Open Planning Architecture and its Application to Logistics", in "Advanced Planning Technology" (ed. A.Tate), pp. 257-264, AAAI Press, Menlo Park, CA. USA. ftp://ftp.aiai.ed.ac.uk/pub/documents/1996/96-arpi-oplan-and-logistics.ps

26. Tate,A. (1996) "The <I-N-OVA> Constraint Model of Plans", Proceedings of the Third International Conference on Artificial Intelligence Planning Systems, (ed. B.Drabble), pp.221-228, Edinburgh, UK, May 1996, AAAI Press. ftp://ftp.aiai.ed.ac.uk/pub/documents/1996/96-aips-inova.ps

A System for Defeasible Argumentation, with Defeasible Priorities

Henry Prakken*[1] and Giovanni Sartor[2]

[1] Computer/Law Institute, Free University, De Boelelaan 1105 Amsterdam
email: henry@rechten.vu.nl
[2] CIRFID, University of Bologna, Via Galliera 3, 40121, Bologna
IDG-CNR, Via Panchiatichi 56/16, Firenze
email sartor@cirfid.unibo.it

Abstract. Inspired by legal reasoning, this paper presents an argument-based system for defeasible reasoning, with a logic–programming–like language, and based on Dung's argumentation–theoretic approach to the semantics of logic programming. The language of the system has both weak and explicit negation, and conflicts between arguments are decided with the help of priorities on the rules. These priorities are not fixed, but are themselves defeasibly derived as conclusions within the system.

1 Introduction

This paper presents an argument–based system for defeasible reasoning, with a logic–programming–like language. Argument–based systems analyze defeasible reasoning in terms of the interactions between arguments for alternative conclusions. Defeasibility arises from the fact that arguments can be defeated by stronger counterarguments.

Argumentation has proved to be a fruitful paradigm for formalising defeasible reasoning (cf. [13, 17, 18]). Not only does the notion of an argument naturally point at possible proof theories, but also do notions like argument, counterargument, attack and defeat have natural counterparts in the way people think, which makes argument–based systems transparent in applications. Especially in legal reasoning these notions are prevalent, which explains why several argument–based systems have been applied to that domain ([14, 10, 8, 16]).

Also the present system is inspired by the legal domain. In particular, we want to capture the following features of legal reasoning (but also of some other domains, such as bureaucracies). The first is that in law the criteria for comparing arguments are themselves part of the domain theory. For instance, in Italy, in town planning regulations we can find a priority rule stating that rules on the protection of artistic buildings prevail over rules concerning town planning.

---

* Henry Prakken was supported by a research fellowship of the Royal Netherlands Academy of Arts and Sciences, and by Esprit WG 8319 'Modelage'. The authors wish to thank Mark Ryan for his comments on an earlier version of this paper.

Apart from varying from domain to domain, priority rules can also be debatable, in the same way as 'ordinary' domain information can be. For instance, if an artistic–buildings rule is of an earlier date than a conflicting town planning rule, the just–mentioned conflict rule is in conflict with the temporal principle that the later rule has priority over the earlier rule. Other conflict rules may apply to this conflict, and this makes that also reasoning about priorities is defeasible.

The second feature is that in law specificity is not the overriding standard for comparing arguments. In most legal systems it is subordinate to the hierarchical criterion (e.g. 'the constitution has priority over statutes') and to the temporal criterion. This means that systems like [7], making specificity the overriding standard for comparison, are for our purposes inadequate.

Finally, we want to model the fact that legal reasoning combines the use of priorities to choose between conflicting rules with the use of assumptions, or 'weak' negation, within a rule to make it inapplicable in certain circumstances. An example of such a rule is section 3:32–(1) of the Dutch Civil Code, which declares every person to have the capacity to perform juridical acts, "unless the law provides otherwise". Accordingly, our language will have both explicit and weak negation, which yields two different ways of attacking an argument: by stating an argument with a contradictory conclusion, or by stating an argument with a conclusion providing an 'unless' clause of the other argument.

It is not our aim to present a general theory of defeasible argumentation. Rather, we will analyse these phenomena within a logic–programming–like setting, in particular Dung's [6] argument–based approach to the semantics of extended logic programming. With the choice for a logic–programming like language we hope to increase the prospects for implementation, while our choice for Dung's approach is motivated by his emphasis on argumentation.

We will present our system in two phases. In the first phase the priorities are still externally given and fixed (section 2) and in the second phase they are derived within the system itself (section 3). After that, the system is compared with related research (section 4). This paper is a revised version of [16], with more emphasis on formal aspects and less attention to legal applications. For an extensive discussion of examples and applications the reader is referred to [16].

2 The Formal System I: Fixed Priorities

As most systems of defeasible argumentation, our system contains the following elements. To start with, it has an underlying formal language and, based on the language, a notion of an argument. Then it has a definition of when an argument is in conflict with, or attacked by other arguments, a way of comparing conflicting arguments and, most importantly, a definition of the ultimate status of an argument, in terms of three classes: arguments with which a dispute can be 'won', respectively, 'lost' and arguments which leave the dispute undecided.

2.1 The Language

The object language of our system is of familiar logic–programming style: it contains a twoplace one–direction connective that forms rules out of literals. The language has two kinds of negation, weak and classical negation. An atomic first-order formula is a *positive* literal; a positive literal preceded by $\neg$ is a *negative* literal; a positive or negative literal is a *weak* literal if preceded by $\sim$; otherwise it is a *strong* literal. For any atom $P(x)$ we say that $P(x)$ and $\neg P(x)$ are the complement of each other; in the metalanguage $\overline{L}$ denotes the complement of L.

Now a *rule* is an expression of the form

$$r : L_0 \wedge \ldots \wedge L_j \wedge \sim L_k \wedge \ldots \wedge \sim L_m \Rightarrow L_n$$

where r is the name of the rule and each L_i $(0 \leq i \leq k)$ is a strong literal. The conjunction at the left of the arrow is the *antecedent* and the literal at the right of the arrow is the *consequent* of the rule. As usual, a rule with variables is a scheme standing for all its ground instances.

The input information of our system does not only contain rules, but also priorities. We call the input an *ordered theory*, which is a pair $(T, <)$, where T is a set of rules, and $<$ is a noncircular ordering on T. That $r < r'$ means that r' is preferred over r.

The rules are intended to express defeasible information. They can be defeasible in two ways: a rule can contain unwarranted assumptions, and it can still be overridden by stronger rules with a contradictory consequent, even if it does not contain assumptions. Note, finally, that the antecedent of a rule can be empty; such rules can be used to express facts. However, being rules, also the facts are subject to defeat.

2.2 Arguments

The basic notion of a system for defeasible argumentation is that of an argument. In general, the idea is that an argument for a certain proposition is a proof of that proposition in the logic of the underlying language. In our system, the simple language gives rise to a simple notion of an argument, viz. as a sequence of rules that can be chained together, and that is 'grounded' in the facts. This is captured by a slight variant of Dung's [6] notion of a 'defeasible proof'.

Definition 1. An *argument* is a finite sequence $[r_n, \ldots, r_m]$ of ground instances of rules such that

1. for every $i, n \leq i \leq m$, for every positive or negative literal L in the antecedent of r_i there is a $j < i$ such that L is the consequent of r_j; and
2. for no r_i its consequent is also the consequent of some r_j $(j < i)$.

An argument A is *based on* the ordered theory $(T, <)$ iff all rules of A are ground instances of rules in T.[3]

---

[3] We will often leave the phrase 'based on $(T, <)$' implicit.

For any ordered theory Γ we will denote the set of all arguments on the basis of Γ with Args_Γ. Likewise, for any set of rules T, Args_T stands for the set of all arguments that consist of only ground instances of rules in T.

We will also use the following notions. For any argument A, an argument A' is a *(proper) subargument* of A iff A' is a (proper) subsequence of A. A literal L is a *conclusion* of A iff it is the consequent of some rule in A. And L is an *assumption* of A iff $\sim \overline{L}$ occurs in some rule in A. The following example illustrates these notions: for the argument $A = [r_1\colon \sim \neg a \Rightarrow b, r_2\colon b \wedge \sim d \Rightarrow c]$ we have that A's conclusions are $\{b, c\}$, its subarguments are $\{[\,], [r_1], [r_1, r_2]\}$, and its assumptions are $\{a, \neg d\}$.

2.3 Relations between Arguments

So far the notions have been fairly standard; now we present the adversarial aspects of our system, starting with the ways in which an argument can attack, i.e. be a counterargument of another argument. This definition does not yet evaluate arguments; it only tells us which arguments are in conflict. As noted in the introduction, the two different kinds of negation give rise to two ways of attacking an argument. We formalise this as follows.

Definition 2. An argument A_1 *attacks*, or, is a *counterargument of* an argument A_2 iff some conclusion of A_1 is the complement of some conclusion or assumption of A_2. If one argument attacks another, they are *in conflict* with each other.

Note that in order to attack an argument, a counterargument can point its attack at that argument itself, but also at one of its proper subarguments, thereby indirectly attacking the entire argument. In fact, since every argument is a subargument of itself, the definition implies that A_1 attacks A_2 iff a subargument of A_1 attacks a subargument of A_2. So, for instance, if we have

$$r_1\colon \Rightarrow a \quad r_2\colon a \Rightarrow b$$
$$r_3\colon \Rightarrow \neg b \quad r_4\colon \neg b \Rightarrow \neg a$$

we have that not only $[r_1, r_2]$ and $[r_3]$ attack each other, and $[r_3, r_4]$ and $[r_1]$ attack each other, but also that $[r_1, r_2]$ and $[r_3, r_4]$ attack each other.

The concept of 'attack/counterargument' is very important, since obviously, any system for defeasible argumentation should say that if two arguments are in conflict with each other, they cannot be accepted together as justified. We will prove that our system fulfils this requirement. To that end, we also need to define when an argument is coherent, and when a set of arguments is conflict-free.

Definition 3. An argument is *coherent* iff it does not attack itself.

Two examples of incoherent arguments are $[r_1\colon \Rightarrow a, r_2\colon a \Rightarrow \neg a]$ and $[r_1\colon \sim a \Rightarrow b, r_2\colon b \Rightarrow a]$.

Definition 4. A set $Args$ of arguments is *conflict-free* iff no argument in $Args$ attacks an argument in $Args$.

Now that we know which arguments are in conflict with each other, the next step is to compare conflicting arguments. To this end we define, in two steps, a binary relation of defeat among arguments. It is important to realise that this comparison does not yet determine with which arguments a dispute can be won; it only tells us something about the relation between two individual arguments (and their subarguments). Note also that the argument relations and properties defined below are relative to an implicitly assumed ordered theory.

To capture the different 'force' of the two ways of attack, we define 'defeat' in terms of two other evaluative notions, depending on whether an attack is on a conclusion or on an assumption of another argument. Only in the first case the priorities will be used. The definition of defeat will state how to use these two notions in combination.

Definition 5. Let A_1 and A_2 be two arguments. Then

- A_1 *rebuts* A_2 iff for some pair of rules r_1 in A_1 and r_2 in A_2:
  - r_1 and r_2 have complementary consequents; and
  - $r_1 \not< r_2$.
- A_1 *undercuts* A_2 iff some conclusion of A_1 is the complement of some assumption of A_2.

This is almost the definition of attack; the only difference is that if arguments have complementary conclusions, they are compared with the help of priorities. Thus, since undercutting will imply defeat, an attack on an assumption always succeeds. This is motivated by our reading of $\sim A$ simply as the assumption that there is no evidence of A.

The way this definition uses the priorities is that it compares arguments with contradictory conclusions on the priority relation between the rules with these conclusions as the consequent.

As with attack, also rebutting and undercutting an argument can be 'direct', or 'indirect', by providing the complement of a conclusion, or assumption, of a proper subargument. Note also that if A rebuts or undercuts B, then A attacks B. Obviously, it does not hold that if A undercuts B, then B undercuts A. However, it neither holds that if A undercuts B, then B does not undercut A. A counterexample is $A = [r_1 : \sim b \Rightarrow a], B = [r_2 : \sim a \Rightarrow b]$. It is also not the case that if A rebuts B, then B rebuts A. Just assume we have $A = [r_1 : \Rightarrow a]$, $B = [r_2 : \Rightarrow \neg a]$, and $r_1 < r_2$. Then B rebuts A but not the other way around. However, rebutting involving a $<$ relation between conflicting rules is not always one-sided. To see this, assume in the above example illustrating attack, that $r_1 < r_4$ and $r_3 < r_2$; then $[r_1, r_2]$ and $[r_3, r_4]$ rebut each other.

Finally, our definition of defeat states how in evaluating arguments the notions of undercutting and rebutting attack are combined. As a boarder case it regards any incoherent argument as defeated by the empty argument. Apart from this, the definition is based on two ideas, of which the first is inherited from the definition of rebutting and undercutting: defeat of an argument can be direct, or indirect, by defeating one of its proper subarguments; this captures that an argument cannot be stronger than its weakest link. The other idea is that our reading of $\sim A$ not only makes attacks on assumptions always succeed, but also makes an attack on an assumption stronger than rebutting: if one argument undercuts the other, and the other does not undercut but only rebut the first, the second does not defeat the first.

Definition 6. Let A_1 and A_2 be two arguments. Then A_1 *defeats* A_2 iff A_1 is empty and A_2 is incoherent, or else if

- A_1 undercuts A_2; or
- A_1 rebuts A_2 and A_2 does not undercut A_1.

We say that A_1 *strictly defeats* A_2 iff A_1 defeats A_2 and A_2 does not defeat A_1.

Corollary 7. *If A_1 attacks A_2, then A_1 defeats A_2 or A_2 defeats A_1. And if A_1 defeats A_2, then A_1 attacks A_2.*

The following example illustrates that undercutting an argument is stronger than rebutting it. Consider $r_1 : \sim \neg Innocent(OJ) \Rightarrow Innocent(OJ)$ and $r_2 : \Rightarrow \neg Innocent(OJ)$ and assume that $<= \emptyset$. Then, although $[r_1]$ rebuts $[r_2]$, $[r_1]$ does not defeat $[r_2]$, since $[r_2]$ undercuts $[r_1]$. So $[r_2]$ strictly defeats $[r_1]$.

Our notion of defeat is a weak one, since for rebutting an argument no $>$ relation is needed between the relevant rules, but only a $\not<$ relation. So, rather than having to be 'really better' than the argument that is to be defeated, a defeating argument only has to be not inferior. This is since we want our notion of 'justified arguments', to be defined next, to really capture only those arguments that, given the premises, are beyond any doubt or challenge. And doubt can already be cast on an argument by providing a counterargument that is at least not inferior to it. For the same reason we also need the notion of strict defeat, which, being asymmetric, captures the idea of 'really being better than'. This notion will be used to ensure that a counterargument fails to cast doubt if it is inferior to at least one counterargument that is itself protected from defeat.

2.4 The Status of Arguments

Since defeating arguments can themselves be defeated by other arguments, compairing just pairs of arguments is not sufficient; what is also needed is a definition that determines the status of arguments on the basis of all ways in which they interact. In particular, the definition should allow for reinstatement of defeated arguments, if their defeater is itself (strictly) defeated by another argument. This definition, then, is the central element of our system. It takes as input the set of all possible arguments and their mutual relations of defeat, and produces as output a division of arguments into three classes: arguments with which a dispute can be 'won', respectively, 'lost' and arguments which leave the dispute undecided. As remarked above, the winning arguments should be only those arguments that, given the premises, are beyond any doubt: the only way to cast doubt on these arguments is by providing new premises, giving rise to new defeating counterarguments. Accordingly, we want our set of justified arguments to be unique, and to be conflict–free.

The intuitive idea is that the set of *justified* arguments is constructed step–by–step (note that everything here is relative to an implicitly assumed input theory). We first collect into $JustArgs_1$ all arguments which are directly justified, by their own strength: those are the ones which are not defeated by any counterargument. Then we add all arguments that are justified indirectly, i.e. with the help of arguments in $JustArgs_1$. More exactly, each argument that has defeating counterarguments, is still added to $JustArgs_1$ if all those counterarguments are strictly defeated by an argument already in $JustArgs_1$. The resulting set is $JustArgs_2$. We repeat this step until we obtain a set $JustArgs_n$ to which no new argument can be added, which, then, is the set of all justified arguments. Then we can define the losing, or 'overruled' arguments as those that are attacked by a justified argument and, finally, the undeciding or 'defensible' arguments as all the arguments that are neither justified nor overruled.

We formalise this with a definition based on Dung's [6] grounded (sceptical) semantics of extended logic programs. It makes use of a variant of Dung's notion of the acceptability of an argument with respect to a set of arguments.

Definition 8. An argument A is *acceptable* with respect to a set $Args$ of arguments iff each argument defeating A is strictly defeated by an argument in $Args$.

Next we use this notion in defining the set of justified arguments.

Definition 9. Let Γ be an ordered theory. Then we define the following sequence of subsets of $Args_\Gamma$.

- $F_\Gamma^0 = \emptyset$
- $F_\Gamma^{i+1} = \{A \in Args_\Gamma \mid A$ is acceptable with respect to $F_\Gamma^i\}$.

Then the set $JustArgs_\Gamma$ of arguments that are justified on the basis of Γ is $\cup_{i=0}^\infty (F_\Gamma^i)$.

In terms of the set of justified arguments we define the overruled and defensible arguments. We also define the corresponding notions for conclusions.

Definition 10. For any ordered theory Γ and argument A we say that on the basis of Γ:

1. A is *overruled* iff A is attacked by an argument in $JustArgs_\Gamma$;
2. A is *defensible* iff A is neither justified nor overruled.

And for any literal L, we say that L is a *justified conclusion* iff it is a conclusion of a justified argument, L is a *defensible conclusion* iff it is not justified and it is a conclusion of some defensible argument, and L is an *overruled conclusion* iff it is not justified or defensible, and a conclusion of an overruled argument.

In the following subsection this definition will be illustrated. Now we state some formal properties. Firstly, by definition the set of justified arguments is unique, as we wanted. Furthermore, Proposition 11 says that the set of justified arguments can be constructed step–by–step by just adding new arguments; at no step arguments are deleted. And Proposition 12 says that the result of the construction is conflict–free.

Proposition 11. *Let $JustArgs_\Gamma = \cup_{i=0}^{\infty}(F_\Gamma^i)$. Then for all i, $F_\Gamma^i \subseteq F_\Gamma^{i+1}$.*

Proposition 12. *For each ordered theory Γ, $JustArgs_\Gamma$ is conflict–free.*

The reader will have noticed that Definition 10 does not explicitly require that all proper subarguments of an argument are justified, as, e.g. [11, 18, 14] do. Instead, as the following proposition states, this requirement is implicit in our definitions, as also in e.g. [13, 17, 7].

Proposition 13. *If an argument is justified on the basis of Γ, all its subarguments are justified on the basis of Γ.*

2.5 Illustration of the Definitions

The first example illustrates the step–by–step construction of $JustArgs$.[4]

$$r_0: \Rightarrow a \qquad r_1: a \Rightarrow b$$
$$r_2: \sim b \Rightarrow c$$
$$r_3: \Rightarrow \neg a$$

where $r_0 < r_3$. First we identify the relations of defeat. The argument $A_1 = [r_0, r_1]$ defeats the argument $A_2 = [r_2]$, since it undercuts it. Furthermore, the argument $A_3 = [r_3]$ defeats A_1, by rebutting its proper subargument $A_0 = [r_0]$ and thereby also rebutting A_1 itself.

With these relations we can construct the set of justified arguments as follows. A_3 is not defeated by any argument, since its only counterargument A_1 is too weak. So $F^1 = \{A_3\}$ How now about A_1? We cannot add it, since it is defeated by A_3, which in turn is not strictly defeated by any argument in F^1. Also A_0 cannot be added, for the same reasons. How then about A_2? Although it is defeated by its only counterargument A_1, we can still add it, since A_1 is in turn strictly defeated by an argument in F^1, viz. A_3. Thus A_3 reinstates A_2 and we have that $F^2 = \{A_3, A_2\}$. Repeating this process adds no new relevant arguments, so we can stop here: $F^3 = F^2$. Thus we obtain that A_2 and A_3 are justified, while A_0 and A_1 are overruled. Note that the weakest link principle is respected: A_1 is overruled since its subargument A_0 is overruled.

Next we illustrate the relation between undercutting and rebutting attack.

---

[4] In the rest of this paper we will leave the empty argument, and combinations of independently justified arguments, implicit.

$$r_1 : \Rightarrow Has\_Porsche \qquad r_2 : Has\_Porsche \Rightarrow Rich$$
$$r_3 : \sim Rich \Rightarrow \neg Has\_Porsche$$

Assume that $r_1 < r_3$. Definition 6 ignores this ordering; $B = [r_3]$ does not defeat $A = [r_1, r_2]$ since A undercuts B. This causes A to be justified, as well as well as its subargument $A' = [r_1]$, although that is defeated by B. A' is reinstated since A strictly defeats its counterargument B.

Finally we illustrate that our definitions respect the 'step–by–step' nature of argumentation: conflicts about conclusions or assumptions earlier in the chains are dealt with before 'later' conflicts.

$$r_1 : \Rightarrow a \qquad r_2 : a \Rightarrow b \qquad r_3 : b \Rightarrow c$$
$$r_4 : \Rightarrow \neg a \qquad r_5 : \neg a \Rightarrow d \qquad r_6 : d \Rightarrow \neg c$$

Assume that $r_4 < r_1$ and $r_3 < r_6$. Then the arguments $[r_1 - r_3]$ and $[r_4 - r_6]$ defeat each other. However, $[r_1]$ (and also $[r_1, r_2]$), strictly defeats $[r_4 - r_6]$ and has no other counterarguments; so $F^1 = \{[r_1], [r_1, r_2]\}$. But then $[r_4 - r_6]$, although defeating $[r_1 - r_3]$, is not in F^2, while $[r_1 - r_3]$ is in F^2, reinstated by $[r_1]$.

3 The Formal System II: Defeasible Priorities

3.1 Definitions

So far we have simply assumed that there is an input ordering on the rules. Now we will study the situation where this ordering is derived from the premises. To this end we assume that our language contains a distinguished twoplace predicate symbol $\prec$, with which information on the priorities can be stated in the object language. This makes the ordering component of an ordered theory redundant, so an *ordered theory* is from now on just a set of rules. Next we change the definition of rebutting and undercutting arguments, to make sure that arguments which together would make the ordering circular cannot be accepted simultaneously.

Definition 14. Let A_1 and A_2 be two arguments. Then

1. A_1 *rebuts* A_2 iff
   - for some pair of rules r_1 in A_1 and r_2 in A_2:
     - r_1 and r_2 have complementary consequents; and
     - $r_1 \not\prec r_2$.
   - or for some sequence of rules $r_1, \ldots, r_n$ in A_1 and some rule r_m in A_2:
     - the consequent of r_m is $x \prec y$ and the consequents of $r_1, \ldots, r_n$ are a chain $y \prec z, \ldots, z' \prec x$; and
     - for all r_i $(1 \leq i \leq n) : r_i \not\prec r_m$.
2. A_1 *undercuts* A_2 iff
   - some conclusion of A_1 is the complement of some assumption of A_2; or
   - A_2 contains an assumption $x \prec y$ and A_1 has a chain of conclusions $y \prec z, \ldots, z' \prec x$.

Note that in priority conflicts between arguments more than one rule of an argument may directly contribute to a conclusion, viz. when the chain of priority conclusions has more than one element. In that case it is natural to require for rebutting that not just the last of those rules, but all of them are not less than the relevant rule of the other argument. To illustrate this with an example, assume we have $r_4: \Rightarrow r_1 \prec r_2$, $r_5: \Rightarrow r_2 \prec r_3$ and $r_6: \Rightarrow r_3 \prec r_1$, and assume that $< = \{r_4 < r_5, r_4 < r_6\}$. With Definition 14 we have that $[r_4]$ is strictly defeated by $[r_5, r_6]$, which itself is not defeated by any argument, so that $r_2 \prec r_3$ and $r_3 \prec r_1$ are justified conclusions, while $r_1 \prec r_2$ is an overruled conclusion. By contrast, if only the last rule of the sequence were taken into account, we would have that $[r_4, r_5]$ defeats $[r_6]$, and all the conclusions would be defensible, which seems a less natural outcome.

We now define the consequences of the extended framework with a revision of the fixpoint definition. The idea is that now with the set of justified arguments also the ordering is 'constructed' step–by–step. The resulting definition is inspired by an earlier version of [4].

Note that we now have to make the dependence of the various notions on a rule ordering explicit, since this ordering now varies with the conclusions that have been drawn so far. To this end we first define the following notation. For any set $Args$ of arguments

$$<_{Args} = \{r < r' \mid r \prec r' \text{ is a conclusion of some } A \in Args\}$$

Then we say for any set $Args$ of arguments and any set T of rules that A (strictly) $Args$–defeats B on the basis of T iff according to Definition 6 A (strictly) defeats B on the basis of $(T, <_{Args})$.[5] Occasionally, we will also use the analogous notion $Args$–rebuts.

Corollary 15. *If A_1 attacks A_2, then for any conflict-free set $Args$ of arguments, A_1 $Args$–defeats A_2 or A_2 $Args$–defeats A_1; and if A_1 $Args$–defeats A_2, then A_1 attacks A_2.*

Next we incorporate the new notation in the definition of acceptability.

Definition 16. An argument A is *acceptable* with respect to a set $Args$ of arguments iff all arguments $Args$–defeating A are strictly $Args$–defeated by some argument in $Args$.

Thus acceptability of an argument with respect to a set $Args$ now depends on the priority conclusions of the arguments in $Args$. With this change, the definition of justified arguments can stay the same (recall that Γ is now a set of rules).

Definition 17. Let Γ be an ordered theory. Then we define a sequence of subsets of $Args_\Gamma$ as follows.

---

[5] Below we will leave the phrase 'on the basis of T' implicit. Note also that now $<_{Args}$ can for arbitrary $Args$ be circular (although not for $JustArgs$: see Corollary 20).

$$- \ G_\Gamma^0 = \emptyset$$
$$- \ G_\Gamma^{i+1} = \{A \in Args_\Gamma \mid A \text{ is acceptable with respect to } G_\Gamma^i\}.$$

Then the set $JustArgs_\Gamma$ of arguments that are justified on the basis of Γ is $\cup_{i=0}^{\infty}(G_\Gamma^i)$. Overruled and defensible arguments are defined as above.

Also for this definition it holds that each new step only adds arguments.

Proposition 18. *Let $JustArgs_\Gamma = \cup_{i=0}^{\infty}(G_\Gamma^i)$. Then for all i, $G_\Gamma^i \subseteq G_\Gamma^{i+1}$.*

Note that this time each step in the construction $JustArgs$ also implicitly extends the ordering on rules; this is because G uses the notion of acceptability, which in turn uses the notion of $Args$–defeat, and the point is that $Args$, and thus also $<_{Args}$, changes with each new step. So what happens is that at each new step the defeat relations are redetermined on the basis of the set of justified arguments that has been constructed thus far.

Finally, we can again prove that the set of justified arguments is conflict–free.

Proposition 19. *For each ordered theory Γ, $\cup_{i=0}^{\infty}(G_\Gamma^i)$ is conflict–free.*

Corollary 20. *For any set of justified arguments, $<_{JustArgs}$ is noncircular.*

3.2   Illustrations

We will illustrate the new definitions with an example in which the abovementioned Italian priority rule on building regulations conflicts with the temporality principle that the later rule has priority over the earlier one. They state contradicting priorities between a town planning rule saying that if a building needs restructuring, its exterior may be modified, and an earlier, and conflicting, artistic–buildings rule saying that if a building is on the list of protected buildings, its exterior may not be modified. In the example we will use a common method for naming rules. Every rule with terms $t_1, \ldots, t_n$ is named with a function expression $r(t_1, \ldots, t_n)$, where r is the informal name of the rule.

Note that rule r_9 states that rule r_3 is later than the Lex Posterior principle T, which implies that r_3 prevails over T, according to T itself. The application of a priority rule to itself (or better, to one of its instances), is an interesting peculiarity of this example.

$r_1(x)$:	x is protected $\Rightarrow \neg\ x$'s exterior may be modified
$r_2(x)$:	x needs restructuring $\Rightarrow x$'s exterior may be modified
$r_3(y, x)$:	x is a rule about the protection of artistic buildings $\wedge$
	y is a town planning rule $\Rightarrow y \prec x$
$T(x, y)$:	x is earlier than $y \Rightarrow x \prec y$
$r_4(r_1(x))$:	$\Rightarrow r_1(x)$ is about the protection of artistic buildings
$r_5(r_2(x))$:	$\Rightarrow r_2(x)$ is a town planning rule
$r_6(r_1(x), r_2(y))$:	$\Rightarrow r_2(x)$ is later than $r_1(y)$
$r_7(Villa_0)$:	$\Rightarrow Villa_0$ is protected
$r_8(Villa_0)$:	$\Rightarrow Villa_0$ needs restructuring
$r_9(r_3(x, y), T(x, y))$:	$\Rightarrow r_3(x, y)$ is later than $T(x, y)$

To maintain readability, we will below only give the function symbol part of the rule names, except when we want to stress that a rule is applied to other rules. We also use the following abbreviations: the fact instance $r_6(r_2, r_1)$, stating that r_2 is later than is r_1, is abridged as r_6'; the rule instance $r_3(r_2, r_1)$, giving precedence to artistical protection rule r_1, is written as r_3', and the rule instance $T(r_1, r_2)$, giving precedence to the later rule r_2, is shortened to T'.

First we collect all arguments which have no G^0– defeating counterarguments (for readability, we do not list subarguments).

$$G^1 = \{[r_4], [r_5], [r_6'], [r_7], [r_8], [r_6(r_3', T')], T(T', r_3')]\}$$

The last argument in G^1 concludes that, as a criterion for solving the conflict between r_1 and r_2, r_3 is better than T itself, i.e., that r_3' is better than T':

$$T(T', r_3'): r_3' \text{ is later than } T' \Rightarrow T' \prec r_3'$$

Hence $<^1 = \{T' < r_3'\}$. With this ordering relation we can solve the conflict between the argument $[r_6', T']$, saying that rule r_2 prevails over r_1, according to temporality, and the argument $[r_4, r_5, r_3']$, saying that rule r_1 prevails over rule r_2, according to r_3: the latter argument now strictly G^1–defeats the first, so $G^2 = G_1 \cup \{[r_4, r_5, r_3']\}$ and $<^2 = \{T' < r_3', r_2 < r_1\}$. With this priority relation added, we can finally solve the conflict between the arguments $[r_7, r_1]$ and $[r_8, r_2]$ in favour of the first: $G^3 = G_2 \cup \{[r_7, r_1]\}$. Having considered all arguments, we can stop here: our set of justified arguments is G^3, which means that the exterior of $Villa_0$ may not be modified.

4 Comparison with Related Work

With respect to related research, we here focus on logic– programming–like systems for defeasible reasoning. Related research in Artificial Intelligence and Law is discussed in [16]. [6] has developed various argumentation based semantics of extended logic programming, based on more abstract research in [2] and [5]. As already said above, we have adapted Dung's version of [12]'s well–founded semantics of extended logic programs. However, there are some differences. Firstly, Dung does not consider reasoning with or about priorities. Moreover, since Dung only reformulates the various semantics of logic progams, in the case of well–founded semantics he inherits some of its features that we find less attractive. In particular, Dung defines arguments as being the set of assumptions of what we define as an argument. For instance, in his terms the program $r_1 : \Rightarrow a, r_2 : \Rightarrow b$, $r_3 : \Rightarrow \neg a$, has only one argument, viz. [ ], which defeats itself: so $F^1 = F^0 = \emptyset$. We, by contrast, have that $F^1 = \{[r_3]\}$ and $F^2 = F^1$, which seems more natural.

Also [1] deviate from well–founded semantics, for similar reasons. Although their system is not argument–based, it has two kinds of negations and prioritized rules, but not reasoning about priorities. It would be interesting to study the relation between [1] and the special case of our framework with fixed priorities.

In [4] Brewka has defined an extension of [12]'s well–founded semantics to programs with defeasible priorities. Since Brewka defines a conservative extension of this semantics, he inherits its features. Another difference with our system is that Brewka reduces rebutting to undercutting defeat, by adding to every rule with consequent L a literal $\sim \overline{L}$ to its antecedent. Although this makes the definitions simpler, it also gives up some expressive power. In particular, the difference between rules like 'If A then B' and 'If A then B, unless the contrary can be shown' cannot be expressed.

Two other relevant logic–programming–like systems also need to be mentioned: 'ordered logic' (see e.g. [9]) and Nute's [11] 'defeasible logic', which both have prioritized rules but no undercutting arguments or reasoning about priorities. Nute also has a second category of so–called 'strict rules', of which the use in an argument cannot cause the argument to be defeated. Currently we are investigating how strict rules can be included in our theory with avoiding some features of Nute's treatment that we find less attractive.

Finally, an alternative approach to reasoning about priorities, suitable for extension– or model–based nonmonotonic logics, was developed by [3] for prioritised default logic, and generalised and slightly revised by [15] for any extension– or model–based system. Roughly, the method checks whether what an extension says about the priorities corresponds to the ordering on which the extension is based. Space limitations prevent a detailed comparison here.

5 Conclusion

Inspired by legal reasoning, and in a logic–programming like setting, this paper has studied the combination of the following features of defeasible argumentation: reasoning with two kinds of negation, reasoning with priorities, and reasoning about priorities. As already indicated, one aim of future research is to extend the language with strict rules, in order to make the expression possible of properties of relations, such as transitivity, and of incompatibility of predicates, like 'bachelors are not married'. We also plan to develop a proof theory, in terms of 'dialectical proof trees'.

6 Proofs

Proposition 11 *Let* $JustArgs_\Gamma = \cup_{i=0}^{\infty}(F_\Gamma^i)$. *Then for all* i, $F_\Gamma^i \subseteq F_\Gamma^{i+1}$.

Proof. The proof is by induction on the definition of $JustArgs_\Gamma$. Clearly $F^0 = \emptyset \subseteq F^1$. Assume next that $F^{i-1} \subseteq F^i$ and consider any $A \in F^i$ and $B \in Args_\Gamma$ such that B defeats A. Then some $C \in F^{i-1}$ strictly defeats B, and since also $C \in F^i$, A is acceptable with respect to F^i and so $A \in F^{i+1}$.

Proposition 12 *For each ordered theory* Γ, $\cup_{i=0}^{\infty}(F_\Gamma^i)$ *is conflict–free.*

Proof. We first prove with induction that each set F^i is conflict–free. Clearly $F^0 = \emptyset$ is conflict–free. Consider next any F^i that is conflict–free, and assume that $A, A' \in F^{i+1}$ and A attacks A'. Then by Corollary 7 A defeats A' or A' defeats A. Assume without loss of generality that A defeats A'. Then, since

$A' \in F^{i+1}$, some $B \in F^i$ defeats A. But then, since $A \in F^{i+1}$, some $C \in F^i$ defeats that B. But then F^i is not conflict–free. Contradiction, so also F^{i+1} is conflict–free.

Now with Proposition 11 it follows that also $\cup_{i=0}^{\infty}(F_{\Gamma}^i)$ is conflict–free.

Proposition 13 *If an argument is justified on the basis of Γ, all its subarguments are justified on the basis of Γ.*

Proof. Suppose $A \in JustArgs_{\Gamma}$, A' is a subargument of A and B defeats A'. Observe first that for some $F^i \subseteq JustArgs_{\Gamma}$ A is acceptable wrt F^i. Then two cases have to be considered. Firstly, if B does not defeat A, this is because A undercuts B. But then A strictly defeats B. Secondly, if B defeats A, then some $C \in F^i$ strictly defeats B. In both cases A' is acceptable with respect to F^i and so $A' \in F^{i+1}$ and by Proposition 11 $A' \in JustArgs_{\Gamma}$.

Proposition 18 *Let $JustArgs_{\Gamma} = \cup_{i=0}^{\infty}(G_{\Gamma}^i)$. Then for all i, $G_{\Gamma}^i \subseteq G_{\Gamma}^{i+1}$.*

Proof. It sufficies to prove the following properties of $Args$–defeat.

Lemma 21. *For any two conflict–free sets of arguments S and S' such that $S \subseteq S'$, and any two arguments A and B we have that*

1. *If A S'–defeats B, then A S–defeats B.*
2. *If A strictly S–defeats B, then A strictly S'–defeats B.*

Proof. Observe first that undercutting is independent of S and S'. Then (1) follows since if no argument in S' has a conclusion $r < r'$, also no argument in S has that conclusion. For (2) observe first that if S contains an argument A with conclusion $r < r'$, also S' contains A and by conflict–freeness S' does not contain an argument for $r' < r$; so for any B and C, if B strictly S–defeats C, then B S'–defeats C. Moreover, by contraposition of (1) C does not S'–defeat B if C does not S–defeat B, so C strictly S'–defeats B.

With this lemma the proof of Proposition 11 can easily be adapted to the present case.

Proposition 19 *For each ordered theory Γ, $\cup_{i=0}^{\infty}(G_{\Gamma}^i)$ is conflict–free.*

Proof. Observe first that for any conflict–free G^{i-1}, $A \in G^{i-1}$ and $B \in Args_{\Gamma}$ attackking A, by Corollary 15 A G^{i-1}–defeats B or B G^{i-1}–defeats A. Then the proof can be completed in the same way as for Proposition 12.

Corollary 20 For any set of justified arguments, $<_{JustArgs}$ is noncircular.

Proof. Assume for contradiction that some conclusions of arguments in $JustArgs$ form a sequence $r_1 \prec r_2, \ldots, r_m \prec r_n, r_n \prec r_1$. Then $JustArgs$ contains an argument A_1 with conclusion $r_n \prec r_1$, and an argument A_2 containing a sequence of conclusions $r_1 \prec r_2, \ldots, r_m \prec r_n$ (A_2 is the combination of the arguments for all atoms in the sequence). Then A_1 and A_2 $JustArgs$–rebut each other and by Lemma 21(1) they also G^i–rebut each other for any $G^i \subseteq JustArgs$. Then by Corollary 15 we have that A_1 and A_2 attack each other, which by Proposition 19 implies a contradiction.

References

1. A. Analyti and S. Pramanik, Reliable semantics for extended logic programs with rule prioritization. *Journal of Logic and Computation* 5 (1995), 303–324.
2. A. Bondarenko, F. Toni, R.A. Kowalski, An assumption–based framework for non-monotonic reasoning. *Proceedings of the Second International Workshop on Logic Programming and Nonmonotonic Reasoning*, MIT Press, 1993, 171–189.
3. G. Brewka, Reasoning about priorities in default logic. *Proceedings AAAI-94*, 247–260.
4. G. Brewka, What does a defeasible rule base with explicit prioritiy information entail? *Proceedings of the second Dutch/German Workshop on Nonmonotonic Reasoning*, Utrecht 1995, 25–32.
5. P.M. Dung, On the acceptability of arguments and its fundamental role in non-monotonic reasoning, logic programming, and n–person games. *Artificial Intelligence* 77 (1995), 321–357.
6. P.M. Dung, An argumentation semantics for logic programming with explicit negation. *Proceedings of the Tenth Logic Programming Conference*, MIT Press 1993, 616–630.
7. H. Geffner and J. Pearl, Conditional entailment: bridging two approaches to default reasoning. *Artificial Intelligence* 53 (1992), 209–244.
8. T.F. Gordon, The pleadings game: an exercise in computational dialectics. *Artificial Intelligence and Law*, Vol. 2, No. 4, 1994, 239–292.
9. E. Laenens and D. Vermeir, A fixed points semantics for ordered logic. *Journal of Logic and Computation* Vol. 1 No. 2, 1990, 159–185.
10. R.P. Loui, J. Norman, J. Olson, A. Merrill, A design for reasoning with policies, precedents, and rationales. *Proceedings of the Fourth International Conference on Artificial Intelligence and Law*, ACM Press, 1993, 202–211.
11. D. Nute, Defeasible logic. In D. Gabbay (ed.) *Handbook of Logic and Artificial Intelligence*, Vol. 3. Oxford University Press, 1994, 353–395.
12. L.M. Pereira and J.J. Alferes, Well–founded semantics for logic programs with explicit negation. *Proceedings ECAI-92*.
13. J.L. Pollock, Defeasible reasoning. *Cognitive Science* 11 (1987), 481–518.
14. H. Prakken, An argumentation framework in default logic. *Annals of Mathematics and Artificial Intelligence*, 9 (1993) 91–131.
15. H. Prakken, A semantic view on reasoning about priorities (extended abstract) *Proceedings of the Second Dutch/German Workshop on Nonmonotonic Reasoning*, Utrecht 1995, 152–159.
16. H. Prakken and G. Sartor, On the relation between legal language and legal argument: assumptions, applicability and dynamic priorities. *Proceedings of the Fifth International Conference on Artificial Intelligence and Law*. ACM Press 1995, 1–9.
17. G.R. Simari and R.P. Loui, A mathematical treatment of defeasible argumentation and its implementation. *Artificial Intelligence* 53 (1992), 125–157.
18. G. Vreeswijk, *Studies in defeasible argumentation*. Doctoral dissertation Free University Amsterdam, 1993.

Handling Uncertainty in Control of Autonomous Robots

Alessandro Saffiotti

Applied Autonomous Sensor Systems
Department of Technology and Science
Örebro University, S-70182 Örebro, Sweden
URL: http://www.oru.se/forsk/aass
E-mail: alessandro.saffiotti@ton.oru.se

Abstract. Autonomous robots need the ability to move purposefully and without human intervention in real-world environments that have not been specifically engineered for them. These environments are characterized by the pervasive presence of uncertainty: the need to cope with this uncertainty constitutes a major challenge for autonomous robots. In this note, we discuss this challenge, and present some specific solutions based on our experience on the use of fuzzy logic in mobile robots. We focus on three issues: how to realize robust motion control; how to flexibly execute navigation plans; and how to approximately estimate the robot's location.

1   I had a dream

It is Monday morning, and it is raining. I enter my office. Edi, my purple personal robot, promptly realizes my presence, and happily rolls out to get me some coffee. Down the corridor, it slips over the water left by somebody's shoes, and has to correct its trajectory by sensing the walls. The cafeteria's main door is closed, so Edi crosses the library and enters the cafeteria by its side door. Having obtained a cup of coffee from Gianni, the barman, it comes back by the same way, moving smoothly in order not to spill the coffee. Three people are smoking in the corridor, and Edi has to maneuver around them, and around a cart hiding behind them. I have just finished reading my mail when Edi comes in with my coffee on its head. It is still hot.

What makes this story a dream? After all, the task performed by Edi may not seem very complex to an outsider; and we know that industrial robots can perform seemingly elaborate tasks with high reliability. Yet, this story is probably close to the best that today's most advanced research robots can do. Having a commercially produced, inexpensive robot to reliably perform tasks of this type in our offices and houses is still a dream. Why?

A crucial observation to understand the difficulties involved is that control programs are typically based on a *model* of the controlled system. Control engineers use a mathematical description of the plant to design their regulators; and

AI planning programs incorporate a symbolic description of the target system, of its dynamics, and of the effects of our actions on it. Now, in the case of robot operation the controlled system is composed of the robot *and* its workspace, and we need to account for both these elements in our models — see Figure 1.

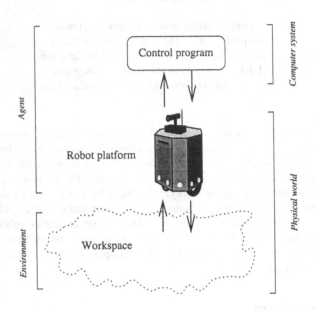

Fig. 1. The two facets of the robotic problem. The external observer sees a physical agent (the robot's body and its software) operating in an environment. The designer sees a control program controlling a physical system (the robot's body and its workspace).

A reasonably accurate model of the robot on its own can usually be obtained. For industrial robots, a complete model of the workspace is also usually available. The workspace is highly engineered and completely determined at design time: we know where the workpiece will be, and we know that there will not be a child standing in front of it (if these assumptions are wrong, the robot fails to perform its task). Unfortunately, the same amount of knowledge cannot be obtained in general for the type of real-world environments where we would like our autonomous robots to operate.

There are two sources of problems in getting a reliable model of the "robot + environment" system. The first one is the environment. Our prior knowledge of unstructured environments is necessarily incomplete, uncertain, and approximate: maps typically omit some details and temporary features, spatial relations between objects may have changed since the map was built, and the metric information may be imprecise and inaccurate. Moreover, the environment dynamics is typically complex and unpredictable: objects can move, other agents can modify the environment, and relatively stable features may change slowly with time (e.g., seasonal variations).

The second problem is that the interaction between the robot and the environment may be extraordinarily difficult to model. The results of the robot's actions are influenced by a number of environmental conditions which are hard to be accounted for: wheels may slip, and a gripper may lose its grasp on an object. And the relation between the perceptual information and the reality is elusive: noise in sensor measurements introduces uncertainty; the limited sensor range, combined with the effect of environmental features (e.g., occlusion) and of adverse observation conditions (e.g., lighting), leads to imprecise data; and errors in the measurement interpretation process may lead to incorrect beliefs.

Several of these sources of difficulties appear in the above dream. Edi must use a map to plan its route to the cafeteria, but this map turns out to be inaccurate (the door is closed) and incomplete (the people who are smoking are not in it). The effect of Edi turning its wheels is modified as a result of the wet floor. And the cart only comes into the sensor's view at the last moment. In general, builders of autonomous robots must face a great challenge: to design robust control programs that reliably perform complex tasks in spite of the large amount of uncertainty[1] inherent to real-world environments. As Lumelsky and Brooks already remarked in 1989 ([24], p. 714.)

> The next big leap of industrial and household automation depends on our ability to overcome the very expensive and often unrealistic requirement of structure and order characteristic of today's "hard" (industrial) automation.

In this note, we present some ways in which we can make it possible to take this leap. In the next section, we analyze the sources of uncertainty in the autonomous navigation task, and discuss how the robotics community has tried to deal with them. In the following sections, we present some possible solutions to the problem of uncertainty in robot navigation, based on the analysis of a test case: the use of fuzzy logic in the SRI International mobile robot Flakey (see [39] for more comprehensive reports on this work). We concentrate on three specific important problems: how to define robust behavior-producing modules; how to flexibly execute complex tasks; and how to reliably establish the robot's position with respect to a map of the environment. We conclude this note by a few remarks on the choice of a "best" way to deal with uncertainty in robotics.

2 The challenge of uncertainty

Consider again Figure 1, and recall our claim that many of the difficulties in modeling the "robot + environment" system come from the inherent uncertainty

---

[1] Throughout this note, we use the term "uncertainty" in its most general flavor; we shall use more specific terms like "imprecision," "vagueness" and "unreliability" when we want to focus on a specific facet of uncertainty.

of real-world environments. We now inspect this claim in deeper detail, and sketch the most common solutions adopted to circumvent this problem.

Suppose for concreteness that we are modeling our system by using the tools from the theory of dynamical systems (similar considerations could be made assuming a logic-based representation in the mainstream of AI). For example, we may model the system by the following pair of equations:

$$x_{t+1} = f(x_t, u_t)$$
$$y_t = g(x_t), \tag{1}$$

where x_t denotes the state of the system "robot + environment" at time t; u_t the control signals sent to the robot at t; and y_t the signals returned by the robot's sensors at t. The f function, usually called the state transition function, accounts for the dynamics of the controlled system; the g function, usually called the output function, accounts for the observability of the system.

Equations (1) do not take any uncertainty into account: we know for sure that whenever we are in state x_t, we will observe the output $g(x_t)$; and that if we apply control u_t in this state, we will end up in state $f(x_t, u_t)$. A possible way to bring uncertainty into the picture is by introducing two random variables v and w that represent the effects of the unknown factors, or *disturbances*. For instance, we might write

$$x_{t+1} = f(x_t, u_t) + v_t$$
$$y_t = g(x_t) + w_t.$$

To use this technique, we must be able to somehow specify the values taken by the v_t and w_t variables, for instance by defining two probability distributions for these variables. In other words, we must provide a *model of the uncertainty* that affects our model. This model can be provided for many physical systems; e.g., errors in the action of many effectors may be effectively modeled by assuming a Gaussian distribution over v_t. Unfortunately, in the case of most of the uncertainty that affects real-world unstructured environments, we are not able to precisely characterize and quantify the disturbances.

As an example of this, consider the uncertainty induced in the environment by the presence of people. People walk around, and they may change the position of objects and furniture. The actions of most persons cannot be described by a deterministic or a stochastic process — we just cannot write a meaningful probability distribution of when I will go to the printer room. As a consequence, we cannot write a meaningful model of the disturbances induced in the state transition function f by the presence of people. A similar observation can be made for the disturbances introduced in the output function g. The reliability of visual recognition, for instance, is influenced by the lighting conditions, which may depend on the cloudiness. And the reliability of the distances measured by a sonar sensor is influenced by the geometry and the reflectance property of the objects in the environment. In each case, a probabilistic (or otherwise) model of uncertainty is either meaningless, or overly complex to obtain.

One possible way to approach this problem is to attack the uncertainty at its very source, by carefully engineering the robot and its workspace so that the uncertainty is minimized and the residual uncertainty can be fully characterized in some way. As we have noticed, this is typically done in industrial robots, where the dynamics of the work-cell is completely determined, and sensing is limited to internal precise sensors that monitor the position of the robot's parts. Some amount of environment engineering has often been applied to autonomous robotics too: from the early days of Shakey [28], where the observation conditions were carefully controlled, and the set of possible "unforeseen" events was known a priori; to the current service robots that patrol hospital floors by following a white or magnetic strip.

Careful engineering can result in good performance, but it has obvious drawbacks. First, adding sophisticated sensors to a robot may enormously increase its cost and fragility; domestic or service robots are expected to use cheap and "easy" sensors (typically, sonar sensors). Second, having to modify the environment is usually undesirable, as it increases the costs and reduces the autonomy of the robot: we do not want an autonomous wheelchair to be restricted to move in selected streets and buildings. Third, sometimes engineering the environment is just impossible: think of a rescue robot going to a disaster area. Fourth, relying on such engineering may reduce the robustness of the robot; for instance, robots that follow a white strip tend to get hopelessly lost if a long portion of the strip is obscured. Finally, and perhaps most importantly, not all sources of uncertainty can be eliminated in this way, and some uncertainty is inherent to the nature of the environment: the actions of humans and the variability of the lighting conditions are typical examples of this.

If we want to build easily available robots that inhabit our homes, offices, or factory floors, we should accept the idea that the platform cannot be overly sophisticated, and that the environment should not be modified. Hence, we should strive to build robust control programs that reliably perform complex tasks in spite of the environmental uncertainties.

A strategy that has been widely employed in the robotics literature has been to abandon the idea to completely model the environment at the design phase, and endow the robot with the capability of building or updating the model on-line. This strategy led to the so-called *hierarchical* architectures, sketched in Figure 2. The robot uses exteroceptive sensors to acquire a model of the environment as it is at the moment when the task must be performed.[2] From this model, a planning program builds a plan that will perform the given task in the given environment. This plan is then passed to a lower-level control program for execution. Typically, execution proceeds "blindly" — the controller may use a model of the robot and monitor the state of the robot's effectors (proprioception), but it does not try to sense or model the environment anymore. In a sense, the hierarchical approach factors the environment out of the controlled system, thus

---

[2] Exteroceptive sensors, like a camera or a sonar sensor, observe the state of the environment; proprioceptive sensors, like a compass or shaft encoders on the wheels, observe the state of the robot's body. Although exteroceptive sensors are usually mounted on the robot, we prefer to draw them as a separate entity to emphasize the difference between exteroceptive and proprioceptive information.

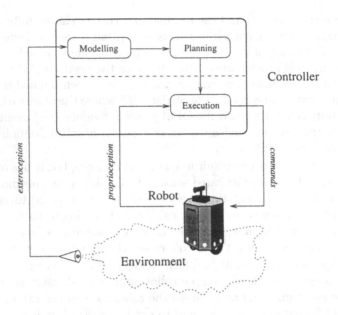

Fig. 2. Hierarchical architecture. The high-level layer builds a model of the environment and generates a plan for action. The low-level blindly executes this plan.

making the control problem tractable. This approach has been extensively used in the robotics literature; in most cases, the plan consists of a path leading to a goal position, and execution consists in tracking this path.

It is not difficult to see the limitations of the hierarchical approach when dealing with real-world environments. The model acquired by the robot is necessarily incomplete and inexact, due to the uncertainty in perception. Moreover, this model is likely to rapidly become out of date in a dynamic environment, and the plan built from this model will then turn out to be inadequate to the situation actually encountered during execution. The fact that the modeling and planning processes are usually complex and time consuming exacerbates this problem. Intuitively, the feedback loop with the environment must pass through all these processes — for this reason, this approach is also known as the "Sense-Model-Plan-Act", or SMPA approach. The complexity of the processes in the SMPA loop makes the response time of the robotic system far too long for dynamic environments (of the order of seconds).

By the mid-eighties technological improvements had caused the cost of mobile platforms and sensors to drop, and mobile robots began to appear in several AI research labs. Research on autonomous navigation was strongly pushed, and a number of new architectures were developed that tried to integrate perception and action more tightly. The general feeling was that planning should make as few assumptions as possible about the environment actually encountered during execution; and that execution should be sensitive to the environment, and adapt

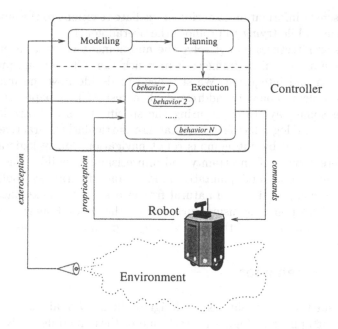

Fig. 3. Hybrid architecture. The lower layer uses perception to dynamically adapt plan execution to the environmental contingencies. Complexity in this layer is managed by a *divide et impera* strategy.

to the contingencies encountered. To achieve this, perceptual data has to be included into the executive layer, as shown in Figure 3 (we'll see the meaning of the "behavior" modules in a moment). Architectures of this type are often called *hybrid* because they combine ideas from hierarchical architectures and from behavior-based architectures [5].

Although a seemingly simple extension, the inclusion of perceptual data in the execution layer has two important consequences. First, it makes robot's interaction with the environment much tighter, as the environment is now included in a closed-loop with the (usually fast) execution layer. Second, the complexity of the execution layer has to be greatly increased, as it now needs to consider multiple objectives: pursuing the tactical goals coming from the planner; and reacting to the environmental events detected by perception.

Following the seminal works by Brooks [5], Payton [31] and Arkin [1], most researchers have chosen to cope with this complexity by a *divide et impera* strategy: the execution layer is decomposed into small independent decision-making processes, or *behaviors*, as shown in Figure 3. Other decompositions of the execution layer are possible: for example, in Khatib's proposal [32], an "elastic" path given by the planner is first modified to avoid collisions with sensed obstacles, and then it is given to a path tracking process. In all cases, the execution layer uses local sensor information to decide immediate reactions to the environmental contingencies, while trying to promote the overall goals.

Hybrid architectures do not solve the autonomous navigation problem, but they provide a convenient framework in which the different sub-problems can be dealt with and integrated. We still need to decide how the uncertainty in each sub-problem should be addressed. The rest of this paper is devoted to illustrating some ways to do so using the specific tools of fuzzy logic. As we shall show, fuzzy logic has features that are particularly attractive in light of the problems posed by autonomous robot navigation. Fuzzy logic allows us to model different types of uncertainty and imprecision; to build robust controllers starting from heuristic and qualitative models; and integrate symbolic reasoning and numeric computation in a natural framework. In the next pages, we shall illustrated these points by using our work on the robot Flakey as a test case. (See [40] for an overview of the uses of fuzzy logic in autonomous robotics.)

3 Robust behavior

The first issue that we consider is the design of the individual behavior-producing modules that appear in Figure 3. Each one of these modules fully implements a control policy for one specific sub-task, or behavior, like following a path, avoiding sensed obstacles, or crossing a door.

Fuzzy control is credited with being an adequate methodology for designing robust controllers that are able to deliver a satisfactory performance in face of large amounts of noise in the input and of variability in the parameters. The key to this robustness is to be found in the interpolation mechanism implemented by fuzzy controllers, which embodies the idea that similar inputs should produce similar actions. In addition to this, the rule format and the use of linguistic variables make fuzzy control an adequate design tool for non-linear systems for which a precise mathematical model cannot be easily obtained, but for which heuristic control knowledge is available. Finally, fuzzy controllers lend themselves to efficient implementations, including hardware solutions. (See, for instance, [18, 22] for a reminder of the basic principles of fuzzy control.)

These characteristics fit well the needs of autonomous robotics, where: (i) a mathematical model of the environment is usually not available; (ii) sensor data is uncertain and imprecise; and (iii) real-time operation is of essence. It is no surprise, then, if fuzzy control has since long attracted the attention of robot developers, and it represents today the most common application of fuzzy logic in the robotics domain. Notable examples include the early fuzzy controller developed in 1985 by Sugeno and Nishida to drive a model car along a track [43]; and the more recent behavior-based fuzzy controllers included in the award-winning robots Flakey [6], Marge [30], and Moria [44]. In the rest of this section, we detail our use of fuzzy control to implement basic behaviors in Flakey. (See [37, 39] for a more complete treatment.)

In our approach, we express desirable behavioral traits as quantitative *preferences*, defined over the set of possible control actions, from the perspective of the goal associated with that behavior. Following the formal semantic characterization of Ruspini [33, 34], we describe each behavior B in terms of a desirability function

$$Des_B : State \times Control \rightarrow [0, 1],$$

where $State$ is the internal state of the robot, including variables that represent relevant quantities in the environment or internal reference points, and $Control$ is the set of possible robot's actions. For each state x and control c, the value of $Des_B(x, c)$ measures the desirability of applying the control c when the state is x *from the point of view of attaining the goal associated with B*. For example, if the value of the state suggest that there is an obstacle on the left of the robot, then right turning control actions will have higher desirability than left turning ones from the point of view of an obstacle avoidance behavior.

A desirability function is given in the form of a set R of fuzzy rules

$$\text{IF } A_i \text{ THEN } C_i, \quad i = 1, \ldots, n,$$

where A_i is a propositional formula in fuzzy logic whose truth value depends on the state, and C_i is a fuzzy set of control values. For each possible control value c, $C_i(c)$ quantifies the extent by which c is a good instance of C_i. From these fuzzy rules, a desirability function Des_R is computed by

$$Des_R(x, c) = [A_1(x) \wedge C_1(c)] \vee \cdots \vee [A_n(x) \wedge C_n(c)], \tag{2}$$

where $\wedge$ and $\vee$ denote fuzzy conjunction and disjunction, respectively (these are min and max in our current implementation, but can be any t-norm / t-conorm pair in the general case). Intuitively, this equation characterizes a control c as being desirable in the state x, if there is some rule in R that supports c and whose antecedent is true in x. This interpretation of a fuzzy rule set is that of a classical (Mamdani type) fuzzy controller [22], generalized so as to allow each antecedent A_i to be an arbitrary fuzzy-logic formula.

```
IF (lane-too-right ∧ ¬lane-angled-left) THEN turn-medium-right
IF (lane-too-left ∧ ¬lane-angled-right) THEN turn-medium-left
IF (lane-angled-right ∧ ¬centerline-on-left) THEN turn-smooth-right
IF (lane-angled-left ∧ ¬centerline-on-right) THEN turn-smooth-left
```

Fig. 4. Fuzzy control rules for the FOLLOW behavior.

Figure 4 shows a set of rules that implement the FOLLOW behavior. This behavior is intended to make the robot proceed along the mid-line of a given lane; it can be used to go down a corridor, of drive on a road. The fuzzy predicates used in the rule antecedents depend on the the current position of the lane with respect to the robot. The consequents of the rules are triangular fuzzy subsets of the space of possible steering (and, in general, velocity) commands.

A desirability function specifies, for each input variable value, a ranking over possible controls rather than a unique control value to apply in that situation. The robot eventually employs this ranking to *choose* one specific control $\hat{c}$ that is sent to the controlled system. A possible mechanism to accomplish that selection is centroid defuzzification:

$$\hat{c} = \frac{\int c \, Des_R(x, c) \, dc}{\int Des_R(x, c) \, dc}, \tag{3}$$

which computes the mean of possible control values, weighted by their degree of desirability. Centroid defuzzification has been found satisfactory in our experiments whenever the rules in a rule set do not suggest dramatically opposite actions. In these cases, centroid defuzzification obviously does not work as averaging of such multi-modal desirability measures might result in selection of a very undesirable choice (e.g., the best trade-off between avoiding an oncoming train by jumping to the left or to the right is hardly to stay on the track!). Our empirical strategy has been to design the rule sets so as to avoid production of multi-modal desirability functions — roughly, we insist that rules that propose opposite controls have mutually exclusive antecedents, so that only unimodal fuzzy sets are produced for every input. Other authors [47] have relied, however, on alternative defuzzification functions.

Up to this point, we have been a little vague on the content of the robot's internal state. In general, the state will contain variables holding the reference values for the controller, related to the behavior's goal. For example, in the FOLLOW behavior above, the state contains the current position of the lane to follow. For a path-tracking behavior, it may contain a representation of the path, or a set of way-points to achieve.

As we have discussed in the previous section, behaviors that rely on pre-computed paths can be ineffective in real-world dynamic environments, as the environment actually encountered during execution may differ significantly from the model used in the planning phase. For this reason, most behaviors in current autonomous robots are sensor-based: the controller takes as input data from the (exteroceptive) sensors, rather than an internal reference, thus moving the robot with respect to the perceived features in the environment. Typical examples include moving along a wall or a contour, reaching a light source or a beacon, and avoiding obstacles. Sensor-based behaviors can be more tolerant to uncertainty, in that they consider the environment as it is during actual execution.

One way to implement sensor-based behaviors is to include data from the sensors in the internal state, and to use these data as input to the controller. For example, to go down a corridor, we could use the sonar sensors to keep sensor contact with the corridor's walls. In our approach, we take a slightly more involved route: we use sensor data to update variables in the state that are related to the goal of the behavior, and then use these variables in the antecedents of the fuzzy rules.

More precisely, each goal-directed behavior in Flakey maintains in the state a *descriptor* of the object relevant to that behavior. For example, the FOLLOW behavior maintains a descriptor of the lane to follow, and uses the rules in Figure 4 with respect to it. An explicit procedure, called *anchoring* [35], is employed to maintain the correspondence between descriptors and environmental features detected by the sensors. Which features should be used for anchoring depends on the specific instance of the behavior. For example, to go down a given corridor, we use the FOLLOW behavior and anchor the lane to the walls of that corridor.

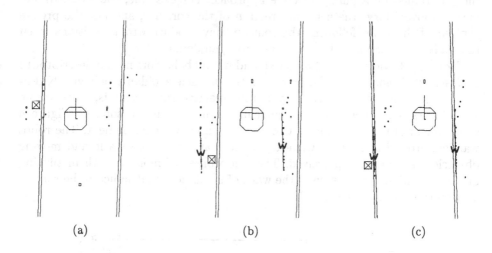

(a)   (b)   (c)

Fig. 5. Anchoring a corridor descriptor to sensor readings during corridor following; (a) the descriptor is used as a starting assumption; (b) the walls are detected; (c) the descriptor is updated.

Figure 5 shows an example of this. Initially (a), the robot is given a descriptor, produced from prior map information, of a corridor to follow (double lines), and FOLLOW operates with respect to this descriptor. After a while (b), enough sonar readings, marked by the small dots in the figure, are gathered to allow the perceptual routines to recognize the existence of two parallel walls, marked by "W." In this example, the descriptor does not match precisely the position of the real corridor: this may be due to errors in the robot's estimate of its own location, or to inaccuracies in the map. Finally (c), the perceived position of the walls is used to update the descriptor — i.e., the descriptor is *anchored* to the sensor data. As the rules of FOLLOW are based on the properties of the descriptor, anchoring implies that the robot will now follow the actual corridor. The corridor descriptor is normally re-anchored at each control cycle whenever the walls are visible. Note that the ability to recover from vague or imprecise assumptions originating from inexact prior knowledge is particularly important in practice, since our maps typically contain only approximate metric information (see Section 5 below).

Descriptors serve several functions. First, they allow us to give a behavior an explicit *goal* by initializing its descriptor using the relevant data (e.g., the position of a specific corridor to follow). Second, descriptors act as sources of credible *assumptions* when perceptual data is not available, as is the case when first engaging a new corridor, or when the walls are momentarily occluded by obstacles. Third, they allow us to *decouple* the problem of control from the problem of interpreting noisy data; the latter problem is confined to the anchoring process. Finally, the use of descriptors results in more *abstract* behaviors than those obtained by a purely reactive approach. For example, the FOLLOW behavior above follows the general direction of the corridor, and not the precise contour of the walls; following the contour may produce wrong decisions when the walls are interrupted by obstacles and open doors.

Not all behaviors are goal-directed, and not all behaviors need a descriptor to represent their goal object. For example, the obstacle avoidance behavior KEEP-OFF is implemented in Flakey by purely reactive rules, that is, rules whose antecedents only depend on the current readings from the sonars.[3] Figure 6 shows a run of this behavior in a completely unknown environment. The robot wanders around at random while trying to stay away from static and moving obstacles as they were perceived. The smoothness of motion, both in turning and acceleration, can be seen in the wake of small dots that indicate the robot's trajectory (one dot per second).

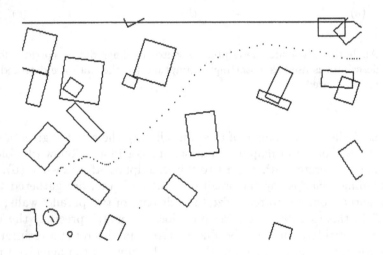

Fig. 6. A run of the obstacle avoidance behavior in an unknown environment.

In our experience, fuzzy behaviors are generally easy to write and to debug, and they perform well in face of uncertainty. We have written a dozen behaviors for Flakey, including behaviors for avoiding obstacles, for facing a given object,

---

[3] This is not entirely true, as KEEP-OFF also uses the last 50 readings in order to improve sonar coverage; this however does not change the essentially reactive nature of the behavior.

for crossing a door, and reaching a near location, and so on. Each behavior typically consists of four to eight rules involving up to a dozen fuzzy predicates. The main difficulty that we have encountered is that the debugging and tuning of the behaviors must be done by trials and errors — this is the price to pay for not using a mathematical model of the controlled system. Although writing most behaviors was very easy, some comparatively complex behavior, like KEEP-OFF, required extensive fine-tuning. In future, we may consider the use of learning techniques (e.g., [4, 14, 25]).

4   Flexible task execution

A behavior is a small unit of control aimed at achieving one simple goal in a restricted set of situations. Autonomous robots need to perform complex tasks, usually requiring the activation and cooperation of a number of behaviors. In this section, we focus on the problem of how to organize and coordinate the execution of basic behaviors in order to perform a given complex task. With respect to Figure 3 above, this means that we focus on the link between the behavior-based execution at the lower level, and the goal-oriented planning activity at the higher level. The simplest example is the coordination of an obstacle avoidance behavior and a target reaching behavior to achieve the goal of safely reaching a given position in the presence of unexpected or moving obstacles.

Since the first appearance of behavior-based approaches in the mid-eighties, authors have noticed the importance of the problem of behavior coordination. Many proposals are based on a simple on-off *switching* scheme: in each situation, one behavior is selected for execution and is given complete control of (some of the) effectors [5, 8, 10, 29, 31]. Unfortunately, this simple scheme may be inadequate in situations where several criteria should be simultaneously taken into account. To see why, consider a robot that encounters an unexpected obstacle while following a path, and suppose that it has the option to go around the obstacle from the left or from the right. This choice may be indifferent to the obstacle avoidance behavior. However, from the point of view of the path-following behavior, one choice might be dramatically better than the other. In most implementations, the obstacle avoidance behavior could not know about this, and would take an arbitrary decision.

To overcome this limitation, several researchers have proposed coordination schemes that allow the parallel execution of different behaviors, and perform a weighted combination of the commands they issue. These schemes bring about the important issue of how to resolve conflicts between the outputs of different concurrent behaviors. Consider the case where several behaviors are simultaneously active. Ideally, we would like the robot to select the controls that best satisfy all the active behaviors. This may not be possible, though, if some behaviors suggest different actions. In the rest of this section, we show how behavior coordination can be obtained by *context-dependent blending* (CDB), the behavior coordination technique that we have implemented in Flakey.

The key observation to CDB is that behaviors are not equally applicable to all situations: for instance, corridor following is most applicable when we are in a corridor and the path is clear, while obstacle avoidance is more applicable when there is an obstacle on the way. Correspondingly, we associate to each behavior a *context* of applicability, expressed by a formula in fuzzy logic. Given a set $\mathcal{B} = \{B_1, \ldots, B_k\}$ of behaviors, we denote by Cxt_i the formula representing the context of B_i. We then define the *context-dependent blending* of the behaviors in $\mathcal{B}$ to be the composite behavior described by the following desirability function:

$$Des_B(s,c) = (Cxt_1(s,c) \wedge Des_1(s)) \vee \cdots \vee (Cxt_k(s,c) \wedge Des_k(s)). \qquad (4)$$

Intuitively, the composite desirability function is obtained by merging the individual recommendations from all the behaviors, each one discounted by the truth value of the corresponding context in the current state.

Equation (4) extends (2) to the meta-level, by merging the outputs of a set of behaviors rather than those of a set of control rules. Correspondingly, context-dependent blending may be expressed by a set of fuzzy meta-rules (or "context-rules") of the form

$$\text{IF } Cxt_j \text{ THEN } B_j, \qquad j = 1, \ldots, m, \qquad (5)$$

where Cxt_j is a formula in fuzzy-logic describing a context, and B_j is a behavior.[4] A set of context-rules of this type can be evaluated to produce a combined desirability function using (4). This desirability function can then be defuzzified by (3) to produce a crisp control. This way to realize context-dependent blending corresponds to using a hierarchical fuzzy controller, as schematized in Figure 7. This is how CDB has been implemented in Flakey.

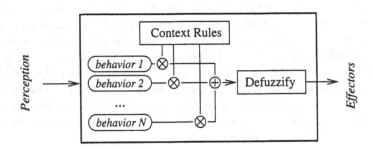

Fig. 7. A hierarchical fuzzy controller that implements Context-Dependent Blending.

A few observations should be made on Figure 7. First, it is essential that the defuzzification step be performed *after* the combination: the decision taken

---

[4] The hierarchical structure is reminiscent of the one previously proposed by Berenji et al. [2]. Context-dependent blending generalizes and extends that proposal by allowing dynamic modification of the degrees of importance of each goal.

from the collective preference can be different from the result of combining the decisions taken from the individual preferences [36]. Second, although in Figure 7 all the context-rules are grouped in one module, the same effect can be obtained by including each context-rule inside the corresponding behavior; this solution would be more amenable to a distributed implementation. Third, CDB can be iterated: we can use the structure in Figure 7 to implement each individual behavior, and combine several such (complex) behaviors using a second layer of context-rules; and so on. (Defuzzification should still be the last step.)

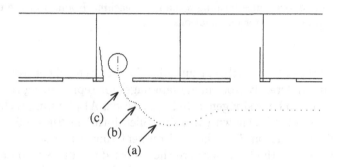

Fig. 8. Context-Dependent Blending of behaviors can compensate for inexact prior knowledge: (a) the CROSS behavior uses a wrong estimate of the door position; (b) KEEP-OFF intervenes to avoid a collision; (c) by blending both behaviors, the robot safely passes through the opening.

The CDB mechanism can be used to combine reactive and goal-directed behaviors. For example, the following context rules determine the blending between the obstacle avoidance behavior KEEP-OFF, and a behavior CROSS for passing through a doorway.

IF obstacle-close THEN KEEP-OFF
IF near-door ∧ ¬(obstacle-close) THEN CROSS

An interesting outcome of this type of combination is an increased tolerance to imprecision in the prior knowledge. Figure 8 illustrates this point. In (a), the CROSS behavior is relying on the estimated position of the door to cross based on map information. This estimate turns out to be off by some 40 centimeters, and the robot is grossly misheaded. In (b), the edge of the door has been detected as a close obstacle, and the preferences of KEEP-OFF begin to dominate, thus causing the robot to slow down and re-orient toward the free space corresponding to the door opening. Later (c), both behaviors cooperate to lead the robot though the office door — i.e., through the sensed opening that is more or less at the assumed position. During these maneuvers, the preferences of both behaviors are considered, through (4), and contribute to the control choices.

Context-dependent blending can also be used to execute full plans. In [36] we have proposed to represent plans as sets of *situation→action* rules of the form

Context	Behavior
obstacle	KEEP-OFF(OG)
¬obstacle ∧ at(Corr-2) ∧ ¬at(Corr-1)	FOLLOW(Corr-2)
¬obstacle ∧ at(Corr-1) ∧ ¬near(Door-5)	FOLLOW(Corr-1)
¬obstacle ∧ near(Door-5) ∧ anchored(Door-5)	CROSS(Door-5)
¬anchored(Corr-2)	SENSE(Corr-2)
¬anchored(Corr-1)	SENSE(Corr-1)
¬anchored(Door-5)	FIND(Door-5)

Fig. 9. A set of context rules forming a plan for reaching Room-5 in the environment of Figure 10 (see the text for explanations).

(5). These rules can be directly executed by the hierarchical controller above; interestingly, and differently from many languages for representing reactive plans, these rules can also be easily generated by classical AI planning techniques. For example, the set of rules shown (in a simplified form) in Figure 9 constitutes a plan to navigate to Room-5 in the environment shown in Figure 10 (top). The arguments passed to the behaviors are the object descriptors to be used to control motion ("OG" denotes the occupancy grid built from the sensor readings and used for obstacle avoidance). This plan has been generated by a simple goal regression planner from a topological map of the environment, and from a description (provided by the behavior designer) of the preconditions and effects of the basic behaviors available to the robot.[5] In this experiment, the map does not contain the position of Door-5, but states that it is the only doorway in Corr-1. Hence, the plan includes the behavior FIND, aimed at detecting the door; it also includes two more perception-oriented behaviors, called SENSE, whose aim is to help perception of the corridor walls when these are not anchored.

The lower part of Figure 10 shows the time evolution of the context values for the behaviors in this plan during the reported run. At (a), Flakey is in Corr-2, and FOLLOW(Corr-2) is active. As the robot approaches Corr-1 (c), the truth value of the context of FOLLOW(Corr-1) increases, and the robot smoothly turns into Corr-1 and follows it. At (g), the side sonars detect the door and Door-5 is anchored, and thus Flakey engages in the door crossing maneuvers. Notice that the perceptual behaviors become inactive once the corresponding feature has been detected and anchored (b, d, f, g), but they may come back to activity if anchoring is lost, like in (e), where a number of boxes occluded the left wall for some length. Also notice that at several occasions in the run the KEEP-OFF behavior blends in to go around unforeseen obstacles.

The above example shows that sets of fuzzy context rules can represent plans that are tolerant to uncertainty. Our plan could accommodate the extremely weak information available at planning time about the position of Door-5. The highly conditional nature of this plan also allows the robot to cope with the

---

[5] The planner uses the preconditions to build the contexts of activation. This is similar to building the triangular tables used in the robot Shakey [28].

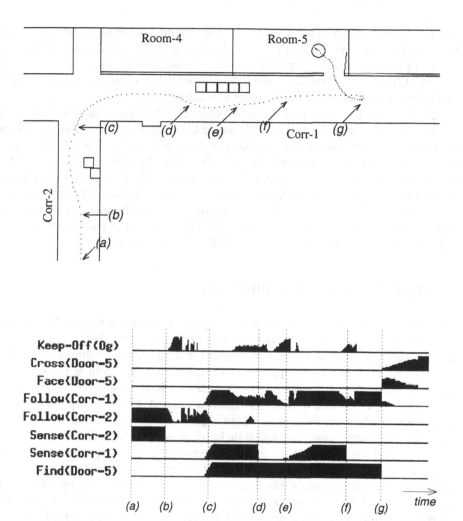

Fig. 10. A run of the plan in Figure 9 (top), and the corresponding evolution over time of the activation of the behaviors (bottom).

uncertainty in the effect of actions. For example, the effect of SENSE is to have the corridor anchored; however, this effect may be undone by later actions — like following the corridor in the area where a wall is occluded. This problem could not be detected at planning time, as the planner does not know about the obstacles in the corridor. However, the context rules just re-activate the SENSE behavior when the need to do so arises. (In this sense, our plans are similar to Schopper's universal plans [41].)

Following its implementation on Flakey [37], CDB has been used by several researchers in autonomous robotics [13, 26, 44–46]. CDB provides a flexible means to implement complex behavior coordination strategies in a modular way using a logical rule format. This modularity simplifies writing and debugging of complex behaviors: the individual behaviors and the coordination rules can be debugged and tuned separately; a few unforeseen interferences may remain, but identifying and correcting these have proved in our experience to be a much easier task than writing and debugging a complex monolitic behavior.

CDB is strictly more general than other coordination schemes commonly used in robotics. It can simulate both on-off behavior switching, and the vector summation scheme used in the popular potential field techniques [16, 20], but it differs from them in the general case. The fact that the same format is used for the control rules and the context rules has several advantages: it allows us to write increasingly complex behaviors in a hierarchical fashion; it facilitates the use of standard AI planning techniques to generate coordination strategies that achieve a given goal; and it allows us to formally analyze the resulting combined behavior. A more detailed analysis of CDB can be found in [36].

5 Approximate self-localization

The approaches that we have discussed up to here cope with uncertainty by *tolerating* it, that is, by building robust control programs that try to achieve their goals despite the presence of errors and inaccuracies in sensing and in prior knowledge. Another way to approach the uncertainty problem is by explicitly *representing* it, and by reasoning about its effects. To see the difference, consider the problem of building a robot navigation plan. A tolerant approach would generate a highly conditional plan, where a good amount of decision is postponed until the execution phase, and which includes provisions for real-time sensing in order to reactively adapt to the execution contingencies. The approach presented in the last section is an example of this. By contrast, an explicit representation approach would try to model the different sources of uncertainty, by estimating the (say) probability that an action will fail, that the position of an object will be different from what is expected, and so on; and would generate a plan that maximizes some measure of certainty of success.

One issue in robotics where an explicit representation of uncertainty is often preferred is reasoning with spatial knowledge. Spatial information about the environment can be obtained from several sources, including different types of sensors, motion history, and prior knowledge. If we have a measure of uncertainty for all items of information, then we can combine them to reduce uncertainty, for instance by synchronously fusing the data from different sensors, and/or by diachronically accumulating these data over time. The result of this process is usually to build a *map* of the environment.

Using a map brings about the important problem of *self-localization*: how to estimate of the robot's position with respect to this map. Knowing one's position is necessary to relate the perceived world to the map, and to decide which actions to perform. Self-localization can use information from the odometric sensors (e.g., wheel encoders) to update the robot's position. Unfortunately, odometry has cumulative errors, and the robot's odometric estimate of its position can

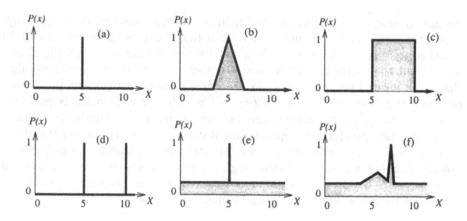

Fig. 11. Representing different types of uncertainty by fuzzy sets: (a) crisp; (b) vague; (c) imprecise; (d) ambiguous; (e) unreliable; (f) combined.

diverge from reality without bounds. Landmark-based techniques are commonly used to correct this problem [19]. A landmark can be any perceptually recognizable feature of the environment that is represented in the robot's map, like doors or walls. The robot uses the difference between the perceived and the expected locations of perceived landmark to correct the estimate of its own position.

Most existing approaches to landmark-based self-localization are based on a probabilistic representation of spatial uncertainty, and use some form of Kalman filter [15, 23, 27, 42] to update the robot's position estimate. These approaches can be very effective, provided that: (1) the underlying uncertainty can be given a probabilistic interpretation; (2) the initial estimate is good enough; and (3) the required data is available. In particular, the latter requirement means that (3a) we have an accurate dynamic model of the robot; (3b) we have an accurate stochastic model of the sensors; (3c) these systems do not change in unpredictable ways with time.

These conditions are pretty demanding, and they may easily be violated in the case of autonomous robots. In these cases, fuzzy logic may offer valuable alternatives which require less demanding assumptions: for example, fuzzy-based localization methods typically need only qualitative models of the system and of the sensors. In what follows, we illustrate this point by discussing the way we have used fuzzy logic for approximate map representation and for self-localization in Flakey (see [38] for more on this).

We represent the approximate location of an object by a fuzzy subset of a given space, read under a possibilistic interpretation [48, 49]: if P_o is a fuzzy set representing the approximate location of object o, then we read the value of $P_o(x) \in [0, 1]$ as the *degree of possibility* that o be actually located at x. This representation allows us to model different aspects of locational uncertainty. Figure 11 shows six approximate locations in one dimension: (a) is a crisp (certain) location; in (b), we know that the object is located at approximately 5 (this is commonly referred to as "vagueness"); in (c), it can possibly be located any-where between 5 and 10 ("imprecision"); in (d), it can be either at 5 or at 10 ("ambiguity"); (e) shows a case of "unreliability": we are told that the object is at 5, but the source may be wrong, and there is a small "bias" of possibility that it be located just anywhere. As an extreme case, we represent total igno-rance by the "vacuous" location $P(x) = 1$ for all x: any location is perfectly possible. Finally, (f) combines vagueness, ambiguity and unreliability. Clearly, the information provided by a measurement device can present any of the above aspects, alone or in combination. It is important to emphasize that a degree of possibility is *not* a probability value: e.g., there is no necessary relation between the observed frequency of a location and its possibility; and degrees of possibility of disjoint locations need not add up to one.

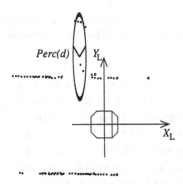

Fig. 12. The approximate location of a perceived door. The radiuses of the ellipsoid are proportional to the width of fuzzy location along the corresponding component. The "V" in the middle indicates the width of the fuzzy set of possible orientations.

We use fuzzy sets to represent the approximate position of objects in the map of the environment. More precisely, our approximate maps contain the approxi-mate positions of the major environmental features (doors, walls, corridors, ...), represented by a fuzzy point in R^3 — that is, a fuzzy subset of the set of (x, y, θ) coordinates in a global Cartesian frame, where θ is the orientation of the object measured with respect to the X axis. We also use fuzzy sets to represent the approximate position of features locally perceived by the sensors. For example, Figure 12 shows the fuzzy position $Perc(d)$ of a door d detected by the sonar sensors.[6] The shape of this fuzzy set is due to the fact that the sonar signature of a door on a side can only give a reliable indication about the position of the door along the longitudinal axis, while the distance and orientation of the

---

[6] In our current implementation, a fuzzy location is encoded by three triangular fuzzy sets representing its projections on the three axes X, Y and Θ. Future implementa-tions will use less restrictive representations.

door remains extremely vague. This set might also include a "bias" to reflect the unreliability of perceptual recognition, as in Figure 11 (e-f).

The above representation can be used by an algorithm for approximate self-localization. In [38] we have proposed a recursive algorithm of this type. Its outline is very simple. At each time-step t, the robot has an approximate hypothesis of its own location in the map, represented by a fuzzy subset H_t of the map frame. During navigation, the robot's perceptual apparatus recognizes relevant features, and searches the map for matching objects using a fuzzy measure of similarity. Each matching pair is used to build a *fuzzy localizer*: a fuzzy set representing the approximate location in the map where the robot *should be* in order to see the object where the feature has been observed. So, each localizer provides one imprecise source of information about the actual position of the robot. All these localizers, plus odometric information, are combined by fuzzy intersection to produce the new hypothesis H_{t+1}, and the cycle repeats.

Figure 13 illustrates the operation of our algorithm. Each screen-dump shows: on the left, the robot's internal view of its local workspace (details of this view are not important for the discussion here); on the right, the internal map of the environment used by the robot; this includes the robot self-location estimate H_t, represented by the ellipsoid around the robot's shape (the narrow cone in front of the robot indicates the uncertainty in orientation). In (a) the robot has some uncertainty as to its position along the X axis; however, there is little uncertainty along the Y axis and in the orientation, due to a previous matching of the corridor's walls. After a while, the sonar sensors detect a door D on the robot's right. By matching this percept to the approximate map, the robot builds the localizer loc_D shown in (b): this indicates that the robot should be located somewhere in the fuzzy set loc_D. The robot also builds the dead reckoning localizer loc_{dr} from the previous H_t using odometric information from the wheel encoders. The loc_D and the loc_{dr} localizers are then intersected to produce the new, narrower estimate H_{t+1} of the robot's position, as shown in (c).

The fuzzy self-localization algorithm above was able to keep Flakey well registered during several navigation experiments in an unstructured office environment. The algorithm was also able to produce a correct location hypothesis starting from a situation of total ignorance — a difficult task for probability-based methods. Finally, fuzzy locations can be smoothly integrated inside fuzzy-logic based controllers as the ones reported above. This is an important issue, as locational information eventually has to be used to take decisions.

6 Concluding remarks

Several factors contribute to make truly autonomous robots still a dream — although a not entirely unrealistic one. For one thing, we do not fully understand the principles that underlie intelligent agency, and the intricate relation between agents and their environments. This is a fundamental problem that has been attracting attention from philosophers and scientists for centuries. On a more practical key, autonomous robotics needs the contributions of a number of differ-

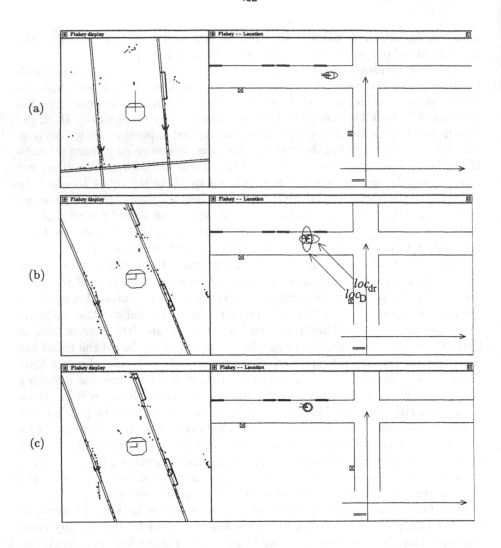

Fig. 13. Fuzzy self-localization. Left: the robot's internal view of its surroundings. Right: the robot's map of the environment, with (a) initial location hypothesis H_t; (b) dead reckoning and door localizers; (c) updated hypothesis H_{t+1}.

ent technologies developed in different fields, including artificial intelligence, control theory, vision, signal processing, mechatronics, and so on. Integrating these technologies in one system is a hard engineering problem. Finally, autonomous robots must operate in face of the large uncertainty which is inherent to the nature of real-world, unstructured environments, and to the robot-environment interaction. It is this last aspect that we have discussed in this note.

As with most problems involving uncertainty, we can take three different attitudes toward the presence of uncertainty in the robotics domain:

1. Get rid of it, by carefully engineering the robot and/or the environment;
2. Tolerate it, by writing robust programs able to operate under a wide range of situations, and to recover from errors; or
3. Reason about it, by using techniques for the representation and the manipulation of uncertain information.

Industrial robots show us that we can achieve remarkable performance taking the first attitude. If we want to build easily available robots that inhabit our homes, offices, or factory floors, though, we must live with the idea that the platform cannot be overly sophisticated, and that the environment should be only minimally modified. Then, we must consider the second or third attitudes to some extent.

By taking the tolerant attitude, we try to build control programs that provide a reasonable performance in face of large variability in the parameters of the model (due to poor prior knowledge), and large uncertainty in the state of the system (due to poor sensor data and errors in actions). We may express this by saying that these programs should rely on a weak model of the "robot + environment" system. By contrast, taking the third attitude we make the model richer, by explicitly including information about the uncertainty and variability of the parameters. The aim here is to build control programs that reason about this uncertainty in order to choose the actions that are more likely to produce the intended results.

Numerous examples of all these attitudes exist in the robotic domain, showing that often the same problem can be attacked with any one of them. It is difficult to say which uncertainty should be better eliminated by engineering the robot or the environment, and which one should be tolerated or explicitly represented. In general, there is a fundamental tradeoff between using better engineering or better programs (see [6] for an illustration of this tradeoff in the context of a robotic competition).

In this note, we have presented embodiments of the second and the third attitudes to address a few important issues in autonomous robot navigation. For the tolerant attitude, we have shown how we can implement robust behaviors that can tolerate uncertainty in sensing and action; and how we can use these behaviors to flexibly execute plans built from uncertain prior knowledge while adapting to the actual contingencies encountered. As for the representation attitude, we have shown how we can represent approximate spatial information, and reason about it in order to infer a good estimate of the robot's location. The solutions that we have presented were originally developed for the mobile robot Flakey, leading to good experimental results. These solutions have since been ported to a second robot, Edi; they have also been included in the general robot architecture Saphira [17], used on several robotic platforms. Two of these solutions are particularly novel: context-dependent blending, and fuzzy self-localization. The former is being increasingly applied in the autonomous robotics field; for the latter, some related work has been independently developed [12].

Needless to say, there are many other issues in autonomous robotics for which we need to take uncertainty into account, and which we have not touched here.

Three omitted issues are particularly worth mentioning. First, perceptual interpretation and modeling. This is a huge field in itself, including a number of subproblems like signal processing, sensor fusion, image interpretation, 3D modeling, and active perception, just to mention a few. Each subproblem is the object of a vast literature, where dealing with uncertainty often plays an important role (see, e.g., [3] for a starting point). Second, planning. Several planning techniques that explicitly take uncertainty into account have been proposed both in the robotics and the AI literature (see, e.g., [7, 21]). Third, learning. Learning techniques can cope with the uncertainty in the model of the system by giving the agent the ability to discover and adaptively modify the model by itself (whether this model is explicitly or implicitly represented is not an issue here). Machine learning techniques have been widely used in autonomous robotics: an interesting sample can be found in two recent special issues [9, 11].

Whatever the issue, the problem of uncertainty needs to be addressed by choosing one of the three attitudes above and, if we opt for an explicit approach, by choosing a specific uncertainty formalism. Although most of the literature on dealing with uncertainty in robotics is based on probabilistic techniques, solutions based on fuzzy logic are being increasingly reported (see [40] for an overview). We have hinted at a few advantages of this choice in the pages above. Still, we emphasize that the choice of the formalism to use depends on the robot-environment-task configuration: there is no "best" way to deal with uncertainty in robotics, but there are as many best ways as there are different robots, environments and tasks.

Acknowledgments

This research was partly supported by the BELON project, founded by the *Communauté Française de Belgique*. The work on Flakey was performed while the author was with the AI Center of SRI International, in strict collaboration with Enrique Ruspini, Kurt Konolige and Leonard Wesley.

References

1. R. C. Arkin. Motor schema based navigation for a mobile robot. In *Proc. of the IEEE Int. Conf. on Robotics and Automation*, pages 264–271, 1987.
2. H. Berenji, Y-Y. Chen, C-C. Lee, J-S. Jang, and S. Murugesan. A hierarchical approach to designing approximate reasoning-based controllers for dynamic physical systems. In *Proc. of the Conf. on Uncertainty in Artif. Intell.*, pages 362–369, Cambridge, MA, 1990.
3. I. Bloch. Information combination operators for data fusion: A comparative review with classification. *IEEE Trans. on Systems, Man, and Cybernetics*, A-26(1):52–67, 1996.
4. A. Bonarini and F. Basso. Learning to compose fuzzy behaviors for autonomous agents. *Int. J. of Approximate Reasoning*, 17(4):409–432, 1997.
5. R. A. Brooks. A robust layered control system for a mobile robot. *IEEE Journal of Robotics and Automation*, RA-2(1):14–23, 1986.

6. C. Congdon, M. Huber, D. Kortenkamp, K. Konolige, K. Myers, E. H. Ruspini, and A. Saffiotti. CARMEL vs. Flakey: A comparison of two winners. *AI Magazine*, 14(1):49–57, Spring 1993.

7. C. Da Costa Pereira, F. Garcia, J. Lang, and R. Martin-Clouaire. Planning with graded nondeterministic actions: a possibilistic approach. *Int. J. of Intelligent Systems*, 12:935–962, 1997.

8. M. Dorigo and M. Colombetti. *Robot shaping: an experiment in behavior engineering*. MIT Press / Bradford Books, 1997.

9. M. Dorigo (Editor). Special issue on: Learning autonomous robots. *IEEE Trans. on Systems, Man, and Cybernetics*, B-26(3), 1996.

10. J. R. Firby. An investigation into reactive planning in complex domains. In *Proc. of the AAAI Conf.*, pages 202–206. AAAI Press, Menlo Park, CA, 1987.

11. J. A. Franklin, T. M. Mitchell, and S. Thrun (Editors). Special issue on: Robot learning. *Machine Learning*, 23(2-3), 1996.

12. J. Gasós and A. Martín. Mobile robot localization using fuzzy maps. In T. Martin and A. Ralescu, editors, *Fuzzy Logic in AI — Selected papers from the IJCAI '95 Workshop*, number 1188 in Lecture Notes in AI, pages 207–224. Springer-Verlag, 1997.

13. S. G. Goodridge, M. G. Kay, and R. C. Luo. Multi-layered fuzzy behavior fusion for reactive control of an autonomous mobile robot. In *Proc. of the IEEE Int. Conf. on Fuzzy Systems*, pages 579–584, Barcelona, SP, 1997.

14. F. Hoffmann and G. Pfister. Evolutionary learning of a fuzzy control rule base for an autonomous vehicle. In *Proc. of the Conf. on Information Processing and Management of Uncertainty (IPMU)*, pages 1235–1238, Granada, SP, 1996.

15. A. H. Jazwinski. *Stochastic processes and filtering theory*. Academic Press, 1970.

16. O. Khatib. Real-time obstacle avoidance for manipulators and mobile robots. *The International Journal of Robotics Research*, 5(1):90–98, 1986.

17. K. Konolige, K.L. Myers, E.H. Ruspini, and A. Saffiotti. The Saphira architecture: A design for autonomy. *Journal of Experimental and Theoretical Artificial Intelligence*, 9(1):215–235, 1997.

18. R. Kruse, J. Gebhardt, and F. Klawonn. *Foundations of Fuzzy Systems*. Wiley and Sons, 1994.

19. B. J. Kuipers. Modeling spatial knowledge. *Cognitive Science*, 2:129–153, 1978.

20. J. C. Latombe. *Robot Motion Planning*. Kluver Academic Publishers, Boston, MA, 1991.

21. A. Lazanas and J. C. Latombe. Motion planning with uncertainty: a landmark approach. *Artificial Intelligence*, 76(1-2):285–317, 1995.

22. C. C. Lee. Fuzzy logic in control systems: fuzzy logic controller (Parts I and II). *IEEE Trans. on Systems, Man, and Cybernetics*, 20(2):404–435, 1990.

23. J. J. Leonard, H. F. Durrant-Whyte, and I. J. Cox. Dynamic map building for an autonomous mobile robot. *Int. J. of Robotics Research*, 11(4):286–298, 1992.

24. V. J. Lumelsky and R. A. Brooks. Special issue on sensor-based planning and control in robotics: Editorial. *IEEE Conference on Robotics and Automation*, 5(6):713–715, 1989.

25. M. Maeda, M. Shimakawa, and S. Murakami. Predictive fuzzy control of an autonomous mobile robot with forecast learning function. *Fuzzy Sets and Systems*, 72:51–60, 1995.

26. F. Michaud. Selecting behaviors using fuzzy logic. In *Proc. of the IEEE Int. Conf. on Fuzzy Systems*, pages 585–592, Barcelona, SP, 1997.

27. P. Moutarlier and R. Chatila. Stochastic multisensory data fusion for mobile robot location and environment modeling. In *5th Int. Symp. on Robotics Research*, pages 207–216, Tokyo, JP, 1989.

28. N. J. Nilsson. SHAKEY the robot. Technical Note 323, SRI Artificial Intelligence Center, Menlo Park, CA, 1984.

29. N. J. Nilsson. Teleo-reactive programs for agent control. *Journal of Artificial Intelligence Research*, 1:139–158, 1994.

30. I. Nourbakhsh, S. Morse, C. Becker, M. Balabanovic, E. Gat, R. Simmons, S. Goodridge, H. Potlapalli, D. Hinkle, K. Jung, and D. Van Vactor. The winning robots from the 1993 robot competition. *AI Magazine*, 14(4):51–62, Winter 1993.

31. D. W. Payton. An architecture for reflexive autonomous vehicle control. In *Proc. of the IEEE Int. Conf. on Robotics and Automation*, pages 1838–1845, San Francisco, CA, 1986.

32. S. Quinlan and O. Khatib. Elastic bands: connecting path planning and robot control. In *Procs. of the Int. Conf. on Robotics and Automation*, volume 2, pages 802–807, Atlanta, Georgia, 1993. IEEE Press.

33. E. H. Ruspini. On the semantics of fuzzy logic. *Int. J. of Approximate Reasoning*, 5:45–88, 1991.

34. E. H. Ruspini. Truth as utility: A conceptual synthesis. In *Proc. of the Conf. on Uncertainty in Artif. Intell.*, pages 316–322, Los Angeles, CA, 1991.

35. A. Saffiotti. Pick-up what? In C. Bäckström and E. Sandewall, editors, *Current Trends in AI Planning — Procs. of EWSP '93*, pages 166–177. IOS Press, Amsterdam, Nederlands, 1994.

36. A. Saffiotti, K. Konolige, and E. H. Ruspini. A multivalued-logic approach to integrating planning and control. *Artificial Intelligence*, 76(1-2):481–526, 1995.

37. A. Saffiotti, E. H. Ruspini, and K. Konolige. Blending reactivity and goal-directedness in a fuzzy controller. In *Proc. of the IEEE Int. Conf. on Fuzzy Systems*, pages 134–139, San Francisco, California, 1993. IEEE Press.

38. A. Saffiotti and L. P. Wesley. Perception-based self-localization using fuzzy locations. In L. Dorst, M. van Lambalgen, and F. Voorbraak, editors, *Reasoning with Uncertainty in Robotics*, number 1093 in LNAI, pages 368–385. Springer-Verlag, Berlin, DE, 1996.

39. A. Saffiotti (maintainer). Fuzzy logic in the autonomous mobile robot Flakey: on-line bibliography. http://aass.oru.se/People/Saffiotti/flakeybib.html. Also ftp://aass.oru.se/pub/saffiotti/robot/.

40. A. Saffiotti (maintainer). Using fuzzy logic in autonomous robotics: web resource collection. http://aass.oru.se/Events/FLAR/index.html.

41. M. J. Schoppers. Universal plans for reactive robots in unpredictable environments. In *Procs. of the Int. Joint Conf. on Artificial Intelligence*, pages 1039–1046, 1987.

42. R. C. Smith and P. Cheeseman. On the representation and estimation of spatial uncertainty. *Int. J. of Robotics Research*, 5(4):56–68, 1986.

43. M. Sugeno and M. Nishida. Fuzzy control of model car. *Fuzzy Sets and Systems*, 16:103–113, 1985.

44. H. Surmann, J. Huser, and L. Peters. A fuzzy system for indoor mobile robot navigation. In *Proc. of the IEEE Int. Conf. on Fuzzy Systems*, pages 83–86, Yokohama, JP, 1995. IEEE Press.

45. E. Tunstel, H. Danny, T. Lippincott, and M. Jamshidi. Autonomous navigation using an adaptive hierarchy of multiple fuzzy behaviors. In *Proc. of the IEEE Int. Sym. on Computational Intelligence in Robotics and Automation*, Monterey, CA, 1997.

46. C. Voudouris, P. Chernett, C. J. Wang, and V. L. Callaghan. Hierarchical behavioural control for autonomous vehicles. In A. Halme and K. Koskinen, editors, *Proc. of the 2nd IFAC Conf. on Intelligent Autonomous Vehicles*, pages 267–272, Helsinki, FI, 1995.

47. J. Yen and N. Pfluger. A fuzzy logic based robot navigation system. In *Procs. of the AAAI Fall Symposium on Mobile Robot Navigation*, pages 195–199, Boston, MA, 1992.

48. L. A. Zadeh. Fuzzy sets. *Information and Control*, 8:338–353, 1965.

49. L. A. Zadeh. Fuzzy sets as a basis for a theory of possibility. *Fuzzy Sets and Systems*, 1:3–28, 1978.

The Event Calculus Explained

Murray Shanahan

Department of Electrical and Electronic Engineering,
Imperial College,
Exhibition Road, London SW7 2BT,
England.
Email: m.shanahan@ic.ac.uk

Abstract

This article presents the event calculus, a logic-based formalism for representing actions and their effects. A circumscriptive solution to the frame problem is deployed which reduces to monotonic predicate completion. Using a number of benchmark examples from the literature, the formalism is shown to apply to a variety of domains, including those featuring actions with indirect effects, actions with non-deterministic effects, concurrent actions, and continuous change.

Introduction

Central to many complex computer programs that take decisions about how they or other agents should act is some form of representation of the effects of actions, both their own and those of other agents. To the extent that the design of such programs is to be based on sound engineering principles, rather than *ad hoc* methods, it's vital that the subject of how actions and their effects are represented has a solid theoretical basis. Hence the need for logical formalisms for representing action, which, although they may or may not be realised directly in computer programs, nevertheless offer a theoretical yardstick against which any actually deployed system of representation can be measured.

This article presents one such formalism, namely the *event calculus*. There are many others, the most prominent of which is probably the *situation calculus* [McCarthy & Hayes, 1969], and the variant of the event calculus presented here should be thought of as just one point in a space of possible action formalisms which the community has yet to fully understand.

The calculus described here is based on first-order predicate calculus, and is capable of representing a variety of phenomena, including actions with indirect effects, actions with non-deterministic effects, compound actions, concurrent actions, and continuous change. It incorporates a straightforward solution to the frame problem which is robust insofar as it works in the presence of each of these phenomena. Although this solution employs a non-monotonic formalism, namely circumscription, in most of the cases of interest here, the circumscriptions reduce to monotonic predicate completions.

The article is tutorial in form, and presents a large number of examples, illustrating how different benchmark scenarios can be represented in the event calculus. No proofs are given of the propositions asserted here, as these, or proofs of similar propositions, can be found elsewhere, mainly in [Shanahan, 1997a]. To make the presentation more digestible, three versions of the formalism, of increasing sophistication, are given in turn — the *simple* event calculus, the *full* event calculus, and the *extended* event calculus. Most of the material is drawn directly from three sources: [Shanahan, 1997a], [Shanahan, 1997b], and [Shanahan, 1999].

1 Event Calculus Basics

The event calculus was introduced by Kowalski and Sergot as a logic programming formalism for representing events and their effects, especially in database applications [Kowalski & Sergot, 1986]. Though still couched in logic programming terms, a later simplified version presented by Kowalski is closer to the one presented here [Kowalski, 1992]. A number of event calculus dialects have sprung up since Kowalski and Sergot's original paper. The one described here, which is expressed in first-order predicate calculus with circumscription, is drawn from Chapter 16 of [Shanahan, 1997a].

1.1 What the Event Calculus Does

Figure 1 summarises the way the event calculus functions. The event calculus is a logical mechanism that infers what's true when given what happens when and what actions do. The "what happens when" part is a *narrative* of events, and the "what actions do" part describes the *effects* of actions. For example, given that eating makes me happy and that I eat at 12:00, the event calculus licenses the conclusion that I'm happy at 12:05.[1]

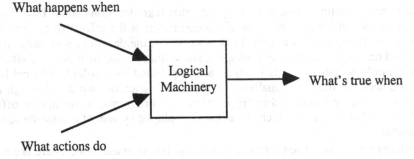

Figure 1: How the Event Calculus Functions

From Figure 1, without fleshing out the formal details, we can see how the event calculus can supply a logical foundation for a number of reasoning tasks. These can be broadly categorised into *deductive* tasks, *abductive* tasks, and *inductive* tasks. In a deductive task, "what happens when" and "what actions do" are given and "what's true when" is required. Deductive tasks include temporal *projection* or *prediction*, where the outcome of a known sequence of actions is sought.

In an abductive task, "what actions do" and "what's true when" are supplied, and "what happens when" is required. In other words, a sequence of actions is sought that leads to a given outcome. Examples of such tasks include temporal *explanation* or *postdiction*, certain kinds of *diagnosis*, and *planning*.

Finally, in an inductive task, "what's true when" and "what happens when" are supplied, but "what actions do" is required. In this case, we're seeking a set of general rules, a theory of the effects of actions, that accounts for observed data. Inductive tasks include certain kinds of *learning*, *scientific discovery*, and *theory formation*.

How can we render an informal characterisation such as that depicted in Figure 1 into something mathematically precise? A variety of design choices confronts us. To begin

---

[1] Of course, the conclusion rests on the assumption that nothing else happens between 12:00 and 12:05 to upset me. The event calculus makes such assumptions by default.

with, we have to make some meta-level decisions. What sort of logic are we going to employ? We could take the modal route, and build a new logic from scratch, defining a special language and semantics for handling actions. On the other hand, we could build on first-order predicate calculus, introducing suitable predicates and functions for representing the kind of action-related information we're interested in, and possibly presenting a set of axioms constraining the set of models we want. The event calculus adopts the latter approach.

1.2 The Ontology and Predicates of the Event Calculus

The first choice to be made in designing a first-order language for representing actions and their effects is the underlying *ontology*, that is to say the types of things over which quantification is permitted. The basic ontology of the event calculus comprises *actions* or *events* (or rather action or event *types*), *fluents* and *time points*.[2] A fluent is anything whose value is subject to change over time. This could be a quantity, such as "the temperature in the room", whose numerical value is subject to variation, or a proposition, such as "it is raining", whose truth value changes from time to time. We'll confine our attention here to propositional fluents.

Going hand in hand with the choice of ontology is the choice of basic *predicates*. In this section, we'll restrict ourselves to a simple event calculus, which has all the fundamental characteristics of the full version we'll study later but is easier to understand. Both versions of the calculus include predicates for saying what happens when, for describing the initial situation, for describing the effects of actions, and for saying what fluents hold at what times. Table 1 introduces the language elements of the simple event calculus.[3]

Formula	Meaning
Initiates(α,β,τ)	Fluent β starts to hold after action α at time τ
Terminates(α,β,τ)	Fluent β ceases to hold after action α at time τ
Initially$_P$(β)	Fluent β holds from time 0
$\tau 1 < \tau 2$	Time point $\tau 1$ is before time point $\tau 2$
Happens(α,τ)	Action α occurs at time τ
HoldsAt(β,τ)	Fluent β holds at time τ
Clipped($\tau 1,\beta,\tau 2$)	Fluent β is terminated between times $\tau 1$ and $\tau 2$

Table 1: Some Event Calculus Predicates

As this table shows, in the event calculus, fluents are *reified*. That is to say, fluents are first-class objects, which can be quantified over and can appear as the arguments to predicates. Formalisms in which fluents are unreified are, of course, possible, as we'll see later.

The commitments we've now made lead to Figure 2, which is the same as Figure 1, but made more precise using the newly introduced predicate symbols.

---

[2] I use the terms action and event interchangeably.

[3] Many-sorted predicate calculus is used throughout this article. Time points are assumed to be interpreted by the reals, and the corresponding comparative predicates and arithmetic functions are taken for granted. Predicate and function symbols always start with an upper-case letter, and variables always start with a lower-case letter.

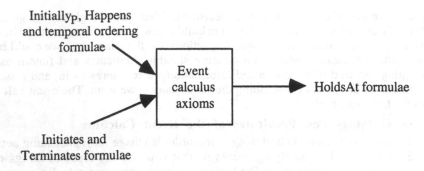

Figure 2: A More Precise Version of Figure 1

1.3 The Axioms of the Simple Event Calculus

We now require a suitable collection of axioms relating the various predicates together. The following three, whose conjunction will be denoted SC, will do the job.[4]

$$\text{HoldsAt}(f,t) \leftarrow \text{Initially}_P(f) \land \neg \text{Clipped}(0,f,t) \tag{SC1}$$

$$\text{HoldsAt}(f,t2) \leftarrow \tag{SC2}$$
$$\text{Happens}(a,t1) \land \text{Initiates}(a,f,t1) \land t1 < t2 \land \neg \text{Clipped}(t1,f,t2)$$

$$\text{Clipped}(t1,f,t2) \leftrightarrow \tag{SC3}$$
$$\exists\, a,t\ [\text{Happens}(a,t) \land t1 < t < t2 \land \text{Terminates}(a,f,t)]$$

Axiom (SC1) says that a fluent holds at a time t if it held at time 0, and hasn't been terminated between 0 and t. Axiom (SC2) says that a fluent holds at time t if it was initiated at some time before t and hasn't been terminated between then and t.

Note that, according to these axioms, *a fluent does not hold at the time of the event that initiates it but does hold at the time of the event that terminates it*. In other words, the intervals over which fluents hold are open on the left and closed on the right.

A superficial look at the logical machinery we've now assembled might be enough to convince someone that it was sufficient for its intended role. But an important issue has been neglected, namely the *frame problem*. In the next section, we'll take a look at the frame problem as it arises with the event calculus.

2 The Frame Problem in the Event Calculus

How do we use logic to represent the effects of actions, without having to explicitly represent all their non-effects? This, in a nutshell, is the frame problem. First brought to light by McCarthy and Hayes in the late Sixties [McCarthy & Hayes, 1969], it has exercised the minds of numerous AI researchers over the years. To see how it arises in the context of the event calculus, let's consider an example, namely the well-known Yale shooting scenario [Hanks & McDermott, 1987]. This will also serve to illustrate the style in which event calculus formulae are usually written.

2.1 The Yale Shooting Scenario

In this version of the Yale shooting domain there are three types of action — a Load action, a Sneeze action, and a Shoot action — and three fluents — Loaded, Alive and

---

[4] Throughout the article, variables are assumed to be universally quantified with maximum possible scope, unless otherwise indicated.

Dead. The effect of a Load action is to make Loaded hold, a Shoot action makes Dead hold and Alive not hold so long as Loaded holds at the time, and a Sneeze action has no effects. The following three Initiates and Terminates formulae describe these effects.

Initiates(Load,Loaded,t) (Y1.1)

Initiates(Shoot,Dead,t) ← HoldsAt(Loaded,t) (Y1.2)

Terminates(Shoot,Alive,t) ← HoldsAt(Loaded,t) (Y1.3)

The Yale shooting scenario comprises a Load action followed by a Sneeze action followed by a Shoot action. Using some arbitrarily chosen time point constant symbols, this can be represented by the following Happens and temporal ordering formulae.

Initially$_P$(Alive) (Y2.1)

Happens(Load,T1) (Y2.2)

Happens(Sneeze,T2) (Y2.3)

Happens(Shoot,T3) (Y2.4)

T1 < T2 (Y2.5)

T2 < T3 (Y2.6)

T3 < T4 (Y2.7)

Now let Σ be the conjunction of (Y1.1) to (Y1.3), and let Δ be the conjunction of (Y2.1) to (Y2.7). The intention is that we should have,

$\Sigma \wedge \Delta \wedge SC \vDash$ HoldsAt(Dead,T4).

Unfortunately this sequent is not valid. This is because we've neglected to describe explicitly the non-effects of actions. In particular, we haven't said that the Sneeze action doesn't unload the gun. So there are, for example, models of $SC \wedge \Sigma \wedge \Delta$ in which Terminates(Sneeze,Loaded,T2) is true, Holds(Alive,T4) is true, and HoldsAt(Dead,T4) is false.

In fact, there's a whole spectrum of annoying possibilities that we must rule out before we have a theory from which the intended conclusions follow. In addition to describing the non-effects of actions, we must describe the non-occurrence of actions. And, more trivially, we must include formulae that rule out the possibility that, say, the Sneeze action and the Shoot action are identical.

The first of these issues is easily dealt with. In general, when describing the effects of actions, we always need to include a set of uniqueness-of-names axioms for fluents and actions. In the present case, we have the following formulae, which use a notation taken from Baker [1991].

UNA[Load, Sneeze, Shoot] (Y3.1)

UNA[Loaded, Alive, Dead] (Y3.2)

These entail that Load ≠ Sneeze, Loaded ≠ Alive, and so on.

2.2 Using Predicate Completion

The non-effects of actions and the non-occurrence of events can be made explicit by supplying the *completions* of the Initiates, Terminates and Happens predicates. Formulae (Y1.1) and (Y1.2) are replaced by the following.

Initiates(a,f,t) ↔ (Y4.1)
[a = Load ∧ f = Loaded] ∨ [a = Shoot ∧ f = Dead ∧ HoldsAt(Loaded,t)]

Terminates(a,f,t) ↔ a = Shoot ∧ f = Dead ∧ HoldsAt(Loaded,t) (Y4.2)

We retain formulae (Y2.1) and (Y2.5) to (Y2.7), but (Y2.2) to (Y2.4) are replaced by the completion of the Happens predicate.

Initially$_P$(Alive) (Y5.1)

Happens(a,t) $\leftrightarrow$ (Y5.2)
    [a = Load $\wedge$ t = T1] $\vee$ [a = Sneeze $\wedge$ t = T2] $\vee$ [a = Shoot $\wedge$ t = T3]

T1 < T2 (Y5.3)

T2 < T3 (Y5.4)

T3 < T4 (Y5.5)

Now let Ω be the conjunction of (Y3.1) and (Y3.2), let Σ be the conjunction of (Y4.1) and (Y4.2), and let Δ be the conjunction of (Y5.1) to (Y5.5). Now, as desired, we have,

$\Sigma \wedge \Delta \wedge SC \wedge \Omega \vDash$ HoldsAt(Dead,T4).

Here we have the seeds of a satisfactory solution to the frame problem. Generally, though, especially in non-trivial domains, it's highly desirable to have some logical mechanism that *automatically* constructs the completions of the Initiates, Terminates and Happens predicates from individual clauses like those in (Y1.1) to (Y1.3) and (Y2.2) to (Y2.4). As well as being notationally more convenient, this allows a theory to be constructed in a more modular fashion. It also makes our theories more *elaboration tolerant* [McCarthy, 1988], in the sense that new actions, new fluents, new effects of actions, and new event occurrences can easily be accommodated by an extant theory.

The usual way to address this issue is to adopt some form of *non-monotonic* formalism, such as *default logic* [Reiter, 1980], or *circumscription* [McCarthy, 1980] to formalise the *common sense law of inertia*, whereby a fluent is assumed to persist unless there is reason to believe otherwise. In doing so, care must be taken to avoid the so-called *Hanks-McDermott problem*, which arises when a formalisation of the common sense law of inertia admits unexpected change [Hanks & McDermott, 1987].

Although the Hanks-McDermott problem dominated research on reasoning about action for some years, there's no need to investigate it too closely here. (For a detailed discussion, see [Shanahan, 1997a].) This is because, in the context of the event calculus, a simple approach suffices to construct the predicate completions of Initiates, Terminates and Happens, and avoids the Hanks-McDermott problem altogether.

2.3 A Circumscriptive Solution to the Frame Problem

This simple approach is based on circumscription [McCarthy, 1980]. The idea of circumscription is to minimise the extensions of certain named predicates. That is to say, the circumscription of a formula Φ yields a theory in which these predicates have the smallest extension allowable according to Φ. The circumscription of Φ minimising the predicate ρ is written,

CIRC[Φ ; ρ].

This is equivalent to the following second-order formula.

$\Phi \wedge \neg \exists q [\Phi(q) \wedge q < \rho]$

where,

- $q = \rho$ means $\forall \bar{x} [q(\bar{x}) \leftrightarrow \rho(\bar{x})]$,
- $q \leq \rho$ means $\forall \bar{x} [q(\bar{x}) \rightarrow \rho(\bar{x})]$,
- $q < \rho$ means $[q \leq \rho] \wedge \neg [q = \rho]$, and
- $\Phi(q)$ is the formula obtained by replacing all occurrences of ρ in Φ by q.

However, there's no need to understand this formula here. For the interested reader, a detailed discussion of circumscription can be found in [Lifschitz, 1994], and an extensive history of its application to the frame problem is presented in [Shanahan, 1997a].

This definition is straightforwardly extended to cover the minimisation of multiple predicates. (For the actual definition, see either of the works just cited). The circumscription of Φ minimising a tuple of predicates $\rho*$ is written,

CIRC[Φ ; $\rho*$].

Now let's return to the event calculus. Given,

- a conjunction Σ of Initiates and Terminates formulae,
- a conjunction Δ of Initially$_P$, Happens and temporal ordering formulae, and
- a conjunction Ω of uniqueness-of-names axioms for actions and fluents,

we're interested in,

CIRC[Σ ; Initiates, Terminates] $\wedge$ CIRC[Δ ; Happens] $\wedge$ SC $\wedge$ Ω.

The minimisation of Initiates and Terminates corresponds to the default assumption that actions have no unexpected effects, and the minimisation of Happens corresponds to the default assumption that there are no unexpected event occurrences. The key to this solution to the frame problem is the splitting of the theory into different parts, which are circumscribed separately. This technique is also employed in [Crawford & Etherington, 1992], [Doherty, 1994], [Kartha & Lifschitz, 1995], and [Lin, 1995], and is akin to what Sandewall calls *filtering* [Sandewall, 1994].

In most of the cases we're interested in here, Σ and Δ will be conjunctions of Horn clauses, and, according to a theorem of Lifschitz [1994], the separate circumscriptions therefore reduce to predicate completions. While we remain within the class of formulae to which Lifschitz's theorem is applicable, this solution is effectively monotonic, and can be likened to the frame problem solution proposed by Reiter [1991] based on the work of Haas [1987] and Schubert [1990].

We can now use the original, uncompleted formulae to formalise the Yale shooting scenario and, in the context of circumscription, we get the desired results. Let Σ be the conjunction of (Y1.1) to (Y1.3), and let Δ be the conjunction of (Y2.1) to (Y2.7). We have,

CIRC[Σ ; Initiates, Terminates] $\wedge$
   CIRC[Δ ; Happens] $\wedge$ SC $\wedge$ Ω $\models$ HoldsAt(Dead,T4).

This is because (Y4.1) and (Y4.2) follow from CIRC[Σ ; Initiates, Terminates], and (Y5.2) follows from CIRC[Δ ; Happens].

3 The Full Event Calculus

The event calculus of Section 1 is very limited in its applicability, and is only really meant to introduce the formalism's basic concepts. This section presents the full version of the formalism, which builds on the simple version of Section 1 in the following ways.

- It includes three new axioms, (EC4) to (EC6), which mirror (SC1) to (SC3), but which describe when a fluent does *not* hold. New predicates Initially$_N$ and Declipped are introduced as counterparts to Initially$_P$ and Clipped.
- It incorporates a three-argument version of Happens. This allows actions with duration, and facilitates the representation of compound actions.

- It incorporates a new predicate, Releases, which is used to disable the common sense law of inertia. This predicate was first introduced in [Kartha & Lifschitz, 1994], and is related to Sandewall's idea of *occlusion* [Sandewall, 1994].

As we'll see, the full formalism can also be used to represent domains involving actions with indirect effects and actions with non-deterministic effects.

3.1 New Predicates and New Axioms

Table 2 describes those predicates used in the full event calculus that weren't part of the simple version.

Formula	Meaning
Releases(α,β,τ)	Fluent β is not subject to inertia after action α at time τ
Initially$_N$(β)	Fluent β does not hold from time 0
Happens($\alpha,\tau1,\tau2$)	Action α occurs starts at time $\tau1$ and ends at time $\tau2$
Declipped($\tau1,\beta,\tau2$)	Fluent β is initiated between times $\tau1$ and $\tau2$

Table 2: Four New Predicates

Here is the new set of axioms, whose conjunction will be denoted EC.

$$\text{HoldsAt}(f,t) \leftarrow \text{Initially}_P(f) \wedge \neg \text{Clipped}(0,f,t) \tag{EC1}$$

$$\text{HoldsAt}(f,t3) \leftarrow \tag{EC2}$$
$$\text{Happens}(a,t1,t2) \wedge \text{Initiates}(a,f,t1) \wedge$$
$$t2 < t3 \wedge \neg \text{Clipped}(t1,f,t3)$$

$$\text{Clipped}(t1,f,t4) \leftrightarrow \tag{EC3}$$
$$\exists \, a,t2,t3 \, [\text{Happens}(a,t2,t3) \wedge t1 < t3 \wedge t2 < t4 \wedge$$
$$[\text{Terminates}(a,f,t2) \vee \text{Releases}(a,f,t2)]]$$

$$\neg \text{HoldsAt}(f,t) \leftarrow \text{Initially}_N(f) \wedge \neg \text{Declipped}(0,f,t) \tag{EC4}$$

$$\neg \text{HoldsAt}(f,t3) \leftarrow \tag{EC5}$$
$$\text{Happens}(a,t1,t2) \wedge \text{Terminates}(a,f,t1) \wedge$$
$$t2 < t3 \wedge \neg \text{Declipped}(t1,f,t3)$$

$$\text{Declipped}(t1,f,t4) \leftrightarrow \tag{EC6}$$
$$\exists \, a,t2,t3 \, [\text{Happens}(a,t2,t3) \wedge t1 < t3 \wedge t2 < t4 \wedge$$
$$[\text{Initiates}(a,f,t2) \vee \text{Releases}(a,f,t2)]]$$

$$\text{Happens}(a,t1,t2) \rightarrow t1 \leq t2 \tag{EC7}$$

The two-argument version of Happens is now defined in terms of the three-argument version, as follows.

$$\text{Happens}(a,t) \equiv_{\text{def}} \text{Happens}(a,t,t)$$

Note that if Releases is always false, then (SC1) to (SC3) follow from (EC1) to (EC7).

The frame problem is overcome in much the same way as with the simple event calculus. Given,

- a conjunction Σ of Initiates, Terminates and Releases formulae,
- a conjunction Δ of Initially$_P$, Initially$_N$, Happens and temporal ordering formulae, and
- a conjunction Ω of uniqueness-of-names axioms for actions and fluents,

we're interested in,

CIRC[Σ ; Initiates, Terminates, Releases] $\wedge$ CIRC[Δ ; Happens] $\wedge$ EC $\wedge$ Ω.

3.2 Using the Full Formalism

To see the full formalism working, let's take a look at the so-called Russian turkey shoot [Sandewall, 1991], an extension of the Yale shooting problem that includes a Spin action instead of a Sneeze, which, as in the "game" of Russian roulette may or may not result in the gun being unloaded. In addition, since we can now reason about when fluents do not hold, we only need the Alive fluent and can dispense with the fluent Dead. (This example doesn't highlight the use of the three-argument Happens predicate, whose primary application is to the representation of compound actions. These will be covered later.) Here are the effect axioms.

Initiates(Load,Loaded,t)	(R1.1)
Terminates(Shoot,Alive,t) $\leftarrow$ HoldsAt(Loaded,t)	(R1.2)
Releases(Spin,Loaded,t)	(R1.3)

Here are the formulae describing the narrative of events.

Initially$_P$(Alive)	(R2.1)
Happens(Load,T1)	(R2.2)
Happens(Spin,T2)	(R2.3)
Happens(Shoot,T3)	(R2.4)
T1 < T2	(R2.5)
T2 < T3	(R2.6)
T3 < T4	(R2.7)

Finally we have,

UNA[Load, Spin, Shoot]	(R3.1)
UNA[Loaded, Alive]	(R3.2)

Let Σ be the conjunction of (R1.1) to (R1.3), let Δ be the conjunction of (R2.1) to (R2.7), and let Ω be the conjunction of (R3.1) and (R3.2). Now, although we have,

CIRC[Σ ; Initiates, Terminates, Releases] $\wedge$
CIRC[Δ ; Happens] $\wedge$ EC $\wedge$ Ω $\vDash$ HoldsAt(Loaded,T2) $\wedge$ HoldsAt(Alive,T3)

we do *not* have either of the following.

CIRC[Σ ; Initiates, Terminates, Releases] $\wedge$
CIRC[Δ ; Happens] $\wedge$ EC $\wedge$ Ω $\vDash$ HoldsAt(Alive,T4)

CIRC[Σ ; Initiates, Terminates, Releases] $\wedge$
CIRC[Δ ; Happens] $\wedge$ EC $\wedge$ Ω $\vDash$ $\neg$ HoldsAt(Alive,T4)

This is because the Spin action has "released" the Loaded fluent from the common sense law of inertia. So in some models the gun is loaded at the time of the Shoot action, while in others it is not.

In fact, this is a somewhat flawed representation of the Russian turkey shoot scenario, since the Loaded fluent, after being released, is completely wild — the axioms permit, for example, models in which it oscillates from true to false many times between T2 and T3. A better formalisation is possible using the techniques described below for representing actions with non-deterministic effects.

3.3 State Constraints

The *ramification problem* is the frame problem for actions with indirect effects, that is to say actions with effects beyond those described explicitly by their associated effect axioms. Although it's always possible to encode these indirect effects as direct effects instead, the use of constraints describing indirect effects ensures a modular representation and can dramatically shorten an axiomatisation. One way to represent actions with indirect effects is through *state constraints*. These express logical relationships that have to hold between fluents at all times. We'll look into other aspects of the ramification problem in a later section, but for now we'll focus solely on state constraints.

In the event calculus, state constraints are HoldsAt formulae with a universally quantified time argument. Here's an example, whose intended meaning should be obvious.

$$\text{HoldsAt(Happy(x),t)} \leftrightarrow \tag{H1.1}$$
$$\neg \,\text{HoldsAt(Hungry(x),t)} \wedge \neg \,\text{HoldsAt(Cold(x),t)}$$

Note that this formula incorporates of fluents with arguments. Actions may also be parameterised, as in the following effect axioms.

$$\text{Terminates(Feed(x),Hungry(x),t)} \tag{H2.1}$$
$$\text{Terminates(Clothe(x),Cold(x),t)} \tag{H2.2}$$

Here's a narrative for this example.

$$\text{Initially}_P\text{(Hungry(Fred))} \tag{H3.1}$$
$$\text{Initially}_N\text{(Cold(Fred))} \tag{H3.2}$$
$$\text{Happens(Feed(Fred),10)} \tag{H3.3}$$

Finally we have the customary uniqueness-of-names axioms.

$$\text{UNA[Feed, Clothe]} \tag{H4.1}$$
$$\text{UNA[Hungry, Cold]} \tag{H4.2}$$

The incorporation of state constraints has negligible impact on the solution to the frame problem already presented. However, state constraints must be conjoined to the theory outside the scope of any of the circumscriptions. Given,

- a conjunction Σ of Initiates, Terminates and Releases formulae,
- a conjunction Δ of Initially$_P$, Initially$_N$, Happens and temporal ordering formulae,
- a conjunction Ψ of state constraints, and
- a conjunction Ω of uniqueness-of-names axioms for actions and fluents,

we're interested in,

$$\text{CIRC}[\Sigma \,; \text{Initiates, Terminates, Releases}] \wedge \text{CIRC}[\Delta \,; \text{Happens}] \wedge \text{EC} \wedge \Psi \wedge \Omega.$$

For the current example, if we let Σ be the conjunction of (H2.1) and (H2.2), Δ be the conjunction of (H3.1) to (H3.3), Ψ be (H1.1), and Ω be the conjunction of (H4.1) and (H4.2), we have,

$$\text{CIRC}[\Sigma \,; \text{Initiates, Terminates, Releases}] \wedge$$
$$\text{CIRC}[\Delta \,; \text{Happens}] \wedge \text{EC} \wedge \Psi \wedge \Omega \vDash \text{HoldsAt(Happy(Fred),11)}.$$

State constraints must be used with caution. As can be seen by inspection, Axioms (EC1) to (EC7) enforce the following principle: *a fluent that has been initiated/terminated directly through an effect axiom cannot then be terminated/initiated indirectly through a state constraint, unless it is released beforehand.* Similarly, a fluent that holds at time 0 because of an Initially$_P$ formula cannot then be terminated indirectly through a state constraint, unless it's released beforehand, and a fluent that does not hold at time 0 because of an Initially$_N$ formula cannot then be initiated indirectly through a state constraint, unless it's released beforehand.

Suppose, in the present example, we introduced an Upset(x) event whose effect is to terminate Happy(x). Then the addition of Happens(Upset(Fred),12) would lead to contradiction. Similarly, the addition of Initially$_N$(Happy(Fred)) would lead to contradiction.

State constraints are most useful when there is a clear division of fluents into *primitive* and *derived*. Effect axioms are used to describe the dynamics of the primitive fluents and state constraints are used to describe the derived fluents in terms of the primitive ones.

3.4 Actions with Non-Deterministic Effects

The full event calculus can also be used to represent actions with non-deterministic effects. There are several different ways to do this. Here we'll confine our attention to the method of *determining fluents*. Some discussion of other techniques can be found in [Shanahan, 1997a]. A determining fluent is one which is not subject to the common sense law of inertia, yet whose value determines whether or not some other fluent is initiated or terminated by an event.

For example, suppose we have an action Toss, which non-deterministically results in either Heads holding or Heads not holding. (Tails could be defined as not Heads, but we don't need a Tails fluent for the examples.) To formalise the Toss action, we introduce a determining fluent, ItsHeads. ItsHeads is never initiated or terminated by an event, and is therefore not subject to the common sense law of inertia. We have the following effect axioms.

$$\text{Initiates(Toss,Heads,t)} \leftarrow \text{HoldsAt(ItsHeads,t)} \tag{C1.1}$$

$$\text{Terminates(Toss,Heads,t)} \leftarrow \neg\,\text{HoldsAt(ItsHeads,t)} \tag{C1.2}$$

Now suppose a series of Toss actions is performed.

$$\text{Initially}_P\text{(Heads)} \tag{C2.1}$$

$$\text{Happens(Toss,10)} \tag{C2.2}$$

$$\text{Happens(Toss,20)} \tag{C2.3}$$

$$\text{Happens(Toss,30)} \tag{C2.4}$$

Since there's just one action, the only uniqueness-of-names axiom we need is for fluents.

$$\text{UNA[Heads, ItsHeads]} \tag{C3.1}$$

Let Σ be the conjunction of (C1.1) and (C1.2), Δ be the conjunction of (C2.1) to (C2.4), and Ω be (C3.1). Now, there are some models of,

CIRC[Σ ; Initiates, Terminates, Releases] $\wedge$ CIRC[Δ ; Happens] $\wedge$ EC $\wedge$ Ω

in which we have, for example,

HoldsAt(Heads,15) $\wedge \neg$ HoldsAt(Heads,25) $\wedge$ HoldsAt(Heads,35)

and others in which we have, for example,

$\neg$ HoldsAt(Heads,15) $\wedge$ HoldsAt(Heads,25) $\wedge \neg$ HoldsAt(Heads,35).

However, in all models, the Heads fluent retains its value from one Toss event to the next, as we would expect.

Here's a variation on this example due to Ray Reiter. Suppose we throw a coin onto a chess board. Before this action, the coin isn't touching any squares, but when it comes to rest on the chess board, it could be touching just a white square, it could be touching just a black square, or it could be touching both. This example exposes flaws in attempts to solve the frame problem which naively minimise the change brought about by an action. Such formalisms are prone to reject the possibility of the coin touching both black and white squares, as this is a non-minimal change. But the following event calculus formalisation, using the determining fluents ItsBlack and ItsWhite, works fine.

Initiates(Throw,OnWhite,t) ← HoldsAt(ItsWhite,t)   (R1.1)

Initiates(Throw,OnBlack,t) ← HoldsAt(ItsBlack,t)   (R1.2)

Initially$_N$(OnWhite)   (R2.1)

Initially$_N$(OnBlack)   (R2.2)

Happens(Throw,10)   (R2.3)

HoldsAt(ItsWhite,t) ∨ HoldsAt(ItsBlack,t)   (R3.1)

UNA[OnWhite, OnBlack, ItsWhite, ItsBlack]   (R4.1)

Let Σ be the conjunction of (R1.1) and (R1.2), Δ be the conjunction of (R2.1) to (R2.3), let Ψ be (R3.1), and Ω be (R3.1). As we would expect, in some models of,

CIRC[Σ ; Initiates, Terminates, Releases] ∧ CIRC[Δ ; Happens] ∧ EC ∧ Ψ ∧ Ω

we have, for example,

HoldsAt(OnWhite,15) ∧ ¬ HoldsAt(OnBlack,15)

while in others we have,

HoldsAt(OnWhite,15) ∧ HoldsAt(OnBlack,15).

In all models at least one of the fluents OnBlack or OnWhite holds after time 10, and in all models these fluents retain their values forever after time 10.

3.5 Compound Actions

The final topic for this section is compound actions, that is to say actions which are composed of other actions. These are particularly useful in hierarchical planning (see [Shanahan, 1997b]). Let's take a look at an example of a compound action definition describing a commuter's daily journey. Suppose we have two atomic actions: WalkTo(x) and TrainTo(x), whose effects are described by the following formulae.

Initiates(WalkTo(x),At(x),t)   (J1.1)

Terminates(WalkTo(x),At(y),t) ← HoldsAt(At(y),t) ∧ x ≠ y   (J1.2)

Initiates(TrainTo(x),At(x),t) ← HoldsAt(At(y),t) ∧ Train(y,x)   (J1.3)

Terminates(TrainTo(x),At(y),t) ← HoldsAt(At(y),t) ∧ Train(y,x)   (J1.4)

There are trains from Herne Hill to Victoria and from Victoria to South Kensington.

Train(HerneHill,Victoria)   (J1.5)

Train(Victoria,SouthKen)   (J1.6)

The following is a flawed example of a compound event definition describing a compound action, GoToWork, in terms of a sequence of WalkTo and TrainTo sub-actions.

Happens(GoToWork,t1,t4) ←
    Happens(WalkTo(HerneHill),t1) ∧ Happens(TrainTo(Victoria),t2) ∧
      Happens(TrainTo(SouthKen),t3) ∧ Happens(WalkTo(Work),t4) ∧
        t1 < t2 ∧ t2 < t3 ∧ t3 < t4

This formula is problematic for the following reason. Normally, in hierarchical planning for example, we would expect to be able to work out the effects of a compound action given the effects of its sub-actions. As it stands, this formula doesn't allow this, as it doesn't exclude the possibility that other events occur in between the sub-events mentioned in the definition, which undo the effects of those sub-events. For example, if I'm arrested at Herne Hill station and taken away by the police, then the

TrainTo(Victoria) action will be ineffective, and the GoToWork action won't have its expected outcome. Here's a modified form of the formula incorporating extra ¬ Clipped conditions that rule out intervening events.

Happens(GoToWork,t1,t4) ←   (J2.1)
    Happens(WalkTo(HerneHill),t1) ∧ Happens(TrainTo(Victoria),t2) ∧
      Happens(TrainTo(SouthKen),t3) ∧ Happens(WalkTo(Work),t4) ∧
      t1 < t2 ∧ t2 < t3 ∧ t3 < t4 ∧ ¬ Clipped(t1,At(HerneHill),t2) ∧
        ¬ Clipped(t2,At(Victoria),t3) ∧ ¬ Clipped(t3,At(SouthKen),t4)

Now, given (J1.1) to (J1.4), we can confidently write the following effect axioms.

Initiates(GoToWork,At(Work),t)   (J3.1)

Terminates(GoToWork,At(x),t) ← HoldsAt(At(x),t) ∧ x ≠ Work   (J3.2)

The only required uniqueness-of-names axiom is for actions.

UNA[WalkTo, TrainTo, GoToWork]   (J4.1)

Now consider the following narrative of actions.

Happens(WalkTo(HerneHill),10)   (J5.1)

Happens(TrainTo(Victoria),15)   (J5.2)

Happens(TrainTo(SouthKen),20)   (J5.3)

Happens(WalkTo(Work),25)   (J5.4)

Let Σ be the conjunction of (J1.1) to (J1.6) plus (J2.1). Let Δ be the conjunction of (J5.1) to (J5.4), and Ω be (J4.1). Notice that (J3.1) and (J3.2) have been omitted. We have,[5]

  CIRC[Σ ; Initiates, Terminates, Releases] ∧
    CIRC[Δ ; Happens] ∧ EC ∧ Ω ⊨ Happens(GoToWork,10,25)

and,

  CIRC[Σ ; Initiates, Terminates, Releases] ∧
    CIRC[Δ ; Happens] ∧ EC ∧ Ω ⊨ HoldsAt(At(Work),30)

The inclusion of (J3.1) and (J3.2) would yield the same logical consequences.

Although not illustrated in this small example, it's worth noting that both conditional and recursive compound action definitions are also possible. Further discussion of compound events can be found in [Shanahan, 1997b], which also includes examples featuring such standard program constructs.

4 The Ramification Problem

As already mentioned, state constraints aren't the only way to represent actions with indirect effects, and often they aren't the right way. To see this, we'll take a look at the so-called "walking turkey shoot" [Baker, 1991], a variation of the Yale shooting problem in which the Shoot action, as well as directly terminating the Alive fluent, indirectly terminates a fluent Walking. The effect axioms are inherited from the Yale shooting problem.

Initiates(Load,Loaded,t)   (W1.1)

Terminates(Shoot,Alive,t) ← HoldsAt(Loaded,t)   (W1.2)

The narrative of events is as follows.

---

[5] Examples with compound actions are among the few useful cases of event calculus formulae that don't reduce straightforwardly to predicate completion. Examples involving recursion are especially tricky.

Initiallyp(Alive)	(W2.1)
Initiallyp(Loaded)	(W2.2)
Initiallyp(Walking)	(W2.3)
Happens(Shoot,T1)	(W2.4)
T1 < T2	(W2.5)

We have two uniqueness-of-names axioms.

UNA[Load, Shoot]	(W3.1)
UNA[Loaded, Alive, Walking]	(W3.2)

Now, how do we represent the dependency between the Walking and Alive fluents so as to get the required indirect effect of a Shoot action? The obvious, but incorrect, way is to use a state constraint.

$$HoldsAt(Alive,t) \leftarrow HoldsAt(Walking,t)$$

The addition of this state constraint to the above formalisation would yield a contradiction, because it violates the rule that a fluent, in this case Walking, that holds directly through an Initiallyp formula cannot be terminated indirectly through a state constraint. (The same problem would arise if the Walking fluent had been initiated directly by an action.)

4.1 Effect Constraints

Instead, the way to represent the relationship between the Walking fluent and the Alive fluent in the walking turkey shoot is through an *effect constraint*. Effect constraints are Initiates and Terminates formulae with a single universally quantified action variable. The constraint we require for this example is the following.

$$Terminates(a,Walking,t) \leftarrow Terminates(a,Alive,t) \qquad (W4.1)$$

Notice that effect constraints are weaker than state constraints: the possibility of resurrecting a corpse by making it walk, inherent in the faulty state constraint, is not inherent in this formula.

Let Σ be the conjunction of (W1.1), (W1.2) and (W4.1). Let Δ be the conjunction of (W2.1) to (W2.5), and Ω be the conjunction of (W3.1) and (W3.2). We have,

$$CIRC[\Sigma ; Initiates, Terminates, Releases] \wedge$$
$$CIRC[\Delta ; Happens] \wedge EC \wedge \Omega \vDash \neg HoldsAt(Walking,T2).$$

Effect constraints can be used to represent a number of other standard benchmarks for the ramification problem. However, there remain certain examples for which they're unsuited, specifically those involving the instantaneous propagation of interacting indirect effects. Fortunately, these can be handled by *causal constraints*, as set out in the next section, which draws on techniques presented in [Shanahan, 1999].

4.2 Causal Constraints

The circuit of Figure 3 illustrates the instantaneous propagation of interacting indirect effects [Thielscher, 1997]. Closing switch 1 activates the relay, in turn opening switch 2, thereby preventing the light from coming on.

To represent examples like this, we introduce several new predicates. The formula Started(β,τ) means that either β already holds at τ or an event occurs at τ that initiates β. Conversely, the formula Stopped(β,τ) means that either β already does not hold at τ or an event occurs at τ that terminates β. The predicates Started and Stopped are defined by the following axioms, which will be conjoined to our theories outside the scope of any of the circumscriptions.

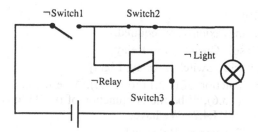

Figure 3: Thielscher's Circuit

Started(f,t) ↔   (CC1)
    HoldsAt(f,t) ∨ ∃ a [Happens(a,t) ∧ Initiates(a,f,t)]

Stopped(f,t) ↔   (CC2)
    ¬ HoldsAt(f,t) ∨ ∃ a [Happens(a,t) ∧ Terminates(a,f,t)]

The formula Initiated(β,τ) means that fluent β either already holds at τ or is about to start holding. Similarly Terminated(β,τ) represents that β either already does not hold at τ or is about to cease holding at τ. These predicates are defined as follows.

Initiated(f,t) ↔   (CC3)
    Started(f,t) ∧ ¬ ∃ a [Happens(a,t) ∧ Terminates(a,f,t)]

Terminated(f,t) ↔   (CC4)
    Stopped(f,t) ∧ ¬ ∃ a [Happens(a,t) ∧ Initiates(a,f,t)]

To represent the dependencies between the fluents in Thielscher's circuit example, we introduce three events LightOn, Open2 and CloseRelay, which are triggered under conditions described by the following formulae.

Happens(LightOn,t) ←   (L1.1)
    Stopped(Light,t) ∧ Initiated(Switch1,t) ∧ Initiated(Switch2,t)

Happens(Open2,t) ←   (L1.2)
    Started(Switch2,t) ∧ Initiated(Relay,t)

Happens(CloseRelay,t) ←   (L1.3)
    Stopped(Relay,t) ∧ Initiated(Switch1,t) ∧ Initiated(Switch3,t)

These formulae represent *causal constraints*. If a fluent is dependent on a number of other fluents, such formulae ensure that an event giving that fluent the right value is triggered whenever the fluents that influence it attain the relevant values. The effects of the new events in this example are as follows. A Close1 event is also introduced.

Initiates(LightOn,Light,t)   (L2.1)

Terminates(Open2,Switch2,t)   (L2.2)

Initiates(CloseRelay,Relay,t)   (L2.3)

Initiates(Close1,Switch1,t)   (L2.4)

The circuit's initial configuration, as shown in Figure 3, is as follows.

Initially$_N$(Switch1)   (L3.1)

Initially$_P$(Switch2)   (L3.2)

Initially$_P$(Switch3)   (L3.3)

Initially$_N$(Relay)   (L3.4)

Initially$_N$(Light)   (L3.5)

The only event that occurs is a Close1 event, at time 10.

Happens(Close1,10) (L3.6)

Two uniqueness-of-names axioms are required.

UNA[LightOn, Close1, Open2, CloseRelay] (L4.1)

UNA[Switch1, Switch2, Switch3, Relay, Light] (L4.2)

Now let Σ be the conjunction of (L2.1) to (L2.4), Δ be the conjunction of (L1.1) to (L1.3) with (L3.1) to (L3.6), Ψ be the conjunction of (CC1) to (CC4), and Ω be the conjunction of (L4.1) and (L4.2). We have,

CIRC[Σ ; Initiates, Terminates, Releases] $\wedge$
    CIRC[Δ ; Happens] $\wedge$ EC $\wedge$ Ψ $\wedge$ Ω $\vDash$
        HoldsAt(Relay,20) $\wedge$ $\neg$ HoldsAt(Switch2,20) $\wedge$ $\neg$ HoldsAt(Light,20).

In other words, this formalisation of Thielscher's circuit yields the logical consequences we require. In particular, the relay is activated when switch 1 is closed, causing switch 2 to open, and the light does not come on.

5 The Extended Event Calculus

This section shows how the full event calculus of Section 3 can be extended to represent concurrent actions and continuous change. The calculus is presented formally first, then two examples are given, one featuring concurrent action, the other featuring continuous change.

Table 3 describes those predicates used in the extended event calculus that weren't part of the full calculus of Section 3. Three new predicates are introduced. The predicates Cancels and Cancelled, as in [Gelfond, et al., 1991] and [Lin & Shoham, 1992], cater for concurrent actions that interfere with each other's effects. The Cancels predicate will be minimised via circumscription, along with Initiates, Terminates and Releases. The Trajectory predicate, first proposed in [Shanahan, 1990], is used to capture continuous change, as in the height of a falling ball or the level of liquid in a filling vessel, for example.

Formula	Meaning
Cancels(α1,α2,β)	The occurrence of α1 cancels the effect of a simultaneous occurrence of α2 on fluent β
Cancelled(α,β,τ1,τ2)	Some event occurs from time τ1 to time τ2 which cancels the effect of action α on fluent β
Trajectory(β1,τ,β2,δ)	If fluent β1 is initiated at time τ then fluent β2 becomes true at time $\tau+\delta$

Table 3: Three More New Predicates

Here is the new set of axioms, whose conjunction will be denoted XC. The first seven axioms correspond to the seven axioms of the calculus of Section 3. The only difference is the incorporation in Axioms (XC2), (XC3), (XC5) and (XC6) of $\neg$ Cancelled conditions that block the applicability of the axiom in the case of the simultaneous occurrence of events which cancel each other's effects.

HoldsAt(f,t) $\leftarrow$ Initially$_P$(f) $\wedge$ $\neg$ Clipped(0,f,t) (XC1)

HoldsAt(f,t3) $\leftarrow$ (XC2)
   Happens(a,t1,t2) $\wedge$ Initiates(a,f,t1) $\wedge$ $\neg$ Cancelled(a,f,t1,t2) $\wedge$
    t2 < t3 $\wedge$ $\neg$ Clipped(t1,f,t3)

$$\text{Clipped}(t1,f,t4) \leftrightarrow \tag{XC3}$$
$$\exists\, a,t2,t3\ [\text{Happens}(a,t2,t3) \wedge t1 < t3 \wedge t2 < t4 \wedge$$
$$[\text{Terminates}(a,f,t2) \vee \text{Releases}(a,f,t2)] \wedge$$
$$\neg\, \text{Cancelled}(a,f,t2,t3)]$$

$$\neg\, \text{HoldsAt}(f,t) \leftarrow \text{Initially}_N(f) \wedge \neg\, \text{Declipped}(0,f,t) \tag{XC4}$$

$$\neg\, \text{HoldsAt}(f,t3) \leftarrow \tag{XC5}$$
$$\text{Happens}(a,t1,t2) \wedge \text{Terminates}(a,f,t1) \wedge \neg\, \text{Cancelled}(a,f,t1,t2) \wedge$$
$$t2 < t3 \wedge \neg\, \text{Declipped}(t1,f,t3)$$

$$\text{Declipped}(t1,f,t4) \leftrightarrow \tag{XC6}$$
$$\exists\, a,t2,t3\ [\text{Happens}(a,t2,t3) \wedge t1 < t3 \wedge t2 < t4 \wedge$$
$$[\text{Initiates}(a,f,t2) \vee \text{Releases}(a,f,t2)] \wedge$$
$$\neg\, \text{Cancelled}(a,f,t2,t3)]$$

$$\text{Happens}(a,t1,t2) \rightarrow t1 \leq t2 \tag{XC7}$$

Axiom (XC8) defines the Cancelled predicate.

$$\text{Cancelled}(a1,f,t1,t2) \leftrightarrow \text{Happens}(a2,t1,t2) \wedge \text{Cancels}(a2,a1,f) \tag{XC8}$$

Axiom (XC9) is the counterpart of Axiom (XC2) for continuous change.

$$\text{HoldsAt}(f2,t3) \leftarrow \tag{XC9}$$
$$\text{Happens}(a,t1,t2) \wedge \text{Initiates}(a,f1,t1) \wedge \neg\, \text{Cancelled}(a,f,t1,t2) \wedge$$
$$t2 < t3 \wedge t3 = t2 + d \wedge \text{Trajectory}(f1,t1,f2,d) \wedge$$
$$\neg\, \text{Clipped}(t1,f1,t3)$$

As before, a two-argument Happens is defined in terms of the three-argument version.

$$\text{Happens}(a,t) \equiv_{\text{def}} \text{Happens}(a,t,t)$$

In addition to the three new predicates introduced above, the extended event calculus employs a new infix function symbol &, which will be used to express the cumulative effects of concurrent actions. The term $\alpha1 \& \alpha2$ denotes a compound action comprising the two actions $\alpha1$ and $\alpha2$. We write $\text{Happens}(\alpha1\&\alpha2,\tau1,\tau2)$ to denote that actions $\alpha1$ and $\alpha2$ occur concurrently, that is to say they both start at $\tau1$ and end at $\tau2$. The final new axiom we require defines the & symbol.

$$\text{Happens}(a1\&a2,t1,t2) \leftarrow \text{Happens}(a1,t1,t2) \wedge \text{Happens}(a2,t1,t2) \tag{CA}$$

The circumscriptive approach to the frame problem employed before extends straightforwardly to the new calculus. Since it constrains the Happens predicate, Axiom (CA) must be included inside the circumscription that minimises Happens. In general, given,

- a conjunction Σ of Initiates, Terminates, Releases, Trajectory and Cancels formulae,
- a conjunction Δ of Initially$_P$, Initially$_N$, Happens and temporal ordering formulae,
- a conjunction Ψ of state constraints, and
- a conjunction Ω of uniqueness-of-names axioms for actions and fluents,

we're interested in,

$$\text{CIRC}[\Sigma\ ;\ \text{Initiates, Terminates, Releases, Cancels}] \wedge$$
$$\text{CIRC}[\Delta \wedge (\text{CA})\ ;\ \text{Happens}] \wedge XC \wedge \Psi \wedge \Omega.$$

Ψ is omitted if there are no state constraints.

If Cancels and Trajectory are everywhere false, then Axioms (EC1) to (EC7) follow from Axioms (XC1) to (XC9). Accordingly, the examples already presented in this article to illustrate the simple event calculus and the full event calculus also work with the extended event calculus.

The next two sections comprise examples of the use of the extended event calculus to deal with concurrent action and continuous change.

5.1 Concurrent Actions

This section formalises the soup bowl scenario from [Gelfond, *et al.*, 1991]. This example features concurrent actions with both *cumulative* and *cancelling* effects. The domain comprises two actions, LiftLeft and LiftRight, which represent respectively lifting the left side of a soup bowl and lifting the right side. Two fluents are involved: Spilled and OnTable. The soup bowl is full of soup. So a LiftLeft action on its own will initiate Spilled, as will a LiftRight action on its own. Carried out together, though, these actions cancel each other's effect on the Spilled fluent. On the other hand, carried out together, a LiftLeft action and a LiftRight action have a cumulative effect, namely to raise the bowl from the table, terminating the OnTable fluent. We have the following Initiates and Terminates formulae.

Initiates(LiftLeft,Spilled,s)	(B1.1)
Initiates(LiftRight,Spilled,s)	(B1.2)
Terminates(LiftLeft&LiftRight,OnTable,s)	(B1.3)

Here are the required Cancels formulae.

Cancels(LiftLeft,LiftRight,Spilled)	(B2.1)
Cancels(LiftRight,LiftLeft,Spilled)	(B2.2)

In the initial situation, the soup bowl is on the table, and there has been no spillage. At time 10, a LiftLeft action and a LiftRight action occur simultaneously.

Initially$_P$(OnTable)	(B3.1)
Initially$_N$(Spilled)	(B3.2)
Happens(LiftLeft,10)	(B3.4)
Happens(LiftRight,10)	(B3.5)

Here are the customary uniqueness-of-names axioms.

UNA[OnTable, Spilled]	(B4.1)
UNA[LiftLeft, LiftRight]	(B4.2)

Now let Σ be the conjunction of (B1.1) to (B1.3) with (B2.1) and (B2.2), Δ be the conjunction of (B3.1) to (B3.4), and Ω be the conjunction of (B4.1) and (B4.2). We have,

CIRC[Σ ; Initiates, Terminates, Releases, Cancels] $\wedge$
 CIRC[$\Delta \wedge$ (CA) ; Happens] $\wedge$ XC $\wedge \Omega \vDash$
  $\neg$ HoldsAt(OnTable,20) $\wedge \neg$ HoldsAt(Spilled,20).

In other words, the formalisation yields the desired conclusion that the bowl is no longer on the table at time 20, but in spite of the occurrence of a LiftLeft and a LiftRight action, the soup has not been spilled.

5.2 Continuous Change

This section demonstrates how the extended calculus copes with continuous change, via an example involving a vessel that fills with water. The example also features *triggered events*, that is to say events that occur when certain fluents reach certain values. These are similar to the events that are used to represent causal constraints in Section 4.2. But in the present case, the event is triggered when a continuously varying quantity attains a particular value, specifically when the water level reaches the rim of the vessel.

The domain comprises a TapOn event, which initiates a flow of liquid into the vessel. The fluent Filling holds while water is flowing into the vessel, and the fluent Level(x) represents holds if the water is at level x in the vessel, where x is a real number. An Overflow event occurs when the water reaches the rim of the vessel at level 10. The Overflow event initiates a period during which the fluent Spilling holds. A TapOff action is also included. Here are the Initiates, Terminates and Releases formulae for the domain.

Initiates(TapOn,Filling,t)	(S1.1)
Terminates(TapOff,Filling,t)	(S1.2)
Releases(TapOn,Level(x),t)	(S1.3)
Initiates(TapOff,Level(x),t) ← HoldsAt(Level(x),t)	(S1.4)
Terminates(Overflow,Filling,t)	(S1.5)
Initiates(Overflow,Level(10),t)	(S1.6)
Initiates(Overflow,Spilling,t)	(S1.7)

Note that (S1.3) has to be a Releases formula instead of a Terminates formula, so that the Level fluent is immune from the common sense law of inertia after the tap is turned on.

Now we have the Trajectory formula, which describes the continuous variation in the Level fluent while the Filling fluent holds. The level is assumed to rise at one unit per unit of time.

Trajectory(Filling,t,Level(x2),d) ← $\qquad$ (S1.8)
$\quad$ HoldsAt(Level(x1),t) $\wedge$ x2 = x1 + d

Next we have a state constraint that ensures that the water always has a unique level.

HoldsAt(Level(x1),t) $\wedge$ HoldsAt(Level(x2),t) $\rightarrow$ x1 = x2 $\qquad$ (S2.1)

The next formulae ensures the Overflow event is triggered when it should be.

Happens(Overflow,t) ← $\qquad$ (S3.1)
$\quad$ HoldsAt(Level(10),t) $\wedge$ HoldsAt(Filling,t)

Here's a simple narrative. The level is initially 0, and the tap is turned on at time 5.

Initially$_P$(Level(0))	(S4.1)
Initially$_N$(Filling)	(S4.2)
Initially$_N$(Spilling)	(S4.3)
Happens(TapOn,5)	(S4.4)

The following uniqueness-of-names axioms are required.

UNA[TapOn, TapOff, Overflow]	(S5.1)
UNA[Filling, Level, Spilling]	(S5.2)

Let Σ be the conjunction of (S1.1) to (S1.8), Δ be the conjunction of (S4.1) to (S4.4) with (S3.1), Ψ be the (S2.1), and Ω be the conjunction of (S5.1) and (S5.2). We have,

$\quad$ CIRC[Σ ; Initiates, Terminates, Releases, Cancels] $\wedge$
$\qquad$ CIRC[$\Delta \wedge$ (CA) ; Happens] $\wedge$ XC $\wedge \Psi \wedge \Omega \vDash$
$\qquad\quad$ HoldsAt(Level(10),20) $\wedge \neg$ HoldsAt(Filling,20) $\wedge$ HoldsAt(Spilling,20).

In other words, the formalisation yields the expected result that the water stops flowing into the vessel (at time 15), when it starts spilling over the rim, and that the level is subsequently stuck at 10.

The Trajectory predicate can be used to represent a large number of problems involving continuous change. But for a more general treatment, in which arbitrary sets of differential equations can be deployed, see [Miller & Shanahan, 1996].

Concluding Remarks

The extended event calculus of the last section is a formalism for reasoning about action that incorporates a simple solution to the frame problem, and is capable of representing a diverse range of phenomena. These phenomena include,

- actions with indirect effects, including interacting indirect effects as in Thielscher's circuit example,
- actions with non-deterministic effects, including examples with non-minimal change such as Reiter's chess-board example,
- compound actions, which can include standard programming constructs such as sequence, choice and recursion,
- concurrent actions, including actions with cumulative and cancelling effects, as in the soup bowl example, and
- continuous change with triggered events, as in the filling vessel example.

Nothing has been said so far about *explanation*, that is to say reasoning from effects to causes, which is isomorphic to *planning*. The logical aspects of this topic are dealt with in Chapter 17 of [Shanahan, 1997a], where it is shown that explanation (or planning) problems can be handled via abduction. In [Shanahan, 1997b], an implementation of abductive event calculus planning is presented, which will also perform explanation. This implementation also forms the basis of a system used to control a robot [Shanahan, 1998], in which sensor data assimilation is also cast as a form of abductive reasoning with the event calculus [Shanahan, 1996].

Acknowledgments

This work was carried out as part of the EPSRC funded project GR/L20023 "Cognitive Robotics". Thanks to all those members of the reasoning about action community whose work has influenced the development of the event calculus.

References

[Baker, 1991] A.B.Baker, Nonmonotonic Reasoning in the Framework of the Situation Calculus, *Artificial Intelligence*, vol. 49 (1991), pp. 5–23.

[Crawford & Etherington, 1992] J.M.Crawford and D.W.Etherington, Formalizing Reasoning about Change: A Qualitative Reasoning Approach, *Proceedings AAAI 92*, pp. 577–583.

[Doherty, 1994] P.Doherty, Reasoning about Action and Change Using Occlusion, *Proceedings ECAI 94*, pp. 401–405.

[Gelfond, *et al.*, 1991] M.Gelfond, V.Lifschitz and A.Rabinov, What Are the Limitations of the Situation Calculus? in *Essays in Honor of Woody Bledsoe*, ed R.Boyer, Kluwer Academic (1991), pp. 167–179.

[Haas, 1987] A.R.Haas, The Case for Domain-Specific Frame Axioms, *Proceedings of the 1987 Workshop on the Frame Problem*, pp. 343–348.

[Hanks & McDermott, 1987] S.Hanks and D.McDermott, Nonmonotonic Logic and Temporal Projection, *Artificial Intelligence*, vol. 33 (1987), pp. 379–412.

[Kartha & Lifschitz, 1994] G.N.Kartha and V.Lifschitz, Actions with Indirect Effects (Preliminary Report), *Proceedings 1994 Knowledge Representation Conference (KR 94)*, pp. 341–350.

[Kartha & Lifschitz, 1995] G.N.Kartha and V.Lifschitz, A Simple Formalization of Actions Using Circumscription, *Proceedings IJCAI 95*, pp. 1970–1975.

[Kowalski, 1992] R.A.Kowalski, Database Updates in the Event Calculus, *Journal of Logic Programming*, vol. 12 (1992), pp. 121–146.

[Kowalski & Sergot, 1986] R.A.Kowalski and M.J.Sergot, A Logic-Based Calculus of Events, *New Generation Computing*, vol. 4 (1986), pp. 67–95.

[Lifschitz, 1994] V.Lifschitz, Circumscription, in *The Handbook of Logic in Artificial Intelligence and Logic Programming, Volume 3: Nonmonotonic Reasoning and Uncertain Reasoning*, ed. D.M.Gabbay, C.J.Hogger and J.A.Robinson, Oxford University Press (1994), pp. 297–352.

[Lin & Shoham, 1992] F.Lin and Y.Shoham, Concurrent Actions in the Situation Calculus, *Proceedings AAAI 92*, pp. 590–595.

[McCarthy, 1980] J.McCarthy, Circumscription — A Form of Non-Monotonic Reasoning, *Artificial Intelligence*, vol. 13 (1980), pp. 27–39.

[McCarthy, 1988] J.McCarthy, Mathematical Logic in Artificial Intelligence, *Daedalus*, Winter 1988, pp. 297–311.

[McCarthy & Hayes, 1969] J.McCarthy and P.J.Hayes, Some Philosophical Problems from the Standpoint of Artificial Intelligence, in *Machine Intelligence 4*, ed. D.Michie and B.Meltzer, Edinburgh University Press (1969), pp. 463–502.

[Miller & Shanahan, 1996] R.S.Miller and M.P.Shanahan, Reasoning about Discontinuities in the Event Calculus, *Proceedings 1996 Knowledge Representation Conference (KR 96)*, pp. 63–74.

[Reiter, 1980] R.Reiter, A Logic for Default Reasoning, *Artificial Intelligence*, vol. 13 (1980), pp. 81–132.

[Reiter, 1991] R.Reiter, The Frame Problem in the Situation Calculus: A Simple Solution (Sometimes) and a Completeness Result for Goal Regression, in *Artificial Intelligence and Mathematical Theory of Computation: Papers in Honor of John McCarthy*, ed. V.Lifschitz, Academic Press (1991), pp. 359–380.

[Sandewall, 1991] E.Sandewall, *Features and Fluents*, Technical Report LiTH-IDA-R-91-29 (first review version), Department of Computer and Information Science, Linköping University, Sweden, 1991.

[Sandewall, 1994] E.Sandewall, *Features and Fluents: The Representation of Knowledge about Dynamical Systems, Volume 1*, Oxford University Press (1994).

[Schubert, 1990] L.K.Schubert, Monotonic Solution of the Frame Problem in the Situation Calculus, in *Knowledge Representation and Defeasible Reasoning*, ed. H.Kyburg, R.Loui and G.Carlson, Kluwer (1990), pp. 23–67.

[Shanahan, 1990] M.P.Shanahan, Representing Continuous Change in the Event Calculus, *Proceedings ECAI 90*, pp. 598–603.

[Shanahan, 1996] M.P.Shanahan, Robotics and the Common Sense Informatic Situation, *Proceedings ECAI 96*, pp. 684–688.

[Shanahan, 1997a] M.P.Shanahan, *Solving the Frame Problem: A Mathematical Investigation of the Common Sense Law of Inertia*, MIT Press, 1997.

[Shanahan, 1997b] M.P.Shanahan, Event Calculus Planning Revisited, *Proceedings 4th European Conference on Planning (ECP 97)*, Springer Lecture Notes in Artificial Intelligence no. 1348 (1997), pp. 390–402.

[Shanahan, 1998] M.P.Shanahan, Reinventing Shakey, *Working Notes of the 1998 AAAI Fall Symposium on Cognitive Robotics*, pp. 125–135.

[Shanahan, 1999] M.P.Shanahan, The Ramification Problem in the Event Calculus, *Proceedings IJCAI 99*, to appear.

[Thielscher, 1997] M.Thielscher, Ramification and Causality, *Artificial Intelligence*, vol. 89 (1997), pp. 317–364.

Towards a Logic Programming Infrastructure for Internet Programming

Paul Tarau[1] and Veronica Dahl[2]

[1] Département of Computer Science
University of North Texas, USA
tarau@cs.unt.edu
[2] Logic and Functional Programming Group
Department of Computing Sciences
Simon Fraser University, Canada
veronica@cs.sfu.ca

Abstract. After reviewing a number of Internet tools and technologies originating in the field of logic programming and discussing promising directions of ongoing research, we describe a logic programming based networking infrastructure which combines reasoning and knowledge processing with flexible coordination of dynamic state changes and computation mobility, as well as and its use for the design of intelligent mobile agent programs.

A lightweight logic programming language, Jinni, implemented in Java is introduced as a flexible scripting tool for gluing together knowledge processing components and Java objects in networked client/server applications and thin client environments as well as through applets over the Web.

Mobile threads, implemented by capturing first order continuations in a compact data structure sent over the network, allow Jinni to interoperate with remote high performance BinProlog servers for CPU-intensive knowledge processing.

A Controlled Natural Language to Prolog translator with support of third party speech recognition and text-to-speech translation allows interaction with users not familiar with logic programming.

Keywords: Logic Programming and Internet technologies, mobile computations, remote execution, metaprogramming, first order continuations, Linda coordination, blackboard based logic programming, mobile code, intelligent mobile agents, controlled natural language

1 Introduction

1.1 Logic Programming and the Web

The intersection between Logic Programming and the Internet is a very new but rapidly growing field. In this section we briefly survey the field, and we argue the necessity of endowing it with Web based interaction as well as natural language processing capabilities, including speech.

Recent logic-based Web applications have been presented at [44,49,41], and a special issue of the Journal of Logic Programming on this subject is currently under preparation. A recent survey of logic programming approaches to web applications in terms of the usual classification into client-based systems, server-side systems, and peer-to-peer systems has been provided in [23].

Depending on the site where (most of) the processing happens, most systems fell in client-side or server-side systems, while peer-to-peer systems tend to have fully symmetric interaction capabilities.

Client-side systems [23,7,5] offer more sophisticated user interfaces than server-side ones, and avoid networking programs that can affect server-side applications. They include HTML extensions to incorporate Prolog code, support libraries for Web applications, Java integrations with Prolog, logic-based Web querying languages (Weblog [21]), W-ACE [29]).

Some server-side systems use libraries which enable Prolog programs to process information from CGI input and generate suitable replies. Others use sockets for communication between the invoked CGI interface scripts and the task process or a higher-level communication layer based on active modules (PiL-LoW/CIAO [7]). Some early server-side systems completely replace the traditional web server by software which combines the functionality of a server with the particular task (e.g. the ECLiPSe HTTP server library [5]) although availability of extensible servers like Apache or Jigsaw allows integrating a Logic Programming component directly in the server.

Peer-to-peer systems (e.g. April [26], LogicWeb [23], LogiMOO [45], Jinni [34]) use other abstractions (message passing or blackboards) but retain the Internet as their underlying communication layer. This allows them to implement multi-agent systems, where all participants must communicate on equal terms, bypassing the intrinsic asymmetry of the client/server model. Their most natural incarnation is the metaphor of communicating Virtual Worlds.

1.2 Social computing- towards natural language interaction

Virtual worlds, which evolved from MUDs and MOOs (Multi User Domains - Object Oriented) in the context of networked games [25,27] have placed new requirements on interface design.

Traditional MOOs use places called *rooms* and chat facilities to put in touch users represented by *avatars* for entertainement or information exchange purposes. The architecture is usually client/server, with users connecting to the server either through conventional telnet sessions or through more special purpose MOO shells.

Their direct descendants, Virtual Worlds, converge towards a common interaction metaphor: an avatar represents each participant in a multi-user virtual world, usually realistically represented by VRML landscapes where avatars move. Once the initial fascination with looking human has faded away, the automation of complex behaviour becomes the next challange. Towards this end, high-level coordination and deductive reasoning abilities are among the most important additions Logic programming promisses to add to virtual world modeling languages.

The only system we know of that uses logic programming for virtual world simulation is [45], although a large number of sophisticated Web-based applications and tools have been implemented in LP/CLP languages, for instance [6,24,7,5,31,22].

Presently, despite their graphical sophistication, virtual worlds do not allow *controlling* behavior and object creation i.e., *programming with words*. Yet their characteristics favor the use of natural language: each virtual world represents a particular domain of interest, so that its associated relevant subset of language is naturally restricted; and the command language into which natural language sentences would have to be parsed is formal and straightforward enough while being already relatively close to natural language.

Endowing virtual worlds with natural language capability would certainly enhance social computing, by allowing a user to communicate in (a controlled form) of his/her own language, to be automatically translated into a logic-based interlingua such as in [45], from which the commands resulting from the language exchange would be executed and could be seen being put in action by all participants.

It is interesting to observe that in order to endow virtual worlds with natural language capabilities, we can exploit interesting features that are present in virtual worlds only, e.g.:

- Since virtual worlds handle mostly commands, outermost sentences will be imperative, with their implicit subject being the avatar that the user is controlling (but embedded sentences, being descriptive rather than imperative, will include a subject).
- Knowledge can be categorized as static (world knowledge that exists before a user's sequence of world-changing commands) or dynamic (the new knowledge that results from those commands, often subject to revision).
- The need to dynamically introduce new concepts into the world (e.g. "craft a gnu" must be accepted even if no gnus exist in the virtual world yet) calls for the capability of infering the function of some words (e.g. nouns) from context rather than from a pre-defined lexicon.

Such characteristics call for a system that can infer the subject of imperative sentences in a multi-user world; that can obtain static knowledge previous to the parsing of a sequence of natural language commands, while creating dynamic knowledge by execution of such commands; and that can evaluate noun phrases on the fly even when they contain, e.g., unknown nouns, and refer to them later as needed (thus the need to build complete formulas decreases, in favour of partially evaluated such formulas, with consequent gain re. disambiguation). Language extensibility can thus be obtained in two senses: that of adapting the system to various natural languages [13], and that of allowing implicitly defined new words within the same language.

1.3 Intelligent Knowledge extraction from the Web

There is presently a growing interest in enhancing the web's role as a universal repository of information by adding computational content to it.

A common example of *active pages* have form based submission mechanisms (the user invokes programs on remote hosts by submitting information via a form document). *Mobile code* [38] can be transmitted across the Internet and executed locally on the other end.

Among the applications made possible by programs which interact with the net, those for information and concept extraction from Web documents are particularly interesting, given that as the web continues to expand, retrieving documents relevant to a user's interests becomes trickier. Since most web documents are in natural language and are fairly unstructured, keyword oriented searches find it difficult to minimize noise (the obtention of irrelevant documents) and silence (the non-obtention of relevant documents). Two families of solutions to this problem are being investigated: having Web documents conform to information forms that are more amenable to sophisticated querying and automatic knowledge extraction and developing extraction tools which are concept-based rather than keyword based. The latter approach, which in our view the most attractive one, is the less explored, partly because computational content web applications are largely dominated by imperative programming (e.g. Java, Tcl) from which inference capabilities are usually missing.

1.4 Towards NL based programming languages

With the advent of accessible speech recognition systems (e.g. Naturally Speaking, Microsoft Agent etc.), there is a very strong move towards the use of natural language as a command language today. Companies such as General Magic, Microsoft, IBM are pioneering its use for major telecomunication applications which routinely use spoken language to interact with the user both for input and output.

We expect that as the domain of intelligent software agents matures, the current emphasis on the interaction will be balanced towards more sophisticated reasoning abilities, with LP in a very good position to provide them.

One of the key design ideas in our own work with LogiMOO [45] was that natural language has a serious potential as an effective programming language, at least as far as end user interaction (scripting) is concerned. Our views are confirmed by programs like the recently released Microsoft Agent (downloadable from www.microsoft.com) or General Magic's upcoming Portico, a voice-only intelligent assistant able to learn and remember the state its interaction with the user.

Interestingly, the web itself is evolving into a stateful new model consisting of a set of connected MOOs. Under this model, methodologies for Prolog-based natural language interaction within a virtual world (as in [45]) can be extended for controlling the web itself through natural language, or at least through some combination of natural language and visual tools.

1.5 Code and computation mobility

Data mobility has been present since the beginning of networked computing, and is now used in numerous applications – from remote consultation of a database, to Web browsing.

Code mobility, which followed, is now well known, mostly due to Java's ability to execute applets directly in client browsers.

More transparently, executables coming over network file systems on intranets as well as self-installing programs are all instances of mobile code. Self-updating software is probably the maximum of functionality which can be expressed in this framework.

Migrating the state of the computation from one machine or process to another still requires a separate set of tools. Java's remote method invocations (RMI) add *control mobility* and a (partially) automated form of *object mobility* i.e. integrated code (class) and data (state) mobility.

The Oz 2.0 distributed programming proposal of [50] makes *object mobility* more transparent, although the mobile entity is still the state of the objects, not "live" code.

Mobility of "live code" is called *computation mobility* [9]. It requires interrupting execution, moving the state of a runtime system (stacks, for instance) from one site to another and then resuming execution. Clearly, for some languages, this can be hard or completely impossible to achieve.

Telescript and General Magic's new Odyssey [16] agent programming framework, IBM's Java based *aglets* as well as Luca Cardelli's Oblique [3] have pioneered implementation technologies achieving *computation mobility*.

We will show that in the context of Logic Programming, full *computation mobility* can be achieved easily through our *mobile threads*. They are implemented by a surprisingly small, source level modification of the BinProlog system, taking advantage of the availability of 'first order' continuations[1] as well as of BinProlog's high level networking primitives.

Mobile threads can be seen as a refinement of *mobile computations* as corresponding to *mobile partial computations* of any granularity. *Mobile agents* can be seen as a collection of synchronized *mobile threads* sharing common state [36].

2 A Logic Programming Based Internet Programming Infrastructure

2.1 Linda based coordination

Our networking constructs are built on top of the popular Linda [10] coordination framework, enhanced with unification based pattern matching, remote execution and a set of simple client-server components merged together into a scalable peer-to-peer layer, forming a 'web of interconnected worlds':

---

[1] I.e. continuations accessible as an ordinary data structure - a Prolog term in this case.

```
out(X): puts X on the server
in(X):  waits until it can take an object
        matching X from the server
all(X,Xs): reads the list Xs matching X
        currently on the server
```

The presence of the `all/2` collector avoids the need for backtracking over multiple remote answers. Note that the only blocking operation is `in/1`. Typically, distributed programming with Linda coordination follows consumer-producer patterns (see Fig. 1) with added flexibility over message-passing communication through associative search. Blocking `rd/1`, which waits until a matching term becomes available, without removing it, is easily emulated in terms of `in/1` and `out/1`, while non-blocking `rd/1` is emulated with `all/2`.

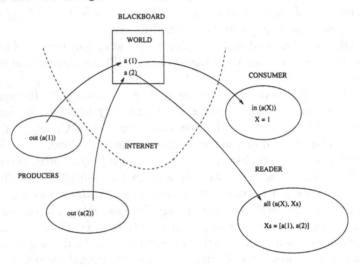

Fig. 1. Basic Linda operations

The MOOs inspired 'web of worlds' metaphor [43] implemented as a set of BinProlog and Java based Linda *blackboards* storing *state information* on servers connected over the the Internet, allows a simple and secure remote execution mechanism through specialized *server-side* interpreters.

A *virtual place* (world) is implemented as a server listening on a port[2] which can spawn clients in the same or separate threads interacting with other servers through a simple question/answer protocol.

A master server on a 'well-known' host/port is used to exchange identification information among peers composed of clients and a server, usually running as threads of the same process.

---

[2] Ports are operating system level abstractions denoting client or server connections over the network.

2.2 Remote Execution Mechanisms

Implementation of arbitrary remote execution is easy in a Linda + Prolog system, due to Prolog's *metaprogramming* abilities. No complex serialization/remote object packages are needed. Our primitive remote call operation is:

```
host(Other_machine)=>>
   remote_run(Answer,RemoteGoal).
```

It implements deterministic *remote predicate calls* with (first)-answer or 'no' returned to the calling site.

For instance, to iterate over the set of servers forming the receiving end of our 'Web of Worlds', after retrieving the list from a 'master server' which constantly monitors them making sure that the list reflects login/logout information, we simply override host/1 and port/1 with intuitionistic implication =>> [33,12]:

```
ask_all_servers(Channel,Servers,Query):-
  member(server_id(Channel,H,P),Servers),
  host(H)=>>port(P)=>>
    ask_a_server(Query,_),
  fail;true.
```

Note that a `Channel` pattern is used to select a subset of relevant servers, and in particular, when `Channel` is a "match all" free logical variable, all of them. By using term subsumption this allows building sophisticated "publish/subscribe" communication patterns hierarchies.

3 Mobile Code

3.1 Mobile threads – are they needed?

Advanced *mobile object* and *mobile agents* agent systems have been built on top of Java's dynamic class loading and its new reflection and remote method invocation classes. IBM Japan's Aglets or General Magic's Odyssey provide comprehensive mobility of code and data. Moreover, data is encapsulated as state of objects. This property allows protecting sensitive components of it more easily. Distributed Oz 2 provides fully transparent movement of objects over the network, giving the illusion that the same program runs on all the computers.

So *why do we need* the apparently more powerful concept of mobile "live code" i.e. mobile execution state?

Our answer to this question is that live mobile code is needed because is still *semantically simpler* than mobile object schemes. Basically, all that a programmer needs to know is that his or her program has moved to a new site and it is executing there. A unique (in our case `move_thread`) primitive, with an intuitive semantics, needs to be learned. When judging about how appropriate a language feature is, we think that the way it looks to the end user is among the most important ones. For this reason, mobile threads are competitive with sophisticated *object mobility* constructs on "end-user ergonomy" grounds, while being fairly simple to implement, as we have shown, in languages in which continuations can be easily represented as data structures.

And *what if the host language does not offer first order continuations*? A simple way around this is to implement in on top of a script interpreter (e.g. a subset of Scheme or Prolog) which does support them. As it is a good idea to limit code migration to lightweight scripts anyway, this is a very practical solution for either C/C++ or Java based mobile code solutions, not requiring complex serialization mechanisms.

3.2 Lazy code fetching

In BinProlog, code is fetched lazily over the network, one predicate at a time, as needed by the execution flow.

Code is cached in a local database and then dynamically recompiled on the fly if usage statistics indicate that it is *not volatile* and it is *heavily used* locally.

The following operations

```
host(Other_machine)=>>rload(File).
host(Other_machine)=>>code(File)=>>TopGoal.
```

allow fetching remote files `rload/1` or on-demand fetching of a predicate at a time from a remote host during execution of `TopGoal`.

This is basically the same mechanism as the one implemented for Java applet code fetching, except that we have also implemented a caching mechanism, at predicate level (predicates are cached as dynamic code on the server to efficiently serve multiple clients).

3.3 Dynamic recompilation

Dynamic recompilation is used on the client side to speed-up heavily used, relatively non-volatile predicates. With dynamically recompiled consulted code, listing of sources and dynamic modification to any predicate is available, while average performance stays close to statically compiled code (usually within a factor of 2-3).

Our implementation of dynamic recompilation for BinProlog is largely motivated by the difficulty/complexity of relying on the programmer to specify execution methods for remote code.

The intuition behind the dynamic recompilation algorithm of BinProlog is that *update* vs. *call* based *statistics* are associated to each predicate declared or detected as dynamic. Dynamic (re)compilation is triggered for relatively non-volatile predicates, which are promoted on the *'speed-hierarchy'* to a faster implementation method (interpreted -> bytecode -> native). The process is restarted from the 'easier to change' interpreted representation, kept in memory in a compact form, upon an update.

We can describe BinProlog's dynamic *'recompilation triggering statistics'* through a simple 'thermostat' metaphor. *Updates* (assert/retract) to a predicate have the effect of increasing its associated 'temperature', while *Calls* will decrease it. Non-volatile ('cool') predicates are dynamically recompiled, while recompilation is avoided for volatile ('hot') predicates. A *ratio* based on cooling factors (number of calls, compiled/interpreted execution speed-up etc.) and heating factors (recompilation time, number of updates etc.) smoothly adjusts for optimal overall performance, usually within a factor of 2 from static code.

4   Engines and Answer Threads

4.1   Engines

BinProlog allows launching multiple Prolog engines having their own stack groups (heap, local stack and trail). An engine can be seen as an abstract data-type which produces a (possibly infinite) stream of solutions as needed. To create a new engine, we use:

```
create_engine(+HeapSize,+StackSize,
              +TrailSize,-Handle)
```

or, by using default parameters for the stacks:

```
create_engine(-Handle)
```

The `Handle` is a unique integer denoting the engine for further processing. To 'fuel' the engine with a goal and an expected answer variable we use:

```
load_engine(+Handle,+Goal,
              +AnswerVariable)
```

No processing, except the initialization of the engine takes place, and no answer is returned with this operation.

To get an answer from the engine we use:

```
ask_engine(+Handle,-Answer)
```

Each engine has its own heap garbage collection process and backtracks independently using its choice-point stack and trail during the computation of an answer. Once computed, an answer is copied from an engine to its "master".

When the stream of answers reaches its end, `ask_engine/2` will simply fail. The resolution process in an engine can be discarded at any time by simply loading another goal with `load_engine/3`. This allows avoiding the cost of backtracking, for instance in the case when a single answer is needed, as well as garbage collection costs.

If for some reason we are not interested in the engine any more, we can free the space allocated to the engine and completely discard it with:

```
destroy_engine(+Handle)
```

The following example [3] in the BinProlog distribution [33] shows a sequence of the previously described operations:

```
?-create_engine(E),
    load_engine(E,append(As,Bs,[1,2]),As+Bs),
    ask_engine(E,R1),write(R1),nl,
    ask_engine(E,R2),write(R2),nl,
    destroy_engine(E).
```

Multiple 'orthogonal engines' as shown in Figure 2 enhance the expressiveness of Prolog by allowing an AND-branch of an engine to collect answers from multiple OR-branches of another engine. They give to the programmer the means to see as an abstract sequence and control, the answers produced by an engine, in a way similar to Java's Enumeration interface.

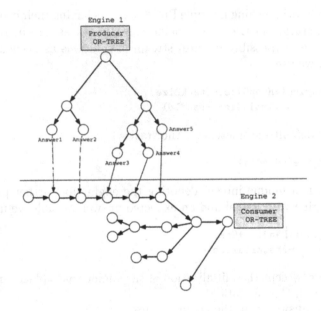

Fig. 2. Orthogonal Engines

4.2 Threads

Engines can be assigned to their own thread by using BinProlog's POSIX thread package. A unique primitive is needed,

```
    ask_thread(E,R)
```

which launches a new thread R to perform the computation of an answer of engine E. On top of this facility each thread can implement a separate server, client or become the base of a mobile agent.

[3] See more in files library/engines.pl, progs/engtest.pl

5 First order Continuations through Binarization

We will shortly explain here BinProlog's continuation passing preprocessing technique, which results in availability of continuations as data structures accessible to the programmer.

The binarization transformation Binary clauses have only one atom in the body (except for some in-line 'builtin' operations like arithmetics), and therefore they need no 'return' after a call. A transformation introduced in [35] allows to faithfully represent logic programs with operationally equivalent binary programs.

To keep things simple, we will describe our transformations in the case of definite programs. We will follow here the notations of [46].

Let us define the *composition* operator $\oplus$ that combines clauses by unfolding the leftmost body-goal of the first argument.

Let $A_0 : -A_1, A_2, \ldots, A_n$ and $B_0 : -B_1, \ldots, B_m$ be two clauses (suppose $n > 0, m \geq 0$). We define

$$(A_0 : -A_1, A_2, \ldots, A_n) \oplus (B_0 : -B_1, \ldots, B_m) = (A_0 : -B_1, \ldots, B_m, A_2, \ldots, A_n)\theta$$

with $\theta = \text{mgu}(A_1, B_0)$. If the atoms A_1 and B_0 do not unify, the result of the composition is denoted as $\perp$. Furthermore, as usual, we consider $A_0 : -\text{true}, A_2, \ldots, A_n$ to be equivalent to $A_0 : -A_2, \ldots, A_n$, and for any clause C, $\perp \oplus C = C \oplus \perp = \perp$. We assume that at least one operand has been renamed to a variant with variables standardized apart.

This Prolog-like inference rule is called LD-resolution and it has the advantage of giving a more accurate description of Prolog's operational semantics than SLD-resolution. Before introducing the binarization transformation, we describe two auxiliary transformations.

The first transformation converts facts into rules by giving them the atom true as body. E.g., the fact p is transformed into the rule p :- true.

The second transformation, inspired by [52], eliminates the metavariables by wrapping them in a call/1 goal. E.g., the rule and(X,Y):-X, Y is transformed into and(X,Y) :- call(X), call(Y).

The transformation of [35] (*binarization*) adds continuations as extra arguments of atoms in a way that preserves also first argument indexing.

Let P be a definite program and *Cont* a new variable. Let T and $E = p(T_1, ..., T_n)$ be two expressions.[4] We denote by $\psi(E, T)$ the expression $p(T_1, ..., T_n, T)$. Starting with the clause

(C) $A : -B_1, B_2, ..., B_n$.

we construct the clause

(C') $\psi(A, Cont) : -\psi(B_1, \psi(B_2, ..., \psi(B_n, Cont)))$.

The set P' of all clauses C' obtained from the clauses of P is called the binarization of P.

The following example shows the result of this transformation on the well-known 'naive reverse' program:

---

[4] Atom or term.

```
app([],Ys,Ys,Cont):-true(Cont).
app([A|Xs],Ys,[A|Zs],Cont):-
  app(Xs,Ys,Zs,Cont).

nrev([],[],Cont):-true(Cont).
nrev([X|Xs],Zs,Cont):-
  nrev(Xs,Ys,app(Ys,[X],Zs,Cont)).
```

The transformation preserves a strong operational equivalence with the original program with respect to the LD resolution rule, which is *reified* in the syntactical structure of the resulting program, i.e. each resolution step of an LD derivation on a definite program P can be mapped to an SLD-resolution step of the binarized program P'.

Clearly, continuations become explicit in the binary version of the program. We have devised a technique to access and manipulate them in an intuitive way, by modifying BinProlog's binarization preprocessor. Basically, the clauses constructed with ::- instead of :- are considered as being already in binary form, and not subject therefore to further binarization. By explicitly accessing their arguments, a programmer is able to access and modify the current continuation as a 'first order object'. Note however that code *referring* to the continuation is also *part* of it, so that some care should be taken in manipulating the circular term representing the continuation from 'inside'.

6 Mobile threads: Take the *Future* and Run

As continuations (describing *future* computations to be performed at a given point) are first order objects in BinProlog, it is easy to extract from them a conjunction of goals representing *future* computations intended to be performed at another site, send it over the network and resume working on it at that site. The natural unit of mobility is a *thread* moving to a server executing multiple local and remotely originated threads. *Threads communicate with their local and remote counterparts, listening on ports through the Linda protocol, as described in [15].* This combination of Linda based coordination and thread mobility is intended to make building complex, pattern based agent scripts fairly easy.

6.1 Capturing continuations

Before moving to another site, the current continuation needs to be captured in a data structure (see Appendix I). For flexibility, a wrapper capture_cont_for/1 is used first to restrict the scope of the continuation to a (deterministic) toplevel Goal. This avoids taking irrelevant parts of the continuation (like prompting the user for the next query) to the remote site inadvertently.

A unique logical variable is used through a backtrackable linear assumption cont_marker(End) to mark the end of the scope of the continuation with end_cont(End).

From inside the continuation, `call_with_cont/1` is used to extract the relevant segment of the continuation. Towards this end, `consume_cont(Closure,Marker)` extracts a conjunction of goals from the current continuation until Marker is reached, and then it applies `Closure` to this conjunction (calls it with the conjunction passed to `Closure` as an argument).

Extracting the continuation itself is easy, by using BinProlog's ability to accept user defined binarized clauses (introduced with ::- instead of :-), accessing the continuation as a 'first order' object:

```
get_cont(Cont,Cont)::-true(Cont).
```

6.2 The Continuation Moving Protocol

Our continuation moving protocol can be described easily in terms of synchronized *source side*[5], and *target side* operations.

Source side operations

- wrap a Goal with a unique terminator marking the end of the continuation to be captured, and call it with the current continuation available to it through a linearly assumed fact[6]
- reserve a free port P for the future code server
- schedule on the target server a sequence of actions which will lead to resuming the execution from right after the `move_thread` operation (see target side operations), return and become a code server allowing the mobile thread to fetch required predicates one a time

Target side operations are scheduled as a sequence of goals extracted from the current continuation at the *source side* , and received over the network together with a small set of synchronization commands:

- schedule as delayed task a sequence of goals received from the source side and return
- wait until the *source side* is in server mode
- set up the back links to the source side as assumptions
- execute the delayed operations representing the moved continuation
- fetch code from the source side as needed for execution of the goals of the moved continuations and their subcalls
- shut down the code server on the source side

Communication between the base and the target side is done with *remote predicate calls* protected with *dynamically generated passwords* shared between the two sides before the migratory component "takes off".

---

[5] which will be also shortly called the *base* of the mobile thread

[6] BinProlog's linear assumptions are backtrackable additions to the database, usable at most once.

Initially the target side waits in server mode. Once the continuation is received on the target side, the source side switches in server mode ready to execute code fetching and persistent database update requests from its mobile counterpart on the target side.

Fig. 3 shows the connections between a mobile thread and its base.

Note that when the base turns into a server, it offers its *own code* for remote use by the moved thread - a kind of virtual "on demand" process cloning operation, one step at a time. As the server actually acts as a code cache, multiple moving threads can benefit from this operation. Note also that only predicates needed for the migratory segment of the continuation are fetched. This ensures that migratory code is kept lightweight for most mobile applications. Synchronized communication, using Linda operations can occur between the mobile thread and its base server, and through the server, bitween multiple mobile threads which have migrated to various places.

As our networking infrastructure, our *mobile threads* are platform independent. As Java, BinProlog is a platform independent emulator based language. As a consequence, a thread can start on a Unix machine and move transparently to a Windows NT system and back. Binaries for various Unix and Windows platforms are freely available at http://clement.info.umoncton.ca/BinProlog . For faster, platform specific execution, BinProlog provides compilation to C of static code using an original partial translation technique described in [48].

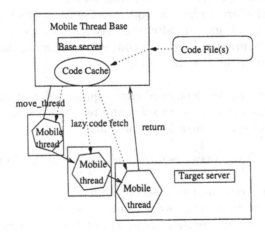

Fig. 3. Launching a mobile thread from its base

6.3 Emulating computation mobility through control mobility

As shown in [40], part of the functionality of *mobile computations* can be emulated in terms of remote predicate calls combined with remote code fetching. An implicit *virtual place* (host+port) can be set as the target of the remote calls.

Then, it is enough to send the top-level goal to the remote side and have it fetch the code as needed from a server at the site from where the code originates.

Note however that this is less efficient in terms of network transactions and less reliable than sending the full continuation at once as with our *mobile threads*.

6.4 Mobile Agents

Mobile agents can be seen as a collection of synchronized *mobile threads* sharing common state [36].

Mobile agents are implemented by iterating *thread mobility* over a set of servers[7] known to a given master server. An efficient pyramidal deployment strategy can be used to efficiently implement, for instance, *push technology* through mobile agents. Inter-agent communication can be achieved either by rendez-vous of two mobile threads at a given site, by communicating through a local Prolog database, or through the base server known to all the deployed agents. Communication with the base server is easily achieved through remote predicate calls with remote_run. Basic security of mobile agents is achieved with randomly generated passwords, required for remote_run operations, and by running them on a restricted BinProlog machine, without user-level file write and external process spawn operations.

7 Jinni: a Java-based Logic Programming Engine

Jinni[8] (Java INference engine and Networked Interactor), a lightweight, multi-threaded, pure logic programming language, intended to be used as a flexible scripting tool for gluing together knowledge processing components and Java objects in networked client/server applications, as well as through applets over the Web.

Mobile threads, implemented by capturing first order continuations in a compact data structure sent over the network, allow Jinni to interoperate with remote high performance BinProlog servers for CPU-intensive knowledge processing and with other Jinni components over the Internet.

These features make Jinni a perfect development platform for intelligent mobile agent systems.

By supporting multiple threads, control mobility and inference processing, Jinni is well suited for the development of intelligent mobile agent programs.

Jinni supports multi-user synchronized transactions and interoperates with the latest version of BinProlog [33].

7.1 The world of Jinni

Jinni is based on a simple **Things**, **Places**, **Agents** ontology, borrowed from MUDs and MOOs [27,1,4,14,47,32].

---

[7] possibly filtered down to a relevant subset using a 'channel'-like pattern

[8] Available at http://clement.info.umoncton.ca/ tarau/netjinni/Jinni.html

Things are represented as Prolog terms, basically trees of embedded records containing constants and variables to be further instantiated to other trees.

Places are processes running on various computers with a server component listening on a port and a blackboard component allowing synchronized multi-user Linda [10,15] and remote predicate call transactions.

Agents are collections of threads executing a set of goals, possibly spread over a set of different Places and usually executing remote and local transactions in coordination with other Agents. Jinni does not provide at this time a single abstract data type for agents or places because it is intended to be an infrastructure on top of which they are built in an application specific way. As crisp abstractions will emerge through development of libraries and applications, a hierarchy of Places and Agents will be built. Place and Agent prototypes will be clonable, support inheritance/sharing of Things and will be easily editable/configurable using visual tools. Agent threads moving between places and agents moving as units will be supported. Places will be used to abstract away language differences between processors, like for instance Jinni and BinProlog. Mobile code will allow very high speed processing in Jinni by delegating heavy inference processing to high-performance BinProlog components.

7.2 Jinni as a Logic Programming Java component

Jinni is intended to be a lightweight, thin client logic programming component, based as much as possible on fully portable, vendor and version independent Java code. Its main features come from this architectural choice:

- a trimmed down, simple, operatorless syntactic subset of Prolog,
- pure Prolog (Horn Clause logic) with leftmost goal unfolding as inference rule,
- multiple asynchronous inference engines each running as a separate thread,
- a shared blackboard to communicate between engines using a simple Linda-style subscribe/publish (in/out in Linda jargon) coordination protocol based on associative search,
- high level networking operations allowing code mobility [3,18,16,8,50,19] and remote execution,
- a straightforward Jinni-to-Java translator allows packaging of Jinni programs as Java classes to be transparently loaded over the Internet
- backtrackable assumptions [42,12] implemented through trailed, overridable undo actions

Jinni's spartan return to (almost) pure Horn Clause logic does not mean it is necessarily a weaker language. Expressiveness of full Prolog (and beyond:-)) is easily attained in Jinni by combining multiple engines. For theoretical CS lovers, the magic is similar to just adding another stack to a Push Down Automaton: this morphs it into a Turing machine! Engines give transparent access to the underlying Java threads and are used to implement local or remote, lazy or eager findall operations, negation as failure, if-then-else, etc. at source level. Inference engines running on separate threads can cooperate through either predicate calls or through an easy to use flavor of the Linda coordination protocol.

Remote or local dynamic database updates (with deterministic, synchronized transactions with immediate update semantics) make Jinni an extremely flexible Agent programming language. Jinni is designed on top of dynamic, fully garbage collectible data structures, to take advantage of Java's automatic memory management.

7.3   Basic agent programming with Jinni

Two simple agents are part of Jinni's standard library:
Window 1: a reactive channel listener

```
?-listen(fun(_)).
```

Window 2: a selective channel publisher

```
?-talk(fun(jokes)).
```

They implement a front end to Jinni's associative publish/subscribe abilities. The more general pattern fun(_) will reach all the users interested in instances of fun/1, in particular fun(jokes). However, someone publishing on an unrelated channel e.g. with ?-talk(stocks(nasdaq)). will not reach fun/1 listeners because stocks(nasdaq) and fun(jokes) channel patterns are not unifiable.

A more realistic stock market agent's buy/sell components look as follows:

```
sell(Who,Stock,AskPrice):-
  % triggers a matching buy transaction
  notify_about(offer(Who,Stock,AskPrice)).

buy(Who,Stock,SellingPrice):-
  % runs as a background thread
  % in parallel with other buy operations
  spawn(try_to_buy(Who,Stock,SellingPrice)).

try_to_buy(Me,Stock,LimitPrice):-
  % this thread connects to a server side constraint and waits
  % until the contstraint is solved to true on the server
  % by a corresponding sell transaction
  wait_for(offer(You,Stock,YourPrice),[ % server side mobile code
    lesseq(YourPrice,LimitPrice),
    local_in(has(You,Stock)),
    local_in(capital(You,YourCapital)), % server side 'local' in/1
    local_in(capital(Me,MyCapital)),    % operations
    compute('-',MyCapital,YourPrice,MyNewCapital),
    compute('+',YourCapital,YourPrice,YourNewCapital),
    local_out(capital(You,YourNewCapital)),
    local_out(capital(Me,MyNewCapital)),
```

```
    local_out(has(Me,Stock))
]).
```

Note that this example also give a glimpse on Jinni's fairly spartan syntax (to be generated through a controlled natural language preprocessor) and it's multi-threaded client/server design, as well as it's mobile code and servers side constraint solving ability. We will now describe these features and Jinni's architecture in more detail.

8 What's new in Jinni

8.1 Engines

Jinni inherits from BinProlog's design the ability to launch multiple Prolog engines having their own stack groups (heap, local stack and trail). An engine can be seen as an abstract data-type which produces a (possibly infinite) stream of solutions as needed. To create an new engine, we use:

```
new_engine(Goal,Answer,Handle)
```

The Handle is a unique Java Object denoting the engine, assigned to its own thread, for further processing.

To get an answer from the engine we use:

```
ask_engine(Handle,Answer)
```

Each engine has its own virtual garbage collection process and backtracks independently using its choice-point stack and trail during the computation of an answer. Once computed, an answer is copied from an engine to the maseter engine which initiated it.

When the stream of answers reaches its end, ask_engine/2 will simply fail. The resolution process in an engine can be discarded at any time with stop_engine/1. This allows avoiding the cost of backtracking, for instance in the case when a single answer is needed.

The following example (see more in file tarau/jinni/lib.pro in the Jinni distribution shows how to extract one solution from an engine:

```
one_solution(X,G,R):-
  new_engine(G,X,E),
  ask_engine(E,Answer),
  stop_engine(E),
  eq(Answer,R).
```

Note that new_engine/3 speculatively starts execution of Goal on a new thread and that either a term of the form the(X) or no is returned by ask_answer. Synchronization with this thread is performed when asking an answer, using a special monitor object. It is quite surprising how simply everything is built on top of this one_solution/3 primitive[9].

```
if(Cond,Then,Else):-
  one_solution(successful(Cond,Then),Cond,R),
  select_then_else(R,Cond,Then,Else).

select_then_else(the(successful(Cond,Then)),Cond,Then,_):-Then.
select_then_else(no,_,_,Else):-Else.

once(G):-one_solution(G,G,the(G)).

not(G):-one_solution(G,G,no).

copy_term(X,CX):-one_solution(X,true,the(CX)).

spawn(Goal):-new_engine(Goal,_,_). % spawns a new background thread
```

Similarly, findall/3 is emulated easily by iterating over ask_engine/2 operations. Note that lazy variants of findall can be implemented as well.

```
find_all(X,G,Xs):-
  new_engine(G,X,E),
  once(extract_answers(E,Xs)).

extract_answers(E,[X|Xs]):-
  ask_engine(E,the(X)),
  extract_answers(E,Xs).
extract_answers(_,[]).
```

In fact, as in BinProlog, by using orthogonal engines, a programmer does not really need to use findall and other similar predicates anymore - why accumulate answers eagerly on a list which will get scanned and decomposed again, when answers can be produced on demand?

8.2 Server-side constraint solving

A natural extension to Linda is to use constraint solving for selection matching terms, instead of plain unification. This is implemented in Jinni through the use of 2 builtins:

Wait_for(Term,Constraint): waits for a Term such that Constraint is true on the server, and when this happens, it removes the result of the match from the server with an in/1 operation. Constraint is either a single goal or a list of goals [G1,G2,..,Gn] to be executed on the server.

---

[9] In fact, for efficiency reasons, now Jinni has a first_solution/3 builtin, which does not require a separate engine. It is implemented simply by throwing a special purpose exception when the first solution is found.

Notify_about(Term): notifies the server to give this term to any blocked client which waits for it with a matching constraint i.e.

```
notify_about(stock_offer(nscp,29))
```

would trigger execution of a client having issued

```
wait_for(stock_offer(nscp,Price),less(Price,30)).
```

The use of server side execution was in fact suggested by a real-life stock market application. It turned out that is just too tricky in pure Linda to do something as simple as triggering an atomic transaction when data verifying a simple arithmetic inequality becomes available. We plan to incorporate in the near future a simple server-side symbolic constraint reducer (FD or interval based).

8.3 Jinni-BinProlog interoperability through Mobile Threads

Jinni's mobile computation is a scaled down, simplified subset of BinProlog's mobile computation facilities. They are both based on the use of *first order continuations* i.e. encapsulated future computations, which can be easily suspended, moved over the network, and resumed at a different site. As continuations are first-order objects both in Jinni and BinProlog, the implementation is straightforward [37] and the two engines can interoperate transparently by simply moving computations from one to the other.

In the case of Jinni a unique **move/0** operation is used to transport computation to the server, together with **there/0** which is used to focus Jinni's attention to the default server[10]. The client simply waits until computation completes, when bindings for the first solution are propagated back:

Window 1: a mobile thread

```
?-there,move,println(hello_on_the_server),member(X,[1,2,3]).
X=1;
no.
```

Window 2: a server

```
?-run_server.
hello_on_the_server
```

Note that mobile computation is more expressive and more efficient than remote predicate calls as such. Basically, it moves once, and executes on the server all future computations of the current AND branch. This can be seen by compare real time execution speed for:

---

[10] **here/0** brings the focus of attention back to local mode.

```
?-there,for(I,1,1000),run(println(I)),fail.

?-there,move,for(I,1000),println(I),fail.
```

While the first query uses `run/1` each time to send a remote task to the server, the second moves once the full computation to the server where it executes without further requiring network communications.

8.4 Application domains

Jinni's client and server scripting abilities are intended to support platform and vendor independent Prolog-to-Java and Prolog-to-Prolog bidirectional connection over the net and to accelerate integration of the effective inference technologies developed the last 20 years in the field of Logic Programming in mainstream Internet products.

The next iteration is likely to bring a simple, plain English scripting language to be compiled to Jinni, along the lines of the LogiMOO prototype, with speech recognizer/synthesizer based I/O. A connection between Jinni and its Microsoft Agent counterpart *Genie* are among the high priority tasks likely to be left to the growing community of Jinni co-developers[11].

Among the potential targets for Jinni based products: lightweight rule based programs assisting customers of Java enables appliances, from Web based TVs to mobile cell phones and car computers, all requiring knowledge components to adjust to increasingly sophisticated user expectations.

A stock market simulator is currently on the way to be implemented based on Jinni, featuring user programmable intelligent agents. It is planned to be connected to real world Internet based stock trade services.

9 Programming with words: a MOO-inspired Controlled Natural Language interface to Logic Programming components

There is a very strong move towards the use of natural language as a command language today, with General Magic, Microsoft, IBM and telecommunication companies pioneering its use for major industrial applications which routinely use spoken language to communicate with the user both for input and output.

We expect that as the domain of intelligent software agents matures, the current emphasis on the interaction will be balanced towards more sophisticated reasoning abilities, with LP in a very good position to provide them.

One of the key design ideas behind our LogiMOO virtual world (on the way to be rewritten as a Jinni component) was that natural language has a serious potential as an effective programming language, at least as far as end

---

[11] Jinni's sustained growth is insured through a relatively unconventional *bazaar* style development process, similar to Linux and more recently Netscape client products.

user interaction (scripting) is concerned. Our views are confirmed by programs like the recently released Microsoft Agent [28] or General Magic's upcoming Portico [17], a voice-only intelligent assistant able to learn and remember the state its interaction with the user.

LogiMOO is one of the very few existing virtual worlds that can be controlled with natural language. The reasons why we wanted to provide LogiMOO with a NL interface are:

1. natural language is the most convenient way for us to communicate;
2. a natural language interface is the first step towards voice-controlled interaction with the virtual world[12];
3. a virtual world is a perfect environment to experiment with natural language because the domain of discourse is limited;
4. natural language is needed for the upcoming speech recognition/generation based human/computer interaction tools

The peculiar features of the world to be consulted- a virtual world- induced novel parsing features which are interesting in themselves: flexible handling of dynamic knowledge, immediate evaluation of noun phrase representations, allowing us to be economic with representation itself, inference of some basic syntactic categories from the context, a treatment of nouns as proper nouns, easy extensibility within the same language as well as into other natural languages. We refer to [45] for a more detailed description of LogiMOO's Natural Language processor.

10 Related work

Multi-user blackboard systems have been described in [11,15]. Among the original features of Jinni and BinProlog is a combination of multi-user blackboards, multi-threading and interoperation with Web protocols (httpd). However, BinProlog is not the only Prolog featuring blackboard processing. Commercial systems like SICStus Prolog also contain Linda subsystems. In fact, this makes Linda based logic programs fairly portable.

Remote execution and code migration techniques are pioneered by [2,19,30]. Support for remote procedure calls (RPC) are part of major operating systems like Sun's Solaris and Microsoft's Windows NT.

A very large number of research projects have recently started on mobile computations/mobile agent programming. Among the pioneers, Kahn and Cerf's Knowbots [20]. Among the most promising recent developments, Luca Cardelli's Oblique project at Digital and mobile agent applications [3] and IBM Japan's aglets [18]. Mobile code technologies are pioneered by General Magic's Telescript

---

[12] With operating systems as OS/2 Warp integrating basic voice recognition and products like Dragon Systems' continuous unrestricted speech recognizer widely available, controlling software as well as programming in a speech-friendly environment becomes increasingly realistic.

(see [16] for their last Java based *mobile agent* product). General Magic's upcoming Serengeti software combines mobile code technologies and voice recognition based command language (MagicTalk) for a new generation of PDAs. Another mobility framework, sharing some of our objectives towards transparent high level distributed programming is built on top of Distributed Oz [50,51], a multiparadigm language, also including a logic programming component. Although thread mobility is not implemented in Distributed Oz 2, some of this functionality can be emulated in terms of network transparent mobile objects. Achieving the illusion of a unique application transparently running on multiple sites makes implementing shared multi-user applications particularly easy. We can achieve similar results by implementing mobile agents (e.g. avatars) as mobile threads with parts of the shared world *visible* to an agent represented as dynamic facts, lazily replicated through our lazy code fetching scheme when the agent moves. Both Distributed Oz 2 and our BinProlog based infrastructure need a full language processor (Oz 2 or BinProlog) to be deployed at each node. However, assuming that a Java processor is already installed, our framework's Java client (see [40,39]) allows this functionality to be available through applets attached to a server side BinProlog thread. A calculus of *mobility* dealing with containers, called *ambients*, is described in [8]. The calculus covers at very high level of generality movement and permissions to move from one ambient to another and show how fundamental computational mechanisms like Turing machines as well as process calculi can be expressed within the formalism. Our *coordination logic* of [36] introduces similar concepts, based on programming mobile avatars in shared virtual worlds. Two classes of containers, *clonable* and *unique* regulate creation of new instances (clones) and non-copiable (unique) entities (like electronic money), as well as their movement.

11   Conclusion

We have described how mobile threads are implemented by capturing first order continuations in a data structure sent over the network. Supported by *lazy code fetching* and *dynamic recompilation*, they have been shown to be an effective framework for implementing mobile agents.

The techniques presented here are not (Bin)Prolog specific. The most obvious porting target of our design is to functional languages featuring first order continuations and threads. A particularily interesting porting target is Java and similar OO languages having threads, reflection classes and remote method invocation.

Future work will focus on intelligent mobile agents integrating knowledge and controlled natural language processing abilities, following our previous work described in [43].

The Jinni project shows that Logic Programming languages are well suited as the basic glue so much needed for elegant and cost efficient Internet programming. The ability to compress so much functionality in such a tiny package shows that building logic programming components to be integrated in emerging tools like Java might be the most practical way towards mainstream recognition and widespread use of Logic Programming technology. Jinni's emphasis on functionality and expressiveness over performance, as well as it's use of integrated multi-threading and networking, hint towards the priorities we consider important for future Logic Programming language design.

Acknowledgment

We thank for support from NSERC (grants OGP0107411 and 611024), and from the FESR of the Université de Moncton and the Radiance Group Inc. Special thanks go to Bart Demoen, Koen De Boschere, Ed Freeman, Don Garrett, Stephen Rochefort and Yu Zhang for fruitful interaction related to the design, implementation and testing of Jinni.

References

1. The Avalon MUD. http://www.avalon-rpg.com/.
2. G. T. Almes, A. P. Black, E. D. Lazowska, and J. D. Noe. The Eden System: A Technical Review. *IEEE Transactions on Software Engineering*, 11(1):43–59, January 1985.
3. K. A. Bharat and L. Cardelli. Migratory applications. In *Proceedings of the 8th Annual ACM Symposium on User Interface Software and Technology*, Nov. 1995. http://gatekeeper.dec.com/ pub/DEC/SRC/research-reports/ abstracts/src-rr-138.html.
4. BlackSun. CyberGate. http://www.blaxxsun.com/.
5. P. Bonnet, L. Bressnan S., Leth, and B. Thomsen. Towards ECLIPSE Agents on the Internet. In Tarau et al. [44]. http://clement.info.umoncton.ca/ lpnet.
6. D. Cabeza and M. Hermenegildo. html.pl: A HTML Package for (C)LP systems. Technical report, 1996. Available from http://www.clip.dia.fi.upm.es.
7. D. Cabeza and M. Hermenegildo. The Pillow/CIAO Library for Internet/WWW Programming using Computational Logic Systems. In Tarau et al. [44]. http://clement.info.umoncton.ca/ lpnet.
8. L. Cardelli. Mobile ambients. Technical report, Digital, 1997. http://www.research.digital.com/ SRC/personal/Luca_Cardelli/Papers.html.
9. L. Cardelli. Mobile Computation. In J. Vitek and C. Tschudin, editors, *Mobile Object Systems - Towards the Programmable Internet*, pages 3–6. Springer-Verlag, LNCS 1228, 1997.
10. N. Carriero and D. Gelernter. Linda in context. *CACM*, 32(4):444–458, 1989.
11. P. Ciancarini. Coordinating Rule-Based Software Processes with ESP. *ACM Transactions on Software Engineering and Methodology*, 2(3):203–227, 1993.
12. V. Dahl, P. Tarau, and R. Li. Assumption Grammars for Processing Natural Language. In L. Naish, editor, *Proceedings of the Fourteenth International Conference on Logic Programming*, pages 256–270, MIT press, 1997.
13. V. Dahl, P. Tarau, S. Rochefort, and M. Scortescu. A Spanish Interface to LogiMoo-towards multilingual virtual worlds. In *International Workshop on Spanish Natural Language Processing and Spanish Language Technologies*, New Mexico, July 1997. invited talk.

14. K. De Bosschere, D. Perron, and P. Tarau. LogiMOO: Prolog Technology for Virtual Worlds. In *Proceedings of PAP'96*, pages 51–64, London, Apr. 1996.
15. K. De Bosschere and P. Tarau. Blackboard-based Extensions in Prolog. *Software — Practice and Experience*, 26(1):49–69, Jan. 1996.
16. GeneralMagicInc. Odissey. 1997. available at http://www.genmagic.com/agents.
17. GeneralMagicInc. Portico. 1998. http://www.genmagic.com/portico/portico.html.
18. IBM. Aglets. http://www.trl.ibm.co.jp/aglets.
19. E. Jul, H. Levy, N. Hutchinson, and A. Black. Fine-Grained Mobility in the Emerald System. *ACM Transactions on Computer Systems*, 6(1):109–133, February 1988.
20. R. E. Kahn and V. G. Cerf. The digital library project, volume i: The world of knowbots. 1988. Unpublished manuscript, Corporation for National Research Initiatives, Reston, Va., Mar.
21. Lakshmanan, L. V. S. and Sadri, F. and Subramanian, I.N. A Declarative Language for Querying and Restructuring the WWW. In *Proc. of the Post-ICDE IEEEWorkshop on Research Issues in Data Engineering*, feb 1996.
22. S. W. Locke, A. Davison, and S. L. Lightweight Deductive Databases for the World-Wide Web. In Tarau et al. [44]. http://clement.info.umoncton.ca/ lpnet.
23. S. W. Loke. *Adding Logic Programming Behaviour to the World Wide Web*. Phd thesis, University of Melbourne, Australia, 1998.
24. S. W. Loke and A. Davison. Logic programming with the world-wide web. In *Proceedings of the 7th ACM Conference on Hypertext*, pages 235–245. ACM Press, 1996.
25. J. Ludewig. Problems in Modeling the Software Development Process as an Adventure Game. In H. Rombach, V. Basili, and R. Selby, editors, *Int. Workshop on Experimental Sw Engineering Issues*, volume 706, pages 23–26, Dagsthul, Germany, Sept 1992. Springer.
26. McCabe, F.G. and Clark, K.L. April- Agent Process Interaction Language. In *Intelligent Agents, (LNAI 890)*. Springer-Verlag, 1995.
27. T. Meyer, D. Blair, and S. Hader. WAXweb: a MOO-based collaborative hypermedia system for WWW. *Computer Networks and ISDN Systems*, 28(1/2):77–84, 1995.
28. MicrosoftCorp. Microsoft Agent. 1998. http://www.microsoft.com/msagent/agentdl.asp/.
29. Pontelli, E. and Gupta, G. W-ACE: A Logic Language for Intelligent Internet Programming. In *Proc. of IEEE 9th ICTAI'97*, pages 2–10, 1997.
30. J. W. Stamos and D. K. Gifford. Remote Evaluation. *ACM Transaction on Programming Languages and Systems*, 12(4):537–565, October 1990.
31. P. Szeredi, K. Molnár, and R. Scott. Serving Multiple HTML Clients from a Prolog Application. In Tarau et al. [44]. http://clement.info.umoncton.ca/ lpnet.
32. P. Tarau. Logic Programming and Virtual Worlds. In *Proceedings of INAP96*, Tokyo, Nov. 1996. keynote address.
33. P. Tarau. BinProlog 5.75 User Guide. Technical Report 97-1, Département d'Informatique, Université de Moncton, Apr. 1997. Available from *http://clement.info.umoncton.ca/BinProlog*.
34. P. Tarau. *Jinni: a Lightweight Java-based Logic Engine for Internet Programming*. Manchester, U.K., June 1998. invited talk.
35. P. Tarau and M. Boyer. Elementary Logic Programs. In P. Deransart and J. Maluszyński, editors, *Proceedings of Programming Language Implementation and Logic Programming*, number 456 in Lecture Notes in Computer Science, pages 159–173. Springer, Aug. 1990.

36. P. Tarau and V. Dahl. A Coordination Logic for Agent Programming in Virtual Worlds. In W. Conen and G. Neumann, editors, *Proceedings of Asian'96 Post-Conference Workshop on Coordination Technology for Collaborative Applications*, Singapore, Dec. 1996.

37. P. Tarau and V. Dahl. Mobile Threads through First Order Continuations. 1997. submitted, http://clement.info.umoncton.ca/ html/tmob/html.html.

38. P. Tarau and V. Dahl. *Mobile Threads through First Order Continuations*. Coruna, Spain, July 1998.

39. P. Tarau, V. Dahl, and K. De Bosschere. A Logic Programming Infrastructure for Remote Execution, Mobile Code and Agents. In *Proceedings of WETICE'97*.

40. P. Tarau, V. Dahl, and K. De Bosschere. Logic Programming Tools for Remote Execution, Mobile Code and Agents. In *Proceedings of ICLP'97 Workshop on Logic Programming and Multi Agent Systems*, Leuven, Belgium, July 1997.

41. P. Tarau, V. Dahl, and K. De Bosschere. Remote Execution, Mobile Code and Agents in BinProlog. In *Electronic Proceedings of WWW6 Logic Programming Workshop, http://www.cs.vu.nl/ eliens/WWW6/papers.html*, Santa Clara, California, Mar. 1997.

42. P. Tarau, V. Dahl, and A. Fall. Backtrackable State with Linear Affine Implication and Assumption Grammars. In J. Jaffar and R. H. Yap, editors, *Concurrency and Parallelism, Programming, Networking, and Security*, Lecture Notes in Computer Science 1179, pages 53–64, Singapore, Dec. 1996. "Springer".

43. P. Tarau, V. Dahl, S. Rochefort, and K. De Bosschere. LogiMOO: a Multi-User Virtual World with Agents and Natural Language Programming. In S. Pemberton, editor, *Proceedings of CHI'97*, pages 323–324, Mar. 1997.

44. P. Tarau, A. Davison, K. De Bosschere, and M. Hermenegildo, editors. *Proceedings of the 1st Workshop on Logic Programming Tools for INTERNET Applications*, JICSLP'96, Bonn, Sept. 1996. http://clement.info.umoncton.ca/ lpnet.

45. P. Tarau, K. De Boschere, V. Dahl, and S. Rochefort. LogiMOO: an Extensible Multi-User Virtual World with Natural Language Control. 1997. accepted for publication, http://clement.info.umoncton.ca/ html/lm/html.html.

46. P. Tarau and K. De Bosschere. Memoing with Abstract Answers and Delphi Lemmas. In Y. Deville, editor, *Logic Program Synthesis and Transformation*, Springer-Verlag, pages 196–209, Louvain-la-Neuve, July 1993.

47. P. Tarau and K. De Bosschere. Virtual World Brokerage with BinProlog and Netscape. In Tarau et al. [44]. http://clement.info.umoncton.ca/ lpnet.

48. P. Tarau, K. De Bosschere, and B. Demoen. Partial Translation: Towards a Portable and Efficient Prolog Implementation Technology. *Journal of Logic Programming*, 29(1–3):65–83, Nov. 1996.

49. P. Tarau, K. De Bosschere, and M. Hermenegildo, editors. *Proceedings of the 2nd International Workshop on Logic Programming Tools for INTERNET Applications*, ICLP'97, Leuven, July 1997. http://clement.info.umoncton.ca/ lpnet.

50. P. Van Roy, S. Haridi, and P. Brand. Using mobility to make transparent distribution practical. 1997. manuscript.

51. P. Van Roy, S. Haridi, P. Brand, G. Smolka, M. Mehl, and R. Scheidhouer. Mobile Objects in Distributed Oz. *ACM TOPLAS*, 1997. to appear.

52. D. H. D. Warren. Higher-order extensions to Prolog – are they needed? In D. Michie, J. Hayes, and Y. H. Pao, editors, *Machine Intelligence 10*. Ellis Horwood, 1981.

Towards Autonomous, Perceptive, and Intelligent Virtual Actors

Daniel Thalmann

Computer Graphics Lab, EPFL - LIG
Lausanne, Switzerland
thalmann@lig.di.epfl.ch

Hansrudi Noser

Multimedia Laboratorium
University of Zurich
noser@ifi.unizh.ch

Abstract.

This paper explains methods to provide autonomous virtual humans with the skills necessary to perform stand-alone role in films, games and interactive television. We present current research developments in the Virtual Life of autonomous synthetic actors. After a brief description of our geometric, physical, and auditory Virtual Environments, we introduce the perception action principles with a few simple examples. We emphasize the concept of virtual sensors for virtual humans. In particular, we describe our experiences in implementing virtual sensors such as vision sensors , tactile sensors, and hearing sensors. We then describe knowledge-based navigation, knowledge-based locomotion and in more details sensor-based tennis.

From Behavioral Animation to Virtual Life

This paper explains methods to provide virtual actors with the skills necessary to perform stand-alone role in films, games (Bates et al. 1992) and interactive television (Magnenat Thalmann and Thalmann 1995).

For the modeling of actor *behaviors*, the ultimate objective is to build *intelligent autonomous* virtual humans with *adaptation*, *perception* and *memory*. These virtual humans should be able to act *freely* and *emotionally*. They should be *conscious* and *unpredictable*. But can we expect in the near future to represent in the computer the concepts of behavior, intelligence, autonomy, adaptation, perception, memory, freedom, emotion, consciousness, and unpredictability ? First, we will try to define these terms. More details may be found in [Magnenat Thalmann and Thalmann 1994).

- **Behavior** for virtual humans may be defined as a manner of conducting themselves. it is also the response of an individual, group, or species to its environment.
- **Intelligence** may be defined as the ability to learn or understand or to deal with new or trying situations.
- **Autonomy** is generally defined as the quality or state of being self-governing.
- **Adaptation**: an artificial organism is adaptive as long as it may "survive" in more or less unpredictable and dangerous environments.
- **Perception** is defined as the awareness of the elements of environment through physical sensation.
- **Memory** is generally defined as the power or process of reproducing or recalling what has been learned and retained especially through associative mechanisms.
- **Emotion** may be defined as the affective aspect of consciousness; this is a state of feeling, a psychic and physical reaction subjectively experienced as strong feeling and physiologically involving changes that prepare the body for immediate vigorous.
- **Consciousness** may be defined as the quality or state of being aware especially of something within oneself or the state of being characterized by sensation, emotion, volition, and thought.
- **Freedom** for a virtual actor may be defined as the extent that his future behaviour is unpredictable to somebody.

As a virtual world is completely generated by computer, it expresses itself visually, with sounds and feelings. Virtual worlds deal with all the models describing physical laws of the real world as well as the physical, biological, and psychological laws of life. Virtual Life is linked to problems in artificial life but differs in the sense that these problems are specific to virtual worlds. It does not deal with physical or biological objects in real life but only with the simulation of biological virtual creatures. Virtual Life is at the intersection of Virtual Reality and Artificial Life (Magnenat Thalmann and Thalmann 1994), it is an interdisciplinary area strongly based on concepts of real-time computer animation, autonomous agents, and mobile robotics. Virtual Life cannot exist without the growing development of Computer Animation techniques and corresponds to the most advanced concepts and techniques of it.

This kind of research is strongly related to the research efforts in behavioral animation as introduced by Reynolds (1987) to study the problem of group trajectories: flocks of birds, herds of land animals and fish schools. This kind of animation using a traditional approach (keyframe or procedural laws) is almost impossible. In the Reynolds approach, each bird of the flock decides its own trajectory without animator intervention. Reynolds introduces a distributed behavioral model to simulate flocks. The simulated flock is an elaboration of a particle system with the simulated birds being the particles. A flock is assumed to be the result of the interaction between the behaviors of individual birds. Working independently, the birds try both to stick together and avoid collisions with one another and with other objects in their environment. In a module of behavioral animation, positions, velocities and orientations of the actors are known from the system at any time. The animator may control several global parameters: e.g. weight of the obstacle avoidance component, weight of the convergence to the goal, weight of the centering of the group, maximum velocity, maximum acceleration, minimum distance between actors. The animator provides data about the leader trajectory and the behavior of other birds relatively to the leader. A computer-generated film has been produced using this distributed behavioral model: Stanley and Stella. Haumann and Parent (1988) describe behavioral simulation as a means to obtain global motion by simulating simple rules of behavior between locally related actors. Lethebridge and Ware (1989) propose a simple heuristically-based method for expressive stimulus-response animation. Wilhelms (1990) proposes a system based on a network of sensors and effectors. Ridsdale (1990) proposes a method that guides lower-level motor skills from a connectionist model of skill memory, implemented as collections of trained neural networks. We should also mention the huge litterature about autonomous agents (Maes 1991) which represents a background theory for behavioral animation. More recently, genetic algorithms were also proposed by Sims (1994) to automatically generate morphologies for artificial creatures and the neural systems for controlling their muscle forces. Tu and Terzopoulos (1994) described a world inhabited by artificial fishes

A Geometrical, Physical, and Auditory Virtual Environment

The environment of the actors is modeled with behavioral L-systems which are timed production systems designed to model the development and behavior of static objects, plant like objects and autonomous creatures. The behavioral L-system we use, is based on a timed, parametric, stochastic and conditional production system, force fields, synthetic vision and audition. More information can be found in [Noser and Thalmann 1993; Noser and Thalmann 1994; Noser and Thalmann 1995; Noser and Thalmann 1996]. The L-system interpreter controls and synchronizes the animation of the actors and the virtual environment that integrates geometric, physical and acoustic elements. Figure 1 shows an example of Virtual Environment.

Geometric modeling

The L-system model associates to its symbols basic geometric primitives as cubes, spheres, trunks, cylinders, line segments, pyramids and imported triangulated surfaces. We define the non generic environment as the ground, the tennis court, or walls directly in the axiom of the production system. The generic parts, as growing plants, are defined by production rules. The actors are represented by a special symbol. Their geometric representation can vary form simple primitives like some cubes and spheres, over a more complicated skeleton structure to a fully deformed triangulated body surface usable in a raytracer. The choice of an actor's shape depends on the purpose of the application which can range from tests to interactive real time simulations or raytraced video productions.

Fig. 1. Autonomous Virtual Humans with L-system-based Virtual Environment

Physical modeling

To model realistic virtual environments we use particle dynamics in force fields based on Newton's equation of movement. Particle dynamics can be used to model behavioral animation [Noser and Thalmann 1993; Reynolds 1987] and for physical simulation. In a force field animation system the 3D world has to be modeled not only geometrically, but also by force fields. Some objects exert repulsion forces on others in case of collisions. Other objects are attractive. There can exist objects being attractive at far distances and repulsive at short distances. Space force fields like gravity or wind can influence trajectories of moving particles. In the tennis game simulation, for example, the particle dynamics serves to animate the ball. With this approach the ball movement in gravitation and wind force fields, including collisions of the ball with the ground, the net and the racket can be simulated. In our dynamic particle system each particle is treated as a point object which can carry a vector force field influencing other objects.

Sound modeling

The acoustic environment is composed of sound sources and a propagation medium. The sound sources can produce sound events composed of a sound file name, a position in the world, a type of sound, and a start and an end time of the sound event. Spoken words and sentences, collision sounds or background music represent sound events. The sounds used are read from a library of numeric AIFF files.

Figure 2 shows the architecture of our sound environment model. The propagation medium corresponds to the sound event handler which controls the sound events and transmits the sounds to the ears of the actors and/or to a user and/or a sound event track file.

Each sound event is emitted to the sound event handler which controls the playback, the update of the sound event log file, the duration of the sound, and the update of the sound source position during the activation time of the sound. By using the sound event handler, each actor can access the currently active sounds. We do sound rendering only for video production. In this case, at each frame, a sound event log file is additionally updated which is rendered at the end of the animation by a sound renderer described in [Noser and Thalmann 1995]. For tests or interactive applications we suppose an infinite sound propagation speed without weakening of the signal. The sound sources are all omni-directional, and the environment is non reverberant.

An acoustic environment can be modeled by using procedures from two modules "sound event handler" and "sound library" shown in Figure 2. The module "sound library" offers the possibility to define a set of sounds and to play them on the SGI hardware.

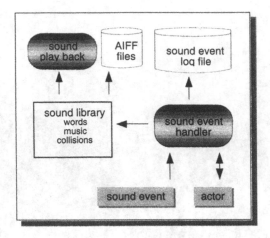

Fig. 2. Sound environment architecture

The Actor – Environment Interface

Perception through Virtual Sensors

The actor-environment interface, or the synthetic sensors, constitute an important part of a behavioral animation system. As sensorial information drastically influences behavior, the synthetic sensors should simulate the functionality of their organic counterparts. Due to real-time constraints, we did not make any attempt to model biological models of sensors. Therefore, synthetic vision only makes efficient visibility tests using SGI's graphics rendering hardware that produces a Z-buffered color image representing an agent's vision. A tactile point-like sensor will be represented by a simple function evaluating the global force field at its position. The synthetic "ear" of an agent will be represented by a function returning the on-going sound events. What is important for an actor's behavior is the functionality of a sensor and how it filters the information flow from the environment, and not the specific model of the sensor.

Another aspect of synthetic sensor design is its universality. The sensors should be as independent as possible from specific environment representations and they should be easily adjustable for interactive users. For example, the same Z-buffer based renderer displays the virtual world for an autonomous actor and an interactive user. The user and the autonomous actors perceive the virtual environment through rendered images, without knowing anything about the internal 3D environment representation or the rendering mechanism.

The sense of touch plays also an important role for humans. In order to model this sense, we use a physically based force field model. This model is close to reality, as the real sense of touch also perceives collision forces. By adding a physically-based animation of objects, we can extend the force field model to a physically based animation system where touch sensors correspond to special functions evaluating the global force field at their current position. This approach also solves the response problem of collisions, as they are handled automatically by the physics-based evolution system if both colliding objects - sensor and touched object - exert for example short range repulsion forces. We opted for a force field-based model to represent the sense of touch, as it integrates itself naturally into the physically-based particle system we already use for physical and behavioral animation. Of course, for real-time applications, the number of sensors and particles should be small, as the evolution of the particle system is computationally expensive. Another disadvantage of this approach is that the touch sensors only "sense" geometrical shapes that are explicitly bounded by appropriate force fields. Another difficulty arising due to the force field model is the fact that the parameterization of the force fields, the numerical integration of the system of differential equations, the time step and the speed of moving objects depend on each other, and that the adaptation of all parameters for a stable animation is not always trivial. All these parameters need to be manually tuned in the L-system definition.

As pointed out above, we use a sound event framework for controlling the acoustic model of the animation system. The sound event handler maintains a table of the on-going sound events. Consequently, one can immediately model synthetic hearing by simple querying of this table of on-going sound events. An interactive user can also produce sound events in the virtual environment via a speech recognition module. Through a sound event, an autonomous actor can directly capture its semantic, position and emitting source.

The Vision System

In our implementation of the vision-based approach to behavioral animation, the synthetic actor perceives its environment through a small window in which the environment is rendered by the computer from the actor's point of view. Rendering is based on Z-buffer techniques. The Z-buffer consists of an array containing the depth values of the pixels of the image. The algorithm uses these Z-buffer values for efficient rendering of 3D scenes. Renault et al. [1990] used the Z-buffering hardware graphics of workstations for efficiently rendering a bitmap projection of the actor's point of view. The color of an object is unique and serves the purpose of identifying the semantics of an object in the image. This synthetic vision was used to create an animation involving synthetic actors moving autonomously in a corridor, and avoiding objects as well as other synthetic actors.

As an actor can access Z-buffer values of the pixels - corresponding to the distances of the objects' pixels to the observer -, their color, and its own position, it can therefore locate visible objects in the 3D environment. This local information is sufficient for some local navigation. For global navigation, however, a visual memory is useful in order to recognize dead-ends problems, such as searching for the exit to a maze. We modeled visual memory by a 3D occupancy octree grid, similar to a technique described in [Roth-Tabak and Jain 1989]. In this space grid, each pixel of an object, transformed back to 3D world coordinates, occupies a voxel. By comparing, in each frame, the rendered voxels in the visual field with the corresponding pixel of the vision window, we can update the visual memory by eliminating voxels having disappeared in the 3D world. Consequently, the visual memory reflects the state of the 3D dynamic world as perceived by the synthetic actor.

The concept of synthetic vision with a voxelized visual memory is independent of 3D world modeling. Even fractal objects and procedurally-defined and rendered worlds without 3D object database can be perceived as long as they can be rendered in a Z-buffer-based vision window. We use synthetic vision in conjunction with a visual memory, for environment recovery, for global navigation, for local navigation optimization and for object recognition through color coding in several behaviors. The reconstruction of the perceived environment by the "visual memory" of an actor, and its use in global navigation is published in [Noser et al. 1993; Noser et al. 1995].

The Hearing Sensors

The hearing sensor of an actor corresponds to the table of the currently active sounds provided by the sound event handler representing the propagation medium. From this table the actor retrieves the complete information regarding each event consisting of the sound identifier, source and position. The same principle as for the other synthetic sensors also applies to the hearing sensor. We need to define special functions usable in the conditions of production rules, and returning useful information. We implemented functions that return on-going identifiers of sound events and sound sources.

The Tactile Sensors

Ideally, geometrical collision detection between surfaces should be used for the modeling of tactile sensors. However, as a typical L-system environment is composed of a large number of objects, and as there is no geometrical database of the 3D objects, traditional collision detection is not the best solution for a tactile sensor model. As we already have a force field environment integrated in the L-system, we use a force field approach to model tactile sensor points. All we need to do is define a function that can evaluate the amount of the global force field at a given position. This amount can be compared with a threshold value that represents, for instance, a collision. With this function, even wind force fields can be sensed. Traditional collision detection between surfaces can cause a large number of collisions, and it will not always be easy to model the behavioral response. With the definition of only one or few sensor points attached to an actor, this behavioral response is easier to control, and calculation time is reduced, which is important for real-time applications. We can also associate a particle having an appropriate force field with a sensor point that will act automatically on other particles. Thus, an actor can "sense" and manipulate other particles.

In order to use tactile information for behavior modeling with production rules, the force field sensing function must be usable under the conditions of the production rules during the derivation phase of the symbolic object. During interpretation of the symbolic using a query symbol, the turtle position can be copied into the parameter space of the symbol. Consequently, the turtle position, given by the x, y, and z coordinates, is available in the parameters x, y, and z of the query symbol for the force field function. This force field function returns the amount of force felt at the position of the turtle. Therefore, the force can be used in conditions that trigger certain behaviors represented by production rules.

When the turtle position is available in the parameter space of a symbol, it can of course also be used for geometrical collision detection, coded within the condition expressions of production rules. If the parameter y corresponds to the y coordinate of the turtle, a condition, such as y<0, for example, detects a collision of the turtle when the ground is situated at y = 0, and gravity is acting in the y down direction.

Speech Recognition

A considerable part of human communication is based on speech. Therefore, a believable virtual humanoid environment with user interaction should include speech recognition. In order to improve real time user interaction with autonomous actors we extended the L-system interpreter with a speech recognition feature that transmits spoken words, captured by a microphone, to the virtual acoustic environment by creating corresponding sound events perceptible by autonomous actors. This concept enables us to model behaviors of actors reacting directly to user-spoken commands.

For speech recognition we use POST, the Parallel Object oriented Speech Toolkit [Hennebert and Delacrétaz 1996], developed for designing automatic speech recognition. POST is freely distributed to academic institutions. It can perform simple feature extraction, training and testing of word and sub-word Hidden Markov Models with discrete and multi Gaussian statistical modeling. We use a POST application for isolated word recognition.

The system can be trained by several users and its performance depends on the number of repetitions and the quality of word capture. This speech recognizing feature was recently added to the system and we don't have much experience with its performance. First tests, however, with a single user training, resulted in a satisfactory recognition rate for a vocabulary of about 50 isolated words.

Actor Behaviors

Action level

Synthetic vision, audition and tactile allow the actor to perceive the environment. Based on this information, his behavioral mechanism will determine the actions he will perform. Actions may be at several degrees of complexity. An actor may simply evolve in his environment or he may interact with this environment or even communicate with other actors. We will emphasize three types of actions: navigation and locomotion, grasping and ball games.

Actions are performed using a common architecture for motion (Boulic et al. 1995). The motion control part includes 5 generators: keyframing, inverse kinematics, dynamics, walking and grasping and high-level tools to combine and blend them.

Behavior control

A high level behavior (see Figure 3) uses in general sensorial input and special knowledge. A way of modeling behaviors is the use of an automata approach. Each actor has an internal state which can change each time step according to the currently active automata and its sensorial input. In the following we use behavior and automata as synonyms. To control the global behavior of an actor we use a stack of automata. At the beginning of the animation the user provides a sequence of behaviors (the script) and pushes them on the actor's stack. When the current behavior ends the animation system pops the next behavior from the stack and executes it. This process is repeated until the actor's behavior stack is empty. Some of the behaviors use this stack too, in order to reach subgoals by pushing itself with the current state on the stack and switching to the new behavior allowing them to reach the subgoal. When this new behavior has finished the automata pops the old interrupted behavior and continues. This behavior control using a stack facilitates to an actor to become more autonomous and to create his own subgoals while executing the original script.

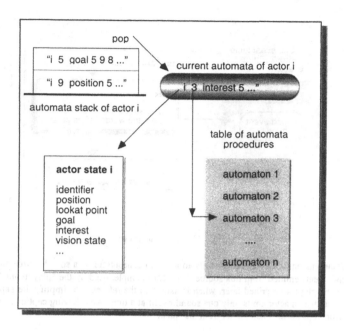

Fig. 3. Architecture of the behavior control

We present three behaviors, which have some "intelligent" aspects: knowledge-based navigation, knowledge-based locomotion, and knowledge-based tennis. They are based on a kind of reasoning on the data obtained from the perception process and some basic knowledge. In the future, it will be possible to increate the complexity of situations and reasoning.

We implemented the behavior stack by a stack of command strings. Each string identifies in its header the actor and the automaton. The rest of the string contains commands that modify the actor's state variables. If an automaton pops a behavior, it is parsed and interpreted. If a state variable is not affected, it maintains the actual value. The following list shows the behaviors used by the tennis players and the referee.

- **Navigation and observe:**

The **"walk_continuously"** automaton allows navigation and path planning for actors based on vision and visual memory. It allows an actor to navigate autonomously to a given goal from its actual position. We described the principles of this automaton already in [Noser et al. 1995]. The **"observe"** automaton is used by actors which have detected a collision in front of them. The vision system turns around by 360 degrees in order to update the visual memory, and to find visible color coded objects. After having turned around once, the next automaton is popped from the stack.

- **Talk and listen:**

A high level behavior, which has to talk at a given moment (see referee), can use the **"talk"** automaton (see Figure 4). It puts n words into the actor's sound event table "wordsToSpeak", pushes itself on the stack, and changes to the "talk" automaton. The "talk" automaton transmits sequentially these events to the sound event handler by taking into account the duration of each word. When it has transmitted the last event, it clears the table and pops the next automaton from the stack.

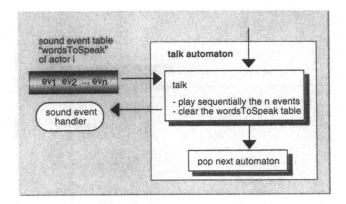

Fig. 4. The "talk" automaton

The **"listen"** automaton (see Figure 5) permits an actor to concentrate on a sound source and to memorize the next n sound events emitted from this source. It is, for example, used by the "play_tennis" automaton of the synthetic tennis players described later, when it listens to the referee. To simplify the capture of spoken words, we suppose that an actor emits only one sound event at a time. After having captured the n events, the "listen" automaton pops the next automaton from the stack.

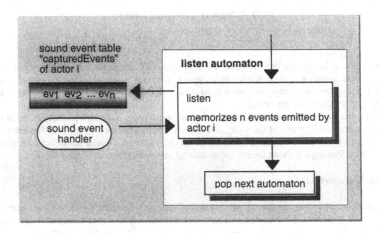

Fig. 5. The "listen" automaton

Knowledge-based Navigation

The task of a navigation system is to plan a path to a specified goal and to execute this plan, modifying it as necessary to avoid unexpected obstacles.

We may distinguish two types of navigation methods: The **local navigation** algorithm uses the direct input information from the environment to reach goals and sub-goals given by the **global navigation** and to avoid unexpected obstacles. The local navigation algorithm has no model of the environment, and doesn't know the position of the actor in the world. In our approach, local navigation is based on the concept of Displacement Local Automata (DLA). These DLAs work as a black box which has the knowledge to create goals and subgoals in a specific local environment. They can be thought of as low-level navigation reflexes which use vision, reflexes which are automatically performed by the adults. Figure 6 shows an example of vision-based navigation.

Fig. 6. Vision-based navigation

The global navigation needs a prelearned model of the environment to perform path-planning. This model is constructed with the information coming from the sensory system. Most navigation systems developed in robotics for intelligent mobile robots are based on the accumulation of accurate geometrical descriptions of the environment. Kuipers and Byun [1988] give a nearly exhaustive list of such methods using quantitative world modeling. In robotics, due to low mechanical accuracy and sensory errors, these methods have failed in large scale area. We don't have this problem in Computer Graphics because we have access to the world coordinates of the actor, and because the synthetic vision or other simulations of perception systems are more accurate. Elfes [1990] proposed a 2D geometric model based on grid but using a Bayesian probabilistic approach to filter non accurate information coming from various sensor positions. Roth-Tabak [1989] proposed a 3D geometric model based on a grid but for a static world. In our approach, we use an octree as the internal representation of the environment seen by an actor because it offers several interesting features. With an octree we can easily construct voxelized objects by choosing the maximum depth level of the subdivision of space. Detailed objects like flowers and trees do not need to be represented in complete detail in the problem of path searching. It is sufficient to represent them by some enclosing cubes corresponding to the occupied voxels of the octree. The octree adapts itself to the complexity of the 3D environment, as it is a dynamic data structure making a recursive subdivision of space. The octree has to represent the visual memory of an actor in a 3D environment with static and dynamic objects. Objects in this environment can grow, shrink, move or disappear as the *view*.

Knowledge-based Locomotion

When the actor evolves in his environment, a simple walking model is not sufficient, the actor has to adapt his trajectory based on the variations of terrain by bypassing, jumping or climbing the obstacles he meets. The bypassing of obstacles consists in changing the direction and velocity of the walking of the actor. Jumping and climbing correspond to more complex motion. These actions should generate parameterized motion depending on the height and the length of the obstacle for a jump and the height and location of the feet for climbing the obstacle. These characteristics are determined by the actor from his perception.

The actor can be directed by giving his linear speed and his angular speed or by giving a position to reach. In the first case, the actor makes no perception (virtual vision). He just walks at the given linear speed and turns at the given angular speed. In the second case, the actor makes use of virtual vision enabling him to avoid obstacles. The vision based navigation can be local or global. With a local navigation, the agent goes straight on to his goal and it is possible that he cannot reach it. With a global navigation, the actor first tries to find a path to his goal and if the path exists, the actor follows it until he reaches the goal position or until he detects a collision by his vision. During global navigation the actor memorizes his perceived environment by voxelizing it, based on his synthetic vision.

We developed a special automata for walking in complex environments with local vision based path optimization. So an actor continues walking even if he detects a future collision in front of him. By dynamically figuring out a new path during walking he can avoid the collision without halting. We also proposed a system for the automatic derivation of a human curved walking trajectory [Boulic et al. 1994] from the analysis provided by its synthetic vision module. A general methodology associates the two low-level modules of vision and walking with a planning module which establishes the middle term path from the knowledge of the visualized environment. The planning is made under the constraint of minimizing the distance, the speed variation and the curvature cost. Moreover, the planning may trigger alternate walking motion whenever the decreasing in curvature cost is higher than the associated increasing in speed variation cost due to the corresponding halt and restart. The Analysis of walking trajectories on a discrete environment with sparse foothold locations has been also completed [Boulic et al. 1993] regarding the vision-based recognition of footholds, the local path planning, the next step selection and the curved body trajectory. The walking model used is based on biomechanical studies of specific motion pattern [Boulic et al. 1990]. Figure 7 shows an example of walking.

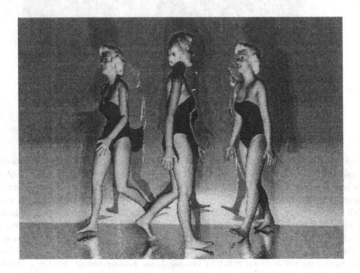

Fig. 7. Biomechanical model for walking

Sensor-based Tennis Playing

Tennis playing is a human activity which is severely based on the vision of the players. In our model, we use the vision system to recognize the flying ball, to estimate its trajectory and to localize the partner for game strategy planning. The geometric characteristics of the tennis court however, make part of the players knowledge. For the dynamics simulation of the ball, gravity, net, ground and the racquet we use the force field approach developed for the L-system animation system. The tracking of the ball by the vision system is controlled by a special automata. A prototype of this automata is already able to track the ball, to estimate the collision time and collision point of ball and racquet and to perform successfully a hit with given force and a given resulting ball direction. In a first step, we have a prototype where only two racquets with synthetic vision can play against each other, in order to develop, test and improve game strategy and the physical modeling (see Figure 8). The integration of the corresponding locomotor system of a sophisticated actor (see Figure 9) has been integrated in the context of Networked Virtual Environments [Molet et al. 1999; Çapin et al. 1999].

In the navigation problem each colored pixel is interpreted as an obstacle. No semantic information is necessary. In tennis playing however, the actor has to distinguish between the partner, the ball and the rest of the environment. The ball has to be recognized, its trajectory has to be estimated and it has to be followed by the vision system. At the beginning of a ball exchange, the actor has to verify that its partner is ready. During the game the actor needs also his partner's position for his play strategy.

To recognize objects in the image we use color coding. The actor knows that a certain object is made of a specific material. When it scans the image it looks for the corresponding pixels and calculates its average position and its approximate size. Thus each actor can extract some limited semantic information from the image.

Fig. 8. Sensor-based tennis

Fig. 9. An articulated tnnis player

Once the actor has recognized the ball, it follows it with his vision system and adjusts at each frame his field of view. To play tennis each partner has to estimate the future racket-ball collision position and time and to move as fast as possible to this point. At each frame (1/25 sec) the actor memorizes the ball position. So, every n-th frame the actor can derive the current velocity of the ball. From this current velocity and the current position of the ball it can calculate the future impact point and impact time. We suppose that the actor wants to hit the ball at a certain height h.

In the next phase the actor has to play the ball. Now he has to determine the racket speed and its orientation to play the ball to a given place. Before playing the ball the actor has to decide where to play. In our simulation approach he looks where his partner is placed and then he plays the ball in the most distant corner of the court.

All the above features are coordinated by a specialized "tennis play" automata. First an actor goes to his start position. There he waits until his partner is ready. Then he looks for the ball, which is thrown into the game. Once the vision system has found the ball, it always follows it by adjusting the field of view angle. If the ball is flying towards the actor, it starts estimating the impact point. Once the ball has passed the net, the actor localizes his partner with his vision system during one frame. This information is used for the game strategy. After playing the ball, the actor goes back to his start point and waits until the ball comes back to play it again.

The evolution of a tennis game can also be described by an automaton with transitions as illustrated in Figure 10. At the beginning the player is in an inactive state. Through the transition t_1 triggered ,for example, through an external event, it changes to the state "at_start" by navigating to its start position. When it arrives there, it goes into the state "look_for_partner", where it waits until its partner has arrived at the start point. It verifies this of course by using synthetic vision. Then, it changes to the state "follow_ball" where it looks for the ball. When it has seen the ball, it tracks it with the vision system, and estimates its speed and position.

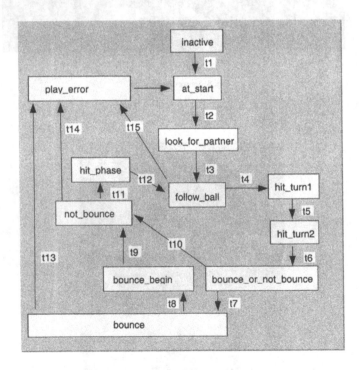

Fig. 10. Actor states during a tennis game

In order to estimate its velocity, each actor maintains the positions of the last n (=3) frames and derives the velocity from them and the frame to frame time increment. If the actor sees the ball approaching, it goes through transition t_4 into the state "hit_turn_one". As the velocity estimation of the ball is still not satisfactory, it waits some time by changing through the intermediate state "hit_turn_two" to the state "bounce_or_not_bounce", where it has to decide whether to let the ball bounce or not. According to its decision, it changes to the state "bounce" or "not_bounce". In the state "bounce", when the ball is close to the ground, it enters the state "bounce_begin". When the ball has collided and starts mounting, it goes to the state not_bounce. If it is close to the racket ball impact point, it enters into the state "hit_phase" where it strikes the ball according to the game strategy described later. After the stroke the player enters the "follow_ball" state, and a new cycle can begin.

During a game the "play_tennis" automaton (see Figure 11) has to control the actor's vision system, the audition system and its internal state of the game. Each of the three systems has its own state variables which can be mutually manipulated. The audition system control checks at each frame the sound events. If the automaton detects the sound event "fault", emitted by the referee, it pushes the actual "play_tennis" automaton on the stack, together with the necessary initializations allowing a new game. Then, it activates the "walk_continuously" automaton in order to move to its start position on the tennis court.

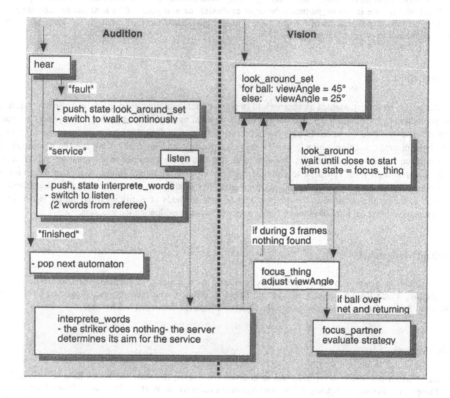

Fig. 11. The "play_tennis" automaton

If the detected sound event is "finished", the whole game is finished, and the actor pops the next automaton from the stack. If it detects the sound event "service", coming from the referee, it pushes the "play_tennis" automaton on the stack with the initial state "interprete_words", and switches to the "listen" automaton which captures the next two words coming from the referee. When the "listen" automaton has captured the two words, it pops the next automaton, being of course the "play_tennis" one, with the initial state "interprete_words". These two words are the name of the server and the server position "left" or "right". The actor recognizes whether it is the server or not. If it is the server, it fixes the correct aim point for its service, changes to the "look_around_set" state, and a new game will begin.

Each actor has a state variable designing its object of interest it is looking for with its vision system. In the state "look_around_set" it initializes its view angle according to the size of its object of interest which can be the ball or its game partner, and it focuses its eyes on the start position of its opponent. Then, it enters the state "look_around". If its object of interest is the ball, it goes to the state "focus_thing" if the ball is visible. If the object of interest, however, is the other player, it waits until it is close to the start point. Only then, it switches to the state "focus_thing". In this state it controls several features. As the name of the state indicates, one task of the actor is to focus the vision system on the object of interest, and to adjust the view angle. When the object of interest or the actor move fast, it can happen that the vision system fails to track it. In this case the state is changed to "look_around_set" where the actor starts again to look for the ball.

If during the impact point estimation the actor estimates the impact point to be outside of its court, it decides to call a let, and to move directly back to its start position, waiting there for a new game. That is why, it pushes the "play_tennis" automaton on the stack, together with the initializations for a new game, and activates the "walk_continuously" automaton with its start point as goal. If the vision state is "focus_thing" and the game state "look_for_partner", the state is reset to "look_around_set", and the ball becomes the object of interest. When the object of interest is the ball, and when the vision state is still "focus_thing", the striker tries to determine its opponents position to use it for its game strategy. That's why, when the ball flies over the net, the player changes its vision state to "focus_partner" after having set its object of interest to its opponent.

If the vision state is "focus_partner", the actor evaluates the aim point of its next stroke according to its strategy and the actual position of the opponent. Then, it goes back into the "focus_thing" state, after having selected the ball as object of interest.

Conclusion

In this paper, we have presented an approach to implement autonomous virtual actors in virtual worlds based on perception and virtual sensors. We believe this is an ideal approach for modeling a behavioral animation and offers a universal approach to pass the necessary information from the environment to an actor in the problems of path searching, obstacle avoidance, game playing, and internal knowledge representation with learning and forgetting characteristics. We also think that this new way of defining animation is a convenient and universal high level approach to simulate the behavior of intelligent human actors in dynamics and complex environments including virtual environments. The intelligence of virtual actors is constrained and limited to the results obtained in the development of new methods of Artificial Intelligence. However, the representation under the form of virtual actors is a way of visually evaluating the progress.

Acknowledgments

The authors are grateful to the people who contributed to this work, in particular Srikanth Bandi, Pascal Bécheiraz, Ronan Boulic, Zhyong Huang, and Serge Rezzonico. The research was supported by the Swiss National Science Research Foundation and the Federal Office for Education and Science.

References

Bates J, Loyall AB, Reilly WS (1992) "An architecture for Action, Emotion, and Social Behavior", Proc. Fourth Europeans Workshop on Modeling Autonomous Agents in a multi Agents World, S. Martino al Cimino, Italy.

Boulic R., Capin T., Kalra P., Lintermann B., Moccozet L., Molet T., Huang Z., Magnenat-Thalmann N., Saar K., Schmitt A., Shen J. and Thalmann D. (1995) "A system for the Parallel Integrated Motion of Multiple Deformable Human Characters with Collision Detection", EUROGRAPHICS' 95, Maastricht.

Boulic R., Noser H., Thalmann D. (1993) "Vision-Based Human Free-Walking on Sparse Foothold Locations", Fourth Eurographics Workshop on Animation and Simulation, Barcelona Spain, Eurographics, pp.173-191

Boulic R., Noser H., Thalmann D. (1994) "Automatic Derivation of Curved Human Walking Trajectories from Synthetic Vision", Computer Animation '94, Geneva, IEEE Computer Society Press, pp.93-103.

Boulic R., Thalmann D, Magnenat-Thalmann N. (1990) "A global human walking model with real time kinematic personification" The Visual Computer, 6(6).

Elfes A. (1990) "Occupancy Grid: A Stochastic Spatial Representation for Active Robot Perception", Proc. Sixth Conference on Uncertainty in AI.

Haumann D.R., Parent R.E. (1988) "The Behavioral Test-bed: Obtaining Complex Behavior from Simple Rules", The Visual Computer, Vol.4, No 6, pp.332-347.

Hennebert J. and Delacrétaz D.P., (1996) *POST: Parallel Object-Oriented Speech Toolkit*, to be published at ICSLP 96, Philadelphia

Kuipers B., Byun Y.T. (1988) "A Robust Qualitative Approach to a Spatial Learning Mobile Robot", SPIE Sensor Fusion: Spatial Reaoning and Scene Interpretation, Vol. 1003.

Lethebridge T.C. and Ware C. (1989) "A Simple Heuristically-based Method for Expressive Stimulus-response Animation", Computers and Graphics, Vol.13, No3, pp.297-303

Maes P. (ed.) (1991) "Designing Autonomous Agents", Bradford MIT Press.

Magnenat Thalmann N., Thalmann D. (1994) "Creating Artificial Life in Virtual Reality" in: (Magnenat Thalmann and Thalmann, eds) Artificial Life and Virtual Reality, John Wiley, Chichester, 1994, pp.1-10

Magnenat Thalmann N., Thalmann D. (1995) "Digital Actors for Interactive Television", Proc. IEEE, July.

Noser N., Pandzic I. S., Capin T. K., Magnenat Thalmann N, Thalmann D., (1996) *Playing Games through the Virtual Life Network*, ALIFE V, Oral Presentations, May 16-18, Nara, Japan, pp. 114-121

Noser H., Thalmann D. (1993) "L-System-Based Behavioral Animation", Proc. Pacific Graphics '93, pp.133-146.

Noser H., Thalmann D. (1994), Artificial Live and Virtual Reality, Chapter: *Simulating Life of Virtual Plants, Fishes and Butterflies* edited by Nadia Magnenat Thalmann and Daniel Thalmann, 1994 John Wiley & Sons, Ltd.

Noser H., Renault O., Thalmann D., Magnenat Thalmann N. (1995) "Navigation for Digital Actors based on Synthetic Vision, Memory and Learning", Computers and Graphics, Pergamon Press, Vol.19, No1, pp.7-19.

Noser H., Thalmann D. (1995), *Synthetic Vision and Audition for Digital Actors*, Computer Graphics forum, Vol. 14. Number 3, Conference Issue, Maastricht, The Netherlands, pp. 325 –336.

Noser H., D. Thalmann, (1996) *The Animation of Autonomous Actors Based on Production Rules*, Proceedings Computer Animation'96, June 3-4, 1996, Geneva Switzerland, IEEE Computer Society Press, Los Alamitos, California, pp 47-57

Renault O., Magnenat Thalmann N., Thalmann D. (1990) "A Vision-based Approach to Behavioural Animation", The Journal of Visualization and Computer Animation, Vol 1, No 1, pp 18-21.

Reynolds C. (1987) "Flocks, Herds, and Schools: A Distributed Behavioral Model", Proc.SIGGRAPH '87, Computer Graphics, Vol.21, No4, pp.25-34

Ridsdale G. (1990) "Connectionist Modelling of Skill Dynamics", Journal of Visualization and Computer Animation, Vol.1, No2, 1990, pp.66-72.

Roth-Tabak Y. (1989) "Building an Environment Model Using Depth Information", Computer, pp 85-90.

Sims K. (1994) "Evolving Virtual Creatures", Proc. SIGGRAPH '94, pp. 15-22.

Tu X., Terzopoulos D. (1994) "Artificial Fishes: Physics, Locomotion, Perception, Behavior", Proc. SIGGRAPH '94, Computer Graphics, pp.42-48.

Wilhelms J. (1990) "A "Notion" for Interactive Behavioral Animation Control", IEEE Computer Graphics and Applications , Vol. 10, No 3 , pp.14-22

Temporally Invariant Junction Tree for Inference in Dynamic Bayesian Network

Y. Xiang

Department of Computer Science
University of Regina
Regina, Saskatchewan, Canada S4S 0A2
Phone: (306) 585-4088, E-mail: yxiang@cs.uregina.ca

Abstract. Dynamic Bayesian networks (DBNs) extend Bayesian networks from static domains to dynamic domains. The only known generic method for *exact* inference in DBNs is based on dynamic expansion and reduction of active slices. It is effective when the domain evolves relatively slowly, but is reported to be "too expensive" for fast evolving domain where inference is under time pressure.

This study explores the *stationary* feature of problem domains to improve the efficiency of exact inference in DBNs. We propose the construction of a temporally invariant template of a DBN directly supporting exact inference and discuss issues in the construction. This method eliminates the need for the computation associated with dynamic expansion and reduction of the existing method. The method is demonstrated by experimental result.

Keywords: probabilistic reasoning, temporal reasoning, knowledge representation, dynamic Bayesian networks.

1 Introduction

Dynamic Bayesian networks (DBNs) [5, 9] extend Bayesian networks (BNs) [10] from static domains to dynamic domains, i.e., domains that change their states with time. A DBN consists of a finite number of "slices" each of which is a domain dependence model at a particular time interval. Slices corresponding to successive intervals are connected through arcs that represent how the state of the domain evolves with time. Collectively, the slices represent the dynamic domain over a period of time.

When inference must be performed over an extended period of time, it is not feasible to maintain all slices accumulated in the past. Kjaerulff [9] proposed a method, which we shall refer to as the *dynamic expansion and reduction* (DER) method, to perform *exact* inference by dynamically adding new slices and cutting off old slices. To the best of our knowledge, it is the only method explicitly designed for exact inference in DBNs. However, as networks become more complex, the method does not provide satisfactory performance in time-critical domains [7].

In this paper, we investigate ways to improve the efficiency of exact run time inference computation when the domain is either *stationary* or close to be stationary. In Section 2, we define the terminology. Graph-theoretic terms that may not be familiar to some readers are included in Appendix. In Section 3, we propose the construction of a temporally invariant representation to support exact run time inference computation. We discuss technical issued involved in the subsequent two sections and demonstrate our method with an experiment in Section 6.

2 Dynamic Bayesian Networks

A DBN [5, 9] is a quadruplet

$$\mathcal{G}^K = (\bigcup_{i=0}^{K} N_i, \bigcup_{i=0}^{K} E_i, \bigcup_{i=1}^{K} F_i, \bigcup_{i=0}^{K} P_i).$$

Each N_i is a set of nodes labeled by variables. N_i represents the state of a dynamic domain at time interval $t = i$ ($i = 0, \ldots, K$). Collectively, $N = \bigcup_{i=0}^{K} N_i$ represents the states of the dynamic domain over $K + 1$ intervals. Each E_i is a set of arcs between nodes in N_i, which represent conditional independencies between domain variables at a given interval. Each F_i is a set of *temporal* arcs each of which is directed from a node in N_{i-1} to a node in N_i ($i = 1, \ldots, K$). These arcs represent the Markov assumption: the future states of the domain is conditionally independent of the past states given the present state. The subset of N_i ($0 \le i < K$)

$$FI_i = \{x \in N_i | (x, y) \in F_{i+1}\}$$

is called the *forward interface* of N_i, where (x, y) is a temporal arc from x to y. The subset of N_i ($0 < i \le K$)

$$BI_i = \{y \in N_i | (x, y) \in F_i\} \cup \{z \in N_i | z \in \pi(y) \ \& \ (x, y) \in F_i\}$$

is called the *backward interface* of N_i, where $\pi(y)$ is the set of parent nodes of y. Arcs of E_i and F_i are so directed that $D_i = (N_i \cup FI_{i-1}, E_i \cup F_i)$ is a directed acyclic graph (DAG). Each P_i is a conditional probability distribution

$$P_i = \begin{cases} P(N_0) & i = 0 \\ P(N_i | FI_{i-1}) & i > 0 \end{cases}$$

specified by a set of probability tables one for each variable x in N_i conditioned on $\pi(x)$. The pair $S_i = (D_i, P_i)$ is called a *slice* of the DBN and D_i is called the structure of S_i. Collectively, the slices of a DBN define a Bayesian network, whose structure is the union of slice structures and whose joint probability distribution (jpd) is the product of probability tables in all slices.

Figure 1 shows the structure of a DBN where $N_1 = \{a_1, b_1, c_1, d_1, e_1, f_1\}$, $E_1 = \{(a_1, b_1), (b_1, c_1), (b_1, d_1), (c_1, e_1), (d_1, e_1), (e_1, f_1)\}$, $F_1 = \{(a_0, b_1), (f_0, f_1)\}$, $FI_1 = \{a_1, f_1\}$ and $BI_1 = \{a_1, b_1, e_1, f_1\}$.

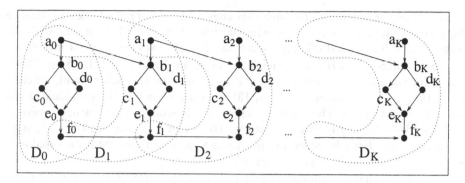

Fig. 1. A dynamic Bayesian network.

At any time $t = j \le K$, the slices $S_0, \ldots, S_{j-1}$ represent the domain history and $S_{j+1}, \ldots, S_K$ predict the future. Evidence (observations obtained in the past and present) may be entered into $S_0, \ldots, S_j$. Limited by computational resource, normally only $S_i, \ldots, S_K$ ($i \le j \le K$) are explicitly maintained, called *active slices* of the DBN.

We assume that the DBN is *connected*. Otherwise the domain can be partitioned into independent subdomains each of which can be represented by a separate DBN.

3 Temporally Invariant Template

Kjaerulff [9] proposed the DER method to perform *exact* inference in DBNs. The method dynamically adds new slices to the front of active slices, converts the expanded slices into a junction tree (JT) [8] representation, reduces the JT by removing the parts corresponding to slices in the most remote history, and uses the reduced JT to process new evidence.

The DER method is effective for domains that evolve relatively slowly, e.g., monitoring the effect of medical therapy [1] or commercial forecasting [3]. However, for fast evolving domains where inference computation is under time pressure, e.g., mobile robot navigation [6] or automated vehicles [7], the computation is "too expensive" as reported in [7].

We attribute the unsatisfactory performance of the DER method partially to the expensive computation during dynamic expansion and reduction. We argue that in many practical applications, the domain is *stationary* or at least is stationary for an extensive period of time before changing to a different (stationary) state. When the domain is stationary, the slices of the DBN are invariant with time. If the number of active slices is also a constant, then dynamic expansion/reduction by the DER method is unnecessarily repeated over and over again.

Forbes et al. [7] recognized this opportunity for improvement. They proposed to precompile the slice of a stationary DBN into a "temporally invariant network". However, since the approach that they took was to replace exact inference by approximate inference using stochastic simulation, they did not deal with the issue of establishing a stable representation directly capable of *exact* inference.

Exact inference in BNs in general has been shown to be NP-hard [2]. Moreover, approximate inference is also NP-hard [4]. On the other hand, efficient algorithms for exact inference [10, 8, 13] are available when the graphical structure of a BN is sparse. The approach taken in this study is to investigate ways to improve the efficiency of exact inference. To this end, we explore the stationary property of the DBN by precompiling a run-time slice representation capable of supporting more efficient exact inference.

We assume that the number of active slices of the DBN is a constant (relaxed in Section 7) $m \geq 1$. Since the domain is stationary, the m active slices at any two time intervals are identical. For the study of inference efficiency, it makes no difference to treat the m slices as one big slice. Therefore, without loss of generality, we can consider only the case $m = 1$.

As stated, we want to precompile some slice representation of a stationary DBN that supports more efficient exact inference. The representation consists of a graphical structure and the associated conditional probabilities. Once such a representation is constructed, a copy of it can be stored as a *template* which we shall denote by T. Inference using the template works as follows:

At any time interval $t = i$, place an active copy T_i of T in the memory. T_i is identical to T except that it has absorbed all evidence acquired when $t < i$. To proceed in time, we evolve T_i into T_{i+1}. First, we cache the belief on some interface (defined below) between T_i and T_{i+1}. Then belief of T is copied into T_i. This effectively makes T_i identical to T without changing the overall data structure of T_i (e.g., the internal representation of the graphical structure). The belief of T_i is then updated using cached belief, which turns (physical) T_i into (logical) T_{i+1}. Now T_{i+1} has emerged and is ready to process new evidence while T_i has vanished.

We emphasize that the above inference uses only two *physical* copies of the template, T and T', and only the belief of T' is modified from interval to interval. Much computation required by DER method is no longer needed.

4 Defining Subnet

In order to construct the template, a portion of the DBN must be selected, which we refer to as a *subnet*. It may or may not be identical to a slice. The subnet may be multiply connected in general. To allow efficient exact inference, we convert it into a JT representation [8] as the run-time template.

Instead of defining the subnet first and then converting to template, we may *conceptually* first convert the DBN into a JT, then select a subtree T of it as the template, and finally determine the corresponding subnet. The subnet/template pair must be such that the template contains exactly the set of variables of the subnet, namely, no clique in T contains variables outside the subnet. When this is the case, we say that the subnet and the subtree template *covers* each other. We will define the subnet in this way.

As in the standard method [8], the process of converting the DBN into a JT consists of moralization, triangulation, organizing cliques into a JT, and assigning belief to each clique. As we shall see, to ensure that the subnet is covered by a subtree, triangulation is the key step in this process.

We define some minimum separator of the moral graph of DBN as the interface between T_i and T_{i+1}, denoted by I_i. This is semantically correct since variables in a separator renders the two groups of variables it separates conditionally independent.

We use node elimination to triangulate (Appendix) the moral graph. The elimination order will be consistent with the order that each T_i emerges and vanishes. That is, for each T_i $(0 < i \le K)$, nodes contained in T_j $(0 \le j < i)$, except I_i, are eliminated before any node of T_i. We shall call any such order a *temporal elimination order*. We show that in the resultant triangulation, the interface I_i is complete.

Proposition 1 *Let $G = \{N, E\}$ be the moral graph of a stationary DBN. Let $I_i \subset N_{i-1} \cup N_i$ $(1 < i \le K)$ be a minimum graph separator of G. Let $\{N_a, I_i, N_b\}$ be a partition of N such that N_a and N_b are separated by I_i. Let G be triangulated into G' by eliminating all nodes in N_a before any node in $I_i \cup N_b$ is eliminated. Then I_i is complete in G'.*

Proof:

We show that an arbitrary pair of nodes in I_i is connected in G'. Since the DBN is stationary, there exists $I_{i-1} \subset N_{i-2} \cup N_{i-1}$ for $i \ge 2$. Consider a pair of nodes x_i and y_i in I_i and the corresponding node x_{i-1} in I_{i-1}.

Since the DBN is connected and I_i is minimum, there exists a path from x_i to x_{i-1} such that all nodes on the path are contained in N_a, except x_i. Otherwise, for every path from x_i to x_{i-1}, there exists a node $z_i \in I_i$. In that case, x_i may be removed from I_i such that I_i is still a separator, which contradicts the assumption that I_i is minimum.

For the similar argument, there exists a path from y_i to x_{i-1} such that all nodes on the path are contained in N_a. Hence, there exists a path from x_i to y_i such that all nodes on the path are contained in N_a. Due to Lemma 4 in Rose et al. [11], the link $\{x_i, y_i\}$ is in G'. $\square$

Proposition 1 implies that I_i is contained in a clique of G' and so is I_{i-1}. If we organize cliques of G' into a JT, then all nodes of the DBN between I_i and I_{i-1} can be covered by a subtree that connects to the rest of the JT through these two cliques. This subtree (a JT) can then be used as the run-time template. This is justified in Theorem 3. Proposition 2 prepares for its proof.

Proposition 2 *Let I be a complete separator between nodes x and y in a triangulated graph G. Let C_x and C_y be two cliques of G such that $x \in C_x$ and $y \in C_y$. Then there exists a JT T of G such that I is either a sepset on the simple path from C_x to C_y in T or is contained in a clique on that path.*

Proof:

The set N of nodes of G can be partitioned into $\{N_x, I, N_y\}$ such that $x \in N_x$, $y \in N_y$, and N_x and N_y are separated by I. Since I is a complete separator, the subgraph G_x spanned by $N_x \cup I$ is triangulated and so is the subgraph G_y spanned by $N_y \cup I$. Hence, a JT T_x of G_x exists and so does a JT T_y of G_y.

The two JTs can be combined into a single JT as follows: Identify a clique Q_x in T_x containing I and a clique Q_y in T_y containing I. If one of the cliques equals I, then join the two JTs by unioning Q_x and Q_y. If none of the cliques equals I, then join the two JTs by a sepset I. The resultant is a JT that satisfies the requirement. □

The following theorem shows that a JT of a DBN can be found that consists of a sequence of (sub)JTs chained together. The subJT will be our template.

Theorem 3 *Let $G = \{N, E\}$ be the moral graph of a stationary DBN. Let $I_i \subset N_{i-1} \cup N_i$ ($1 < i \leq K$) be a minimum graph separator of G. Let $\{N_a, I_{i-1}, N_b, I_i, N_c\}$ be a partition of N, where N_a and N_b are separated by I_{i-1}, and N_b and N_c are separated by I_i.*

Then there exists a temporal elimination order triangulating G into G', and there exists a JT T of G' that satisfies the following conditions:

1. *There exists a subtree T_i connected to the rest of T through two cliques $C_{i-1} \supseteq I_{i-1}$ and $C_i \supseteq I_i$ such that every clique in T_i is a subset of $I_{i-1} \cup N_b \cup I_i$ except that C_{i-1} may contain nodes in N_a and C_i may contain nodes in N_c.*
2. *For each $y \in N_b$, y is contained in nowhere in T except in T_i.*

Proof:

It suffices to show that for any $x \in N_a$ and $y \in N_b$ where x is contained in a clique C_x and y is contained in a clique C_y, it must be the case that $C_x \neq C_y$ and C_{i-1} is on the path between C_x and C_y in some T obtained by some temporal elimination order.

According to a temporal elimination order, x is eliminated before y. They are in a same clique of G' iff they are connected when x is eliminated. Since I_{i-1} is the separator between x and y, y is not in the adjacency of x, and hence they are not connected at the time x is eliminated. Hence $C_x \neq C_y$.

By Proposition 1, since I_{i-1} is a minimum separator, I_{i-1} is complete in G' using any temporal elimination order. Hence C_{i-1} exists in G'. By Proposition 2, it follows that C_{i-1} is on the path between C_x and C_y. □

We can now define the subnet based on such a template.

Definition 4 *Let I_i be a minimum separator in the moral graph of a DBN. Let $\{N_a, I_{i-1}, N_b, I_i, N_c\}$ be a partition of N such that N_a and N_b are separated by I_{i-1}, and N_b and N_c are separated by I_i. The subgraph spanned by $I_{i-1} \cup N_b \cup I_i$ defines the structure of a subnet relative to separator I_i.*

Through previous *conceptual* analysis, we have understood what the structure of a subnet should be. In *practice*, the subnet obtained by Definition 4 will be the starting point in the construction of a template.

5 Choosing Separator

Given the moral graph of a DBN, there are many minimum separators. We first consider two immediate choices: the forward and backward interface. The following propositions show that both can be used as the basis in choosing the separator.

Proposition 5 *Backward interface BI_i is a separator in the moral graph of DBN.*

Proof:

BI_i contains the head of each temporal arc and the parents of the head. In the moral graph, every simple path from a node in N_{i-1} to a node in N_i must contain either a temporal link or a moral link. Hence, deletion of BI_i renders them separated. $\square$

Proposition 6 *Forward interface FI_i is a separator in the moral graph of DBN.*

Proof:

FI_i contains the tail of each temporal arc. In the moral graph, every simple path from a node in N_{i-1} to a node in N_i must pass the tail of a temporal arc, and then either the corresponding temporal link or a moral link. Hence, deletion of BI_i renders them separated. $\square$

It should be noted that both forward and backward interface may not be minimum separators. For example, let $x \in N_i$ be the head of a temporal arc, and $y \in N_i$ be a parent of x. If y has no parent nor other child, then the minimum separator based on BI_i includes x but not y.

Similarly, if the tail of a temporal arc has no parent nor other child, then the minimum separator based on the forward interface does not include this node.

Construction of the template requires assignment of belief to cliques of the template JT. This is performed by assigning each node in the subnet to a unique clique in the JT that contains the family of the node. The belief of a clique C is initialized to the product of $P(x|\pi(x))$ for each x assigned to C. The family of a node in the subnet may not be identical to its family in the DBN. This may or may not cause problem in the belief assignment as discussed below:

First, consider a subnet defined based on forward interface FI_{i-1} and FI_i. The family of each node in this subnet is identical to that in the DBN except for nodes in FI_{i-1}. Since during inference, the belief on FI_{i-1} will be *replaced* by the belief on FI_{i-1} from the previously active template, the belief on these nodes can be left unassigned (equivalent to a constant belief). Hence, difference of family size for nodes in separator FI_{i-1} causes no problem to belief assignment.

On the other hand, if the subnet is defined based on backward interface BI_{i-1} and BI_i, the situation is different. For example, let $x \in N_i$ be the head of a temporal arc, and $y \in N_i$ be a parent of x. The parents of y in the DBN may not be contained in the subnet. Therefore, $P(y|\pi(y))$ as specified in the DBN cannot be included in the belief assignment. Without this piece of knowledge, a correct belief assignment of the template cannot be accomplished. Therefore, the belief assignment of a template cannot be performed *locally* using only the subnet defined by backward interface.

Since forward interface separator allows local belief assignment and thus simplifies the implementation of the template constructor, it is generally preferred over backward interface separator. We shall call forward interface a *self sufficient* separator. In fact, it is not the only self sufficient separator. We characterize such separators as follows:

Definition 7 *Let I_i be a minimum separator in a DBN and S be a subnet defined by separators I_{i-1} and I_i. I_i is* self sufficient *if for each node in S, its family is identical to that in the DBN except nodes in I_{i-1}.*

Since self sufficient separators simplify template constructor, they are generally preferred over separators that are not self sufficient.

Among self sufficient separators, different separators may produce templates of different run-time computational complexity. It is known that the amount of inference computation in a JT of a BN increases as the size of the total state space (STSS) of the JT [12]. Hence a template of smaller STSS is preferred. As finding a JT with the minimum STSS is NP-hard [12], we have to settle for heuristic methods.

According to Proposition 1, the separator will be completed during triangulation. Therefore, a larger separator creates a larger clique and tends to increase the STSS of the resultant template. Furthermore, a larger separator needs more fill-ins to complete. These fill-ins may cause additional cycles which in turn require more fill-ins to triangulate the graph. The result is the additional increase of the STSS. Therefore, one useful heuristics is to choose the separator of the smallest state space, which we shall term as a *minimal* separator.

6   Experimental Demonstration

The method proposed has been implemented and tested in WEBWEAVR-III environment, a research testbed that supports many aspects of representation and inference with uncertain knowledge. The modules involved in this work include a Bayesian network editor for specifying a slice or subnet, a template constructor, and a dynamic inference engine. In the following, we demonstrate the method proposed using our implementation.

We shall demonstrate using the monitoring of a digital counter since understanding the problem requires very little domain knowledge. The counter consists of three D flip-flops (DFFs). The first DFF is driven by an external clock signal. Its output is used to drive the second DFF, whose output is in turn used to drive the third DFF. The circuit, a clock input and its normal output are shown in Figure 2.

The counter cannot be modeled using standard Bayesian networks. This is because the input and output of each DFF are changing with time. The state of each DFF can also change with time. A DFF may be initially normal but becomes abnormal. However, the topology of the circuit is fixed. The state of each DFF

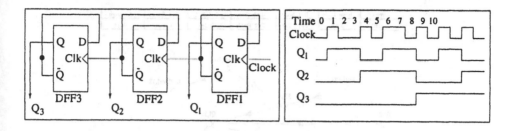

Fig. 2. Left: a digital counter made of three D flip-flops. Right: the input and output of the counter.

can be modeled as temporally changing between two types of behavior: normal and abnormal. Each type can be described without reference to time. Hence the domain is *stationary* and our proposed method is applicable.

The first DFF toggles at the positive edge (not positive level) of the clock. The edge monitoring can be modeled by a variable GotLow. At each time interval, GotLow = true if the input clock level is negative. The value implies that the next positive level will be a positive edge. When the input clock level is positive, two possible previous clock levels should be considered. If the previous clock level has been positive, then GotLow should be false since the negative level has not been seen yet. If the previous clock level has been negative, then the current positive level represents a positive edge. The value of GotLow should be reset to start the next cycle of monitoring. Hence, GotLow = false whenever the input clock level is positive. We have $P(GotLow = true|Clock = 0) = 1$ and $P(GotLow = true|Clock = 1) = 0$.

The toggling decision is made based on both GotLow value and the current clock level. This decision can be modeled by a variable Flip. Flip = yes if and only if GotLow = true and Clock = 1.

The output Q_1 is determined by the previous value of Q_1 and the Flip decision. Q_1 toggles if and only if Flip = yes.

To model the abnormal behavior of a DFF, we assume that if the DFF is abnormal, it will not toggle when it should 80% of the time. It may toggle when it shouldn't 10% of the time.

The other two DFFs can be similarly modeled. Since each of them is driven by $\overline{Q}$ of another DFF, it toggles at the negative edge of Q of the other DFF. Hence the variable GotHigh is used to model the edge monitoring.

We model the persistence of the state of a DFF as follows: If a DFF is normal at $t = i$, it may become abnormal at $t = i + 1$ with 1% probability. If it is abnormal at $t = i$, it will stay abnormal. A subnet of the DBN specified using the Bayesian network editor is shown in Figure 3, where each node is labeled by the variable name followed by the index of the node. The subnet is defined based on the forward interface. FI_{i-1} contains nodes 0, 2, 3, 4, 6, 7, 8, 10 and 11. FI_i contains nodes 13 through 21.

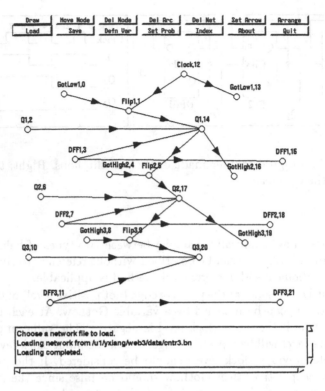

Fig. 3. A subnet of DBN for digital counter.

Once the subnet is specified, we use the template constructor to generate the template. The constructor module converts subnet into a template JT with belief assigned and initialized. The template JT generated based on the subnet is shown in Figure 4, where each clique is labeled by the indexes of member variables. The clique C_8 contains FI_{i-1} and is used to propagate evidence from the previous active template into the current template during inference. The clique C_0 contains FI_i and is used to propagate evidence from the current template into the next active template.

After the template is generated, inference can be performed using the dynamic inference engine. In our experiment, we assume that all DFFs are normal at $t = 0$. At $t = 4$, DFF2 breaks down and did not toggle. Since DFF3 is driven by the output of DFF2, the output of DFF3 is also affected. The corresponding output of DFF2 and DFF3 are shown in Figure 5. Note the difference from Figure 2.

We assume that the initial values of all variables at $t < 0$ are known, e.g., $Q_i = 0$, $GotLow1 = false$, $DFF1 = good$, etc. We assume that clock can be cheaply observed and is observed at every time interval. The observation of output of each DFF incurs a cost, and hence only one DFF is observed at a time

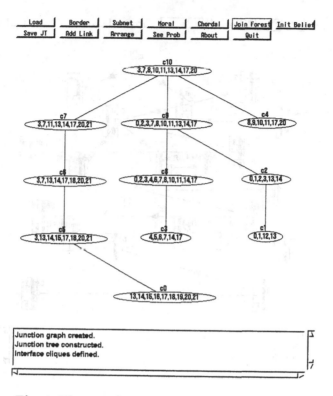

Fig. 4. The template of DBN for digital counter.

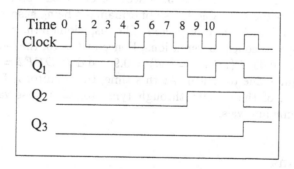

Fig. 5. Incorrect output due to breading down of DFF2 at $t = 4$.

interval. The first observation is made on Q_1 at $t = 4$. At $t = 5$, 6 and 7, Q_2, Q_3 and Q_1 are observed respectively, and so on. No other variables are observable after $t = 0$.

Figure 6 shows the belief at $t = 3$. Since no observation has been made except on clock, the inference engine has simulated the expected output of each DFF from $t = 0$ to $t = 3$ essentially based on their normal behavior. The first observation on Q_1 is made at $t = 4$ (not shown in figures due to space limit). Although Q_2 becomes abnormal and does not toggle at this interval, the observation on Q_1 does not reflect the problem yet.

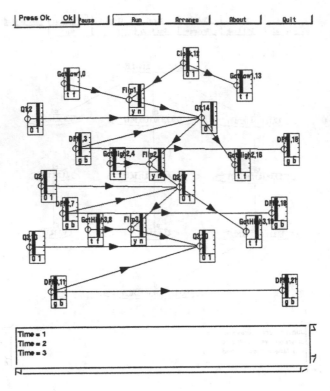

Fig. 6. The belief at $t = 3$.

Figure 7 shows the belief at $t = 5$. Since the observed value of Q_2 is inconsistent with the expected value 1, its abnormality is being suspected. Due to limited observation, DFF1 is also suspected. The suspicion on the abnormality of DFF1 is denied by subsequent observations. Hence at $t = 10$, the belief becomes $P(DFF1 = bad) = 0.05$, $P(DFF2 = bad) = 0.98$, and $P(DFF2 = bad) = 0.08$ (not shown in figures due to space). At this time, the monitor is fairly certain about the problem of the counter through tying together observations made across different time intervals.

7 Conclusions

In this work, we explore the stationary feature of problem domains to improve the efficiency of exact inference in DBNs. We propose the construction of a temporally invariant template of a DBN which can be reused at run time. This saves the run time computation associated with dynamic expansion and reduction by the DER method.

We show that once a slice of DBN is specified, the forward and backward interface form direct basis to select a minimum separator in the moral graph of the DBN. A subnet can then be defined from which the template is constructed. Unlike backward interface and other non-self sufficient separators, forward interface and other self sufficient separators allow local belief assignment using the

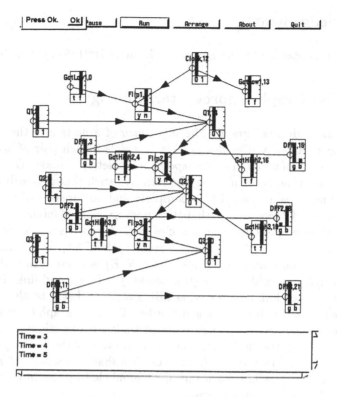

Fig. 7. The belief at $t = 5$.

subnet only. Thus self sufficient separators should be preferred as they simplify template construction.

Besides the property of self sufficiency, using a minimal separator appears to be a useful heuristics in order to reduce the size of total state space of the resultant template. Further experimental study is being conducted to test this heuristics.

Our approach can be extended to close-to-stationary domains. If the DBN can be expressed by a small number of distinct slices, several templates may be created for each distinct slice, one for each distinct preceding slice. The assumption of a constant number of active slices (Section 3) can also be lifted in the same way.

Our presentation has focused on inference that supports *estimation* (estimating the current state of some unobserved variables) and *forecast* (predicting the future state of the domain). The template constructed can also support *backward smoothing* (re-estimating the past state of some unobserved variables). The extension is straightforward.

Acknowledgement

This work is supported by the Research Grant OGP0155425 from NSERC.

Appendix: Graph-theoretic terminology

Let G be an undirected graph. The *adjacency* of a node x is the set of nodes adjacent to x. A set X of nodes in G is *complete* if each pair of nodes in X is adjacent. A set S of nodes in G is a *separator* if deleting S makes G disconnected. S is *minimum* if no node in S may be removed such that S is still a separator. A set C of nodes is a *clique* if C is complete and no superset of C is complete. G is *connected* if there is a path between every pair of nodes. G is *multiply* connected if there exists undirected cycles in G. A *chord* is a link connecting two nonadjacent nodes. G is *triangulated* if every cycle of length > 3 has a chord.

A node x in an undirected graph $G = (N, E)$ is *eliminated* if its adjacency is made *complete* by adding links (if necessary) before x and links incident to x are removed. Each link thus added is called a *fill-in*. Let ρ be the set of fill-ins added in eliminating all nodes in some order. Then the graph $G' = (N, E \cup \rho)$ is triangulated. Let T be a graph whose nodes are labeled by cliques of G' such that intersection of any two nodes are contained in every node on the path between them. Then T is a *junction tree* (JT) of G'. We shall call a node of T as a clique if no confusion is possible. Each link in T is labeled by the intersection of the two end nodes and is called a *sepset*.

Let D be a directed graph. For any arc (x, y) (from x to y), x is called the *tail* and y is called the *head* of the arc. The *family* of a node is the union of the node and its parent nodes. The *moral* graph of D is obtained by completing parents of each node and dropping the direction of each arc. Each link added is called a *moral link*. The process of obtaining the moral graph from D is called *moralization*.

References

1. S. Andreassen, R. Hovorka, J. Benn, K.G. Olesen, and E.R. Carson. A model-based approach to insulin adjustment. In *Proc. 3rd Conf. on Artificial Intelligence in Medicine*, pages 239–248. Springer-Verlag, 1991.
2. G.F. Cooper. The computational complexity of probabilistic inference using Bayesian belief networks. *Artificial Intelligence*, 42(2-3):393–405, 1990.
3. P. Dagum, A. Galper, and E. Horvitz. Dynamic network models for forecasting. In D. Dubois, M.P. Wellman, B. D'Ambrosio, and P. Smets, editors, *Proc. 8th Conf. on Uncertainty in Artificial Intelligence*, pages 41–48, Stanford, CA, 1992.
4. P. Dagum and M. Luby. Approximating probabilistic inference in Bayesian belief networks is NP-hard. *Artificial Intelligence*, 60(1):141–153, 1993.
5. T.L. Dean and K. Kanazawa. A model for reasoning about persistence and causation. *Computational Intelligence*, (5):142–150, 1989.
6. T.L. Dean and M.P. Wellman. *Planning and Control*. Morgan Kaufmann, 1991.

7. J. Forbes, T. Huang, K. Kanazawa, and S. Russell. The batmobile: towards a bayesian automated taxi. In *Proc. Fourteenth International Joint Conf. on Artificial Intelligence*, pages 1878–1885, Montreal, Canada, 1995.

8. F.V. Jensen, S.L. Lauritzen, and K.G. Olesen. Bayesian updating in causal probabilistic networks by local computations. *Computational Statistics Quarterly*, (4):269–282, 1990.

9. U. Kjaerulff. A computational scheme for reasoning in dynamic probabilistic networks. In D. Dubois, M.P. Wellman, B. D'Ambrosio, and P. Smets, editors, *Proc. 8th Conf. on Uncertainty in Artificial Intelligence*, pages 121–129, Stanford, CA, 1992.

10. J. Pearl. *Probabilistic Reasoning in Intelligent Systems: Networks of Plausible Inference*. Morgan Kaufmann, 1988.

11. D.J. Rose, R.E. Tarjan, and G.S. Lueker. Algorithmic aspects of vertex elimination on graphs. *SIAM J. Computing*, 5:266–283, 1976.

12. W.X. Wen. Optimal decomposition of belief networks. In *Proc. 6th Conf. on Uncertainty in Artificial Intelligence*, pages 245–256, 1990.

13. Y. Xiang, D. Poole, and M. P. Beddoes. Multiply sectioned Bayesian networks and junction forests for large knowledge based systems. *Computational Intelligence*, 9(2):171–220, 1993.

Author Index

Lecture Notes in Artificial Intelligence (LNAI)

Lecture Notes in Computer Science